Genealogical Books In Print

A catalogue of in-print titles, useful and interesting to those doing genealogical research; including prices and complete ordering information for over 5000 items

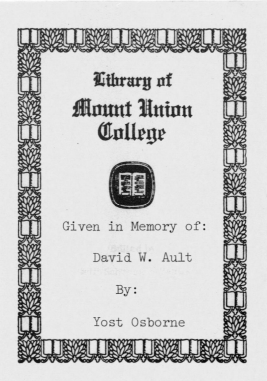

Library of Congress Catalog Number 75-4225
International Standard Book Number 0-89157-015-2

Printed in the United States of America

Original printing .... May 1975
Second printing ... November 1975

Braceland Press, Inc.
6304 F Gravel Ave.
Franconia, Virginia

This volume may be ordered from:

Netti Schreiner-Yantis
6818 Lois Drive
Springfield, Virginia 22150

Price: $4.00

This volume of GENEALOGICAL BOOKS IN PRINT will be available until approximately August 1977. A supplement may be issued in January 1976 - if demand
warrants. A new catalogue will be issued early in 1978. If you would like to be
notified when the supplement (if issued) and the new catalogue are released,
please send your indication to the above address. [Individuals who have ordered
this catalogue will automatically be informed of the availability of new issues.
They need comply with the above only if they have changes of address.]

ii

Table of Contents

General Reference

Lesson Assignments For Fundamentals of Genealogical Research, by Jaussi & Chaston [12 lessons for self study; workshops; correspondence and university classes; private instruction] 20pp. ..... .75 (241)

Your Family Tree, Being a Glance at Scientific Aspects of Genealogy, by Jordan & Kimball 11.50 ..... (130)

The Genealogist's Guide, by Marshall (repr. of 1903 ed.)996pp. 47.50 45.00 (546)

Don't Cry "Timber"!, by Michael (3rd ed.) [Instructions on all phases of research & where to get records] 75pp. 3.85 (183)

Creative Imagination in Research (in NGSQ, v.55, #4) 10pp. 3.00 (616)

Help is Available, by Nichols [Defines needs of the family researcher and explains how & where to find the answer.] 168pp..... 4.45 (538)

The Genesis of Your Genealogy, by Nichols [Instruction book for beginner, a work book with basic instructions.] 175pp. 4.45 (538)

Genealogist's Encyclopedia, by Pine 2.95 (734)

Teach Yourself Heraldry& Genealogy, by Pine 2.50 (852)

Records & Record Searching: A Guide to the Genealogist and Topographer, by Rye 254pp. 9.50 ..... (233)

An"Quest"ors, A Guide to Tracing Your Family Tree, by St. Louis Genealogical Society 95pp. 2.85 (29)

A Basic Course in Genealogy, by Shaw [Includes all forms needed by beginners. Designed for class or individuals] 3.25 (838)

Search & Research: The Researcher's Handbook, A Guide to Official Records and Library Sources For Investigators, Historians, Genealogists, Lawyers, & Librarians, by Stevenson (rev. ed.) 365pp. 3.50 (689)

Making A Pedigree, by Unett 7.50 ..... (130)

Know Your Ancestors: A Guide to Genealogical Research, by Williams 6.75 ..... (657)

Building An American Pedigree, by Norman E. Wright [Step-by-step guide to effective genealogical research.] 639pp. 9.95 (702)

How to Grow Your Family Tree, by Courtney & Gerlene York [Beginner genealogy instruction book with starting kit.] 105pp 6.00 (497)

Texts, Manuals, Handbooks for Special Subjects

The Handy Book for Genealogists, by George B. Everton, Sr. (6th ed.) Lists all counties in U.S., shows date formed and parent county. Also types of records available in each.] 7.75 6.90 (538)

Where to Write for Divorce Records ..... .35 (401)

Where to Write for Birth & Death Records ..... .35 (401)

Where to Write for Marriage Records ..... .35 (401)

Handbook for Genealogical Correspondence, by Cache Br. Lib. 6.45 ..... (538)

How to Decipher and Study Old Documents: Being a Guide to the Reading of Ancient Manscripts, by Cope 10.00 ..... (233)

Handwriting of American Records for a Period of 300 Years, by Kirkham 6.00 ..... (538)

Handy Guide to Record-Searching in the Larger Cities of the United States, by Kirkham [Includes maps of wards] 9.45 ..... (538)

The Old Germanic Principles of Name-Giving, by Woolf 17.50 15.00 (546)

Dutch Systems in Family Naming [N.Y. & N.J.] by Bailey 2.00 (616)

The Library Handbook: Simplified Methods & Terms for the Genealogist, by Radewald [Includes illustrated examples.] 2.75 (24)

Establishing a Library (Technical Leaflet #27), by ASSLH ..... .50 (890)

Organizing a Local Historical Society (2nd ed.), by ASSLH 2.00 (890)

Cemetery Transcribing (Technical Leaflet #9), by ASSLH ..... .50 (890)

Planning Local Workshops (Technical Leaflet #43), by ASSLH ..... .50 (890)

Stranger Stop and Cast An Eye, by Jacobs [Instructions in 4 basic methods in stone rubbings, plus historic background on stones. 4.95 ..... (662)

Lest We Forget, by Babbel [A Guide to Genealogical Re-
search in Wash. D. C.] (4th ed. to be available in 1975)   .... (783)
Guide to the National Archives of the United States, by Nation-
al Archives and Records Services (1974)   12.30   ..... (401)
Guide to Genealogical Records in the National Archives 1.30 (401)
Guide to the Archives of the Government of the Confederate
States of America, by Beers   5.00   ..... (403)
Tracing Your Civil War Ancestor, by Groene   5.95   ..... (496)
Research in Archives: The Use of Unpublished Primary
Sources, by Brooks   5.75   ..... (810)
Introduction to the Use of the Public Records, by Galbraith 6.25 ..... (937)
Historian as Detective: Essays on Evidence, by Winks 2.95 (992)
Beneath the Footnote: A Guide to the Use & Preservation of
American Historical Sources, by Burnett (1969)   10.00   ..... (811)
Aids to Historical Research, by Vincent   8.75   ..... (636)
The Historic Notebook, by Brewer   29.95   ..... (981)
Writing the History Paper, by Sanderlin 2.25 (994)
In Pursuit of American History: Research & Training in the
United States, by Rundell   7.95   ..... (664)
Historical Research: An Outline of Theory & Practice, by
Vincent   16.50   ..... (625)
Professional Techniques and Tactics in American Genealogical
Research, by Kirkham   6.00   ..... (538)

Filing Systems, Data Processing Retrieval

Search and Retrieval, by Marsh [The application of data
processing to genealogical research.] 5.65 (527)
Information Storage and Retrieval Systems for Individual
Researchers, by Jahoda   12.75   ..... (695)
Order, by Pehrson [Filing systems, numbering systems,
genealogical research filing system.] 4.95 (538)

Care & Repair of Old Manuscripts, Old Letters, etc.

Guide to the Care and Administration of Manuscripts, by
Kane (2nd ed.) 2.50 (890)
Manuscripts & Documents: Their Deterioration & Restora-
tion, by Barrow (rev. ed.)   7.95   ..... (713)

Publishing Your Own Book or Newsletter

A Manual of Style, by Univ. of Chicago Pr. (12th ed.) (1969) 12.50 ..... (810)
Style Sheet for Authors, by Inst. of Early Am. Hist. & Cult.
[Guide to their style in quotations, footnote citations, etc.
Explicit guidance on form for historical documentation] 50 (740)
Creating a Worthwhile Family Genealogy, by Colket 1.50 (616)
The Lackor Family, by Middleton [This book won the first award
in a contest sponsored by The American Society of Genealogists for excellence in genealogical arrangement, proper ci-
tation of sources, thoughtful evaluation of the evidence, and
careful research; it is thus useful as a model.] 205pp   6.00   ..... (591)
How to Publish, by Barnett [Tips on compiling, typesetting,
kinds of printing and binding, marketing.] 1.00 (688)
Publish it Yourself: A Manual, by Schreiner-Yantis [Everything
you need to know about publishing and marketing a book (including how to prepare camera-ready copy); with stress on
keeping cost low and quality high.] Illustrated. 100pp   7.50   4.00 (289)
Manual on the Printing of Newsletters, by ASSLH 3.50 (890)
Bookbinding by Hand for Students & Craftsmen, by Town   9.50   ..... (790)
Basic Bookbinding, by Lewis 1.75 (852)

Historian's Handbook: A Key to the Study & Writing of History, by Gray, Wood, et al (2nd ed.)	.....	4.25	(703)
Indexes and Indexing, by Collison (4th ed.) (1972)	8.95	.....	(684)
Indexing Books, by Collison (1962)	.....	2.95	(684)
Indexing Your Book: A Practical Guide For Authors, by Spiker (2nd ed.) (1963)	.....	1.00	(690)
General Information on Copyright, by Copyright Office	.....	free	(784)

Biographical Encyclopedias

Appletons' Cyclopaedia of American Biography, by Wilson & Fiske (1887-89) [20,000 biograhies of citizens of U.S. Canada, Mexico, and South America] 7 vols. Set:	168.00	.....	(233)
The Twentieth Century Biographical Dictionary of Notable Americans, by Johnson & Brown (1897-1903) 10 vols. Set:	130.00	.....	(233)
Dictionary of American Biography, Including Men of the Time; Containing Nearly Ten Thousand Notices of Persons of both Sexes, of Native and Foreign Birth, Who Have Been Remarkable or Prominently Connected with the Arts, Sciences, Literature, Politics, or History, of the American Continent, by Drake (1872) 2 vols. Set:	42.50	.....	(233)
Biographical Dictionaries and Related Works, by Slocum (1967) [A bibliography of 4,829 collections of biographical info.]	25.00	.....	(233)
Biographical Dictionaries and Related Works Supplement, by Slocum (1972) [Adds 3,442 citations.]	25.00	.....	(233)
General Biographical Dictionary, by Chalmers (1812-1817) [Acct. of the lives and writings of the most eminent persons in every nation.] 32 vols. Set:	800.00	.....	(624)
American Women: Fifteen Hundred Biographies with Over 1,400 Portraits . . . of Am. Women During the 19th Century, by Willard & Livermore (1897) 2 vols. Set:	35.00	.....	(233)
Woman on the American Frontier. . . Heroism, Adventures, Privations, Captivities, Trials, etc., by Fowler (1878)	16.50	.....	(233)
American Women, by Stein & Baxter. 44 vols. Set:	765.00	.....	(629)

Portraits

A.L.A. Portrait Index, by Lane & Browne (repr. of 1906 ed.) 3 vols. Set:	55.00	.....	(625)
Yale University Portrait Index, 1701-1951, by Yale U. (1951)	10.00	.....	(764)
Paintings & Miniatures at the Historical Society of Pennsylvania, by Wainwright (1974)	20.00	.....	(1005)

Surnames & Given Names [Origin, meaning, etc.]

Theory of Names, by American Name Society (1955)	8.50	6.00	(546)
What's Your Name?, by Adamic (1942)	17.50	15.00	(546)
The Surnames of Scotland; Their Origin, Meaning, and History, by Black	10.00	.....	(729)
Surnames in the United States Census of 1790, by Am. Council of Learned Soc. [On the national origins of the population]	15.00	.....	(130)
An Etymological Dictionary of Family and Christian Names; With an Essay on Their Derivation and Import, by Arthur	9.50	.....	(233)
British Family Names, Their Origin and Meaning, With Lists of Scandinavian, Frisian, Anglo-Saxon & Norman, by Barber	10.00	.....	(130)
A Dictionary of English and Welsh Surnames, With Special American Instances, by Bardsley	20.00	.....	(130)
Family Names and Their Story, by Baring-Gould (1910)	8.00	.....	(233)
Ludus Patronymicus; Or, The Etymology of Curious Surnames, by Charnock (1868) [4,000 names, unusual forms]	9.50	.....	(233)
Homes of Family Names in Great Britain, by Guppy	16.50	.....	(130)
Family Names of Huguenot Regugees to America, by Lawton	.....	3.00	(130)

References to English Surnames in 1601 and 1602, by Hitching 10.00 ..... (130)
A History of Surnames of the British Isles. A Concise Acct. of
    Their Origin, Evolution, Etyonology & Legal Status, by Ewen 14.00 ..... (130)
Irish Names & Surnames: Sloinnte Gaedheal Is Gall, by Woulfe 21.50 ..... (130)
Surnames in the United Kingdom: A Concise Etymological
    Dictionary, by Harrison 17.50 ..... (130)
An Index to Changes of Name; Under Authority of Act of Par-
    liament or Royal License, and Including Irregular Changes
    from I George III to 64 Victoria, 1760 to 1901, by Philli-
    more & Fry (1905) 10.50 ..... (233)
Baptismal Names: Embodying the Various Baptismal Names
    Used in America, England, Scotland, and Ireland, Togeth-
    er with Their Synonyms, Their Variants, Their Deriva-
    tives, Their Pet Forms, Their Abbreviations, Their Con-
    tractions and Their Corruptions, by Weidenhan (4th ed.) 13.75 ..... (233)
Dutch Systems in Family Naming, by Bailey 2.00 (616)
The Old Germanic Principles of Name-Giving, by Woolf (1936) 17.50 15.00 (546)

Place Names & Gazetteers

Sixth Report of the United States Geographic Board, 1890 to
    1932, by U.S. Geog. Board (1933) [32,000 place names.] 19.00 ..... (233)
The Origin of Certain Place Names in the U.S., by Gannett 11.00 ..... (130)
    "   "   "   "   " 9.00 ..... (233)
The American Gazetteer, Exhibiting, in Alphabetical Order,
    A Much More Full and Accurate Account, Than has been
    Given of the States, Provinces, Counties, Cities, Towns,
    Villages, Rivers . . . Mountains, Forts, Indian Tribes,
    and New Discoveries on the American Continent . . . With
    Particular Description of the Georgia Western Territory,
    by Morse (repr. of 1797 ed.) [Arrangement of streets,
    etc. are given for Marietta, Lexington, Louisville, Pitts-
    burgh, Cincinnati, Limestone, Nashville, and many other
    western settlements. Maps.] 26.00 ..... (629)

Maps & Atlases

A List of Geographical Atlases in the Library of Congress,
    With Bibliographical Notes, by Lib. of Cong. (repr. of
    1909-1920 ed.) 4 vols. Set: 345.00 ..... (630)
A List of Maps of America in the Library of Congress, by
    Lib. of Cong. Map Div. (repr. of 1902 ed.) 2v. in 1. 35.00 ..... (625)
Index to Maps in Books & Periodicals, First Supplement,
    by American Geographical Society Map Dept. 75.00 ..... (843)
Maps & Charts Published in America Before 1800, A Bibli-
    ography, by Yale Univ. Pr. .... (764)
American & Foreign Maps Published by the U.S. Congress,
    1789-1861: Historical Catalog & Index, by Claussen & Friis 30.00 (732)
Guide to Cartographic Records in the National Archives 3.25 ..... (401)
SL #29 - List of Selected Maps of States & Territories ..... free (402)
SL #26 - Pre-Federal Maps in the National Archives: An An-
    notated List, by McLaughlin ..... free (402)
British Maps of Colonial America, by Cuming 10.95 ..... (810)
The British Cartography of 18th Century North America, by
    Cumming (1973) .... (810)
Book of Old Maps, by Fite & Freeman (repr. of 1927)
    [Facsimile reproductions of old maps.] 100.00 ..... (629)
American Maps & Map Makers of the Revolution, by Guthorn 7.95 ..... (1018)
Book of Old Maps Delineating American History From the Ear-
    liest Days Thru Revolutionary War, by Fite & Freeman 7.00 (852)

Lewis Evans: His Map of the Middle British Colonies in Amer-
ica; A Comparative Account of 18 Different Editions Publish-
ed Between 1755 & 1814, by Stevens (1920) [24 facsimiles.]   6.00   ..... (629)
The American Revolution, 1775-1783; An Atlas of 18th Century
Maps & Charts, by Greenwood [Detailed maps of: Boston,
Narragansett Bay, New York City, The Hudson-Lake Cham-
plain-Lake George Waterways, Delaware Bay, Chesapeake
Bay, Charleston, Savannah; two easternmost sections of Fry
& Jefferson Map of Virginia (1777). Pamphlet indexes over
10,000 place names shown on the maps. 20 maps.] 8.50 (401)
SL #19 - List of Cartographic Records of the General Land Off.   ..... free (402)
SL #13 - Cartographic Records of thr Bureau of Indian Affairs   ..... free (402)
Panoramic Maps of Anglo-American Cities, by Hebert [List of
approx. 1000 maps in the Lib. of Cong. covering period
c1865 to 1920.] 2.20 (401)
Southeast in Early Maps, by Cumming (2nd ed.) [States south
of Virginia & north of Florida.]   19.95   ..... (650)
Civil War Maps in the National Archives (1964)   ..... .75 (403)

Roads & Trails

Early Emigrant Trails East of the Mississippi, by Lewis 3.00 (616)
The Great Wagon Road From Philadelphia to the South, by Rouse 8.95   ..... (741)
The Old Glade (Forbe's) Road, by Hulbert [Pa. state rd. Maps.] 12.95   ..... (630)
Boone's Wilderness Road, by Hulbert [Includes maps.]   12.95   ..... (630)
Waterways of Westward Expansion. The Ohio River and Its
Tributaries, by Hulbert [With maps.]   12.95   ..... (630)
The Bozeman Trail: Historical Accounts of the Blazing of the
Overland Routes Into the Northwest, and the Fights with
Red Cloud's Warriors, by Hebard & Brininstool. 2v.   Set: 63.50   ..... (630)
The Road to Oregon, A Chronicle of the Great Emigrant Trail
With 32 Illustrations & a Map, by Ghent   10.00   ..... (630)
Development of the Potomac Route to the West, by Bacon-Foster 16.50   ..... (625)
Oregon Trail, by Parkman   ..... .75 (967)
Turnpike Road System, 1663-1840, by Albert (1972)   18.50   ..... (836)

Exploration & Travel - [Diaries, letters, journals, private papers.]

Voyage to Hudson's Bay, By the Dobbs Galley & California,
in the Years 1746-1747, by Ellis   15.00   ..... (1000)
Chronicles of the Hudson: Three Centuries of Travelers'
Accounts, by Van Zandt   20.00   ..... (950)
Christopher Gist's Journals, by Darlington (repr. of 1893 ed.) 17.50   ..... (629)
Travels Through the Middle Settlements in North America in
the Years 1759-1760, With Observations Upon the State of
the Colonies, by Burnaby [Maine to Virginia.] 1.75 (835)
The Papers of Henry Bouquet, by Stevens, et. al. 2 vols.
[Vol. 1, 1756-1758; Vol. 2, Forbes Expedition]   Each: 12.00   ..... (916)
Narrative Journals of Travels Through the Northwestern Re-
gions of the U.S. Extending From Detroit Through the Great
Chain of American Lakes to the Sources of the Mississippi
River, by Schoolcraft (repr. of 1821 ed.)   16.00   ..... (629)
Letters From Illinois & Notes of a Journey in America, by
Birkbeck (3rd ed.) (repr. of 1818 ed.)   12.50   ..... (738)
George Rogers Clark Papers, 1771-1784, ed by James. 2 vols.
(repr. of 1912-1926 ed.)   Set: 62.50   ..... (630)
Travels in America Performed in 1806, for the Purpose of
Exploring the Rivers Alleghany, Monongahela, Ohio, & Mis-
sissippi, and Ascertaining the Produce and Condition of
Their Banks and Vicinity, by Ashe (repr. 1808) 3v.   Set: 67.50   ..... (630)

Original Journals of the Lewis & Clark Expedition, ed. by
Thwaites (repr. of 1904 ed.) 8 vols. Set: 135.00 ..... (629)
Men & Manners in America, by Hamilton (repr. of 1843 ed.)
[Based on travels in New York, Massachusetts, New England, Wash. D.C., North Carolina & Quebec. The author
comments on social conditions, political institutions.] 12.00 ..... (988)
American Diaries: An Annotated Bibliography of American
Diaries Written Prior to the Year 1861, by Matthews (1945) 10.00 ..... (673)
American Diaries in Manuscript 1580-1954 [Publication, 1975] 12.50 ..... (917)
The Papers of Robert Morris, 1781-1784, Vol. 1 (1973), ed.
by Ferguson [Banker in Philadelphia. Signer of Declaration
of Independence. Land speculator.] 17.50 ..... (991)
Travels in North America in the Years 1780, 1781, & 1782, by
The Marquis de Chastellux [Chastellux, one of the three major generals who accompanied Rochambeau and the French
Expeditionary Forces to America, was a man of letters & a
member of the French Academy. This journal is a deeply
etched portrait of a country and its people.] 17.95 ..... (650)
Memorable Days in America. Being a Journal of a Tour to the
United States, Principally Undertaken to Ascertain, by Positive Evidence, the Condition and Probable Prospects of
British Emigrants, Including Accounts of Mr. Birkbeck's
Settlement in the Illinois; And Intended to Shew Men and
Things as They are in America., by Faux (repr. 1823) 14.50 ..... (630)
Scenes and Adventures in the Army: Or Romance of Military
Life, by Cooke [Personal acct. of an army officer briefly
stationed at Fort Snelling and Fort Leavenworth, then at Ft.
Gibson from 1827-1840's. Fought briefly in Black Hawk
War. In 1845 led an expedition to Green River country.] 20.00 ..... (629)
Letters From the Battlefields of the Mexican War, by Zachariah Taylor (repr. of 1908 ed.) 12.00 ..... (624)
Over the Alleghanies and Across the Prairies. Personal Recollections of the Far West One and Twenty Years Ago, by
Peyton (repr. of 1869 ed.) 12.50 ..... (630)

Land & Land Companies

Beginnings of the American Rectangular Land Survey System,
1784-1800, by Pattison (1970) [A study of the conception,
execution, and results of rectangular land surveys.] 4.80 ..... (888)
PI #22 - Preliminary Inventory of the Land-Entry Papers of
the General Land Office, by National Archives ..... free (402)
A List of References for the History of the Farmer & the Revolution, 1763-1790, by Bowers (1971) [Bibliography, with
many entries annotated, of each of 13 colonies, plus Maine
and Vermont. Section on "Land & the Westward Movement",
with titles referring to military bound lands, land grants,
land office business, and land policy & speculation.] ..... free (542)
History of the James River & Kanawha Company, by Dunaway 12.50 ..... (630)
Holland Land Company, by Evans (repr. of 1924 ed.) 15.00 ..... (738)
Federal Land Series: A Calendar of Archival Materials on the
Land Patents Issued by the U.S. Govt. With Subject, Tract,
And Name Indexes, by Smith. 2 vols.
Vol. 1 - 1788-1810
Vol. 2 - 1799-1835 [Bounty-land warrants in Military Dist.
of Ohio - Coshocton, Delaware, Franklin, Guernsey,
Holmes, Knox, Licking, Marion, Morrow, Muskingum,
Tuscarawas Cos.- tells to whom land was issued.] Each: 20.00 ..... (297)

Hudson's Bay Record Society. Publications. [1670-1840]
    Vols. 1-12 (1938-1949) Per vol., paperbound: $36.00 Set: 504.00 432.00 (624)
    Vols. 13, 14, 16, 18, 23. (1950-1961)   Each: 36.00 (624)
George Mercer Papers, Relating to the Ohio Company of
    Virginia, ed. by Mulkearn   12.95 ..... (991)
The Sesquehannah Company Papers, ed. by Boyd, et. al.
    Vol. 1-4, ed. by Boyd   Set: 45.00 ..... (835)
    Vol. 5 & 6, ed. by Taylor   Each: 27.50 ..... (835)
    Vol. 7, 8, 9, 10, 11, ed. by Taylor   Each: 20.00 ..... (835)

Research aids

Major Genealogical Record Sources in the U.S., by LDS ..... .85 (845)
Genealogist's Encyclopedia, by Pine (1969) 12.50 ..... (945)
Find Your Ancestor, by Criswell [Condensed compilation of
    genealogical & historical facts arranged in chronological
    order (1453-1890) to provide handy desk reference. Maps.] 10.00 (307)
Dictionary of U.S. History; Alphabetical, Chronological, Sta-
    tistical; From Earliest Exploration to the Present Time,
    by Jameson (repr. of 1893 ed.) 24.00 ..... (233)
Check List of Historical Records Survey Publications, by
    Child & Holmes 8.50 ..... (130)
General Aids to Genealogical Research, by NGS [Reprints of
    articles which appeared in the National Genealogical Society
    Quarterly.]   Titles include:
        "Pitfalls in Genealogical Research"
        "Genealogy and American Scholarship"
        "County Atlases for Genealogical Use"
        "How the National Archives Can Aid Genealogists"
        " The Territorial Papers as a Source for the Genealogist"
        "The William Wade Hinshaw Index to Quaker Meeting
            Records"
        "Brief Summary of the County Records on Microfilms in
            Harrisburg, Pennsylvania"
        " German Reformed Church Records in Pennsylvania"
        "Schwenckfelder Genealogical Records"
        "Trailing Ancestors Through Pennsylvania"
    Individual authors. Bound in one volume. 3.75 (616)

Bibliographies, Catalogs, & Inventories

Milton Rubincam: A Bibliographical Record, 1935-1960, by
    Pennsylvania Junto   [List of articles and monographs written by
    by one of America's foremost genealogists.] 2.00 (681)
Books About Early America, by the Institute Staff   [Over 700
    titles. Pre-1815.] (4th ed.) 1.00 (740)
Writings on American History, ed. by Griffin, et.al. (repr.
    of 1902-1940 eds.) (1904-05 not publ.)   Set: 708.00 ..... (624)
General Index to Writings on Am. Hist. 1902-40 (above) 78.00 ..... (624)
List of American Doctoral Dissertations, by Lib. of Cong. Cat-
    alog Div. [27v. covering years 1912-1938]   Set: 430.80 ..... (624)
American Genealogical Periodicals: A Bibliography With a
    Chronological Finding List, by Cappon 1.75 (729)
Catalog of Maps, Ships' Papers, & Logbooks, by Mariners
    Museum Library, Newport News, Va. (1964) 50.00 ..... (843)
Catalogue of the Genealogical and Historical Library of the
    Colonial Dames of the State of New York [7,500 items.] 28.50 ..... (233)
Catalog of National Archives Microfilm Publications, by N.A.
    [General guide to the more than 104,000 rolls of microfilm
    which the National Archives has produced since 1940.] ..... free (402)

PI #157 - Preliminary Inventory of the General Records of the
    Department of State, by National Archives   .....   free   (402)
Sources of Genealogical Research in State Department Records
    (in NGSQ, v. 52, #4) 10pp. 3.00   (616)
SL #7 - List of Documents Relating to Special Agents of the
    Department of State, 1789-1906, by National Archives   .....   free   (402)
PI #168 - Preliminary Inventory of the Records of the Post
    Office Department, by National Archives   .....   free   (402)
PI #113 - Preliminary Inventory of the Records of the United
    States House of Representatives, 1789-1946. 2v.   .....   free   (402)
PI #17 - Preliminary Inventory of the Records of the Adjutant
    General Office, by National Archives   .....   free   (402)
SL #31 - List of Pre-1840 Federal District & Circuit Court
    Records, by National Archives   .....   free   (402)

INDEXES

General indexes

Grassroots of America [Index to American State Papers: Land
    Grants & Claims 1789-1837.]   27.95   .....   (1150)
Dissertations in History: An Index to Dissertations Completed
    in History Departments of United States & Canadian Univer-
    sities, by Kuehl. Vol. 1, 1873-1960; Vol. 2, 1961-1970 Set: 37.50   .....   (126)

Indexes to Periodicals

General Index to Journal of American History, Vols. 1-45,
    1914/15-1959/60   45.00   40.00   (624)
Topical Index to National Genealogical Society Quarterly,
    Volumes 1-50 [1912-1962], by Fisher   13.25   .....   (616)
Index of Persons, Subjects, Places in New England Historical
    Genealogical Register, Vols. 1-50, by Rayne & Chapman   60.00   .....   (130)
Index to Genealogical Periodicals, by Jacobus   12.50   .....   (130)
Genealogical Periodical Annual Index, by Russell. 3 v.
    (1967, 1968, & 1969) [Topical, subject, author, locality
    index to all materials published each year in all English-
    language genealogical periodicals, journals, magazines,
    etc.] Set of 3: $15.00.   Each: 5.50   (178)

Indexes to Local Histories

Local Histories in the Library of Congress: A Bibliography,
    by Kaminkow. 4 vols.   Set: 250.00   .....   (622)
The Bibliographer's Manual of American History, Contain-
    ing an Account of all State, Territory, Town, and County
    Histories Relating to the United States of North American,
    by Bradford. 5v. (repr. 1907) [6,056 items.]   Set: 68.00   .....   (233)
Consolidated Bibliography of County Histories in Fifty States,
    by Peterson   8.50   .....   (130)
Dictionary Catalog of the Local History of Genealogy Division
    of New York Public Library. 18 vols.   Set: 1,420.00   .....   (843)

Indexes to Published Genealogies

Genealogies in the Library of Congress: A Bibliography,
    by Kaminkow. 2 vols.   125.00   .....   (622)
American & English Genealogies in the Library of Congress   27.50   .....   (130)
Index to American Genealogies. And to Genealogical Material
    Contained in All Works, Such as Town Histories, County
    Histories, etc. [and] Supplement, by Munsell's Sons   13.50   .....   (130)
Catalogue of American Genealogies in the Library of the Long
    Island Historical Society, by Toedleberg   16.50   .....   (130)

A List of Some American Genealogies Which Have Been Printed
in Book Form, by Glenn   8.50   .....   (130)
Index to American Genealogies; And to Genealogical Material
Contained in All Works Such as Town Histories, County Histories, etc. (5th ed.) [Index to 50,000 references; over
8,000 American families.]   18.00   .....   (233)
The American Genealogist. Being a Catalogue of Family His-
tories, by Munsell's Sons   [Bibliography.]   12.50   .....   (130)

Guide to Manuscripts & Archives in the United States

The National Union Catalog of Manuscript Collections, by the
Library of Congress
    Vol. 1959-61   9.75   .....   (1159)
    Vol. 1962   13.50   .....   (823)
    Vol. 1963-1964   10.00   .....   (1158)
    Vol. 1965, 1966, & 1967   Each: 15.00   .....   (1158)
    Vol. 1968   25.00   .....   (1158)
    Vol. 1969, 1970, 1971, 1972, & 1973/4 Each: 50.00 ..... (1158)
Guide to Photocopies of Historical Materials in the United
States and Canada, by Hale   10.00   .....   (835)
Guide to the Manuscript Materials for the History of the
United States to 1783, by Andrews & Davenport (1908) 20.00   (624)
Guide to Archives & Manuscripts in the United States, by
Hamer (1961)   17.50   .....   (764)
Ten Centuries of Manuscripts in the Huntington Library, by
Schultz, et. al. 1.50   (832)
Guide to the Manuscript Collections in the Duke University
Library, by Tilley & Goodwin (1947) 10.00   (630)
Calendar of Papers in Washington Archives Relating to the
Territories of the United States to 1873, by Parker (1911) 19.20 (624)
Roads to Research: Distinguised Library Collections of the
Southeast, by English   4.50   2.75   (917)

Guide to Manuscripts & Archives in Foreign Countries

Guide to the Manuscript Materials for the History of the United
States to 1783, in the British Museum, in Minor London Ar-
chives, and in the Libraries of Oxford & Cambridge (1908) 20.00 (624)
Guide to the Materials in London Archives for the History of
the United States Since 1783, by Paulin & Paxson 30.00   (624)
Guide to the Materials for American History to 1783 in the Pub-
lic Record Office of Great Britain, by Andrews. 2v.   Set: 30.00 (624)
Guide to Materials for American History in the Libraries and
Archives of Paris, by Leland. 2v.   Set: 54.00 (624)
Guide to the Materials for the History of the United States in
Swiss & Austrian Archives, by Faus (repr. of 1916 ed.) 14.40 (624)
Guide to Manuscript Materials Relating to American History in
the German State Archives, by Learned (1912) 16.80   (624)
Guide to British West Indian Archive Materials, in London and
in the Islands, for the History of the U.S., by Bell, et.al. 19.20 (624)
Report on American Manuscripts in the Royal Institution of
Great Britain, by Gr.Br.Hist.MSS Comm. 4v.   Set: 90.00 ..... (854)
English Wills: Probate Records in England & Wales, by Walne 2.00 (244)
List of Manuscripts Concerning American History Preserved
in European Libraries, by Matteson 12.00   (624)
Index to Facsimiles of Manuscripts in European Archives Re-
lating to America, 1773-1783, by Stevens (repr. 1898) 40.00   .....   (630)
Guide to Materials for the History of the United States in
Principal Archives of Mexico (1913) 24.00   (624)

A List of Documents in Spanish Archives Relating to the History of the U.S., which have been printed or of which transcripts are preserved in American Libraries, by Robertson (1910)	.....	16.80	(624)
Guide to Materials for American History in Russian Archives, by Golder. 2v. (repr. 1917-1937) Set:	.....	14.40	(624)
A Guide to the Materials for American History in Roman & Other Archives, by Fish	.....	14.40	(624)
Colonial Settlers & English Adventurers. Abstracts of Legal Proceedings in 17th Century English and Dutch Courts Relating to Immigrant Families.	17.50	.....	(130)
Tentative Guide to Historical Materials of the Spanish Borderlands, by Steck (repr. of 1943 ed.)	12.50	.....	(625)
American Colonists in English Records, by Sherwood .	10.00	.....	(130)

Newspapers

American Newspapers, 1821-1936, by Bibliographical Society of America (1937) [A Union List of Files Available in the United States and Canada, nearly 5,700 depositories.]	90.00	.....	(624)
A Checklist of American Eighteenth Century Newspapers in the Library of Congress	24.50	.....	(881)
Checklist of Newspapers & Official Gazettes in the New York Public Library, by N.Y. Lib.	o.p.	.....	
An Historical Digest of the Provincial Press: Being a Collection of All Items of Personal and Historic Reference Relating to American Affairs Printed in the Newspapers . . . Beginning 1689 . . . and Ending . . . 1783, by Weeks & Bacon. 1 vol. (all publ.) (repr. 1911 ed.)	20.00	.....	(630)
Genealogical Data From the Pennsylvania Chronicle, 1767-1774, by Scott	13.25	.....	(616)
Genealogical Abstracts From the American Weekly Mercury, 1719-1746, by Scott	10.00	.....	(130)
Abstracts From Ben Franklin's Pennsylvania Gazette, 1728-1748, by Scott	20.00	.....	(130)
Virginia Gazette From 1736-1780. 6 reels. Microfilm:	72.00		(740)
Index to the Virginia Gazette, 1736-1780 (above), 2v. Set:	65.00	.....	(740)

Records

Journals of the Continental Congress 1774-1789. 34v. Set:	850.00	725.00	(1000)
" " " " " Each:	.....	22.00	(1000)
The Territorial Papers of the United States, ed. by Carter 26 vols. bound in 25. (repr. 1934-1962) Set:	1,400.00	.....	(630)
The New American State Papers: Exploration Series, ed. by Cochran. [More comprehensive than old series.]			
Public Lands Subject. 8 vols. Set:	372.00	.....	(816)
Commerce Subject. 47 vols. Set:	2,290.00	.....	(816)
Labor & Slavery Subject. 7 vols. Set:	334.00	.....	(816)
Indian Affairs. 13 vols. Set:	540.00	.....	(816)
Explorations. 15 vols. Set:	560.00	.....	(816)
American Marriage Records Before 1699, by Clemens	10.00	.....	(130)
Marriage Notices, 1785-1794, For Whole U.S., by Bolton	10.00	.....	(130)
Family Bible Records, by Tally-Frost. 4 vols. Each:	.....	5.25	(294)
County Court Note-Book & Ancestral Proofs and Probabilities, by Ljungstedt	28.00	.....	(130)

Census

United States Census Compendium, by Stemmons [List of census, and other records used as substitute for the census, and where they are located.]	7.45	.....	(538)

A Century of Population Growth From the First Census of the
United States to the Twelfth, 1790-1900, by Census Bureau   17.50   .....   (130)
SL #24 - Federal Population & Mortality Schedules, 1790-1890,
in the National Archives & the States: Outline of a Lecture
on Their Availability, Content, and Use, by Franklin   .....   free   (402)
SL #8 - Population Schedules, 1800-1870: Volume Index to
Counties & Major Cities   .....   free   (402)
PI #161 - Prelimianry Inventory of the Records of the Bureau
of the Census, by Davidson & Ashby   .....   free   (402)
SL #24 - Public and Private Depositories of Census Microfilm
Throughout the United States, by National Archives   .....   free   (402)
Microfilm Catalogue of Federal Population Census 1790 thru
1890, by National Archives (1974) 1.00   (403)
Working Paper #39: Population & Housing Inquiries in the U.S.
Decennial Censuses, 1790-1970. by Census Bureau [Tells
what information was asked in each.] 2.50   (404)

Military

History of Military Pension Legislation in the United States,
by Glasson (repr. 1900 ed.)   12.50   .....   (630)
Biographical Register of the Officers and Graduates of the
U.S. Military Academy at West Point, N.Y., from Its Es-
tablishment, in 1802, to 1890 . . . Complete With Supple-
ments, by Cullum, et al. (repr. 1891-1950) 9v. in 10 Set: 927.00   .....   (630)
Volumes 1-10.   Each: 94.50   .....   (630)
Volume 8 of the above set (only) [1930-1940]   47.50   45.00   (546)
List of Officers of the Navy of the United States and of the
Marine Corps, 1775-1900, by Callahan (repr. of 1901 ed.) 34.95   .....   (642)
Historical Register and Dictionary of the United States Army
1789-1903, by Heitman. 2 vols.   Set: 20.00   .....   (678)
Alphabetical List of Battles, 1754-1900; War of the Rebellion,
Spanish-American War, Philippine Insurrection, and All
Old Wars with Dates, by Strait (repr. of 1905 ed.)   6.75   .....   (233)
Arms For Empire: A Military History of the British Colonies
in North America, 1607-1763, by Leach   14.95   .....   (734)
Historical Journal of the Campaigns in North America for the
Years 1757, 1758, 1759 & 1760, by Knox. 3 vols.
        Vol. 1   34.75   .....   (881)
        Vol. 2   46.50   .....   (881)
        Vol. 3   44.50   .....   (881)
Navies in the Mountains: The Battles on the Waters of Lake
Champlain & Lake George, 1609-1814, by Bird (1962)   7.95   .....   (937)
Five Forts, by Andenbruck [Wilderness wars for the Old North-
west, and the people who established and held forts at Fort
Wayne, 1721-1819.] 1.95   (93)
Fort Wayne, Gateway of the West, 1802-1913: Garrison Orderly
Books; Indian Agency Account Book, by Griswold (1927)   24.50   .....   (630)
Digested Summary and Alphabetical List of Private Claims
Which Have Been Presented to the House of Rep. 3 vols.
[Land grants, Revolutionary War and War of 1812 records.] 85.00   .....   (130)
George Rogers Clark Papers, 1771-1784, ed. by James. 2v.
(repr. 1912-1926) [Leader of Vincennes Expedition.]   Set: 62.50   .....   (630)
A Census of Pensioners for Revolutionary or Military Services
[1840] With their Names, Ages, and Places of Residence . . .
by U.S. Dept. of State [Bound with a general index.]   20.00   .....   (130)
The Women of the American Revolution, by Ellet (repr. of
1848-50 ed.) 3 vols.   Set: 49.95   .....   (642)

DAR Patriot Index [Names of persons upon whose service
  members have been eligible to join the Society.]   11.00   .....   (785)
DAR Patriot Index, Supplement #1   .....   1.00   (785)
DAR Patriot Index, Supplement #2   .....   1.50   (785)
A General Index to a Census of Pensioners for Revolutionary
  or Military Service, 1840, by LDS 10.00   (130)
Index of Revolutionary War Pension Applications, by Hoyt
  [Key to the over 2,000 reels of microfilm produced by the Na-
  tional Archives (Series M804) which contain the applications
  for pension & bounty land warrants made by veterans & their
  widows.] Revised, enlarged ed. available fall 1975.   ....   (616)
The History of the American Revolution, by Ramsay (repr. of
  1789 ed.) [Ramsay was a delegate to Cont. Cong.fr. S.C.]   20.00   .....   (988)
American Prisoners of the Revolution, by Dandridge   14.00   .....   (130)
The American Revolution: A Bibliography, by Shy 2.95   (1013)
Reminiscences and Memorials of Men of the Revolution and
  Their Family, by Muzzey (repr. of 1883 ed.)   22.50   .....   (233)
Seventeen Hundred and Seventy-six; Or, the War of Indepen-
  dence, by Lossing (repr. 1847) [Am.Rev., 1763-1789.]   15.00   .....   (233)
Eyewitness Accounts of the Am. Revolution. 101v.   Set: 1,190.00   .....   (629)
Battle Maps & Charts of the Am. Revolution, by Carrington   35.00   .....   (629)
Some Accounts of the British Army Under the Command of Gen-
  eral Howe, & the Battle of Brandywine, by Townsend (1846)   4.50   .....   (629)
The Organization of the British Army in the American Revolu-
  tion, by Curtis (repr. of 1926 ed.)   7.50   .....   (630)
The Provincial Committees of Safety in the American Revolu-
  tion, by Hunt (repr. of 1904 ed.)   11.95   .....   (642)
Known Military Dead During the American Revolutionary
  War, 1775-1783, by Peterson   10.00   .....   (130)
Diary of the American Revolution; From Newspapers & Orig-
  inal Documents, by Moore & Decker. 2v. (1860 ed.) Set: 38.00   .....   (629)
The American Revolution 1775-1783: An Atlas of 18th Century
  Maps & Charts: Threatres of Operations, by Greenwood   8.50   .....   (401)
Naval Documents of the American Revolution, Vol. 5. Ed. by
  Morgan [Covers period fr. May 1776 to July 1776.]   13.25   .....   (401)
Naval Documents of the American Revolution, Vol. 5. Ed. by
  Morgan [Covers period fr. Aug. 1776 to Nov. 1776.]   18.40   .....   (401)
PI #144 - Preliminary Inventory of the War Dept. Collection
  of Revolutionary War Records, by National Archives   .....   free   (402)
Orderly Book of the Northern Army, at Ticonderoga & Mt. In-
  dependence, from Oct. 17, 1776 to Jan. 8, 1777, With Bio-
  graphical and Explanatory Notes, by Munsell (1859)   17.50   15.00   (546)
The King's Mt. Men. The Story of the Battle, With Sketches
  of the American Soldiers Who Took Part, by White   10.00   .....   (130)
King's Mt. & Its Heroes, by Draper   15.00   .....   (130)
The German Allied Troops in the North American War of In-
  dependence, 1776-1783, by Eelking   12.00   .....   (130)
The Commander-in-Chief's Guard: Rev. War, by Godfrey   12.50   .....   (130)
Historical Register of Officers of the Continental Army During
  the War of the Revolution . . . , Heitman   16.50   .....   (130)
Rejected or Suspended Applications for Revolutionary War Ap-
  plications, by U.S. Dept. of the Int.   13.50   .....   (130)
Pensioners of the Revolutionary War - Struck off the Roll   7.50   .....   (130)
Pierce's Register. Register of the Certificates Issued by John
  Pierce, Esq., Paymaster General & Comm. of Army Accts.   16.00   .....   (130)
Revolutionary Pensioners. A Transcript of the Pension List of
  the United States for 1813, by U.S. War Dept. 5.00   (130)

The Story of the Continental Army 1775-1783, by Montross	10.00	.....	(817)
Hessians in the Revolutionary War, by Lowell (repr. 1884)	10.00	.....	(979)
German-American Genealogical Research Monograph No. 1: Brunswick Deserter-Immigrants of the American Revolution, by Smith [Deserters in the U.S. & Canada from the Brunswick contingent of mercenaries serving with the British forces. Gives birthplace; age; how, where, and when he left the service.]	6.00	.....	(752)
German- American Genealogical Research Monograph No. 2: Mercenaries from Ansbach & Bayreuth, Germany, who Remained in America After the Rev., by Smith	6.00	.....	(752)
King's Friends: The Composition & Motives of the American Loyalist Claimants, by Brown (1965)	12.50	.....	(1016)
Royal Commission on the Losses & Services of the American Loyalists 1783-1785, by Coke (repr. of 1915 ed.)	25.00	.....	(629)
Loyalism in New York During the American Revolution, by Flick (repr. of 1901 ed.)	10.00	.....	(630)
The Loyalists in Revolutionary America, 1760-1781, by Calhoon (1973)	17.50	.....	(1019)
Biographical Sketches of Loyalists of the American Revolution, by Sabine. (repr. of 1864 ed.) 2v. Set:	25.00	.....	(637)
Index of the Rolls of Honor (Ancestor's Index) in the Lineage Books of the National Society of the D.A.R.	45.00	.....	(130)
Official Letters of the Military & Naval Officers of the U.S. During the War with Great Britain 1812-1815, by Brannan	20.00	.....	(629)
1812 Ancestor Index, by N.S. Daughters of 1812 [Approx. 20,000 1812 ancestors with service betw. 1784 & 1815.]	22.50	.....	(872)
The Military Heroes of the War of 1812; With a Narrative of the War, by Peterson (repr. of 1848 ed.)	12.50	10.00	(546)
The Creek War of 1813 & 1814, by Halbert, et al	8.00	.....	(788)
The Pension Roll of 1835, by U.S. War Dept. 4 vols.	80.00	.....	(130)
History of the Mormon Battalion 1846-1848, by Tyler	o.p.	.....	(755)
Military Bibliography of the Civil War, Vol. 1, by Dornbusch	25.00	.....	(629)
Confederate Veteran Magazine Index, 1893-1932 [A listing of each of 40 years of the deaths as reported in C.V.M.]	25.00	.....	(848)
Guide to Archives of the Government of the Confederate States of America, by Beers	5.00	.....	(401)
PI #101 - Preliminary Inventory of the War Department Collection of Confederate Records, by National Archives	.....	free	(402)
PI #169 - Preliminary Inventory of the Treasury Department Collection of Confederate Records, by National Archives	.....	free	(402)
Guide to Federal Archives Relating to the Civil War, by Munden & Beers	5.00	.....	(401)
Tracing Your Civil War Ancestor, by Groene [Textbook.]	5.95	.....	(496)
Regimental Losses in the American Civil War, 1861-1865, by Fox [The statistics of the Union Army, and a chapter on losses in the Confederate Army.]	35.00	.....	(848)
Confederate Soldiers & Sailors Who Died as Prisoners of War at Camp Butler, Illinois, 1862-1865, by Praws [Name, rank, company, regt., date of death, place of burial of 809 men.]	.....	6.00	(290)
Confederate Soldiers, Sailors & Civilians Who Died As Prisoners of War at Camp Douglas, Chicago, Illinois, 1862-1865, by Praws [Name, rank, company, regt., date of death and place of burial of 4,454 men.]	.....	6.00	(290)
Behind the Old Brick Wall - A Cemetery Story, by Moore & Baber [Tombstone inscriptions from the Old City Cemetery in Lynchburg, Virginia. Includes names of 2,701 Confed-			

erate soldiers from Ala, Ark, Fla, Ga, Ky, La, Md, Miss,
Mo, NC, SC, Tenn, Tex, & Va. giving company, regiment,
and state of each; also approx. 187 Union soldiers from
Conn, Del, Ind, Me, Md, Mass, Mich, NH, NJ, NY, O,
Pa, RI, Vt, Va, & Wisc. temporarily interred in this ceme-
tery giving the company, regiment, & state of each.]   7.50   ..... (569)
List of Pensioners on the Roll, January 1, 1883. 5 vols. Set: 97.50   ..... (130)
Military Affairs - General Index to Volumes 1-32 [Includes
articles on war prisoners.]   23.00   18.00 (624)

Law

Legal Terminology [Technical leaflet #55], by AASLH 50 (890)
English Common Law in the Early American Colonies, by
Reinsch (repr. of 1899 ed.)   6.50   ..... (928)
Commentaries on the Laws of England: First American Edition,
Philadelphia, 1771-1772, by Blackstone   125.00   ..... (878)

Religious and ethnic groups

Survey of American Church Records, by Kirkham. Vol. 1
[Bibliography of church records available from the major
denominations before the Civil War.]   6.00   ..... (538)
The History of the Reformation and Other Ecclesiastical Trans-
actions in, and About, the Low-Countries, from the Beginning
of the Eighth Century Down to the End of the Famous Synod of
Dort in Which All the Revolutions that Happened in Church &
State on Account of the Division Between the Protestants and
the Catholics, the Arminians and Calvinists, are Fairly Care-
fully Represented, by Brandt. 4v. (repr. 1720-1733) Set: 110.00   ..... (630)
A List of Emigrant Ministers to America, by Fothergill   7.50   ..... (130)
National Index of Parish Registers: Sources of Births, Marri-
ages & Deaths Before 1837, by Steel. Vol. 1 (1967)   12.50   ..... (657)
The History of the Society of Friends in America, by Bowden
(repr. of 1854 ed.) 2 vols. in 1   39.00   ..... (629)
Americans of Jewish Descent, by Stern [A ten page pamphlet,
documented and highly informative study of the early settle-
ments of Jews in America.] 2.00 (616)
Americans of Jewish Descent, by Stern [A book, illustrating
lineages, etc.]   40.00   ..... (676)
An American Jewish Bibliography, Being a List of Books &
Pamphlets by Jews or relating to them, printed in the U.S.
. . . until 1850, by Rosenbach (repr. 1926)   16.80   ..... (624)
Jewish Immigration to the United States 1881-1910, by Joseph 10.00   ..... (630)
American Jewish Historical Quarterly [Periodical of the
American Jewish Historical Society, published since 1893.] $15/yr (440)
American Jewish Historical Quarterly
        Vols. 1-55 & General index to vols. 1-20   1,051.20 715.20 (624)
        Vols. 1-37   Each: 12.00 (624)
        Vols. 38-55   Each: 14.40 (624)
        General Index to vols. 1-20   .....   12.00 (624)
        Vols. 56-58, 1965/66-1967/68. 3 vols.   Each: 14.40 (624)
Catholics in Colonial Days, by Phelan (repr. of 1935 ed.)   12.50   ..... (233)
The Catholic Church on the Kentucky Frontier (1785-1812),
by Mattingly (repr. of 1936 ed.)   10.00   ..... (630)
Catholic Historical Review. Vols. 1-17 & Gen. Ind. 1-20 Set: 605.00 515.00 (624)
        Vols. 1-17 (1915/16-1931/32)   Each: 30.00 (624)
        General Index to volumes 1-20   .....   4.80 (624)
        Vols. 18-55 (1932/33-1969/70)   Set: 1,272.00 1,044.00 (624)
        Vols. 18-47   Each: 30.00 (624)
        Vols. 48-55   Each: 18.00 (624)

The Trail of the Huguenots in Europe, the United States, South
Africa, and Canada, by Reaman   10.00 ..... (130)
Huguenot Pedigress, by Lart   10.00 ..... (130)
History of the Huguenot Emigration to America, by Baird   16.50 ..... (130)
The Huguenots: Their Settlements, Churches and Industries
in England & Ireland, by Smiles   13.50 ..... (130)
The Huguenots in France and America, by Lee   15.00 ..... (130)
The Huguenots: Their Settlements, Churches and Industries
in England and Ireland, by Smiles   13.50 ..... (130)
Catalogue or Bibliography of the Library of the Huguenot
Society of America, by Morand   11.50 ..... (130)
History of the Church: History of Joseph Smith, by Smith
8 Vols. & Index   Set: 35.00 ..... (689)
8 Vols.   Each: 4.50 ..... (689)
Index only   5.50 ..... (689)
William Clayton's Journal: A Daily Record of the Journey of
the Original Company of "Mormon" Pioneers from Nauroo,
Illinois, to the Valley of the Great Salt Lake. (repr. 1921) 18.00 ..... (629)
Latter-Day Saint's Emigrants' Guide, by Clayton 2.00 (829)
Frontier Mission: A History of Religion West of the Southern
Appalachians to 1861, by Posey   9.00 ..... (126)
A History of the Church Known as the Moravian Church, or, the
Unitas Fratrum, or, the Unity of the Brethren, During the
18th and 19th Centuries, by Hamilton (repr. of 1900 ed.)   25.50 ..... (630)
Communal Pietism Among Early American Moravians, by
Sessler (repr. of 1933 ed.)   12.00 ..... (630)
The Great Revival, 1787-1805: The Origins of the Southern
Evangelical Mind, by Boles   10.00 ..... (126)
Encyclopedia of Southern Baptists, by Cox. Vol. 1 & 2 Set: 20.00 ..... (638)
Sources for Genealogical Research in Methodist Records
(in NGSQ, v.50, #4) 6pp. 3.00 (616)
Isaac Backus on Church, State, & Calvinism: Pamphlets
1754-1789, by Backus   15.00 ..... (948)
Presbyterians in the South, by Thompson. Vol. 1, 1607-1861   15.00 ..... (731)
The Establishment of the English Church in Continental
American Colonies, by Davidson (repr. of 1936 ed.)   7.50 ..... (630)
Historical Collections Relating to the American Colonial Church,
by Perry. 5 parts in 4 v. (repr. 1870-1878)   Each: 37.50 ..... (630)
Magnalia Christi Americana, Or the Ecclesiastical History of
New England From the Year 1620 to 1698, by Mather (1702) 48.00 ..... (629)
The Faithful Shepherd: A History of the New England Ministry
in the 17th Century, by Hall   11.95 ..... (650)
Religion and Trade in New Netherland: Dutch Origins and
American Development, by Smith   12.50 ..... (835)
Seventh Day Baptists in Europe & America, by Randolph. Vols.
1 & 2. [Denomination history since the Reformation, chief-
ly in U.S.A. and England, to about 1900.] 1500pp. Set: 9.00 ..... (397)
Seventh Day Baptists in Europe & America, by Rogers. Vol. 3
[History since 1900, with biographical sketches.]   6.00 ..... (397)
European Origins of the Brethren, by Durnbaugh   10.00 ..... (751)
The Brethren in Colonial America, by Durnbaugh   10.00 ..... (751)
A History of the German Baptist Brethren in Europe & America,
Brumbaugh (repr. of 1899 ed.)   24.00 ..... (630)
One Hundred Fifty Years [of the Evangelical United Brethren
Church], by Ness   5.95 ..... (813)
History of the Anabaptists in Switzerland, by Burrage (1881) 13.50 ..... (625)
Anabaptists in Hesse, by Franz (1951)   6.00 ..... (925)
The Schwenkfelders in Pennsylvania, by Kriegel (repr. 1904) 12.50 ..... (630)

The German Pietists of Provincial Pennsylvania, 1694-1708,
  by Sachse (repr. of 1895 ed.)   25.00   ..... (630)
Biographical Directory of Clergyman of the American Lutheran
  Church   15.00   ..... (911)
History of the Evangelical Lutheran Church in the United States,
  by Jacobs (repr. of 1893 ed.)   22.50   ..... (625)
History of the Evangelical & Reformed Church, by Dunn (1961)   o.p.   ..... (772)
The German & Swiss Settlements of Colonial Pennsylvania:
  A Study of the So-called Pennsylvania Dutch, by Kuhns (1901)   8.75   ..... (630)
History of the German Settlements & of the Lutheran Church in
  North & South Carolina, by Bernheim (repr. of 1872 ed.)   18.00   ..... (663)
Luthern Church in New York & New Jersey, 1722-1760, by Hart
  [Translation of Lutheran correspondence pertaining to these
  colonies and now housed in the staatsarchiv at Hamburg.]   10.00   ..... (1021)
The Scotch-Irish, by Leyburn [Describes their life in Scotland,
  when the essentials of their character and culture were
  shaped, their removal to Northern Ireland; and their mi-
  gration to America.]   8.95   ..... (650)

Colonial families

Ancestral Records & Portraits. A Compilation From the Ar-
  chives of Chapter I, Colonial Dames of America. 2 vols.   30.00   ..... (130)
English Wills of Colonial Settlers, by Currer-Briggs [Col-
  lection of 17th century wills.]   12.50   ..... (580)
Surname Index to Sixty-five Volumes of Colonial & Revolution-
  ary Pedigrees, by Crowther [Index to the following:]
        Colonial Families of America
        Colonial & Revolutionary Lineages of America
        American Colonial Families
        American Family Antiquity
        Armorial Families of America
        Ancestral Roots of Sixty Colonists Who Came to
            New England Between 1623 & 1650
        Historic Families of America
        The Magna Charta Sureties, 1215
        Patten, Buchanan, and Allied Families
        The Prominent Families of the U.S.A. 6.75   (616)
Colonial Families of the United States of America, by
  Mackenzie. 7 vols.   125.00   ..... (130)
Ancestral Roots of Sixty Colonists Who Came to New England
  1623-1650, by Farmer   12.50   ..... (130)
The Magna Charta Sureties, 1215: The Barons Named in the
  Magna Charta and Some of Their Descendants Who Settled
  in America, 1607-1650, by Adams & Weis   8.50   ..... (130)
American Ancestry, Giving the Name and Descent in the Male
  Line of Americans Whose Ancestors Settled in the U.S.
  Previous to the Declaration of Independence, A.D. 1776,
  by Munsell's Sons. 12 vols.   Each: 9.00   ..... (130)
Genealogical Guide to the Early Settlers of America [Surnames
  Abby through Prior.], by Whittemore   20.00   ..... (130)
The Compendium of American Genealogy. The Standard Gene-
  alogical Encyclopedia of the First Families of America,
  ed. by Virkus. 7 vols.   Set: 150.00   ..... (130)
Immigrants to America Before 1750. An Alphabetical List
  . . . Surnames A-Bat. (all publ.), by Virkus   10.00   ..... (130)
Bristol & America. A Record of the First Settlers in the
  Colonies of North America, 1654-1685, by Hargreaves   10.00   ..... (130)
Colonial Families of the Southern States of Am., by Hardy   18.50   ..... (130)

Indians

Major Genealogical Sources of Indians in the U.S., by LDS	.....	.85 (845)
Dictionary of Indian Biography, by Buckland (repr. of 1906 ed.) [Contains 2,600 concise biographies.]	19.95	..... (642)
Dictionary of Indian Biography, by Buckland (repr. of 1906 ed.)	28.50	..... (233)
Indian Affairs 1789-1827, by U.S. Congress. 2 vols. [American State Papers, Documents, Legislative & Executive, of the Congress of the U.S.] (repr. of 1832-34 ed.)	140.00	..... (630)
PI #163 - Preliminary Inventory of the Records of the Bureau of Indian Affairs, by National Archives. 2 vols.	.....	free (402)
Select Catalog of National Archives Publications on the American Indian, by National Archives & Records Service	.....	free (402)
Rolls of Certain Indian Tribes, by McChesney, et al [Partly depositions given in 1913 by Chinook Indians - hundreds of Indian names, some pictures.]	10.00	..... (829)
The Eastern Cherokee, by Siler [1851 census of Cherokees in N.C., Tenn., Ala., & Ga.]	15.00	..... (580)
Old Frontiers: The Story of the Cherokee Indians from the Earliest Times to Their Removal to the West, 1838, by Brown	27.00	..... (629)

Indian Captivity

New England Captives Carried to Canada: Between 1677 & 1760; During the French & Indian Wars, by Coleman. 2 v. Set:	39.50	..... (636)
Memoirs of a Captivity Among the Indians of North America, From Childhood to the Age of Nineteen, by Hunter (1823 ed.)	15.00	..... (1000)
Selection of Some of the Most Interesting Narratives of Outrages Committed by the Indians in Their Wars with the White People, by Loudon (1808 ed.) 2v. [Firsthand accounts.] Set:	30.00	..... (629)
White into Red. A Study of the Assimilation of White Persons Captured by Indians, by Heard	6.00	..... (920)

Black people

Select Catalog of National Archives Microfilm Publications on Black Studies, by National Archives	.....	free (402)
Reminiscences of Levi Coffin, the Reputed President of the Underground Railroad; Being a Brief History of the Labors of a Lifetime in Behalf of the Slave, with the Stories of Numerous Fugitives, Who Gained Their Freedom..., by Coffin	15.00	..... (630)
Missing Pages in American History. Revealing the Services of Negroes in the Early Wars in the U.S. 1641-1815, by Wilkes (repr. of 1919 ed.)	7.50	..... (630)
Services of Colored Americans in the Wars of 1776 & 1812, by Nell (repr. of 1851 ed.)	10.00	..... (630)

Immigration, emigration, & migration

Colonial Immigration Laws: A Study of the Regulation of Immigration by the English Colonies in Am., by Proper	6.00	..... (630)
Locating Your Immigrant Ancestor, by Neagles & Lee	5.95	..... (538)
Atlantic Migration 1607-1860, by Hansen	.....	3.25 (992)
A Bibliography of Ship Passenger Lists 1538-1825; Being a Guide to Published Lists of Early Immigrants to North America, by Lancour (rev. & enl. by Wolfe)	5.00	..... (729)
Migration, Emigration, Immigration, by Miller [Sources.]	.....	6.95 (538)
Some Early Emigrants to America & Emigrants From Liverpool	7.50	..... (130)
Immigration in Colonial Times, by Clarke (1973)	3.95	..... (864)
SL #22 - List of American-Flag Merchant Vessels That Received Certificates of Enrollment of Registry at the Port of N.Y., 1789-1867, by Holdcamper. 2 vols.	.....	free (402)

English Convicts in Colonial America, by Coldham. Vol. 1	20.00	.....	(580)
British-American Genealogical Monograph No. 1: British Deportees to America, Pt. 1, 1760-1763		8.00	(752)
German-American Genealogical Research Monograph No. 1: Brunswick Deserter-Immigrants of the American Revolution, by Smith [Deserters in the U.S. & Canada from the Brunswick contingent of mercenaries serving with the British forces. Gives birthplace; age; how, where, and when they left the service.]		6.00	(752)
German-American Genealogical Research Monograph No. 2: Mercenaries from Ansbach & Bayreuth, Germany, Who Remained in America After the Revolution, by Smith [Gives company, when deserted; sometimes data on birthplace and parentage.]		6.00	(752)
Manual for Emigrants to America, by Colton (repr. 1832)	4.50	.....	(629)
Emigrant's Guide to the U.S. of America, Containing all Things Necessary to be Known by Every Class of Persons Emigrating to That Continent, by Collins (repr. of 1830 ed.)	7.50	.....	(721)
Dutch Emigration to North America, 1624-1860, by Wabeke	11.00	.....	(636)
Americans From Wales, by Hartman [History of Welsh emigrations and settlements in the United States.] (1967)	6.50	.....	(998)
Germany & the Emigration, 1816-1885, by Walker	11.00	.....	(948)
The German Element in the U.S.: With Special Reference to Its Political, Moral, Social, and Educational Influence, by Faust 2 vols. [Vol. 1 covers from before Rev. through 19th century. Vol. 2 discusses Ger. influences, with specific references to German settlements in various parts of U.S.] Set:	37.50	.....	(629)
Ireland & the American Emigration, 1850-1900, by Schrier (repr. of 1958 ed.) [Discusses conditions in Ireland that led to mass emigration & position of the immigrant in the U.S.]	9.50	.....	(988)
Ulster Emigration to Colonial America: 1718-1775, by Dickson	11.75	.....	(976)
Scotch Irish Pioneers in Ulster and America, by Bolton [Passenger lists.]	12.00	.....	(130)
The Scotch-Irish in America, by Ford [Full story of Ulster plantation, a study of causes which led to emigration, description of settlements in U.S., and recital of frontier experiences.] (repr. of 1915 ed.)	15.00	.....	(629)
Irish Immigration in the United States: Immigrant Interviews, by O'Donovan [Interviews with author's countrymen, with acct. of parts of Emerald Isle whence they emigraed together with a direct reference to their present location in the land of their adoption, during his travels in various states in 1854 and 1855.]	11.50	.....	(629)
Passenger Lists From Ireland, by Hackett & Early	.....	5.00	(130)
Norwegian Migration to America: 1825-1860, by Blegen 2v. Set:	32.95	.....	(642)
Norwegian Settlement in the United States, by Qualey	12.00	.....	(629)
The Background of Swedish Immigration, 1840-1930, by Janson	21.50	.....	(629)
Lists of Swiss Emigrants in the 18th Century to American Colonies, by Faust & Brumbaugh	17.50	.....	(130)
The Religious As Aspects of Swedish Immigration; A Study of Immigrant Churches, by Stephenson (repr. of 1932 ed.)	14.00	.....	(630)
Who's Who in Polish America: A Biograhical Directory of Polish-American Leaders . . . , by Bolek [5,000 sketches.]	23.50	....	(629)
The Poles in America, by Fox (repr. of 1922 ed.)	6.00	.....	(629)
The Russian Immigrant, by Davis	7.00	.....	(629)
Immigrant Ancestors. A List of 2500 Immigrants to America Fefore 1750, by Virkus	.....	5.00	(130)
Passenger Arrivals, 1819-1820, by U.S. Dept. of State	15.00	.....	(130)

American Colonists in English Records, by Sherwood	10.00	.....	(130)
The Original Lists of Persons of Quality: Emigrants, etc. Who Went From Great Britain to American Plantations, 1600-1700, by Hotten	15.00	.....	(130)
List of Emigrants to America From Liverpool, by French	.....	5.00	(130)
Two Early Passenger Lists, 1635-1637, by Putnam	.....	3.50	(130)
The Latter-Day Saints' Emigrants Guide, by Clayton	.....	2.25	(777)
Naturalization of Foreign Protestants in the American & West Indian Colonies, by Giuseppi [Huguenots, passenger lists.]	11.00	.....	(130)
Mingling of the Canadian & American Peoples, Vol. 1, by Hansen (repr. of 1940 ed.)	12.00	.....	(629)
History of Immigration to the United States . . . Compiled From Official Data: With An Introductory Review of the Progress and Extent of Immigration to the United States Prior to 1819 & An Appendix Containing the Naturalization And Passenger Laws of the United States . . . Relative to Immigrants . . ., by Bromwell [Statistical. Covers 64 years.]	6.50	.....	(629)
The Legislative History of Naturalization in the United States: From the Revolutionary War to 1861, by Franklin	9.00	.....	(629)

Foreign in America

Account of the European Settlements in America, by Burke (repr. of 1777 ed.) 2 vols. in 1	40.00	.....	(629)
An Account of the European Settlements in America, by Burke (repr. of 1808 ed.) 6 pts. in 2 vols. Set:	30.00	.....	(630)
An Account of the Spanish Settlements in America, by Campbell (repr. of 1762 ed.) [Includes map of America.]	25.00	.....	(630)
The Irish in America, by Wittke	.....	1.50	(762)
The Irish in America, by O'Brien	.....	5.00	(130)
History of the Irish Settlers in North America From the Earliest Period to the Census of 1850, by McGee	10.00	.....	(130)
Scotch Irish Pioneers in Ulster & America, by Bolton	12.00	.....	(130)
The Scotch-Irish or the Scot in North Britain, North Ireland & North America, by Hanna. 2 vols. Set:	27.50	.....	(130)
A Historical Account of the Settlement of Scotch Highlanders in America Prior to the Peace of 1783, by MacLean	13.50	.....	(130)
The Huguenots in France & America, by Lee	15.00	.....	(130)
The French Blood in America, by Fosdick	14.00	.....	(130)
England in America, 1580-1752, by Tyler (repr. of 1904 ed.)	16.95	.....	(642)
The Germans in America, by Wittke	.....	1.50	(762)
The Finns in America, by Kolehmainen	.....	1.50	(762)
Swedes in America, 1638-1938, by Benson (repr. of 1938)	29.95	.....	(642)
History of the Scandinavians and Successful Scandinavians in the United States, by Nelson. 2 vols. Set:	39.95	.....	(642)
The Greeks in America, by Saloutos	.....	1.50	(762)
The Mexicans in America, by McWilliams	.....	1.50	(762)
Hispanic American Historical Review. Vols. 1-49	1,646.40	1,352.40	(624)
Vols. 1-49 (1918-1969)	.....	27.60	(624)
Guide to the Hispanic American Historical Review, Vols. 1-25	.....	14.40	(624)
Guide to the Hispanic American Historical Review, Vols. 26-35	.....	12.00	(624)
The Pilgrim Fathers from a Dutch Point of View, by Plooij	5.00	.....	(630)

Royal Descent

Pedigrees of Some of the Emperor Charlemagne's Descendants, Vol. 11, by Langston & Buck [American Ancestry preceeded by a Foreword by Beard helpful to those seeking a Charlemagne or Royal descent.]	20.00	.....	(929)
A Royal Lineage: Alfred the Great, 901-1901, by Watson(1901)	12.50	10.00	(546)

Baronia Anglica Concentrata: Or, A Concentrated Account Of
All the Baronies Commonly Called Baronies In Fee; Deriv-
ing Their Origin From Writ of Summons, and Not From Any
Specific Limited Creation . . ., by Banks (repr. 1843 ed.)
2 vols.   Set: 45.00   40.00   (546)
Royal Genealogies: Or, The Genealogical Tables of Emperors,
Kings, and Princes, From Adam to These Times . . ., by
Anderson (repr. of 1736 ed.)   47.50   45.00   (546)
Families Directly Descended From All the Royal Families in
Europe (495-1932) and Mayflower Descendants, by Leach   17.50   15.00   (546)
Pedigrees of Some of the Emperor Charlemagne's Descen-
dants, by Redlich. Vol. 1 (all publ.)   12.50   .....   (130)
The Magna Charta Sureties, 1215: The Barons Named in the
Magna Charta & Some of Their Descendants Who Settled in
America, 1607-1650, by Adams & Weis   8.50   .....   (130)
Magna Charta Barons & Their American Descendants . . . ,
by Browning   15.00   .....   (130)
The Magna Charta Barons & Their American Descendants, To-
gether With the Pedigrees of the Founders of the Order of
Runnemede, by Browning   15.00   .....   (130)
Family Origins & Other Studies, by Round   12.50   .....   (130)
Index of Baronetage Creations, by Parry   17.50   .....   (130)
Dictionary of Royal Lineage of Europe and Other Countries,
From the Earliest Period to the Present Date, by Allstom
2 Vols.   Set: 50.00   45.00   (546)
Studies in Peerage & Family History, by Round   15.00   .....   (130)
Living Descendants of Blood Royal (in America), by
d'Angerville. Vol. 3   25.00   .....   (130)
Americans of Royal Descent. Collection of Genealogies Show-
ing the Lineal Descent From Kings of Some American
Families, by Browning   15.00   .....   (130)
Americans of Gentle Birth & Their Anc., by Pittman. 2v. Set: 67.50   .....   (130)
Some "Colonial Dames" of Royal Descent. Pedigrees Showing
the Lineal Descent From Kings of Some Members of the Na-
tional Society of the Colonial Dames of Am., by Browning   12.50   .....   (130)
The Institution, Laws and Ceremonies of the Most Noble Order
of the Garter, by Ashmole   50.00   .....   (130)
Memorials of the Most Noble Order of the Garter From Its
Foundation to the Present Time. Including the History of
the Order; Biographical Notices of the Knights in the Reigns
of Edward III and Richard II, the Chronological Succession
of the Members, by Beltz (repr. of 1841 ed.)   35.00   .....   (630)
Bolton's American Armory. A Record of Coats-of-Arms Which
Have Been in Use Within the Present Bounds of the U.S.,
by Bolton   8.50   .....   (130)
Catalog of Kings, by Milles   15.00   .....   (580)

Heraldry

Encyclopaedic Dictionary of Heraldry, by Franklyn & Tanner   32.00   .....   (694)
Handbook of Heraldry; With Instructions for Tracing Pedigrees
and Deciphering Ancient Mss.; Rules for the Appointment
of Liveries, etc., by Cussans. 4th ed. (1893)   15.00   .....   (233)
The Manual of Heraldry. A Concise Description of the Several
Terms Used and Containing a Dictionary of Every Descrip-
tion in the Science, by Grant   7.50   .....   (130)
Intelligible Heraldry, by Lynch-Robinson   8.50   .....   (130)
Scottish Heraldry Made Easy, by Johnson   9.95   .....   (973)
A Glossary of Terms Used in Heraldry, by Gough & Parker   6.50   .....   (233)

The History, Principles & Practice of Heraldry, by Hulme ..... 13.95 ..... (642)
A Dictionary of Heraldry, by Elvin ..... 18.50 ..... (130)
Guide to Printed Books and Manuscripts Relating to English &
Foreign Heraldry & Genealogy, Being a Classified Catalogue
of Works of Those Branches of Literature, by Gatfield (repr.
of 1892 ed.) [Classified bibliography of 17,500 items.] ..... 19.50 ..... (233)
Use of Coats of Arms by Americans (in NGSQ, v.50, #3) 4pp. 3.00 (616)
Heraldry for the American Genealogist, by Stephenson 2.50 (616)
Heraldry in America, by Zieber. 2nd ed. (1909) ..... 27.95 ..... (642)
Beasts in Heraldry, by Angel & Brooke-Littel [The most wide-
ly known animals in heraldry, rendered in full color by a
master.] ..... 20.00 ..... (662)
Heraldic Designs & Engravings Manuel, by Bergling (rev. ed.) ..... 14.95 ..... (954)
Heraldic Design, by Child ..... 12.50 ..... (130)
Historic Devices, Badges, and War-Cries, by Palliser (1870) ..... 22.50 ..... (233)
A Hand-Book of Mottoes, by Elvin ..... 8.50 ..... (130)
A Hand-Book of Mottoes Borne by the Nobility, Gentry, Cities,
Public Companies, etc., by Elvin (repr.of 1860 ed.)
[10,000 mottoes.] ..... 8.00 ..... (233)
A Genealogical & Heraldic History of the Colonial Gentry, by
Burke & Burke ..... 21.00 ..... (130)
The General Armory of England, Scotland, Ireland & Wales,
by Burke ..... 32.50 ..... (130)
General Armory Two. Alfred Morant's Additions & Corrections
to Burke's General Armory, by Morant ..... 21.50 ..... (130)
A Roll of Arms, by Order of the Crown of Charlemagne in Am.
[135 full page drawings of arms, with a biographical sketch
of the armiger.] ..... 15.00 ..... (368)
The College of Arms, by Godfrey & Wagner ..... 40.00 ..... (130)
An Heraldic Alphabet, by Brooke-Little ..... 8.95 ..... (680)
An Alphabetical Dictionary of Coats of Arms Belonging to
Families of Great Britain & Ireland, by Papworth ..... 30.00 ..... (130)
A Dictionary of Heraldry & Related Subjects, by Puttock ..... 11.00 ..... (130)
An Index of Hereditary English, Scottish & Irish Titles of
Honour, by Solly ..... 11.00 ..... (130)
Crozier's General Armory: A Registry of American Fami-
lies Entitled to Coat Armor, by Crozier ..... 8.50 ..... (130)
The Heraldic Journal. Recording the Armorial Bearings and
Genenealogies of American Families, by Whitmore ..... 20.00 ..... (130)
Costumes & Brasses. A Manual of Costume as Illustrated by
Monumental Brasses, by Druitt ..... 16.00 ..... (130)
Fairbairn's Book of Crests of the Families of Great Britain
& Ireland, by Fairbairn ..... 30.00 ..... (130)
The Bearing of Coat-Armour By Ladies, by Franklin ..... 8.50 ..... (130)
Shield and Crest. An Account of the Art and Science of
Heraldry, by Franklyn ..... 17.50 ..... (130)
The Armorial Who is Who, 1966-1969, by Gayre of Gayre ..... 15.00 ..... (130)
Armorial General, by Rietstap ..... 55.00 ..... (130)
Illustrations to the Rietstap's Armorial General (above),
by Rolland & Rolland ..... 75.00 ..... (130)
Supplement to Rietstap's Armorial General, by Rolland ..... 150.00 ..... (130)
Biblioteca Heraldica Magnae Britanniae, by Moule ..... 15.00 ..... (130)
New Extinct Peerage, 1884-1971. Containing Extinct, Abeyant,
Dormant & Suspended Peerages With Genealogies and Arms,
by Pine ..... 27.00 ..... (130)
Peerage and Pedigree. Studies in Peerage Law and Family
History, by Round ..... 25.00 ..... (130)
Motley Heraldry, By the Fool of Arms, by Scott-Giles ..... 4.00 ..... (130)

Scot's Heraldry, by Innes	12.50	..... (130)
An Ordinary of Arms Contained in the Public Register of All Arms and Bearings in Scotland, by Paul	13.50	..... (130)
Eight 13th-Century Rolls of Arms in French & Anglo-Norman Blazon, by Corard	15.00	..... (915)
Prominent Families in America With British Ancestry, by Burke's Peerage [Includes illustrations.]	25.00	..... (742)

Miscellaneous

The American Genealogist, ed. by McCracken. [A genealogical quarterly of national scope. Includes genealogical methods, corrections of material in print, compiled genealogies, European ancestry of American families, queries, book reviews, and varied articles.] Subscription per year:	.....	7.00 (712)
Taxation in the United States From 1789 to 1816, by Adams (repr. of 1884 ed.)	10.25	6.25 (1000)
The Quit Rent System in the American Colonies	6.00	..... (804)
Ancestor Hunting, by Watkins [Reprint of articles & queries which appeared in "The Shreveport Journal", 1963-1968]	15.00	..... (960)
The Story of the Pony Express: An Account of the Most Remarkable Mail Service Ever in Existence . . . , by Bradley	9.50	..... (233)
Colonists in Bondage: White Servitude & Convict Labor in America, 1607-1776, by Smith	.....	3.45 (875)
Ark of Empire: The American Frontier 1784-1803, by Every	.....	.75 (967)
Westward Expansion: A History of the American Frontier, by Billington	12.95	..... (734)
Forth to the Wilderness: The First American Frontier, 1754-1774, by Van Every	6.00	..... (927)
All the Western States & Territories, From the Alleghanies to the Pacific & From the Lakes to the Gulf, Containing Their History From the Earliest Times, by Barber (repr. 1867)	o. p.	.....
New Governments West of the Alleghenies Before 1780: Introduction to a Study of the Organization & Admission of New States, by Alden (repr. of 1897 ed.)	6.00	..... (629)
Our Western Border, Its Life, Combats, Adventures, Forays, Massacres, Capitivities, Scouts, Red Chiefs, Pioneer Omen, One Hundred Years Ago, Carefully Written & Compiled, by McKnight (repr. of 1876 ed.)	27.50	..... (1000)
The American Territorial System, ed. by Bloom	10.00	..... (879)
A Hidden Phase of American History. Ireland's Part in America's Struggle for Liberty, by O'Brien	15.00	..... (130)
The Cymry of '76; or, Welshmen & Their Descendants of the American Revolution, by Jones	8.50	..... (130)
Genealogy, Handmaid of History, by Cappon	.....	2.00 (616)
Brief Guide to American Genealogical Societies & Publications, by Harvey, Kapphahan & Morgan [Publication date, May 1975]....		3.40 (595)
Bibliography of American Historical Societies (The United States and the Dominion of Canada), by Griffin. 2nd ed. (1907)	35.00	..... (233)
Independent Historical Societies: An Enquiry into Their Research & Publication Functions & Their Financial Future, by Whitehill	15.00	..... (948)
Ancient & Modern Genealogies, by Tinney [Numbering Genealogically of Bible with European Royalty and Miscellaneous records.]	15.00	..... (147)
The Grand-Families of America 1776-1976, by Kolb [Origins, colonial settlements, and growth of families of America's prevelent surnames with maps & frequency tables.]	.....	6.50 (223)

A Few Titles Concerning Foreign Research

Irish and Scotch-Irish Ancestral Research, by Margaret D.
  Falley, F.A.S.G. 2 vols. Over 1100 pp.   Set: 35.00   ..... (615)
O'Kief, Coshe Mang, Slieve Lougher & Upper Blackwater in
  Ireland and photoprint of Historical & Topographical Notes on
  Buttevant, Castletownroche, Doneraile, Mallow & Vicinity,
  by Casey, et al [3,000,000 indexed names; census, military
  lists, archives, tithe lists, wills, probate, church registers
  (Catholic & non-catholic), abs. of nearly all important his-
  torical books including the Annals of the Four Masters.
  15 vols.   Set:452.00   ..... (488)
Scotch-Irish Family Research Made Simple, by Campbell 3.00 (165)
Irish Family Research Made Simple, by Collins 3.00 (165)
Ancient Ireland & Its Kings Before the Coming of the English, by
  Kearney [Chart - 32" x 42" - dates from time of Christ to
  1171 AD with High Kings & lesser kings, father to son rela-
  tionships shown, plus chronology of history during the period]..... 7.00 (537)
Key to the Parochial Registers of Scotland, by Bloxham 6.95 (702)
A Genealogical Gazetteer of Scotland, by Smith   6.45   ..... (538)
Johnston's Clan Histories [22 separate histories.]   Each clan: 2.50 (742)
Tartans of the Clans & Families of Scotland, by Innes   15.00   ..... (742)
Irish Family Names, by Grehan   10.95   ..... (742)
The Atlantic Bridge to Germany, Vol. 1, by Charles M. Hall
  [Genealogical atlas for state of Baden-Wuerttemberg, Ger.] 6.95 (539)
German Family Research Made Simple, by Collins 3.00 (165)
Palatine Pamphlet, by Hall [Sample origins of German immi-
  grants 1727-1775.] 3.95 (539)
Genealogical Research in German-Speaking Land: A Symposium
  [Articles on research in Germany, Austria, Switzerland, and
  a paper on the ancestry passport of Nazi Germany.] 2.00 (616)
Cradled in Sweden, by Johansson [Language, jurisdictions, ar-
  chives, naming systems, geography & history of Sweden.] 7.45 ..... (538)
The Danish Genealogical Helper, by Kowallis & Poulsen [Pro-
  bate, parish and other Danish records, plus many maps.] 6.00 (538)
Major Genealogical Record Sources in Denmark, by LDS 85 (845)
Genealogical Guidebook and Atlas of Norway, by Smith et al 5.95 ..... (538)
Studies in Asian Genealogy, by Palmer [A collection of orig-
  inal papers on academic uses of traditional materials and
  the preservation of records.]   12.50   ..... (702)
A Guide to Source Materials for the Study of Barbados History,
  1627-1834, by Handler   12.50   ..... (757)
Canadian-American Query Exchange [To help searchers who
  have lost Canadian ancestors (and Canadians searching in
  the U.S.) get together, along with some general articles.]
  Four issues/yr.;   Subscription/yr: 6.00 (224)
Acadia & Nova Scotia, by Akins   17.50   ..... (580)
1770 Census of Nova Scotia, by Richard 3.50 (857)
Major Genealogical Sources for Canada, Quebec, & Acadia 85 (845)
Pre-1858 English Probate Jurisdictions for Counties (or
  Shires) of England, by The Genealogical Society-LDS Each: ..... .85 (845)
[Note: An extensive list of research papers has been published
by the Genealogical Society (LDS). Among these are papers on
sources in England, Wales, Ireland, Scotland, Isle of Man, New
Zealand, Australia, Samoa, Germany, Switzerland, Netherlands,
Austria, Hungary, Norway, Iceland, Sweden, Finland, Denmark,
France, Italy, Guatemala, Mexico, Japan, Taiwan, & the United
States. Each research paper sells for 85¢. A complete list of
the titles which are available will be sent free upon request. En-
close a self-addressed stamped envelope, please.]   .....   free (845)

Research Sources By Locality

Alabama

STATEWIDE REFERENCES

	Cloth	Paper	
Southern Genealogist's Exchange (A genealogical quarterly covering several southern states), Ed., A.C. Shaw. Subscription:	.....	$ 8.50	(838)
Reminiscences of Public Men in Alabama, by Wm. Garrett	$30.00	.....	(663)
Alabama: Her History, Resources, War Record, and Public Men From 1540 to 1872, by Willis Brewer	27.00	.....	(663)
History of Alabama and Incidentally of Georgia and Mississippi, by Albert J. Pickett	27.00	.....	(663)
History of Alabama and Incidentally of Georgia and Mississippi, From the Earliest Period, by A.J. Pickett (repr. of 1851 ed.)	35.00	.....	(629)
Formative Period in Alabama, 1815-1828	7.50	.....	(788)
Early Settlers of Alabama With Notes & Genealogies by Elizabeth S. B. Stubbs, by James E. Saunders	15.00	.....	(130)
Alabama Portraits Prior to 1870, by Colonial Dames of Alabama	.....	.....	(672)
Letters From Alabama, 1817-1822, by Anne N. Royall	7.50	.....	(788)

In process:

	Cloth	Paper	
The Journals of Thomas Hubbard Hobbs, 1840-1862 [refers to hundreds of persons in Alabama and the Southeast] 1975	.....	.....	(788)
Alabama Settlers, 1780-1813 [Census, land grant, church, brand records of Spanish Mobile District], by J.D.L. Holmes. 1975	.....	.....	(483)

Research Aids

	Cloth	Paper	
Alabama: Its Development & Records (in National Genealogical Society Quarterly, Vol. 57, No. 1) 12pp.	.....	.....	(616)
Historical Records Survey: Check List of Alabama Imprints, 1807-1840 (repr. of 1939 ed.)	.....	6.00	(624)

Records

	Cloth	Paper	
Alabama Census Returns, 1820, and an Abstract of Federal Census of Alabama, 1830	10.00	.....	(130)
Alabama, An Index to the 1830 United States Census	.....	18.00	(28)
Index to Alabama Wills, 1808-1870, by Alabama Society DAR	15.00	.....	(130)
Marriage Notices From Alabama Newspapers 1846-1890	.....	10.00	(688)
Death Notices From Alabama Newspapers 1846-1890	.....	20.00	(688)
About People . . . [Newspaper notices other than deaths and marriages from 1846-1890] by Helen S. Foley	.....	.....	(688)

Military

	Cloth	Paper	
Index to Compiled Service Records of Alabama Units in the Creek War, by Achee & Wright. 2 volume set	.....	12.00	(825)
Index for Compiled Service Records of Alabama Units in Florida War [Indian War fought in late 1830's], Achee & Wright	.....	7.50	(825)

Religious

	Cloth	Paper	
Some Early Alabama Churches, by Mabel P. Wilson	$10.00	5.00	(778)

BARBOUR COUNTY

First Marriage Records, 1838-1849, by Helen S. Foley	.....	5.00	(688)
Marriage Records, 1850-1860, by Helen S. Foley	.....	5.50	(688)
Marriage Records, 1860-1869, by Helen S. Foley	.....	5.00	(688)
Abstracts of Wills & Estates, Vol. I (1835-1847), by Foley	.....	5.00	(688)
Abstracts of Wills & Estates, Vol. II (1847-1851), by Foley	.....	6.50	(688)

COOSA COUNTY

Horse & Buggy Days on Hatchet Creek, by Mitchell B. Garrett	7.50	.....	(788)
Index of the History of Coosa County by Rev. George E. Brewer	.....	10.00	(461)

ESCAMBIA COUNTY

Headstones & Heritages [Compilation of headstones in 106 cemeteries of Escambia Co.; with added genealogical information]	17.50	.....	(494)

HENRY COUNTY

1840 Census Record, by Courtney & Gerlene York	.....	3.50	(497)
The War Between the Union & the Confederacy [A roster of every soldier of the 15th Alabama Infantry, by William C. Oates	20.00	.....	(848)

JEFFERSON COUNTY

A History of the Pioneer Settlement of Roupes Valley, by Walker	.....	.....	(768)
Early Days in Birmingham, by Pioneers Club of Birmingham	5.95	2.95	(763)
1840 Federal Census, by Courtney & Gerlene York	.....	3.50	(497)

MADISON COUNTY

Historic Huntsville: 1804 to 1870, by Edward C. Betts	.....	.....	(763)
Orphans Court Minutes, 1810-1817 [Guardianships, wills, estate settlements, etc.], by Dorothy Scott Johnson	.....	5.00	(159)
Cemeteries, Vol. I [Covers west half of county - 122 cemeteries]	.....	15.00	(159)

MARSHALL COUNTY

Marriage Records, 1836-1848, Vol. I, by Christine P. Jones	.....	10.00	(953)

MOBILE COUNTY

1837 & 1839 Mobile City Directory	.....	10.50	(511)
1842 Mobile City Directory	.....	5.50	(511)
Names of Persons in Missing Files in Probate Court, Nov. 1889	.....	2.00	(511)
Bay & Bayou Burials, Vol. I [Cemetery listings-south Mobile Co.]	.....	12.50	(511)
Bay & Bayou Burials, Vol. II [Listings of western Mobile Co.]	.....	12.50	(511)
Burial Records, Mobile, Alabama — 1857-1870	.....	5.00	(666)

MONTGOMERY COUNTY

Marriage Records, 1817-1850, by Pauline Jones Gandrud	.....	13.00	(855)

ST. CLAIR COUNTY

Genealogical Notes, by Mildred S. Wright, C.R.S. [Marriage Bk. 1855-64; CSA Veterans; 8 old cemetery inventories]	.....	7.95	(431)

WASHINGTON COUNTY

	Cloth	Paper	
Early Marriages 1826-1873 & Early Deeds 1818-1838	......	10.50	(511)

Arizona

STATEWIDE REFERENCES

Arizona: A Student's Guide to Localized History, by Pare 1.50 (762)
Index to the 1880 Census of the Territory of Arizona — 4 rolls of Microfilm: 55.00 (1002)

COCHISE COUNTY

The Last Chance: Tombstone's Early Years, by John Myers 1.75 (760)

MARICOPA COUNTY

One Hundred Yesterdays [Stories of early-day Mesa & neigh-
  boring towns] by W. Earl Merrill   8.00 ..... (390)
One Hundred Echoes From Mesa's Past [More accounts of local
  happenings & people] by W. Earl Merrill] 1975   8.00 ..... (390)

PIMA COUNTY

Spanish Colonial Tucson, by Henry F. Dobyns. 1975 .... (792)

Arkansas

STATEWIDE REFERENCES

Pioneers and Makers of Arkansas, by Josiah H. Shinn   12.50 ..... (130)
The Arkansas Waterway 1817-1971: People, Places, Events in
  the Valley, by Ruth B. Mapes   8.25 ..... (454)
History of the Ozarks [Accurate information on many people in
  Ozark Mts., which includes Arkansas], by Eunice Pennington   5.00   2.00 (733)
Biographical Index to Centennial History of Arkansas by Herndon 2.00 (324)
Index to Biographical & Historical Memoirs of Ark., by Goodspeed 20.00 (324)
Index to Biog. & Hist. Memoirs of Central Ark., by Goodspeed 3.00 (324)
Index to Biog. & Hist. Memoirs of West Ark. & Conway Co. 3.00 (324)
Index to Biog. & Hist. Memoirs of South Ark., by Goodspeed 5.00 (324)
Index to Biog. & Hist. Memoirs of NW Ark., by Goodspeed 5.00 (324)
Index to Biog. & Hist. Memoirs of NE Ark., by Goodspeed 5.00 (324)
Index to Biog. & Hist. Memoirs of Eastern Ark., by Goodspeed 5.00 (324)

Research Aids

Historical Records Survey: Check List of Arkansas Imprints,
  1821-1876   .....   8.50 (624)
Survey of the County Records of Arkansas, by James Morgan 1.00 (706)

Records

1830 Federal Census of Arkansas Territory, by Presley 15.00 (324)
Index to the 1830 Census of Arkansas Territory, by McLane 7.50 (28)

1840 Federal Census - Indexed by county, by Mrs. L. E. Presley 20.00   (324)
Index to the 1840 Census, by Inez E. Cline & Bobbie J. McLane 10.00   (28)
Surname Index to 1850 Census, by Mrs. Leister E. Presley 20.00   (324)
1850 Mortality Schedules, by Capitola Glazner & Bobbie McLane 7.50   (28)
1860 Mortality Schedules, by Capitola Glazner & Bobbie McLane 10.00   (28)
1870 Mortality Schedules, by Capitola Glazner & Bobbie McLane 10.00   (28)
1880 Mortality Schedules, by Capitola Glazner & Bobbie McLane 15.00   (28)
Marriages & Divorces of Arkansas, 1808-1830 [From all existing
   court & newspaper records], by James Logan Morgan 5.00   (706)
Genealogical Records of Arkansas, 1804-1830 [Probate records,
   chancery records, wills, administrations, obituaries from all
   existing court and newspaper records for the period, by Morgan 10.00   (706)
Newspaper Abstracts: Arkansas Advocate, 1830-1832, by Morgan 2.00   (706)
Newspaper Abstracts: Arkansas Gazette, 1819-1822, by Morgan 2.00   (706)

Military

Arkansas Military Bounty Grants (War of 1812), by Christensen 10.00   (28)
Fort Smith: Little Gibraltar on the Arkansas, by Bears & Gibson   6.95   .....   (664)

ARKANSAS COUNTY

1830 Census - Indexed, by Mrs. L. E. Presley 1.00   (324)
1840 Census - Indexed, by Mrs. L. E. Presley 1.00   (324)
Surname List of 1850 Census, by Mrs. L. E. Presley 1.00   (324)
Probate & Chancery Records , 1819-1833, by James L. Morgan 2.50   (706)
Wills & Administrations, 1814-1819, by James L. Morgan 2.00   (706)
Wills & Administrations, 1819-1833, by James L. Morgan 3.00   (706)
Marriages, 1808-1819, by James L. Morgan 2.50   (706)
Marriages, 1839-1846, by James L. Morgan 2.50   (706)

ASHLEY COUNTY

Surname List of 1850 Census, by Mrs. L. E. Presley 1.00   (324)

BENTON COUNTY

1840 Census - Indexed, by Mrs. L. E. Presley 1.00   (324)
Surname List of 1850 Census, by Mrs. L. E. Presley 1.00   (324)
Reprint of the Biography Section of Goodspeed's 1889 Ed. - Indexed 4.00   (497)

BRADLEY COUNTY

Surname List of 1850 Census, by Mrs. L. E. Presley 1.00   (324)

CALHOUN COUNTY

Jurors, 1860-1861 (in Gen. Ref. Builders, Vol. 3, No. 4) 2pp. 1.50   (931)

CARROLL COUNTY

1840 Census - Indexed, by Mrs. L. E. Presley 1.00   (324)
Surname List of 1850 Census, by Mrs. Leister E. Presley 1.00   (324)
Reprint of Biography Section of Goodspeed's 1889 Ed. - Indexed 3.50   (497)

CHICOT COUNTY

1830 Census - Indexed, by Mrs. L. E. Presley 1.00   (324)
1840 Census - Indexed, by Mrs. L. E. Presley 1.00   (324)
Surname List of 1850 Census, by Mrs. L. E. Presley 1.00   (324)

CLARK COUNTY

1830 Census - Indexed, by Mrs. L. E. Presley	1.00	(324)
1840 Census - Indexed, by Mrs. L. E. Presley	1.00	(324)
Surname List of 1850 Census, by Mrs. L. E. Presley	1.00	(324)
Marriages, 1821-1837, by James Logan Morgan	3.00	(706)
Marriage Records, 1821-1879, by Bobbie Jones McLane	15.00	(28)

CONWAY COUNTY

1830 Census - Indexed, by Mrs. L. E. Presley	1.00	(324)
1840 Census - Indexed, by Mrs. L. E. Presley	1.00	(324)
Surname List of 1850 Census, by Mrs. L. E. Presley	1.00	(324)
Genealogical Records, 1837-1845, by James L. Morgan	3.50	(706)

CRAIGHEAD COUNTY

Craighead County Historical Quarterly - 13 vols. [Most back issues available. Contents basically historical, but many family articles. Inquiries invited.]	.....	(581)

CRAWFORD COUNTY

1830 Census - Indexed, by Mrs. L. E. Presley	1.00	(324)
1840 Census - Indexed, by Mrs. L. E. Presley	1.00	(324)
Surname List of 1850 Census, by Mrs. L. E. Presley	1.00	(324)

CRITTENDEN COUNTY

1830 Census - Indexed, by Mrs. L. E. Presley	1.00	(324)
1840 Census - Indexed, by Mrs. L. E. Presley	1.00	(324)
Surname List of 1850 Census, by Mrs. L. E. Presley	1.00	(324)
Marriage Records, Vol. A (1843-1859), by Pat Isabel Brown	3.00	(138)
Wills & Administrations, 1826-1845, by James L. Morgan	3.50	(706)

CROSS COUNTY

Wills, 1864-1869, by James L. Morgan	2.00	(706)

DALLAS COUNTY

Surname List of 1850 Census, by Mrs. L. E. Presley	1.00	(324)

DESHA COUNTY

1840 Census - Indexed, by Mrs. L. E. Presley	1.00	(324)
Surname List of 1850 Census, by Mrs. L. E. Presley	1.00	(324)

DREW COUNTY

Surname List of 1850 Census, by Mrs. L. E. Presley	1.00	(324)
Wills, 1847-1861, by James L. Morgan	2.00	(706)
Administrations & Guardianships, 1847-1852, by James Morgan	2.00	(706)

FRANKLIN COUNTY

1840 Census - Indexed, by Mrs. L. E. Presley	1.00	(324)
Surname List of 1850 Census, by Mrs. L. E. Presley	1.00	(324)

FULTON COUNTY

1850 Census, by James L. Morgan	3.00	(706)
Surname List of 1850 Census, by Mrs. Leister E. Presley	1.00	(324)

GARLAND COUNTY

Tombstone Inscriptions, Vol. I [Eastern Garland Co.]	7.50	(28)
Tombstone Inscriptions, Vol. II [Western Garland Co.]	7.50	(28)
Tombstone Inscriptions, Vol. III [City]	10.00	(28)
Tombstone Inscriptions, Vol. I, II, & III [Set of above]	20.00	(28)

GREEN COUNTY

1840 Census - Indexed, by Mrs. L. E. Presley	1.00	(324)
Surname List of 1850 Census, by Mrs. L. E. Presley	1.00	(324)
Tax Records, 1834-1840, by James L. Morgan	2.00	(706)

HEMPSTEAD COUNTY

1830 Census - Indexed, by Mrs. L. E. Presley	1.00	(324)
1840 Census - Indexed, by Mrs. L. E. Presley	1.00	(324)
1850 Census [With notes concerning 110 families], by McLane	7.50	(28)
Surname List of 1850 Census, by Mrs. L. E. Presley	1.00	(324)
1860 Census, by Capitola Glazner & Bobbie J. McLane	10.00	(28)
Marriage Records 1817-1875, by Glazner & McLane	12.50	(28)
Wills & Administrations 1820-1837, by James L. Morgan	2.50	(706)

HOT SPRING COUNTY

1830 Census - Indexed, by Mrs. L. E. Presley	1.00	(324)
1840 Census - Indexed, by Mrs. L. E. Presley	1.00	(324)
Surname Index of 1850 Census, by Mrs. L. E. Presley	1.00	(324)
Marriage Records 1825-1880, by Bobbie J. McLane	12.50	(28)
Genealogical Records 1833-1845, by James L. Morgan	3.00	(706)

INDEPENDENCE COUNTY

1830 Census - Indexed, by Mrs. L. E. Presley	1.00	(324)
1840 Census - Indexed, by Mrs. L. E. Presley	1.00	(324)
1850 Census, by James L. Morgan	7.50	(706)
Surname List of 1850 Census, by Mrs. L. E. Presley	1.00	(324)
Marriage Records 1826-1877, by M.S. Harris & B. J. McLane	15.00	(28)
Genealogical Records 1845-1850, by James L. Morgan	4.00	(706)
Inventory of Maple Springs Cemetery, by James L. Morgan	1.50	(706)
Genealogical Records of NE Arkansas 1816-1830, by J.Morgan	3.00	(706)
Genealogical Records of NE Arkansas 1830-1838, by J. Morgan	4.00	(706)
Genealogical Records of Independence County 1838-1845	3.50	(706)

IZARD COUNTY

1830 Census - Indexed, by Mrs. L. E. Presley	1.00	(324)
1840 Census - Indexed, by Mrs. L. E. Presley	1.00	(324)
1850 Census, by James L. Morgan	4.00	(706)
Surname List of 1850 Census, by Mrs. L. E. Presley	1.00	(324)

JACKSON COUNTY

1830 Census - Indexed, by Mrs. L. E. Presley	1.00	(324)
1840 Census - Indexed, by Mrs. L. E. Presley	1.00	(324)
1850 Census, by James L. Morgan	4.00	(706)
Surname List of 1850 Census, by Mrs. L. E. Presley	1.00	(324)
County Court Records I (1830-1837), by James L. Morgan	2.00	(706)
Marriage Returns 1834-1846, by James L. Morgan	2.00	(706)
Early Business Ledgers 1834-1839, by James L. Morgan	2.00	(706)
Genealogical Records of NE Arkansas 1830-1838, by J. Morgan	4.00	(706)

JEFFERSON COUNTY

1830 Census - Indexed, by Mrs. L. E. Presley	.....	1.00	(324)
1840 Census - Indexed, by Mrs. L. E. Presley	.....	1.00	(324)
1850 Census & Marriage Books A & B, by Glazner & McLane	.....	10.00	(28)
Surname List of 1850 Census, by Mrs. L. E. Presley	.....	1.00	(324)
Genealogical Records 1830-1842, by James L. Morgan	.....	4.00	(706)

JOHNSON COUNTY

1840 Census - Indexed, by Mrs. L. E. Presley	.....	1.00	(324)
Surname List of 1850 Census, by Mrs. L. E. Presley	.....	1.00	(324)

LAFAYETTE COUNTY

1830 Census - Indexed, by Mrs. L. E. Presley	.....	1.00	(324)
1840 Census - Indexed, by Mrs. L. E. Presley	.....	1.00	(324)
Surname List of 1850 Census, by Mrs. L. E. Presley	.....	1.00	(324)

LAWRENCE COUNTY

1830 Census - Indexed, by Mrs. L. E. Presley	.....	1.00	(324)
1840 Census - Indexed, by Mrs. L. E. Presley	.....	1.00	(324)
1850 Census, by James L. Morgan	.....	6.00	(706)
Surname List of 1850 Census, by Mrs. L. E. Presley	.....	1.00	(324)
Marriages 1821-1836, by James L. Morgan	.....	2.50	(706)
Genealogical Records of NE Arkansas 1816-1830, by J. Morgan	.....	3.00	(706)
Genealogical Records of NE Arkansas 1830-1838, by J. Morgan	.....	4.00	(706)
Genealogical Records of Lawrence County 1838-1845, by Morgan	.....	3.50	(706)
Wills and Administrations 1816-1834, by James L. Morgan	.....	2.00	(706)
Wills and Administrations 1845-1855, by James L. Morgan	.....	2.50	(706)

LONOKE COUNTY

Wills 1873-1880, by James L. Morgan	.....	2.00	(706)

MADISON COUNTY

1840 Census - Indexed, by Mrs. L. E. Presley	.....	1.00	(324)
Surname List of 1850 Census, by Mrs. L. E. Presley	.....	1.00	(324)

MARION COUNTY

1840 Census - Indexed, by Mrs. L. E. Presley	.....	1.00	(324)
1850 Census, by Courtney & Gerlene York	.....	5.00	(497)
Surname List of 1850 Census, by Mrs. L. E. Presley	.....	1.00	(324)

MILLER COUNTY

1830 Census - Indexed, by Mrs. L. E. Presley	.....	1.00	(324)

MISSISSIPPI COUNTY

History of Mississippi County, by Goodspeed [Reprint of 1889 edition. New comprehensive index.]	12.50	.....	(19)
1840 Census - Indexed, by Mrs. L. E. Presley	.....	1.00	(324)
Surname List of 1850 Census, by Mrs. L. E. Presley	.....	1.00	(324)
1860 Census, by Ophelia Richardson Wade	.....	5.00	(19)
Vital Records [Land entry book beg. 1826, index to will books, postoffice history, complete 1840 census, 1850 & 1860 slave records, mortality schedules.], by Mrs. Jeff Wade, Jr.	.....	6.00	(19)
Wills and Administrations 1862-1866, by James L. Morgan	.....	2.00	(706)

MISSISSIPPI COUNTY (cont.)

The Heritage of Blytheville [A collection of church, census, cemetery, Bible and post office records. Memoirs of Bert Richardson. Extracts from Goodspeed, & newspapers.] by O. R. Wade 10.00 (19)
Blytheville Cemetery Inscriptions, by Ophelia R. Wade 10.00 (19)

MONROE COUNTY

1830 Census - Indexed, by Mrs. L. E. Presley	.....	1.00 (324)
1840 Census - Indexed, by Mrs. L. E. Presley	.....	1.00 (324)
Surname List of 1850 Census, by Mrs. L. E. Presley	.....	1.00 (324)
Genealogical Records 1830-1852, by James L. Morgan	.....	6.00 (706)

MONTGOMERY COUNTY

Surname List of 1850 Census, by Mrs. L. E. Presley 1.00 (324)

NEWTON COUNTY

Surname List of 1850 Census, by Mrs. L. E. Presley 1.00 (324)

PERRY COUNTY

1850 Census, by Courtney & Gerlene York	.....	5.00 (497)
Surname List of 1850 Census, by Mrs. L. E. Presley	.....	1.00 (324)

PHILLIPS COUNTY

1830 Census - Indexed, by Mrs. L. E. Presley	.....	1.00 (324)
1840 Census - Indexed, by Mrs. L. E. Presley	.....	1.00 (324)
Surname List of 1850 Census, by Mrs. L. E. Presley	.....	1.00 (324)
Genealogical Records 1821-1833, by James L. Morgan	.....	4.00 (706)

PIKE COUNTY

1840 Census - Indexed, by Mrs. L. E. Presley	.....	1.00 (324)
1850 Census, by Courtney & Gerlene York	.....	5.00 (497)
Surname List of 1850 Census, by Mrs. L. E. Presley	.....	1.00 (324)
Reprint of biography section of Goodspeed's 1889 ed. - Indexed	.....	4.00 (497)

POINSETT COUNTY

1840 Census - Indexed, by Mrs. L. E. Presley	.....	1.00 (324)
1850 Census, by Courtney & Gerlene York	.....	5.00 (497)
Surname List of 1850 Census, by Mrs. L. E. Presley	.....	1.00 (324)
Wills 1875-1892, by James L. Morgan	.....	2.00 (706)

POLK COUNTY

1850 Census, by Courtney & Gerlene York	.....	5.00 (497)
Surname List of 1850 Census, by Mrs. L. E. Presley	.....	1.00 (324)

POPE COUNTY

1830 Census - Indexed, by Mrs. L. E. Presley	.....	1.00 (324)
1840 Census - Indexed, by Mrs. L. E. Presley	.....	1.00 (324)
1850 Census & Marriage Book A, by Glazner & McLane	.....	7.50 (28)
Surname List of 1850 Census, by Mrs. L. E. Presley	.....	1.00 (324)
1860 Census & Marriage Books B & C, by Glazner & McLane	.....	10.00 (28)
Marriage Records 1860-1892, by Glazner & McLane	.....	12.50 (28)

PRAIRIE COUNTY

1850 Census, by Courtney & Gerlene York	..... 5.00	(497)
Surname List of 1850 Census, by Mrs. L. E. Presley	..... 1.00	(324)
Wills 1855-1860, by James L. Morgan	..... 2.00	(706)

PULASKI COUNTY

1830 Census - Indexed, Mrs. L. E. Presley	..... 1.00	(324)
1840 Census - Indexed, Mrs. L. E. Presley	..... 1.00	(324)
Surname List of 1850 Census, by Mrs. L. E. Presley	..... 1.00	(324)
Wills 1820-1841, by James L. Morgan	..... 2.50	(706)
Genealogical Records 1839-1845, by James L. Morgan	..... 4.00	(706)

RANDOLPH COUNTY

1840 Census - Indexed, by Mrs. L. E. Presley	..... 1.00	(324)
1850 Census - Indexed, by Barbara Ferree Barden	..... 4.00	(800)
Surname List of 1850 Census, by Mrs. L. E. Presley	..... 1.00	(324)
Wills and Administrations 1838-1852, by James L. Morgan	..... 5.00	(706)
Genealogical Records of NE Arkansas 1830-1838, by J. L. Morgan	4.00	(706)

ST. FRANCIS COUNTY

1830 Census - Indexed, by Mrs. L. E. Presley	..... 1.00	(324)
1840 Census - Indexed, by Mrs. L. E. Presley	..... 1.00	(324)
Surname List of 1850 Census, by Mrs. L. E. Presley	..... 1.00	(324)
Wills 1865-1881, by James L. Morgan	..... 2.50	(706)

SALINE COUNTY

1840 Census - Indexed, by Mrs. L. E. Presley	..... 1.00	(324)
Surname List of 1850 Census, by Mrs. L. E. Presley	..... 1.00	(324)
Genealogical Records 1836-1845, by James L. Morgan	..... 4.00	(706)

SCOTT COUNTY

1840 Census - Indexed, by Mrs. L. E. Presley	..... 1.00	(324)
Surname List of 1850 Census, by Mrs. L. E. Presley	..... 1.00	(324)

SEARCY COUNTY

1840 Census - Indexed, by Mrs. L. E. Presley	..... 1.00	(324)
Surname List of 1850 Census, by Mrs. L. E. Presley	..... 1.00	(324)

SEVIER COUNTY

1830 Census - Indexed, by Mrs. L. E. Presley	..... 1.00	(324)
1840 Census - Indexed, by Mrs. L. E. Presley	..... 1.00	(324)
1850 Census & Available Marriage Records Thru 1852	..... 7.50	(28)
Surname List of 1850 Census, by L. E. Presley	..... 1.00	(324)
1860 Census & Marriage Book Two, by Glazner & McLane	..... 10.00	(28)

SHARP COUNTY

Genealogical Records 1868-1880, by James L. Morgan	..... 5.00	(706)

UNION COUNTY

1830 Census - Indexed, by Mrs. L. E. Presley	..... 1.00	(324)
1840 Census - Indexed, by Mrs. L. E. Presley	..... 1.00	(324)
Surname List of 1850 Census, by Mrs. L. E. Presley	..... 1.00	(324)

VAN BUREN COUNTY

1840 Census - Indexed, by Mrs. L. E. Presley	.....	1.00	(324)
Surname List of 1850 Census, by Mrs. L. E. Presley	.....	1.00	(324)

WASHINGTON COUNTY

1830 Census - Indexed, by Mrs. L. E. Presley	.....	1.00	(324)
1840 Census - Indexed, by Mrs. L. E. Presley	.....	1.00	(324)
Surname List of 1850 Census, by Mrs. L. E. Presley	.....	1.00	(324)

WHITE COUNTY

1840 Census - Indexed, by Mrs. L. E. Presley	.....	1.00	(324)
1850 Census - Indexed, by Mrs. L. E. Presley	.....	1.00	(324)
Genealogical Records of NE Arkansas 1830-1838, by J. Morgan	.....	4.00	(706)
Genealogical Records of White County 1838-1855, by J. Morgan	.....	3.50	(706)

WOODRUFF COUNTY

Wills 1865-1873, by James L. Morgan	.....	2.00	(706)

YELL COUNTY

Surname List of 1850 Census, by Mrs. L. E. Presley	.....	1.00	(324)

California

STATEWIDE REFERENCES

History of California, by Bancroft, 7 vols.	150.00	.....	(741)
Frontier Settlement in Mexican California: The Hijar - Padres Colony & Its Origins, 1769-1835, by Hutchinson	12.50	.....	(764)
The History of California: The Spanish Period, by Chapman	29.50	.....	(899)
Early Emigration to California, by Packard (1971)	.....	1.50	(829)
Bigler's Chronicle of the West: The Conquest of California, Discovery of Gold, & Mormon Settlement as Reflected in Henry William Bigler's Diaries, by Gudde	5.95	.....	(831)
Admission of the 31st State by the 31st Congress: Annotated Bibliography of Speeches, by Robert G. Cowan	6.50	.....	(442)

Goldrush

Diary of a Forty-Niner, by Canfield (repr. of 1906 ed.)	10.50	.....	(854)
California As it is & As it May Be: Or a Guide to the Gold Region, by Wierzbicki (repr. of 1849 ed.)	14.50	.....	(625)
The California Gold Rush Diary of a German Sailor, Jackson W. Turrentine, by A. Windeler	7.50	.....	(892)
The Gold Hunters: A First-Hand Picture of Life in California Mining Camps in the Early Fifties, by Borthwick	17.50	.....	(233)
Journal of the Overland Route to California & the Gold Mines, by Aldrich (repr. of 1851 ed.)	.....	4.55	(546)
Sea Routes to the Goldfields, by Lewis	.....	1.25	(947)
Gold Rush Diary, Being the Journal of Elisha D. Perkings on the Overland Trail in the Spring & Summer of 1849, by Perkins	10.00	.....	(831)
Foreigners in the California Goldrush, by Sylva	.....	7.00	(802)
Echoes of the Past: An Account of the First Emigrant Train to California, Fremont in the Conquest of California, the Discovery of Gold & Early Reminiscences, by Bidwell (repr.)	7.00	.....	(629)

Research Aids

California: A Student's Guide to Local History	.....	1.50	(762)
A Bibliography of the History of California, 1510-1930, 4 vols. in 1, by Robert E. & Robert G. Cowan	25.00	.....	(442)
The First Hundred Years: Bibliography of California History Society Publications 1871-1971, by Evans	10.00	.....	(842)
Who's Who in California, 10th Edition, by Dr. Alice Catt Armstrong [20% discount to libraries]	45.00	.....	(299)

Records

Index to 1850 Census of California, by Alan P. Bowman	25.00	.....	(130)
California Wagon Train Lists, Vol. I, by Rasmussen	10.25	.....	(789)
California Pioneer Register and Index, 1542-1848, by Bancroft	11.00	.....	(130)
Northern California Marriages, 1850-1860 (in National Genealogical Quarterly, Vol. 54, Nos. 2, 3 & 4) 79pp. total.		Each: 3.00	(616)

ALAMEDA COUNTY

The History of Alameda County, by Wood (repr. of 1883 ed.)	22.50	.....	(824)

FRESNO COUNTY

History of Fresno Calif., by Elliott & Co. (repr. of 1882 ed.)	22.50	20.00	(546)

KERN COUNTY

A California Middle Border: The Kern River County, 1772-1880 [Approx. 700 pioneers mentioned, with references to their roles in development of the county], by Wm. H. Boyd, Ph.D.	8.00	.....	(278)

LOS ANGELES COUNTY

Los Angeles: A Student's Guide to Local History	.....	1.50	(762)
Pomona Cemeteries, Vol. I [Primarily contains burial and tombstone records for Pomona Cemetery (on Franklin Ave., Pomona) 1877 to 1910. Some records for Palomares & Spadra Cem.]	.....	7.50	(177)
Pomona Cemeteries, Vol. II [Primarily contains burial and tombstone records for Pomona Cemetery, 1911-1925. Some additional records for Spadra Cem.] by Pomona Valley Gen. Soc.	.....	7.50	(177)
Some Early Southern California Burials [Earliest burials to 1920 in Long Beach Muncipal, Wilmington, & Sunnyside Cemeteries]	.....	5.25	(472)
First Los Angeles City & County Directory, 1872 (repr.)	17.50	.....	(841)
History of Los Angeles Co. & Orange Co., by Thompson & Vest	17.50	.....	(892)

MARIN COUNTY

History of Marin County, by Munro-Fraser (repr. of 1880 ed.) [Land grants, early history, names of pioneers, biographical sketches. Separate history of townships.]	25.40	.....	(228)

MONTEREY COUNTY

Monterey: Adobe Capitol, by Van Nostrand	14.95	.....	(842)
Monterey: The Presence of the Past, by Fink	9.95	.....	(798)

NEVADA COUNTY

History of Nevada County, by Wells (repr. of 1880 ed.)	20.00	.....	(892)

SACRAMENTO COUNTY

The Sacramento Valley: A Student's Guide to Local History	.....	1.50	(762)

SAN DIEGO COUNTY

San Diego Leaves & Saplings [A quarterly published by the San Diego Genealogical Society which contains records of the area, etc. Received by members as part of their membership privilege. There is an annual index.] Yearly subscription: 7.50 (619)

SAN JOAQUIN COUNTY

Marriage Records, Vol. I (1850-1865) [Includes bride's index] 5.00 (551)
Marriage Records, Vol. II (1866-1884) [Includes bride's index] 5.00 (551)
Index to Probate Records 1850-1900, by San Joaquin Gen. Soc. 5.00 (551)
Old Cemeteries, Vol. I [Alphabetical listings for Rural Cemetery, Stockton, California to 1920], by San Joaquin Gen. Soc. 5.00 (551)
Old Cemeteries, Vol. III [Small family, county & private cemeteries, mausoleums & crematoriums to 1920] 5.00 (551)

SONOMA COUNTY

History of Sonoma County, by Munro-Fraser (repr. of 1880 ed.) [Full record of Mexican grants; early history; names of pioneers; biographical sketches; history of townships, etc.] 25.40 ..... (228)

TULARE COUNTY

Land of the Tules: The Early Years of Tulare County, by Mitchell 4.95 (809)

Colorado

STATEWIDE REFERENCES

Experiments in Colorado Colonization: 1869-1872, by Willard 20.00 ..... (899)
The Mines of Colorado, by Hollister (repr. of 1867 ed.) 21.00 ..... (629)
Colorado Gold Rush: Contemporary Letters & Reports 1858-59' 20.00 ..... (909)

Research Aids

Colorado: A Student's Guide to Local History 1.50 (762)
Colorado Area Key [A comprehensive guide to genealogical records in Colorado], by Florence Clint 6.00 (552)
Index to Colorado Genealogist - Vols. I - X (1939-1949) [A publication of the Colorado Genealogical Society] 10.00 (464)
Index to Colorado Genealogist - Vols. XI - XX (1950-1959) 12.50 (464)

BOULDER COUNTY

Area Key [A comprehensive guide to the genealogical records] 6.00 (552)

CLEAR CREEK COUNTY

My Rocky Mountain Valley, by James G. Rogers (1968) 8.95 ..... (753)

FREMONT COUNTY

From Trappers to Tourists: Fremont County 1830-1950 9.50 6.95 (747)

LARIMER COUNTY

Marriage Bk. A (in Gen. Ref. Builder, Vol. 8, No. 4) 10pp. 2.00 (931)

PUEBLO COUNTY

Some Genealogical Sources in Pueblo Co., by Barbara J. Brown 3.00 (282)

Connecticut

STATEWIDE REFERENCES

Complete History of Connecticut, Civil & Ecclesiastical, From the
Immigration of its First Planters, From England in the Year
1630 to 1764, by Trumbull (repr. of 1818 ed.) 2 vols. in 1   65.00   .....   (629)
A General History of Connecticut, From its First Settlement Under
George Fenwick to its Latest Period of Amity with Great Brit-
tain Prior to the Revolution, by Peters (repr. of 1781 ed.)   11.00   .....   (854)
Connecticut in Transition: 1775-1818 (rev. ed.), by Purcell   10.00   .....   (858)
Connecticut Town Origins, by Sellers [Names boundaries, histor-
ies and founding families of all 169 Connecticut towns.] 2.95 (812)
Genealogical Notes, or Contributions to the Family History of the
First Settlers of Connecticut & Massachusetts, by Goodwin   13.50   .....   (130)
The Refugees of 1776 From Long Island to Connecticut, by Mather   30.00   .....   (130)
A Brief History of the Pequot War: Especially of the Taking of
Their Fort at Mistick in Conn. in 1637, by Mason (repr. 1736) 3.55 (546)

Records

1790 Census, by U.S. Census Bureau   10.00   .....   (663)
1790 Census, by U.S. Census Bureau   12.50   .....   (130)
Index to 1800 Census, by Lowell Volkel [3 vols. in 1]   20.00   .....   (752)
A Catalogue of the Names of the First Puritan Settlers of the
Colony of Connecticut; With the Time of Their Arrivals in
the Colony, etc., by Hinman   12.50   .....   (130)

FAIRFIELD COUNTY

Index to 1800 Census of Fairfield & Hartford Cos., by Volkel 5.00 (752)
Stamford Revolutionary War Damage Claims 5.00 (812)
They Face the Rising Sun, by Beach [Unity Burial Ground in Trum-
bull, Conn., illustrations & index]   6.00   .....   (812)

HARTFORD COUNTY

Index to 1800 Census of Fairfield & Hartford Cos., by Volkel 5.00 (752)
The Private Journal of Abraham Joseph Warner [He entered Trinity
College in Hartford in 1838. Comments on people he met.]   11.00   .....   (83)

LITCHFIELD COUNTY

Index to 1800 Census of Litchfield, New Haven, Tolland & Windham Cos, Conn., by Lowell Volkel 6.00 (752)

MIDDLESEX COUNTY

Index to 1800 Census of Middlesex & New London Cos., by Volkel 5.00 (752)

NEW HAVEN COUNTY

Index to 1800 Census of Litchfield, New Haven, Tolland & Windham Cos, Conn, by Lowell Volkel 6.00 (752)
Families of Ancient New Haven, by Jacobus [With cross-index]
9 vols. in 3.   85.00   .....   (130)
New Haven Town Records, Vol. 3 (1684-1769) 15.50 (932)
1786: Centenary of Hamden, Conn., by Hamden town (repr. 1886)   22.50   20.00 (546)

NEW HAVEN COUNTY (cont.)

Madison's Heritage, edited by Philip S. Platt [A collection of historical sketches about people, places and events in Madison's long history dating back 325 years when it was East Guilford.]   4.50   ..... (577)

The Private Journal of Abraham Joseph Warner, by Col. Herbert B. Enderton [Journal covers period from 1838 through Civil War. He was in New Haven County part of this time.]   11.00   ..... (83)

NEW LONDON COUNTY

Index to 1800 Census of Middlesex & New London Cos., by Volkel 5.00 (752)

Lyme Records 1678-1730, by Burr   17.50   ..... (812)

A History of the Town of Stonington From its First Settlement in 1649 to 1900, by Wheeler (1966)   25.00   ..... (866)

TOLLAND COUNTY

Index to 1800 Census of Litchfield, New Haven, Tolland & Windham Cos., by Lowell Volkel 6.00 (752)

WINDHAM COUNTY

Index to 1800 Census of Litchfield, New Haven, Tolland & Windham Cos., by Lowell Volkel 6.00 (752)

The Old Fulling Mill of Pomfret, Connecticut, by Olive Wetherbee [Sixty years of trade - beginning in 1786.- This is an authentic account taken from day book & ledgers. Names over 1,000 customers, and their odd payments: a pig, taters, etc.]   10.00   ..... (422)

Delaware

STATEWIDE REFERENCES

The Maryland & Delaware Genealogist, edited by Raymond B. Clark, Jr. [A genealogical quarterly containing transcriptions of primary material, queries, etc. Annual index. Subscription per year: 6.00 (212)

A History of the Original Settlements of the Delaware From Its Discovery . . . to the Colonization Under Penn, by Ferris (repr.)   12.50   ..... (637)

English on the Delaware: 1610-1682, by Weslager (1967)   7.50   ..... (950)

Dutch Explorers, Traders & Settlers in the Delaware Valley, by Weslager (1964)   10.00   ..... (989)

The Gallant Men of the Delaware River Forst - 1777, by Mackey   5.95   ..... (926)

Narratives of Early Pennsylvania, West New Jersey, & Delaware 1630-1707, by Myers [Original narratives] (repr. of 1912 ed.)   5.75   ..... (643)

The Swedish Settlements on the Delaware, 1638-1664, by Johnson   27.50   ..... (130)

[Swedish] Delaware Settlers, 1693 (in National Genealogical Society Quarterly, Vol. 53, No. 3) 2pp. 3.00 (616)

Illustrated Map of Delaware Historic Sites, by Good 3.00 (980)

An Outline of the Maryland Boundary Disputes & Related Events, by Charles Morrison [Outlines the origin, development, and culmination of the dispute between the Calverts and the Penns over the Province of Delaware] 3.00 (325)

The Delaware Loyalists, by Hancock (repr. of 1940 ed.)   9.00   ..... (854)

Research Aids

Delaware: A Student's Guide to Local History 1.50 (762)

Military

Revolutionary Soldiers of Delaware, by Whitely 2.25 (900)
Delaware Continentals, by Ward 15.50 ..... (900)

Records

Reconstructed 1790 Census of Delaware, by de Valinger [Re-
places the missing 1790 census, using tax lists.] 4.25 (616)
Delaware Public Archives - 5 vols. (repr. of 1911 ed.) set: 187.50 ..... (630)
Records of Holy Trinity (Old Swedes) Church, 1697-1810,
translated by Burr 15.50 ..... (900)

KENT COUNTY

Marriages & Births in Deed Books (in Md. & Del. Genealogist,
Vol. 10/11, No.) 5pp. 2.00 (212)

NEW CASTLE COUNTY

Calendar of Wills, 1682-1800, by Colonial Dames of Delaware 10.00 ..... (130)

District of Columbia

STATEWIDE REFERENCES

L'Enfant & Washington 1791-1792: Published & Unpublished Documents Brought Together for First Time, by Kite (repr. 1929) 8.00 ..... (629)

Research Aids

Records of the Columbia Historical Society of Wash. D.C., ed.
by Rosenberger 20.00 ..... (897)
Lest We Forget: A Guide to Genealogical Research in the Nations's Capital, by June Andrew Babbel [Step by step direc-
tions on research in the National Archives, Library of Congress, D.A.R. Library, National Genealogical Society, &
other places for research in the area.] This book is currently being revised, and price of new edition not yet set. .... (783)
Guide to the National Archives of the United States, by the
National Archives & Records Service 12.30 ..... (401)
A Guide to Genealogical Records in the National Archives 1.30 (401)

Records

Marriages & Deaths, National Intelligencer, Wash. D.C.,
1800-1820 [This newspaper contains information, not only
of D.C., but all parts of America & foreign countries.] 15.75 ..... (616)
Original Patentees of Land at Wash. Prior to 1700, by Gahn 8.50 ..... (130)

Florida

STATEWIDE REFERENCES

Historical Collections of Louisiana & Florida: Including Transla-
tions of Original Manuscripts Relating to their Discovery & Set-
tlement, by French (repr. of 1869 ed.) 2 vols. Each: 18.50 ..... (630)
Loyalists in East Fla, 1774-1785, by Fla. St. Hist. Soc. - Vol. I 17.50 15.00 (546)
Loyalists in East Fla, 1774-1785, by Fla. St. Hist. Soc. - Vol. II 27.50 25.00 (546)
Historical Sketches of Colonial Fla., by Campbell (repr. of 1892) 12.00 ..... (819)

East Florida as a British Province, 1763-1784, by Mowat (1943)   7.50   .....   (819)

British West Florida, 1763-1783, by Johnson (repr. of 1943 ed.)   8.00   .....   (823)

"Re-Discover Florida", by Hampton Dunn [Florida landmarks, historical sites, & contemporary offbeat attractions.]   5.95   2.95   (470)

Florida Sketches, by Hampton Dunn [Vignettes of Florida historical landmarks, sites, & contemporary offbeat attractions.]   5.95   (470)

"Accent Florida", by Hampton Dunn [Collection of author's columns on Florida history from the Tampa Tribune & Tampa Times] 2.50   (470)

Religious

Catholic Hist. of Ala. & the Floridas, by Carroll (repr. 1908)   11.75   .....   (630)

Cross in the Sand: The Early Catholic Church in Florida, 1613-1870, by Gannon   7.50   3.45   (819)

Records

Colonial Records of Spanish Florida; Letters & Reports of Governors and Secular Person, by Connor (1925-1930) 2v.   Set: 55.00   .....   (630)

United States Territorial Papers, by U.S. Govt. 26v. (repr.) Territory of Florida: Vol. 22, 1821-1824; Vol. 23, 1824-1828; Vol. 24, 1828-1834; Vol. 25, 1834-1839.   Each: 57.50   .....   (630)

Index to 1830 Census of Florida, by Aurora C. Shaw 5.00   (838)

Index to 1840 Census of Florida, by Mallon & Taylor 5.50   (511)

Index to 1840 Census of Florida, by Aurora C. Shaw 5.00   (838)

HILLSBOROUGH COUNTY

"Yesterday's Tampa", by Hampton Dunn [Pictorial history with capsule narrative.]   7.95   .....   (470)

LEON COUNTY

"Yesterday's Tallahassee", by Hampton Dunn [Pictorial history with narrative.]   7.95   .....   (470)

PINELLAS COUNTY

"Yesterday's St. Petersburg", by Hampton Dunn [Pictorial history of St.Petersburg & surrounding communities with narrative.]   7.95   .....   (470)

"Yesterday's Clearwater", by Hampton Dunn [Pictorial history of Clearwater & surrounding upper Pineallas communities.]   8.95   .....   (470)

Georgia

STATEWIDE REFERENCES

Georgia Pioneers Genealogical Magazine, edited by Mary Carter [Genealogical quarterly. Approx. 50 pages per issue. Single issues: $2.50. Subscription per year: 9.50   (427)

Atlas for Georgia History, by Bonner [Over 30 maps showing original counties, Indian land cessions, history of counties, etc.] 5.00   (688)

Men of Mark in Georgia, Vol. 1 [Prior to 1800] Index to all vols.   21.00   .....   (663)

Men of Mark in Georgia, Vol. 2 [1800 to Civil War]   "   "   21.00   .....   (663)

Men of Mark in Georgia, Vol. 3 [During Civil War]   "   "   24.00   .....   (663)

Men of Mark in Georgia, Vol. 4, 5, 6, 7 [Civil War to 1912] [A new consolidated index to all vols. is in each vol.]   Each: 21.00   .....   (663)

The History of Georgia, by C.C. Jones. 2 vols.   Each: 17.50   .....   (663)

The Dead Towns of Georgia, by C. C. Jones, Jr.   15.00   .....   (663)

Biographical Sketches of the Delegates From Georgia to the Continental Congress, by C. C. Jones   12.00   .....   (663)

. . . .

Savannah River Plantations, by Granger	18.00	.....	(663)
Georgia, Comprising Sketches of Counties, Towns, Events, Institutions, and Persons, Arranged in Cyclopedic Form, by Candler & Evans. 4 vols. [Vol. 1 (A-E); Vol. 2 (F-N); Vol. 3 (O-Z); Vol. 4 (Supplemental vol. with biog. sketches)] Each:	27.00	.....	(663)
History of Alabama, & Incidentally of Georgia & Mississippi, From the Earliest Period, by Pickett (repr. of 1851 ed.)	35.00	.....	(629)
Debatable Land: A Sketch of the Anglo-Spanish Contest for the Georgia Country, by Bolton & Ross (repr. of 1925 ed.)	7.00	.....	(988)
Sketches of Some of the First Settlers of Upper Georgia, of the Cherokees, and the Author, by Gilmer	13.50	.....	(130)
Historic Georgia Families, by Rigsby	13.50	.....	(130)
The Story of Georgia & the Georgia People, 1732 to 1860, by Smith	18.50	.....	(130)
Georgia Plan, 1732-1752, by Taylor	6.50	.....	(831)
Georgia's Last Frontier, by Bonner	7.50	.....	(917)
Georgia: A Short History (rev. ed.), by Coulter	8.95	.....	(650)
Georgia History in Outline, by Coleman	.....	1.95	(917)
Georgia Speculation Unveiled, by Bishop (repr. of 1798 ed.)	.....	3.55	(546)
The Golden Isles of Georgia, by Lovell [Hist. of Golden Isles off Georgia coast, plus data on prominent families.]	10.00	.....	(287)

Research Aids

Genealogical Research in Georgia, by Ga. Dept. of Ar. & Hist.	.....	free	(914)
Primer for Georgia Genealogical Research, by B. Hathaway	.....	4.35	(562)
Georgia: A Student's Guide to Local History	.....	1.50	(762)
Tracing Family Trees in Eleven States [one of which is Ga.]	.....	5.50	(29)
Georgia Bibliography: County History [Map of Ga. counties, which created from, etc.], by Ga. Dept. of Education	.....	.....	(896)

Records

Colonial Records of the State of Georgia 1732-1782, by Candler (repr. of 1904 ed.) 26 vols. Each:	42.50	.....	(630)
Abstracts of Colonial Wills of the State of Georgia, 1733-1777, compiled by Georgia Dept. of Ar. & Hist.	.....	7.50	(914)
Authentic List of All Land Lottery Grants Made to Veterans of the Revolutionary War by the State of Georgia, by Hitz [2nd ed., 1966]	.....	1.50	(914)
Passports Issued by Governors of Georgia, 1785-1809, by Bryan	.....	4.25	(616)
Passports Issued by Governors of Georgia, 1810-1820 [Continuation of the above work, with an index to both] by Bryan and Dumont	.....	4.25	(616)
List of the Early Settlers of Georgia, by Saye & Coulter	6.00	.....	(917)
1805 Georgia Land Lottery, by Virginia S. Wood	15.00	.....	(175)
1807 Georgia Land Lottery, by Lucas	12.50	.....	(658)
Index to 1820 Georgia Census, by Ga. Hist. Soc.	.....	8.50	(924)
Official Register of 1827 Georgia Land Lottery, by Houston	15.00	.....	(130)
Index to 1830 Census of Georgia, by Alvaretta K. Register	18.50	.....	(130)
The Cherokee Land Lottery [1832], by James E. Smith	16.50	.....	(130)
1850 Georgia Mortality Census - Indexed, by Aurora C. Shaw	.....	5.00	(838)
Historical Collections of the Joseph Habersham Chap., Vol. I	12.00	.....	(130)
Historical Collections of the Joseph Habersham Chap., Vol. II	21.00	.....	(130)
Historical Collections of the Joseph Habersham Chap., Vol. III	11.00	.....	(130)
Historical Collections of Georgia, by George White	17.50	.....	(130)

Military

Roster of Confederate Soldiers of Georgia, 1861-1865, 6 vols. Each:	.....	7.50	(914)

Military

British Drums on the Southern Frontier: The Military Coloni-
zation of Georgia, 1733-1749, by Ivers   12.50   ..... (650)
Memoirs of the Am. Revolution, by Drayton (repr. of 1821 ed.) 30.00 set .... (629)
Recollections of a Georgia Loyalist, by Johnston   12.00   ..... (663)
Revolutionary Records of the State of Ga., 1769-1784, by Ga.
General Assembly. 3 vols.   Each: 47.50   ..... (630)
Georgia's Roster of the Revolution, by Knight   16.00   ..... (130)
Roster of Revolutionary Soldiers in Ga., by McCall. Vol. I   12.50   ..... (130)
Roster of Revolutionary Soldiers in Ga., by McCall. Vol. II 12.50   ..... (130)
Roster of Revolutionary Soldiers in Ga., by McCall. Vol. III 15.00   ..... (130)
Confederate Records of the St. of Ga. 1860-1868. 6 vols. Each: 58.00   ..... (630)

Religious

Catholicity in the Carolinas & Georgia, by O'Connell   21.00   ..... (663)
The Moravians in Georgia, 1735-1740, by Fries   11.50   ..... (130)
Detailed Report on the Salzburger Emigrants Who Settled in
America, 1736, by Samuel Urlsperger   10.00   ..... (917)
Detailed Report on the Salzburger Emigrants Who Settled in
North America, 1734-1735, by Urlsperger, Vol. 2   7.50   ..... (917)

APPLING COUNTY

1820 Federal Census - Indexed, by Aurora Shaw 3.00 (838)
1850 Federal Census - Indexed, with additions by F. Huxford 5.50 (838)

BULLOCH COUNTY

Marriage Records, 1796 (origin of county) thru 1875, by Register 7.50 (515)

BURKE COUNTY

"Burke County, Georgia" (article in National Genealogical Society
Quarterly, Vol. 54, No. 1) 54pp. 3.00 (616)
1850 Census, by Rhea Cumming Otto 6.75 (853)

CAMDEN COUNTY

Special Aids to Genealogical Research on Southern Families [Con-
tains Land Journal, 1787-1790 & Camden Co. Archives - as
well as material on other areas.] 5.50 (616)

CATOOSA COUNTY

History in Catoosa County, by Wm. H. H. Clark [County history,
also 65 pp. genealogical information on approx. 600 of the 1835-
1860 settlers of NW Ga. History through Civil War period.] 9.50 ..... (518)

CHATHAM COUNTY

Abstracts and Wills, 1773-1817   .....   5.50 (616)
The Siege of Savannah - 1779, by Franklin B. Hough   12.00   ..... (663)

CLARKE COUNTY

Strolls About Athens During the Early Seventies, by S. Morris
(repr. of 1912 ed.) [Author discusses the houses he passes,
telling anecdotes about present - 1870's - & previous owners.] 2.50 (612)
Oconee Hill Cemetery: Tombstone Inscriptions for that Part of the
Cemetery West of Oconee River and Index to Record of Inter-
ments, by Marshall [Burials c1856 to 1963- over 3400. Map.] 6.50 (612)
1874 Map of Athens, Ga., by Thomas (reprint) [35 x 45] [Streets,
churches, Univ. of Ga. bldgs, some property owners by name.] 6.00 (612)

COLUMBIA COUNTY

Early Marriage Records [binding damaged]	.....	5.00	(427)
A Century of Columbia County Wills [binding damaged]	.....	5.00	(427)
Georgia Cemetery Inscriptions - "Neath Georgia Sod" [damaged]	10.00	.....	(427)

DADE COUNTY

History In Catoosa County, by Clark [Some data on Dade settlers]	9.50	.....	(518)

DECATUR COUNTY

Early Marriage Records & Abstracts of Wills [damaged]	.....	4.00	(427)

DOOLY COUNTY

Historical & Genealogical Collections of Dooly County, by Powell	15.00	.....	(647)

ELBERT COUNTY

History of Elbert County, 1790-1935, by McIntosh [In addition to history, contains extensive genealogical data]	20.00	.....	(287)

FLOYD COUNTY

A History of Rome & Floyd County, by Battey	25.00	.....	(287)
History In Catoosa County, by Clark [Some data on Floyd settlers]	9.50	.....	(518)

GLASCOCK COUNTY

Neath Georgia Sod: Georgia Cemetery Inscriptions [damaged]	10.00	.....	(427)

GLYNN COUNTY

Our Todays & Yesterdays, A Story of Brunswick & the Coastal Islands, by Cate	15.00	.....	(663)

GREEN COUNTY

Preface to Peasantry: A Tale of Two Black Belt Counties, by Raper [Studies in American Negro Life]	.....	3.45	(952)

GWINNETT COUNTY

Gone to Georgia, by Stewart [1820 Census enumeration of Gwinnett with numerous annotations & genealogical notes on families.]	15.75	.....	(616)

JACKSON COUNTY

Gone to Georgia, by Stewart [1820 Census enumeration of Jackson with numerous annotations & genealogical notes on families.]	15.75	.....	(616)

McDUFFIE COUNTY

Neath Georgia Sod: Georgia Cemetery Inscriptions [damaged]	10.00	.....	(427)

McINTOSH COUNTY

McIntosh County Academy, 1820-1875, by Wood [Minutes of Commissioners, 1820-1875; Acct. Bk. of Students, 1821-1834; Genealogical Notes; Indexed.]	.....	13.95	(175)

NEWTON COUNTY

The Glory of Covington, by Williford [History of antebellum houses with extensive data on owners for 150 years. Illustrated.]	12.00	.....	(287)
Marriages Performed in Newton County 1822-1912, by Boyd	.....	15.00	(1010)

RICHMOND COUNTY

Autobiograhy of a County: The First Half-Century of Augusta, Georgia, by Fleming	12.00	.....	(663)
Memorial History of Augusta, Georgia, by Jones & Dutchen	17.50	.....	(663)
Neath Georgia Sod: Georgia Cemetery Inscriptions [damaged]	10.00	.....	(427)

SUMTER COUNTY

Americus Through the Years: A Georgia Town and Its People, 1831-1956, by Wm. B. Wllliford (rev. ed.)	15.00	.....	(287)

TALIAFERRO COUNTY

Neath Georgia Sod: Georgia Cemetery Inscriptions [damaged]	10.00	.....	(427)

TATTNALL COUNTY

1820 Census - Indexed, by Aurora C. Shaw	.....	3.00	(838)

TELFAIR COUNTY

1820 Census - Indexed, by Aurora C. Shaw	.....	3.00	(838)

WARREN COUNTY

Early Marriage Records [damaged]	.....	5.00	(427)
A Century of Warren County, Georgia, Wills 1790-1890 [damaged]	.....	5.00	(427)
Neath Georgia Sod: Georgia Cemetery Inscriptions [damaged]	10.00	.....	(427)

WASHINGTON COUNTY

Newspaper Notices of Deaths & Marriages	.....	10.00	(936)

WILKINSON COUNTY

Wilkinson Co, Georgia - Historical Collections, by Joseph T. Maddox [All peoples of Wilkinson County during 19th century and their relationships.]	15.75	.....	(74)

Hawaii

STATEWIDE REFERENCES

America's Only Royal Family: Genealogy of the Former Hawaiian Ruling House, by Milton Rubincam	.....	1.50	(616)
Hawaii: A Student's Guide to Local History	.....	1.50	(762)

Idaho

STATEWIDE REFERENCES

An Illustrated History of the State of Idaho . . . From the earliest Period . . . , by Lewis Pub. Co. (repr. 1899 ed.)	47.50	45.00	(546)
History of Idaho Territory, by Elliott & Co. (repr. 1884 ed.)	25.00	.....	(829)
History of Washington, Idaho, & Montana, by Bancroft	20.00	.....	(741)

Research Aids

Idaho: A Student's Guide to Local History	.....	1.50	(762)
Historical Records Survey: Check List of Idaho Imprints 1839-1890	.....	4.50	(624)

BENEWAH COUNTY

The Coeur D'Alene Indian Reservation [Contains many names]	5.00	.....	(829)

IDAHO COUNTY

An Illustrated History of North Idaho, Embracing Nez Perces, Idaho, Latah, Kootenai and Shoshone Cos. (repr. 1903)	47.50	45.00	(546)

KOOTENAI COUNTY

An Illustrated History of North Idaho, Embracing Nez Perces, Idaho, Latah, Kootenai and Shoshone Cos. (repr. 1903)	47.50	45.00	(546)
Northwest Notebook, Vol. I, by Elaine Walker [Early marriages, cemetery records, court house records in Kootenai & Shoshone Counties.]	.....	5.00	(931)

LATAH COUNTY

An Illustrated History of North Idaho, Embracing Nez Perces, Idaho, Latah, Kootenai and Shoshone Cos. (repr. 1903)	47.50	45.00	(546)

LEMHI COUNTY

History of Leesburg Pioneers, by Kirkpatrick (1934)	12.50	10.00	(546)

NEZ PERCES COUNTY

An Illustrated History of North Idaho, Embracing Nez Perces, Idaho, Latah, Kootenai and Shoshone Cos. (repr. 1903)	47.50	45.00	(546)

ONEIDA COUNTY

History of Weston, Idaho, by Frederickson	.....	3.00	(696)

SHOSHONE COUNTY

Northwest Notebook, Vol. I, by Elaine Walker [Early marriages, cemetery records, court house records in Kootenai & Shoshone Counties.]	.....	5.00	(931)
An Illustrated History of North Idaho, Embracing Nez Perces, Idaho, Latah, Kootenai and Shoshone Cos. (repr. 1903)	47.50	45.00	(546)

Illinois

STATEWIDE REFERENCES

Historical Encyclopedia of Illinois & History of Coles County, by Munsell Pub. Co. (repr. of 1906 ed.)	47.50	45.00	(546)
The Illinois Country 1673-1818, by Alvord	7.00	.....	(771)
Great Britain & the Illinois Country 1763-1774, by Carter (1910 ed.)	9.25	.....	(637)
Settlement of Illinois 1778-1830, by Boggess	9.75	.....	(636)
Illinois in 1818, by Buck (repr. of 1918 ed.)	7.50	.....	(678)
Letters From Illinois, by Birkbeck (repr. of 1818 ed.)	12.50	.....	(863)
Memoirs of the Lower Ohio Valley, by Fed. Pub. Co. (repr.1905) [Data on hundreds of people who lived along the shores of the Ohio R. from head in Pa. to mouth at Mississippi]	12.50	.....	(818)
Illinois Historical Atlas 1876, by Warner & Beer (repr.)	.....	3.95	(850)
Historical Encyclopedia of Illinois (repr. of 1908 ed.)	25.00	.....	(867)
Land Betweens the Rivers: The Southern Illinois Country, by Horrell et. al.	15.00	.....	(757)
Trade Tokens of Illinois, by Vacketta [Tokens issued by saloons, cigar stores, billiard parlors, general merchants, etc.]	12.50	.....	(495)

Research Aids

Sources For Genealogical Searching in Illinois, by McCay		2.25	(417)
Tracing Family Trees in Eleven States, by St. Louis Gen. Soc.		5.50	(29)
Bibliography of Illinois Imprints, 1814-1858, by Byrd	12.50		(810)
Illinois, by Federal Writer's Project (repr. 1947)	34.00		(939)
Illinois: A Student's Guide to Localized History		1.50	(762)
Descriptive Bibliography of Civil War Manuscripts in Illinois, by Burton		8.50	(749)
Guide to the Microfilm Publication of the Pierre Menard Collection in the Ill. St. Hist. Lib., by Seineke, (new ed.)		2.00	(749)
General Index to Journal of the Ill. St. Hist. Soc.-Vols.1-25	20.00		(749)
Cumulative Index " " " " " " 26-50	20.00		(749)
Cumulative Index " " " " " " 51-60	8.00		(749)

Records

Illinois Census Returns, 1810 and 1818, by Norton	12.50		(130)
Illinois Census Returns, 1820, by Norton	15.00		(130)
Index to 1820 Census of Illinois, by Volkel & Gill	8.00	5.00	(752)
Index to 1830 Census of Illinois, by Gill & Gill, 4 vols.	24.00		(752)
Vol. 1 - Alexander, Pope, Union, Johnson, Jackson, Franklin, Perry, Randolph, Monroe, Washington, Marion, Jefferson, Hamilton and Gallatin Cos.		5.00	(752)
Vol. 2 - Crawford, Edgar, Clark, Schuyler, McDonough, Vermilion, Macon, Shelby, Tazewell, Montgomery, and Macoupin Cos.		5.00	(752)
Vol. 3 - Greene, Morgan, Sangamon, Calhoun, Pike, Fulton, Knox, Henry, Adams, Hancock, Warren, Mercer, Peoria, Putnam and JoDaviess Cos.		5.00	(752)
Vol. 4 - White, Edwards, Wabash, Wayne, Clay, Clinton, St. Clair, Madison, Bond, Fayette, Lawrence Cos.		5.00	(752)
Index to 1840 Census of Illinois, by Wormer			
Vol. 1 - Counties Adams through DuPage		6.50	(752)
Vol. 2 - Counties Edgar throught Jefferson		6.50	(752)
1850 Mortality Schedule, by Volkel, 3 vols.	24.50		(752)
Vol. 1 - Counties Adams through Iroquois		6.95	(752)
Vol. 2 - Counties Jackson through Ogle		6.95	(752)
Vol. 3 - Counties Peoria through Woodford		6.95	(752)

Military

Col. George Rogers Clark's Sketch of His Campaign in the Illinois in 1778-1779, by Geo. Rogers Clark, (repr. 1869)	8.00		(629)
Revolutionary Soldiers Buried in Illinois, by Walker	11.00		(130)
The Black Hawk War, 1831-1832, Vol. 1, by Whitney [Gives names of Illinois volunteers]	20.00		(749)
The Black Hawk War, 1831-1832, Vol. 2, by Whitney [Letters and papers, Pt. 1, April 30, 1831-June 23, 1832]	25.00		(749)
Black Hawk's War of 1832, by Hollmann & Mitchum (new ed.)	6.95		(669)
Behind the Guns: The History of Battery One, Second Regt., Illinois Light Artillery, by Putney [ed. by Walton]	15.00		(757)
Admissions to the Soldiers & Sailors Home in Quincy, Illinois, 1878-1889 [Veterans of Mexican & Civil Wars living in Illinois at time of admission, but had served from many states. Data includes this information], by Volkel		7.25	(752)

Religious and Ethnic Groups

Narrative of Riots at Alton, by E. Beecher (repr. of 1838 ed.)		9.95	(642)
The Catholic Church in the Meeting of Two Frontiers: The Southern Illinois Country 1763-1793, by Walker (repr. 1935)	7.50		(630)
Nauvoo: Kingdom on the Mississippi, by Flanders	6.50		(678)

ALEXANDER COUNTY

An Index to History of Alexander, Union & Pulaski Cos. (1883 ed.)	9.00	6.00	(752)
1850 Federal Census - Indexed, by Wormer	.....	5.00	(752)

BOND COUNTY

Excerpts from Bond Co., Ill. Biographies, 1915 [Alphabetical listing of biographical sketches - indexed.]	.....	2.00	(264)
1850 Federal Census - Indexed [Projected publication, 1975]	.....	.....	(264)

BOONE COUNTY

Cemetery Inscriptions, Vol. 1, by Hyde & Decker [Cemeteries in Flora & Manchester Twps.]	.....	5.00	(752)

BROWN COUNTY

1882 Brink's History of Schuyler & Brown Cos. (reprint)	20.00	.....	(867)
Index to Brink's History of Schuyler & Brown Cos.	.....	2.00	(867)
1892 Biographical Review of Schuyler, Cass & Brown	30.00	.....	(867)

CALHOUN COUNTY

1850 Federal Census - Indexed, by Decatur Gen. Soc.	.....	5.00	(264)

CARROLL COUNTY

The History of Carroll County . . . , by Kett & Co.	27.50	25.00	(546)
1850 Federal Census - Indexed, by Smith	.....	5.00	(752)

CASS COUNTY

1892 Biographical Review of Schuyler, Cass & Brown Cos.	30.00	.....	(867)

CHAMPAIGN COUNTY

Friends [Quakers] in Illiana in 1826 [Abstracts of the Vermilion Quarterly Meeting in Vermilion Grove, Ill.]	.....	10.00	(526)
1850 Federal Census, by Swartz	.....	5.00	(857)
Burials GAR Cemetery, Homer, Champaign Co., 1886-1970	.....	2.00	(264)

CHRISTIAN COUNTY

1850 Federal Census - Indexed, by Decatur Gen. Soc.	.....	5.00	(264)
Cemetery Inscriptions, Vol. 1: Edinburg, Hunter, Kelsay, Long, Furrow, Milligan, Old Walnut Hill, Simpson, Stafford, Bethel Baptist, Durbin, Traylor, Tovey, Ponting, Harper's Ferry, Millersville	.....	6.00	(264)
Cemetery Inscriptions, Vol. 2: Achenbach, Adams-Jordon, Bilyew, Buckeye, Buchart, Carmen, Dalbey, Donner, Harris, Hays, Kettelkamp, Leachman, Morrisonville, Mt. Zion, New Walnut Hill, Ralson, St. Joseph, Stokes	.....	6.00	(264)
Cemetery Inscriptions, Vol. 3: Anderson, Antioch, Bethan, Blueville, Center Grove, Clark, Cloyd, Darmer, Fairview, Finley, Goode, Hawk, Hinkle, Jacobs, Langley, Mt. Auburn, Old Stonington.	.....	6.00	(264)
Cemetery Inscriptions, Vol. 4: Grove City, Linwood, Mound Chapel, Ohlman, Owaneco, Poor Farm, Young	.....	5.00	(264)
Berea Cemetery, Mosquito Twp. [includes genealogical notes]	.....	1.50	(264)

CLAY COUNTY

1850 Federal Census - Indexed, by Wormer	.....	6.00	(752)
Gleanings From Old Newspapers of Clay & Richland Cos, by Taylor [Marriages, Obits, Divorces, etc. to 1915] Available in 1975	.....	.....	(449)

CLINTON COUNTY

1850 Federal Census - Indexed, by Wormer	6.50	(752)

COLES COUNTY

Marriage Records, Vol. 1 [1831-1853]	5.00	(971)
Assessor's Book, 1866, Morgan Twp. [List of R.E. & P.P. tax]	2.00	(264)

COOK COUNTY

The Chicago Genealogist [Quarterly publication of the Chicago Gen.
Soc.] Back numbers available. Write for list & prices. ..... (857)
Vital Records from Chicago Newspapers, Vol. I, 1833-1839 ..... 5.00 (857)
Vital Records from Chicago Newspapers, Vol. II, 1840-1842 ..... 6.00 (857)
Vital Records from Chicago Newspapers, Vol. III, 1843-1844 ..... 6.00 (857)
  [The above volumes contain items for other counties in Northern
  Illinois and in New York State - as well as in Chicago.]
List of Letters Remaining in the Post Office, Chicago and Vicinity.
  Jan. 1834-July 1836. [Notices were in post offices in Chicago,
  DuPage, Juliet (Joliet), Naperville, Ottawa, Paw Paw, & Plain-
  field], compiled by the Chicago Gen. Soc. 5.00 (857)
General Directory of the City of Chicago for the Year 1844 [Map] 3.50 (857)
1888-89 West Hammond (now Calumet City) directory and also Hege-
  wisch (now a part of Chicago), by Gero (reprint) 3.00 (505)
1891-92 West Hammond City Directory, by Gero (reprint) 3.00 (505)
Directory of Austin, Illinois (1897) [Austin is now part of Chicago] 3.50 (857)
Abstract of Birth, Marriage & Death Notices from Chicago Tribune
  1860-1871, by Boyd [30,000 entries in index] Available in 1975. ..... (94)

CRAWFORD COUNTY

1850 Federal Census - Indexed, by Decatur Gen. Soc.	6.00	(264)

CUMBERLAND COUNTY

1850 Federal Census - Indexed, by Decatur Gen. Soc.	5.00	(264)

De KALB COUNTY

1850 Federal Census - Indexed, by Richard	6.00	(651)

De WITT COUNTY

1850 Federal Census - Indexed, by Decatur Gen. Soc. 5.00 (264)
Patron Index - Landowners - 1875 Plat Book 4.00 (264)
Patron Index - Landowners - 1894 Plat Book 3.00 (264)
Cemetery Inscriptions, Vol. 1: Baptist, Barnett, Hays, Rucker
  Chapel, Tunbridge, Old Union, Hill, Pleasant Valley, Randolph,
  Rock Creek, Rose, & one near Jenkins Switch - Indexed 5.00 (264)
Cemetery Inscriptions, Vol. 2: Union, Camel Hump, Evergreen,
  Lisenby, Sugar Grove, Cru, McClimans, Willmore, St. Patrick 6.00 (264)
Cemetery Inscriptions, Vol. 3: Woodlawn, Memorial Park, Maus-
  oleum Park (all in Clinton, Ill.) - Indexed 8.00 (264)
Cemetery Inscriptions, Vol. 4: Camp Ground, Greenleaf, St. Jo-
  seph's Catholic, DeWitt, Long Point, Texas Christian, Barnett,
  Hall, Weaver, McCord, John, Troutman, Walden, Fairview 6.00 (264)
Cemetery Inscriptions, Vol. 5: Weldon, Nixon Twp., Maple Grove,
  Santa Anna Twp., City Cemetery - Indexed 6.00 (264)

DOUGLAS COUNTY

Friends [Quakers] in Illiana 1826 [Abstracts of records of Vermilion Quarterly Meeting in Vermilion Grove, Ill.] 10.00 (526)

Du PAGE COUNTY

A History of the County of Du Page . . . by Richmond (repr.1857)	12.50	10.00	(546)
An Index to the Names of Persons appearing in 1882 History of Du Page County, by Blanchard	9.00	6.00	(752)
List of Letters Remaining in the Post Office, Chicago & Vicinity, Jan. 1834-July 1836	.....	5.00	(857)

EDGAR COUNTY

Friends [Quakers] in Illiana 1826 (see Champaign Co.)	.....	10.00	(526)
1830 Federal Census - Alphabetical, by Decatur Gen. Soc.	.....	1.25	(264)
1850 Federal Census - Indexed, by Smith	.....	5.00	(752)
Cemetery Inscriptions, Vol. 1: Bennington, Old Carney, Densmore, Old Greathouse, Earl Ibbotson, Old Johnson, Macedonia, Miller, Original Pleasant Hill, Samsville, Original Shiloh, Yetke	.....	4.00	(264)

EFFINGHAM COUNTY

1850 Federal Census - Indexed, by Decatur Gen. Soc.	.....	5.00	(264)
Funeral Home Records, Altamont 1900-1922, by Decatur Gen. Soc.	.....	2.00	(264)

FAYETTE COUNTY

Patron Index - Landowners - Plat Book, 1891	.....	5.00	(264)
Excerpts from Fayette Co. History Biographies	.....	2.00	(264)
Persons Mentioned in Twps., 1910 History of Fayette County	.....	1.25	(264)
1830 Federal Census - Indexed	.....	2.50	(264)
1840 Federal Census - Indexed	.....	3.00	(264)
1850 Federal Census - Indexed	.....	6.75	(264)
Marriage Index, 1821-1874	.....	5.00	(264)

FRANKLIN COUNTY

1840 Federal Census - Indexed, by Rademacher & Rademacher	.....	3.50	(752)
1860 Federal Census - Indexed, by Rademacher & Rademacher	.....	8.00	(752)
Marriage Records, First Book 1836-1848 (and some earlier)	.....	4.00	(752)

FULTON COUNTY

A History of Fulton County in Spoon River Country 1818-1968	16.00	.....	(586)
Historic Fulton County: Sites and Scenes - Past and Present	13.00	.....	(586)
1825 State Census	.....	3.30	(586)
Index to the 1830 Federal Census	.....	.90	(586)
Index to the 1840 Federal Census	.....	2.90	(586)
Burials in Randall Cemetery - Bernadotte Twp.	.....	.60	(586)
Cemetery Inscriptions, Vol. 1: Deerfield Twp., Ellisville Twp., & Young Hickory Twp. [all known cemeteries in each & map]	.....	5.50	(586)
Cemetery Inscriptions, Vol. 2: Kerton, Isabel & Waterford Twps. [All known cemeteries and burial plots, with map of each twp.]	.....	4.50	(586)

GALLATIN COUNTY

Index to History of Gallatin, Saline, Hamilton, Franklin & Williamson Counties, pub. by Goodspeed, 1887	9.00	6.00	(752)
1850 Federal Census - Indexed	.....	5.00	(222)
Cemeteries [90], a short history and original land owners - Indexed	.....	8.00	(752)

HAMILTON COUNTY

1840 Federal Census - Indexed	.....	3.50	(752)
1860 Federal Census - Indexed	.....	8.00	(752)
Cemetery Inscriptions, Vol. 1: Bethel, Braden's Valley, Brush Harbor, Cartwright, Cherry Grove, Cook, Council Farm, Crescent Hill, Digby, Lanham, McLeansboro, Newman, Old Family, Pleasant Hill, Preston, Stull, Sullivan, Woolf - Indexed	.....	4.00	(264)

HARDIN COUNTY

Biographical Review of Johnson, Massac, Pope & Hardin Cos.,
by Biographical Pub. Co. (1893 ed.)   37.50   35.00 (546)

HENRY COUNTY

The Bishop Hill Colony, A Religious Communistic Settlement
in Henry County, Illinois, by Mikkelsen   10.25   6.25 (1000)

JACKSON COUNTY

Residents in 1850 - Indexed, by Wright 5.25 (752)

JASPER COUNTY

Cemeteries, Vol. 1: Backbone, Chapman, Cline's Harper, Miller,
Wheeler, Beckers, Cummins, Lancaster, Woods, Cook, De-
vore, Foster, Freeman, McQueen, Worthey, Collins, Bowers,
Burford, Higgins, Poor Farm, Jasper, Jones, Eidson, Selby 4.00 (752)
Cemeteries, Vol. 2: Grandville, Smallwood, South Muddy & Wil-
low Hill Twps. 5.50 (752)
Cemeteries, Vol. 3: Crooked Creek & Fox Twps. 5.50 (752)
Cemeteries, Vol. 4: Hunt, North Muddy & Ste. Marie Twps. 7.00 (752)

JEFFERSON COUNTY

1850 Federal Census - Indexed 7.50 (752)

JERSEY COUNTY

Abandoned Cemeteries of, by Witt 5.00 (752)

JoDAVIESS COUNTY

Index to 1878 History of Jo Daviess County, by Kett & Co. 9.00   6.00 (752)
Prairie Farmers' Directory of Jo Daviess Co.[Lists farmers,
wife's given & maiden name, children, etc.] (repr. 1917) 3.00 (752)

JOHNSON COUNTY

Biog. Review of Johnson, Massac, Pope, & Hardin (repr.1893) 37.50 35.00 (546)
1850 Federal Census - Indexed 5.00 (222)

LAKE COUNTY

Index to 1912 History of Lake County, by Halsey   9.00   6.00 (752)

La SALLE COUNTY

History of La Salle Co, by Baldwin (repr. 1877 ed.)   32.50   30.00 (546)

LEE COUNTY

1850 Federal Census - Indexed 5.00 (752)

LOGAN COUNTY

Notes from the Centennial Edition of the Lincoln Evening Courier 2.00 (264)
1850 Federal Census - Indexed 5.00 (264)
Records of the Lincoln Circuit Methodist Churches, 1866-1920 ..... 5.00 (264)
G. H. Tuttle Funeral Home Records, 1862-1918, Atlanta, Ill. 4.00 (264)
Cemetery Inscriptions, Vol. 1: Edgell-Barnes, Jolly, Blue Grass,
Kline, Braucher, Lawrence, Mt. Pulaski - Indexed 6.00 (264)
Cemetery Inscriptions, Vol. 2: Green Hill, Bethel, Union Station,
Lawndale, Elkhart, Hartsburg, Carlyle - Indexed 6.00 (264)
Cemetery Inscriptions, Vol. 4: Walnut Hill, Zion, Thomas, Pool
Hill, Stephens, Latham-Thompson, Donnan, Pleasant Valley,
Lucas Chapel, Musick, Baker, Skelton, Perry, Carlock, Reed,
Spring Bank, Laenna, Turley, Richmond Grove - Indexed 6.00 (264)

Cemetery Inscriptions, Vol. 5: Old Union (Lincoln) inscriptions,
    burial records, Ill. Vet. Comm. records, purchasers of lots 8.00 (264)
Cemetery Inscriptions, Vol. 6: St. Mary's, West Lincoln Twp., S
    St. Patrick's, Broadwell Twp., Atlanta and records 6.00 (264)

McLEAN COUNTY

1850 Federal Census - Indexed	.....	7.50	(752)
Marriage Records Abstracted from Lexington Newspapers	.....	3.00	(752)
Burials in Lexington Cemetery	.....	5.00	(752)
Pleasant Hill Cemetery Records	.....	5.00	(752)

MACON COUNTY

The Centennial History of Blue Mound, Illinois, by Matthew [References to over 200 families.]	6.00	.....	(609)
History of Macon County (repr. of 1880 ed., with new index)	15.00	.....	(264)
Patron's Biog. Notes from 1903 Atlas of Macon County - Indexed	.....	3.00	(264)
1830 Federal Census - Indexed	.....	1.25	(264)
1850 Federal Census - Indexed	.....	5.00	(264)
Marriage Records, Vol. I 1829-1850 - Indexed	.....	3.00	(264)
Marriage Records, Vol. II 1851-1860 - Indexed	.....	4.00	(264)
Marriage Records, Vol. III 1861-1870 - Indexed	.....	6.00	(264)
Marriage Records, Vol. IV 1871-1880 - Indexed	.....	6.00	(264)
Marriage Records, Vol. V 1881-1890 - Indexed	.....	6.00	(264)
Abstracts of Circuit Court, Record Book A, 1831-1839 - Indexed	.....	4.00	(264)
Abstracts of Probate Records, 1831-1847 - Indexed	.....	4.00	(264)
Antebellum Decatur & Macon County, 1816-1860, by Brockway	.....	1.10	(264)
Cemetery Inscriptions, Vol. 1: Emery, Brown, Hall, in Austin, Blue Mound, Pleasant View & Whitmore Twps.	.....	6.00	(264)
Cemetery Inscriptions, Vol. 2: Boiling Springs, Hays Family, Peach Orchard, Cross, Frantz, Peck, Ritchie, Wheeler [in Hickory Point & Oakley Twps.]	.....	6.00	(264)
Cemetery Inscriptions, Vol. 3: Illini, Long Grove & Macon cemeteries in Illini and South Macon Twps.	.....	6.00	(264)
Cemetery Inscriptions, Vol. 4: Friends Creek, Long and Long Point Cem. in Niantic & Friends Creek Twps.	.....	6.00	(264)
Cemetery Inscriptions, Vol. 5: Florey, North Fork, Point Pleasant, Ridge, Maroa, Wrights Grove [in Long Creek & Maroa Twps.]	.....	6.00	(264)
Cemetery Inscriptions, Vol. 6: Calvary Catholic Cem., Decatur Twp	.....	6.00	(264)
Cemetery Inscriptions, Vol. 7: Mt. Gilead, Salem, Walnut Grove, Turpin [also obits & history of S. Wheatland Twp.]	.....	6.00	(264)
Cemetery Inscriptions, Vol. 8: Mt. Zion Presby., Mt. Zion, Gibson, Turpin, Harristown, Whitley, Gouge, Swarts, St. Johannes, Sharon, Spangler	.....	6.00	(264)
Cemetery Inscriptions, Vol. 9: Macon Co. Memorial Park Cem.	.....	5.00	(264)

MACOUPIN COUNTY

1850 Federal Census - Indexed	9.95	6.00	(141)

MADISON COUNTY

1830 Federal Census - Indexed	.....	3.00	(264)
Alton Trials - of Winthrop S. Gilman, Enoch Long, & Others, by Lincoln (repr. of 1838 ed.)	9.00	.....	(629)
Narrative of Riots at Alton, by Beecher (repr. of 1838 ed.)	.....	9.95	(642)

MARION COUNTY

1850 Federal Census - Indexed	.....	7.00	(752)

MASSAC COUNTY

Biog. Review of Johnson, Massac, Pope & Hardin Cos. (1893 ed.) 37.50 35.00 (546)

MENARD COUNTY

1850 Federal Census and a brief county history, by Galvez 3.85 (29)

MONTGOMERY COUNTY

Special Aids to Genealogical Research in NE & Central States [One
   article concerns settlers in Mont. Co. before 1840] 4.25 (616)

MOULTRIE COUNTY

1881 History of Shelby & Moultrie Cos. [repr. with new index] 17.50 ..... (411)
1850 Federal Census - Indexed 5.00 (264)
Cemetery Inscriptions, Vol. 1: Bracken (Bolin) Family, Camfield,
   Graham's Chapel, Hampton (Shiels), Mitchell, New Hope, Oak
   Grove, Seass, St. Isadore's Catholic, Strain (Dedman), Turner,
   Waggoner, Walker 6.00 (264)
Cemetery Inscriptions, Vol. 2: Branch Side, Franch, Ginn (Ellis),
   Selby, Hagerman, Liberty, Otto Farm, Pea, Thomason (Cook),
   Taylor (Hudson), First Waggoner, Wright, Yarnell, Turner 6.00 (264)
Cemetery Inscriptions, Vol. 3: Lynn Creek, Cunningham, Daugh-
   erty, Munson-McCormick, Todd's Point, Wright, Marrowbone
   (Bethant), Snyder, Selby, Hostetler, McDaniels, "unnamed" 6.00 (264)
Cemetery Inscriptions, Vol. 4: Greenhill & Jonathan Creek 6.00 (264)
Cemetery Inscriptions, Vol. 5: Purvis, Souther's, Ill. Masonic
   Home, Smyser, Whitfield, Hewitt 6.00 (264)

OGLE COUNTY

1850 Federal Census - Indexed 7.00 (651)

PERRY COUNTY

1850 Federal Census - Indexed 6.50 (752)
Marriages, 1827-1850, With Genealogical Notes, by Spurgeon 5.00 (752)

PIKE COUNTY

Marriages, Vol. I 1827-1845, by Keller & Zachary 5.00 (355)
Marriages, Vol. II 1846-1853, by Keller & Zachary 5.00 (355)

POPE COUNTY

1850 Federal Census - Indexed 5.00 (752)
Marriages, 1816-1839 - Indexed 5.00 (752)

PULASKI COUNTY

Index to 1883 History of Alexander, Union & Pulaski Cos. 9.00 6.00 (752)
1850 Federal Census - Indexed 5.00 (752)

RANDOLPH COUNTY

1825 State Census 3.00 (1027)

RICHLAND COUNTY

Early Marriages, 1840-1899, by Taylor 12.50 ..... (449)
Gleanings from Old Newspapers of Clay & Richland Cos. [Marri-
   ages, obits, births, divorces, real estate transfers to 1916]
   [To be published in 1975] .... (449)
Cemetery Inscriptions, Vol. 1: Oleny Twp. 6.25 (752)
Cemetery Inscriptions, Vol. 2: other eight twps. 6.25 (752)
Cemetery Inscriptions, Vol. 1 & 2 (above) 15.00 ..... (752)

ST. CLAIR COUNTY

1840 Federal Census - Indexed, by Buecher	5.50	(752)
Marriages 1791-1845, by Buecher	3.85	(29)

SALINE COUNTY

1850 Federal Census - Indexed	5.00	(222)

SANGAMON COUNTY

Early Settlers of Sangamon County, by Power (repr. of 1873 ed.)	35.00		(16)
Cemetery Inscriptions, Vol. 1: Riverside, Calvary, Wilcox, Eckel, Bethel Church, Etter, Cass, Buffalo Hart Twp., Constant, Martin, Taylor, in Illiopolis, Lanesville, Buffalo Hart, Cooper, & Clear Lake Twps.		6.00	(264)
Records of the Meth. Ep. Ch., Illiopolis, 1875-1907		5.00	(264)

SCHUYLER COUNTY

Historical Enclopedia (repr. of 1908 ed.)	25.00		(867)
1872 Atlas of Schuyler Co. [100 biographies] (repr.)	30.00		(867)
1892 Biog. Review of Schuyler, Cass & Brown Cos. (repr.)	30.00		(867)
1882 History of Schuyler & Brown Cos., by Brink (repr.)	20.00		(867)
Index to 1882 Hist. of Schuyler & Brown Cos. (above)		2.00	(867)
History of Bainbridge Twp. [Twp. where most first settlers came]		5.00	(867)
1850 Federal Census - Indexed		12.50	(867)
1850-1860-1870-1880 Mortality Schedules		5.00	(867)
Naturalization & Citizenship [partial list of applicants]		1.50	(867)
Records of Wills, Bks. A & B 1866-1887; Index to Bks. A & B 1857-1879 of Administrator's Bonds [4 vols. in 1]		5.00	(867)
Wills-Letters of Adm.-Guardian Bonds, Vols.1,2,3, 1827-1849		5.00	(867)
Wills and Estates - Order Bk. A, Jan. 1850-Aug. 1868		5.00	(867)
School Schedules 1838-1839 [Lists students, teachers, directors]		3.00	(867)
Marks & Brands in Schuyler County		1.50	(867)
"The Schuylerite" [Quarterly whose contents include Bible records, Cemetery lists, family history, etc.] Subcription per year:		5.00	(867)

SHELBY COUNTY

1881 Hist. of Shelby & Moultrie Cos. [reprint with new index]	17.50		(411)
Here and There in Shelby County, by Gordon		3.20	(411)
Patron List from 1875 Plat Book [name, date settled, etc.]		1.50	(264)
Excerpts from Shelby Co. History Biographies		5.00	(264)
Supplement to Shelby Co. History Biographies		3.00	(264)
Listing of Persons Mentioned in Shelby Co. 1910 History		1.50	(264)
1830 Federal Census - Indexed		3.00	(264)
1840 Federal Census - Indexed		3.00	(264)
1850 Federal Census - Indexed		7.00	(264)
Probate Journal #1 (1839-1849), by Lloyd		4.75	(411)
Probate Journal #2, pt. 1 (1843-1850), by Lloyd		2.75	(411)
Probate Journal #2, pt. 2 (1843-1850), by Lloyd		4.75	(411)
Cemetery Inscriptions, Vol. 1: Coal Creek (Conner), Ludwig (Salem), Tolly, Austin, Hamilton, Little Flock, Snyder-Traughber, West New Hope, Prairie Home, Masonic		5.00	(264)
Cemetery Inscriptions, Vol. 2: Bethan, Center, Clark, Corley, Henderson, I.O.O.F., Mt. Olive, Wm.Price, Wilborn Creek, Tennessee		5.00	(264)
Cemetery Inscriptions, Vol. 3: Jacob Swallow, Eiler, Quigley, Mud Run, Pleasant Grove, Oak Grove, Neil (Johnson), Mt. Zion		5.00	(264)

STARK COUNTY

Index to 1876 History of Stark Co. & Its Pioneers, by Shellenberger	9.00	6.00	(752)
Marriages 1839-1866 - Indexed, by Leeson	.....	4.00	(752)
1850 Federal Census - Indexed	.....	5.00	(857)

STEPHENSON COUNTY

History of Stephenson County	14.00	.....	(934)
1850 Federal Census, by Haver & Morgan	.....	8.50	(176)

VERMILION COUNTY

Index to 1879 History of Vermilion Co., by Beckwith	9.00	6.00	(752)
1833 Tax List & Original Land Records	.....	.....	(752)
Vermilion Co. Pioneers: Biographies from the Danville newspaper	.....	5.00	(752)
Vermilion Co. Pioneers: Biographies from the Danville newspaper	.....	3.00	(752)
Friends [Quakers] in Illinana 1826 (see Champaign County)	.....	10.00	(526)
History of the Hopewell Primitive Baptist Church & Cemetery Records 1829-1968	.....	3.00	(526)
Mann's Chapel Cemetery Inscriptions	.....	2.50	(526)
1850 Federal Census	.....	7.50	(526)

WABASH COUNTY

1850 Federal Census	.....	6.00	(857)

WASHINGTON COUNTY

Index to 1879 History of Washington County by Brink, etc.	9.00	6.00	(752)
1850 Federal Census - Indexed	.....	7.00	(752)

WAYNE COUNTY

Newspaper Gleanings, 1855-1875 [Birth, death, marriage, etc.]	.....	8.40	(192)
Cemetery Inscriptions [total of 86 cem.] 4 vols. Each vol:	.....	7.35	(192)

WHITE COUNTY

1850 Federal Census - Indexed	.....	7.50	(264)

WHITESIDE COUNTY

Marriages, 1856-1881 [Exerpted from newspapers, mainly concern Whiteside couples, but some from neighboring counties.]	.....	10.00	(388)
Deaths, 1856-1881 [Exerpted from newspapers - as above]	.....	10.00	(388)
The Private Journal of Abraham Joseph Warner [Episcopal Missionary of Sterling, Rock Falls & vicinity c1845 to ? . [Comments on everyone he met and describes living conditions of the era.]	11.00	.....	(83)

WILLIAMSON COUNTY

1850 Federal Census - Indexed	.....	6.00	(264)

WINNEBAGO COUNTY

History of Rockton, Winnebago County, 1820-1898, by Carr (1898)	12.50	10.00	(546)
Index to 1877 History of Winnebago County by Kett & Co.	9.00	6.00	(752)
Cemetery Inscriptions, Vol. 1: New Milford, Cherry Valley, Powell and Dodge	.....	4.00	(752)
Cemetery Inscriptions, Vol. 2: Durand, St. Mary, Crane School, Davis and Carman	.....	5.00	(752)
Cemetery Inscriptions, Vol. 3: Pecatonica Cemetery	.....	5.00	(752)
1850 Federal Census, by Richard	.....	8.00	(857)

Indiana

STATEWIDE REFERENCES

History of Indiana from Its Earliest Exploration by Europeans to the Close of Territorial Government in 1816, by Dillon (1859)	28.00	.....	(629)
Topographical Description of the State of Ohio, Indiana Territory, & Louisiana, by Cutler (repr. of 1812 ed.)	10.00	.....	(629)
Indiana: A History, by Wilson	7.50	.....	(744)
Indiana Canals, by Fatout	10.50	.....	(675)
Furniture Makers of Indiana, 1793-1850, by Walters	.....	2.00	(288)
Indiana Ancestors - Index # 1 [Index to genealogy column which appears in Indianapolis Sunday Star - about 7,000 names]	.....	2.50	(417)

Records

The Territorial Papers of the U.S. - Indiana Territory 1800-1816, Vols. 7 & 8 [Microfilm Series M721, Roll # 5]	Microfilm:	12.00	(402)
The Territorial Papers of the U.S. - Territory Northwest of the Ohio River (Ohio & Ind.) 1787-1803, Vol. 2 [Microfilm Series M721, Roll # 2]	Microfilm:	12.00	(402)
Index to Towns, Townships, & Counties as Shown in the 1876 "Illustrated Historical Atlas of the State of Indiana."	......	6.00	(269)
Index to Towns as Shown in the 1876 "Illustrated Historical Atlas of the State of Indiana."	.....	5.00	(269)
Maps of Indiana Counties in 1876 [92 maps reprinted from the "Illustrated Historical Atlas of the State of Indiana"]	.....	5.00	(288)
1850 Mortality Schedules: [Deaths betw. June 1849 & June 1850]			
Vol. 1: Adams through Harrison counties	.....	7.50	(752)
Vol. 2: Hendricks through Posey counties	.....	7.50	(752)
Vol. 3: Pulaski through Whitley counties	.....	7.50	(752)
Revolutionary Soldiers Buried in Indiana, with Supplement	15.00	.....	(130)

Research aids

Sources for Genealogical Searching in Indiana, by McCay	.....	3.25	(417)
Tracing Family Trees in Eleven States (includes Indiana)	.....	5.50	(29)
Indiana: A Guide to the Hoosier State (repr.) Fed. Writer's	17.50	.....	(939)

Religious

Catholic Church in Indiana, 1789-1834, by McAvoy	12.50	.....	(630)

BOONE COUNTY

Abstracts of the Records of the Society of Friends in Indiana, Pt. 5, by Willard Heiss	17.50	15.00	(288)

CARROLL COUNTY

Carroll County History, by Helm [1882 reprint, new index]	15.00	.....	(850)
Carroll County Atlas (repr. of 1863 ed.)	.....	6.00	(850)
Carroll County - Delphi, Indiana, Its Heritage, by Mayhill	.....	1.00	(850)
Carroll County - Wabash & Erie Canal, by Mayhill [new index]	.....	3.75	(850)

CASS COUNTY

Biog. & Genealogical Hist. of Cass, Miami, Howard, & Tipton Cos., by Lewis Pub. Co. (repr. of 1898 ed.)	22.50	.....	(468)
1840 Federal Census - Indexed	.....	3.00	(289)

CLAY COUNTY

The Encyclopedic Directory . . . (repr. of 1896 ed.) [Name, post
    office, # acres owned, school district, section #, etc.] 3.00 (303)

DEARBORN COUNTY

History of Dearborn & Ohio Cos., Ind., by Weakley & Co. (1885)   47.50   45.00 (546)
Sparta Twp. Early Settlers, 1814-1837 & Real Estate Owners,
    1875-1899, by Fletcher [alphabetical listing] 1.50 (264)

DEKALB COUNTY

Pioneer Sketches; Containing Facts & Incidents of the Early History
    of DeKalb County, by Widney (repr. of 1859, with index) 3.25 (554)

DELAWARE COUNTY

Delaware County Atlas of 1887 (repr.) 3.00 (850)

FOUNTAIN COUNTY

Marriage Records - Book 1, 1826-1839, by Luke 3.00 (752)
Marriage Records - Book 2, 1839-1848, & Letters of Administra-
    tion, 1832-1846, by Luke 5.00 (752)
Abstract of Will Bk. 1 (1827-1851) & Original Land Records 5.00 (752)
Biog. Abstracts [from 1881 Hist. of Fountain Co. by Beckwith] 5.00 (752)

FULTON COUNTY

1883 Historical Atlas of Fulton Co, by Kingman [contains history,
    and 305 biographical sketches.] (repr.)   13.00   ..... (418)
Fulton County Folks, Vol. 1: Stories of 66 families, hotels, etc.   8.50   ..... (418)
Fulton County Historical Society Quarterly:
    Vol. 4, No. 1 - The Story of Bigfoot, 12pp. 1.00 (418)
    Vol. 5, No. 1 - How Kewanna Got Its Name, 12pp. 1.00 (418)
    Vol. 5, No. 1 - Historical Sketch of Fulton County, 5pp. 1.00 (418)
    Vol. 5, No. 2 - Hist. of Athens & W. Pt. of Henry Twp., 16pp. 1.00 (418)
    Vol. 7, No. 1 - History of Kewanna & Chief Kewanna, 20pp. 1.00 (418)
    Vol. 8, No. 1 - History of Fulton (town), 24pp. 1.00 (418)
    Vol. 8, No. 2 - History of Mt. Zion, 28pp. 1.00 (418)
    Vol. 8, No. 3 - Richland Township 1833-1933, 42pp. 1.00 (418)
    Vol. 9, No. 1 - History of Green Oak, 10pp. 1.00 (418)
    Vol. 9, No. 1 - Fulton Co's 1st Railroad & Depot -Museum 1.00 (418)
    Vol. 9, No. 1 - Prill School, 3pp. 1.00 (418)
    Vol. 9, No. 3 - History of Akron, 38pp. 1.00 (418)
    Vol. 10, No. 1 - Aubbeenaubbe Twp's. One-Room Schools, 13pp 1.00 (418)
    Vol. 10, No. 1 - History of Leiters Ford, 16pp. 1.00 (418)
    Vol. 10, No. 1 - Eleven Yrs. of Fulton Co. Hist. Soc., 3pp. 1.00 (418)
    Vol. 10, No. 2 - Newspaper Records of Fulton County, 2pp. 1.00 (418)
    Vol. 10, No. 2 - Underground Railroad in Fulton County, 5pp. 1.00 (418)

GRANT COUNTY

Abstracts of the Records of the Society of Friends in Indiana, Pt. 3
    by Willard Heiss   15.00   12.50 (288)
Early Friends [Quakers] in Grant County (1825-1913), by Ellis 1.50 (303)

HENDRICKS COUNTY

One Hundred Years, A Masonic History of Eminence, Indiana, by
    Littell [Biog. sketch on each of the 69 Past Masters & some gen-
    ealogical data on each member. 1871-1971   10.00   ..... (274)
A Brief History of Western Yearly Mtg. of Conservative Friends
    and the Separation of 1877, by Willard Heiss 1.00 (303)

HENRY COUNTY

Henry County History (repr. of 1884 ed.)	9.95	.....	(850)
Henry County History, by Pleas (reprint of 1871 ed. - new index)	4.95	.....	(850)
Original Land Entry Atlas 1821-49, by Mayhill (not a reprint)	.....	12.00	(850)
Atlas of 1875 (reprint)	.....	4.00	(850)
Abstracts of the Records of the Society of Friends in Indiana, Pt. 4 by Willard Heiss	15.00	12.50	(288)
Pictorial Souvenir of the Dunreith Train Wreck	.....	1.50	(850)
Wayne Twp. Early Cemetery Records, by Mayhill	.....	4.00	(850)
Greensboro & Harrison Twps. Cemetery Records, by Mayhill	.....	3.20	(850)
Wayne-Greensboro-Harrison Twp. Cemetery Rec. (see above)	7.50	.....	(850)

HOWARD COUNTY

Abstracts of the Records of the Society of Friends in Indiana, Pt. 3 by Heiss	15.00	.....	(288)

JAY COUNTY

Index to the 1870 Federal Population Census, by Neeley [To be published in 1975]	.....	.....	(184)

KNOX COUNTY

"Post Vincennes 1749-1784" (article in Genealogical Reference Builders "Newsletter", Vol. 9, No. 1, 32pp.	.....	2.00	(931)
Early Land Records & Court Indexes 1783-1815, by Barekman	.....	12.50	(252)

LAKE COUNTY

1888-89 Hammond & East Chicago City Directory. Also includes West Hammond (now Calument City) & Hegewisch, Ill., by Gero	.....	3.00	(505)
1891-92 Hammond City Directory [includes history of Hammond]	.....	3.00	(505)
1904 Reprint of Hammond Daily News [Contains 50 pages of history of Hammond, 1850-1904, with pictures, names, etc.]	.....	2.00	(505)

MADISON COUNTY

Early Settlement of the Wabash Valley, by Cox (repr. of 1860 ed.)	4.95	.....	(303)

MARSHALL COUNTY

Rev. Arthur Bradley's Journal (abstracted) (Article in National Genealogical Society Quarterly, Vol. 55, No. 1) 11pp.	.....	3.00	(616)

MIAMI COUNTY

Abs. of the Rec. of the Soc. of Friends in Ind., Pt. 3, by Heiss	15.00	12.50	(288)

MONTGOMERY COUNTY

Old Settlers of the Wabash Valley, by Cox (repr. of 1860 ed.)	4.95	.....	(303)
Wills [1823-1852] & Marriages [1823-1837], Vol. 1	.....	5.00	(752)
Wills [1837-1847] & Marriages [1837-1847], Vol. 2	.....	6.00	(752)
Wills [1868-1883] & Marriages [1847-1852], Vol. 3	.....	6.00	(752)

MORGAN COUNTY

One Hundred Years, A Masonic History of Eminence, Indiana, by Littell [A biographical-genealogical sketch of each of the 69 Past Masters. Some gen. data on each member. 1871-1971]	10.00	.....	(274)
Abs. of the Rec. of the Soc. of Friends in Ind., Pt. 5, by Heiss	17.50	15.00	(288)
One Hundred Men, A Legislative History of Morgan County, by Littell [Biog.-genealogical sketch on the 100 men who have represented this county in the State Legislature, 1822-1970.]	10.00	.....	(274)

ORANGE COUNTY

Abs. of the Rec. of the Soc. of Friends in Ind., Pt. 5, by Heiss   17.50   15.00 (288)

PARKE COUNTY

Abs. of the Rec. of the Soc. of Friends in Ind., Pt. 5, by Heiss   17.50   15.00 (288)
Marriage Records - Bk. A (1833-1844) by Sanders 3.00 (752)

PORTER COUNTY

1850 Federal Census - Indexed, by Hiday 6.00 (752)

POSEY COUNTY

Angel & the Serpent: The Story of New Harmony, by Wilson   10.95   ..... (744)

PUTNAM COUNTY

Biog. & Hist. Records, by Lewis Pub. Co. (repr. of 1887 ed.)   9.75   ..... (850)
Index to Biog. & Hist. Records of Putnam (above) 3.00 (850)
Combined price of above - Biog. & Hist. Rec. & index   11.50   ..... (850)
One Hundred Yrs., A Masonic Hist. . . (see Morgan Co.)   10.00   ..... (274)

RANDOLPH COUNTY

Randolph County History, by Tucker (repr. of 1882 ed.)   24.00   ..... (850)

RIPLEY COUNTY

Marriage Records, 1821-1840, by Fletcher 3.00 (264)
Marriage Records, 1841-1850, by Fletcher 3.00 (264)

RUSH COUNTY

Rush County History, by Brant & Fuller (repr. of 1888 ed.)   9.95   ..... (850)
Rush County & Rushville, Ind., by Johnson & Campbell   8.75   6.75 (850)
Abs. of the Rec. of the Soc. of Friends in Ind., Pt. 4, by Heiss   15.00   12.50 (288)

SHELBY COUNTY

Shelby County History, by Brant & Fuller (1887 ed., new index)   11.20   ..... (850)

SPENCER COUNTY

Early Wills & Est. Settlements 1818-1831, Wills 1833-1839   .....   5.00 (752)
Marriages 1818-1855   .....   10.00 (752)
Cemeteries: Vols. 1, 2, 3, 4   Each: 5.00 (752)
Cemeteries: Vol. 5 - Sunset Hill Cemetery 7.50 (752)
Cemeteries: Vol. 6, 7, 8, 9, 10, 11, 12, 13   Each: 5.00 (752)
Surname Index to above 13 vols. of cemeteries 2.00 (752)

TIPPECANOE COUNTY

Recollections of the Early Settlement of the Wabash Valley, by Cox
(repr. of 1860 ed.) [Chiefly Tippecanoe, some Madison, Mont.]   4.95   ..... (303)

VERMILLION COUNTY

Original Land Owners and Marriages, 1838-1844, by Volkel 4.00 (752)
Marriage Records - Vol. 3, 1844-1861, by Volkel 4.00 (752)
History of the Hopewell Primitive Baptist Church & Cemetery
Records 1829-1968   .....   3.00 (526)
Friends [Quakers] in Illiana 1826 [Abs. of Vermilion Quart. Mtg.] 10.00 (526)

VIGO COUNTY

Honey Creek Monthly Meeting of Friends, Vigo Co., Ind. 1820, by
Heiss [Pt. one: 1820-1829; Pt. two: Hicksite Records 1829-1874   .....   1.50 (303)

WABASH COUNTY

Complete Index to Wabash County History, by Helm [13,000 entries].....	7.50	(363)
Cemetery Records for Pleasant, Chester, & Paw Paw Twps.	15.00	(363)
Abstracts of the Records of the Society of Friends in Ind. , Pt. 3 15.00	12.50	(288)

WARREN COUNTY

Will Abstracts, 1830-1858, by Leath	3.00	(752)

WASHINGTON COUNTY

Abstracts of Records of the Society of Friends in Indiana, Pt. 5 17.50	15.00	(288)

WAYNE COUNTY

Wayne County History, by Young (repr. of 1872 ed.) 12.00	.....	(850)
Abstracts of Records of the Society of Friends in Indiana, Pt. 1	7.50	(288)
Abstracts of Records of the Society of Friends in Indiana, Pt. 4 15.00	12.50	(288)
Annals of Pioneer Settlers on the Whitewater & Its Tributaries, in the Vicinity of Richmond, Indiana, from 1804-1830 (1875)	2.00	(303)
Tombstone Inscriptions, by Yount 4 vols.[1600pp. total] Set:	34.00	(910)

WHITE COUNTY

Idaville United Presbyterian Church Records & Cemeteries, by Kay [Baptisms, membership, where buried, history.]	7.00	(152)

WHITLEY COUNTY

Index to Landowners of Whitley County, 1862 (w/plat map)	5.00	(269)

Iowa

STATEWIDE REFERENCES

Hawkeye Heritage [Quarterly of the Iowa Genealogical Society. Contains records of Iowa counties, census, cemeteries, military, land, historical background, Bible, abandoned towns, maps, tax lists, etc.] 50pp/issue. Subscription/yr.:	5.00	(208)
Notes on the Wisconsin Territory, by Lea (repr. of 1836 - book that gave Iowa its name)	5.00	(1001)
Autobiography . . . Formative Years, by Tatum [Tatum's Circulating Letter.' Genealogical notes by Willard Heiss]	1.50	(303)
A History of Iowa, by Sage 9.95	.....	(990)
Cartographic Records - Territory of Iowa, 1838-46 [SL #27]	free	(402)

Research aids

Hist. Records Survey: Check List of Iowa Imprints, 1838-1860	4.50	(624)
A Surname Index, by the Iowa Gen. Soc. [Approx. 21,000 names submitted by members from foreign countries - 1500's to everywhere U.S.A. 1972. Iowa maps included with county & county seat; contributor's name & address.]	7.50	(209)

APPANOOSE COUNTY

Records: 1850-52 Census, early marriages, cemeteries, land patents, probate records, etc. (in Hawkeye Heritage, Vol. 2, Nos. 1 & 2.) 46pp. Each No.:	2.00	(208)

CALHOUN COUNTY

Records: 1857 tax list, 1860 census, GAR records, 1st marriages (in Hawkeye Heritage, Vol. 5, No. 4) 24pp.	2.00	(208)

CHEROKEE COUNTY

Records: History, map, birth records before 1880, 1860-70 census, towns, cemeteries, probate records, mgs. 1856-80 (in Hawkeye Heritage, Vol. 8, No. 2) 38pp. 2.00 (208)

CLARKE COUNTY

Records: Wills, marriages, cemetery, Bible (in Hawkeye Heritage, Vol. 4, No. 1) 30pp. 2.00 (208)

DALLAS COUNTY

Records: Civil War & 1812 soldiers, original land entries, wills, cemeteries (in Hawkeye Heritage, Vol. 3, No. 1) 35pp. 2.00 (208)

DES MOINES COUNTY

Records: 1836 census, Mgs. 1835-39, abandoned towns, history (in Hawkeye Heritage, Vol. 1, No. 4) 13pp. 2.00 (208)

DUBUQUE COUNTY

Records: History, 1836 census, Mgs. 1835-38, Andreas Atlas Patrons List-1875 (in Hawkeye Heritage, Vol. 1, No. 3) 13pp. 2.00 (208)

FREMONT COUNTY

1870 Federal Census, by Harrison 8.50 (1029)

HENRY COUNTY

Records: 1854 census, GAR records, 1860 mortality & 1883 pension lists, 1st mgs (Hawkeye Heritage, Vol. 4, No. 3 & 4) 53pp. 4.00 (208)

JASPER COUNTY

Some Cemeteries of SE Wayne Co., Ky. & Jasper Co., Ia., by Young [all of Rock Creek, part of Our Silent City in Jasper Co.] 3.00 (722)
Land Owners - 1887 - Des Moines Twp. (in MCGS Reporter, Vol. 5, No. 4) 3pp. ..... .75 (596)

JEFFERSON COUNTY

Records: 1840 census, 1840 pioneers, 1st mgs 1839-43, abandoned towns (in Hawkeye Heritage, Vol. 2, No. 3) 19pp. 2.00 (208)
Some Ohio & Iowa Pioneers - Their Friends & Descendants, by Koleda [Collection of letters, bills, deeds, etc. from 1811-1947] 10.00 (3)

JOHNSON COUNTY

Records: History, map, 1st census, 1st map, 1st tax list, cemeteries, old settlers (in Hawkeye Heritage, Vol. 7, No. 3) 31pp. 2.00 (208)

LEE COUNTY

Illinois - Iowa - Missouri Searcher [Quarterly of the Lee County Genealogical Society - write for information] .... (603)
Keokuk Death Records, Vol. 1, 1867-1872 - Indexed, by Kay 5.00 (263)
Keokuk Death Records, Vol. 2, 1873-1878 - Indexed, by Kay 5.00 (263)

LINN COUNTY

History of Linn County, by Brewer & Wick [1st settlers, marriage records, Civil War soldiers, biographies. Every-name index.] 30.00 ..... (605)
Records: History, early settlers, cemeteries, map, 1840 census, early marriages (in Hawkeye Heritage, Vol. 7, No. 1) 31pp. 2.00 (208)

MADISON COUNTY

Records: Maps, 1st mgs., early mgs., Will Bk. A, Ky. settle-
ment, abandoned towns (Hawkeye Heritage, Vol. 5, No. 1) 25pp. 2.00   (208)

MARION COUNTY

Records: 1847 census, 1st mgs., Probate Bk. A, Dutch settlers,
abandoned towns (in Hawkeye Heritage, Vol. 3, No. 2) 15pp. 2.00   (208)

MARSHALL COUNTY

Records: History, map, cemeteries, mgs. 1849-64, Will Bk. 1,
Death Register (in Hawkeye Heritage, Vol. 8, No. 1 & 3) 63pp. 4.00   (208)

POLK COUNTY

Polk County Association of Early Settlers, 1840-1850-1860 (in
Hawkeye Heritage, Vol. 4, No. 2) 19pp. 2.00   (208)

SCOTT COUNTY

Records: History, Probate Bks. 1 & 2, Marriages 1831-51, Bible
rec., Marriages 1852-54 (Hawkey Heritage, Vol. 6, No. 1) 29pp. 2.00   (208)

STORY COUNTY

Records: History, Will Bk. 1, Mgs - Bks. 1 & 2, Early deaths,
probate records, 1854 census, Bible records (in Hawkeye Heritage, Vol. 6, No. 3) 40pp. 2.00   (208)

TAYLOR COUNTY

Records: History, maps, 1860 census, Will Bk. A, 1st Patent Bk.,
1st mgs. (in Hawkeye Heritage, Vol. 5, No. 2) 19pp. 2.00   (208)

VAN BUREN COUNTY

Records: History, abandoned towns, 1838 census, 1847 census
(in Hawkeye Heritage, Vol. 1, No. 1) 24pp. 2.00   (208)

WAPELLO COUNTY

Records: History, 1846 census, 1847 census index, abandoned
towns (in Hawkeye Heritage, Vol. 2, No. 1) 15pp. 2.00   (208)

Kansas

STATEWIDE REFERENCES

History of the State of Kansas, by Andreas (1883)   47.50   45.00   (546)

The Beginning of the West: Annals of the Kansas Gateway to the
West, 1540-1854, by Barry (1972)   14.75   .....   (903)

The Northwest Route [A history of a railroad crossing Kansas
from 1887-1919] by Lowry 2.00   (491)

Research aids

    List of Voters in Territorial Census of 1855   .....   1.95   (850)
    Kansas: A Student's Guide to Localized History 1.50   (762)

DOUGLAS COUNTY

The German Methodist Episcopal Church of Lawrence, Kansas
1859-1918 [History of the church & biographical sketches] 3.25   (697)

SHAWNEE COUNTY

Surname Index to 1860 Shawnee Co., Kansas Territorial Census 5.50   (946)

Kentucky

STATEWIDE REFERENCES

The Kentucky Genealogist, edited by Martha Porter Miller [A genealogical quarterly containing primary source material, compiled genealogies, queries, etc.] Subscription per yr:	.....	5.00	(8)
Valley of the Ohio, by Butler [Covers period from 1748-1791]	5.00	.....	(821)
Discovery, Settlement & Present State of Kentucky, by Filson	.....	4.25	(804)
History of Kentucky, by Collins (repr. of 1847 ed.)	12.50	.....	(930)
Filson's Kentucke: A Facsimile (repr. of 1930 ed.)	12.00	.....	(625)
Kentucky's Last Frontier (2nd ed., 1972)	7.35	.....	(970)
A History of Kentucky, by Allen (1872)	27.50	25.00	(546)
History of Kentucky, edited by Kerr. By Connelley et al (1922)			
Vol. 1	37.50	35.00	(546)
Vol. 2	37.50	35.00	(546)
Vol. 3	47.50	45.00	(546)
Vol. 4	47.50	45.00	(546)
Vol. 5	47.50	45.00	(546)
Set of 5 above volumes:	217.50	205.00	(546)
Liberal Kentucky, 1780-1828, by Sonne [Traces the conflict between liberal and Calvinist forces in Kentucky.]	.....	2.75	(126)
The County Courts in Antebellum Kentucky, by Ireland	9.00	.....	(126)
Kentucky: A Pictorial History (2nd ed.), by Coleman	8.95	.....	(126)
Sketches of Western Adventure, by M'Clung (repr. of 1832 ed.) [West of Applacians, 1755-1794, incidents of conflicts between settlers & Indians in the late 18th century.]	13.00	.....	(629)
Kentucky Bourbon: The Early Years of Whiskeymaking, by Crowgey [Studies not only Ky., but early yrs. in Va., Tenn., etc.]	9.75	.....	(126)
The Long Hunters of Skin House Branch, by Burdette & Berley [Acct. of Long Hunters & early history of Green R. country.]	.....	.....	(882)
Andre Michaux's Travels into Kentucky, 1792-1796, by Thwaites	18.00	.....	(630)
Colonial Men and Times; containing the journal of Col. Daniel Trabue, some account of his ancestry, life and travels in Virginia and the present state of Kentucky during the revolutionary period; the Huguenots, genealogy, etc., by Lillie DuPuy Harper	37.50	35.00	(546)
A Topographical Description of the Western Territory of North America, by Imlay (repr. of 1797 ed.) [Describes early stages of settlement in Kentucky & portions of Mississippi Valley.]	10.00	.....	(1000)
Boone's Wilderness Road, by Hulbert	11.50	.....	(630)
Wilderness Road: Description of the Routes of Travel by Which the Pioneers First Came to Kentucky, by Speed (repr. 1886)	10.00	.....	(625)
Kentucky Pioneers & Their Descendants, by Fowler	13.50	.....	(130)

Eastern, Southeastern, Northeastern Kentucky

The Big Sandy Valley, by Ely	13.50	.....	(130)
The Big Sandy Valley: A Regional History Prior to the Year 1850, by Jillson	8.50	.....	(130)
Pioneers of Eastern Kentucky: Their Feuds & Settlements, by Caudill	.....	.....	(923)
Talley's Kentucky Papers, by Talley	15.00	.....	(688)
Talley's Northeastern Kentucky Papers, by Talley	18.00	.....	(688)
[The 2 above Talley books purchased as a set:]	25.00	.....	(688)
Early Families of Eastern & Southeastern Kentucky, by Kozee	17.50	.....	(130)
Pioneer Families of Eastern & Southeastern Ky., by Kozee	10.00	.....	(130)

Research aids

Kentucky Genealogical Research Sources, by Hathaway	.....	6.45	(562)
Inventory of County Records of Kentucky, by Hathaway	.....	6.45	(562)
Tracing Family Trees in Eleven States [Kentucky is included]	.....	5.50	(29)
Sources For Genealogical Researching in Kentucky, by McCay	.....	2.50	(417)
Kentucky: A Student's Guide to Localized History	.....	1.50	(762)
Map tracing lineages of each county, parent counties, etc.			
[23 x 35, shows approximated county lines of 1790]	.....	5.00	(679)
An Historical Atlas of Kentucky & Her Counties, by Rone	.....	.....	(886)
A Guide to Kentucky Place Names, by Field	.....	.....	(898)

Records

Kentucky Family Records, Vol. I - 36 Bible records, 31 cemetery records, will abstracts, early marriages of Breckinridge Co., obituaries, pension, postal & family articles, 1810 census of Grayson Co. [Includes material on: Breckinridge, Caldwell, Daviess, Grayson, Hancock, Logan, McLean, Muhlenberg, Ohio, Todd, Trigg & Warren Cos.	.....	7.50	(471)
Kentucky Family Records, Vol. II - 19 Bible records, 25 cemetery records, will abstracts, Index to Will Bk. 1 of McLean Co., Ky., pension records & lists, family articles, marriages, military warrants, etc. [Contains data on: Breckinridge, Christian, Daviess, Grayson, Hancock, Henderson, Hopkins, Logan, McLean, Muhlenberg, Todd, Ohio, Warren & Webster Cos.	.....	7.50	(471)
Kentucky Family Records, Vol. III - 17 Bible records, Index to 1830 Census of Hancock Co., Index to Will Bks. 1-4 (1830-94) of Hancock Co., Early map of Hancock Co., 17 family articles, church records of Ohio Co., Estates & Adms., 1815-1864, of Daviess Co. [Contains data on: Allen, Daviess, Grayson, Green, Hancock, Hart, Henderson, McLean, Muhlberg, Ohio, Simpson & Union Cos.	.....	7.50	(471)
Land on the Western Waters, by Schreiner-Yantis [Includes preemption certificates showing dates of settlement before 1778] [Publication date 1976]	.....	.....	(289)
The Territorial Papers of the US - Territory south of the Ohio R. (Ky. & Tenn.) 1790-1796 [Microfilm Ser. M721, Roll 3]	Microfilm:	12.00	(402)
"First Census" of Kentucky, by Heinemann [Tax lists]	10.00	.....	(130)
"Second Census" of Kentukcy, by Clift [Tax lists]	16.50	.....	(130)
Index to the 1810 Census of Kentucky, by Volkel			
Vol. 1: Counties Adair - Cumberland	.....	6.00	(752)
Vol. 2: Counties Estill - Hopkins	.....	6.00	(752)
Vol. 3: Counties Jefferson - Muhlenberg	.....	6.00	(752)
Vol. 4: Counties Nelson - Woodford	.....	6.00	(752)
Volumes 1, 2, 3, & 4 bound together in one book	28.00	.....	(752)
Index to the 1820 Census of Kentucky, by Volkel			
Vol. 1: Counties Adair - Cumberland	.....	7.00	(752)
Vol. 2: Counties Daviess - Hopkins	.....	7.00	(752)
Index to the 1830 Census of Kentucky, by Smith			
Vol. 1: Counties Adair - Campbell	.....	6.00	(752)
Vol. 2: Counties Casey - Gallatin	.....	6.00	(752)
Vol. 3: Counties Garrard - Hopkins	.....	6.00	(752)
Vol. 4: Counties Jefferson - Meade	.....	6.00	(752)
Vol. 5: Counties Mercer - Russell	.....	6.00	(752)
Vol. 6: Counties Scott - Woodford	.....	6.00	(752)
Volumes 1, 2, & 3 bound together in one book	22.00	.....	(752)
Volumes 4, 5, & 6 bound together in one book	22.00	.....	(752)

A Surname Index for the 1850 Federal Census, by McDowell
[This will be a 33 volume surname index. Each volume is
one microfilm roll and is indexed by county. Three vols.
completed - listed under counties.]   .... (276)
Kentucky Bible Records, Vol. 1, by Ky. Rec. Res. Comm. DAR 5.00 (560)
Kentucky Bible Records, Vol. 2,   "   "   "   "   " 5.00 (560)
Kentucky Bible Records, Vol. 3,   "   "   "   "   " 7.50 (560)
Kentucky Bible Records, Vol. 4,   "   "   "   "   " 7.50 (560)
Kentucky Bible Records, Vol. 5,   "   "   "   "   " 8.50 (560)
Kentucky Cemetery Rec., Vol. 1,   "   "   "   "   " 10.00 (560)
Kentucky Cemetery Rec., Vol. 2,   "   "   "   "   " 8.50 (560)
Kentucky Cemetery Rec., Vol. 3,   "   "   "   "   " 8.50 (560)
Kentucky Cemetery Rec., Vol. 4,   "   "   "   "   " 10.00 (560)
Kentucky Records, Early Wills and Marriages, Old Bible Re-
cords and Tombstone Inscriptions, by Ardery. Vol. 1 10.00 ..... (130)
Kentucky Court & Other Records, Wills, Deeds, Orders, Suits,
Church Minutes, Marriages, Old Bibles and Tombstone
Records, by Ardery. Vol. 2   10.00 ..... (130)
Kentucky Pioneer & Court Records, by McAdams [Abstracts
of early wills, deeds, and marriages.]   11.50 ..... (130)
Old Kentucky Entries and Deeds: A Complete Index to All of the
Earliest Land Entries, Military Warrants, Deeds, and Wills
of the Commonwealth of Kentucky, by Jillson   15.00 ..... (130)
Kentucky Land Grants: A Systematic Index to All of the Land
Grants Recorded in the State Land Office at Frankfort, Ken-
tucky, 1782-1924, by Jillson   37.50 ..... (130)
Kentucky Marriages, 1797-1865, by Clift   15.00 ..... (130)
Abstract of Early Kentucky Wills and Inventories, by King 16.50 ..... (130)

Military

Revolutionary Soldiers in Kentucky, by Quisenberry   13.50 ..... (130)
Kentucky in the War of 1812, by Quisenberry   12.50 ..... (130)
Kentucky Soldiers in the War of 1812, by Ky. Adj.-Gen. Off. 37.50 ..... (130)
Kentucky Pension Roll for 1835, by U.S. War Dept.   7.50   5.00 (130)
History of the Orphan Brigade, 1861-1865, by Thompson
[Biog. sketches & photos of many of the Conf. Ky. men] 32.50 ..... (848)

Religious

Sketches of the Early Catholic Missions of Kentucky: From Their
Commencement in 1787 to 1826-7, by Spalding (repr. 1844) 15.00 ..... (629)

ADAIR COUNTY

Methodist History of Adair County, 1782-1969, by Allison 7.63   ..... (648)
Kentucky Genealogy & Biography, Vol. 5, ed. Westerfield   14.95 ..... (579)
1810 Tax List, by Simmons 3.00 (531)
1810 Federal Census, by Simmons 3.00 (531)

ALLEN COUNTY

Kentucky Genealogy & Biography, Vol. 2, ed. Westerfield 11.95 ..... (579)

ANDERSON COUNTY

Early Wills [first 63 wills in Will Bk. A] (in The Ridge Runners,
Vol. 3, No. 1] 2.00 (670)

BALLARD COUNTY

Ballard's Brave Boys, by Magee [Civil War records & genealogy
of 1200 soldiers; also names of 4,000 more in the area.] 12.00 7.50 (358)

BARREN COUNTY

Kentucky Genealogy & Biography, Vol. 2, ed. by Westerfield   11.95   .....   (579)

BOONE COUNTY

Surname Index to 1850 Census of Boone, Bourbon & Boyle Cos. 3.50   (276)

BOURBON COUNTY

Surname Index to 1850 Census of Boone, Bourbon & Boyle Cos. 3.50   (276)

BOYLE COUNTY

Surname Index to 1850 Census of Boone, Bourbon & Boyle Cos. 3.50   (276)
Kentucky Genealogy & Biography, Vol. 5, ed. by Westerfield   14.95   .....   (579)

BRECKINRIDGE COUNTY

Roman Catholic Cemeteries of Breckinridge & Meade Cos., Vol. 1   .....   7.50   (88)
Church Cemeteries [31] of Breckinridge & Meade Cos., Vol. 2   .....   7.50   (88)
Church Cemeteries [23] of Meade, Breckinridge & Hancock Cos.,
   Vol. 3 [All above cemetery listings are complete & indexed.] 7.50   (88)
Deed Bk. A, 1800-1803, (in The Kentucky Genealogist, Vol. 16,
   Nos. 1, 2, & 3)   8-5-7pp.   Each no. - $1.50.   Total: 4.50   (8)
Kentucky Family Records, Vol. 1 [Early marriages included] 7.50   (471)
Kentucky Genealogy & Biography, Vol. 1, ed. by Westerfield   11.95   .....   (579)

BULLITT COUNTY

Fort Knox Cemeteries in Bullitt, Hardin & Meade Cos., with His-
   torical and Genealogical Notations,   [Publication date, 1975]   ....   (276)

BUTLER COUNTY

Kentucky Genealogy & Biography, Vol. 3, ed. by Westerfield   11.95   .....   (579)
Butler Co. Cemeteries, Pt. 1, by Haun 5.00   (1007)

CALDWELL COUNTY

Kentucky Genealogy & Biography, Vol. 4, ed. by Westerfield   14.95   .....   (579)

CALLOWAY COUNTY

Jackson Purchase Census 1830, by Simmons 4.50   (531)
1840 Federal Census, by Simmons 4.00   (531)

CHRISTIAN COUNTY

Tax Lists 1797-1798-1799 [Gives real estate, slaves, horses] 2.50   (531)
1810 Federal Census, by Simmons 3.00   (531)

CRITTENDEN COUNTY

Kentucky Genealogy & Biography, Vol. 4, ed. by Westerfield   14.95   .....   (579)

CUMBERLAND COUNTY

Kentucky Genealogy & Biography, Vol. 5, ed. by Westerfield   14.95   .....   (579)

DAVIESS COUNTY

Estates & Adms. 1815-1864 (included in Ky. Fam. Rec., Vol. 3) 7.50   (471)
1850 Federal Census, Annotated, by Ford 12.75   (471)

EDMONSON COUNTY

Kentucky Genealogy & Biography, Vol. 1, ed. by Westerfield   11.95   .....   (579)

FAYETTE COUNTY

The History of Pioneer Lexington: 1779-1806, by Staple (repr.)   10.50   .....   (996)
Ante Bellum Houses of the Bluegrass: . . . Architecture in Fay-
   ette County, by Lancaster   12.50   .....   (126)

FLEMING COUNTY

Abstracts of Deed Books A-G (1797-1818) [All data indexed]	36.00	.....	(304)
" " " " " Each book sold separately:	.....	4.50	(304)

FLOYD COUNTY

1850 Federal Census, by Parrish		.....	5.00	(302)

FRANKLIN COUNTY

History of Franklin County, by Kohnson (repr. of 1912 ed.)	13.50	.....	(870)
Franklin County Atlas, 1870-1880 (reprint)	.....	9.95	(821)

FULTON COUNTY

1850 Federal Census, by Simmons		.....	6.00	(531)

GARRARD COUNTY

Kentucky Genealogy & Biography, Vol. 5, ed. by Westerfield	14.95	.....	(579)

GRAVES COUNTY

Jackson Purchase Tax Lists 1822-1823-1824 [Includes taxpayers, children 4-14, slaves, horses, etc.]	.....	4.50	(531)
Jackson Purchase Census 1830, by Simmons	.....	4.50	(531)
1840 Federal Census, by Simmons	.....	3.00	(531)
1850 Federal Census, by Simmons [Added genealogical facts.]	.....	9.00	(531)
Marriage Records 1852-1859 [from the Vital Statistics - includes residence, birthplace, age, etc.]	.....	3.50	(531)

GRAYSON COUNTY

Surname Index to 1850 Census of Grayson, Greene, Greenup, & Hancock Counties, by McDowell	.....	3.50	(276)
1810 Census (in Kentucky Fam. Rec., Vol. 1)	.....	7.50	(471)
Kentucky Genealogy & Biography, Vol. 1, ed. by Westerfield	11.95	.....	(579)
1850 Federal Census, by West-Central Fam. Res. Assoc.	.....	.....	(471)

GREEN COUNTY

Brick Union Christian Graveyard (in Kentucky Genealogist, Vol. 14, No. 3) 5pp.	.....	1.50	(8)
Kentucky Genealogy & Biography, Vol. 5, ed. by Westerfield	14.95	.....	(579)
Surname Index to 1850 Census of Grayson, Greene, Greenup, & Hancock Cos., by McDowell	.....	3.50	(276)

HANCOCK COUNTY

Early map; Index to 1830 Federal Census; Index to Will Bks. 1-4 [1830-1894] (in Kentucky Family Records, Vol. 3)	.....	7.50	(471)
Kentucky Genealogy & Biography, Vol. 1, ed. by Westerfield	11.95	.....	(579)
Cemeteries, Vol. 1, by Leftwich	.....	10.00	(471)
Church Cemeteries [23] of Meade, Breckinridge & Hancock Cos., Vol. 3, by Bolin	.....	7.50	(88)
1850 Federal Census	.....	.....	(471)

HARDIN COUNTY

Chronicles of Hardin County, 1766-1974, by Winstead	8.00	.....	(984)
Kentucky Genealogy & Biography, Vol. 1, ed. by Westerfield	11.95	.....	(579)
Marriage Bonds 1792-1812, by Stancliff	.....	7.50	(250)
Fort Knox Cemeteries in Bullitt, Hardin, and Meade Counties, with Historical and Genealogical Notations, by McDowell	.....	.....	(276)

HARLAN COUNTY

My Appalachia, by Caudill	4.95	.....	(974)
1850 Federal Census, by Hiday	.....	5.00	(752)

HART COUNTY

Kentucky Genealogy & Biography, Vol. 1, ed. by Westerfield   11.95 ..... (579)

HICKMAN COUNTY

Jackson Purchase Tax Lists 1822, 1823, 1824 [Taxpayers, children 4-14, slaves, horses, etc.] 4.50 (531)
1840 Federal Census, by Simmons 4.00 (531)
1850 Federal Census, by Simmons 6.50 (531)

HOPKINS COUNTY

Kentucky Genealogy & Biography, Vol. 4, ed. by Westerfield   14.95 ..... (579)

JEFFERSON COUNTY

Tomstone Inscriptions from Small Cemeteries in Jefferson Co. (in The Kentucky Genealogist, Vol. 14, No. 4; Vol. 15, Nos. 1, 2, 3, 4) 11, 8, 6, 7, 6 pp. Each No.: $1.50.   Total: 7.50 (8)
The Louisville Directory For the Year 1832 (repr.) 4.95 (963)

JOHNSON COUNTY

1850 Federal Census, by Parrish 5.00 (302)

LaRUE COUNTY

Kentucky Genealogy & Biography, Vol. 1, ed. by Westerfield   11.95 ..... (579)

LETCHER COUNTY

1850 Federal Census, by Griffith 3.35 (29)
1880 Federal Census, by Griffith 3.35 (29)

LINCOLN COUNTY

Order Books, 1781-1791 (in The Kentucky Genealogist, Vol. 6, #1, 2, 3, 4; Vol. 7, #1, 2, 3, 4; Vol. 8, #1, 3; Vol. 9, #2, 4; Vol. 10, #2, 3, 4; Vol. 11, #1, 2, 3, 4; Vol. 12, #1, 2, 3, 4; Vol. 13, #1, 2, 3, 4; Vol. 14, #1, 2, 3, 4; Vol. 15, #2, 3, 4) Each # contains 3 to 11pp. Total: 221pp. Each #: $1.50   Total: 51.00 (8)
Kentucky Genealogy & Biography, Vol. 5, ed. by Westerfield   14.95 ..... (579)

LIVINGSTON COUNTY

Kentucky Genealogy & Biography, Vol. 4, ed. by Westerfield   14.95 ..... (579)
1810 Census, by Simmons 2.00 (531)

LOGAN COUNTY

Kentucky Genealogy & Biography, Vol. 4, ed. by Westerfield   14.95 ..... (579)

LYON COUNTY

Kentucky Genealogy & Biography, Vol. 4, ed. by Westerfield   14.95 ..... (579)

McCRACKEN COUNTY

Index to Will Book #1 (included in Ky. Fam. Rec., Vol. 2) 7.50 (471)
Jackson Purchase Census 1830, by Simmons 4.50 (531)
1850 Federal Census, by Simmons 6.50 (531)

McLEAN COUNTY

Kentucky Genealogy & Biography, Vol. 3, ed. by Westerfield   11.95 ..... (579)

MADISON COUNTY

Kentucky Genealogy & Biography, Vol. 5, ed. by Westerfield   14.95 ..... (579)
Militia Officers, 1786-1791 (in Ky. Genealogist, Vol. 15, #2) 5pp. 1.50 (8)

....

MARION COUNTY

Kentucky Genealogy & Biography, Vol. 5, ed. by Westerfield   14.95   .....   (579)

MARSHALL COUNTY

1850 Federal Census, by Simmons 8.00   (531)

MASON COUNTY

Abstracts of Deed Book A-L, 1789-1810 [Fully indexed abstracts of neighbors, witnesses, apprentices, as well as principals.]	29.50	.....	(304)
Abstracts of Deed Book A, B, C, D, E, F, G, H, I, J, K, or L (above)	.....	3.95	(304)
Abstracts of Deed Books M- [to be available at a later date]	.....	.....	(304)

MEADE COUNTY

All Roman Catholic Cemeteries of Breckinridge & Meade Cos.	.....	7.50	(88)
31 Church Cemeteries of Breckinridge & Meade Cos., Indexed	.....	7.50	(88)
23 Church Cemeteries of Meade, Breckinridge & Hancock Cos.	.....	7.50	(88)
[Each of 3 above books has complete listings & is indexed.]			
Fort Knox Cemeteries in Bullitt, Hardin, & Meade Cos., with Historical & Genealogical Notations [available in 1975]	.....	.....	(276)
Kentucky Genealogy & Biography, Vol. 1, ed. by Westerfield	11.95	.....	(579)

MERCER COUNTY

Cemetery Records, Vol. 1, 2, 3, & 4 [Each: $8.50] Set of 4:	.....	30.00	(463)
Bible Records of Mercer County Families, Vol. 1	.....	13.00	(463)
Records of Bethel Baptist Church, Wash. [now Mercer] 1817-1875	.....	5.00	(1139)
Militia Officers before 1792 (in The Ky. Genealogist, Vol. 16, #4)	.....	1.50	(8)

METCALFE COUNTY

Kentucky Genealogy & Biography, Vol. 2, ed. by Westerfield   11.95   .....   (579)

MONROE COUNTY

Pioneer Families of Sullivan Co., Mo. With Related Families of St. Charles Co., Mo. & Monroe Co., Ky., by Sears	15.00	.....	(22)
Kentucky Genealogy & Biography, Vol. 2, ed. by Westerfield	11.95	.....	(579)

MONTGOMERY COUNTY

Index to Estates, 1797-1823   (in The Kentucky Genealogist, Vol.
   14, #1 & 2) 3, 5pp. Total: 8pp. Each #: $1.50   Total: 3.00   (8)

MUHLENBURG COUNTY

Kentucky Genealogy & Biography, Vol. 3, ed. by Westerfield   11.95   .....   (579)

NELSON COUNTY

Marriage Bonds, 1785-1832, Vol. 1 [Grooms' surnames A-J]	.....	10.00	(250)
Marriage Bonds, 1785-1832, Vol. 2 [Grooms' surnames K-Z]	.....	10.00	(250)
Will Book 1784-1790 (in The Ky. Genealogist, Vol. 15, #1 & 2) 6pp each. Total: 12pp. Each #: $1.50 Total:	.....	3.00	(8)
Kentucky Genealogy & Biography, Vol. 5, ed. by Westerfield	14.95	.....	(579)

NICHOLAS COUNTY

Marriages 1831-1835 (in The Ky. Genealogist, Vol. 15, #1 & 2)
   4pp each. Total: 8pp. Each #: $1.50   Total: 3.00   (8)

OHIO COUNTY

Kentucky Genealogy & Biography, Vol. 3, ed. by Westerfield	11.95	.....	(579)
Ohio County, Ky. in the Olden Days: A Series of Old Newspaper Sketches of Fragmentary History, by Taylor	10.00	.....	(130)

Some Church Records of Ohio County (included in Kentucky Family Records, Vol. 3) 7.50 (471)
Some Cemeteries (in The Kentucky Genealogist, Vol. 16, #3) 4pp. 1.50 (8)
1850 Federal Census, by West-Central Ky. Fam. Res. Assn. 10.00 (471)

PENDLETON COUNTY

Will Abstracts 1841-1871 (in Genealogical Reference Builders "Newsletter", Vol. 7, #3) 16pp. 2.00 (931)

PULASKI COUNTY

Marriage Records, Book I (1797-1850) 6.00 (1142)
Graves of the Lake Cumberland Basin, by Young (see Wayne Co.) 7.50 (722)

RUSSELL COUNTY

Graves of the Lake Cumberland Basin, by Young (see Wayne Co.) 7.50 (722)

SHELBY COUNTY

Marriages 1792-1800 (in Gen. Ref. Builders, Vol. 6, #3) 8pp. 2.00 (931)

SIMPSON COUNTY

Kentucky Genealogy & Biography, Vol. 4, ed. by Westerfield 14.95 ..... (579)

TAYLOR COUNTY

Kentucky Genealogy & Biography, Vol. 5, ed. by Westerfield 14.95 ..... (579)

UNION COUNTY

Kentucky Genealogy & Biography, Vol. 4, ed. by Westerfield 14.95 ..... (579)

WARREN COUNTY

Kentucky Genealogy & Biography, Vol. 2, ed. by Westerfield 11.95 ..... (579)

WASHINGTON COUNTY

Records of Bethel Baptist Church, 1817-1875 [Minutes, lists of members, death dates, etc.] Church now located in Mercer Co. 5.00 (1139)
Kentucky Genealogy & Biography, Vol. 5 14.95 ..... (579)

WAYNE COUNTY

1830 Census, by Carter 3.50 (1146)
Wayne County Pioneers, by Bork [Biographical Sketches & Civil Court Records] 19.50 ..... (35)
Marriages & Vital Records, 1801-1860, by Bork [Marriages A-J; Cemetery Lists; 1820 Census; Delinquent Tax Lists; Old Letters; many other items - completely indexed] 14.50 (35)
Marriages & Vital Records, 1801-1860, by Bork [Marriages K-Z; Cemetery Lists; Birth & Death Records; 1830 Census; Revolutionary War Pension Applications; Early Doctors; Midwives; Minsters; Extra's - completely indexed] 17.50 (35)
Vital Records, Vol. 3, by Bork [1850 Census; Cemetery Lists; Bible Records; Cumberland Co. Marriages; Wills] 12.50 (35)
Wayne County Records, Vol. 4, by Bork [Available, fall 1975]

Marriages, 1801-1860, by Nutter 12.50 (102)
Wills, 1802-1909, by Nutter 12.50 (102)
Some Cemeteries of Southeastern Wayne Co., Ky. & Jasper Co., Ia, by Young [13 complete & 6 partial listings of Wayne Co. - all of Rock Creek & part of Our Silent City in Jasper Co.] 3.00 (722)
Graves of the Lake Cumberland Basin, [Name of persons disinterred and where reinterred - with map showing location of the cemeteries. List prepared by U.S. Corps. of Engineers.] 7.50 (722)

···

WEBSTER COUNTY

Kentucky Genealogy & Biography, Vol. 4, ed. by Westerfield   14.95   .....   (579)

WOODFORD COUNTY

History of Woodford, Kentucky, by Railey   ....   (130)

Louisiana

STATEWIDE REFERENCES

A History of French Louisiana, Vol. 1: The Reign of Louis XIV by Giraud	15.00	.....	(935)
Louisiana in French Diplomacy: 1759-1804, by Lyon (repr. 1934)	8.95	.....	(664)
A Guide to Spanish Louisiana, 1762-1806, by Holmes	.....	3.95	(483)
The Canary Islands Migration to Louisiana, 1778-1783 , by Villeré	10.00	.....	(130)
Voyage to Louisiana 1803-1805, by Robin	12.50	.....	(859)
History of Louisiana, by Gayarree	75.00	.....	(960)
History of Louisiana, by Fortier (rev. ed.) 2 vols. Each:	15.00	.....	(960)
Story of Louisiana, by Davis 4 vols. Set:	79.50	.....	(960)
Southwest Louisiana, by Perrin	15.00	.....	(960)
Louisiana Under the Rule of Spain, France & the United States 1785-1807, by Robertson	38.50	.....	(636)
Boundaries of the Louisiana Purchase: A Historical Study, by Houck (repr. of 1901 ed.)	6.00	.....	(629)
Sketches of Early Texas & Louisiana, by Gaillariet	6.50	1.95	(640)
Pioneer Leaders & Early Institutions in La. Education, by Cline	7.95	.....	(960)
Louisiana Leaders, by Louisiana Pen Women	12.50	.....	(960)
Biographies of the Judges of Louisiana, ed. by Fruge	12.50	.....	(960)
Attempt to Re-assemble the Old Settlers in Family Groups, by Marchand	6.00	.....	(960)
First Families of Louisiana, by Conrad 2 vols.	25.00	.....	(960)
Old Families of Louisiana, by Arthur & Kernion	12.50	.....	(960)

Research aids

Louisiana: A Student's Guide to Localized History, by Taylor	.....	1.50	(762)
Those Strange Louisiana Names, by Parkerson	.....	1.25	(960)
Index to Louisiana Historical Quarterly, Vols. 1-33, by Cruise	.....	20.00	(859)

Records

The Notarial Acts of Estevan De Quinones 1785-1786, by Gianelloni [Abstracts, La. Spanish colonial records, mostly marriage applications giving age, occupation, parents, etc.]	.....	6.95	(700)
Selected Acadian & Louisiana Church Records, by Bodin [Abs. of Catholic records of Acadians - various areas of La.] 2 vols......	.....	.....	(547)
The New Orleans French, 1720-1733: A Collection of Marriage Records Relating to the First Colonists of the Louisiana Province, by DeVille	12.50	.....	(130)
The Census Tables for the French Colony of Louisiana From 1699 Through 1732, by Maduell	12.50	.....	(130)
Some Late 18th Century La. Census Records 1758-1796	.....	.....	(865)
The Territorial Papers of the U.S. - Louisiana & Missouri 1803-1820 [Microfilm Series M721, Roll # 9] Microfilm:	12.00		(402)
1810 Census of Louisiana, by Accelerated Index	15.00	.....	(677)
Index to Louisiana 1860 Mortality Schedule, by Achee & Wright [Those who died in year prior to 1860 Census - gives name, sex, nativity, month died, cause of death, etc.]	.....	12.50	(825)

Religious and ethnic groups

The Early Jews of New Orleans, by Korn	12.50	.....	(440)
The Jews in the South, ed. by Dinnerstein & Palsson	12.50	.....	(935)
Yugoslavs in Louisiana, by Vujnovich [Starting 1830's]	12.50	.....	(859)

Military

Honor and Fidelity: Louisiana Infantry Regiment and the Louisiana Militia Companies, 1766-1821, by Holmes   10.00   .....   (483)

Louisiana Troops, 1720-1770, by DeVille 10.00   (130)

A Southern Record, 3rd Louisiana Infantry, by Tunnard [A complete roster & service rec. of over 2,000 soldiers]   15.00   .....   (848)

"Try Us": The Story of the Washington Artillery in WW II, by Casey [Narrative acct. of New Orleans Regt. + names of 5000 WW II dead from La. & 4000 from other states. Maps.]   15.00   .....   (493)

ACADIA PARISH

Southwest La. Records - 1756 to 1810, by Hebert [All civil & ecclesiastical records of genealogical value in the 13 civil parishes of SW La. - marriages, baptisms, deaths, successions]   25.00   .....   (234)

ATTAKAPAS DISTRICT

Records of Attakapas District, Vol. 1 (1739-1811), by Sanders	.....	10.00	(688)
Records of Attakapas District, Vol. 2 (1811-1860), by Sanders	.....	10.00	(688)

Marriage Contracts of the Attakapas Post, 1760-1803 & The 1774 Census of Attakapas, by DeVille, Guillory & David   x   (547)

AVOYELLES PARISH

Colonial Louisiana Marriage Contracts, by Winston DeVille	10.00	.....	(960)
Census Records, Vol. I [of Avoyelles & St. Landry, 1810 & 1820]	11.50	.....	(130)

CALDWELL PARISH

History of Caldwell Parish, by Wood   6.95   .....   (960)

EVANGELINE PARISH

The Opelousas Country, by Gahn   6.95   .....   (960)

FLORIDA PARISHES

[Included West Feliciana, East Feliciana, East Baton Rouge, St. Helena, Livingston, Tangipahoa, Washington, & St. Tammany]

Amite County, Mississippi & Florida Parishes, Louisiana, by Casey et al, 4 vols. [Marriages, wills, adms., abs. of church records, deeds, tax lists, censuses, military records, land grants, maps, genealogies, Spanish claims, land plats (photocopies), etc.]   71.00   .....   (488)

An Index to the 1820 Census of Florida Parishes & 1812 St. Tammany Parish Tax List, by Sanders 5.00   (195)

GRANT PARISH

History of Grant Parish, by Harrison & McNeely   10.00   .....   (960)

IBERVILLE PARISH

Census Records, Vol 2 [of Iberville, Natchitoches, Pointe Coupee, and Rapides Parishes, 1810 & 1820 by Ardoin   14.00   .....   (130)

LAFAYETTE PARISH

The Attakapas Country: A History of Lafayette Parish, by Griffin [Accts. of early settlers, church records, biographies, etc.]   15.00   .....   (859)

NATCHITOCHES PARISH

Census Records, Vol. 2   (see Iberville Parish)   14.00   .....   (130)

ORLEANS PARISH

Creole Families of New Orleans, by King	12.50	.....	(960)
New Orleans & Bayou Country, by Bridaham	.....	.....	(743)

OUACHITA PARISH

Index to Ouachita Parish, Louisiana Probates 1800-1870, by Achee	6.00	(825)

POINTE COUPEE PARISH

First Settlers of Pointe Coupee: 1737-1750, by DeVille	.....	10.00	(580)
Colonial Louisiana Marriage Contracts, by DeVille	10.00	.....	(960)
Louisiana Census Records, Vol. 2 (see Iberville Parish)	14.00	.....	(130)

RAPIDES PARISH

Reprint of the Rapides Parish section of Biog. & Hist. Memoirs of Northwest Louisiana - with new index [Available, 1975]	.....	.....	(825)
Louisiana Census Records, Vol. 2 (see Iberville Parish)	14.00	.....	(130)
Once Upon a River: History of Pineville, La., by Brister	6.00	.....	(960)

ST. HELENA PARISH

Hunting For Bears, by Murray [Reprints of Newspaper Genealogical column - marriage records, queries, censuses, etc.] Each:	.....	1.50	(277)

ST. JOHN THE BAPTIST PARISH

Asint-Jean-Baptiste Des Allemands: Abstract of Civil Records of St. John the Baptiste Parish, With Genealogies, 1753-1803	.....	.....	(865)

ST. LANDRY PARISH

Census Records, Vol. 1 [of Avoyelles & St. Landry, 1810 & 1820]	11.50	.....	(130)
St. Landry Parish Successions Index, 1807-1865	.....	4.50	(688)

ST. MARTIN PARISH

Records of Attakapas Dist., Vol. 3: St. Martin Parish, 1808-1860	.....	10.00	(195)

ST. MARY PARISH

"St. Mary Parish Heirship Series" , by Sanders			
Vol. 1: Annotated Abstracts of Successions, 1811-1834	xxx	.....	(195)
Vol. 2: Annotated Abstracts of Marriage Bk. 1, 1811-1829	8.50	.....	(195)
Vol. 3: Abstracts of Marriage Bk. 2, 1830-1837	10.00	.....	(195)
Vol. 4: Abstracts of Successions, 1834-1837 & Misc. Records	10.00	.....	(195)

TANGIPAHOA PARISH

Hunting For Bears, by Murray (see St. Helena Parish) Each:	.....	1.50	(277)

VERNON PARISH

A Brief History of Vernon Parish, by Cupit	7.50	.....	(960)

WEST CARROLL PARISH

Between the Rivers, by McKoin	7.95	.....	(960)

Maine

STATEWIDE REFERENCES

The Pioneers of Maine & New Hampshire, 1628 to 1660, by Pope	10.00	.....	(130)
Beginnings of Colonial Maine 1603-1658, by Burrage (repr.)	19.50	.....	(625)
History of the State of Maine, by Williamson	30.00	.....	(876)

Research aids

Research in Maine (in NGS Quarterly, Vol. 55, #2) 6pp. 3.00 (616)
Collections of the Maine Historical Society, 10 vols.   Set: 295.00 ..... (630)

Records

Pioneers of Maine Rivers, With Lists to 1651, by Spencer 12.50 ..... (130)
Maine Wills, 1640–1760, by Sargent 22.50 ..... (130)
1790 Federal Census, by U.S. Census Bureau 7.50 ..... (663)
1790 Federal Census, by U.S. Census Bureau 10.00 ..... (130)
1800 Federal Census, by Accelerated Indexing Systems 21.00 ..... (677)
Province & Court Records of Maine, by Moody 18.00 ..... (724)
Names of Soldiers of the American Revolution [from Maine]
  Who Applied for State Bounty, by House 7.50 ..... (130)
An Alphabetical Index of Rev. Pensioners in Maine, by Flagg 8.50 ..... (130)
The Maine Hist. & Gen. Recorder, Vols. 1–9 [repr. in 3 vols.] 100.00 ..... (130)
Genealogical Dictionary of Maine & N.H., by Noyes, et al 17.50 ..... (130)

ANDROSCOGGIN COUNTY

Franklin & Androscoggin Counties, by Chadbourne 1.95 (876)

AROOSTOOK COUNTY

Maine & Her People, Supplement on Aroostook Co., by Clifford 6.00 ..... (876)
A History of Three Corners [Aroostook, Penobscot & Washington
  Counties] by Storms 10.00 ..... (966)

FRANKLIN COUNTY

FRANKLIN & ANDROSCOGGIN COUNTIES, by Chadbourne 1.95 (876)

HANCOCK COUNTY

Peninsula, by Rich [concerns Gouldsboro] 2.95 (781)

KENNEBEC COUNTY

History of Vassalborough, Maine 1771–1971, by Robbins [Lists
  names of original settlers] 2.75 (479)

PENOBSCOT COUNTY

An Illustrated History of Bangor, Maine 1769–1969, by Vickery 5.00 2.50 (958)
A History of Three Corners (see Aroostook County) 10.00 ..... (966)

WALDO COUNTY

Cemetery Inscriptions from Mt. Repose Cemetery, by Lundberg 2.00 (949)

WASHINGTON COUNTY

History of Kennebunkport, Maine, by Bradbury 10.00 ..... (662)
History of York, Maine, by Banks 30.00 ..... (130)
A History of Three Corners (see Aroostook County) 10.00 ..... (966)

Maryland

STATEWIDE REFERENCES

The Maryland & Delaware Genealogist, ed. by Clark [A genealogical quarterly containing primary source material, queries,
  etc. Annual index.]   Subscription per year: 6.00 (212)
An Historical View of the Government of Maryland, From Its Colonization to the Present Day (1831), by McMahon (repr.) 17.50 ..... (663)

The Provisional Government of Md. (1774-1777), by Silver (repr.) 10.25   6.25   (1000)
Maryland: The Federalist Years, by Renzulli   15.00   .....   (736)
Old Maryland Manors, With the Records of a Court Leet & a Court
    Baron, by Johnson (repr. of 1883 ed.)   10.25   6.25   (1000)
Maryland: A History 1632-1974, ed. by Walsh & Fox   12.50   .....   (506)
History of Maryland From the Earliest Period to the Present
    Day, by Scharf (repr. of 1879 ed. - new index) 3 vols.   Set: 55.00   .....   (233)
New Index Prepared for (and bound into) the above 5.00   (233)
Maryland Main & the Eastern Shore, by Footner   8.00   .....   (233)
History of Maryland: Province and State, by Andrews (1929 repr.) 17.50   .....   (233)
The Maryland Original Research Soc. of Baltimore, by Richardson 11.50   .....   (130)
Narratives of Early Maryland, 1633-1684, by Hall (repr. 1910 ed.) 5.75   .....   (643)
His Lordship's Patronage: Offices of Profit in Colonial Maryland,
    by Owings [Studies in Maryland history]   7.50   .....   (506)
An Outline of the Maryland Boundary Disputes and Related Events,
    by Morrison [All disputes between 1635-1910] 3.00   (325)
Colonial families & Their Descendants, by Emory (repr. 1900) 17.50   15.00   (546)
Historic Graves of Maryland & the Dist. of Columbia, by Ridgely 12.50   .....   (130)

Research aids

Genealogical Research in Maryland, by Meyer 4.50   (506)
An Index to the Source Records of Maryland, by Passano   18.50   .....   (130)
Index Holdings of Maryland Hall of Records - Bulletin No. 17   .....   free   (266)
The County Courthouses & Records of Maryland, Part Two: The
    Records [Tells records available in courthouses - and also
    at the Hall of Records in Annapolis]   5.00   .....   (266)
Maryland: A Student's Guide to Localized History 1.50   (762)
The Manuscript Collections of the Maryland Historical Society
    [2 million mss in 1750 collections; much genealogy]   15.00   .....   (506)
Sources for Genealogical Searching in Maryland, by McCay 3.25   (417)

Records

Calendar of Maryland State Papers, No. 1: The Black Books
    [Abs. of papers, 1636-1785 - all name index.]   13.50   .....   (130)
Calendar of Maryland State Papers, No. 3: The Brown Books
    [Abs. of military papers of Revolutionary period - indexed]   6.00   .....   (266)
Calendar of Maryland State Papers, No. 4, Pt. 1, The Red Bks.
    [Abs. of military & civil papers, revolutionary period]   6.00   .....   (266)
Calendar of Maryland State Papers, No. 4, Pt. 2, The Red Bks.
    [Continuation of Pt. 1 - both indexed]   3.00   .....   (266)
Calendar of Maryland State Papers, No. 4, Pt. 3, The Red Bks.
    [Continuation of Pt. 1 & Pt. 2 - indexed]   3.00   .....   (266)
Calendar of Maryland State Papers, No. 5, Executive Miscellanea
    [Abs. of papers, same period & series but omitted in above]   3.00   .....   (266)
The Early Settlers of Maryland: An Index to Names of Immigrants
    Compiled From Land Patents, 1663-1680, by Skordas   15.00   .....   (130)
Divorces and Names Changed in Maryland, 1634-1854, by Meyer xx   .....   (506)
The Maryland Calendar of Wills from 1635-1743, 8 vols.   85.00   .....   (130)
Directory of Maryland Legislatures, 1635-1789, by Papenfuse 3.00   (1147)
Original Patentees of Land at Washington Prior to 1700, by Gahn 8.50   .....   (130)
1752 Maryland Account Book #33, by Carothers 5.00   (459)
Marriages & Deaths From the Md. Gazette, 1727-1839, Barnes 10.00   .....   (130)
1776 Census of Maryland, by Carothers 10.50   (459)
1790 Federal Census, by U.S. Census Bureau (repr.)   10.00   .....   (663)
1790 Federal Census, by U.S. Census Bureau (repr.)   11.50   .....   (130)
Index to 1800 Federal Census of Maryland, by Volkel et al, 4 v.
    Vol. 1: Allegheny, Anne Arundell, Calvert & Baltimore City 5.00   (752)
    Vol. 2: Caroline, Cecil, Charles, Frederick, & Kent 5.00   (752)

Vol. 3: Dorchester, Harford, Montgomery, Prince Georges & Queen Annes	.....	5.00	(752)
Vol. 4: St. Mary's, Somerset, Talbot, Washington, Worchester	.....	5.00	(752)
Vols. 1, 2, 3, & 4 [bound together in one book]	24.00	.....	(752)
Index to 1800 Census of Maryland, by Accelerated Indexing	23.00	.....	(677)
Land Office & Prerogative Court Records of Colonial Maryland, by Hartsook & Skordas	8.50	.....	(130)

Maps and roads

Cumberland Road, by Hulbert	11.50	.....	(630)
The Fry & Jefferson Map of Virginia & Maryland: Facsimiles of the 1754 & 1794 Printings Boxed:	.....	35.00	(713)

Military

Causes of the Maryland Revolution of 1689, by Sparks (repr.)	12.50	8.50	(1000)
Revolutionary Records of Maryland, Pt. 1, by Brumbaugh	7.50	.....	(130)
Maryland Revolutionary Records, by Newman	8.00	.....	(130)
Muster Rolls and Other Records of Service of Maryland Troops in the American Revolution, 1775-1783, by Md. Hist. Soc.	30.00	.....	(130)
Maryland Revolutionary Soldiers Entitled to Lands West of Fort Cumberland, by Carothers	.....	5.00	(459)
The British Invasion of Maryland, 1812-1815, by Marine [With and appendix of 11,000 names]	13.50	.....	(233)
Maryland in World War II, by Md. Hist. Soc. 4 vols. Vol. 1 - Participation; Vol. 2 - Industry & Agriculture; Vol. 3 - [op]; Vol. 4 - Gold Star Honor Roll Each:	.....	3.25	(506)
Maryland in World War II - Register of Service Personnel, by Md. Hist. Soc. 5 vols. Each:	20.00	.....	(506)
[Also see Calendar of Md. State Papers under "Records".]			

Religious and ethnic groups

Parish Institutions of Maryland, With Illustrations From Parish Records, by Ingle (repr. of 1883 ed.)	10.25	6.25	(1000)
The Germans in Colonial Times, by Bittinger (repr. of 1901 ed.) [Settlements in Md., Pa., N.J., Va., N.C., & S.C.]	8.50	.....	(988)
The Pa. German in the Settlement of Md.[&]Wayside Inns of the Lancaster Roadside Betw. Philadelphia & Lancaster	.....	10.50	(1144)
Maryland Germans: A History, by Cunz (repr. of 1948 ed.)	17.50	.....	(637)
Quakerism of the Eastern Shore, by Carroll	12.50	.....	(506)
Quaker Records in Md., by Jacobsen [Explanation of meetings, location of meetings, what records are available - & where]	5.00	.....	(266)
Church and State in Early Maryland, by Petrie (repr., 1892 ed.)	10.25	6.25	(1000)
Early Presbyterianism in Maryland, by McIlvain (repr. 1890)	15.25	11.25	(1000)
A Puritan Colony in Maryland, by Randall (repr. of 1886 ed.)	10.25	6.25	(1000)
Desc. of Godfrey Gatch . . . with Material on Early Methodist History in Md., Va., & Ohio, by Markham	18.00	.....	(430)

ALLEGHANY COUNTY

A History of Allegany County With a Biog. & Genealogical Record of Representative Families, by Thomas & Williams 2 vols.	60.00	.....	(130)
Orphan's Ct. Proceedings (in Md. & Del. Genealogist Vols. 10 & 11)	.....	.....	(212)
Marriage Records of Rev. W. Welch (in Gen. Ref. Builders "Newsletter" Vol. 3, No. 5) 6pp.	.....	1.50	(931)
1800 Federal Census, by Maryland Genealogical Society	.....	4.00	(885)

ANNE ARUNDEL COUNTY

Quakers in the Founding of Anne Arundel County, by Kelly	5.50	.....	(506)
The Founders of Anne Arundel & Howard Counties, by Warfield	15.00	.....	(130)

Oaths of Fidelity to Maryland During the Revolution, Vol. 1:
Anne Arundel, Cecil, Charles, Washington, Harford, Mont-
gomery, Pr. Georges, Queen Anne, Frederick, Somerset,
& Talbot , by Carothers 6.00 (459)
Maryland Slave Owners & Superintendents - 1798, Vol. 1: Anne
Arundel, Caroline, Baltimore city, Charles, & Harford 6.00 (459)
Anne Arundel Wills (in Md. & Del. Genealogist, Vol. 8, #1, 2, 3,
& 4; Vol. 9, #1, 2, 3, & 4) 16pp. Each #: 2.00 (212)

BALTIMORE COUNTY

Md. Slave Owners & Superintendents - 1798 (see Anne Arundel Co.) 6.00 (459)
Oaths of Fidelity to Maryland During the Revolution, Vol. 2: Baltimore, Dorchester, Caroline, & Calvert Cos., by Carothers 6.00 (459)
Tax Lists, 1699-1706, by Clark [Earliest extant record of the county. Complete name index.] 5.00 (212)
Genealogy & Biography of Leading Families of the City of Baltimore
and Baltimore County, by Chapman Pub. Co., (repr. 1897 ed.) 47.50 45.00 (546)
History of Baltimore City & County, Including Biographical Sketches of Their Representative Men, by Scharf 52.50 ..... (130)

CALVERT COUNTY

Wills, 1654-1700, by Clark & Clark [Completely indexed] 10.00 (212)
Oaths of Fidelity During Rev., Vol. 2 (see Baltimore Co.) 6.00 (459)

CAROLINE COUNTY

History of Caroline County From Its Beginning, by Cochrane 13.50 ..... (130)
Oaths of Fidelity During Rev., Vol. 2 (see Baltimore Co.) 6.00 (459)
1778 Census of Md. [Includes Caroline, Charles, & Queen Anne] 5.00 (459)
Md. Slave Owners & Superintendents - 1798 (see Anne Arundel Co.) 6.00 (459)
1820 Federal Census - Indexed, by Wright 4.50 (534)
1860 Federal Census & Slaveholder Schedule - Indexed, by Wright 9.00 (534)
Marriage Licenses, 1774-1825 [&] A History of Caroline County 7.50 (212)
Abstracts of Marriages & Deaths in Caroline County Newspapers,
1830-1874 [&] Mortality Schedules for 1850, 1860, 1870 ..... 5.50 (534)

CARROLL COUNTY

History of Western Maryland: Frederick, Montgomery, Carroll,
Washington, Allegany, & Garrett Cos., by Scharf, 2 vols. Set: 57.50 ..... (130)

CECIL COUNTY

History of Cecil County, by Johnston 21.00 ..... (130)
Marriage Licenses, 1777-1840, by Capt. J. Baker Chapt., DAR 5.00 (130)
Oaths of Fidelity During Rev., Vol. I (see Anne Arundel Co.) 6.00 (459)

CHARLES COUNTY

Charles County Gentry, by Newman 12.50 ..... (130)
Oaths of Fidelity During Rev., Vol. 1 (see Ane Arundel Co.) 6.00 (459)
Md. Slave Owners & Superintendants - 1798 (see Anne Arundel) 6.00 (459)
1778 Census of Md. [Includes Caroline, Charles, & Queen Anne] 5.00 (459)

DORCHESTER COUNTY

Oaths of Fidelity During Rev., Vol. 2 (see Baltimore Co.) 6.00 (459)

FREDERICK COUNTY

History of Frederick County From the Earliest Settlements to 1861,
by Williams; Also from 1861-1910, by McKinsey 2 vols. Set: 55.00 ..... (130)
Fireign-Born in Frederick County (in National Genealogical Society
Quarterly, Vol. 56, No. 2) 12pp. 3.00 (616)

Frederick County Naturalizations, 1799-1850, by Clark [Gives date
  naturalized, country & principality of nativity, witnesses, etc.] 7.50 (212)
Oaths of Fidelity During Rev., Vol. 1 (see Anne Arundel Co.) 6.00 (459)
History of Western Maryland: Frederick, Montgomery, Carroll,
  Washington, Allegany, & Garrett Cos., by Scharf. 2 vols. Set: 57.50 ..... (130)
Marriages & Burials From the Frederick, Md., Evangelical Lu-
  theran Church, 1743-1811, by Weiser [Burial records often date
  & place of birth in Germany, other genealogical data.]   13.25 ..... (616)

GARRETT COUNTY

History of Western Maryland: Frederick, Montgomery, Carroll,
  Washington, Allegany, & Garrett Cos., by Scharf. 2 vols. Set: 57.50 ..... (130)

HARFORD COUNTY

History of Harford County From 1608 to the Close of the War of
  1812, by Preston   13.00 ..... (130)
Oaths of Fidelity During the Rev., Vol. 1 (see Anne Arundel Co.) 6.00 (459)
Maryland Slave Owners & Superintendents - 1798 (see Anne Arundel)..... 6.00 (459)

HOWARD COUNTY

Founders of Anne Arundel & Howard Cos., by Warfield   15.00 ..... (130)

KENT COUNTY

Old Kent: The Eastern Shore of Maryland, by Hanson   12.50 ..... (130)
Marriage Licenses, 1796-1850 & Lists of Ministers, by Clark 7.50 (212)

MONTGOMERY COUNTY

History of Montgomery County, 1650-1879, by Boyd (repr.)   8.50 ..... (130)
History of Western Maryland: Frederick, Montgomery, Carroll,
  Washington, Allegany, & Garrett Cos. 2 vols. Set: 57.50 ..... (130)
Oaths of Fidelity During Rev., Vol. 1 (see Anne Arundel Co.) 6.00 (459)
Orphans Court Proceedings (in Md. & Del. Gen., Vols. 11 & 12) .... (212)

PRINCE GEORGES COUNTY

Across the Years in Prince George's County, by Bowie   30.00 ..... (130)
Inventories (in Md. & Del. Gen., Vols. 10 & 11)   .... (212)
Oaths of Fidelity During Rev., Vol. 1 (see Anne Arundel Co.) 6.00 (459)
Index of Marriage Licenses, 1777-1886, by Brown   10.00 ..... (130)

QUEEN ANNES COUNTY

Marriage Licenses, 1817-1858, by Clark & Clark 5.00 (212)
Oaths of Fidelity During Rev., Vol. 1 (see Anne Arundel Co.) 6.00 (459)
1778 Census of Md. [Of Caroline, Charles & Queen Annes Cos.] 5.00 (459)

SOMERSET COUNTY

Old Somerset on the Eastern Shore: A Study in Foundations and
  Founders, by Torrence   16.00 ..... (130)
Oaths of Fidelity During the Rev., Vol. 1 (see Anne Arundel Co.) 6.00 (459)
Wills (in Md. & Del. Gen., Vols. 10 & 11)   .... (212)
1850 Federal Census & Mortality Schedule - & Family Notes 10.00 (396)

TALBOT COUNTY

History of Talbot County, 1661-1861, by Tilghman   28.50 ..... (130)
Marriage Licenses - For Scattered Colonial Years & 1794-1850,
  by Clark [Hist. of churches, biog. of ministers, map, lists of
  ministers, index to brides.] 3 vols., Each: $5.00   Set: 15.00 (212)
Wills (in Md. & Del. Gen., Vols. 11 & 12)   .... (212)
Oaths of Fidelity During Rev., Vol. 1 (see Anne Arundel Co.) 6.00 (459)

WASHINGTON COUNTY

The History of Washington County, by Williams. 2 vols.	Set: 65.00	.....	(130)
History of Western Maryland: Frederick, Montgomery, Carroll, Washington, & Garrett Cos., by Scharf. 2 vols.	Set: 57.50	.....	(130)
1800 Census - Indexed, by Clark [Also short hist. of co.]	.....	5.00	(212)
Oaths of Fidelity During Rev., Vol. 1 (see Anne Arundel Co.)	.....	6.00	(459)

WORCESTER COUNTY

Marriage Licenses (in Md. & Del. Gen., Vols. 11 & 12) 15pp.	.....	.....	(212)

Massachusetts

STATEWIDE REFERENCES

Wonder-Working Providence of Sions Saviour in New-England (1654), [also] Good News from New-England (1648). Repr. 2 vols. in 1. [The first general history of New England.]	15.00	.....	(922)
Chronicles of the First Planters of the Colony of Massachusetts Bay, from 1623 to 1636, by Young (repr. of 1846 ed.) [Collected from original records & contemporaneous Manuscripts.]	32.50	30.00	(546)
Chronicles of the Pilgrim Fathers of the Colony of Plymouth from 1602-1625, by Young (2nd ed.)	17.50	.....	(130)
History of the Colony of Massachusetts Bay, by Hutchinson (repr. of 1764 ed.) 3 vols.	Set: 100.00	.....	(629)
Commonwealth History of Massachusetts, Colony, Province, & State, by Hart (repr. of 1927-30 ed.) [Covers 1605-1930]	125.00	.....	(988)
Nova Scotia's Massachusetts: A Study of Massachusetts - Nova Scotia Relations, 1630-1784, by Rawlyk	12.50	.....	(737)
Maritime History of Massachusetts, 1783-1860, by Morrison	.....	2.35	(703)
Genealogical Notes, or Contributions to the Family History of the First Settlers of Connecticut & Massachusetts, by Goodwin	13.50	.....	(130)
Winthrop's Journal, History of New England, 1630-1649, by Winthrop (repr. of 1908 ed.) 2 vols.	Set: 11.50	.....	(643)
The Rich Men of Massachusetts: Containing a Statement of the Reputed Wealth of about Fifteen Hundred Persons, with Brief Sketches of More Than One Thousand, by Forbes (repr. 1851)	12.50	10.00	(546)
The Pioneers of Massachusetts [1820-1650], by Pope	16.00	.....	(130)
The Genealogical Advertiser, by Greenlaw [A quarterly magazine of family history.]	21.50	.....	(130)
The English Ancestry and Homes of the Pilgrim Fathers, by Banks	8.50	.....	(130)

Research aids

Massachusetts: A Student's Guide to Localized History	.....	1.50	(762)
Massachusetts Magazine [Devoted to Mass. History, Genealogy, Biography] Vols. 1-11 (all published). Repr. 1908-1918. May be purchased separately, paperbound: $13.75.	Set: 170.00	150.00	(1000)
Massachusetts Historical Society, Boston, Collections			
Series 1. Vols. 1-10, 1792-1809. Cloth, each $20.00.	Set: 200.00	.....	(1000)
Series 2. Vols. 1-10, 1814-1823.	Set: 205.00	.....	(1000)
Separately: Vols. 1-5, & 7-9	Each: 20.00	.....	(1000)
Vols. 6, & 10	Each: 24.75	.....	(1000)
Series 6. Vol. 8 [Historical Index to the Pickering Papers. 1896.]	24.75	.....	(1000)
[Note, Vol. 10 of each series contains index.]			
Microfilms of the Harbottle Dorr Collection of Annotated Mass. Newspapers, 1765-1776. 4 reels with manuscript index.	Microfilm: 80.00+		(951)

Records

The Planters of the Commonwealth, 1620-1640, by Banks [Passenger lists.]	11.50	.....	(130)
The Winthrop Fleet of 1630, by Banks [Passenger lists.]	8.50	.....	(130)
Records of the Court of Assistants of the Colony of the Massachusetts Bay, 1630-1692. 3 vols. Each: $32.50 Set:	97.50	.....	(630)
Peirce's Colonial Lists: Civil, Military, and Professional Lists of Plymouth & Rhode Island Colonies . . . 1621-1700	8.50	.....	(130)
The Massachusetts Civil List for the Colonial & Provincial Periods, 1630-1774, by Whitmore (repr. 1870) [Names & dates of appt. of all civil officers.]	12.50	10.00	(546)
The Massachusetts Civil List for the Colonial & Provincial Periods, 1630-1774, by Whitmore	11.50	.....	(130)
Port Arrivals and Immigrants ot the City of Boston, 1715-1716 and 1762-1769, by Whitmore	8.50	.....	(130)
Cambridge University Historical Register, Inclusive to 1910	6.50	.....	(836)
The Loyalists of Massachusetts, Their Memorials, Petitions, and Claims, by Jones	15.00	.....	(130)
Loyalists of Massachusetts & the Other Side of the American Revolution, by Stark	18.50	.....	(738)
Early Massachusetts Marriages Prior to 1800 [with] Plymouth County Marriages, 1692-1746, by Bailey	16.00	.....	(130)
Lists of Persons Whose Names Have Been Changed in Massachusetts, 1780-1892, by Mass. Sect'y of the Commonwealth	14.50	.....	(130)
1790 Federal Census, by U.S. Bureau of the Census (repr.)	17.50	.....	(130)
1790 Federal Census, by U.S. Bureau of the Census (repr.)	15.00	.....	(663)
1800 Federal Census, by Accelerated Indexing Systems	30.00	.....	(677)
A List of Alien Passengers, Bonded From January 1, 1847 to January 1, 1851, for the Use of the Overseers of the Poor, in the Commonwealth, by Munroe	7.50	.....	(130)
An Index of Pioneers From Massachusetts to the West, Especially the State of Michigan, by Flagg	7.50	.....	(130)

Military

Boston Under Military Rule 1768-1769, by Dickerson (1936 ed.)	9.50	.....	(899)
The Siege of Boston, by Allen	15.00	.....	(663)
The Day of Concord and Lexington, the 19th of April, 1775, by Allen	12.50	.....	(663)
The Nineteenth of April, 1775, by Murdock	10.50	.....	(663)
Bunker Hill, Notes & Queries on a Famous Battle, by Murdock	10.50	.....	(663)
Western Massachusetts in the Revolution, by Taylor	10.00	.....	(624)

Mayflower

Lineage Books, General Society of Mayflower Descendants			
Texas Mayflower Descendants, Vol. 1	15.00	.....	(1154)
Texas Mayflower Descendants, Vol. 2	5.75	.....	(1154)
District of Columbia Desc. [1970 ed. bound with 1973 supp.]	17.50	.....	(1151)
Supplement only	....	5.00	(1151)
Mayflower Descendants and Their Marriages For Two Generations After the Landing, by Landis	.....	5.00	(130)
Signers of the Mayflower Compact, by Haxtun	10.00	.....	(130)
History and Genealogy of the Mayflower Planters and First Comers to Ye Olde Colonie, by Hills [2 vols in 1]	15.00	.....	(130)
Mayflower Remembered: A History of the Plymouth Pilgrims, by Gill	8.50	.....	(799)
The Women of the Mayflower and Women of Plymouth Colony, by Noyes	10.00	.....	(233)

Religious and ethnic groups

Harvard Theological Studies, Vol. 25: An Inventory of the
Particulary (Congregational) Churches of Massachusetts
Gathered 1620-1805, by Worthley   10.00   ..... (978)
Church & State in Massachusetts From 1740-1833, by Meyer   8.50   ..... (988)
The Life and Character of the Rev. Benjamin Colman, D.D.,
by Turell (repr. of 1749 ed.) [Puritan. Colman has been
credited with a major role in shaping the tone of colonial
New England society in the early 1700's.]   12.50   ..... (922)
Puritanism in 17th Century Massachusetts, by Hall 2.60 (974)

BARNSTABLE COUNTY

A History of Chatham, Massachusetts, Formerly the Constable-
wick or Village of Monomoit, by Smith (repr. of 1909-1947 ed.) 10.00 ..... (993)
The History of Cape Cod: the Annals of Barnstable County, and of
its Several Towns, Including the Dist. of Mashpee, by Freeman 45.00 ..... (993)
Barnstable: Three Centuries of a Cape Cod Town, by Traysen
(repr. of 1939 ed.)   10.00   ..... (993)
A History of Harwich, Barnstable County, Massachusetts, 1620-
1800, by Paine (repr. of 1937 ed.)   10.00   ..... (993)
Truro, Massachusetts Vital Records to 1850   .....   6.00 (1152)
History of Old Yarmouth, comprising the present towns of Yarmouth and Dennis. From Settlement to the Division in 1794
with the History of Both Towns to 1884, by Swift. Ed. by
Holbrook. [Publication date about July 1975.]   xx   ..... (993)

BERKSHIRE COUNTY

Jews in Berkshire County, by Horwitt   .... (834)

DUKES COUNTY

Vital Records of Edgartown, Mass. to the Year 1850 (repr.)   17.50   15.00 (546)
Papers relating to the Island of Nantucket, With Documents Re-
lating to the Original Settlement of that Island, Martha's Vine-
yard, and other islands adjacent, known as Dukes County,
While Under the Colony of New York, by Hough (repr. 1856)
[From official records in the Office of Sec. of St. at Albany]   12.50   10.00 (546)
History of Martha's Vineyard, Duke's County, Mass, by Banks   30.00 ..... (130)

ESSEX COUNTY

Ship Registers of the District of Gloucester, Mass, 1789-1875,
by House   6.00   ..... (957)
The Probate Records of Essex County, 1635-1681, by Essex Inst.
Vol. 1, 1635-1664; Vol. 2, 1665-1674; Vol. 3, 1675-1681 Each: 32.50   30.00 (546)
The Records of the First Church in Salem, 1629-1747, by Pierce   30.00 ..... (957)
Vital Records of Salem to 1850, by Essex Inst. (repr.)
Vols. 1 & 4   Each: 32.50   30.00 (546)
Vols. 5 & 6   Each: 22.50   20.00 (546)
Vol. 2   27.50   25.00 (546)
Vol. 3   37.50   35.00 (546)
Vols. 1, 2, 3, 4, 5, & 6   Set: 175.00   160.00 (546)
Records and Files of the Quarterly Courts of Essex County, by
Essex Inst. (repr. 1911 ed.) Vol. 1, 1636-1656   27.50   25.00 (546)
Town Records of Salem, Vol. 1, 1634-   17.50   15.00 (546)
Trades & Tradesmen of Essex County, Chiefly of 17th Century,
by Belknap   10.00   ..... (957)
The Old Families of Salisbury & Amesbury, With Some Related
Families of Newbury, Haverhill, Ipswich & Hampton, Vol. 1   22.50   22.00 (546)
The Old Families of Salisbury & Amesbury, With Some Related

Families . . ., by Hoyt [related families of adjoining towns and of York County, Maine] Vol. 2	27.50	25.00	(546)
The Old Families of Salisbury & Amesbury . . . by Hoyt [With some related families of adjoining towns and of York County, Maine] Vol. 3	12.50	10.00	(546)
Vital Records of Ipswich, Mass to 1850, by Essex Inst. (repr.)			
Vol. 1	22.50	20.00	(546)
Vol. 2	42.50	40.00	(546)
Vol. 3	8.50	6.00	(546)
Marblehead Town Records, Annotated by Bowden, by Essex Inst.	12.60	10.10	(546)
Vital Records of Rowley, Mass. to 1850, by Essex Inst. (repr.)			
Vol. 1	32.50	30.00	(546)
Vol. 2	8.50	6.00	(546)

FRANKLIN COUNTY

The Puzzle of Catamount Hill, by Davenport [A study of Catamount Hill in Colrain, of its families who came there after the Rev., why they came and why they left.]	.....	2.50	(519)
A History of Deerfield: The times when and the people by whom it was settled, unsettled and resettled: with a special study of the Indian Wars in the Connecticutt valley, by Sheldon (repr.) Vol. 2 (only)	42.50	40.00	(546)
As You Were Shelburne, by Davenport [A complete scholar's hist. including early families and industries using water power.]	.....	2.25	(519)

HAMPSHIRE COUNTY

Granby Bicentennial 1768-1968, by Town of Granby	.....	3.00	(944)

MIDDLESEX COUNTY

Theatrum Majorum, The Cambridge of 1776: Diary of Dorothy Dudley (repr. of 1876 ed.) [Eyewitness acct., Am. Rev.]	7.00	.....	(629)
Carlisle, Composite Community, by Lapham [Colonial history of the town, plus genealogical section of settlers] Repr., 1975	.....	.....	(360)
Vital Records of Chelmsford, to the Year 1850, by Essex Inst.	27.50	25.00	(546)
History of the Town of Concord, Mass, by Shaituck (repr. 1835)	12.50	.....	(318)
Vital Records of Dunstable to the Year 1850, by Essex Inst.	17.50	15.00	(546)
Vital Records of Groton to the Year 1850. 2 vols. Each:	17.50	15.00	(546)
The Golden Threads: New England's Mill Girls & Magnates, by Josephson [Twenty yrs. in the hist. of the textile mills est. at Lowell in 1823, and the women operatives.]	10.00	.....	(988)
Mill & Mansion: A Study of Architecture & Society in Lowell, 1820-1865, by Coolidge (repr. of 1942 ed.)	15.00	.....	(988)
Lowell, As It Was, & As It Is, by Miles (repr. of 1845 ed.)	11.00	.....	(629)
Vital Records of Tyngsboro to the Year 1850, by Essex Inst.	.....	5.00	(957)

NANTUCKET COUNTY

Nantucket Island - A Bibliography of Source Material With Index, by Coffin [Listing of all known sources of important books, documents.]	10.00	.....	(590)
The History of Nantucket, by Macy (repr. of 1835 ed.)	15.00	.....	(854)

NEW PLYMOUTH COUNTY

Records of the Colony of New Plymouth . . . by Shurtleff [Printed by order of legislature of the Comm. of Mass. in 1855-61]			
Vols. 1 & 2 Each:	12.50	10.00	(546)
Vols. 3, 4, 6, 8, 9, 11, & 12 Each:	17.50	15.00	(546)
Vols. 5 & 7 Each:	22.50	20.00	(546)
Vol. 10	27.50	25.00	(546)
Pilgrim Colony: A Hist. of New Plymouth, 1620-1691, by Langdon	7.50	.....	(764)

PLYMOUTH COUNTY

Early Massachusetts Marriages Prior to 1800 [with] Plymouth County Marriages, 1692-1746, by Bailey	16.00	.....	(130)
History of Plymouth Plantation, 1620-1647, by Bradford (1912 ed.)	50.00	.....	(988)
Plymouth Church Records, 1620-1850	30.00	.....	(130)
Genealogical Register of Plymouth Families, by Davis	15.00	.....	(130)
History of the Town of Plymouth From Its Earliest Settlement in 1620, To The Present Time, by Thacher (repr. of 1835 ed.)	12.50	.....	(993)
Marshfield, Mass. Vital Records to 1850	.....	10.00	(1153)
Wright's History of Plympton, 1640-1945, ed. by Bricknell	.....	10.00	(56)
Historical Sketches of Plympton, ed. by Bricknell [A collection of short histories, data, statistics, charts, maps, etc.]	.....	10.00	(56)
Plympton Town & Parish Records , 1701-1734, by Bricknell	.....	10.00	(56)
Plympton Town Records, 1731-1781, by Bricknell, Bk. 2, v. 1	.....	10.00	(56)
Plympton Town Records, 1781-1802, by Bricknell, Bk. 2, v. 2	.....	10.00	(56)
Plympton Town Records, 1802-1815, by Bricknell, Bk. 2, v. 3	.....	10.00	(56)
Plympton Town Records, by Bricknell, Bk. 2 v. 4 [Vital records, town mtgs., marriages, genealogies, etc. 1700's & 1800's]	.....	10.00	(56)
Plympton Town Records, by Bricknell, Bk. 2, v. 5 [cont. of v. 4]	.....	10.00	(56)
Plympton Town Records, 1827-1838, by Bricknell, Bk. 3, v. 1	.....	10.00	(56)
Plympton Town Records, 1838-1863, by Bricknell, Bk. 3, v. 2	.....	10.00	(56)

SUFFOLK COUNTY

An Index to the Vital Records of Boston, 1630-1699, by Gladden	10.00	.....	(797)
Records Relating to the Early History of Boston, by Boston Registry Dept. 39 vols. (repr. 1876-1909 ed.) Each:	30.00	.....	(630)
Letters & Diary of John Rowe, Boston Merchant 1759-1762, 1764-1779, ed. by Cunningham (repr. of 1903 ed.)	16.00	.....	(629)
Vital Records of Roxbury to 1850, by Essex Inst., Vol. 1	22.50	20.00	(546)
Vol. 2	37.50	35.00	(546)

WORCESTER COUNTY

1870 Atlas of Worcester Co.- From Actual Surveys, by Beers	25.00	.....	(657)
1870 Atlas of the City of Worcester - " ", by Beers	17.50	.....	(657)

Michigan

STATEWIDE REFERENCES

A History of the Northern Peninsula, by Sawyer (repr. of 1911)	37.50	35.00	(546)
The Traverse Region . . . With Portraits & Biog. Sketches of Some of Its Prominent Men, by Page & Co. (repr. of 1884 ed.)	27.50	25.00	(546)

Research aids

Evolution of Michigan Townships	.....	2.40	(595)
Directory of Historical Collections & Historical Societies in Michigan, by Hist. Soc. of Mich.	.....	.75	(918)
Michigan Civil War History: An Annotated Bibliography, by May	.....	2.95	(902)
The Counties & Townships of Michigan Past & Present, by Williams [Dates of organization & pertinent facts about each co.]	.....	5.00	(912)

Records

The Territorial Papers of the U.S. - Michigan Territory, 1805-1837 [Microfilm Series M721, Roll # 5] Microfilm:	12.00		(402)
An Index of Pioneers From Massachusetts to the West - Especially the State of Michigan, by Flagg	7.50	.....	(130)

Military

Michigan Military [Revolutionary] Records, by Silliman   10.00   .....   (130)
Record of Service of Michigan Volunteers in the Civil War,
    1861-1865, by Adj-Gen. Office.   Vols. 16 & 24   Each: 12.50   10.00   (546)
Reminiscences, Incidents, Battles, Marches & Camp Life of
    the Old 4th Michigan Inf. . . 1861-1864, by Barrett (1888)   8.50   6.00   (546)

Religious

The Marriage & Funeral Records of Rev. M. F. Nash, compiled
    by Nash [Rev. Nash was a Methodist minister of the Michigan
    Conference from 1923 to 1955. Her records cover ten towns
    and surrounding areas - not whole counties. The towns in which
    she recorded marriages and funerals are:
      Boyne Falls - Charlevoix Co.; Gladwin - Gladwin Co., Far-
      well - Clare Co.; Fife Lake & Odgensburg - Grand Traverse
      Co.; Winn - Isabella Co.; Fulton - Kalamazoo Co.; White
      Cloud - Newaygo Co.; Bloomingdale - Van Buren Co.; &
      Mooretown - Missaukee Co.]

ALLEGAN COUNTY

The Kalamazoo Valley Family Newsletter, Allegan County Issue
    [Maps of all 24 twps. Locations & addresses where official re-
    cords are kept. Varied genealogical references.]   60pp. 3.00   (210)

BARRY COUNTY

The Kalamazoo Valley Family Newsletter, Barry County Issue
    [Maps of all 16 twps. Location of official records, Varied
    genealogical references.]   60pp. 3.00   (210)

BRANCH COUNTY

The Kalamazoo Valley Family Newsletter, Branch County Issue
    [Maps of all twps. Location of records, Varied genealogical
    references. Data on early settlers.]   60pp. 3.00   (210)

CALHOUN COUNTY

The Kalamazoo Valley Family Newsletter, Calhoun County Issue
    [Same type material listed in Allegan, Barry, etc.] 72pp. 3.00   (210)

EATON COUNTY

The Kalamazoo Valley Family Newsletter, Eaton County Issue
    [Maps, location of records, libraries, cemeteries, newspapers,
    all genealogical data they were able to obtain of the county.] 84pp. 3.00   (210)
Cemeteries of Eaton Rapids Twp., by Mid Mich. Gen. Soc. 2.40   (595)

HILLSDALE COUNTY

The Kalamazoo Valley Family Newsletter, Hillsdale County Issue
    [Same type material as listed in Allegan, etc. Cos. 60pp.] 3.00   (210)

INGHAM COUNTY

Death & Marriage Items Reported in Lansing State Republican
    1855-1860, by Druse 2.40   (595)
North Cemetery Burial, Delhi Twp., by Harvey & Martin 2.40   (595)

JACKSON COUNTY

The Kalamazoo Valley Family Newsletter, Jackson County Issue
    (Same type material as listed in Allegan, Barry, etc.] 60pp. 3.00   (210)

KALAMAZOO COUNTY

The Kalamazoo Valley Family Newsletter, Kalamazoo County Issue
[Same type material as listed in Allegan, Barry, etc.] 68pp. 3.00 (210)

LIVINGSTON COUNTY

History of Livingston County, With Illustrations and Biog. Sketches
of Its Prominent Men & Pioneers, by Everts & Abbott (1880) 37.50 35.00 (546)

MACOMB COUNTY

History of Macon County . . . , by Leeson & Co. (repr. 1882) 47.50 45.00 (546)

MANISTEE COUNTY

History of Manistree, Mason & Oceana Cos., by Page & Co. (1882) 17.50 15.00 (546)

MASON COUNTY

History of Manistree, Mason & Oceana Cos., by Page & Co. (1882) 17.50 15.00 (546)

MONROE COUNTY

History of Monroe County, by Wing (repr. 1890) 47.50 45.00 (546)

NEWAYGO COUNTY

The First White Pathfinders of Newaygo Co., by Spooner (1954) 22.50 20.00 (546)

OCEANA COUNTY

History of Manistee, Mason & Oceana Cos., by Page & Co. (1882) 17.50 15.00 (546)

OTTOWA COUNTY

The Early History of Jamestown Twp., by Gitchel [Lists settlers
and locations - about 800 names with relationships.] 5.00 ..... (394)

SAINT JOSEPH COUNTY

The Kalamazoo Valley Family Newsletter, Saint Joseph Co. issue
[Map of each twp., complete state census of 1845, location of
official records, various types genealogical references.] 68pp. 3.00 (210)

WAYNE COUNTY

History of Detroit & Wayne County & Early Michigan, by Farmer
(repr. of 1890 ed.) 17.50 ..... (233)
First Land Owners of Wayne County 5.00 (912)

Minnesota

STATEWIDE REFERENCES

The Northland Newsletter [Quarterly of the Range Genealogical
Society. Contains all kinds of records: marriage, cemetery,
tax rolls, plat books, etc. covering entire state.] Subscription: ..... 4.00/yr(977)
Steamboats and Steamboatmen of the Upper Mississippi, by Mer-
rick [Series of articles first pub. in Saturday Evening Post of
Burlington, Ia. 1913-1920] 1 reel Microfilm: 15.00 (532)

Research aids

Reference Guide to Minnesota History: A Subject Bibliography
of Books, Pamphlets, and Articles, by Brook [Over 3,700
entries under 32 subject headings. Indexed.] 7.50 (532)
Minnesota Geographic Names: Their Origin & Historic Signifi-
cance, by Upham (repr. of 1920 ed.) 10.50 ..... (532)
Minnesota: A Student's Guide to Localized History 1.50 (762)

Records

    1850 Minnesota Territorial Census, by Harpole & Nagle
    [Indexed and annotated version. Appendix of known resi-
    dents not listed in the census.] 5.00 (532)
    Index to Rosters in Minnesota in the Civil and Indian Wars,
    1861-1865 [Microfilm ed. of 2 vol. work] 1 reel   Microfilm: 10.00 (532)
    Minnesota Congressmen, Legislators, and Other Elected
    Officials, 1849-1971, by Toensing [4,628 names] 3.75 (532)

ANOKA COUNTY

History of Bethel Township and East Bethel Village That Became
the City of East Bethel, by Lyon [From earliest settlements
in 1850 to 1974 - how developed.] 2.75 (837)

NOBLES COUNTY

An Illustrated History of Nobles County, by Rose (repr. 1908)   37.50   35.00 (546)

OTTER TAIL COUNTY

Patrons of the 1874 Atlas (in MCGS Reporter, Vol. 5, #6) 2pp. 75 (596)

Mississippi

STATEWIDE REFERENCES

A History of Mississippi, ed. by McLemore. 2 vols.   Set: 25.00   ..... (938)
Random Recollections of Early Days in Mississippi, by Fulkerson   7.50   ..... (960)

Research aids

    Survey of Mississippi Court Houses, by Miss. Gen. Soc. 15.00 (868)
    Mississippi: A Student's Guide to Localized History 1.50 (762)

Records

    Honor and Fidelity: Louisiana Infantry Regiment and the Loui-
    siana Militia Companies, 1766-1821, by Holmes   10.00   ..... (483)
    Mississippi Provincial Archives, by Rowland & Sanders (repr.)
    3 vols.   Set: 90.00   ..... (630)
    Mississippi Court Records, 1799-1835, by King   14.00   ..... (130)
    Mississippi County Court Records From the May Wilson McBee
    Papers, by McBee   12.50   ..... (130)
    Mississippi Territory in the War of 1812, by Rowland   14.00   ..... (130)
    The Territorial Papers of the U. S. - Mississippi Territory,
    1809-1817 [Microfilm Series M721, Roll # 4]   Microfilm: 12.00 (402)
    1820 Federal Census, by Accelerated Indexing Systems   13.00   ..... (677)

ADAMS COUNTY

William Johnson's Natchez, (repr. of 1951 ed.) 2 vols.   Set: 34.50   ..... (637)

AMITE COUNTY

Amite County, Mississippi - Florida Parishes, La., by Casey et al
    [Marriages, wills, adms., abs. of church rec., deeds, tax
    lists, censuses, military records, land grants, maps, geneal-
    ogies, Spanish claims, land plats (photocopies)] 4 vols. Set: 71.00   ..... (488)
Surname Index to 1860 Federal Census, by Burns 4.00 (820)

CLAIBORNE COUNTY

Surname Index, 1860 Federal Census, by Burns   4.00   ..... (820)

COPIAH COUNTY
Surname Index to 1860 Federal Census, by Burns 4.00 (820)

HINDS COUNTY
Marriage Records, Vol. 1 (1823-1848) & Will Book 1 (1822-1859),
  by Forrest .... (38)
Surname Index to 1860 Federal Census, by Burns 5.00 (820)

JEFFERSON COUNTY
Mississippi & Louisiana Border Country: History of Rodney, Mississippi & Environs, by Logan 9.95 ..... (664)

LAWRENCE COUNTY
Marriages, 1818-1879, by Gillis 14.00 11.00 (1140)

MADISON COUNTY
Madison County, Mississippi Territory [later Alabama] 1810-1815
  Tax Lists (in Valley Leaves, Vol. 4, #4) 3.00 (959)

MARSHALL COUNTY
Dear Darling Loulie: Letters Written During the Civil War by Cor-
  delia Lewis Scales, a teenager in Marshall County, ed. by Lum-
  kin [Some names mentioned in the letters were: Anderson, Ar-
  thur, Banks, Beauregard, Clayton, Cottrell, Crump, Flynn,
  Gilmore, Grant, Gray, Hull, Humphries, Irby, Lamar, Lenow,
  McPherson, Maury, Meriman, Meriwether, Mickle, Minor,
  Moon, O'Meara, Pemberton, Pitts, Saunders, Scales, Stuart/
  Steward, Tilghman, Top, & VanDorn. Historical notes added by
  compiler] 8.00 (614)

MONROE COUNTY
1860 Federal Census - Indexed, by Fears [Over 7,500 names] 12.50 (377)

NESHOBA COUNTY
Surname Index to 1860 Federal Census, by Burns 3.00 (820)

NEWTON COUNTY
Surname Index to 1860 Federal Census, by Burns 3.00 (820)

WEBSTER COUNTY
1880 Federal Census, by Wade 8.00 (19)

WINSTON COUNTY
The Centennial History of Winston County, by Lewis 10.95 ..... (674)

Missouri

STATEWIDE REFERENCES
Spanish Regime in Missouri: A Collection of Papers & Documents
  Relating to Upper Louisiana Principally within the Present
  Limits of Missouri During the Dominion of Spain, From the
  Archives of the Indies at Seville, by Houck (2 vols. in 1) 38.00 ..... (629)
History of Missouri From the Earliest Explorations & Settlements
  Until the Admission of the State into the Union, by Houck (repr) 51.00 ..... (629)
History of Missouri, Vol. 1: 1673-1820, by Foley 9.50 ..... (758)
History of Missouri, Vol. 2: 1820-1860, by McCandlesss 9.50 ..... (758)

A History of Missouri, Vol. 3: 1860-1875, by Parrish 9.50 ..... (758)
History of the Ozarks, by Pennington [Accurate information on
many people & places in geographical upland known as Ozarks.] 5.00 2.00 (733)
A History of the Pioneer Families of Missouri, by Bryan & Rose 12.50 ..... (130)

Research aids

Tracing Family Trees in Eleven States [Missouri is included.] 5.50 (29)
Missouri: A Student's Guide to Localized History 1.50 (762)
Resources for Genealogical Research in Missouri, by Williams 5.00 (293)
Genealogical Tour Through the Courthouses and Libraries in
Missouri, by Williams [Supplement to above] 1.75 (293)
A Bibliography of Missouri County Histories & Atlases, by Selby..... ..... (767)

Records

Land Claims in Missouri Territory, 1798-1814 (in Mo. Pioneers,
Vol. 1-50pp. & Vol. 2-22pp.) Each vol.: $5.00 Total: 10.00 (106)
The Territorial Papers of the U.S. - Louisiana & Missouri Ter-
ritory, 1803-1820 [Microfilm Series M721, Roll #9] Microfilm: 12.00 (402)
Missouri Obituaries, from Alexander Campbell's "Millenial
Harbinger", 1841-1860 (in Mo. Pion., Vol. 6 - 8pp.) 5.00 (106)
Missouri Obituaries & Death Notices, from St. Louis Christain
Advocate, M.E. Church, South, 1851-1860 (in Mo. Pion.,
v.5, 1851-54; v.10, 1855; v.13, 1856; v.18, 1857; v. 26,
1858; v. 30, 1860 Each vol.: $5.00. Aver.pp: 20 Total: 30.00 (106)
Missouri Pioneers - Indexed by Counties (in Mo. Pion. v.30) 11pp..... 5.00 (106)
Missouri Pioneers, 30 vols., by Woodruff & Hodges [Each vol.
contains material on 7 or 8 different counties, is complete in
itself, and is indexed.] Each: $5.00 Set: 150.00 (106)
Missouri Cousins, by Coppage [Genealogies and vital records
on Missourians born before 1850, where they settled and
sometimes from whence they came. Some obits, news, etc. 10.00 (80)
Some Cemeteries of the Ozarks (in NGSQ v.56, #1) 12pp 3.00 (616)
Index to the 1830 Census of Missouri, by Glazner & McLane 12.50 (28)
Biographical Index to the Centennial History of Missouri 2.00 (324)

Military

Environs of St. Louis, by Parkin [St. Louis during Rev. War,
and list of soldiers living and dying in Mo.] 1.25 (29)
Missouri's Confederate Dead (in Mo. Pion., v.8) 27pp. 5.00 (106)
Campaigns of First Missouri Brigade Memoirs: Hist. & Personal
by Anderson [Many notes by E.C. Bearss giving Conf. Hist.] 15.00 ..... (848)

ADAIR COUNTY

Abstracts of Wills & Adms., 1857-1865 (in Mo. Pion., v.30) 7pp. 5.00 (106)

ANDREW COUNTY

Abstracts of Wills &Adms., 1841-1856 (in Mo. Pion., v.7) 34pp. 5.00 (106)

ATCHISON COUNTY

Marriage Book A, 1845-1863 (in Mo. Pion., v. 5) 28pp. 5.00 (106)
Abstracts of Wills, Book A, 1845-1871 (in Mo. Pion., v. 21) 10pp. 5.00 (106)

AUDRAIN COUNTY

Abstracts of Wills & Admr. Bonds, 1838-1856 (in Mo. Pion., v.25) 5.00 (106)

BARRY COUNTY

Abs. of Wills, Bonds & Admrs., 1835-1855 (in Mo. Pion., v. 21) 5.00 (106)

....

BARTON COUNTY

History of Hickory, Polk, Cedar, Dade & Barton Cos., by Good-
    speed (repr. of 1889 ed. - with added index)   25.50   .....   (563)
Marriage Book A, 1862-1880 (in Mo. Pion., v. 27) 33pp. 5.00   (106)

BATES COUNTY

Marriage Book A, 1860-1871 (in Mo. Pion., v. 28) 19pp. 5.00   (106)
Abstracts of Wills & Admrs., 1843-1872 (in Mo. Pion., v. 9) 10pp 5.00   (106)

BENTON COUNTY

History of Benton County, by White & Miles. 3 vols. [Very com-
    prehensive. Contains many obits. Indexed.]   Set: 42.50   .....   (318)
History of Benton County, by Lay (repr. of 1876 ed.) 2.50   (318)
Marriage Records, 1839-1861, by Williams 5.00   (293)
Records of Benton Co: Marriages, 1862-1872; Index to Wills &
    Estates, 1839-1875; Early Land Entries, 1836-1839; Settlers 10.00   (293)
1876 State Census, by Williams & Williams 7.50   (293)

BOLLINGER COUNTY

Bits of History, Bollinger County, by Hahn   5.00   .....   (770)
Marriage Book A, 1866-1872 (in Mo. Pion., v. 25) 19pp. 5.00   (106)

BOONE COUNTY

History of Boone County, by Switzler (repr. of 1882 ed.)   16.00   .....   (770)
Index to History of Boone County, by Switzler (above) 4.00   (770)
1821 Tax List (in Mo. Pion., v. 11) 4pp. 5.00   (106)

BUCHANAN COUNTY

Abs. of Wills & Adms, Books A & B, 1839-1857, by Woodruff 5.00   (105)
1860 Federal Census of Buchanan County - excluding Washington   .....
    Twp. and the city of St. Joseph, by Nelson [Indexed] 10.00   (271)
1860 Federal Census of Washington Twp. & St. Joseph City, 2 vols.
    [Index in vol. 2]   Set: 15.00   (271)

BUTLER COUNTY

Marriage Book A, 1849-1865 (in Mo. Pion., v. 8) 10pp. 5.00   (106)

CALDWELL COUNTY

History of Caldwell County, by Nat. Hist. Co. (repr. 1886-Indexed) 25.00   .....   (318)

CALLAWAY COUNTY

History of Callaway County, by Nat. Hist. Co. (repr. 1884 ed.)   25.00   .....   (318)
Abs. of Wills & Adms., 1821-1836 (in Mo. Pion., v. 17) 17pp. 5.00   (106)
1823 Tax List (in Mo. Pion., v. 6) 4pp. 5.00   (106)
Marriage Book B, 1840-1850 (in Mo. Pion., v. 22) 25pp. 5.00   (106)

CAMDEN COUNTY

Before the Dam Water, by Jeffries [Story & pictures of Old Linn
    Creek, a county seat town, destroyed and under 65 feet of water
    of the Lake of the Ozarks, dam constructed in 1930] 3.00   (776)
Tombstone Inscriptions, Vol. 1 [39 cemeteries] 5.00   (293)
Tombstone Inscriptions, Vol. 2 [26 cemeteries] 5.00   (293)
Tombstone Inscriptions, Vol. 3 [22 cem. & list of settlers] 5.00   (293)

CAPE GIRARDEAU COUNTY

A Belated Census of Earliest Settlers of Cape Girardeau County,
    by Gammon [Not really a census, rather approx. 3,200 tomb-
    stone inscriptions - 1829-1935 - from nearly 100 cemeteries] 4.25   (616)
Marriages, 1805-1854 (in Mo. Pion., v. 12) 31pp. 5.00   (106)

1850 Federal Census of Cape Girardeau, Mo.	..... 5.35	(29)
1876 State Census of Cape Girardeau, Mo., by Keller	..... 3.35	(29)

CARTER COUNTY

History of Carter County, by Pennington (1966)	..... 1.00	(733)
Guardian & Curator Bonds, 1861-1890 (in Mo. Pion., v. 20) 6pp.	..... 5.00	(106)
Marriages, 1861-1881 (in Mo. Pion., v. 28) 10pp.	..... 5.00	(106)

CASS COUNTY

Marriage Books A & B, 1836-1865, by Woodruff	..... 4.00	(105)
Abs. of Wills & Admrs., 1835-1865 (in Mo. Pion., v. 5) 10pp.	..... 5.00	(106)

CEDAR COUNTY

History of Hickory, Polk, Cedar, Dade & Barton Cos., by Good-speed (repr. of 1889 ed. - with added index]	25.50	(563)
Marriage Book A, 1845-1874 (in Mo. Pion., vol. 13) 25pp.	..... 5.00	(106)
Abstracts of Wills, 1846-1876 (in Mo. Pion., vol. 18) 10pp.	..... 5.00	(106)

CHARITON COUNTY

1821 Tax List (in Mo. Pion., v. 5) 8pp.	..... 5.00	(106)

CHRISTIAN COUNTY

Marriage Records 1864-1874 [&] Wills and Adms. 1865-1885	..... 7.50	(293)
Tombstone Inscriptions, by Williams & Williams	..... 5.00	(293)
Missouri Circuit Ct. Rec. #1 (in Ridge Runners, v. 2, #4) 7pp.	..... 2.00	(670)
Cemetery Inscriptions (in the Ozark Quarterly, v. 4, #2) 4pp.	..... 1.50	(670)

CLARK COUNTY

Marriages, 1837-1854 (in Mo. Pion., v. 6) 32pp.	..... 5.00	(106)
Marriages, Vol. 1 (1837-1865), by Dunlap & Walker	..... 8.50	(263)
Marriages, Vol. 2 (1866-1884), by Dunlap & Walker	..... 8.50	(263)
Marriages, Vol. 3 (1885-1911), by Dunlap & Walker	..... 12.50	(263)
Marriages, Vol. 4 (1911-1929), by Dunlap & Walker	..... 8.50	(263)
Cemetery Inscriptions, 4 vols. bound in 1 Set:	..... 60.00	(263)
[Above contains all the cemeteries in the county. Single ceme-teries may be purchased upon request for 10¢ per page.]		
Abs. of Wills, Bonds & Admrs., 1837-1854 (in Mo. Pion., v. 18)	..... 5.00	(106)
1850 Federal Census - Indexed, by Dunlap	..... 5.00	(263)

CLAY COUNTY

Index to Original Land Grants, by Bushman	..... 4.95	(248)

CLINTON COUNTY

1840 Federal Census - Complete - Indexed (in Mo. Pion., v. 16)	..... 5.00	(106)

COOPER COUNTY

Circuit Court Minutes, 1819-1820 (in Mo. Pion., v. 4) 16pp.	..... 5.00	(106)
Marriages, 1850-1857 (in Mo. Pion., v. 23) 25pp.	..... 5.00	(106)

CRAWFORD COUNTY

First Marriage Book & A, 1829-1855, by Woodruff	..... 4.00	(105)
Abstracts of Wills, 1832-1868 (in Mo. Pion., v. 13) 13pp.	..... 5.00	(106)

DADE COUNTY

History of Dade County & Her People, by States-Young (repr. of 1917 ed.) 2 vols. repr. as 1. Complete new index added.	25.50	(563)
History of Hickory, Polk, Cedar, Dade & Barton Cos., by Good-speed (repr. of 1889 ed. - with added index)	25.50	(563)

Marriages, 1863-1873, by Dade Co. Hist. Soc.	7.00	(563)
Marriages, 1871-1881, by Dade Co. Hist. Soc.	7.00	(563)
Marriages, 1863-1873; Also, Abs. of Wills & Adms., 1841-1867	5.00	(105)
1850 Federal Census - Indexed, by Dade Co. Hist. Soc.	5.00	(563)
1860 Federal Census - Indexed, by Dade Co. Hist. Soc.	7.50	(563)
1870 Federal Census - Indexed, by Dade Co. Hist. Soc.	10.00	(563)
1880 Federal Census - Indexed, by Dade Co. Hist. Soc. [Map included. Western part of Dade Co. settled after 1870.]	12.50	(563)
Arcola - Hickory Grove Cemetery [Includes history of the cemetery, much additional family information, & index]	3.50	(563)
Buchanan, Cantrell, & Hampton Cemeteries [Includes history of the cemetery, additional family information, & index.]	3.50	(563)
Daughtrey Cemetery	1.75	(563)
Ray Springs Cemetery	2.25	(563)
Pennsboro Cemetery [Very old cem. Approx. burials, 1100. Family data added. Plat of grounds. Indexed.]	8.00	(563)
Rice Cemetery [Map of cem. Family history added. Indexed.]	3.00	(563)
Stockton Cemetery	1.25	(563)
Weir Cemetery	1.25	(563)
Wetzel Cemetery [Dates from 1845. History, map, family data.]	1.50	(563)
An Ozark Boy's Story, by Hulston [Story of Dade Co. area. Includes info. about many people there, including author's family] 5.00		(563)

DALLAS COUNTY

Marriage Books A & B, 1867-1880, by Woodruff	4.00	(105)
Abs. of Wills, Bonds & Admrs., 1871-1883 (in Mo. Pion., v.20)	5.00	(106)
Tombstone Inscriptions, by Williams & Williams	5.00	(293)

DeKALB COUNTY

Marriages, 1845-1867 (in Mo. Pion., v.10) 24pp.	5.00	(106)

DENT COUNTY

Marriages, 1851-1870 [&] Abstracts of Wills, 1866-1893	4.00	(105)

DOUGLAS COUNTY

Spring Creek Cemetery (in The Ridge Runners, v.2, #2) 6pp.	2.00	(670)

DUNKLIN COUNTY

Abs. of Wills, Bonds & Admrs., 1872-1883 (in Mo. Pion., v.29)	5.00	(106)
1850 Federal Census, by Downing & Wade	3.50	(19)
1850, 1860, 1870, & 1880 Mortality Schedules [&] 1850, 1860 Slaveowners and their slaves, by Wade & Downing	3.50	(19)
1880 Federal Census, by Wade & Downing	10.00	(19)

FRANKLIN COUNTY

Centennial Biog. Directory of Franklin Co., by Kiel (repr.1925) 27.50	25.00	(546)
1819 Territorial & County Tax (in Mo. Pion., v.9) 6pp.	5.00	(106)
Abstracts of Wills & Admrs., 1819-1854 (in Mo. Pion., v. 14) 35pp.	5.00	(106)
Marriage Books A & B, by Woodruff	6.00	(105)

GASCONADE COUNTY

Marriage Book A, 1822-1841 (in Mo. Pion., v. 2) 16pp.	5.00	(106)
Marriage Book B, 1842-1855 (in Mo. Pion., v. 24) 20pp.	5.00	(106)
Abs. of Wills, Bonds, & Admrs., 1821-1860 (in Mo. Pion., v.15)	5.00	(106)

GREENE COUNTY

History of Greene County, by West. Hist. Co. (repr. 1883 ed.) 25.00		(318)
Guardian & Curator Bonds, 1834-1864 (in Mo. Pion., v. 9) 11pp.	5.00	(106)

Springfield, Greene Co., Mo., Inhabitants in 1880, by Hall   15.00   .....   (793)
Wills, 1840-1856 (in The Ridge Runners, v.3, #2) 7pp. 2.00   (670)
Marriage Books A & B, 1833-1860, by Woodruff 6.00   (105)
Abs. of Wills & Admrs., 1856-1862 (in Mo. Pion., v.15) 12pp. 5.00   (106)

HENRY COUNTY

History of Henry & St. Clair Cos., by Nat. Hist. Co. (repr. 1883)   25.00   .....   (318)
Wills and Administrations, Vol. 1 (1835-1854), by Williams 5.00   (293)
Wills and Administrations, Vol. 2 (1854-1865), by Williams 5.00   (293)
Tombstone Inscriptions, Vol. 1, by Williams 3.50   (293)
Tombstone Inscriptions, Vol. 2, by Williams 3.50   (293)
Marriage Records, 1835-1861, by Williams 5.00   (293)
Abstracts of Deeds, 1838-1840 (in Mo. Pion., v.8) 12pp. 5.00   (106)

HICKORY COUNTY

History of Hickory, Polk, Cedar, Dade & Barton Cos., by Goodspeed (repr. of 1889 ed. - with added index)   25.50   .....   (563)
Tombstone Inscriptions, by Williams & Williams 5.00   (293)

HOLT COUNTY

Marriages, 1846-1852 & 1853-1860 (in Mo. Pion., v. 2 & 7) Set: 10.00   (106)
Wills & Admr. Bonds, 1841-1860 (in Mo. Pion., v. 22) 10pp. 5.00   (106)

HOWARD COUNTY

History of Howard & Cooper Cos., by Nat. Hist. Co. (repr. of 1883
   ed. with new index)   25.00   .....   (318)
County Court Book B, 1822-1823 (in Mo. Pion., v. 18) 12pp. 5.00   (106)
Marriage Book C, 1850-1860 (in Mo. Pion., v.16) 20pp. 5.00   (106)

HOWELL COUNTY

Marriage Book A, 1867-1871 (in Mo. Pion., v.14) 8pp. 5.00   (106)
Marriage Records 1871-1882, by Williams & Williams 5.00   (293)
Abstract of Deed Book "D" [Pre 1870 deeds], by Williams 5.00   (293)
Index to Circuit Court Cases 1858-1882, by Williams & Williams 5.00   (293)
Personal Property Tax Books of 1875 & 1885, by Williams 5.00   (293)

IRON COUNTY

Marriage Book A, 1857-1872 (in Mo. Pion., v.30) 23pp. 5.00   (106)
Abstracts of Will Book A, 1857-1888 (in Mo. Pion., v.23) 11pp. 5.00   (106)

JACKSON COUNTY

Abs. of Wills, Bonds & Admrs., 1827-48 (in Mo. Pion., v.3) 40pp. 5.00   (106)
Abs. of Wills, Bonds & Admrs., 1849-54 (in Mo. Pion., v.4) 42pp. 5.00   (106)
Abs. of Wills, Bonds & Admrs., 1855-60 (in Mo. Pion., v.21) 20pp 5.00   (106)
Records of Land Patents, 1832-1850 (in Mo. Pion., v.14) 9pp 5.00   (106)

JASPER COUNTY

Marriage Books A & B (1841-1861) [Also brief county history & 25
   biographies.], by Bottens & Harrington 5.00   (1136)
Marriage Books A & B (1865-1874) [History & biographies] 5.00   (1136)
Marriage Book C, by Mary M. Curry 5.00   (1137)
Marriage Book D, by Mary M. Curry 5.00   (1137)
Marriage Book E, by Mary M. Curry 5.00   (1137)
Will Books A & B (1841-1892), by Bottens & Harrington 5.00   (1136)

JEFFERSON COUNTY

1850 Federal Census, by St. Louis Gen. Soc. 3.85 (29)

JOHNSON COUNTY

History of Johnson County, by Kan. City Hist. Pub. Co. (repr. of
    1881 ed. - including a new every-name index) 15.00 ..... (293)
History of Johnson County, by Kan. City Hist. Pub. Co. (1881 ed.-
    indexed) 25.00 ..... (318)
Index to 1881 History of Johnson County (above), by Williams 5.00 (293)
Marriage Records, 1835-1866, by Williams 5.00 (293)
Abstract of Wills & Administrations 1835-1855, by Williams 5.00 (293)
Tombstone Inscriptions, 6 vols.   Each: $3.50   Set: 21.00 (293)
1840 Federal Census [&] Index to Original Entry Book 7.50 (293)
1850 Federal Census 6.00 (293)
1860 Federal Census 7.50 (293)
Pettis, Lafayette & Johnson Cos. Guardian, Curator & Minor's
    Bonds to 1855 [Includes apprentice records & data on minors] 7.50 (293)
Abstracts of Deeds, 1835-1837 (in Mo. Pion., v. 10) 9pp. 5.00 (106)

KNOX COUNTY

Marriage Book A, 1845-1867 (in Mo. Pion., v. 11) 35pp. 5.00 (106)
Abstracts of Wills, Book A, 1849-1872 (in Mo. Pion., v. 22) 13pp. 5.00 (106)

LACLEDE COUNTY

Marriage Book A, 1855-1870 (in Mo. Pion., v. 22) 28pp. 5.00 (106)
Tombstone Inscriptions [from 15 cemeteries], by Williams 5.00 (293)

LAFAYETTE COUNTY

Marriage Records 1850-1865, by Williams & Williams 6.00 (293)
Abstracts of Deeds, 1820-1825 (in Mo. Pion., v. 9) 9pp. 5.00 (106)
Abstracts of Wills & Adms., Vol. 1 (1821-1850) 5.00 (293)
Abstracts of Wills & Adms., Vol. 2 (1850-1865) 6.00 (293)
Early Tombstone Inscriptions [from 29 cemeteries] 5.00 (293)
Pettis, Lafayette & Johnson Cos. Guardian Curator and Minor's
    Bonds to 1855 [Includes apprentice records & data on minors] 7.50 (293)

LAWRENCE COUNTY

Abstracts of Wills, 1846-1884 (in Mo. Pion., v. 6) 15pp. 5.00 (106)
Tombstone Inscriptions, Vol. 1 ..... 7.50 (1137)
Red Oak Cemetery, Red Oak, Mo. [Caretaker's & tombstone data] 2.50 (1137)

LEWIS COUNTY

Marriage Records, Vol. 1 (1833-1868), by Dunlap 8.50 (263)
Marriage Records, Vol. 2 (1869-1883), by Dunlap 8.50 (263)
Marriage Books A & B, 1833-1863 (in Mo. Pion., v. 17) 28pp. 5.00 (106)
First Land Entries 1819-1840 [&] Marriages 1833-1863 [&] Probate
    Index 1833-1850 [&] Index to 1850 Census, by Williams 10.00 (293)

LINCOLN COUNTY

History of Lincoln County, by Goodspeed (repr. 1888, indexed) 25.00 ..... (318)
Abstracts of Wills, 1825-1864 (in Mo. Pion., v. 23) 22pp. 5.00 (106)
Marriages, 1844-1859 (in Mo. Pion., v. 29) 40pp. 5.00 (106)

LINN COUNTY

Abstracts of Wills & Admr. Bonds, 1840-1860 (in Mo. Pion., v. 30) 5.00 (106)

LIVINGSTON COUNTY

Abstracts of Wills & Admr. Bonds, 1857-1863 (in Mo. Pion., v. 19) 5.00 (106)

McDONALD COUNTY

Marriage Book A, 1865-1878, by Woodruff	.....	4.00	(105)
Abstracts of Will Book A, 1860-1891 (in Mo. Pion., v.25) 7pp.	.....	5.00	(106)

MACON COUNTY

Marriages, 1854-1860 (in Mo. Pion., v.20) 20pp.	.....	5.00	(106)

MADISON COUNTY

Marriages, 1818-1850 (in Mo. Pion., v.21) 25pp.	.....	5.00	(106)
Abstracts of Wills, 1822-1855 (in Mo. Pion., v.6) 6pp.	.....	5.00	(106)

MARIES COUNTY

History of Maries County, by King (rev. ed.)	12.50	.....	(770)
Abstracts of Wills, Bonds, Adms, 1866-1888 (in Mo. Pion., v.28)	.....	5.00	(106)

MARION COUNTY

1827 Tax List (in Mo. Pion., v.7) 4pp.	.....	5.00	(106)
Marriage Books A & B, 1827-1856, by Woodruff	.....	5.00	(105)
Abstracts of Wills & Adms., 1827-1837 (in Mo. Pion., v.24) 12pp.	.....	5.00	(106)

MERCER COUNTY

Will Bk. B, 1853-1863 & Bonds A, 1847-1863 (in Mo. Pion., v.10)	.....	5.00	(106)

MILLER COUNTY

Marriage Book A, 1837-1857 (in Mo. Pion., v.19) 20pp.	.....	5.00	(106)
Abstracts of Wills & Adms., 1839-1872 (in Mo. Pion., v.10) 10pp.	.....	5.00	(106)

MISSISSIPPI COUNTY

Marriage Book A, 1845-1865 (in Mo. Pion., v. 18) 15pp.	.....	5.00	(106)

MONITEAU COUNTY

Abstracts of Wills & Adms., 1845-1863 (in Mo. Pion., v.25) 37pp	.....	5.00	(106)

MONROE COUNTY

Marriage Book A, by Woodruff	.....	4.00	(105)
Abs. of Guardianship Bonds, 1831-1866 (in Mo. Pion., v.21) 20pp	.....	5.00	(106)
Abs. of Wills & Adms., 1850-1856 (in Mo. Pion., v.26) 19pp.	.....	5.00	(106)

MONTGOMERY COUNTY

1819 Tax List & Original Land Entries thru 1820 (in Mo. Pion, v.8)	.....	5.00	(106)

MORGAN COUNTY

Abstracts of Will Book A, 1833-1857 (in Mo. Pion., v.30) 7pp.	.....	5.00	(106)

NEW MADRID COUNTY

Abstracts of Wills & Adms., 1832-1846 (in Mo. Pion., v.11) 20pp	.....	5.00	(106)
1850, 1860, 1870, & 1880 Mortality Schedules	.....	3.50	(19)

NEWTON COUNTY

Abstracts of Deeds, 1839-1842 (in Mo. Pion., v.19) 12pp.	.....	5.00	(106)
Tombstone Inscriptions, Vol. 1, by Curry & Belk	.....	7.50	(1137)

NODAWAY COUNTY

On the Banks of the Elkhorn [History of the settlement of Hughes Twp. with 71 family histories. Pictures.] by Graham Hist. Soc.	.....	7.50	(469)
On the Banks of the Elkhorn, Vol. 2 [160 more family histories, newly available info about area, 240 pictures.]	.....	11.50	(469)
Cemetery Inscriptions, Hughes Twp., by Graham Hist. Soc.	.....	3.00	(469)

. . . .

OREGON COUNTY

Marriage Book A, 1845-1869 (in Mo. Pion., v.19) 10pp. 5.00 (106)

OSAGE COUNTY

Marriage Book A, 1841-1861, by Woodruff 4.00 (105)
Abs. of Wills & Adms., 1841-1861 (in Mo. Pion., v. 17) 20pp. 5.00 (106)

OZARK COUNTY

Marriage Book A, 1858-1878 (in Mo. Pion., v.24) 24pp. 5.00 (106)
Abstracts of Wills & Adms., 1865-1895 (in Mo. Pion., v.28) 5.00 (106)

PEMISCOT COUNTY

Pemiscot Pioneers: Land Records 1853-1880; Newspaper excerpts
1891-1895; Gazetter of 1890 Special Census; Plat of Little Prairie 1806; History of Bakerville storebuilding.], by Wade 5.00 (19)
Marriage Records, 1882-1898, by Wade 5.00 (19)
Cemetery Inscriptions, 5 vols., by Pemiscot Hist. Soc.   Each: 5.00 (75)

PERRY COUNTY

Marriage Book A, 1825-1841, by Woodruff 4.00 (105)
Abstracts of Wills & Adms., 1835-1845 (in Mo. Pion., v.24) 17pp 5.00 (106)

PETTIS COUNTY

History of Pettis County, by North (repr. of 1882 ed., indexed) 25.00 . . . . . (318)
Marriage Records, 1865-1877, by Williams & Williams 7.50 (293)
Marriage Records, 1877-1885, by Williams & Williams 10.00 (293)
Pettis, Lafayette & Johnson Counties, Guardian, Curator and
Minor's Bonds to 1855 [Includes apprentice records.] 7.50 (293)
Abstracts of Wills & Adms., 1833-1860 (in Mo. Pion., v.29) 14pp 5.00 (106)

PHELPS COUNTY

Marriage Book A, 1857-1867 (in Mo. Pion., v.18) 16pp. 5.00 (106)
Abstracts of Wills, Bonds & Adms., 1859-1870 (in Mo.Pion.,v.29) 5.00 (106)

PIKE COUNTY

Court Records, 1821-1825 (in Mo. Pion., v.20) 10pp. 5.00 (106)
Marriages 1818-1839 (in Mo. Pion., v.14) 23pp. 5.00 (106)
Marriages 1840-1851 (in Mo. Pion., v. 9) 31pp. 5.00 (106)
Abstracts of Wills & Adms., 1825-1835 (in Mo. Pion., v. 9) 13pp 5.00 (106)

PLATTE COUNTY

Abstracts of Wills & Admr. Bonds, Books A & B, 1841-1861 . . . . . 5.00 (105)

POLK COUNTY

History of Hickory, Polk, Cedar, Dade & Barton Cos., by Good-
speed (repr. of 1889 ed. - with new index added) 25.50 . . . . . (563)
Marriage Book A, 1836-1859, by Woodruff 4.00 (105)
Abstracts of Wills & Adms., 1837-1854 (in Mo. Pion., v.11) 5.00 (106)

PULASKI COUNTY

Abstracts of Wills, Bonds & Adms., 1833-1875 (in Mo.Pion.,v.16) 5.00 (106)

RALLS COUNTY

Marriage Books A & B, 1821-1866, by Woodruff 5.00 (105)

RANDOLPH COUNTY

History of Randolph & Macon Cos., by Nat.Hist.Co. (repr.1884) 25.00 . . . . . (318)
History of Randolph County, by Waller (repr. 1920) 47.50 45.00 (546)
Abstracts of Probates, 1829-1836 (in Mo. Pion., v.23) 13pp. 5.00 (106)

RAY COUNTY

History of Ray County, by Mo.Hist.Co. (repr. 1881 - new index)   25.00   ..... (318)
1821 Tax List (in Mo. Pion., v.2) 4pp. 5.00   (106)
Abstracts of Wills, Bonds & Adms., 1821-1852 (in Mo. pion.,v.8) 5.00   (106)

REYNOLDS COUNTY

History of Reynolds County, by Pennington [Contains many names
of early settlers. Every-name index. Available June 1975]   5.00   3.00   (733)
Pinedale & Dobbins Cem. Inscriptions (in Ridge Run., v.2, #1) 2pp.......   2.00   (670)

RIPLEY COUNTY

Marriages, 1835-1860 (in Mo. Pion., v.10) 20pp. 5.00   (106)
Marriages, 1860-1881 [&] 1850, 1860, 1870, 1880 Mortality Sched-
ules, by McManus [Includes many marriages fr.Randolph Co.] 5.50   (14)
Marriages, 1881-1887 [some names annotated] 5.00   (14)
Cemetery Listings, Pt. 1 [Includes Bethany (Methodist), Girtman,
Pulaski (Catholic), Woolard, Pope's Chapel, Shiloh, Elizabeth,
Wilson, Rosson. Indexed] 5.00   (14)
1840 Federal Census - Indexed, by McManus 3.50   (14)
1850 Federal Census & Slave Census - Indexed, by McManus 4.00   (14)
1870 Federal Census - Indexed, by McManus 5.00   (14)

ST. CHARLES COUNTY

Pioneer Families of Sullivan Co., Missouri, With Related Families
of St. Charles Co. and Monroe Co., Ky., by Sears   15.00   ..... (22)

ST. CLAIR COUNTY

History of Henry & St. Clair Cos., by Nat.Hist.Co. (repr. 1883)   25.00   ..... (318)
Abstracts of Wills & Adms., 1865-1872 (in Mo.Pion., v.24) 17pp 5.00   (106)
Records: Marriages 1855-1866; Index to Probate, through 1870;
Early Settlers; Civil War Muster Rolls, by Williams 7.50   (293)
1850 Federal Census, by St.Louis Genealogical Society 3.35   (29)

ST. FRANCOIS COUNTY

Marriage Books A & B, 1836-1866, by Woodruff 4.00   (105)
Abstracts of Wills, Bonds & Adms., 1825-1852 (in Mo.Pion.,v.20) 5.00   (106)
1850 Federal Census, by St.Louis Genealogical Society 3.35   (29)

STE. GENEVIEVE COUNTY

Marriage Book A, 1807-1827 & 1842-1866, by Woodruff 5.00   (105)
Abstracts of Wills & Adms., 1807-1855 (in Mo. Pion., v.19) 26pp 5.00   (106)

ST. LOUIS COUNTY & CITY

Marriages, 1804-1859, by St. Louis Genealogical Society 11.00   (29)
Marriages, 1860-1876, by St. Louis Genealogical Society 11.00   (29)
Fee Fee Cemetery Inscriptions, by St. Louis Genealogical Soc. 1.00   (29)
Index to 1850 Federal Census of St. Louis County & City 10.50   (29)

SALINE COUNTY

Abstracts of Deeds, 1820-1835 (in Mo. Pion., v. 7) 11pp. 5.00   (106)

SCHUYLER COUNTY

Marriages, 1845-1860 & Abs. of Wills, Bonds & Adms., 1845-
1860 (in Mo. Pion., v.16) 27pp. 5.00   (106)

SCOTLAND COUNTY

Marriage Records, Vol. 1 (1841-1867), by Dodge	..... 8.50	(263)
Marriage Records, Vol. 2 (1868-1882), by Dodge	..... 8.50	(263)
Marriage Records, Vol. 3 (1883-1895), by Dodge	..... 8.50	(263)
Marriages, 1841-1857 [&] Abs. of Wills, 1846-1867 (in Mo. Pion., v. 13) 32pp.	..... 5.00	(106)
Cemetery Inscriptions, by Dodge. 3 vols. Each: $15.00 Set:	..... 45.00	(263)
1860 Federal Census, by Dunlap	..... 5.00	(263)

SCOTT COUNTY

Marriages, 1840-1855 [&] Wills, 1832-1848 (in Mo. Pion., v.7) 5.00 (106)

SHELBY COUNTY

Abstracts of Bond Book A, 1844-1853 (in Mo. Pion., v.12) 23pp 5.00 (106)

STODDARD COUNTY

Wills, 1837-1860 [&] Adms., 1847-1860 (in Mo. Pion., v.22) 13pp 5.00 (106)

STONE COUNTY

Wills & Adms., 1851-1898 [&] Marriages, 1851-1879, by Williams 7.50 (293)

SULLIVAN COUNTY

Pioneer Families of Sullivan County & Related Families of St. Charles County, Missouri, & Monroe County, Kentucky, by Sears [Contains dozens of individual family histories.]   15.00 ..... (22)

TANEY COUNTY

Tombstone Inscriptions, by Williams. 3 vols. Each: $3.50 Set:	..... 10.50	(293)
1840 Federal Census [complete] (in Mo. Pion., v.15) 18pp.	..... 5.00	(106)

TEXAS COUNTY

Record of Adms., 1845-1866 (in Mo. Pion., v.27) 10pp. 5.00 (106)

VERNON COUNTY

Marriage Book A, 1855-1869 (in Mo. Pion., v.20) 15pp.	..... 5.00	(106)
Newspaper Abstracts (in Ridge Runners, v.2, #1) 4pp.	..... 2.00	(670)

WARREN COUNTY

Marriage Books A & B, 1833-1860, by Woodruff	..... 4.00	(105)
Abstracts of Deeds, 1833-1835 (in Mo. Pion., v.27) 7pp.	..... 5.00	(106)
Abstracts of Wills & Adms., 1833-1844 (in Mo. Pion., v.12) 12pp	..... 5.00	(106)

WASHINGTON COUNTY

Marriages, 1825-1850 (in Mo. Pion., v.26) 39pp.	..... 5.00	(106)
Abs. of Wills, Bonds & Adms., 1816-1853 (in Mo. Pion., v.27)	..... 5.00	(106)

WAYNE COUNTY

1840 Federal Census [complete] (in Mo. Pion., v.11) 15pp. 5.00 (106)

WEBSTER COUNTY

Abs. of Wills, Bonds & Adms., 1856-1863 (in Mo. Pion., v.12)	..... 5.00	(106)
Cemetery Inscriptions of Watts, Mountain Dale, & Zion Lutheran Cemeteries (in Ridge Runners, v.2, #3) 9pp.	..... 2.00	(670)

WORTH COUNTY

Marriages, 1861-1873; Wills & Adms., 1861-1875 (in Mo. Pion., v.15) 5.00 (106)

WRIGHT COUNTY

Probate Records, 1864-1874 (in Mo. Pion., v.25) 13pp. 5.00 (106)

Montana

STATEWIDE REFERENCES

Northwest Notebook [New genealogical series. Contains primary source material, etc. on Idaho & Montana.]	.....	5.00	(931)
Montana As It Is, by Stuart (repr. of 1865 ed.)	9.00	.....	(629)
Ghost Towns of Montana, by Miller	17.50	.....	(753)
Montana Genesis, by Stevensville Hist. Soc.	8.50	.....	(782)
History of Montana: From Wilderness to Statehood, 1805-1900, by Milton (2nd rev. & enl. ed.)	10.00	.....	(626)

Research aids

Montana: A Student 's Guide to Localized History	.....	1.50	(762)

Records

Montana Historical Society Contributions (repr. of 1876 ed.) 10 vols. Each: $25.00 Set:	245.00	.....	(673)

BLAINE COUNTY

In the Land of the Chinook, Or the Story of Blaine County, by Noyes (repr. of 1917 ed.)	13.50	10.00	(814)

SILVERBOW COUNTY

A Brief History of Butte, Montana, by Freeman (1969)	7.50	.....	(919)

Nebraska

STATEWIDE REFERENCES

Journal of Mollie Dorsey Sanford in Nebraska & Colorado Territories, 1857-1866, by Sanford	5.00	.....	(760)

Research aids

Nebraska Place-Names, by Fitzpatrick & Fairclough	.....	1.50	(760)
Nebraska: A Guide to the Cornhusker State, Federal Writer's Project (repr. of 1939 ed.)	17.50	.....	(939)
A Guide to the Manuscript Division of the Nebraska State Archives, by James Potter (1974)	10.00	.....	(759)

Military

Fort McPherson, Nebraska Territory, by Holmes	7.50	....'.	(1000)

OTOE COUNTY

For the Record: A Centennial History of Syracuse, Nebraska, by Masters	.....	6.25	(805)

Nevada

STATEWIDE REFERENCES

Adventures in the Apache Country: A Tour Through Arizona & Sonora, With Notes on the Silver Regions of Nevada, by Browne (repr. of 1871 ed.)	26.00	.....	(629)
History of Nevada, by Elliott	.....	.....	(730)

98 - Nevada, New Hampshire

Research aids

Nevada's Newspapers: A Bibliography, A compilation of Nevada History, 1854-1964, by Folkes (1964) .... (730)

New Hampshire

STATEWIDE REFERENCES

Three Centuries of Freemasonry in New Hampshire with Biographical Dictionary, by Foss [97 chapters of historical events and biographies connected with N.H. Masons from 1735 to 1971.] 9.95 ..... (723)
History of New Hampshire, by Belknap. (repr. of 2nd ed., 1813)
  3 vols. Each: $20.00   Set: 67.50 60.00 (546)
History of New Hampshire, by Belknap (repr. 1792) 3 vols. Set: 90.00 ..... (629)
The Pioneers of Maine and New Hampshire, 1628-1660, by Pope 10.00 ..... (130)
Vermont in the Making, 1750-1777, by Jones [N.H. grants] 15.00 ..... (823)

Research aids

New Hampshire Genealogical Research Guide, by Towle [Describes records which are extant, specifies their location and availability to the public, and is a guide to their use.] 3.50 (161)
Hammond's Check List of New Hampshire History (rev. ed.) 10.00 (724)
New Hampshire: A Student's Guide to Localized History 1.50 (762)

Records

Genealogical Dictionary of Maine & New Hampshire, by Noyes 17.50 ..... (130)
New Hampshire State Legislature: Provincial & State Papers,
  by Bouton & Hammond. 18 vols. Set: 775.00 ..... (630)
Notices From the N.H. Gazette, 1765-1800, by Hammond 10.00 ..... (739)
Colonial Gravestone Inscriptions in the State of N.H., by Goss 10.00 ..... (130)
1790 Census of N.H., by U.S. Bureau of Census (repr.) 11.00 ..... (130)
1790 Census of N.H., by U.S. Bureau of Census (repr.) 7.50 ..... (663)
Index to 1800 Census of New Hampshire, by Gill & Gill
  Vol. 1: Index to Cheshire County 4.00 (752)
  Vol. 2: Index to Grafton & Hillsborough Counties 6.00 (752)
  Vol. 3: Index to Rockingham & Strafford Counties 6.00 (752)
  Vol. 1, 2, & 3 [Bound together in one book] 20.00 ..... (752)

Military

The Military History of the State of New Hampshire, From Its Settlement in 1623 to the Rebellion in 1861, by Potter 24.00 ..... (130)
Tories of New Hampshire in the War of the Rev., by Hammond 8.00 ..... (854)
History of the First N.H. Regt. in the War of the Rev., by Kidder
  [Only regimental history for any state for Revolutionary War. Lists men & officers who served. Repr. of 1868 ed.] 10.50 ..... (439)

CARROLL COUNTY

History of Carroll County, by Merrill (repr. of 1889 ed.) 47.50 45.00 (546)

CHESHIRE COUNTY

Keene, N.H. Cemetery Headstone Inscriptions, by Gill 3.50 (752)
History of the First Congregational Church, Keene, by Proper 5.50 (727)

COOS COUNTY

Historical Sketches of the Discovery, Settlement & Progress of Events in the Coos County & Vincinity, 1754-1785, by Powers 35.00 ..... (726)

HILLSBORO COUNTY

History of Manchester, formerly Derryfield, by Potter (repr. 1851) 47.50   45.00 (546)

ROCKINGHAM COUNTY

Rambles About Portsmouth, by Brewster [Sketches of persons,
localities, and incidents of two centuries, principally from tra-
dition & unpublished documents. 2 vols.   Set: 45.00   40.00 (546)
History of the Town of Hampton From Its Settlement in 1638 to the
Autumn of 1892, by Dow (2nd. ed., 1970)   35.00   ..... (439)

New Jersey

STATEWIDE REFERENCES

Narratives of Early Pennsylvania, West New Jersey, & Delaware
1630-1707, by Myers (repr. of 1912 ed.) [Original narratives.] 5.75 ..... (643)
The Province of West New Jersey, 1609-1702, by Pomfret 13.00 ..... (894)
Historical Collections of New Jersey, by Barber & Howe 17.50 ..... (663)
The History of the Colony of Nova-Caesaria [or N.J.], by Smith 17.50 ..... (663)
"Ye Charte of Six Generations of ye Earlie Settlers of Nova Caesar-
ia, Knowne to some as ye Province of New Jersey", by Kearney
[Approx. 32" x 42" - intended for framing - suitable artistic bor-
der. First of 6 generations starts with 99 immigrant families of
1600's and shows intermarriages with other families for 5 addi-
tional generations (to 1800's). Several thousand people.] 8.00 (537)
Historical & Genealogical Miscellany. Data Relating to the Settle-
ment and Settlers of New York & New Jersey, by Stillwell 75.00 ..... (130)
New Jersey Biographical & Genealogical Notes, by Nelson 10.00 ..... (130)
A Study of Slavery in New Jersey, by Cooley 10.25 6.25 (1000)
New Jersey Proprietors & Their Lands, by Pomfret (1964) 6.00 ..... (950)

Research aids

Index to the Genealogical Magazine of New Jersey, by Stryker-
Rodda. 2 vols.   Set: 40.00 ..... (580)
Index to the New Jersey Genesis 1953-1971, by Nissen 16.00 ..... (871)
New Jersey in Traveler's Accounts, 1524-1970: A Descriptive
Bibliography, by Coad 6.00 ..... (920)
New Jersey: A Student's Guide to Localized History 1.50 (762)
Narrative & Descriptive Bibliography of New Jersey, by Burr 6.00 ..... (950)

Records

New Jersey Archives. First Series. 42v. & index. [Colonial,
Rev., & post-Rev. history.] Index: $10. Other vols. each: 37.50 ..... (630)
New Jersey Archives. Second Series. 5v. [Documents relat-
ing to Revolutionary history.]   Each: 37.50 ..... (630)
Revolutionary Census of N.J. 1773-1784, by Stryker-Rodda ,17.50 ..... (580)
New Jersey Marriage Records, 1665-1800, by Nelson 17.50 ..... (130)
Index of Wills, Inventories, Etc., in the Office of the Secretary
of State Prior to 1901, by N.J. Dept. of State. 3 vols. Set: 50.00 ..... (130)
The Loyalists of New Jersey: Their Memorials, Claims, Pe-
titions, etc. From English Records, by Jones (repr. 1927) 16.00 ..... (854)

Maps & Gazetteers

New Jersey Road Maps of the 18th Century 4.00 2.00 (1006)
Gazetteer of the State of N.J., by Gordon 15.00 ..... (580)

Military

The Battles of Trenton & Princeton, by Stryker	15.00	..... (663)
Records of Officers and Men of N.J. in Wars, 1791-1815	25.00	..... (130)
Official Register of the Officers and Men of N.J. in the Revolutionary War, by Stryker	18.50	..... (130)
Index of the Official Reg. . . (above), by Stryker	8.50	..... (130)
Journal & Order Book of Capt. Robert Kirkwood of the Delaware Regiment of the Continental Line [1st Regt., Del. Inf. 1776-1783] (repr. of 1910 ed.)	12.50	..... (637)

Religious and ethnic groups

The Germans in Colonial Times, by Bittinger (repr. of 1901 ed.) [Settlements in Pa., Md., N.J., Va., N.C., & S.C.]	8.50	..... (988)
The Swedish Settlements on the Delaware, 1638-1664, Johnson	27.50	..... (130)
Quaker Miscellany: New Jersey, by Heiss [Six articles reprinted which were originally published in 1800's in Quaker publications "The Friend", "Friends Intelligencer & Journal" & "An Account of . . . Meetings . . . "]	.....	3.00 (303)
Encyclopedia of American Quaker Genealogy, by Hinshaw Vol. 2 [New Jersey & Pennsylvania Monthly Meetings]	50.00	..... (130)
The Early Germans of New Jersey: Their History, Churches, and Genealogies, by Chambers	18.50	..... (130)

ATLANTIC COUNTY

1850 Census of Atlantic, Bergen, & Burlington Cos. [&] List of Revolutionary pensioners appearing in those Cos. in 1840	.....	25.00 (111)

BERGEN COUNTY

1850 Census of Atlantic, Bergen & Burlington Counties [&] List of Revolutionary pensioners in 1840 - Indexed, by Tanco	.....	25.00 (111)
Revolutionary War in the Hackensack Valley: The Jersey Dutch & the Neutral Ground, 1775-1783, by Leiby	10.00	..... (950)
Map of OLD Bergen County [5 sheets]	.....	5.00 (913)

BURLINGTON COUNTY

1850 Census of Atlantic, Bergen, Burlington Counties [&] List of Revolutionary pensioners in 1840 - Indexed, by Tanco		
"Stewart's Genealogical & Historical Miscellany, No. 2" [Burlington Co. birth records from 1753-1773, Bible records, Rev. War incidents, genealogies, etc.] (repr. of 1918 ed.)	.....	3.25 (1141)

CUMBERLAND COUNTY

1850 Census - and 1840 List of Rev. War Pensioners - of Sussex, Ocean, & Cumberland Counties, by Tanco [Indexed]	.....	25.00 (111)

GLOUCESTER COUNTY

1850 Census - and 1840 List of Rev. War Pensioners - of Gloucester, Hunterdon, & Hudson Counties, by Tanco [Indexed]	.....	25.00 (111)

HUDSON COUNTY

1850 Census - and 1840 List of Rev. War Pensioners - of Gloucester, Hunterdon, & Hudson Counties, by Tanco [Indexed]	.....	25.00 (111)

HUNTERDON COUNTY

1850 Census - and 1840 List of Rev. War Pensioners - of Gloucester, Hunterdon, & Hudson Counties, by Tanco [Indexed]	.....	25.00 (111)

MERCER COUNTY

An Historical & Genealogical History of the First United Methodist
Church of Pennington, 1774-1974, by D'Autrechy [Besides a
history of the church, contains all baptisms, births, marriages
and genealogical miscellaney from the church records, 1833-
1898. Record of the cemetery, 1744-1935.]   5.00   .....   (26)

MIDDLESEX COUNTY

Ira Dunn's Coffin Records, 1817-1834 (in NGSQ, v.56, #1) 3.00   (616)

MONMOUTH COUNTY

History of Monmouth County, by Ellis (repr. of 1885 ed.)   26.00   .....   (644)
Index to History of Monmouth County, by Ellis (above)   12.00   .....   (644)
Historical and Genealogical Miscellany, by Stillwell, Vol. 6
[Unrecorded wills & inv. of late 1600's and 1700's]   15.00   .....   (644)
This Old Monmouth of Ours, by Hornor [1,932 old newspaper ar-
ticles on early families – colonial, rev., & Civil War periods] 18.00   .....   (218)
The History of Old Tennent Church, by Symmes (repr. of 1905 ed.)
[Includes membership lists, burial records, etc.] 15.00   (801)
Burial Records of the Old First United Methodiest Church, West
Long Branch, N.J., by Martin 1.00   (1132)

OCEAN COUNTY

1850 Census - and 1840 List of Rev. War Pensioners - of Sussex,
Ocean, & Cumberland Counties, by Tanco 25.00   (111)

SALEM COUNTY

Old Deeds Belonging to the Salem County Historical Society, With
Index of 666 Deeds Not of Record, by Salem Co. Hist. Soc. 3.25   (955)
History & Genealogy Catalogue Containing Inventories of Documents
Surveys, Maps, Mss., Deeds, Microfilms Belonging to the Soc. 4.00   (955)

SUSSEX COUNTY

1850 Census - and 1840 List of Rev. War Pensioners - of Sussex,
Ocean, & Cumberland Counties, by Tanco 25.00   (111)

New Mexico

STATEWIDE REFERENCES

History of Arizona & New Mexico, by Bancroft   20.00   .....   (741)

Research aids

New Mexico: A Student's Guide to Localized History 1.50   (762)
Origins of New Mexico Families in the Spanish Colonial Period;
In Two Parts: The Seventeenth (1598-1693 and the Eighteenth
(1693-1821) Centuries, by Chavez [Biographical dictionary
of families who resided in N.M. during this period]   12.50   .....   (803)

LINCOLN COUNTY

Violence in Lincoln County, by Keleher   9.50   3.45   (803)
History of the Lincoln County War, by Fulton   8.50   .....   (792)

SAN JUAN COUNTY

Aztec: Anasazi to Statehood, by Koogler & Whitney [Follows each
family entering Aztec from 1876 to statehood.]   10.00   .....   (232)

New York

STATEWIDE REFERENCES

Yesteryears Magazine, ed. by Grifone [A quarterly magazine for the appreciation and study of N.Y. regional history. 18 vols. now completed. All 18v. can be purchased in microfilm or xerox copies.] $2.50 single issue. 50+pp. Subscription/yr:	8.00	(445)
Disposition of Loyalist Estates in the Southern District of the State of New York, by Yoshpe	12.50	(630)
History of New Netherland, or New York under the Dutch, by O'Callaghan. Vol. 1 - $15.00; Vol. 2 - $17.50 Set:	32.50	(663)
Colonial Days in Old New York, by Earle (repr. of 1896 ed.)	8.50	(233)
Joseph Ellicott and the Holland Land Company, the Opening of Western New York, by Chazanof	9.00	(808)
Bloody Mohawk, by Clarke (repr. of 1940 ed.) [History of the Mohawk Valey up to the end of the Revolution.]	11.00	(641)
Canadian & Nova Scotia Refugees to New York (in NGSQ, v.53, #2)	3.00	(616)

Research aids

Guide to the Principal Sources for Early American History, 1600-1800, in the City of New York, by Greene & Morris	14.00	(982)
New York: A Student's Guide to Localized History	..... 1.50	(762)
New York City: A Student's Guide to Localized History	...... 1.50	(762)
Aboriginal Place Names of New York, by Beauchamp (1907)	17.50	(233)
PI #116 - Preliminary Inventory of the Records of the U.S. District Court for the Southern District of N.Y., by Nat.Arch.	..... free	(402)
Calendar of Historical Manuscripts in the Office of the Sec. of State, Albany, N.Y., by O'Callaghan. Pt. 1 (repr. 1865)	27.50 25.00	(546)

Records

True and Authentic Register of Persons Who in the Year 1709 Journeyed From Germany to America, by Simmendinger	..... 3.00	(130)
Documents Relative to the Colonial History of the State of New York . . . , Weed, Parsons & Co. (repr. 1863-1887)		
Vols. 1, 2, & 12 Each:	42.50 40.00	(546)
Vols. 3, 4, 5, 6, 7, 8, 9, 10, & 14 Each:	47.50 45.00	(546)
Vols. 11, 13, & 15 Each:	37.50 35.00	(546)
Vols. 1 through 15 Set:	667.50 630.00	(546)
Petition of Protestants of New York 1701 (in Genealogical Reference Builders "Newletter", v.8, #1) 8pp.	..... 2.00	(931)
Genealogical Data From the New York Post Boy, 1743-1773, by Scott	13.25	(616)
Genealogical Data From New York Administration Bonds, 1753-1799, & Hitherto Unpublished Letters of Adm., by Scott	..... 15.00	(901)
New York Marriages Previous to 1784	17.50	(130)
1790 Federal Census, by U.S. Census Bureau (repr.)	12.50	(663)
1790 Federal Census, by U.S. Census Bureau (repr.)	15.00	(130)
Genealogical Records: Manuscript Entries of Births, Deaths, and Marriages, Taken From Family Bibles 1581-1917, by Robison & Bartlett	12.50	(130)
Registers of Births, Marriages and Deaths of the "Eglise Francoise a la Nouvelle York" From 1688-1804, by Wittmeyer	16.00	(130)
Calendar of Wills on File and Recorded in the Office of the Clerk of the Court of Appeals, of the County Clerk at Albany, and of the Secretary of State, 1626-1836, by Fernow	18.50	(130)
New York Historical Manuscripts: Dutch, by Van Laer, 4 vols.	75.00	(130)

The Argyle Patent and Accompanying Documents, by Patten 5.00 (130)
Vessel, 'The Guiding Star'; Copenhagen to New York City, June
  1869, by Barekman [List of passengers on board] 6.00 (252)

Miscelleanous

Historical & Genealogical Miscellany, by Stillwell [Data relating to the settlement & settlers of N.Y. &N.J.] 5 vols. Set: 75.00 ..... (130)
Genealogical Notes of N.Y. & New England Families, by Talcott 15.00 ..... (130)

Military

Minutes of the Commissioners for Detecting & Defeating Conspir-
  acies in the St. of N.Y. by Paltsits & Billias [Revolution -
  Committes of Safety] 3 vols. in 2 Set: 45.00 ..... (854)
The Refugees of 1776 From Long Island to Conn., by Mather 30.00 ..... (130)
Orderly Book of the Three Battalions of Loyalists Commanded
  by Brig. Gen. DeLancey, 1776-1778, by N.Y. Hist. Soc. 7.50 ..... (130)
The Road to Independence: The Revolutionary Movement in New
  York, 1773-1777, by Mason 7.50 ..... (126)
Personal Recollections of the Am. Rev., by Post (repr. 1859) 8.25 ..... (637)
New York in the Revolution, by Fernow 25.00 ..... (580)
Index of Awards on Claims of the Soldiers of the War of 1812 37.50 ..... (130)
Camp Fires of the 23rd: Sketches of . . . 23rd Regt., N.Y.V.,
  by Sterling [pseud. Maxsom] (repr. of 1863 ed.) 12.50 10.00 (546)
Const. & By-Laws of B Company Spaulding Guards, 74th Regt.
  N.G.S.N.Y., Organized Aug. 12, 1854, by Freeman (1877) 8.50 6.00 (546)
History of the 13th Regt., N.G.S.N.Y., by Mandeville (1894) 12.50 10.00 (546)
History of the 7th Regt., N.G.S.N.Y., by Swinton (1870) 32.50 30.00 (546)
History . . . 12th Regt., N.G.S.N.Y., by Dowley (1869) 17.50 15.00 (546)
The Seventy-ninth Highlanders, N.Y. Volunteers in the War
  of the Rebellion, 1861-1865, by Todd (repr. 1886) 32.50 30.00 (546)
New York Infantry, 83rd Regt., 1861-1864, by Swrds (1887) 8.50 6.00 (546)
The Men of the 189th Regt. of N.Y. Volunteers (Civil War) (in
  MCGS Reporter, Vols. 5, #6; 6, #1,2,3) 2pp. each Total: 3.00 (596)
Berdan's U.S. Sharpshooters in the Army of the Potomac,
  1861-1865, by Stevens 15.00 ..... (848)
Albany Zouave Cadets, esto vigilans, Fifty Years Young, July
  23, 1860-1910, by Manning (repr. 1910?) 17.50 15.00 (546)

Religious and ethnic groups

History of New Paltz, N.Y. & Its Old Families 1678-1820, by
  LeFevre [Huguenots] 18.00 ..... (130)
Early 18th Century Palatine Emigration, by Knittle 11.50 ..... (130)
Wills of Early New York Jews (1704-1799), by Hershkowitz 6.00 ..... (440)
The Lee Max Friedman Collection of American Jewish Colon-
  ial Correspondence: Letters of the Franks Family, 1733-
  1748, by Hershkowitz & Meyer, by Am. Jewish Hist. Soc. 10.00 ..... (440)
Records of the Dutch Reformed Church in New Amsterdam &
  New York, by Purple 50.00 ..... (981)
Batisims From 1639-1800 in the Reformed Dutch Church,
  New York, by Evans (repr. of 1901 ed.) 2 vols. 79.00 ..... (854)
Religion & Trade in the New Netherlands, Dutch Origins &
  American Development, by Smith 15.00 ..... (835)
Settlers of Rensselaerswyck, 1630-1658, by van Laer 6.00 (130)
Scandinavian Immigrants in New York, 1630-1674, by Evjen 15.00 ..... (130)
Encyclopedia of Am. Quaker Gen., by Hinshaw. Vol. 3 [N.Y.] 25.00 ..... (130)
History of the Parish of Trinity Church in N.Y.C., by Morgan
  4 vols. Each: $12.50 Set: 50.00 ..... (630)
Moravian Journals Relating to Central N.Y., 1745-66, ed. by
  Beauchamp for Onondaga Hist. Assoc. 12.50 ..... (630)

Maps & Gazetteers

A Check List of New York State County Maps Published 1779-
1945, by Wright .... (1024)
Gazetteer of the State of New York, by French 25.00 ..... (637)

ALBANY COUNTY

The History of the City of Albany (in Yesteryears, v.16,#63 +)
[In 10 installments, approx. 75pp. total] 20.00 (445)
1800 Census Transcript/Index , by Wood [35mm. only] Microfilm: 4.00 (175)

BROOME COUNTY

Index of Names appearing in 1885 ed. of Smith's Broome County
History, by Tyne 12.00 (349)

CAYUGA COUNTY

The Pioneer Stagecoach Line (in Yesteryears, v.16, #62 +) Total: 4.00 (445)
Diana - A Haven for Joseph Bonaparte (in Yesteryears, v.18, #69) 2.50 (445)
1800 & 1810 Census Transcripts/Index [35mm. only] Microfilm: 4.75 (175)

CHAUTAUQUA COUNTY

Chautauqua County: A History, by McMahon (1959) 6.95 ..... (906)

CHENANGO COUNTY

Index of Names appearing in 1880 ed. of Smith's Chenango & Madison Counties, by Tyne 18.00 (349)

CHEMUNG COUNTY

Our County and Its People: A History of the Valley and County
of Chemung . . . , by Towner (repr. 1892) 47.50 45.00 (546)

CLINTON COUNTY

Uriah Cross and His Participation in the Revolutionary War (in
Yesteryears, v. 17, #68) 5pp. 2.50 (445)

COLUMBIA COUNTY

Settlers & Residents, Vol. 1, Town of Germantown, 1710-1899,
by Kelly [1878 history reprint; Livingston ledger records; Reformed, Lutheran, & Methodist Church communion, member-
ship & death lists; cemetery records; federal & state census,
1790-1875] 32.50 ..... (507)
Baptism & Marriage Record of the Reformed Churches of Upper
Red Hook, Tivoli, Mellenville, & Linlithgo, 1766-1899 24.85 ..... (507)
Baptism & Marriage Record of the Reformed Churches of Ghent,
West Ghent, Mt. Pleasant, & Stuyvesant Falls, 1775-1899 29.50 ..... (507)
Baptism Record of Reformed Church of West Copake, N.Y.,
1783-1899, by Kelly 29.55 ..... (507)
Marriage Record of the Four Lutheran Congregations of Manor-
ton, Churchtown, Germantown, & Barrytown, N.Y.,1794-1899 19.35 ..... (507)
Marriage Record of the Four Reformed Cong. in the Towns of Ger-
mantown, Gallatin, Copake, & Hillsdale, N.Y., 1736-1899 19.35 ..... (507)
Marriage Record of Linlithgo Ref. Ch., Livingston, 1723-1899 11.60 ..... (507)
Marriage Record of Ref. Church, Claverack, 1727-1899 30.80 ..... (507)
Baptism Record of St. John's Luth. Ch., Manorton, 1765-1872 41.40 ..... (507)
Baptism Record of St. Thomas' Luth. Ch., Churchtown, 1760-1899 46.65 ..... (507)
Baptism Record of Ref. Ch., Claverack, 1727-1899 67.40 ..... (507)
Baptism Record of Christ Luth. Ch., Germantown, 1746-1899 24.00 ..... (507)
Baptism Record of Ref. Dutch Ch., Hillsdale, 1776-1849 10.50 ..... (507)
Baptism Records of Gallatin Ref. Ch., Gallatinville, 1748-1899 26.55 ..... (507)

Baptism Record of Ref. Church, Germantown, 1729-1898   52.65   .....   (507)
Baptism Record of Linlithgo Ref. Ch., Livingston, 1722-1899   35.70   .....   (507)
   [Note: All above church records have been transcribed by
   Arthur C. M. Kelly. Names of parents, sponsors, witnesses,
   etc. have been included - and all are completely indexed.]
Revolutionary War Veterans Buried in Columbia County, N.Y.,
   Vol. I, by French (for Hendrick Hudson Chap. NSDAR, Inc.)
   [Name, service record, dates of veteran & wife (where avail-
   able), exact location of burial, index of cemeteries.] 10.00   (419)
   Vol. II [To be published in late 1975]   ....   (419)

CORTLAND COUNTY

The Settlement of the Town of Virgil (in Yesteryears, v.16, #64 +)
   [Two installments, approx. 12 pages]   Total: 4.00   (445)

DELAWARE COUNTY

Index of Names appearing in 1898 ed. of Murray's Delaware
   County History, by Tyne 6.00   (349)

DUTCHESS COUNTY

Little Nine Partners, A History of Pine Plains, by Huntting
   (reprint - with new 50pp. index)   29.50   .....   (507)
Documentary History of Rhinebeck, by Smith (repr.-new index) 17.50   .....   (507)
Baptism & Marriage Record of the Reformed Churches of Upper
   Red Hook, Tivoli, Mellenville, & Linlithgo, 1766-1899   24.85   .....   (507)
Marriage Record of the Three Lutheran Congregations of Rhine-
   beck, 1746-1899   23.85   .....   (507)
Baptism Record of St. Paul's Luth. Ch. of Wurtemburg, Rhine-
   beck, N.Y., 1760-1899   18.15   .....   (507)
Marriage Record of the Four Reformed Congregations of Old
   Rhinebeck, 1731-1899   26.55   .....   (507)
Baptism Record of St. Peter's Luth. Ch., Rhinebeck, 1733-1899 37.60   .....   (507)
Baptism Record of St. Paul's (Zion's) Luth. Ch., Red Hook,
   1730-1899   46.50   .....   (507)
Baptism Record of the Eight Episcopal Congregations of Old
   Rhinebeck, 1816-1899   28.50   .....   (507)
Baptism Record of Ref. Church, Rhinebeck, 1731-1899   35.70   .....   (507)
Dutchess County, comp. by Federal Writers' Project (1937)   12.50   10.00   (546)
Historical & Genealogical Record, Dutchess & Putnam Counties,
   by Oxford Pub. Co. (repr. 1912 ed.)   32.50   30.00   (546)
The Records of Christ Church, Poughkeepsie, Vol. 2   22.50   20.00   (546)

ERIE COUNTY

1870 Federal Census of the 4th Ward, City of Buffalo, by Day
   [Completely indexed. To be published in 1975]   ....   (7)

FRANKLIN COUNTY

A History of St. Lawrence & Franklin Counties, by Hough   15.00   .....   (130)

GREENE COUNTY

History of Greene County (repr. of 1884 ed.)   12.50   .....   (693)
Baptism Record of Zion Lutheran Ch., Athens, 1704-1899   39.70   .....   (507)
Notables of the Town of Athens (in Yesteryears, v.15, #57) 10pp. 2.00   (445)
The Settlement of the Town of Coxsackie (in Yesteryears, v.15,
   #60) 20pp. 2.00   (445)
Old Times in Windham, by Prout (repr. 1869) 8.50   (693)

HERKIMER COUNTY
Mohawk Valley Early Families (in Yesteryears, v. 18, #69) 2.00   (445)

[Six installments, approx. 50pp. total] Each: $2.50 ..... 15.00 (445)
1800, 1810, & 1820 Federal Census - Indexed , by Wood 7.25 (175)

JEFFERSON COUNTY

The Organization of Jefferson County (in Yesteryears, v.16, #61)
[Six installments, approx. 35pp. total] Each: $2.00 ..... 12.00 (445)
The North Country - Diana, a Haven for Joseph Bonaparte (in
Yesteryears, v.18, #69) [Three installments, 25pp. total] 7.50 (445)

KINGS COUNTY

Early Settlers in Kings County, Long Island, N.Y., by Bergen 15.00 ..... (580)

LONG ISLAND "AREA"

Check List of Imprints of Sag Harbor, 1791-1820, by McMurtrie 5.40 (624)
Documents and Letters Intended to Illustrate the Revolutionary In-
cidents of Queens County, by Onderdonk (repr. of 1846 ed.) 8.00 ..... (641)
Revolutionary Incidents of Suffolk, Kings Counties, by Onderdonk
(repr. of 1849 ed.) 8.00 ..... (641)
Indexes to Onderdonk's Revolutionary Incidents of Long Island
[2 vols. (see above), pub. in 1846 & 1849], by Stryker-Rodda 5.00 (649)
Sketches From Local History, Long Island (2nd ed.), by Halsey
[About Bridgehampton, Southampton, Sag Harbor, Suffolk] 12.50 ..... (773)
Long Island Before the Revolution [Original title: Early Long Is-
land], by Flint (repr. of 1896 ed.) 8.50 ..... (641)
Stories of Old Long Island, by Jackson 5.00 ..... (641)
Long Island Genealogical Source Material [A Bibliography], by
Seversmith & Stryker-Rodda [Over 800 items] 5.50 (616)
Catalogue of American Genealogies in the Long Island Historical
Society, by Toedteberg 15.00 ..... (1008)

MADISON COUNTY

History of Madison County, by Hammond (repr. 1872) 42.50 40.00 (546)
Index of Names appearing in 1880 ed. of Smith's Chenango & Madi-
son County History, by Tyne 18.00 (349)
Oneida Community (in NGSQ, v. 54, #3) 18pp. 3.00 (616)

MONROE COUNTY

The Private Journal of Abraham Joseph Warner, ed. by Enderton
[Episcopal Priest. Was on a fund-raising trek in 1851 through
N.Y. St. Comments on those he met.] 11.00 ..... (83)
The Organization of Monroe Co. (in Yesteryears, v. 16, #62 +)
[Five installments, approx. 60 pp. total] 10.00 (445)
The Lost Villages of Carthage & Dublin (in Yesteryears, v. 17, #68) 2.50 (445)

NIAGARA COUNTY

Under the Mountain, by Robson [Lewiston] 3.75 (906)

ONEIDA COUNTY

The City of Utica (in Yesteryears, v.15, #58 +) [Four installments, approx. 30 pp. total] 8.00 (445)
1800 Federal Census - Indexed, by Wood 4.00 (175)
1810 Federal Census - Indexed, by Wood [35mm. only] Microfilm: 3.50 (175)

ONTARIO COUNTY

1800 Federal Census - Indexed, by Wood 2.50 (175)
1810 Federal Census - Indexed, by Wood 6.25 (175)

ORANGE COUNTY

Orange County, New York: A Reader's Guide and Bibliography,
  by Gocek [Evaluates books related to Orange County history] 2.45 (405)
Tom Quick "The Indian Slayer" [Orange Co. folk hero] (in Yesteryears, v. 18, #69+) [Four installments, approx. 40pp. total] 10.00 (445)

OTSEGO COUNTY

Early Days in Otigo (in Yesteryears, v. 18, #69 +) 25pp. 7.50 (445)
The Settlement of Unadilla River (in Yesteryears, v. 16, #64) 4.00 (445)
1800 Federal Census - Indexed, by Wood 3.75 (175)

PUTNAM COUNTY

Old Gravestones of Putnam County, Together With Information
  From 10 Adjacent Dutchess County Burying Grounds, by Buys
  [11,800 inscriptions of persons born up to and including 1850 -
  maps showing locations of 79 Putnam Co. cem. - indexed] 25.00 ..... (1156)
Historical & Genealogical Record, Dutchess & Putnam Cos, by
  Oxford Pub. Co. (repr. 1912 ed.) 32.50 30.00 (546)

QUEENS COUNTY

History of Queens County, by Munsell & Co., (repr. 1882 ed.) 32.50 30.00 (546)

RENSSELAER COUNTY

A History of the Troy Citizens Corps, by Judson (repr. 1884 ed.) 17.50 15.00 (546)
The Establishment of the City of Troy (in Yesteryears, v. 15, #59 +)
  [Eight installments, approx. 60pp. total] Each: $2.00 ..... 16.00 (445)

RICHMOND COUNTY

History of Richmond County (Staten Island), by Bayles (1887) 47.50 45.00 (546)

ROCKLAND COUNTY

History of Rockland County, by Cole (repr. 1884 ed.) 32.50 30.00 (546)

SAINT LAWRENCE COUNTY

A History of St. Lawrence and Franklin Cos. , by Hough 15.00 ..... (130)
1810 & 1820 Federal Census - Indexed - of St. Lawrence &
  Jefferson Counties, by Wood 8.75 (175)

SCHOHARIE COUNTY

Baptismal Records of the First (or Woestina) Reformed Church
  of Rotterdam, 1800-1838 (in NGSQ, v. 52, #2) 9pp. 3.00 (616)

SCHUYLER COUNTY

Between the Lakes Cemeteries, by Fischer & Swick [Contains
  about 45,000 names in index from gravestones, with maps] 50.00 35.00 (335)

SENECA COUNTY

Between the Lakes Cemeteries, by Fischer & Swick [Contains
  about 45,000 names in index from gravestones, with maps] 50.00 35.00 (335)
The Presbyterian Church of Hector (in Yesteryears, v. 15, #59) 2.00 (445)
Centennial Historical Sketch of the Town of Fayette, by Willers 12.50 10.00 (546)

STEUBEN COUNTY

History of the Settlement of Steuben County, New York Including
  Notices of the Old Pioneer Settlers . . ., by McMaster (1853) 12.50 10.00 (546)

TIOGA COUNTY

Jacob Willsey's Journal, 1831-1860 (Willseyville, N.Y.), ed. by
Bell. [Complete transcription of the personal diary of the found-
er of Willseyville. Contains many marriages & burials, since
its writer was a JP.] 4.50   (18)
1820 Federal Census, by Hiday 3.50   (752)

TOMPKINS COUNTY

Between the Lakes Cemeteries, by Fischer & Swick [Contains
about 45,000 names in the index, of gravestones, with maps]   50.00   35.00 (335)

ULSTER COUNTY

Baptismal and Marriage Registers of the Old Dutch Church of
Kingston, Ulster County for 150 Years from Their Commence-
ment in 1660, by Hoes (repr. of 1891 ed.)   42.50   40.00 (546)
Ulster County Freeholders, 1798-1812 (in NGSQ, v.53, #1) 24pp. 3.00 (616)

WESTCHESTER COUNTY

Bedford Historical Records, ed. by Marshall
    Vol. 1: Town minutes, 1680-1737; 1710 Census; related doc. 3.00   (452)
    Vol. 2: Land records, 1680-1704; John Copp's records of
       West Purchase, 1700-1740   .....   3.50   (452)
    Vol. 3: Land records, 1687-1741; genealogical entries; map 3.50   (452)
    Vol. 4: Land records, 1689-1800; from town, county, historical
       societies and other sources 5.00   (452)
    Vols. 1, 2, 3, & 4   Set: 12.50   (452)
Records of the Town of Eastchester, 1664-1835, by Eastchester
    Hist. Soc. [Official town min.-land, birth, mar., etc.]   Set: 30.00   (387)
The Book of Strays & The Alteration of Roads, 1761-1862   .....   5.00   (387)
Overseers of the Poor, 1788-1824, by Eastchester Hist. Soc. 5.00   (387)
Minutes of the Trustees of Public Land, 1878-1899, by Eastchester
    Hist. Soc. [Burial records, land records, shipping records] 7.50   (387)
Town Property 1855-1856 & 1858, by Eastchester Hist. Soc. [As-
    sessment rolls - including City of Mt. Vernon & Upper Bronx] 10.00   (387)
Minutes of Town of Eastchester, 1835-1870   .....   10.00   (387)
Misc. Records of Town of Eastchester, 1794-1834 [Includes book
    of colored people (1795), Westchester Co. oaths (1813), etc. 10.00   (387)
Records of St. Paul's Church, 1787-1834   .....   7.50   (387)
Records of St. Paul's Church, 1787-1809: Deacon's Book, 1816-1841
    & Sexton's Books, 1816-1851 [Death records] 10.00   (387)
Burial Records of St. Paul's, 1664-1909 [6500 burial records] 30.00   (387)
History of Westchester County From Its Earliest Settlement to the
    Year 1900, by Shonnar & Spooner   29.50   .....   (667)

WYOMING COUNTY

The Settlement of Wyoming County (in Yesteryears, v. 18, #69+)
    [Ten installments, approx. 100pp.] Each: $2.50   .....   25.00   (445)

North Carolina

STATEWIDE REFERENCES

North Carolina Genealogy, ed. by Johnson [Genealogical periodical. Published semi-annually. Primary source material, no queries or advertising] 52pp/issue - 8 1/2 x 11. Subscription:	.....	10.00	(489)
The Carolina Pirates and Colonial Commerce, 1670-1740, by Hughson	14.00	10.00	(1000)
Historical Sketches of N.C. From 1584-1851, by Wheeler	21.50	.....	(130)
Reminiscences and Memoirs of North Carolina and Eminent North Carolinians, by Wheeler	16.50	.....	(130)
History of North Carolina, by Ashe, Vol. 1	25.00	.....	(663)
History of North Carolina, by Ashe, Vol. 2	35.00	.....	(663)
History of North Carolina, by Hawks, Vol. 1	10.50	.....	(663)
History of North Carolina, by Hawks, Vol. 2	17.50	.....	(663)
Slavery and Servitude in the Colony of North Carolina, by Bassett	10.25	6.25	(1000)
North Carolina History Told by Contemporaries, by Lefler	8.50	.....	(650)
Colonial North Carolina in the 18th Century: A Study in Historical Geography, by Merrens	9.25	.....	(650)
Travels to North & South Carolina, Georgia, East & West Florida, by William Bartram (repr. of 1792 ed.)	.....	.....	(995)
The Outer Banks of North Carolina, 1584-1958, by Stick	6.95	.....	(650)
Chronicles of the Cape Fear River, 1660-1916, by Sprunt	27.00	.....	(663)
The Regulators in North Carolina: A Documentary History, 1759-1776, by Powell, et al [Documents pertaining to uprising of regulators against provincial govt's. fee system & alleged abuses, culminating in Battle of Alamance in 1771]	12.50	.....	(659)
Carolina Backcountry on the Eve of the Revolution: The Journal & Other Writings of Charles Woodmason, Anglican Itinerant, by Woodmason	8.25	.....	(650)
Carolina Cradle: Settlement of the Northwest Carolina Frontier, by Ramsey	8.25	.....	(650)
Sketches of Western North Carolina, Historical & Biographical, by Hunter	11.50	.....	(130)
Western North Carolina: A History From 1730-1913, by Arthur	27.00	.....	(663)
Books From Chapel Hill, 1922-1972: A Complete Catalog of the University of N.C. Press [All printed, even those out of print]	.....	3.95	(650)
For History's Sake: The Preservation and Publication of North Carolina History 1663-1903, by Jones (1966)	8.25	.....	(650)
The John Gray Blount Papers, ed. by Keith [Letters, reports, other papers relating to activities of John Gray, Thomas, & William Blount, members of influential family in politics, shipping, land spectulation in late 18th & early 19th centuries.] 3 vols. Vol. 1, 1764-1789; Vol. 2, 1790-1795; Vol. 3, 1796-1802. Each: $10.00	.....	30.00	(659)
North Carolina Court of Law & Equity Prior to 1868 [Briefly discusses the jurisdiction, function & records of the 6 county-level courts and eleven higher courts in N.C., 1670-1868] 17pp.	.....	.25	(659)

Research aids

North Carolina Genealogical Reference, by Draughon & Johnson [A research guide to county, state, church, etc. records]	15.00	.....	(489)
Guide to Research Materials in the N.C. State Archives [Item by item listing of original & microfilm county records in the North Carolina State archives, Raleigh.]	.....	3.50	(659)
Formation of the N.C. Counties, 1663-1943, by Corbitt	10.00	.....	(659)

Sources for Genealogical Searching in North Carolina, by McCay 2.00 (417)
Tracing Family Trees in Eleven States [N.C. is included] 5.50 (29)
North Carolina: A Student's Guide to Localized History 1.50 (762)
Guide to the Manuscript Collections in the Duke University Library, by Tilley & Goodwin 10.00 ..... (630)
N.C. Newspapers on Microfilm: A Checklist [Over 1,000] 2.00 (659)
N.C. Local History: A Select Bibliography, by Stevenson [Bibliography of county and local histories.] 85pp. 2.00 (659)
Index to N. C. Historical Review, 1st 40 vols. (1924-1963) 5.00 (659)
A Guide to the Study & Reading of N.C. History, by Lefler 5.95 (650)

Records

The Colonial Records of North Carolina, ed. by Parker - Price
Vol. 2, N.C. Higher Court Records, 1670-1696 11.00 ..... (659)
Vol. 3, N.C. Higher Court Records, 1697-1701 12.00 ..... (659)
Vol. 4, N.C. Higher Court Records, 1702-1708 16.00 ..... (659)
N.C. Colonial & State Records; With Index. 10+16+4 Set: 2,105.00 ..... (630)
North & South Carolina Marriage Records, From the Earliest Colonial Days to the Civil War, by Clemens 8.50 ..... (130)
North Carolina Land Grants in Tennessee 1778-1791, by Gardiner & Cartwright [Substitute for 1790 census of the part of N.C. which became Tennessee in 1796] 15.00 ..... (30)
State Census of North Carolina 1784-1787, by Register (2nd rev. ed.) 12.50 ..... (130)
1790 Federal Census, by U.S. Bureau of the Census (repr.) 14.00 ..... (130)
1790 Federal Census, by U.S. Bureau of the Census (repr.) 12.50 ..... (663)
1800 Federal Census, by Accelerated Indexing Systems 35.00 ..... (677)
Index to 1820 Census, Supplemented by Tax Lists & other Sources, by Potter 30.00 (100)
Marriage & Death Notices From the Raleigh Register and North Carolina State Gazette, 1799-1825, by Broughton 10.00 ..... (130)
Marriage & Death Notices . . . (as above), 1826-1845 11.50 ..... (130)
An Abstract of North Carolina Wills From About 1760 to About 1800, by Olds 12.50 ..... (130)
North Carolina Wills & Inventories, by Grimes 15.00 ..... (130)
Abstracts of N.C. Wills [1663-1760], by Grimes 18.50 ..... (130)
Index to North Carolina Wills 1663-1900, by Johnson. 4 vols. [Alamance thru Columbus. Vols. may be purchased sep.] Set: 35.00 (489)
The North Carolina Gazette, Abstracts from 1784-1798 issues (pub. New Bern, N.C.), by Brazeal 8.00 (108)
North Carolina Death Notices taken from "The Free Press" 1824-1826 (in Northampton Cousins, v.1974, #27) 2pp. 1.50 (108)
N.C. Hist. & Gen. Register, by Hathaway. 11 nos. Set: 50.00 (130)
Ray's Index and Digest to Hathaway's "Register" (above) 9.50 ..... (130)

Maps

Research maps of 80 of 100 N.C. counties, by Stout [Large maps on plastic coated paper showing current roads, with historical sites, cemeteries, obsolete names of streams, old towns, etc. superimposed. Narrative accompanies the map explaining when names were used, discontinued, etc.] Cost varies by county - see county wanted. .... (653)
Outline Map of N.C. Giving Names of the Cos., 9 x 18 ..... .10 (659)
Maps & other Cartographic Records in N.C. St. Archives, 7pp ..... .25 (659)
Chart Showing the Origin of N.C. Counties ..... .10 (659)
Map Showing the Formation of N.C. Counties [12 maps, showing counties from 1700-1912] ..... .15 (659)

Map of N.C., 1861-1865, by Gunter. 8 3/4 x 23.	.....	.10	(659)
North Carolina in Maps, by Cumming [15 maps: includes White 1585 MS, White-Debry 1590, Mercator-Hondius 1606, Comberford 1657 MS, Ogilby-Moxon ca. 1672, Moseley 1733, Collet 1770, Mouzon 1775, Price-Strother 1808, MacRae-Brazier 1833, Colton 1861, Bachmann 1861, U.S. Coast Survey 1865, Kerr-Cain 1882, Post Route 1896. Four maps, descriptive and explanatory matter in booklet. Do not order Individual Maps - Sold in sets only!	.....	10.00	(659)

Military

The Loyalists in N. C. During the Revolution, by DeMond	7.50	.....	(823)
North Carolina's Revolutionary War Pay Records [Discussion of pay vouchers & certificates, also mil. land warrants.]	.....	.25	(659)
Indian Wars in North Carolina, 1663-1763, by Lee	.....	.50	(659)
The North Carolina Continentals, by Rankin	12.50	.....	(650)
North Carolina, 1780-1781. Being a History of the Invasion of the Carolinas by ... Cornwallis, by Schenck	15.00	.....	(663)
A History of the Campaigns of 1780-1781, in the Southern Provinces of North America, by Tarleton	15.00	.....	(663)
The Narrative of Colonel David Fanning, Giving an Account of his Adventures in N.C., 1775-1783 [Fanning was a Tory]	10.50	.....	(663)
King's Mt. & Its Heroes, by Draper	15.00	.....	(130)
King's Mt. & Its Heroes, by Draper	15.00	.....	(663)
Roster of Soldiers From N.C. in the American Rev.	16.50	.....	(130)
North Carolina Troops, 1861-1865: A Roster, by Manarin & Jordan. 4 vols. [Projected - 13 vols.] Each:	12.00	.....	(659)
Historical Sketches, 7th Regt., N.C. Troops, by Harris	8.50	6.00	(546)
N.C. Civil War Records: An Intro. to Printed & Mss. Sources	.....	.25	(659)

Religious and ethnic groups

The Religious Development in the Province of N.C., by Weeks	10.25	6.25	(1000)
Early Methodism in the Carolinas, by Chreitzberg	15.00	.....	(663)
Race Elements in the White Population of North Carolina, by Connor [Consideration of the racial characteristics of the English, Scots, and German strains in N.C.-no individuals]	10.50	.....	(663)
Catholicity in the Carolinas and Georgia, by O'Connell	21.00	.....	(663)
History of the German Settlements & of the Lutheran Church in North & South Carolina, by Bernheim	18.00	.....	(663)
Records of the Moravians in N.C., ed. by Fries et al. 11vols. Vol. 1, 1752-1771; Vol. 2, 1752-1775; Vol. 3, 1776-1779; Vol. 4, 1780-1783; Vol. 5, 1784-1792; Vol. 6, 1793-1808; Vol. 7, 1808-1822; Vol. 8, 1823-1837; Vol. 9, 1838-1847; Vol. 10, 1841-1856, Vol. 11, 1852-1879 Each:	10.00	.....	(659)
The Moravian Potters in North Carolina, by Bivins	12.95	.....	(650)
The Moravians in North Carolina, by Reichel	10.00	.....	(130)
Road to Salem, by Fries	6.50	.....	(650)
Encyclopedia of Am. Quaker Gen., by Hinshaw, Vol. 1 [N.C.]	50.00	.....	(130)
The Highland Scots of N.C., by Meyer [Influence during Revolution of Scots who settled in N.C.] 75pp.	.....	.50	(659)
The Highland Scots of North Carolina,1732-1776, by Meyer	8.25	.....	(650)

Miscellaneous

Cyclopedia of Eminent & Representative Men of the Carolinas of the 19th Century, by Ashe. Vol. 2	24.00	.....	(663)
The North Carolina Portrait Index, 1700-1860, by MacMillan	15.00	.....	(650)

ALAMANCE COUNTY

Map, by Stout [See explanation under "Maps" - N.C. Statewide] 6.25 (653)
Index to Wills, Vol. 1 [Includes Alamance, Alexander, Alleghany,
Anson, Ashe, & Beaufort Counties] 10.00 (489)
The Dreamer: Archibald DeBow Murphey 1777-1832, by Turner
[Biography of Murphey, who lived in Alamance County] 7.95 ..... (207)

ALBEMARLE COUNTY

Some Pioneers of North Carolina, 1674-1701 (in NGSQ, v.53, #3) 3.00 (616)
Ye Countie of Albemarle in Carolina: A Collection of Documents,
1664-1675, by Powell 1.50 ..... (659)
Old Albemarle and Its Absentee Landlords, by Ray 8.50 ..... (130)

ALEXANDER COUNTY

Index to Wills, Vol. 1 [see Alamance County] 10.00 (489)
Map, by Stout [See explanation under "Maps" - N.C. Statewide] 6.25 (653)

ALLEGHANY COUNTY

Index to Wills, Vol. 1 [See Alamance County] 10.00 (489)
Map, by Stout [See explanation under "Maps" - N.C. Statewide] 6.25 (653)

ANSON COUNTY

Index to Wills, Vol. 1 [See Alamance County] 10.00 (489)
Map, by Stout [See explanation under "Maps" - N.C. Statewide] 6.25 (653)
Deed Abstracts, Vol. 1: 1749-1757, by Holcomb 12.50 (701)
1820 Federal Census, Vol. 1, by Potter 10.25 (100)

ASHE COUNTY

Index to Wills, Vol. 1 [See Alamance County] 10.00 (489)
Map, by Stout [See explanation under "Maps" - N.C. Statewide] 6.75 (653)
1820 Federal Census, by Potter 3.25 (100)

AVERY COUNTY

Map, by Stout [See explanation under "Maps" - N.C. Statewide] 6.50 (653)

BEAUFORT COUNTY

Map, by Stout [See explanation under "Maps" - N.C. Statewide] 9.25 (653)
Index to Wills, Vol. 1 [See Alamance County] 10.00 (489)
Some Colonial History of Beaufort County, by Cooper 1.25 ..... (650)
Abs: of Original Wills 1729-1868 (in Northampton Cousins, #27
[2pp.] & #28 [3pp.] Each #: $1.50 Total: 3.00 (108)
1820 Federal Census, by Potter 7.25 (100)

BERTIE COUNTY

Map, by Stout [See explanation under "Maps" - N.C. Statewide] 8.50 (653)
Index to Wills, Vol 2 [Includes Bertie, Bladen, Brunswick, Bun-
combe, & Burke Counties] 10.00 (489)
Grace Episcopal Church Cem, Woodville (in Northampton Cousins, #26) 4pp. 1.50 (108)
1820 Federal Census, by Potter 5.25 (100)

BLADEN COUNTY

Map, by Stout [See explanation under "Maps" - N.C. Statewide] 7.50 (653)
Index to Wills, Vol 2 [See Bertie County] 10.00 (489)
1810 Federal Census, by York 3.50 (497)
1820 Federal Census, by Potter 5.25 (100)

BRUNSWICK COUNTY

Map, by Stout [See explanation under "Maps" - N.C. Statewide]	.....	10.00	(653)
Index to Wills, Vol. 2 [See Bertie County]	.....	10.00	(489)
1820 Federal Census, by Potter	.....	3.25	(100)

BUNCOMBE COUNTY

Index to Wills, Vol. 2 [See Bertie County]	.....	10.00	(489)
A History of Buncombe County, by Sondley (repr. of 1930 ed.)	47.50	45.00	(546)
1820 Federal Census, by Potter	.....	9.25	(100)

BURKE COUNTY

Index to Wills [See Bertie County]	.....	10.00	(489)
1820 Federal Census, by Potter	.....	8.25	(100)

BUTE COUNTY

[Discontinued in 1779 - See Warren County & Franklin County]

CABARRUS COUNTY

Map, by Stout [See explanation under "Maps" - N.C. Statewide]	.....	6.25	(653)
Index to N.C. Wills, 1663-1900, by Johnson. Vol. 3 [Includes Cabarrus, Caldwell, Camden, Carteret, Caswell, Catawba, Chatham, Cherokee Counties]	.....	10.00	(489)
1820 Federal Census, by Potter	.....	6.25	(100)

CALDWELL COUNTY

Index to N.C. Wills, 1663-1900, Vol. 3 [See Cabarrus Co.]	.....	10.00	(489)

CAMDEN COUNTY

Map, by Stout [See explanation under "Maps" - N.C. Statewide]	.....	6.25	(653)
Index to N.C. Wills, 1663-1900, Vol. 3 [See Cabarrus Co.]	.....	10.00	(489)
Tombstones & Epitaphs of Northeastern N.C., by Spence	15.00	.....	(308)
1820 Federal Census, by Potter	.....	6.25	(100)

CARTERET COUNTY

Map, by Stout [See explanation under "Maps" - N.C. Statewide]	.....	10.00	(653)
Index to N.C. Wills, 1663-1900, Vol. 3 [See Cabarrus Co.]	.....	10.00	(489)
1820 Federal Census, by Potter	.....	3.25	(100)
1850 Federal Census, by Simpson & Taylor	10.00	.....	(130)

CASWELL COUNTY

Map, by Stout [See explanation under "Maps" - N.C. Statewide]	.....	6.25	(653)
Index to N.C. Wills, 1663-1900, Vol. 3 [See Cabarrus County]	.....	10.00	(489)
1820 Federal Census, by Potter	.....	8.25	(100)

CATAWBA COUNTY

Map, by Stout [See explanation undder "Maps" - N.C. Statewide	.....	6.25	(653)

CHATHAM COUNTY

Map, by Stout [See explanation under "Maps" - N.C. Statewide]	.....	9.00	(653)
Index to N.C. Wills, 1663-1900, Vol. 3 [See Cabarrus County]	.....	10.00	(489)
1820 Federal Census, by Potter	.....	9.25	(100)

CHEROKEE COUNTY

Index to N.C. Wills, 1663-1900, Vol. 3 [See Cabarrus County]	.....	10.00	(489)

CHOWAN COUNTY

Map, by Stout [See explanation under "Maps" - N.C. Statewide]	.....	6.25	(653)
Index to N.C. Wills, 1663-1900, Vol 4 [Includes Chowan, Clay, Cleveland & Columbus Counties], by Johnson	.....	10.00	(489)

Tombstones & Epitaphs of Northeastern North Carolina, by Spence 15.00 ..... (308)
1820 Federal Census of Chowan County, by Potter 5.25 (100)

CLAY COUNTY

Index to Wills of N.C., 1663-1900, Vol. 4 [See Chowan County] 10.00 (489)

CLEVELAND COUNTY

Map, by Stout [See explanation under "Maps" - N.C. Statewide] 6.25 (653)
Index to Wills of N.C., 1663-1900, Vol. 4 [See Chowan County]

COLUMBUS COUNTY

Map, by Stout [See explanation under "Maps" - N.C. Statewide] 10.00 (653)
Index to Wills of N.C., 1663-1900, Vol. 4 [See Chowan County] 10.00 (489)
1810 Federal Census, by York & York 3.50 (497)
1820 Federal Census, by Potter 3.25 (100)

CRAVEN COUNTY

Map, by Stout [See explanation under "Maps" - N.C. Statewide] 10.00 (653)
Christoph Von Graffenried's Account of the Founding of New Bern,
by Todd 18.00 ..... (663)
1820 Federal Census, by Potter 7.25 (100)
1850 Federal Census, by Gwynn 12.50 ..... (130)

CUMBERLAND COUNTY

Map, by Stout [See explanation under "Maps" - N.C. Statewide] 6.25 (653)
1820 Federal Census, by Potter 10.25 (100)

CURRITUCK COUNTY

Map, by Stout [See explanation under "Maps" - N.C. Statewide] 10.00 (653)
The Journal of Curritick County Historical Society, Vol. 1, No. 2
by Pub. Comm. [Historic sites; development of education;
personal histories; study of John Gibbs] 4.00 (621)
Report of the Historical Committee on Outstanding Citizens,
1670-1970 [Biog. sketches of 100 men, including founders of
Mercer Univ., & a president of Pierce-Arrow Motor Car Co.] 2.00 (621)
Tomstones & Epitaphs of Northeastern North Carolina, by Spence 15.00 ..... (308)
Abstracts of Wills & Other Records, Currituck & Dare Counties,
North Carolina, 1663-1850, by Jones 10.00 ..... (130)

DARE COUNTY

Map, by Stout [See explanation under "Maps" - N.C. Statewide] 10.00 ..... (653)
Abstracts of Wills & Other Records, Currituck & Dare Counties,
North Carolina, 1663-1850, by Jones 10.00 ..... (130)

DAVIDSON COUNTY

Map, by Stout [See explanation under "Maps" - N.C. Statewide] 9.00 (653)
Cemetery Records of Davidson (Old Rowan), by Koch [From re-
cords gathered by Reeves - 56 cemeteries] 10.00 (874)

DAVIE COUNTY

Map, by Stout [See explanation under "Maps" - N.C. Statewide] 6.25 (653)
Will Abstracts 1836-1900 & Deed Abstracts 1836-1850, by Linn 15.00 (631)

DUPLIN COUNTY

Map, by Stout [See explanation under "Maps" - N.C. Statewide] 8.00 (653)
1820 Federal Census, by Potter 6.25 (100)

DURHAM COUNTY

Map, by Stout [See explanation under "Maps" - N.C. Statewide]	.....	6.25 (653)
Raleigh-Durham-Chapel Hill: A Student's Guide to Localized Hist.	.....	1.50 (762)
History of the Church of Jesus Christ of Latter-day Saints in North Carolina, by Draughon	10.00	..... (746)

EDGECOMBE COUNTY

Map, by Stout [See explanation under "Maps" - N.C. Statewide]	.....	8.00 (653)
Abstracts of Deeds 1759-1772, by Watson	15.00	..... (54)
Abstracts of Deeds 1772-1788, by Watson	15.00	..... (54)
Estate Records 1730-1820, by Watson	17.50	..... (54)
1820 Federal Census, by Potter	.....	9.25 (100)

FORSYTH COUNTY

Map, by Stout [See explanation under "Maps" - N.C. Statewide]	.....	6.25 (653)
Road to Salem, by Fries [About Moravians]	6.50	..... (650)

FRANKLIN COUNTY

Map, by Stout [See explanation under "Maps" - N.C. Statewide]	.....	9.00 (653)
Land Plats & Land Entries, by Holcomb	.....	15.00 (701)
1810 Federal Census, by Brazeal	.....	2.50 (108)

GASTON COUNTY

Map, by Stout [See explanation under "Maps" - N.C. Statewide]	.....	6.25 (653)

GATES COUNTY

Map, by Stout [See explanation under "Maps" - N.C. Statewide]	.....	6.25 (653)
1820 Federal Census, by Potter	.....	5.25 (100)

GRANVILLE COUNTY

Map, by Stout [See explanation under "Maps" - N.C. Statewide]	.....	6.25 (653)
Colonial Granville County & Its People, by Ray	7.50	..... (130)
Along the Border: A History of Virgilina, Virginia and the Surrounding Area in Halifax and Mecklenburg Counties in Virginia, and Granville and Person Counties in N.C., by Mathis	8.00	..... (123)
Abstracts of the Early Deeds 1746-1765, by Gwynn	19.00	..... (54)
Abstracts of the Wills & Estate Records, 1746-1808, by Gwynn	18.00	..... (54)
1820 Federal Census, by Potter	.....	10.25 (100)

GREENE COUNTY

Map, by Stout [See explanation under "Maps" - N.C. Statewide]	.....	6.25 (653)
1820 Federal Census, by Potter	.....	3.25 (100)

GUILFORD COUNTY

Map, by Stout [See explanation under "Maps" - N.C. Statewide]	.....	9.00 (653)
1820 Federal Census, by Potter	.....	12.25 (100)

HALIFAX COUNTY

Map, by Stout [See explanation under "Maps" - N.C. Statewide]	.....	10.00 (653)
1820 Federal Census, by Potter	.....	8.25 (100)

HARNETT COUNTY

Map, by Stout [See explanation under "Maps" - N.C. Statewide]	.....	10.00 (653)

HAYWOOD COUNTY

1820 Federal Census, by Potter	.....	4.25 (100)

....

HERTFORD COUNTY

Map, by Stout [See explanation under "Maps" - N.C. Statewide]	.....	6.25	(653)
County Court Minutes 1830-1833, by Brazeal	.....	6.50	(108)
Abstracts from "The Citizen" (pub. Murfreesboro) (in Northampton County Cousins, v.3, #1) 1pp.	.....	1.50	(108)
Inscriptions from Liverman Cemetery (in North. Cous., v.5, #4)	.....	1.50	(108)
Hertford County Newspaper Items & Abstracts From "The Hornet's Nest" (1812/13) and "The North Carolina Chronicle" (1827)	.....	2.50	(108)
1810 Federal Census, by Brazeal	.....	2.00	(108)
1820 Federal Census, by Brazeal	.....	2.00	(108)
Ancient Maritime Hist. of Murfreesborough, 1787-1825, Paramore	.....	4.95	(1020)

HOKE COUNTY

Map, by Stout [See explanation under "Maps" - N.C. Statewide]	.....	6.25	(653)

HYDE COUNTY

Map, by Stout [See explanation under "Maps" - N.C. Statewide]	.....	8.00	(653)
In Memory of . . . An Index of Hyde County Cemeteries, by Swindell & Spencer [Approximately 6,000 inscriptions]	20.00	.....	(314)
1800 Federal Census, by Brazeal	.....	2.00	(108)
1820 Federal Census, by Potter	.....	3.25	(100)

IREDELL COUNTY

Prospect Presbyterian Church Cemetery Directory, 1803-1970 [Located in Mooresville]	.....	3.00	(1026)
1820 Federal Census, by Potter	.....	10.25	(100)

JOHNSTON COUNTY

Map, by Stout [See explanation under "Maps" - N.C. Statewide]	.....	10.00	(653)
Will Abstracts 1746-1825, by Ross [Approx. 400 wills. Indexed; also index of slaves willed to heirs]	.....	15.00	(692)
1820 Federal Census, by Potter	.....	7.25	(100)

JONES COUNTY

Map, by Stout [See explanation under "Maps" - N.C. Statewide]	.....	9.00	(653)
1820 Federal Census, by Potter	.....	3.25	(100)
Abstracts of the Records of Jones County, by Gwynn	30.00	.....	(130)

LEE COUNTY

Map, by Stout [See explanation under "Maps" - N.C. Statewide]	.....	6.25	(653)

LENOIR COUNTY

Map, by Stout [See explanation under "Maps" - N.C. Statewide]	.....	8.00	(653)
1820 Federal Census, by Potter	.....	4.25	(100)

LINCOLN COUNTY

Map, by Stout [See explanation under "Maps" - N.C. Statewide]	.....	6.25	(653)
Annals of Lincoln County, by Sherrill	12.50	.....	(130)
1820 Federal Census, by Potter	.....	13.25	(100)

MARTIN COUNTY

Map, by Stout [See explanation under "Maps" - N.C. Statewide]	.....	9.00	(653)
Martin & Pitt County Migrations, by Brazeal [Abs. from deeds making reference to persons living in other states]	.....	3.50	(108)
The Williams Chapel Cemetery (in North. Cous., v.7, #1) 1pp.	.....	1.50	(108)
Joseph Williams Cemetery & annotations (in North. Cous., v.6 #1)	.....	1.50	(108)
The Three Cemeteries of Hamilton [Stones dating from 1845]	.....	2.50	(108)

Martin County Will Book 1 Abstracts, by Brazeal	.....	7.00 (108)
Abstracts of Deeds 1774-1775 (in North. Cous., Apr. 1974, #28)	.....	1.50 (108)
Spring Green Primitive Baptist Ch. Cem. (in North. Cous., #28)	.....	1.50 (108)
1800 Federal Census, by Brazeal	.....	2.00 (108)

MECKLENBURG COUNTY

The Mecklenburg Signers And Their Neighbors, by Ray	12.00	..... (130)
1820 Federal Census, by Potter	.....	11.25 (100)

MONTGOMERY COUNTY

Map, by Stout [See explanation under "Maps" - N.C. Statewide]	.....	9.00 (653)

MOORE COUNTY

Map, by Stout [See explanation under "Maps" - N.C. Statewide]	.....	9.00 (653)
1820 Federal Census, by Potter	.....	6.25 (100)

NASH COUNTY

Map, by Stout [See explanation under "Maps" - N.C. Statewide]	.....	8.00 (653)
Early Marriages of Nash County, by Williams & Griffin	12.50	..... (54)
Abstracts of Will Book 1, 1778-1868, by Williams & Griffin	12.50	..... (54)
1820 Federal Census, by Potter	.....	5.25 (100)

NEW HANOVER COUNTY

Map, by Stout [See explanation under "Maps" - N.C. Statewide]	.....	6.25 (653)
New Hanover County: A Brief History, by Lee	.....	1.00 (659)
A History of New Hanover County and the Lower Cape Fear Region 1723-1800, by Waddell (repr. of 1909 ed.)	17.50	15.00 (546)
1820 Federal Census, by Potter	.....	7.25 (100)

NORTHAMPTON COUNTY

Map, by Stout [See explanation under "Maps" - N.C. Statewide]	.....	8.00 (653)

Note: The following are all articles which appeared in 'Northampton County Cousins', a genealogical periodical edited by Brazeal, Separate issues may be purchased for $1.50 each:

1817 Court Minutes (v.1, #4 - 6pp; v.2, #1- 5pp; v.2, #2 - 4pp; v.2, #3 - 4pp; v.2, #4 -5pp; v.3, #1 - 4pp; v.3, #3 -3pp)	.....	10.50 (108)
Hebron Church Cemetery, Annotated (v.4, #1)	.....	1.50 (108)
Abstracts of Will Book 1 (v.1, #3 - 6pp; v.1, #4 - 6pp; v.2, #1 - 4pp; v.2, #2 - 4pp; v.2, #3 - 4pp; v.2, #4 - 5pp; v.3, #1 - 4pp; v.3, #2 - 1pp)	.....	12.00 (108)
Abstracts of Will Book 2 (v.4, #1 - 4pp; v.4, #2 - 4pp)	.....	3.00 (108)
Abstracts of Will Book 3 (v.5, #1 - 2pp; v.5, #2 - 4pp; v.5, #3, 4pp; v. 5, #4 - 5pp)	.....	6.00 (108)
Division of Estates 1781-1802 (v.5, #2 - 6pp)	.....	1.50 (108)
Abstracts From Deed Book 3 (v.2, #4; v.3, #1,2,3,4; v. 4, #1,2,4; v.5, #1,2,3; v.6, #2,4) Average of 3pp/issue.	.....	19.50 (108)
Inventories & Accounts of Sale of Real Estate 1797-1801(v.7, #1)	.....	1.50 (108)
Guardian Accounts, Book A, 1782-1802 (1974, #27) 4pp.	.....	1.50 (108)
Early Baptist in Northampton County (v.1, #1) 2pp	.....	1.50 (108)
Abstracts from "The North Carolina Journal" (pub. Halifax) (v.5, #1,2,3,4; v.7, #1; 1973, #26; 1974, #27) 6pp/issue	.....	10.50 (108)
1790 Federal Census, by York & York	.....	3.00 (497)
1810 Federal Census, by York & York	.....	3.50 (497)
1820 Federal Census, by Potter	.....	7.25 (100)

ONSLOW COUNTY

Map, by Stout [See explanation under "Maps" - N.C. Statewide]	.....	9.00 (653)
Abstracts of Records of Onslow County, by Gwynn	50.00	..... (130)
1820 Federal Census, by Potter	.....	6.25 (100)

ORANGE COUNTY

Map, by Stout [See explanation under "Maps" - N. C. Statewide] 6.25 (653)
Map - Showing Land Grants to Early Settlers of Old Orange County 10.40 (1003)
Abstracts of Wills, 1752-1800 & 1800-1850, by DAR, N. C. 15.00 ..... (130)
1820 Federal Census, by Potter 16.25 (100)

PAMLICO COUNTY

Map, by Stout [See explanation under "Maps" - N. C. Statewide] 8.00 (653)

PASQUOTANK COUNTY

Map, by Stout [See explanation under "Maps" - N. C. Statewide] 8.00 (653)
Tombstones & Epitaphs of Northeastern North Carolina, by Spence 15.00 ..... (308)
1820 Federal Census, by Potter 6.25 (100)

PENDER COUNTY

Map, by Stout [See explanation under "Maps" - N. C. Statewide] 10.00 (653)

PERQUIMANS COUNTY

Map, by Stout [See explanation under "Maps" - N. C. Statewide] 6.25 (653)
History of Perquimans County, by Winslow 17.50 ..... (130)
Tombstones & Epitaphs of Northeastern North Carolina, by Spence 15.00 ..... (308)
1820 Federal Census, by Potter 5.25 (100)

PERSON COUNTY

Map, by Stout [See explanation under "Maps" - N. C. Statewide] 6.25 (653)
Along the Border: A History of Virgilina, Virginia and the Surrounding Area in Halifax & Mecklenburg Counties in Virginia &
Person & Granville Counties in North Carolina, by Mathis 8.00 ..... (123)
1820 Federal Census, by Potter 6.25 (100)

PITT COUNTY

Map, by Stout [See explanation under "Maps" - N. C. Statewide] 8.00 (653)
Martin & Pitt County Migrations, by Brazeal [Abs. from deeds
making reference to persons living in other states] 3.50 (108)
Deaths from Red Banks Primitive Church Minutes (in Northampton
County Cousins, v.6, #3 - 1pp; v.6, #4 - 2pp; v.7, #1 -2pp) 4.50 (108)
Members of Galloways Meeting House 1828 & Deaths Taken From
Church Minutes (v.1973, #26) 1pp. 1.50 (108)
1820 Federal Census, by Potter 7.25 (100)

RANDOLPH COUNTY

Map, by Stout [See explanation under "Maps" - N. C. Statewide] 10.00 (653)
1850 Federal Census, by Simpson 15.86 (393)

RICHMOND COUNTY

Map, by Stout [See explanation under "Maps" - N. C. Statewide] 8.00 (653)
From a Mustard Seed: A History of the First Baptist Church of
Hamlet, N.C. [Organized in 1878] 5.00 (1148)
1820 Federal Census, by Potter 5.25 (100)

ROBESON COUNTY

Map, by Stout [See explanation under "Maps" - N. C. Statewide] 10.00 (653)
1820 Federal Census, by Potter 6.25 (100)

ROCKINGHAM COUNTY

Map, by Stout [See explanation under "Maps" - N. C. Statewide] 6.25 (653)
Deed Abstracts, 1785-1800, by Webster [Index to names & places] 15.00 (320)
Will Abstracts, 1785-1865 - Vol. 1, by Webster 15.00 (320)
1820 Federal Census, by Potter 9.25 (100)

ROWAN COUNTY

Map, by Stout [See explanation under "Maps" - N. C. Statewide]	.....	8.00	(653)
A History of Rowan County, by Rumple	17.50	.....	(130)
Carolina Cradle, Settlement of the Northwest Carolina Frontier			
1747-1762, by Ramsey	7.50	.....	(650)
Deed Abstracts 1753-1762, by Linn	.....	15.00	(631)
Deed Abstracts 1762-1772, by Linn	.....	15.00	(631)
Will Abstracts 1753-1805, by Linn	.....	15.00	(631)
Will Abstracts 1805-1850, by Linn	.....	15.00	(631)
1820 Federal Census, by Potter	.....	21.25	(100)

RUTHERFORD COUNTY

1782 Tax List & 1790 Census, by Old Tryon Co. Gen. Soc.	.....	3.00	(1143)
1810 Federal Census, by York & York	.....	3.50	(497)
1820 Federal Census, by Potter	.....	13.25	(100)

SAMPSON COUNTY

Map, by Stout [See explanation under "Maps" - N. C. Statewide]	.....	10.00	(653)
1820 Federal Census, by Potter	.....	6.25	(100)

SCOTLAND COUNTY

Map, by Stout [See explanation under "Maps" - N. C. Statewide]	.....	6.25	(653)

STANLY COUNTY

Map, by Stout [See explanation under "Maps" - N. C. Statewide]	.....	8.00	(653)

STOKES COUNTY

Map, by Stout [See explanation under "Maps" - N. C. Statewide]	.....	6.25	(653)
1820 Federal Census, by Potter	.....	11.25	(100)

SURRY COUNTY

Map, by Stout [See explanation under "Maps" - N. C. Statewide]	.....	6.25	(653)
Deed Abstracts, 1771-1774 (in Ridge Runners, v. 3, #2) 7pp.	.....	2.00	(670)
Will Abstracts 1771-1827, by Linn [Contains wills, inv., sales of			
estates, deeds, indentures, powers of atty., etc.]	.....	15.00	(631)
1820 Federal Census, by Potter	.....	10.25	(100)

TRANSYLVANIA COUNTY

Beginnings: A History of the Founding of Baptist Churches in			
Transylvania, by Gavin	.....	4.00	(353)

TYRELL COUNTY

Map, by Stout [See explanation under "Maps" - N. C. Statewide]	.....	6.25	(653)
1820 Federal Census, by Potter	.....	3.25	(100)

UNION COUNTY

Map, by Stout [See explanation under "Maps" - N. C. Statewide]	.....	8.00	(853)

VANCE COUNTY

Map, by Stout [See explanation under "Maps" - N. C. Statewide]	.....	6.25	(853)

WAKE COUNTY

Map, by Stout [See explanation under "Maps" - N. C. Statewide]	.....	10.00	(853)
History of Wake County, by Chamberlain (repr. 1922)	17.50	15.00	(546)
The Raleigh Register, 1799-1863, by Elliott	1.25	.....	(650)

WARREN COUNTY

Map, by Stout [See explanation under "Maps"- N.C. Statewide]	..... 6.25	(653)
Records, Vol 1, by Kerr [Abstracts of wills, etc. of Warren Co., also - Marriage bonds of Bute County 1764-1779. Maps.]	..... 10.00	(444)
Records, Vol 2, by Kerr [Abstracts of Deed Book A (1764-1766), also - 1st Deed Book of Bute County (1764-). Maps.]	..... 5.00	(444)
Records, Vol 2 - Supplement, by Kerr [Abstracts of Deed Books 1766-1779, containing deeds of Bute County which was divided into Warren & Franklin Counties in 1779. Maps.]	..... 12.50	(444)
Records, Vol 3, by Kerr [Abstracts of 16 record books of Wills & Accounts 1779-1814. Maps.]	..... 18.00	(444)
Bute County Land Grant Plats & Land Entries, by Holcomb	..... 15.00	(701)
1790 Federal Census, by York & York	..... 3.00	(497)
1810 Federal Census, by York & York	..... 3.50	(497)
1820 Federal Census, by Potter	..... 5.25	(100)

WASHINGTON COUNTY

Map, by Stout [See explanation under "Maps" - N.C. Statewide]	..... 6.25	(653)
Passengers Arriving at Ports of Plymouth & Washington, N.C. (in Northampton County Cousins, v.6, #4) 2pp	..... 1.50	(108)
1820 Federal Census, by Potter	..... 3.25	(100)

WATAUGA COUNTY

Map, by Stout [See explanation under "Maps" - N.C. Statewide]	..... 7.00	(653)

WAYNE COUNTY

Map, by Stout [See explanation under "Maps" - N.C. Statewide]	..... 8.00	(653)
Abstracts of Deed Books 1 & 2, 1780-1785, by Ham	..... 5.00	(530)
Abstracts of Deed Book 3, 1785-1787, by Ham	..... 5.50	(530)
1820 Federal Census, by Potter	..... 6.25	(100)

WILKES COUNTY

Map, by Stout [See explanation under "Maps" - N.C. Statewide]	..... 10.00	(653)
Wilkes Genealogical Society BULLETIN [Quarterly published by Wilkes Genealogical Soc. All back issues available. Each:	..... 1.00	(328)
Historical Sketches of Wilkes County, by Crouch (repr. of 1902 ed) [Copied, with permission, from 50th Anniv. ed. of newspaper]	..... 5.00	(328)
Wilkes County Land Entry Book 1778-1781 [1944 original entries]	..... 10.00	(328)
Wilkes County Deed Book A-1 (1778-1795) [1st deed bk. - indexed]	..... 5.00	(328)
Wilkes County Deed Book B-1 (1778-1797) [2nd deed bk.- indexed]	..... 5.00	(328)
Wilkes County Deed Book C-1 (1782-1803) [3rd deed bk.- indexed]	..... 7.50	(328)
Wilkes County Deed Book D (1784-1800) [4th deed bk. - indexed]	..... 10.00	(328)
Wilkes County Deed Book F-1 (1778-1807) [5th deed bk. - indexed]	..... 8.00	(328)
Wilkes County Deed Book G-H (1782-1815) [6th deed bk. - indexed]	..... 8.50	(328)
Court Minutes Vol. 1 (1778-1783) [1,200 names - indexed]	..... 6.00	(328)
Court Minutes Vol. 2 (1784-1788) [1,050 names - indexed]	..... 6.00	(328)
Will Books 1 & 2 (1778-1811) [Wills, inv., adm., etc.- indexed]	..... 5.00	(328)
Will Books 3 & 4 (1811-1848) [Wills, inv., adm., etc.- indexed]	..... 5.00	(328)
Marriages Prior to 1800 [From Old Marriage Bond Index]	..... 3.00	(328)
The Levi Absher Ledger [Diary of over 500 deaths prior to 1911; also list of Mulberry District Civil War Soldiers]	..... 2.00	(328)
Abstracts of Reddies River Church Minutes (1798-1899)	..... 2.00	(328)
Cemetery Inventories, Vol. 1 [Of 107 cemeteries in Wilkes area]	..... 10.00	(328)
1782 Tax List	..... 2.00	(328)
1787 State Census [Copied from original in N.C. State Archives]	..... 3.00	(328)
1810 Federal Census, by Phillips	 x	(698)
1820 Federal Census, by Potter	..... 10.25	(100)
1850 Federal Census, by Wilkes Genealogical Society	..... 10.00	(328)
1860 Federal Census, by Wilkes Genealogical Society	..... 15.00	(328)

WILSON COUNTY

Map, by Stout [See explanation under "Maps" - N.C. Statewide] 6.25   (653)

YADKIN COUNTY

Map, by Stout [See explanation under "Maps" - N.C. Statewide] 6.25   (653)

North Dakota

STATEWIDE REFERENCES

The Northland Newsletter [Quarterly of the Range Genealogical
    Society. Contains all kinds of records: marriage, cemetery,
    tax rolls, plat books, etc. for Dakota Territory] Subscription: 4.00/yr   (977)
Outlines of History of the Territory of Dakota: And Emigrants
    Guide to the Free Lands of the Northwest, by Foster (repr.
    of 1870 ed.)   7.00   .....   (636)

BUFORD COUNTY

1885 Territorial Census (in Gen. Ref. Builders, v. 7, #1) 11pp. 2.00   (931)

BURLEIGH COUNTY

1885 Territorial Census (in Bismarck-Mandan Hist. & Gen. Soc.
    Quarterly, v. 3 & 4 - 6 issues total) Each issue: $1.00.   Total: 6.00   (750)

Ohio

STATEWIDE REFERENCES

Ohio Records & Pioneer Families [Genealogical quarterly publish-
    ed by Ohio Genealogical Society.]   Subscription per year: 8.00   (1134)
Wilderness Politics & Indian Gifts: The Northern Frontier 1748-
    1763 [Orig. title: Anglo-French Rivalry Along the Ohio & North-
    west Frontier 1748-1763], by Jacobs 1.65   (760)
Two Years Residence in the New Settlements of Ohio, by Griffiths
    (repr. of 1835 ed.) 6.75   (546)

Research aids

    Evolution of Ohio County Boundaries, by Downes 2.40   (888)
    Ohio: A Student's Guide to Localized History 1.50   (762)
    Tracing Family Trees in Eleven States [Ohio is one state] 5.50   (29)
    Sources For Genealogical Searching in Ohio, by McCay 2.25   (417)
    Guide to Ohio Newspapers, 1793-1973 [Lists over 3,000 Ohio
        newspapers coded to 240 Ohio repositories]   20.00   .....   (888)
    Guide to Manuscripts at the Ohio Historical Society & Ruther-
        ford B. Hayes Library 10.00   (888)
    Guide to the Manuscripts & Archives of the Western Reserve
        Historical Society, by Pike   10.50   .....   (962)
    A Guide to Manuscripts Repositories and Institutional Records
        in Ohio, by Soc. of Ohio Archivists (1974)   ....   (646)
    A Bibliography of the State of Ohio, by Thomson (repr. 1890) Set:25.00   .....   (629)

Records

    The Territorial Papers of the U.S. - Territory Northwest of
        the Ohio River 1787-1803 [Series M721, Reel 2] 35mm Microfilm: 12.00   (402)
    First Ownership of Ohio Lands, by Dyer   7.50   .....   (130)

Federal Land Series: Revolutionary War Bounty-Land Warrants
    of the Federal Govt. 1799-1835, Vol 2, by Smith   20.00 ..... (297)
Early Ohio Tax Records, by Powell   19.50 ..... (71)
Index to the 1800 Census of Northwest Territory [Ohio] &
    Early Ohio Marriages 1791-1803, by Maxwell 5.95 (1009)
Cincinnati Miscellany, or Antiquities of the West: Pioneer
    History & General & Local Statistics Compiled From the
    'Western General Advertiser' (repr. of 1845 ed.) 2v. in 1   30.00 ..... (629)
Index to the 1850 Federal Census, by Ohio Family Historians   75.00 ..... (570)

Maps & Gazetteers

The Heckewelder Map, 1796 [Facsimile reproduction 18 x 27
    accompanied by a 27pp booklet. Northeastern Ohio & north-
    western Pennsylvania. Heckewelder was a moravian] 8.00 (962)
1868 Atlas of Ohio, by Stebbins [To be published in 1975]   .... (850)

Military

Five Forts, by Ankenbruck [The battles for the Old Northwest,
    including the Ohio campaigns aimed at Fort Wayne, Indiana,
    and the early pioneers.] 1.95 (93)
Roster of Ohio Soldiers in the War of 1812, by Adj. Gen. Off.   8.50 ..... (130)
History of the 48th Ohio Vet. Vol. Inf. . . . by Bering (1880)   17.50 15.00 (546)

Religious and ethnic groups

Memoranda of the Early Settlement of Friends in the Northwest
    Territory . . . by Perdue 3.00 (265)
Encyclopedia of American Quaker Genealogy, by Hinshaw.
    Vol. 5 [Ohio]   45.00 ..... (130)
Encyclopedia of American Quaker Genealogy, by Hinshaw.
    Vol. 4 [Ohio]   55.00 ..... (130)

Roads and trails

Ohio Indian Trails, by Wilcox   15.00 ..... (661)
Principal Roads Across the State of Ohio in 1830 (in ORPF,
    v.8, #4) 4pp. 2.00 (214)

ASHTABULA COUNTY

1874 Atlas of Ashtabula County, by Lake (repr.) 10.00 (850)

BELMONT COUNTY

Tombstone Inscriptions & Family Records, by Powell   22.50 ..... (71)
Ohio Valley Genealogies, by Hanna   8.00 ..... (130)

BUTLER COUNTY

1807 Census, by Mayhill & Heiss 1.50 (850)

CLARK COUNTY

1875 Atlas of Clark County, by Everts & Co. (repr.) 12.00 (850)

CLERMONT COUNTY

Index to History of Clermont County, Ohio 1775-1880, by Rockey
    & Bancroft (repr. of 1880 ed.)   12.50 10.00 (546)
Desc. of Godfrey Gatch . . . With Material on Early Methodist
    History in Maryland, Virginia & Ohio, by Markham   18.00 ..... (430)

CLINTON COUNTY

Clinton County Ohio Newspapers Death and Obituary Abstracts,
    1838-1867, by Mart 5.00 (807)

COLUMBIANA COUNTY

Index to the 1870 Atlas of Columbiana County, by Morris 6.00 (933)
1850 Federal Census - Indexed, by Bell 14.00 ..... (214)
Index to 1860 Federal Census, by Bell 5.00 (18)

COSHOCTON COUNTY

St. John's Lutheran Church, New Bedford, Ohio, by White
[Contains family, baptism, confirmation, marriage and
death records.] 10.00 (718)

CRAWFORD COUNTY

History of Crawford County and Ohio, by Baskin & Battey (repr) 47.50 45.00 (546)

CUYAHOGA COUNTY

The German-Speaking Element of Greater Cleveland: A Cultural
History, by Ward, Sinnema & Rumpf 13.95 10.95 (587)

DELAWARE COUNTY

Tombstone Inscriptions & Other Records of Delaware County,
by Powell [Includes parts of Morrow & Marion Cos.] 18.50 ..... (71)

ERIE COUNTY

A History of Sandusky & Erie County, by Frohman 1.20 (888)
The Town of Milan, by Ryan (repr. of 1923 ed.) [Moravian missions, canals, map of Indian trails] 3.00 (888)

FRANKLIN COUNTY

History of Franklin County, by Martin (repr. of 1858 ed.) 7.50 ..... (214)
Index to Martin's History of Franklin County (above) 1.50 (214)

GALLIA COUNTY

The French Five Hundred, by Sibley [Settlement of Gallipolis] 2.40 (888)
Scioto Speculation & The French Settlement at Gallipolis, by
Belote (repr. of 1907 ed.) 12.50 ..... (625)

GEAUGA COUNTY

Pioneer & General History of Geauga County, by Geauga Co. Hist.
Soc. (repr. of 1880 ed.) [New every-name index added] 16.50 ..... (214)

GREENE COUNTY

1874 Atlas of Greene County, by Everts & Co. (repr.) 12.00 (850)

GUERNSEY COUNTY

Guernsey County to Oregon in the Summer of 1853, by Longsworth 2.50 (829)

HAMILTON COUNTY

Cincinnati: A Student's Guide to Localized History 1.50 (762)
Cincinnati Miscellany, or Antiquities of the West: Pioneer
History & General & Local Statistics Compiled from the
'Western General Advertiser' (repr. of 1845 ed.) 30.00 ..... (629)

HARRISON COUNTY

Historical Collections of Harrison County, by Hanna (repr. of 1900
ed.) [Early land, marriage, cemetery records. New index.] 16.50 ..... (214)
Historical Collections of Harrison County, by Hanna 17.50 ..... (130)
Ohio Valley Genealogies, by Hanna 8.00 ..... (130)

HOLMES COUNTY

St. John's Lutheran Church, New Bedford, by White [Family,
  baptism, confirmation, marriage & death records] 10.00 (718)

HURON COUNTY

Newspaper Abstracts, Huron County, 1822-1835, by Tinman
  [Marriage & death notices] 6.00 (639)
The History of Willard, Ohio, by Dush 17.95 (415)
Reprint of Souvenir of Bellevue, Ohio, by Wood [History during
  1800s] 1.00 (599)
1815-1915, Bellevue Centennial Premium List & Home-Coming
  Week [Acct. of Amstens Corners & how it became Bellevue] 1.00 (599)
Pioneer's Progress - The First 25 Years of Lyme Twp. and
  Strong's Ridge, by Wright [1810-1835] 2.00 (599)
The World Grows Smaller - The Second 25 Years of Lyme Twp.
  and Strong's Ridge, by Mittower [1835-1860] 2.00 (599)

JACKSON COUNTY

Index to 1820 Census (in ORPF, v.11, #4) 6pp. 2.00 (214)

JEFFERSON COUNTY

Ohio Valley Genealogies, by Hanna 8.00 ..... (130)
Early Marriages, 1797-1803 (in The Report, v.14, #1) 2pp. 2.00 (214)

KNOX COUNTY

1871 Atlas of Knox County, by Caldwell & Starr (repr) 2.95 (850)

LAKE COUNTY

Probate Court, Marriage Reocrds (1840-1841) (1842-1843)
  (in The Report, v.11, #3 & 4) 18pp. total 4.00 (214)

LICKING COUNTY

Hill's History of Licking County (repr. of 1881 ed.) 15.50 ..... (1023)
Index to Hill's History of Licking County (above) 4.00 (1023)
Licking County History, by Everts (1875) [To be reprinted soon]   .... (850)
Licking County - Atlas of 1866 (Beers) & 1875 (Everts) 2.95 (850)
  [Individual village & twp. maps from above two atlases] Each: ..... .60 (850)
Memorial Record of Licking County, by Record Pub. Co. (1894) 32.50 30.00 (546)
Cemetery Inscriptions:
  Granville Township 5.50 (1023)
  Newton Township 6.50 (1023)
  Mary Ann & Madison Townships 2.50 (1023)
  Washington & Eden Townships 2.75 (1023)
  Fallsbury & Perry Townships 2.50 (1023)
  Hanover Township 2.50 (1023)
  Lima Township 3.00 (1023)
  Harrison & Etna Townships 3.00 (1023)
  Bowling Green & Franklin Townships 2.50 (1023)
  Licking Township 2.50 (1023)
  Hopewell Township 2.50 (1023)
  Jersey Township 2.25 (1023)
  Bennington & McKean Townships 2.50 (1023)
  Burlington Township 2.50 (1023)
  Union Township 2.50 (1023)
  Hartford Township 2.25 (1023)
  St. Albans Township 2.50 (1023)
  Liberty Township 2.25 (1023)
  Monroe Township 3.50 (1023)

Cemetery Inscriptions of Licking County, cont.

Newark Township (except Newark Cedar Hill)	.....	2.75	(1023)
Newark Cedar Hill Cemetery (Dec. 16, 1850-Aug.27, 1909)	.....	8.50	(1023)
Newark Cedar Hill Cemetery (Aug. 27, 1909-May 11, 1946)	.....	8.50	(1023)
Newark Cedar Hill Cemetery (May 13, 1946-Feb. 24, 1971)	.....	5.50	(1023)
Report of the Great Re-union of the Veteran Soldiers & Sailors Held at Newark, July 22, 1878, Under the Auspices of "The Society of the Soldiers & Sailors of Licking County, Ohio", by Miller (repr. of 1879 ed.)	17.50	15.00	(546)

LORAIN COUNTY

History of Lorain County, by Williams Bros. (repr. 1879 ed.) [New every-name index added]	16.50	.....	(623)
1874 Atlas of Lorain County, by Titus [New every-name index]	12.50	.....	(623)
Index to the 1850 Federal Census, by Lorain Co. Hist. Soc.	.....	4.50	(623)

MAHONING COUNTY

1845 Tax List of Original Landowners, by Bell [Listing by twp. of those paying Personal Property & Real Estate taxes.]	.....	6.00	(18)
The Private Journal of Abraham Joseph Warner, by Enderton [Rev. Warner was Rector of St. James Church, Boardman, Ohio in 1864. He comments on those he met.]	11.00	.....	(83)

MARION COUNTY

Abstracts of Deeds, Vol. 2 (in ORPF, v.11, #3) 5pp.	.....	2.00	(214)
Tombstone Incriptions of Delaware Co. & Parts of Morrow & Marion Cos. & Other Records, by Powell	x	.....	(71)

MONROE COUNTY

1850 Federal Census - Indexed, by Davis [Includes map of twps.]	.....	7.50	(121)
1860 Federal Census - Indexed, by Davis [Includes map of twps.]	.....	12.50	(121)
Death Records, 1870-1871 (in ORPF, v.11, #2) 5pp.	.....	2.00	(214)

MONTGOMERY COUNTY

Atlas of Individual Townships - Montgomery County	.....	7.50	(850)

MORROW COUNTY

Tombstone Inscriptions of Delaware Co. & Parts of Morrow & Marion Cos. & Other Records, by Powell	x	.....	(71)

MUSKINGUM COUNTY

1816 Tax List (in ORPF, v.11, #1) 5pp.	.....	2.00	(214)
Muskingum County Atlas of 1866, by Beers & Soule	.....	10.00	(850)

NOBLE COUNTY

History of Noble County, by Watkins & Co. (repr. 1887)	37.50	35.00	(546)

PICKAWAY COUNTY

Some Ohio & Iowa Pioneers Their Friends & Descendants, by Koleda [A collection of letters, bills, deeds, etc., 1811-1945]	.....	10.00	(3)

PREBLE COUNTY

Plat Book of Preble County, 1912 [Loose leaf]	.....	10.00	(313)
1850 Federal Census, by Shilt & Short	14.00	.....	(214)

PUTNAM COUNTY

Putnam County Pioneer Assoc. Centennial History, 1873-1973, by Carroll [Early settlers, locations of cem., veterans all wars, reminiscences, etc. - completely indexed]	.....	5.50	(441)

RICHLAND COUNTY

Abstracts of Wills 1813-1873, by Budd   19.50   .....   (214)
Naturalization Intention Papers, 1875-1896 (in Report, v. 11, #3) 2.00   (214)

ROSS COUNTY

1875 Landowner's Atlas of Ross County, by Gould [New index] 11.50   (850)

SANDUSKY COUNTY

Souvenir of Bellevue, by Wood [Hist. of Bellevue during 1800s] 1.00   (599)
Bellevue Centennial Premium List & Home-Coming Week [Early
    accts. of Amstens Corners and how it became Bellevue] 1.00   (599)

STARK COUNTY

Early Church Records & Cemeteries, by Powell   17.50   .....   (71)

SUMMIT COUNTY

Revolutionary Soldiers of Summit Co. (in Report, v. 12, #1) 9pp. 2.00   (214)

TRUMBULL COUNTY

1874 Atlas of Trumbull County, by Everts & Co. [New index] 17.00   (850)

TUSCARAWAS COUNTY

History of Tuscarawas County, by Warner, Beers & Co. (1884)   21.55   .....   (416)
Historical Atlas of Tuscarawas, 1875, by Everts & 1908, by
    Rhodes - combined. Bound as one.   21.55   .....   (416)
Reminiscences of Dover, by Harmount, Slingluff, & Scott [Set-
    tlers and earlier residents of Dover] 1.81   (416)

VINTON COUNTY

Land Grant Records (in ORPF, v. 12, #2) 4pp 2.00   (214)

WASHINGTON COUNTY

Life & Times of Ephraim Cutler: Prepared From His Journals &
    Correspondence . . . , by Cutler [Firsthand story of the estab-
    lishment and development of the first Am. settlement north of
    the Ohio R. - at Marietta.]   16.00   .....   (629)
1875 Atlas of Washington County, by Titus 3.95   (850)
1875 Atlas of Washington County, by Titus - with index 5.75   (850)

WAYNE COUNTY

History of Wayne County, by Douglass (1878 repr.) [New index]   16.50   .....   (331)
1873 Wayne County Atlas, by Caldwell 8.00   (850)
Atlases of Wayne County (repr. of 1874 & 1897 eds. in one vol.)   16.00   .....   (331)
First Purchasers of Land from the U.S. (in ORPF, v.15, #2) 7pp 2.00   (214)

WILLIAMS COUNTY

Land Grants [Disputed Territory], (in ORPF, v. 12, #2 & 4) Total: 4.00   (214)

WOOD COUNTY

Early Settlers (in ORPF, v. 13, #4) 4pp. 2.00   (214)

Oklahoma

STATEWIDE REFERENCES

Oklahoma: A Student's Guide to Localized History 1.50   (762)
Oklahoma Place Names, by Shirk 5.95   (997)

Records

    Our People And Where They Rest, by Tyner & Timmons [Identi-
        fication of over 65,000 graves in 800 burial plots Indian Ter-
        ritory & Cherokee Nation. Eighteen tribes.] 8 vols. Each: 5.95 (409)
    Where They Cried, by Tyner [1835 Cherokee Census] 7.50 (409)

OKLAHOMA COUNTY

Peters Colonists, Their Descendents & Others (Who settled North
    Texas), by Young. Vol. 3 [To be published in 1975]   .... (433)

STEPHENS COUNTY

Peters Colonists, Their Descendents & Others (Who settled North
    Texas), by Young. Vol. 3 [To be published in 1975]   .... (433)

Oregon

STATEWIDE REFERENCES

A History of Oregon, 1792-1849, by Gray	28.00	.....	(629)
The Old Oregon Country, by Winther	18.00	.....	(624)
On the Oregon Trail (in Gen. Ref. Builders, v. 6, #2) 4pp.	.....	2.00	(931)
To Oregon By Ox Team in '47, by Lockley	3.25	1.25	(814)

Research aids

    Oregon Historical Society Microfilm Guide: Includes manuscripts,
        censuses, land claims, church records, federal & state rec-
        ords, genealogical material, newspapers, etc.] 7.50 (887)
    Guide to the Manuscript Collections of the Oregon Historical
        Society [Approx. 8,000 entries]   20.00   ..... (887)
    Catalogue of Manuscripts in the University of Oregon Library 7.50 (632)

Records

    Genealogical Material in Oregon Donation Land Claims, Vol. 1   .....   6.50 (191)
    Genealogical Material in Oregon Donation Land Claims, Vol. 2   .....   6.50 (191)
    Genealogical Material in Oregon Donation Land Claims, Vol. 3   .....   6.50 (191)
    Genealogical Material in Oregon Donation Land Claims, Vol. 4   .....   9.00 (191)
    1850 Territorial Census of Oregon 10.00 (961)
    Oregon Soldiers During the Civil War , by Genealogical Forum
        of Portland [Indian fighters, no officers] 1.00 (191)
    Catholic Church Records of the Pacific Northwest, by Warner
        & Munnick [Vancouver records, Vol. 1 & 2 & Stellamaris
        Mission - all in one book]   10.00   ..... (665)

BAKER COUNTY

An Illustrated History of Baker, Grant, Malheur, & Harney Cos.	47.50	45.00	(546)
Yesterdays Roll Call, Vol. I [Cemetery records, other data]	.....	11.50	(191)

BENTON COUNTY

History of Benton County, by Fagan (repr. 1885)   32.50   30.00 (546)

COOS COUNTY

History of Southern Oregon, by Walling (repr. 1884)   42.50   40.00 (546)

CROOK COUNTY

An Illustrated History of Central Oregon, Embracing Wasco, Sher-
    man, Gilliam, Wheeler, Brook, Lake & Klamath Cos. (1905)   47.50   45.00 (546)

CURRY COUNTY

History of Southern Oregon, comprising Jackson, Josephine, Douglas, Curry & Coos Cos., by Walling (repr. 1884 ed.)	42.50	40.00	(546)

DOUGLAS COUNTY

History of Southern Oregon, by Walling [See Curry County]	42.50	40.00	(546)
1860 Federal Census, by Hiday	.....	3.00	(191)
1880 Federal Census, by Hiday	.....	6.50	(191)

GILLIAM COUNTY

An Illustrated History of Central Oregon [See Crook County]	47.50	45.00	(546)

GRANT COUNTY

An Illustrated History of Baker, Grant, Malheur & Harney Counties, by Western Historical Publishing Co. (repr. 1902 ed.)	47.50	45.00	(546)

HARNEY COUNTY

An Illustrated History . . . of Harney Co. [See Grant County]	47.50	45.00	(546)

JACKSON COUNTY

History of Southern Oregon . . . [See Curry County]	42.50	40.00	(546)
Marriages. Vol. 1, 1853-1877; Vol. 2, 1877-1888 Each:	.....	5.00	(883)
1860 Federal Census, by Gen. Forum of Portland	.....	2.00	(191)
1870 Federal Census, by Gen. Forum of Portland	.....	2.00	(191)
1880 Federal Census, by Gen. Forum of Portland	.....	4.00	(191)

JOSEPHINE COUNTY

History of Southern Oregon . . . [see Curry County]	42.50	40.00	(546)
1870 Federal Census, by Hiday	.....	2.00	(191)

KLAMATH COUNTY

An Illustrated History of Central Oregon [See Crook County]	47.50	45.00	(546)
History of Klamath County, by Sisemore (repr. of 1941 ed.)	47.50	45.00	(546)

LAKE COUNTY

An Illustrated History of Central Oregon [See Crook County]	47.50	45.00	(546)

LANE COUNTY

An Illustrated History of Lane County, by Walling (repr. 1884 ed.)	37.50	35.00	(546)

LEWIS COUNTY

Old Lewis County, Oregon Territory, by Coffman	5.50	3.50	(814)

MALHEUR COUNTY

An Illustrated History of . . . Malheur County [see Grant Co.]	47.50	45.00	(546)

MULTNOMAH COUNTY

1870 Federal Census [Excluding the city of Portland], by Hiday	.....	3.00	(191)
1870 Federal Census of the City of Portland, by Hiday	.....	6.00	(191)

SHERMAN COUNTY

An Illustrated History of Central Oregon [See Crook County]	47.50	45.00	(546)
Yesterdays Roll Call, Vol. 1 [Cem. records, with other data]	.....	11.50	(191)

UMATILLA COUNTY

An Illustrated History of Umatilla County, by Shiach (repr. 1902)	37.50	35.00	(546)
Yesterdays Roll Call, Vol. 1 [Cem. records, with other data]	.....	11.50	(546)

UNION COUNTY

An Illustrated History of Union & Wallowa Cos., by Western Historical Publishing Company (repr. of 1902 ed.)	42.50	40.00	(546)

WALLOWA COUNTY

An Illustrated History of . . . Wallowa Co. [See Union County]	42.50	40.00	(546)

WASCO COUNTY

An Illustrated History of Central Oregon [See Crook County]	47.50	45.00	(546)
1880 Federal Census, by Hiday	.....	6.50	(191)

WASHINGTON COUNTY

Marriages 1842-1880, by Lepschat & Balfour	.....	4.50	(191)
1880 Federal Census, by Hiday	.....	5.00	(191)

WHEELER COUNTY

An Illustrated History of Central Oregon [See Crook County]	47.50	45.00	(546)

Pennsylvania

STATEWIDE REFERENCES

The Pennsylvania Traveler-Post [A genealogical quarterly] Approx. 210pp./yr. Subscription:	.....	7.75	(109)
Historical Review of the Constitution & Government of Pennsylvania From Its Origin, by Franklin (repr. of 1759 ed.)	28.00	.....	(629)
The History of Pennsylvania, From Its Discovery By Europeans to the Declaration of Independence in 1776, by Gordon	17.50	.....	(663)
The History of Pennsylvania, by Proud. 2 vols. Each:	15.00	.....	(663)
An Outline of the Maryland Boundary Disputes and Related Events, by Morrison [A schematic study - not a text]	.....	3.00	(325)
Penn's Colony, Vol. 2: The Welcome Claimants Proved, Disproved and Doubtful, With an Account of Some of Their Descendants	22.00	.....	(130)
The Life & Public Services of Arthur St. Clair: The St. Clair Papers, ed. by Smith. 2 vols. Set:	38.50	.....	(636)
White Servitude in Pennsylvania: Indentured & Redemption Labor in Colony & Commonwealth, by Herrick (repr. of 1926 ed.)	12.50	.....	(847)
Fair Play Settlers of the West Branch Valley, 1769-1784: A Study in Frontier Ethnography, by Wolf	3.50	2.50	(916)
Conrad Weiser & the Indian Policy of Colonial Pennsylvania, by Walteon (repr. of 1900 ed.)	19.00	.....	(629)

Research aids

County Government & Archives in Pennsylvania, by Pa. Hist. & Mus. [Studies evolution, structure, & kinds of records of the various county offices. No actual records.]	.....	4.00	(916)
Pennsylvania Area Key, by Clint [A comprehensive guide to genealogical records in Pennsylvania]	.....	6.00	(552)
Guide to Genealogical & Historical Research in Pennsylvania, by Hoenstine	11.00	8.50	(298)
Tracing Family Trees in Eleven States [Pa. is included]	.....	5.50	(29)
Pennsylvania Place Names, by Espenshade	11.50	.....	(130)
Pennsylvania: A Student's Guide to Localized History	.....	1.50	(762)
Sources For Genealogical Searching in Pennsylvania, by McCay	.....	3.00	(417)
Bibliography of Pennsylvania History, by Wilkinson (1957)	7.00	.....	(916)
Historical Manuscript Depositories in Pennsylvania, by Richman	.....	1.00	(916)

Guide to the Published Archives of Pennsylvania, by Eddy
[Key to the several series of Col. Rec. & Pa. Archives] 2.00 (916)
PI #124 - Preliminary Inventory of the Records of the U.S. Dis-
trict Court for the Eastern District of Pennsylvania ..... free (402)
Historical Collections of the State of Pa., by Day (repr. 1843) 27.50 ..... (641)
Pennsylvania Magazine of History & Biography, by Pa. Hist. Soc.
Vols. 30-67. Philadelphia 1906-1943 Set: 905.00 755.00 (1000)
Vols. 30-59, 1906-1935 Each: 20.00 (1000)
Vols. 60-67, 1936-1943 Each: 22.50 (1000)
Index to Pennsylvania Magazine of History & Biography, by Doll
Vols. 1-75, 1877-1951 ..... 60.00 (1005)

Records

Colonial Records of Pennsylvania. 16 vols. Each: 32.50 ..... (630)
Pennsylvania Archives. Series 1-9 in 121 vols. Set: 6,100.00 ..... (630)
1st Ser., 12v; 2nd Ser., 19v; 3rd Ser., 31v;
7th Ser., 5v. Each volume: 47.50 ..... (630)
4th Ser., 12v; 5th Ser., 8v; 6th Ser., 16v;
8th Ser., 8v; 9th Ser., 10v. Each volume: 55.00 ..... (630)
The Statutes at Large of Pennsylvania. 1682-1801. 17v. Each: 51.50 ..... (630)
Names of Persons for Whom Marriage Licenses Were Issued
in the Province of Pa. Previous to 1790, by Linn & Egle 8.50 ..... (130)
Record of Pa. Marriages Prior to 1810, by Linn & Egle 31.50 ..... (130)
Pennsylvania German Pioneers, by Strassburger & Hinke (repr.
1934) [Lists of immigrants arriving in the Port of Philadel-
phia from 1727-1808 - mostly from the Palatinate] 2v. Set: 26.00 ..... (1144)
Emigrants From the Palatinate to the American Colonies in the
18th Century, by Krebs & Rubincam [Supplement to Pennsyl-
vania German Pioneers (above)] 3.50 (1144)
A Collection of Upwards of 30,000 Names of German, Swiss,
Dutch, French & Other Immigrants, by Rupp 17.50 ..... (130)
Names of Persons Who Took the Oath of Allegiance to the State
of Pennsylvania, 1777-1789, by Westcott 9.00 ..... (130)
Index to Pennsylvania Warrants & Surveys 3.00 (850)
Persons Naturalized in Pennsylvania, 1740-1773, by Linn & Egle 11.00 ..... (130)
Penn's Colony. Vol. 1: Passengers & Ships Prior to 1684 14.50 ..... (130)
Record of Indentures [1771-1773] of Individuals Bound Out . . . 15.00 ..... (130)
Minutes of the General Assembly of Pennsylvania, 1777-1778
(in Your Family Tree, vols. 15-20) Each Vol.: $5.00 .... (298)
1790 Federal Census of Pa., by U.S. Census Bureau (repr.) 15.00 ..... (130)
1790 Federal Census of Pa., by U.S. Census Bureau (repr.) 15.00 ..... (663)
1800 Federal Census of Pa., by Acc. Indexing Sys. 2v. Set: 34.00 ..... (677)

Military

Pennsylvania Women in the American Revolution, by Egle 10.00 ..... (580)
Muster Rolls of the Pa. Vol. in the War of 1812, by Linn & Egle 17.50 ..... (130)
Pennsylvania and the War of 1812, by Sapio 7.95 ..... (126)
History of the 83rd Regt., Pa. Vol., by Judson (repr. 1865) 12.50 10.00 (546)
History of Company F, 140th Regt., Pa. Vol., by White (1908) 8.50 6.00 (546)
History of Company K, 140th Regt., Pa. Vol., by Powelson 8.50 6.00 (546)

Religious and ethnic groups

Register of Marriages & Baptisms Performed by Rev. John Cuth-
bertson, Covenanter Minister, 1751-1791, With Index to Loca-
tions & Persons Visited, by Fields (repr. 1934) 12.50 10.00 (546)
Encyclopedia of American Quaker Genealogy, by Hinshaw
Vol. 2 [New Jersey & Pennsylvania Monthly Meetings] 50.00 ..... (130)
Quaker Arrivals at Philadelphia, 1682-1750, by Myers 8.50 ..... (130)

Quakers & Politics: Pennsylvania, 1681-1726, by Nash	12.50	.....	(943)
Immigration of the Irish Quakers Into Pa., 1682-1750, by Myers	16.00	.....	(130)
William Penn & the Dutch Quaker Migration to Pa., by Hull	14.00	.....	(130)
Quakers in Pennsylvania, by Applegarth (repr. 1892)	10.25	6.25	(1000)
Early 18th Century Palatine Emigration, by Knittle	11.50	.....	(130)
Historic Background & Annals of the Swiss & German Pioneer Settlers of South-Eastern Pennsylvania, and of Their Remote Ancestors, by Eshleman	12.50	.....	(130)
The German & Swiss Settlements of Colonial Pennsylvania: A Study of the So-Called Pa. Dutch, by Kuhns (new ed. 1901)	8.75	.....	(233)
The Story of the Pa. Germans: Embracing an Account of their Origin, their History, & their Dialect, by Beidelman (1898)	10.00	.....	(233)
Life & Letters of the Rev. John Philip Boehm: Founder of the Reformed Church in Pa., 1683-1749, by Hinke (1916)	26.00	.....	(629)
Settlement of Germantown, Pennsylvania, & the Beginning of German Emigration to N. Am., by Pennypacker (1899 ed.)	12.50	.....	(844)
Memorials of the Huguenots in America, With Special References to Their Emigration to Pennsylvania, by Stapleton	10.00	.....	(130)
Merion in the Welsh Tract, by Glenn [Hist. & gen. collections concerning the Welsh barony in the Province of Pa. settled by the cymric Quakers in 1682]	13.50	.....	(130)
Welsh Founders of Pennsylvania, by Glenn	16.50	.....	(130)
The Swedish Settlements on the Delaware, 1638-1664, Johnson	27.50	.....	(130)

Maps, trails, and roads

The Heckewelder Map, 1796 [Facsimile reproduction (18 x 27) accompanied by 27pp. booklet. Of the northwestern part of Pennsylvania. Heckewelder was a Moravian missionary]	.....	8.00	(962)
Map of Pennsylvania - 1846 [17 x 14]	.....	2.22	(987)
Indian Paths in Pennsylvania, by Wallace (1971)	6.00	.....	(916)
Old Canals & Roads in Penn's Land, by Faris (repr. 1927 ed.)	10.00	.....	(641)

Miscellaneous

Pennsylvania: Genealogies Chiefly Scotch-Irish & German, by Egle	22.50	.....	(130)
Notes & Queries - Historical, Biographical, & Genealogical - Relating Chiefly to Interior Pa., by Egle. 12 vols. Set:	130.00	.....	(130)
Index to Main Families, Persons, Places & Subjects in Egle's Notes & Queries (above), by Egle	8.50	.....	(130)
1955 Year Book, Pennsylvania Society, S.A.R., by Hoenstine [Gen. data fr. appl. of members accepted fr. 1893-1956]	15.00	.....	(298)

WESTERN PENNSYLVANIA

Fort Ligonier and Its Times: A History of the First English Fort West of the Allegheny Mountains . . . , by Sipe (1932)	30.00	.....	(629)
History of Col. Henry Bouquet & the Western Frontiers of Pennsylvania, 1747-1764, by Darlington (repr. 1920 ed.)	11.00	.....	(629)
A History of the Region of Pennsylvania North of the Ohio & West of the Allegheny River, by Agnew (repr. of 1887 ed.)	11.00	.....	(629)
Planting of Civilization in Western Pa., by Buck & Buck	.....	4.45	(987)
Pioneer Life in Western Pa., by Wright & Corbett	.....	2.95	(991)
History of the Insurrection in Western Pennsylvania, Commonly Called the Whiskey Insurrection, 1794, by Brackenridge (1859)	12.00	.....	(629)
Whiskey Rebels: The Story of a Frontier Uprising, by Baldwin	.....	2.95	(991)
Revolution on the Upper Ohio 1775-1777, by Thwaites & Kellogg	11.00	.....	(637)
Frontier Defense on the Upper Ohio: 1777-1778, by Thwaites	15.60	.....	(624)
Frontier Advance on the Upper Ohio, by Kellogg (repr. 1916)	17.50	.....	(863)
Frontier Retreat on the Upper Ohio, by Kellogg	19.50	.....	(863)

SOUTHWESTERN PENNSYLVANIA

Virginia Court Records in Southwestern Pa: Records of the Dist. of W. Augusta, Ohio, & Yohogania Cos., Va., by Crumrine	20.00	.....	(130)
Notes on the Settlement & Indian Wars of the Western Parts of Va. & Pa. From 1763-1783, by Doddridge (repr. 1876)	16.50	.....	(625)
The Old and the New Monongahela, by Van Voorhis	20.00	.....	(130)
Monongahela of Old - Or Historical Sketches of Southwestern Pennsylvania to the Year 1800, by Veech (repr. of 1892 ed.)	15.00	.....	(796)

ADAMS COUNTY

Adams County Area Key: Guide to Genealogical Records	.....	6.00	(552)
History of Cumberland & Adams Cos., by Beers [New index]	21.00	.....	(905)
Guide to Adams Co. Lutheran Ch. Records, by Pastor Weiser	.....	3.00	(1145)

ALLEGHENY COUNTY

Fort Pitt & Letters From the Frontier, by Darlington [Collection of documents, 1749-1799, including an acct. of the organization of Allegheny County. Maps] (repr. 1892 ed.)	14.00	.....	(629)
Pittsburgh: The Story of a City, 1750-1865, by Baldwin	.....	3.31	(987)

ARMSTRONG COUNTY

Armstrong County Area Key: Guide to Genealogical Records	.....	6.00	(552)

BEAVER COUNTY

Beaver County Area Key: Guide to Genealogical Records	.....	6.00	(552)

BEDFORD COUNTY

Bedford County Area Key: Guide to Genealogical Records	.....	6.00	(552)
Orphans Court Abstracts, 1771-1805 (in Your Family Tree, v.17-20) 87pp. total. Each vol: $5.00	.....	20.00	(298)

BERKS COUNTY

Berks County Area Key: Guide to Genealogical Records	.....	6.00	(552)
Baptismal Records of Jerusalem Lutheran & Reformed Church, by Kistler [Translation of entries 1768-1863]	.....	3.00	(616)
Index of Wills & Administration Records, by Williams & Williams	.....	15.00	(109)

BLAIR COUNTY

Blair County Area Key: Guide to Genealogical Records	.....	6.00	(552)
Hollidaysburg Newspaper Items, 1836-1845 (in Your Family Tree, v.15-20) 96pp. total. Each vol: $5.00	.....	30.00	(298)
Soldiers of Blair County, by Hoenstine [Over 12,000 soldiers from Revolutionary War to World War 1 named]	12.00	.....	(298)

BRADFORD COUNTY

Bradford County Area Key: Guide to Genealogical Records	.....	6.00	(552)
Pioneer & Patriot Families of Bradford County, 1770-1800, Including History (1615-1800), Marriages (1776-1850, Soldiers, etc., by Heverly. 2 vols. Set:	55.00	50.00	(546)

BUCKS COUNTY

Bucks County Area Key: Guide to Genealogical Records	.....	6.00	(552)
A Genealogical & Personal History of Bucks County, by Davis	30.00	.....	(130)
Oaths of Allegiance, 1776-1786, by Williams	.....	10.50	(109)
1779 Tax Transcript, by Williams	.....	10.50	(109)
Index of Wills & Administration Records, 1684-1850, by Williams	.....	15.00	(109)
Pioneers of the 18th Century [Extracted fr. Davis's "History of Bucks County" pub. in 1905]	.....	10.00	(109)

BUTLER COUNTY

Butler County Area Key: Guide to Genealogical Records 6.00 (552)

CAMBRIA COUNTY

Cambria County Area Key: Guide to Genealogical Records 6.00 (552)

CAMERON COUNTY

Cameron County Area Key: Guide to Genealogical Records 6.00 (552)

CARBON COUNTY

Carbon County Area Key: Guide to Genealogical Records 6.00 (552)
History of Northampton, Lehigh, Monroe, Carbon & Schuykill
Counties: Containing a Brief History of the First Settlers,
etc., by Rupp (repr. of 1845 ed.) 24.00 ..... (629)

CENTRE COUNTY

Centre County Area Key: Guide to Genealogical Records 6.00 (629)
1800 Federal Census for Mifflin & Centre Counties, by James 3.85 (779)

CHESTER COUNTY

Chester County Area Key: Guide to Genealogical Records 6.00 (552)
History of Chester County, With Gen. & Biog. Sketches, by Cope 47.50 45.00 (546)
History of the Underground Railroad in Chester & the Neighbor-
ing Counties of Pennsylvania, by Smedley (repr. of 1883 ed.) 14.00 ..... (847)

CLARION COUNTY

Clarion County Area Key: Guide to Genealogical Records 6.00 (552)

CLEARFIELD COUNTY

Clearfield County Area Key: Guide to Genealogical Records 6.00 (552)

CLINTON COUNTY

Clinton County Area Key: Guide to Genealogical Records 6.00 (552)

COLUMBIA COUNTY

Columbia County Area Key: Guide to Genealogical Records 6.00 (552)

CRAWFORD COUNTY

Crawford County Area Key: Guide to Genealogical Records 6.00 (552)

CUMBERLAND COUNTY

Cumberland County Area Key: Guide to Genealogical Records 6.00 (552)
History of the Courts of Cumberland, by Cumberland Hist. Soc. ..... .50 (905)
Will Abstracts, 1750-1777 (in Your Family Tree, v.17-20) 20.00 (298)
History of the Middle Spring Presbyterian Church, 1738-1900,
by Swope (repr. of 1900 ed.) 17.50 15.00 (546)

DAUPHIN COUNTY

Dauphin County Area Key: Guide to Genealogical Records 6.00 (552)

DELAWARE COUNTY

Delaware County Area Key: Guide to Genealogical Records 6.00 (552)
Index to Ashmeade's 1884 History of Delaware County 5.00 (779)
Index to Wills & Administrations, by Williams & Williams 12.50 (109)

ELK COUNTY

Elk County Area Key: Guide to Genealogical Records 6.00 (552)

ERIE COUNTY

Erie County Area Key: Guide to Genealogical Records	.....	6.00	(552)

FAYETTE COUNTY

Fayette County Area Key: Guide to Genealogical Records	.....	6.00	(552)
History of Fayette County, by Ellis (repr. of 1882 ed.)	47.50	45.00	(546)
Fayette County Landowners Atlas, by Hopkins & Co. (repr. 1872)	17.00	10.00	(1130)
1810 Federal Census, by Morgan	.....	9.00	(200)
Ohio Valley Genealogies, by Hanna	8.00	.....	(130)

FOREST COUNTY

Forest County Area Key: Guide to Genealogical Records	.....	6.00	(552)

FRANKLIN COUNTY

Franklin County Area Key: Guide to Genealogical Records	.....	6.00	(552)
Guide to Franklin & Fulton Lutheran Ch. Records, by Weiser	.....	3.00	(1145)

FULTON COUNTY

Fulton County Area Key: Guide to Genealogical Records	.....	6.00	(552)
Guide to Franklin & Fulton Co. Lutheran Ch. Records, by Weiser	.....	3.00	(1145)

GREENE COUNTY

Greene County Area Key: Guide to Genealogical Records	.....	6.00	(552)
Surname Index to Bates' 1888 History of Greene County - With Supplemental Data from Census 1800 through 1880, by Adams [To be published about 1976]	.....	.....	(319)
1810 Federal Census, by Morgan	.....	5.00	(200)

HUNTINGDON COUNTY

Huntingdon County Area Key: Guide to Genealogical Records	.....	6.00	(552)
Will Abstracts, 1787-1825 (in Your Family Tree, v.15-20) 96pp.	.....	30.00	(298)

INDIANA COUNTY

Indiana County Area Key: Guide to Genealogical Records	.....	6.00	(552)

JEFFERSON COUNTY

Jefferson County Area Key: Guide to Genealogical Records	.....	6.00	(552)

JUNIATA COUNTY

Juniata County Area Key: Guide to Genealogical Records	.....	6.00	(552)

LACKAWANNA COUNTY

Susquehanna & Lackawanna Area Keys: Guide to Genealogical Rec.	.....	6.00	(552)

LANCASTER COUNTY

Lancaster County Area Key: Guide to Genealogical Records	.....	6.00	(552)
Deed Abstracts & Oaths of Allegiance, by Mayhill	22.50	.....	(850)
An Index to the Will Books & Intestate Records of Lancaster County, 1729-1850, by Fulton & Mylin	10.00	.....	(130)
Lancaster County Tax Lists, 1751, 1756, 1757, & 1758	.....	3.00	(616)
Lancaster County Historical Society, Journal. Vols. 1-15, 1896/7-1911 [Local genealogy, history, & biography]	213.00	178.00	(624)
A Biographical History of Lancaster County: Being a History of Early Settlers and Eminent Men of the County, by Harris	16.50	.....	(130)
Guide to Lancaster Co. Lutheran Ch. Records, by Pastor Weiser	.....	3.00	(1145)
Marriages Performed at the Evangelical Luthern Church of the Holy Trinity, 1748-1767, by Braun & Weiser	13.00	.....	(1144)

LAWRENCE COUNTY

Lawrence County Area Key: A Guide to Genealogical Records	.....	6.00	(552)

LEBANON COUNTY

Lebanon County Area Key: A Guide to Genealogical Records	.....	6.00	(552)
Guide to Lebanon Co. Lutheran Ch. Records, by Pastor Weiser	.....	3.00	(1145)

LEHIGH COUNTY

Lehigh County Area Key: A Guide to Genealogical Records	.....	6.00	(552)
History of Northampton, Lehigh. . . [See Carbon County]	24.00	.....	(629)
Baptismal Records of Jerusalem Lutheran & Reformed Ch., Berks Co. 1768–1863. [Many of those mentioned lived in Lehigh]	.....	3.00	(616)
Index of Wills & Adm. Records of Northampton Co. 1752-1850 & Lehigh Co. 1812-1850, by Williams & Williams	.....	12.50	(109)

LUZERNE COUNTY

Luzerne County Area Key: A Guide to Genealogical Records	.....	6.00	(552)
Index to the 1850 Census of Luzerne & Wyoming Cos., by Bentley	.....	10.00	(130)

LYCOMING COUNTY

Lycoming County Area Key: A Guide to Genealogical Records	.....	6.00	(552)

McKEAN COUNTY

McKean County Area Key: A Guide to Genealogical Records	.....	6.00	(552)

MERCER COUNTY

Mercer & Venango County Area Keys: A Guide to Genealogical Records	.....	6.00	(552)

MIFFLIN COUNTY

Mifflin County Area Key: A Guide to Genealogical Records	.....	6.00	(552)
1800 Federal Census for Mifflin & Centre Counties, by James	.....	3.85	(779)
The People of Mifflin County, 1755-1798, by Bell & Stroup	.....	3.50	(1014)
Will Abstracts, 1789-1833 (in Your Family Tree, v.16-20) 91pp.	.....	25.00	(298)

MONROE COUNTY

Monroe County Area Key: A Guide to Genealogical Records	.....	6.00	(552)
History of Northampton . . . Monroe, etc. [See Carbon Co.]	24.00	.....	(629)

MONTGOMERY COUNTY

Biographical Annals of Montgomery County , Containing Genealogical Records . . ., by Roberts (1904) 2vols.	Vol. 1:	42.50	40.00	(546)
	Vol. 2:	47.50	45.00	(546)
Montgomery County Area Key: A Guide to Genealogical Records		.....	6.00	(552)
Index of Wills & Estate Settlements 1784-1850, by Williams		.....	15.00	(109)

MONTOUR COUNTY

Montour County Area Key: A Guide to Genealogical Records	.....	6.00	(552)
My Danville: Where the Bright Waters Meet, by Foulke [1850-date]	9.75	.....	(998)
Danville, Montour County, Pennsylvania, by Brower (repr. 1881)	17.50	15.00	(546)

NORTHAMPTON COUNTY

Northampton County Area Key: A Guide to Genealogical Records	.....	6.00	(552)
History of Northampton . . . [See Carbon County]	24.00	.....	(629)
Some of the First Settlers of "The Forks of the Delaware" & Their Descendants, by Kieffer [Reformed church records 1763-1823]	14.00	.....	(130)
Index to the 1850 Federal Census, by Bentley	.....	6.50	(130)
Northampton County Guide, by Northampton Co. Hist. & Gen. Soc.	12.50	.....	(630)

NORTHUMBERLAND COUNTY

Genealogical & Biographical Annals of Northumberland County, by Floyd & Co. (repr. 1911)	47.50	45.00	(546)

PERRY COUNTY

Perry County Area Key: A Guide to Genealogical Records	.....	6.00	(552)

PHILADELPHIA COUNTY

Descriptive Inventory of the Archives of the City of Philadelphia, by Daly	.....	.....	(1011)
Index of Wills & Administrations, Book 1, 1682-1782	.....	15.00	(109)
Index of Wills & Administrations, Book 2, 1782-1810	.....	15.00	(109)
Index of Wills & Administrations, Book 3, 1811-1831	.....	15.00	(109)
Index of Wills & Administrations, Book 4, 1832-1850	.....	15.00	(109)
Early Marriage Records of Christ Church, 1709-1810	.....	6.50	(109)
Early Marriage Records of Old Swede's Church, 1750-1810	.....	6.50	(109)

PIKE COUNTY

Pike & Wayne Counties Area Key: A Guide to Genealogical Rec.	.....	6.00	(552)

POTTER COUNTY

Potter & Tioga Counties Area Key: A Guide to Genealogical Rec.	.....	6.00	(552)

SCHUYLKILL COUNTY

Schuylkill County Area Key: A Guide to Genealogical Records	.....	6.00	(552)

SNYDER COUNTY

Snyder & Union Counties Area Key: A Guide to Genealogical Rec.	.....	6.00	(552)
The Snyder County Pioneers, by Fisher (repr.)	.....	15.50	(851)

SOMERSET COUNTY

Somerset County Area Key: A Guide to Genealogical Records	.....	6.00	(552)

SULLIVAN COUNTY

Sullivan & Wyoming Counties Area Key: A Guide to Genealogical Records	.....	6.00	(552)

SUSQUEHANNA COUNTY

Susquehanna & Lackawanna Area Key: A Guide to Genealogical Records	.....	6.00	(552)
Centennial History of Susquehanna County, by Stocker	25.00	.....	(130)

TIOGA COUNTY

Potter & Tioga Area Key: A Guide to Genealogical Records	.....	6.00	(552)

UNION COUNTY

Snyder & Union Area Key: A Guide to Genealogical Records	.....	6.00	(552)

VENANGO COUNTY

Mercer & Venango Area Key: A Guide to Genealogical Records	.....	6.00	(552)

WARREN COUNTY

Warren County Area Key: A Guide to Genealogical Records	.....	6.00	(552)

WASHINGTON COUNTY

Washington County Area Key: A Guide to Genealogical Records	.....	6.00	(552)
History of Washington County, by Crumrine (repr.)	22.00	.....	(1028)
History of Cross Creek Graveyard & Cemetery, by Simpson et al	6.00	.....	(588)

History of Mt. Prospect Graveyard & Cemetery, Washington
    County, Pa., by White & Caldwell   5.00   ..... (588)
The History of the Cross Creek Presbyterian Church, by White   6.00   ..... (588)
Ohio Valley Genealogies, by Hanna   8.00   ..... (130)

WAYNE COUNTY

Pike & Wayne Counties Area Key: A Guide to Genealogical Records 6.00   (552)

WESTMORELAND COUNTY

Westmoreland County Area Key: A Guide to Genealogical Records 6.00   (552)
Tax Lists, 1786-1810, by Dumont 4.25   (616)
St. James Lutheran Church of Unity Township, by Huffman
    [Births & baptisms 1820-1832, 1864-1950; Deaths 1836-1974] 15.00   (499)
Ohio Valley Genealogies, by Hanna   8.00   ..... (130)

WYOMING COUNTY

Sullivan & Wyoming Area Key: A Guide to Genealogical Records 6.00   (552)
Index to the 1850 Census of Luzerne & Wyoming Cos., by Bentley 10.00   (130)

YORK COUNTY

York County Area Key: A Guide to Genealogical Records 6.00   (552)
The Beginnings of the German Element in York County, by Wentz .....-   10.50   (1144)

Rhode Island

STATEWIDE REFERENCES

History of the State of Rhode Island and Providence Plantations,
    by Arnold. 2 vols. Each: $20.00   Set: 40.00   ..... (663)

Research aids

    Rhode Island: A Student's Guide to Localized History 1.50   (762)
    Index of Rhode Island History, v.1-5, 1942-1946, by R.I. Hist.
        Soc. [Index to anything genealogical in this quarterly] 1.50   (478)
    Index of Rhode Island History, v.6-15, 1947-1956, by R.I. Hist.
        Soc. [Index to anything genealogical] 3.50   (478)

Records

    Records of the Colony of Rhode Island & Providence Planta-
        tions, by Bartlett. 10 vols. Each: $32.50   Set: 320.00   ..... (630)
    Rhode Island Colonial Records, by Farnham [Genealogical
        sources in Rhode Island explained] 1.00   (478)
    Harris Papers (Collections of R.I. Hist. Soc., v.10) ed. by
        Brigham [Documents relating to career of Wm. Harris, a
        founder of R.I., & life-long antagonist of Roger Williams.]   10.50   ..... (478)
    Rhode Island Land Evidences, v. 1, 1648-1696, by R.I. Hist.
        Soc. [Abstracts of oldest book of land evidences]   5.50   ..... (478)
    Peirces's Colonial Lists: Civil, Military, and Professional
        Lists of Plymouth & Rhode Island Colonies, 1621-1700   8.50   ..... (130)
    Census of the Inhabitants of the Colony of Rhode Island and
        Providence Plantations Taken by Order of the General
        Assembly in the Year 1774, by R.I. Gen. Ass.   16.00   ..... (130)
    1790 Federal Census, by U.S. Census Bureau (repr.)   7.50   ..... (663)
    1790 Federal Census, by U.S. Census Bureau (repr.)   8.50   ..... (130)
    Index to the 1800 Census of Rhode Island, by Volkel   6.00   10.00   (752)
    Civil & Military List of Rhode Island, 1647-1850. 3v.
        Vol. 1 - Civil to 1800; Vol. 2 - Civil -1800 to 1850 &
        Military 1776-1850; Vol. 3 - Index to 1 & 2.   Set: 122.00   ..... (630)

Military

A Rhode Islander Reports on King Philip's War, by Harris
[2nd Wm. Harris letter, 1676 - major source on the war]   8.25   .....   (478)
Spirit of '76 in Rhode Island, by Cowell   16.00   .....   (130)

Religious and ethnic groups

The Times of Stephen Mumford, by McGeachy [Brief descrip-
tion of religious persecution in Eng., and his move to R.I.] 50   (397)
Memoir Concerning the French Settlements and French Settlers
in the Colony of Rhode Island, by Potter   8.50   .....   (130)

Miscellaneous

The Genealogical Dictionary of Rhode Island; Comprising Three
Generations of Settlers Who Came Before 1690, by Austin   50.00   .....   (130)
Counterfeiting in Colonial Rhode Island, by Scott [Many indi-
viduals mentioned, based chiefly on unpublished records]   4.25   .....   (478)
American Paintings in the Rhode Island Historical Society, by
Goodyear   15.50   .....   (478)

PROVIDENCE COUNTY

Map of the Town of Providence, From Actual Survey, 1823, by
Anthony (repr.) [23 1/2 x 34 1/2] 4.00   (478)
Early Records of the Town of Providence, v. 21 [1661-1712/3]   3.50   .....   (478)
Index to the Early Records of the Town of Providence, Vols. 1-21   .....   3.50   (478)
The Private Journal of Abraham Joseph Warner, by Enderton
[Epis. Priest. Was in Providence & Newport in 1850, com-
ments on those he met.]   11.00   .....   (83)
Ethnic Survey of Woonsocket, by Wessel (repr. of 1931 ed.)   12.50   .....   (629)

WASHINGTON COUNTY

South County Studies: Of Some 18th Century Persons, Places, &
Conditions, in That Portion of R.I. Called Narragansett, by
Carpenter   12.00   .....   (636)
Block Island Cemetery Records, by Mansfield 4.50   (478)

South Carolina

STATEWIDE REFERENCES

The South Carolina Magazine of Ancestral Research, ed. by
Wells [Covers all regions of the state. Emphasis on pri-
mary sources, by some compiled genealogies, book reviews,
and queries] 56pp/issue. 8 1/2 x 11. Subscription/yr: 10.00   (477)
History of South Carolina, From Its First Settlement in 1670 to
the Year 1808, by Ramsay. 2 vols. Each: $12.50   Set: 25.00   .....   (663)
Colonial South Carolina: A Political History, 1663-1763, by
Sirmans   10.95   .....   (650)
Colonial and Revolutionary History of Upper S.C., by Landrum   12.50   .....   (663)
The History of South Carolina Under the Proprietary Government,
1670-1719, by McCrady (repr. of 1897 ed.)   17.50   .....   (988)
The History of South Carolina Under the Royal Government,
1719-1776, by McCrady (repr. of 1899 ed.)   20.00   .....   (988)
The History of South Carolina in the Revolution, 1775-1780, by
McCrady, (repr. of 1901 ed.)   20.00   .....   (988)
The History of South Carolina in the Revolution, 1780-1783, by
McCrady, (repr. of 1902 ed.)   17.50   .....   (988)

Men of the Time, Sketches of Living Notables, by Garlinton (1902)	18.00	.....	(663)
Cyclopedia of Eminent and Representative Men of the Carolinas of the Nineteenth Century, Intr. by McCrady. Vol. 1	24.00	.....	(663)
The Letterbook of Eliza Lucas Pinckney, by Pinckney	9.95	.....	(650)
Royal South Carolina, 1719-1763, by Bargar	.....	1.95	(877)
South Carolina Colonial Land Policies, by Ackerman	.....	.....	(877)
The Last Foray: The South Carolina Planters of 1860: A Sociological Study, by Davidson [S.C. families with 100 + slaves]	14.95	.....	(877)
Travels to North & South Carolina, Georgia, East & West Florida, by Bartram (repr. of 1792 ed.)	.....	.....	(995)
Narratives of Early Carolina, 1640-1708, by Salley (repr. 1911)	6.50	.....	(643)
The First Settlers of South Carolina, 1670-1680, by Baldwin	.....	1.95	(877)
History of the Old Cheraws. With Notieces of Families and Sketches of Individuals, by Gregg	16.50	.....	(130)
South Carolina Memorials, by Esker	12.50	.....	(580)
Traditions and Reminiscences Chiefly of the American Revolution in the South: Including Biographical Sketches . . . Particularly of Residents of the Upper Country, by Johnson	21.00	.....	(663)

Research aids

Research Materials in South Carolina, by Moore	7.95	.....	(877)
Tracing Family Trees in Eleven States [S.C. is included]	.....	5.50	(29)
Palmetto Place Names, Federal Writers's Project [History of Place Names in South Carolina]	10.50	.....	(663)
Books & Articles on S.C.: A List for Laymen, by Jones (1970)	.....	1.95	(877)
Historical Collections of South Carolina: Embracing Many Rare & Valuable Pamphlets, by Bartholomew (repr. 1836) 2v. Set:	60.00	.....	(630)

Records

The Journal of the Commons House of Assembly, by Easterby 10 vols. Each:	47.50	.....	(877)
Records of the Secretary of the Province & Register of the Province of South Carolina, 1671-1675, by Salley	.....	2.25	(877)
Warrants for Lands in S.C., by Salley (repr. of 1910-15 ed.)	25.00	.....	(877)
Journals of the Commissioners of the Indian Trade, September 20, 1710 to August 29, 1718, by McDowell	47.50	.....	(877)
Journals of the Privy Council, 1783-1789, by Edwards (1972)	47.50	.....	(877)
Biographical Directory of the South Carolina House of Representatives, Vol. 1, Session Lists 1692-1973, by Edgar	25.00	.....	(877)
Abstracts of Wills of the State of S.C. 1670-1740, by Moore	25.00	.....	(421)
Abstracts of Wills of the State of S.C. 1740-1760, by Moore	25.00	.....	(421)
Abstracts of Wills of the State of S.C. 1760-1784, by Moore	25.00	.....	(421)
Abstracts of Wills of Charleston District 1783-1800 - And Other Wills Recorded in the District, by Moore	25.00	.....	(421)
Indexes to the County Wills of South Carolina, by Houston	12.00	.....	(130)
Marriage Notices in the South Carolina Gazette and Its Successors, 1732-1801, by Salley	8.50	.....	(130)
A Compilation of the Original Lists of Protestant Immigrants to South Carolina 1763-1773, by Revill	8.00	.....	(130)
North and South Carolina Marriage Records From the Earliest Colonial Days to the Civil War, by Clemens	8.50	.....	(130)
South Carolina Cemeteries (in Gen. Ref. Build., v.3 #5) 7pp.	.....	.....	(931)
1790 Federal Census, by U.S. Census Bureau (repr.)	10.00	.....	(663)
1790 Federal Census, by U.S. Census Bureau (repr.)	11.50	.....	(130)
1800 Federal Census, by Accelerated Indexing Systems	21.00	.....	(677)
Index to 1830 Federal Census, by Hazlewood et al	.....	60.00	(376)
Statutes at Large of S.C. (repr. 1836-41) 12v. Each:$54 Set:	648.00	.....	(630)

Military

Colonial Forts in South Carolina, by Ivers	.....	1.95	(877)
Documentary History of the American Revolution, by Gibbes 3v., Vol. 1, 1764-76; Vol. 2, 1777-80; Vol. 3, 1781-82 Each:	12.50	.....	(663)
King's Mountain and Its Heroes, by Draper	15.00	.....	(663)
Anecdotes of the Revolutionary War in American, With Sketches of Character of Persons . . . in the Southern States, For Civil and Military Services, by Garden	15.00	.....	(663)
South Carolinians in the Revolution, by Ervin	11.00	.....	(130)
Copy of the Original Index Book Showing the Revolutionary Claims in South Carolina, 1783-1786, by Revill	12.50	.....	(130)
Stub Entries to Indents Issued in Payment of Claims Against S.C., Vol. L-N; Vol. O-Q; Vol. R-T; Vol. U-W Each:	7.95	2.95	(877)
History of Kerswhaw's Brigade, by Dickert [Roster and campaigns of South Carolina's best-known brigade]	20.00	.....	(848)
Company K, 14th S.C. Volunteers, by Tompkins & Tompkins	8.50	6.00	(546)

Religious and ethnic groups

History of the Huguenots of South Carolina, by DuBose & Porcher [Sketches of Craven Co., St. Stephen's Parish, St. John's Berkeley Parish, list of Huguenots, etc.] (repr. 1887)	10.00	.....	(41)
The Annals and Parish Register of St. Thomas and St. Denis Parish, in South Carolina, From 1680 to 1884, by Clute	.....	5.00	(130)
Minutes of the Vestry of St. Helena's Parish, South Carolina 1726-1812, by Salley (repr. 1958 ed.)	9.95	.....	(877)
Scotch-Irish Migration to South Carolina, 1772, by Stephenson [Rev. William Martin and five shiploads of settlers (identifying 468 by name) giving their grants which show where they settled, plus any deeds, wills, etc. which show descendants]	6.75	.....	(15)
The History of Methodism in South Carolina, by Shipp	21.00	.....	(663)
Catholicity in the Carolinas and Georgia, by O'Connell	21.00	.....	(663)
The Jews of S.C., From Earliest Times to Present, by Elzas	15.00	.....	(663)
History of the German Settlements and of the Lutheran Church in North and South Carolina, by Bernheim	18.00	.....	(663)
South Carolina Baptists, 1670-1805, by Townsend	15.00	.....	(130)
A Contribution to the History of the Huguenots in S.C.	.....	.....	(907)

ABBEVILLE COUNTY

Two 1787 Tax Lists from 96 District, by Holcomb	.....	7.50	(701)
1800 Federal Census - Indexed, by Phillips	.....	3.50	(698)
Index to 1830 Federal Census, by Hazlewood	.....	5.00	(376)

ANDERSON COUNTY

History of Old Pendleton District with a Genealogy of Its Leading Citizens, by Simpson (repr. of 1913 ed.)	.....	10.00	(373)
Revised Index to Simpson's History of Old Pendleton Dist. (above)	.....	2.25	(114)
Pendlton Historic District, by Badders (1973) [Directory and pictures of structures and families in Town of Pendleton]	.....	5.00	(373)
The Old Stone Church, by Brackett [History, with updated burial list, of pioneer church in Old Pendleton District]	10.00	.....	(373)
Index to 1830 Federal Census, by Hazlewood	.....	5.00	(376)

BARNWELL COUNTY

Index to 1830 Federal Census, by Hazlewood	.....	4.25	(376)

BEAUFORT COUNTY

Index to 1830 Federal Census, by Hazlewood	.....	3.00	(376)

BERKLEY COUNTY

Register of St. Philip's Parish, Charles Town, or Charleston, 1720-1758, by Salley	25.00	.....	(877)
Register of St. Philip's Parish, Charles Town, or Charleston, 1754-1810, by Smith & Salley	25.00	.....	(877)
Death Notices in the South Carolina Gazette, 1732-1775, by Salley	.....	2.25	(877)
"Liste des Francois et Suisses" From an Old Manuscript List of French and Swiss Protestants Settled in Charleston . . . Probably About 1695-6, by Ravenel	6.50	.....	(130)
The Siege of Charleston - 1780, by Hough	12.00	.....	(663)
Marriages Notices in Charleston Courier, 1803-1808, by Salley	.....	2.25	(877)
The Letterbook of Robert Pringle (1732-1745) 2vols. Set:	47.50	.....	(877)
Letters of Eliza Wilkinson During the Invasion & Possession of Charleston, S.C. by the British in the Revolutionary War, ed. by Gilman & Decker (repr. of 1839 ed.)	4.50	.....	(629)
Charleston Business on the Eve of the Am. Revolution, by Sellers	10.00	.....	(629)
Abstracts of Wills of Charleston District, 1783-1800, by Moore	25.00	.....	(421)
Index to Wills of Charleston County, 1671-1868, by Charleston Lib.	15.00	.....	(130)
Index to 1830 Federal Census, by Hazlewood	.....	12.00	(376)

CHEROKEE COUNTY

History of Grindal Shoals and Some Early Adjacent Families, by Bailey (repr. of 1927 ed.)	8.50	6.00	(546)

CHESTER COUNTY

Index to 1830 Federal Census, by Hazlewood	.....	4.00	(376)

CHESTERFIELD COUNTY

Index to 1830 Federal Census, by Hazlewood	.....	2.50	(376)

COLLETON COUNTY

Scotch-Irish Migration to South Carolina, 1772, by Stephenson [Rev. Wm. Martin and 468 known immigrants, giving known data on each. Some received grants in Colleton County.]	6.75	.....	(15)
Index to 1830 Federal Census, by Hazlewood	.....	2.75	(376)

CRAVEN COUNTY

Scotch-Irish Migration to South Carolina, 1772, by Stephenson [Rev. Wm. Martin and 468 known immigrants, giving known data on each. Many received grants in Old Craven County.]	6.75	.....	(15)
History of the Huguenots of South Carolina, by DuBose & Porcher	10.00	.....	(41)

DARLINGTON COUNTY

1800 Federal Census, by Ham	.....	3.00	(530)
Index to 1830 Federal Census, by Hazlewood	.....	3.00	(376)

EDGEFIELD COUNTY

Two 1787 Tax Lists from 96 District, by Holcomb	.....	7.50	(701)
Index to 1830 Federal Census, by Hazlewood	.....	5.00	(376)

FAIRFIELD COUNTY

Index to 1830 Federal Census, by Hazlewood	.....	4.00	(376)

GEORGETOWN COUNTY

History of Georgetown County, South Carolina, by Rogers	19.50	.....	(877)
Index to 1830 Federal Census, by Hazlewood	.....	2.00	(376)

....

GREENVILLE COUNTY

1800 Federal Census - Indexed, by Phillips	.....	3.50	(698)
Index to 1830 Federal Census, by Hazlewood	.....	4.50	(376)

GREENWOOD COUNTY

Greenwood County Sketches: Old Roads and Early Families, by Watson [Informal history, genealogical data on 133 families who settled in the area before 1850 - Indexed.]	.....	12.50	(119)
Tombstone Inscriptions from Family Graveyards in Greenwood County [101 family & 6 church cem., maps, index.]	.....	3.95	(119)

HORRY COUNTY

Index to 1830 Federal Census, by Hazlewood	.....	2.00	(376)

KERSHAW COUNTY

Index to 1830 Federal Census, by Hazlewood	.....	2.50	(376)

LANCASTER COUNTY

Index to 1830 Federal Census, by Hazlewood	.....	2.50	(376)

LAURENS COUNTY

A Laurens County Sketch Book, by Foy	13.00	.....	(908)
Index to 1830 Federal Census, by Hazlewood	.....	5.00	(376)

LEXINGTON COUNTY

1800 Federal Census, by Holcomb	.....	4.00	(701)
Index to 1830 Federal Census, by Hazlewood	.....	2.50	(376)

MARION COUNTY

Index to 1830 Federal Census, by Hazlewood	.....	3.00	(376)

MARLBORO COUNTY

Index to 1830 Federal Census, by Hazlewood	.....	2.00	(376)
A History of Marlboro County, With Traditions and Sketches of Numerous Families, by Thomas	12.50	.....	(130)

NEWBERRY COUNTY

The History of Newberry County, by Pope. Vol. 1, 1749-1860	19.50	.....	(877)
The Annals of Newberry, by O'Neall & Chapman	21.00	.....	(130)
1800 Federal Census - Indexed, by Phillips	.....	3.50	(698)
Index to 1830 Federal Census, by Hazlewood	.....	4.00	(376)

OCONEE COUNTY

History of Old Pendleton District with a Genealogy of Its Leading Citizens, by Simpson	.....	10.00	(373)
Revised Index to Simpson's Hist. of Old Pendleton Dist. (above)	.....	2.25	(114)
The Old Stone Church, by Brackett [History, updated burial list.]	10.00	.....	(373)
Historic Oconee In South Carolina, by Doyle	.....	1.50	(373)

OLD CHERAWS DISTRICT

History of the Old Cheraws, by Gregg [Included present counties of Chesterfield, Darlington, Florence, Georgetown, Horry, Marion, Marlboro, & Williamsburg.]	15.00	.....	(663)

ORANGEBURG COUNTY

The History of Orangeburg County, South Carolina, From Its Settlement to the Close of the Revolutionary War, by Salley	15.00	.....	(130)
Index to 1830 Federal Census, by Hazlewood	.....	3.25	(376)
Index to 1850 Federal Census, by Bronson	.....	8.40	(540)

PENDLETON DISTRICT

Pendleton Legacy: An Illustrated History of the District, by Klosky	12.50	.....	(1025)
History of Old Pendleton District with a Genealogy of Its Leading Citizens, by Simpson	.....	10.00	(373)
Revised Index to Simpson's Hist. of Old Pendleton Dist. (above)	.....	2.25	(114)
1800 Census of Pendleton District, by Stewart [Annotations identify individuals and families and trace their migrations from Va. & N.C. - included Anderson, Pickens, & Oconee Counties.]	.....	8.00	(616)
The Diary of Clarissa Adger Bowen, Ashtabula Plantation, 1865, With Excerpts from Other Family Diaries and Comments by her Granddaughter, Clarissa Walton Taylor, and Many Other Accounts of the Pendleton-Clemson Area, S.C. 1776-1889, compiled by Stevenson [Contains genealogical information about the family of James Adger (1777-1858), especially his dau., Clarissa, with portraits. Also maps and much regional history.]	.....	7.50	(420)
The Old Stone Church, by Brackett [History, with updated burial list, of pioneer church in old Pendleton District.]	10.00	.....	(373)

PICKENS COUNTY

Index to 1830 Federal Census, by Smith	.....	4.50	(376)
Index to 1850 Federal Census, by Bronson	.....	12.40	(540)

RICHLAND COUNTY

A History of Richland County, Vol. 1, 1732-1805. by Green	17.50	.....	(130)
Columbia, 1786-1936: Capital City of S.C., by Hennig	6.50	.....	(893)
Index to 1830 Federal Census, by Hazlewood	.....	2.50	(376)

SPARTANBURG COUNTY

History of Spartanburg County, by Landrum	15.00	.....	(663)
Index to 1830 Federal Census, by Hazlewood	.....	6.00	(376)

SUMTER COUNTY

Index to 1830 Federal Census, by Hazlewood	.....	4.00	(376)

UNION COUNTY

1800 Federal Census - Indexed, by Phillips	.....	x	(698)
Index to 1830 Federal Census, by Hazlewood	.....	4.25	(376)

WILLIAMSBURG COUNTY

Index to 1830 Federal Census, by Hazlewood	.....	2.00	(376)

YORK COUNTY

A City Without Cobwebs: A History of Rock Hill, South Carolina, by Brown	15.00	.....	(663)
Index to 1830 Federal Census, by Hazlewood	.....	4.50	(376)

South Dakota

STATEWIDE REFERENCES

The Northland Newsletter [Quarterly of the Range Genealogical Society. Contains all kinds of records: marriage, cemetery, tax rolls, plat books, etc. for Dakota Territory] Subscription:	.....	4.00/yr	(977)
South Dakota: A Student's Guide to Localized History	.....	1.50	(762)
History of Dakota Territory, by Kingsbury. Ed. by Smith. 5vols.			
Vol. 1	12.50	10.00	(546)
Vol. 2, 3, 4, & 5 [Vol. 4 & 5 contain biog. sketches] Each:	47.50	45.00	(546)

South Dakota Historical Collections, Vol. 1 (repr. of 1902 ed.)
[History of North & South Dakota, by Blackburn; Radisson &
Grossiliers' Travels in the West, & other material.]   8.00 ..... (1004)

CLAY COUNTY

South Dakota Historical Collections, Vol. 13 [Contains Pioneers
of Dakota; Our First Family; & The Early Hist. of Clay Co.]   5.00 ..... (1004)

LYMAN COUNTY

Early Settlers in Lyman County, by Lyman Co. Hist. Soc. (1974)
[Histories of towns, churches, schools, and life stories of
pioneers and homesteaders from 1900 through 1930's.]   14.00 ..... (571)

Tennessee

STATEWIDE REFERENCES

The Civil and Political History of the State of Tennessee: From Its Earliest Settlement Up to the Year 1796; Including the Boundaries of the State, by Haywood (repr. of 1823 ed.) [Eye-witness accts. of Indian wars, the State of Franklin, etc.]	20.00	.....	(629)
The Rear-Guard of the Revolution, by Gilmore [An acct. of the earliest settlers of Tennessee]	15.00	.....	(663)
Western North Carolina: A History From 1730-1913, by Arthur	27.00	.....	(663)
History of Middle Tennessee: Or, Life & Times of General James Robertson, by Putnam (repr. of 1859 ed.)	28.00	.....	(629)
Surname Index to over 5,000 Biographical Sketches in Goodspeed's Histories of Eastern, Middle, & Western Tennessee (1887)	.....	14.00	(324)
Surname Index to over 1,900 Biographical Sketches in Goodspeed's History of Western Tennessee, by Presley	.....	6.00	(324)
Surname Index to over 1,300 Biographical Sketches in Goodspeed's History of Eastern Tennessee, by Presley	.....	4.00	(324)
Surname Index to over 2,600 Biographical Sketches in Goodspeed's History of Middle Tennessee, by Presley	.....	6.00	(324)
Seedtime on the Cumberland, by Arnow (1960)	8.95	.....	(734)
Flowering of the Cumberland, by Arnow (1963)	6.95	.....	(734)
Tennessee Cousins: A History of Tennessee People, by Ray	20.00	.....	(130)

Research aids

Tracing Family Trees in Eleven States [Tennessee is one.]	.....	5.50	(29)
Sources For Genealogical Searching in Tennessee, by McCay	.....	2.25	(417)
Historical Records Survey: Check List of Tennessee Imprints, 1793-1840	.....	18.00	(752)
Tennessee County Records in Print: A Bibliography (in The Ridge Runners, v. 3, #3) 7pp.	.....	2.00	(670)
Tennessee: A Student's Guide to Localized History [#1002-4]	.....	1.50	(762)
Introduction to the Resources of Tennessee, by Killebrew	36.00	.....	(663)
Records Relating to Tennessee in the N. C. State Archives, by Coker [Describes early records; map] 8pp.	.....	.25	(659)
Tennessee Gazetteer, by Morris (repr.)	20.00	.....	(880)
Tennessee History: A Bibliography, by Smith (1974)	17.50	.....	(873)

Records

The Territorial Papers of the United States, by U.S. Govt.			
Vol. 4: The Territory South of the River Ohio, 1790-1796	57.50	.....	(630)
Vol. 4: (as above) Microfilm Series M721, Reel #3	Microfilm: 12.00		(402)

North Carolina Land Grants in Tennessee 1778-1791, by
    Gardiner & Cartwright [Substitute for 1790 Census]   15.00 ..... (30)
The Blount Journal, 1790-1796 [Wm. Blount was the Territorial
    Gov. for the Territory South of the River Ohio.]   6.95 ..... (873)
Index to the Blount Journal, 1790-1796 [Included with above] 2.50 (873)
Tennessee Records: Bible & Marriage Bonds, by Ackley et al 16.50 ..... (130)
The Annals of Tennessee, by Ramsey (repr.) [Includes a new
    analytical index, annotations, and biog. sketch of author.] 25.00 ..... (243)
Tennessee Records, Tombstone Inscriptions, & Manuscripts,
    Historical & Biographical, by Acklen   14.00 ..... (130)

Military

Twenty-four Hundred Tennessee Pensioners: Revolution &
    War of 1812, by Armstrong 6.50 (130)
King's Mountain and Its Heroes, by Draper 15.00 ..... (663)
The Campaigns of Lt. Gen. Forrest and of Forrest's Cavalry,
    by Jordan & Pryor [Roster of officers & campaigns of men.] 20.00 ..... (848)
The Loyal Mountaineers of Tennessee, by Humes [An account
    of the Tennessee Unionists during the Civil War.] 18.00 ..... (663)
The Military Annals of Tennessee - Confederate, by Lindsley
    [Regimental histories & memorial rolls.] 30.00 ..... (663)
Tennesseans in the Civil War: A Military History of Confeder-
    ate and Union Units with Available Rosters of Personnel,
    Vol. 1 - Military History; Vol. 2 - Rosters   Each: 15.00 ..... (873)

Religious and ethnic groups

A People Called Cumberland Presbyterians 10.00 ..... (635)
History of Luthern Church in Virginia & Tennessee 3.50 ..... (717)

BEDFORD COUNTY

Bedford County Historical Society Quarterly, Subscription per yr: 6.00 (528)
The Minutes of the William Frierson Bivowac No. 8, Shelbyville
    [1888 to 1912 Confederate Veterans Organization.] 10.00 ..... (528)
Doors to the Past [Pictures of 80 pre-1900 Bedford Co. homes.] 2.25 (528)
Old Times in Bedford County, by Hutson (repr.) 1.25 (528)
Old City Cemetery Records, Shelbyville, 1812-1973 ..... 1.25 (528)

BLOUNT COUNTY

Free Taxable Inhabitants, 1805 (in Watauga Assoc. Bull., v.2,#1) 5.00 (617)
County Court of Pleas & Quarter Sessions Index - 1795-1818 ..... 12.80 (851)

BRADLEY COUNTY

Historical Cemetery Records of Bradley County, by Ross [Read-
    ing of ALL cemeteries - Indexed.] 18.00 ..... (833)

CARTER COUNTY

1799 Tax Lists (in Watauga Assoc. BULLETIN, v. 1, #2) 5.00 (617)

COFFEE COUNTY

1850 Federal Census, by Porch 8.50 (884)
Marriage Books A & C, 1853-1870, by Potter 8.25 (100)

CUMBERLAND COUNTY

Cumberland County's First Hundred Years, by Bullard & Krechniak
    [Comprehensive history, including 45 family tree designs of
    families in the county in 1856.] 6.70 (683)

DAVIDSON COUNTY

Donelson, Tennessee: Its History and Landmarks, by Aiken
  [Early history of Donelson (Nashville); early families, Col.
  John Donelson, etc. Photos, maps, index, bibliography.]   15.00   .....   (392)
The Advance-Guard of Western Civilization, by Gilmore [An
  acct. of the earliest settlers in the Nashville area.]   15.00   .....   (663)
1850 Federal Census of Davidson County (except Nashville) 15.00   (688)
1850 Federal Census of City of Nashville, by Porch 7.50   (688)

DICKSON COUNTY

1820 Federal Census - Indexed, by Rowe 2.00   (324)

FAYETTE COUNTY

Cemetery Records , by Morton [Inscriptions from 90 cemeteries.] 10.00   (582)

FENTRESS COUNTY

History of Fentress County, by Hogue   10.00   .....   (130)

FRANKLIN COUNTY

1820 Federal Census - Indexed, by Presley 2.50   (324)

GILES COUNTY

1820 Federal Census - Indexed, by Presley 2.00   (324)

GRAINGER COUNTY

List of Insolvents Living Within the Indian Boundary, 1797 (in
  Watauga Assoc. BULLETIN, v.1, #2) 5.00   (617)

GREENE COUNTY

Marriage Records, Vol. 1, 1783-1818, by Soderberg 15.00   (235)
Marriage Records, Vol. 2, 1819-1838, by Soderberg
  [Publication date, 1975-6.]   ....   (235)
Marriages, 1821-1824 (in The Ridge Runners, v. 3, #3) 8pp. 2.00   (670)
Court Minutes, 1783-1796 (in Wautaga Assoc. Bull., v. 2, #1 & 2) 10.00   (617)

HARDEMAN COUNTY

Cemetery Records, Vol. V (excluding Grand Junction Cemetery &
  Hopewill in Miss.), by Owens, Boyd, & Davidson 6.35   (779)

HAWKINS COUNTY

New Providence Presbyterian Church Cemetery Inscriptions; Rey-
  nolds Graveyard; Naturalizations (in Watauga Bull., v. 2, #2) 5.00   (617)
Will Book I (A-K); Richardson's Creek & Hickory Cove Baptist
  Churches (in Watauga Assoc. BULLETIN, v. 1, #2) 5.00   (617)
Will Book I (L-M) (in Watauga Assoc. BULLETIN, v. 2, #1) 5.00   (617)
Newspaper Abstracts (in The Ridge Run., v.2, #3 & 4) 2 + 3pp Both: 4.00   (670)

KNOX COUNTY

The French Broad - Holston Country: A History of Knox County,
  by Rothrock   20.00   .....   (243)
Knoxville's First Graveyard, 1800-1879 [Inscriptions from the
  First Presbyertian Church Cemetery.] 3.00   (243)
Oldest Methodist Cem. in Knoxville (in BULLETIN, v. 2, #2) 5.00   (617)
Occupation of East Tennessee & the Defense of Knoxville, by Poe
  [Civil War in East Tennessee.] 2.00   (243)

LAWRENCE COUNTY

1820 Federal Census - Indexed, by Presley 1.50   (324)

McMINN COUNTY

Newspaper Abstracts (in The Ridge Runners, v.3, #3) 5pp. 2.00 (670)

MAURY COUNTY

1820 Federal Census - Indexed, by Presley 2.50 (324)

MONTGOMERY COUNTY

Along the Warioto, A History of Montgomery County, by Beach
   [History from geologic times to present, economic, social, etc.] 10.00 ..... (710)
Picturesque Clarksville, Past & Present, by Titus (repr. 1887) 15.00 .....or { 503
   [Hist. from 1770's to 1887; includes biog. sketches.]   { 710
A Commenorative History of First Christian Church, Clarksville,
   Tennessee: 1842-1972, by Beach 2.50 (710)
Note: The following are all articles which appeared in The Mont-
   gomery County Genealogical Journal. Price per issue: 1.50 (503)
     McAdow Cumberland Presby. Ch. Register-Apr. 1853, v.3, #2 ..... 1.50 (503)
     Index to Confederate Pension Applications [from Montgomery
      County], v.2, #4; v. 3, #1. 3pp. each. 1.50 (503)
     History of New Providence, v. 2, #2. 5pp. 1.50 (503)
     Soldiers From Montgomery County in the Revolutionary and
      War of 1812 [continuing article with 2 or more in each.] 1.50 (503)
     Bethlehem Methodist Ch. Register-(c1880-1900), v.1, #2 & 3 ..... 3.00 (503)
     Index to Deed Book A (1788-1796) (v.1, #4 thru v.2, #3) Each: 1.50 (503)
     1850 Mortality Schedule (v.1, extra) 3pp. 1.50 (503)
     1860 Mortality Schedule (v.1, #4) 4pp. 1.50 (503)
     1880 Mortality Schedule (v. 2, #1 & 3) 5pp. + 1pp. Each: 1.50 (503)
     Marriage Book 1 [continuing article - 3 to 4 pp /issue] 1.50 (503)
     Burials in Riverview Cemetery [continuing article] 1.50 (503)
     Minute Book 1 [continuing article - average 4pp/issue] 1.50 (503)
     Early Marriages [fragmentary, ones not bound in books]
      (v.1, #1; v.4, #1) 4 + 2 pp. Each: 1.50 (503)
     Liberty Cumberland Presbyterian Church Roll, 1841 (v.1,#1) 1.50 (503)
1798 Personal Property Tax List & 1820 Federal Census 10.00 (503)
1850 Federal Census, by Alley & Beach 10.00 (503)

PERRY COUNTY

1820 Federal Census, by Presley 1.00 (324)

ROBERTSON COUNTY

Cemetery Records, by Durrett 7.00 (167)
1820 Federal Census, by Presley 2.00 (324)

RUTHERFORD COUNTY

Index to 1810 Federal Census, by Presley 1.00 (324)
1820 Federal Census - Indexed, by Presley 2.00 (324)
1840 Federal Census - Indexed, by Rutherford Co. Hist. Soc. 5.25 (707)

SHELBY COUNTY

Raleigh Scrapbook, by Hunt [1838 map, photos, family sketches,
   deeds - Sesquicentennial edition, 1973] 4.00 (891)
Map Showing the Original 362 Town Losts of Memphis 1.00 (891)
Memphis Town Reserve. 1819 Plat [Some names of purchasers.] 1.00 (891)
Elmwood Cemetery [plat of lots] 1.00 (891)
Memphis in 1872, Map 17 x 22 - Includes Street Index 1.50 (891)
Marriage Bonds 1819-1850, by Tennessee Genealogical Society 10.00 (190)
1820 Federal Census, by Presley 1.00 (324)

STEWART COUNTY

Marriage Records 1838-1848 (repr. of WPA Project, new index) 4.00 (531)
Marriage Records 1849-1866 (repr. of WPA Project, new index) 5.50 (531)
Marriage Records 1865-1881 (repr. of WPA Project, new index) 5.50 (531)

SULLIVAN COUNTY

Tennessee Soldiers in the Revolution: A Roster of Soldiers Living
During the War in the Counties of Wash. & Sullivan, by Allen 5.00 (130)
First Land Owners of Sullivan County, by Vineyard [Index to gran-
tee deeds, 1780-c1820 & gen. & hist. data from deeds.] 6.50 (860)
Probate Records 1780-1784; Deed Book 1 (part); Tax Lists 1811-
1812 (in Watauga Assoc. BULLETIN, v.1 # 2; v.2, #1)   Each: 5.00 (617)
1850 Federal Census, by Watauga Association 10.00 (617)

SUMNER COUNTY

Abstracts of Will Books 1 & 2 (1779-1842), by Whitley   8.50   6.00 (546)
1820 Federal Census - Indexed, by Presley 2.50 (324)

WASHINGTON COUNTY

Watauga Association BULLETIN [Bi-annual publication of Watauga
Assoc. Primary records of old Watauga area; Queries] Sub/yr: 10.00 (617)
1814 Tax Lists (in Watauga BULLETIN, v. 2, #2) 5.00 (617)
1830 Tax Lists (in Watauga BULLETIN, v. 1, #2) 5.00 (617)
Tennessee Soldiers in the Revolution: A Roster of Soldiers Living
During the War in the Cos. of Washington & Sullivan, by Allen 5.00 (130)
Marriage Records, 1787-1840, by Grammer & Mullins 5.00 (130)
1830 Federal Census - Heads of Families only, alphabetical 2.50 (264)

WEAKLEY COUNTY

1850 Federal Census, by Porch 10.00 (688)

WHITE COUNTY

History of White County, by Seals   10.50   . . . . . (663)

WILLIAMSON COUNTY

Marriages 1800-1850, by Gardiner & Bejoch 12.50 (30)
Direct Tax List 1816, Franklin (in Gen. Ref. Build., v.5,#3) 7pp. 2.00 (931)
1820 Federal Census - Indexed, by Presley 2.50 (324)

WILSON COUNTY

Sugg's Creek Cumberland Presbyterian Church: An Early History
1800-1900, by Partlow [Names of members going back to 1802,
as well as a list of 310 persons buried in the church cemetery.] 10.00 (704)
Minutes United Confederate Veterans Camp # 941, 1897-1928, by
Partlow [Regt., rank, etc. 1100 soldiers fr. Wilson Co.] 20.00 . . . . . (704)

Texas

STATEWIDE REFERENCES

History of Texas 1673-1779, by Morfi (repr. of 1935 ed.)   25.00   . . . . . (629)
Papers Concerning Robertson's Colony in Texas, Vol. 1: 1788-1822
[Counties included are: Bastrop, Bell, Bosque, Brazos, Brown,
Burleson, Burnet, Callahan, Comanche, Coryell, Eastland,
Erath, Falls, Hamilton, Hill, Hood, Jack, Johnson, Lampasas,
Lee, Limestone, McLennan, Milam, Mills, Palo Pinto, Parker,
Robertson, Somervell, Stephens, & Williamson.] Gives Tennes-
see background of the Texas settlement.   20.00   . . . . . (671)

Sixty Years on the Brazos: The Life & Letters of Dr. John Washington Lockhart, 1824-1900, by Wallis (repr. of 1930 ed.)   20.00 ..... (629)

Frontier of Northwest Texas, 1846-1876, by Richardson   12.00 ..... (794)

The Texan Emigrant, by Texian Press Staff (repr. 1840 ed.)   6.95 ..... (745)

Early Settlers & Indian Fighters of Southwest Texas, by Sowell 2 vols. (repr. 1900 ed.)   Set: 27.50 ..... (964)

Migration into East Texas, 1835-1860: A Study From the United States Census, by Lathrop 3.50 (645)

Texas in 1840, Or the Emigrant's Guide to the New Republic: Being the Result of Observation, Enquiry and Travel in That Beautiful Country. By an Emigrant. (repr. of 1840 ed.)   13.00 ..... (629)

Texas: Observations, Historical, Geographical and Descriptive. In a Series of Letters, Written During a Visit to Austin's Colony, with a View to a Permanent Settlement in that Country, by Mary Austin Holley (cousin of Stephen F. Austin) (repr. 1833)   9.00 ..... (629)

The Austin Papers, ed. by Barker [Papers of Stephen & Moses Austin, of Austin's Colony, Bolivar, Tex.] 3v. in 4.   Set: 265.00 ..... (630)

A Digest of the Laws of Texas; to Which is Subjoined an Appendix Containing the Acts of the Congress of the U.S. on the Subjects of the Naturalization of Aliens, and the Authentication of Records, . . . , by Hartley (repr. of 1850 ed.)   87.50 ..... (630)

Research aids

Cumulative Index of the Southwestern Historical Quarterly, Vols. 1-40 (1950)   12.50 ..... (645)

Vols. 41-60 (1960)   17.50 ..... (645)

Checklist of Texas Imprints, 1846-1860, by Winkler (1949)   12.50 ..... (645)

A Guide to the Historical Manuscripts Collections in the University of Texas Library, by Kielman (1968)   25.00 ..... (640)

Records

Athanase de Mezieres and the Louisiana-Texas Frontier, 1768-1780, by Bolton [Documents from the original Spanish & French Mss., chiefly in the archives of Mexico & Spain; tr. into Eng., ed. and annotated.] 2 v. in 1 (repr. of 1914 ed.)   30.00 ..... (624)

The First Census of Texas, 1829-1836, by Day 4.25 (616)

1840 Census [Tax Lists] of the Republic of Texas, by White   15.00 ..... (514)

Republic of Texas: Poll Lists for 1846, by Mullins   15.00 ..... (130)

Military

Touched With Valor: Civil War Papers and Casualty Reports of Hood's Texas Brigade, by Robertson (repr. 1964 ed.)   12.50 10.00 (546)

Religious and ethnic groups

The Germans in Texas: A Study in Immigration, by Benjamin   12.95 ..... (668)

ANDERSON COUNTY

Early Texas Birth Records, 1838-1878, Vol. 2, by Gracy et al   7.39 ..... (201)

ATASCOSA COUNTY

Probate Records [Index of cases 1856-1939 with history of county, map, table of territorial changes, location & availability of rec.]..... 5.00 (688)

AUSTIN COUNTY

Marriage by Bond in Colonial Texas, by Smith [History of bonds & copy of records for Austin, Brazoria, & Gonzales Counties.]   15.00 ..... (533)

BASTROP COUNTY

Austin Colony Pioneers, Including History of Bastrop, Fayette,
   Grimes, Montgomery, & Washington Cos., by Ray   12.50   .....   (130)
Salt Pork to Sirloin, The History of Baylor County, by Baylor Co.
   Hist. Soc. [County hist. & early setters & others histories.]   13.50   .....   (543)

BOWIE COUNTY

WPA Index to Probate Records 1840-1939, With History of County,
   Map, Location & Availability of Records 5.00   (688)

BRAZORIA COUNTY

WPA Index to Probate Records 1836-1939, With History of County,
   Map, Location & Availability of Records 5.00   (688)
Marriage By Bond In Colonial Texas, by Smith [History of bonds &
   copy of records for Austin, Brazoria, & Gonzales Counties.]   15.00   .....   (533)

BRAZOS COUNTY

WPA Index to Probate Records 1841-1939, With History of County,
   Map, Location & Availability of Records 5.00   (688)

CAMERON COUNTY

Early Texas Birth Records, 1838-1878, Vol. 2, by Sumner et al   7.39   .....   (201)

CASS COUNTY

People of Cass County, by Bowman [History, pictures, dates, etc.]   13.00   10.00   (601)
#3 - Quarterlies of Cass County Genealogical Society, by Bowman
   & Stanley (1974) [Various genealogical data.] 7.50   (601)
Cass County, Texas, Recipes of Pioneer Women [Includes a picture
   of each woman, birth, death, parents & her favorite reciepe.] 5.00   (601)
Early Texas Birth Records, 1838-1878, Vol. 2, by Gentry et al   7.39   .....   (201)

CHEROKEE COUNTY

Early Texas Birth Records, 1838-1878, Vol. 2   7.39   .....   (201)

CHILDRESS COUNTY

They Followed the Rails: History of Childress County, by The Chil-
   dress Reporter [1000 photos of early scenes, families, indiv.]   15.00   .....   (543)

CLAY COUNTY

Peters Colonists, Their Descendents & Others (Who Settled North
   Texas), by Young. Vol. 3 [To be published in 1975]   ....   (433)
Cemeteries of Clay County, by Speakman & Speakman   27.50   .....   (525)

COLLIN COUNTY

Peters Colonists, Their Descendents & Others (Who Settled North
   Texas), by Young. Vol. 3 [To be published in 1975]   ....   (433)

COOKE COUNTY

Peters Colonists, Their Descendants & Others (Who Settled North
   Texas), by Young. Vol. 2 [Cem. lists; 1850 census Texas Cos;
   29 short family genealogies from arrival date to present; historical family pictures, Navy documents of general interest.]   12.35   9.10   (433)

DALLAS COUNTY

Peters Colonists. . ., by Young, Vol. 2 (see Cooke County)   12.35   9.10   (433)
Early Texas Birth Records, 1838-1878, Vol. 2, by Sumner et al   7.39   .....   (201)
Lisbon West of the Trinity, by Anthony [History of pioneer com-
   munity of Lisbon (now inside the Dallas city limits); including

a history of four churches, a collection of 26 pioneer family histories, & list of tombstone inscriptions from Lisbon Cemetery.] 6.95 ..... (137)
Pleasant Mound Cemetery, East Dallas Texas, by Mesquite Gen. Soc..... 5.00 (572)

DENTON COUNTY

Marriage Register, Vol. 1, 1875-1884, by Davis 5.00 (688)
Peters Colonists, Their Descendents & Others (Who Settled North
Texas), by Young. Vol. 1 [Old cemetery lists; Confederate ser-
vice records; sample "proofs" of citizenship in Republic of Texas;
Name index for Cates' History of Wise Co.; Indian Cemetery in
Big Thicket Nat. Pk.; Land grants; Affidavit of name change.] 10.15 5.90 (433)
Marriage Register, Vol. 2, 1885-1894, by Davis 5.00 (688)

DICKENS COUNTY

History of Dickens County, Ranches and Rolling Plains, by Arring-
ton [200 families; stories of Spur, Matador, Pitchfork ranches] 13.50 ..... (543)

DONLEY COUNTY

Donley County: Land O' Promise, by Browder 15.00 ..... (543)

ELLIS COUNTY

Peters Colonists . . . , by Young. Vol. 1 (see Denton County) 10.15 5.90 (433)

FANNIN COUNTY

Peters Colonists . . . , by Young. Vol. 3 (see Clay County) .... (433)
Early Texas Birth Records, 1838-1878, Vol. 2 7.39 ..... (201)

FAYETTE COUNTY

Austin Colony Pioneers; Including History of Bastrop, Fayette,
Grimes, Montgomery & Washington Counties, by Ray 12.50 ..... (130)

FOARD COUNTY

They Loved the Land, The History of Foard County, by Phelps
[Including history of communities, churches, 263 families.] 15.00 ..... (543)

GONZALES COUNTY

Marriage by Bond in Colonial Texas, by Smith [History of bonds &
copy of records for Austin, Brazoria, & Gonzales Counties.] 15.00 ..... (533)

GRAYSON COUNTY

Peters Colonists . . . , by Young. Vol. 1 (see Denton County) 10.15 5.90 (433)

GREGG COUNTY

Early Texas Birth Records, 1838-1878, Vol. 2 7.39 ..... (201)

GRIMES COUNTY

Austin Colony Pioneers; Including History of Bastrop, Fayette,
Grimes, Montgomery & Washington Counties, by Ray 12.50 ..... (130)

GUADALUPE COUNTY

WPA Index to Probate Records 1846-1939, With History of County,
Map, Location & Availability of Records 5.00 (688)

HARDEMAN COUNTY

The Last Frontier, The History of Hardeman County, by Neal
[200 family histories, and history of the county.] 12.50 ..... (543)

HARRIS COUNTY

Houston: A Student's Guide to Localized History [#1384-8] 1.50 (762)
German Colonists & Their Descendants in Houston, by Justman 15.00 ..... (543)

••

JACK COUNTY

Peters Colonists . . . , by Young. Vol. 1 (see Denton County)	10.15	5.90	(433)

JACKSON COUNTY

1880 Federal Census, by Hazlewood	.....	7.50	(376)

JASPER COUNTY

Early Texas Birth Records, 1838–1878, Vol. 2	.....	7.39	(201)
1880 Federal Census, by Hazlewood	.....	15.00	(376)

JOHNSON COUNTY

Peters Colonists . . . , by Young. Vol. 2 (see Cooke County)	12.35	9.10	(433)

JONES COUNTY

1880 Federal Census, by Hazlewood	.....	2.00	(376)

KAUFMAN COUNTY

Early Texas Birth Records, 1838–1878, Vol. 2	7.39	.....	(201)
Marriage Records, 1848–1870, by Mesquite Genealogical Soc.	.....	5.00	(572)

KNOX COUNTY

History of St. Joseph's Parish, by Church Committee [Story of a lovely Gothic style church & ornate altar in West Texas prairie]	10.00	.....	(543)

LAMAR COUNTY

Early Texas Birth Records, 1838–1878, Vol. 2	7.39	.....	(201)

LEE COUNTY

History of Lee County, by Lee Co. Hist. Survey Comm. [Earliest period thru Reconstruction; 100 family histories; 230 photos.]	16.50	.....	(543)

LIBERTY COUNTY

WPA Index to Probate Records 1836–1939, With History of County, Map, Location & Availability of Records	.....	5.00	(688)

McLENNAN COUNTY

Marriages, Vol. 1, 1850–1870, by Central Texas Gen. Soc.	.....	4.00	(428)
Cemetery Records, 2 vols. Each:	10.00	.....	(428)

MARION COUNTY

Early Texas Birth Records, 1838–1878, Vol. 2	7.39	.....	(201)

MITCHELL COUNTY

1880 Federal Census, by Hazlewood	.....	1.00	(376)

MONTAGUE COUNTY

Peters Colonists . . . , by Young. Vol. 1 (see Denton County)	10.15	5.90	(433)

MONTGOMERY COUNTY

Austin Colony Pioneers; Including History of Bastrop, Fayette, Grimes, Montgomery & Washington Counties, by Ray	12.50	.....	(130)

MOTLEY COUNTY

Of Such As These, A History of Motley County, by Traweek [General history, family histories, hundreds of photos.]	15.00	.....	(543)

NACOGDOCHES COUNTY

1880 Federal Census - Indexed, by Hazlewood	.....	20.00	(376)

NAVARRO COUNTY

Early Texas Birth Records, 1838-1878, Vol. 2   7.39 ..... (201)

NEWTON COUNTY

WPA Index to Probate Records 1846-1939, With History of the
County, Map, Location & Availability of Records 5.00 (688)

NUECES COUNTY

The History of Nueces County, by Nueces Co. Hist. Soc.   9.50 ..... (668)
Early Texas Birth Records, 1838-1878, Vol. 2   7.39 ..... (201)

PALO PINTO COUNTY

Peters Colonists . . . , by Young. Vol. 2 (see Cooke County)   12.35   9.10 (433)

PANOLA COUNTY

Marriage Records, 1846-1890, by Phillips   8.00 ..... (698)
1860 Federal Census - Indexed, by Phillips .... (698)

PARKER COUNTY

Peters Colonists . . ., by Young. Vol. 3 (see Clay County) .... (433)

PARMER COUNTY

A History of Parmer County, by Lewis [Gen. & family histories;
complete repr. of pioneer newspaper supplement.]   16.00 ..... (543)

POTTER COUNTY

In the Cattle Country, History of Potter County, 1887-1966, by
Key [Only complete history of Amarillo & Potter County.]   9.95 ..... (543)

ROBERTSON COUNTY

Papers Concerning Robertson's Colony in Texas, Vol. 1: 1788-1822
ed. by McLean [Tenn. background of the Texas settlement.]   20.00 ..... (671)
Papers Concerning Robertson's Colony in Texas, Vol. 2: 1823-1826,
The Leftwich Grant [Available in 1975-1976.] .... (671)
WPA Index to Probate Records 1837-1939, With History of the
County, Map, Location & Availability of Records 5.00 (688)

ROCKWALL COUNTY

Marriage Records, 1876-1894, by Mesquite Gen. Soc. 7.50 (572)

RUSK COUNTY

Early Texas Birth Records, 1838-1878, Vol. 2   7.39 ..... (201)
WPA Index to Probate Records 1843-1939, With History of the
County, Map, Location & Availability of Records 5.00 (688)

SAN SABA COUNTY

WPA Index to Probate Records 1856-1939, With History of the
County, Map, Location & Availability of Records 5.00 (688)

SHELBY COUNTY

WPA Index to Probate Records 1836-1939, With History of the
County, Map, Location & Availability of Records 5.00 (688)

SOMERVELL COUNTY

Early Texas Birth Records, 1838-1878, Vol. 2   7.39 ..... (201)

STEPHENS COUNTY

Peters Colonists . . . , by Young. Vol. 2 (see Cooke County)   12.35   9.10 (433)

TARRANT COUNTY

Peters Colonists . . . , by Young. Vol. 2 (See Cooke County)   12.35   9.10 (433)

TAYLOR COUNTY

Potosi, The First One Hundred Years, by Zachry [Tells of the
    progress of the area - backed by historical research.]   5.95   ..... (434)

TRAVIS COUNTY

1860 Federal Census - All Five Schedules: Population, Slave, Mor-
    tality, Agriculture, and Products of Industry. [Indexed by sur-
    name. Includes county map, sample pages of each schedule.]   5.39   ..... (201)
Marriage Records, 1840-1882, by Price [Includes officiants.]   12.50   ..... (142)

UPSUR COUNTY

Cemeteries of Upshur County, by Hogg & Stanley [All data copied]   25.00   ..... (601)
Early Texas Birth Records, 1838-1878, Vol. 2   7.39   ..... (201)

VAN ZANT COUNTY

Every First Monday, The History of Canton, Texas, by Wren
    [The story of Canton trades days (over 100 years old).]   4.95   ..... (543)

WASHINGTON COUNTY

Austin Colony Pioneers, Including History of Bastrop, Fayette,
    Grimes, Montgomery, & Washington Counties, by Ray   12.50   ..... (130)
Early Texas Birth Records, 1838-1878, Vol. 2   7.39   ..... (201)

WEBB COUNTY

Early Texas Birth Records, 1838-1878, Vol. 2   7.39   ..... (201)

WICHITA COUNTY

History of Wichita Falls, by Morgan (repr.)   5.95   ..... (543)

WILBARGER COUNTY

An Early History of Wilbarger County, by Ross & Rouse   7.95   ..... (543)

WILLIAMSON COUNTY

WPA Index to Probate Records 1848-1939, With History of the
    County, Map, Location & Availability of Records 5.00 (688)

WISE COUNTY

Peters Colonists . . . . , by Young. Vol. 1 (See Denton County)   10.15   5.90 (433)
Wise County History, by Wise Co. Hist. Committee   15.00   ..... (543)

WOOD COUNTY

History of Mineola, by Jones   6.95   ..... (543)

YOUNG COUNTY

Peters Colonists . . . , by Young. Vol. 1 (See Denton County)   10.15   5.90 (433)

Utah

STATEWIDE REFERENCES

History of Utah, by Bancroft   7.00   ..... (1015)
Utah Black Hawk War: Lore & Reminiscences of Participants, by
    Culmsee   5.00   3.00 (696)

William Clayton's Journal: A Daily Record of the Journey of the
Original Company of Mormon Pioneers From Nauveo, Illinois
to the Valley of the Great Salt Lake, by Clayton (repr. 1921) 18.00 ..... (629)

Research aids

Handy Guide to the Genealogical Library and Church Historical
Department, by Evans & Cunningham [To help users of the
unique LDS library to utilize its services.] 2.95 (538)
Handy Index to the Holdings of the Genealogical Society of Utah,
by Brown [Tells what records are on microfilm in Salt Lake
City for each county of the United States.] 6.00 (538)
Genealogical Records of Utah, by Jaussi & Chaston [Details on
Utah church & civil records: boundary changes, courts,
indexes, bibliographies.] 5.95 ..... (241)
Register of LDS Records, by Jaussi & Chaston [Genealogical
Society call numbers for Fundamentals of Genealogical
Research and Genealogical Records of Utah. 4.95 ..... (241)
Utah: A Student's Guide to Localized History 1.50 (762)

Vermont

STATEWIDE REFERENCES

Vermont History, The Proceedings of the Vermont Historical
Society [Quarterly of the Vermont Hist. Soc. - included in
membership to Society. Historical, rather than genealogi-
cal, inscope.] Membership: $7.50/yr. Individual issues: 2.00 (564)
The Reluctant Republic: Vermont 1724-1791, by De Water 6.95 (1017)
Migration From Vermont: 1776-1860, by Stilwill (repr. 1937 ed.) 14.50 ..... (899)
Vermonters, by Kent [List of the famous sons from the towns of
Vermont with profession, dates, and data about each.] 187pp. 1.00 ..... (564)

Research aids

Vermont Imprints, by McCorison 15.00 ..... (713)

Records

Records of the Governor and Council of the State of Vermont,
pub. by authority of the State. [Maps.] 8v. Each: $37.50 Set: 300.00 ..... (630)
1790 Federal Census, by U.S. Census Bureau (repr.) 7.50 ..... (663)
1790 Federal Census, by U.S. Census Bureau (repr.) 15.00 ..... (130)

Military

Soldiers of the Revolutionary War Buried in Vt., by Crockett 5.00 (130)
A List of Pensioners of the War of 1812, by Clark 8.50 ..... (130)
Berdan's U.S. Sharpshooters in the Army of the Potomac,
1861-1865, by Stevens 15.00 ..... (848)

CALEDONIA COUNTY

People of Peacham, by Watts & Choate [A genealogical book deal-
ing with the inhabitants of Peacham from settlement to 1945.] 16.00 ..... (564)

CHITTENDEN COUNTY

Vermont Marriages, Vol. 1: Montpelier, Burlington, Berlin 8.50 ..... (130)

ORANGE COUNTY

A History of Bradford, Vermont Covering the Period From Its
Beginning in 1765 to the Middle of 1968, by Haskins .... (728)

RUTLAND COUNTY

A History of the Town of Poultney, Vermont, From Its Settlement
   to 1875, With Family & Biog. Sketches, by Joslin et al   22.50   20.00   (546)

WASHINGTON COUNTY

Green Mountain Heritage: The Chronicle of Northfield, Vermont,
   by Northfield Town History Committee   11.50   .....   (975)
Vermont Marriages, Vol. 1: Montpelier, Burlington, Berlin   8.50   .....   (130)

Virginia

STATEWIDE REFERENCES

The Virginia Genealogist, edited by Dorman [A genealogical quar-
   terly containing compiled genealogies, primary source mater-
   ial, research helps, and queries.]   Subscription per year: 10.00   (500)
The First Republic in America: An Account of the Origin of This
   Nation, Written from the Records then (1624) Concealed by the
   Council, Rather than from the Histories then Licensed by the
   Crown, by Brown (rep. of 1898 ed.)   17.50   .....   (988)
A True Discourse of the Present State of Virginia. Reprinted from
   the London Edition, 1615, with an introduction by A. L. Rowse.
   (Virginia State Library Publications, No. 3), by Hamor 3.00   (244)
The Old Dominion in the Seventeenth Century: A Documentary
   History of Virginia, 1606-1789, by Billings   12.95   4.95   (650)
History of the Colony and Ancient Dominion of Va., by Campbell   20.00   .....   (663)
Colonial Virginia: Its People and Customs, by Stanard (1917)   15.00   .....   (233)
The Virginia Plutarch: Vol. 1- The Colonial & Revolutionary Eras;
   Vol. 2 - The National Era, by Bruce (repr. of 1929 ed.) [Sketches
   of eminent Virginians forming a continuous narrative of deeds
   running from early in the Colonial age to 1920's.]   Set: 32.50   .....   (988)
Virginia and Virginians, by Brock. 2 vols.   Each: 18.00   .....   (663)
Sketches of Virginia, by Foote   12.50   .....   (731)
The History and Present State of Virginia, by Wright   8.25   .....   (650)
White Servitude in the Colony of Virginia: A Study of the System
   of Indentured Labor in the American Colonies, by Ballagh   11.75   7.75   (1000)
An Outline of the Maryland Boundary Disputes and Related Events,
   by Morrison [Outlines and relates the various boundary disputes
   including the Northern Neck Proprieatary of Lord Fairfax.] 3.00   (325)
Tour Through Part of Virginia in the Summer of 1808, by Caldwill 2.00   (725)
The Old Dominion and the New Nation, 1788-1801, by Beeman
   [Study of Republican & Federalist parties in early Virginia.] 11.00   .....   (126)
A Hornbook of Virginia History (Va. St. Lib. Pub., No. 25) 2.00   (244)
Virginia Beyond the Blue Ridge, by Gowing (1974) [A compilation -
   heavily illustrated - tying the history of the area to today's
   scenes.]   12.95   .....   (660)
Trans-Allegheny Pioneers, by Hale (3rd rev. ed., with new index)
   [Sketches of the first white settlements west of the Alleghenies;
   Battle of Point Pleasant; many pioneer families.]   15.00   7.50   (485)

Research aids

Genealogical Research in the Virginia State Library   .....   free   (244)
Tracing Family Trees in Eleven States [Virginia is included.] 5.50   (29)
Sources For Genealogical Searching in Va. & W. Va., by McCay 3.50   (417)
Virginia Local History; A Bibliography, by Hummel 1.00   (244)

Selected Bibliography of Virginia, 1607-1699, by Swem, et al 1.25 (713)
Travelers in Tidewater Virginia, 1700-1800: A Bibliography, by
    Carson 2.00 (713)
VBAPPA - Virginia Books and Pamphlets Presently Available
    [A descriptive listing of all worth while Virginia books and pam-
    phlets available in reprint or in the original edition.] 22.50 ..... (123)
Published County Records of Virginia: A Bibliography (in The
    Ridge Runners, v.3, #4) 15pp. 2.00 (670)
A Bibliography of Virginia. Part 4. (Bulletin of Va. St. Lib.,
    v. 18, #2, June 1932), by Hall 1.00 (244)
Virginia Land Office Inventory, by Gentry [Complete accounting
    of all records pertaining to land grants, land surveys, land
    patents, etc. which are in the Virginia State Library repository,
    with explanation of each type, whether they have been indexed,
    etc. An introduction by the compiler thoroughly explains the
    methods of taking up land in Virginia from the earliest period
    to the present day.] 2.00 (244)
The British Public Record Office; History, Description, Record
    Groups, Finding Aids, and Materials for American History,
    with Special Reference to Virginia (Va. St. Lib. Pub. #12) 5.00 (244)
Huntington Library Data [1607-1850], Vol. 30 of Virginia Colonial
    Abstracts, by Fleet 5.00 (130)
Index to Printed Virginia Genealogies, by Stewart 10.00 ..... (130)
Virginia Genealogies: A Trial List of Printed Books and Pam-
    phlets, by Brown 20.00 ..... (123)
A List of Places Included in 19th Century Virginia Directories,
    by Hummel (Va. St. Lib. Pub. #11) 3.00 (244)
A Gazetteer of Virginia & West Virginia, by Gannett 12.50 ..... (130)
Parish Lines, Diocese of Virginia, by Cocke (Va. St. Lib. Pub. #28) 5.00 (244)
Parish Lines, Diocese of Southern Virginia, by Cocke (Va. St.
    Lib. Pub. #22) [Maps & narrative indicating each change in
    parish boundaries from 1634-1964.]
Virginia Historical Index, by Swem (repr. of 1934 ed.) [Index to:
    Calendar of Virginia State Papers; Hening's Statutes of Virginia;
    Lower Norfolk County Virginia Antiquary; Virginia Historical
    Register; Tyler's Historical and Genealogical Quarterly; Vir-
    ginia Magazine of History and Biography; 1st & 2nd Series of
    William & Mary College Quarterly Historical Magazine] 100.00 ..... (804)

Records

Calendar of Virginia State Papers, and Other Manuscripts
    Preserved in the Capitol at Richmond, 1652-1869. 11v. Set: 420.00 ..... (624)
Statutes At Large, Being a Collection of All the Laws of Vir-
    ginia From the First Session of the Legislature in the
    Year 1619, by Hening. 13v. Set: 175.00 ..... (713)
Laws of Virginia; Being a Supplement to Hening's "The
    Statutes at Large", com. by Winfree (Va. St. Lib.) (1971)
    [Virginia laws which were forwarded to England at the time
    of their enactment-transcribed from English records.] 15.00 ..... (244)
The Statutes-at-Large of Virginia, From October Session 1792,
    to December Session 1806 [i.e. 1807] Inclusive in Three Vol-
    umes (New Series), Being a Continuation of Hening, by
    Shepherd. (repr. of 1835-1836 ed.) 3v. Each: $25.00 Set: 75.00 ..... (630)
Personal Names in Hening's Statutes at Large & Shepherd's
    Continuation, by Casey 8.50 ..... (130)
Tyler's Quarterly Historical and Genealogical Magazine. 33v.
    Vols. 1-33 (1919-1952) Each, paperbound: $15.60 Set: 712.80 514.80 (624)
The Virginia Historical Register, by Maxwell. 6v. in 3. Each: 18.00 ..... (663)

Virginia Magazine of History and Biography. 38v.			
Vols. 1-38 (1893-1930) Part in original edition.	Set: 957.60	729.60	(624)
Vols. 1-38	Each:	19.20	(624)
William and Mary Quarterly.			
Series 1: Vols. 1-27 (all publ.) (1892-1919)	Set: 499.20	421.20	(624)
" " " " "	Each:	15.60	(624)
Series 2: Vols. 1-23 (all publ.) (1921-1943)	Set: 625.20	529.20	(624)
" " 1-7	Each:	18.00	(624)
" " 8-15	Each:	21.60	(624)
" " 16-23	Each:	28.80	(624)
Series 3: Vols. 1-25 (1944-1968) Part original ed.	Set: 841.20	691.20	(624)
" " 1-3, 23-25	Each:	24.00	(624)
" " 4-22	Each:	28.80	(624)
William and Mary Quarterly Index [to 3rd Series, Vol. 1-15 (1944-1958), by Neiman		6.15	(740)
William and Mary Quarterly Index [to 3rd Series, Vol. 16-30 (1959-1973), by Sheppard		8.00	(740)
The Records of the Virginia Company of London, 4v.	Set: 230.00	.....	(630)
" " " "	Each: 57.50	.....	(630)
The Official Records of Robert Dinwiddie, Lieut-Gov. of the Colony of Virginia, 1751-1758. 2v.	Set: 60.00	.....	(630)
Journals of the House of Burgesses of Virginia, 1619-1776, ed. by Kennedy & McIlwaine. 13v.	Set: 450.00	.....	(244)
Virginia Gazette From 1736-1780. 6 reels.	Microfilm:	72.00	(740)
Virginia Gazette Index, 1736-1780. 2v. 1,314pp.	Set: 65.00	.....	(740)
Colonial Records of Virginia, by Va. Gen. Ass. [Census]	7.50	.....	(130)
Virginia Settlers and English Adventurers: Abstracts of Wills, 1484-1798, and Legal Proceedings, 1566-1700, Relating to Early Virginia Families, by Currier-Briggs	21.00	.....	(130)
Virginia Wills Before 1799, by Clemens [Abstract of over 600]	7.50	.....	(130)
Cavaliers and Pioneers: Abstracts of Land Patents and Grants, 1623-1666, by Nugent	18.50	.....	(130)
Virginia Valley Records, by Wayland	13.50	.....	(130)
Annals of Southwest Virginia, 1769-1800, by Summers. 2v. Set:	32.50	.....	(130)
Some Emigrants to Virginia, by Stanard [Passenger lists]	.....	5.00	(130)
Early Virginia Immigrants, 1632-1666, by Greer	11.50	.....	(130)
Virginia Court Records in Southwestern Pennsylvania, by Crumrine [Records of Dist. of W.Augusta, Ohio & Yohogania Co.]	20.00	.....	(130)
Virginia Ancestors and Adventurers, by Hamlin. 3v. in 1	20.00	.....	(130)
Virginia County Records, by Crozier. 11v. Each:$15.00 Set:	165.00	.....	(630)
" " ", Vol.4: Early Virginia Marriages	10.00	.....	(130)
" " ", Vol.6: Miscellaneous County Records	12.50	.....	(130)
" " ", Vol.7: " " "	10.00	.....	(130)
" " ", Vol.9: " " "	8.50	.....	(130)
" " ", Vol.10: " " "	7.50	.....	(130)
Virginia Wills & Administrations, 1632-1800, by Torrence	11.50	.....	(130)
Index to Obituary Notices in the Richmond Enquirer 1804-1828, and the Richmond Whig 1824-1838, by McIlwaine	.....	5.00	(130)
In combination these books constitute the Virginia "1790 Census" { Virginia Tax Payers, 1782-1787, by Fothergill & Naugle	12.50	.....	(130)
Heads of Families at the First Census of Virginia: State Enum., 1782-1785	10.00	.....	(663)
In combination cover the entire state { Index to the 1810 Virginia Census, by Crickard	15.00	.....	(47)
Supplement to the 1810 Census of Virginia, by Schreiner-Yantis	15.00	10.00	(289)

Virginia

al Days in the Land that Became Pulaski Co., by Smith
blication date: May 1975.] .... (597)
Beverly Patent - 1736, by Hildebrand 2.00 (709)
n the Western Waterns, by Schreiner-Yantis [Settlement of
Va. 1745-1790;Tax, military, survey records, land grants,
; Map.] Publication date: 1976. .... (289)
by the Long Grey Trail, by Harrison 20.00 ..... (130)
Early Augusta County Marriages (in Gen. Ref. Builders, Each issue:
#4; v.6, #1 & 2) Average 6pp/issue. 2.00 (931)
County, Virginia, in the History of the United States, by
ap (repr. of 1918 ed.) 8.50 6.00 (546)
he following are all articles which appeared in The Augusta
Historical Society BULLETIN. Price per issue: 3.00 (322)
tory Behind the Stone (Beverley Manor Grant), by Sprunt
n v.6, #1) 6pp. 3.00 (322)
eyan Female Institute, by Hamrick (in v.6, #1) 19pp. 3.00 (322)
Loyal Land Company, by Bushman (reprint - 17pp.) 3.00 (322)
ime Life in Augusta County (in v.6, #1) 9pp. 3.00 (322)
ourts of Augusta County, by Moffett (in v.7, #1) 6pp. 3.00 (322)
th Century Tax Aid (Hemp certificates 1764-1769)(v.8,#2) 3.00 (322)
tery Committee Report: A List of Recorded Family Cem-
ries and Church Cemeteries (in v.9, #1) 2pp. 3.00 (322)
Pleasant Claims [Over 200 names] (in v.9, #1) 10pp. 3.00 (322)
rations of Intention to Become U.S. Citizens 1844-1859
v.9, #2) 4pp. 3.00 (322)
er Forts of Old Augusta, by Clemmer (in v.10, #1) 3.00 (322)
umb Dutch of the Shenandoah Valley (in v.1, #1) 16pp. 3.00 (322)
a County's Relation to the Revolution (in v.2, #1) 16pp. 3.00 (322)
a County During the Civil War, by Brice (v.1, #2) 15pp. 3.00 (322)
ections of Augusta County, by Tams (in v.1, #1) 22pp. 3.00 (322)
mes of Augusta County (v.7, #2-20pp; v.9, #2-16pp) Each: 3.00 (322)
Potteries, & Potting in Augusta 1800-1870 (v.9, #1) 12pp 3.00 (322)
y of Stuart Hall, by Jones (in v.5, #1) 20pp. 3.00 (322)
ral Census, by Crickard 7.00 (47)

BEDFORD COUNTY

ry of Bedford County, 1754-1954, by Parker (1954) 12.50 10.00 (546)
dford County, 1750-1865, by Hildebrand 2.00 (709)
Bonds, by Dennis & Smith 6.00 (130)
of Wills, Inventories, & Accounts 1754-1787, by Whitten 10.00 (550)
ral Census, by Crickard [Partial list] 3.50 (47)

BLAND COUNTY

the Middle New River Settlements, by Johnston (repr.
ed.) [Early settlements, family genealogies, Indian cap-
military rosters. New every-name index.] 17.50 ..... (289)

BOTETOURT COUNTY

ounty, Its Men of 1770-1777, by Burton [Taken from
tax lists, etc.] 5.00 (2)
Tithables, 1770-1773, by Kegley [Tax list of residents
River and its branches.] 4.34 (268)
Census Enumeration for Botetourt, by Burton [Names
of families, # of white persons in each, indexed.] 5.00 (2)
axable Property in the District of John Robinson, For-
e Upper Dist. of Botetourt and Now the Lower of Mont-
or the Yr. 1790 [Part annexed by Mont. in 1789.] 2.00 (289)

Virginia - 159

Military

List of the Colonial Soldiers of Virginia, by Eckenrode 5.00 (130)
Virginia Colonial Militia, 1651-1776, by Crozier. 7.50 ..... (130)
Memoir of Indian Wars, and Other Occurrences: By the Late
Colonel Stuart of Greenbriar (repr. of 1833 ed.) [Firsthand
acct. of the Battle of Point Pleasant.] 6.00 ..... (629)
Western Lands & the American Revolution, by Abernethy (repr.
of 1937 ed.) [Western lands as cause for revolution.] 15.00 ..... (988)
The Valley of Virginia in the American Revolution 1763-1789,
by Hart (repr. of 1942 ed.) 13.00 ..... (988)
Virginia Soldiers of 1776, by Burgess. 3v. Set: 40.00 ..... (130)
"   "   " - Vol. 1, 2, & 3 Each: 21.00 ..... (663)
Colonel George Rogers Clark's Sketch of His Campaign in the
Illinois in 1778-1779, by Clark (repr. of 1869 ed.) 8.00 ..... (629)
Loyalism in Virginia; Chapters in the Economic History of the
Revolution, by Harrell (repr. of 1926 ed.) 10.00 ..... (630)
Frontier Advance on the Upper Ohio, by Kellogg (repr. of 1916
ed.) [Revolution in Southwestern Virginia; tories.] 17.50 ..... (863)
Frontier Retreat on the Upper Ohio, by Kellogg [Tories.] 19.50 ..... (863)
A History of the Campaigns of 1780 & 1781, in the Southern
Provinces of North American, by Tarleton 15.00 ..... (663)
King's Mountain and Its Heroes, by Draper 15.00 ..... (663)
The Yorktown Campaign and the Surrender of Cornwallis, by
Johnston 12.00 ..... (663)
Historical Register of Virginians in the Revolution; Soldiers,
Sailors, Marines, by Gwathmey 20.00 ..... (130)
Records of the Revolutionary War [bound with] Index to Saffell's
List of Virginia Soldiers of the Revolution, by Saffell 16.00 ..... (130)
Revolutionary War Records, by Brumbaugh. Vol. 1 (all pub.) 20.00 ..... (130)
Catalogue of Revolutionary Soldiers and Sailors of the Common-
wealth of Virginia to Whom Land Bounty Warrants Were
Granted by Virginia for Military Services in the War of In-
dependence, vy Wilson 8.50 ..... (130)
Revolutionary War Pension Applications, by Dorman. 20v.
[Detailed abstract of each Virginia applicant's papers. Index
to all persons named in the papers, plus all place names.]
    Vol. 1: Aaron to Almy 5.00 (500)
    Vol. 2: Alsop to Arnold, J. 5.00 (500)
    Vol. 3: Arnold, L. to Bailey, T. 5.00 (500)
    Vol. 4: Bailey, W. to Barr 5.00 (500)
    Vol. 5: Barram to Beazeley 5.00 (500)
    Vol. 6: Beazley to Biggs, J. 5.00 (500)
    Vol. 7: Bigg, J. to Bly 5.00 (500)
    Vol. 8: Board to Bowles 5.00 (500)
    Vol. 9: Bowling to Brayhill 5.00 (500)
    Vol. 10: Breckinridge to Brooks 5.00 (500)
    Vol. 11: Broom to Broyles; and A & B additions 5.00 (500)
    Vol. 12: Bruce to Burger 5.00 (500)
    Vol. 13: Burgess to Butler, P. 5.00 (500)
    Vol. 14: Butler, R. to Camp; and A & B additions 5.00 (500)
    Vol. 15: Campbell to Carper 5.00 (500)
    Vol. 16: Carr to Cashwell 5.00 (500)
    Vol. 17: Cason to Chappell 5.00 (500)
    Vol. 18: Charity to Chunn 5.00 (500)
    Vol. 19: Church to Clemens 5.00 (500)
    Vol. 20: Clement to Cole, John 5.00 (500)
(continuing series)

A Guide to Virginia Military Organizations 1861-65, by Wallace
[A "blue book" of Virginia Confederate officers.]   15.00   ..... (123)

Make Me a Map of the Valley: Journal of Jedediah Hotchkiss
[Stonewall Jackson's topographer], ed. by McDonald [Civil
war journal, 1862-1865 - notes on many people he met.]   12.50   ..... (685)

Religious and ethnic groups

Encyclopedia of American Quaker Genealogy, by Hinshaw
Vol. 6 [Virginia records.]   45.00   ..... (130)

The Douglas Register. Being a Detailed Record of Births,
Marriages & Deaths . . . 1750-1797, by Jones [Huguenots]   11.50   ..... (130)

Documents, Chiefly Unpublished, Relating to the Huguenot Emigration to Virginia, by Brock [Passenger lists.]   10.00   ..... (130)

Memoirs of a Huguenot Family, by Fontaine   16.00   ..... (130)

History of Mennonites in Virginia, 1727-1900, by Brunk   7.00   ..... (1133)

The Brethren in Virginia, by Sappington   7.00   ..... (344)

History of the Baptists in Virginia, by Semple   15.00   ..... (580)

Old Churches, Ministers and Families of Virginia [with] Digested Index and Genealogical Guide, by Meade   25.00   ..... (130)

Antebellum Virginia Disciples: An Account of the Emergence
and Early Development of the Disciples of Christ in Virgin-
ia, by Darst [History, & individual churches & leaders.]   5.00   ..... (17)

The Struggle of Protestant Dissenters for Religious Toleration
in Virginia, by McIlwaine (repr. of 1894 ed.)   10.25   6.25   (1000)

The Lexington Presbytery Heritage, by Wilson [The history of
Virginia Presbyterians pioneering to the Ohio River frontier.
Details on local churches (10,000 officers listed-1700's to
1971). Maps. Every-name index. Documented.]   8.50   ..... (523)

Maps

The Fry & Jefferson Map of Virginia & Maryland: Facsimiles
of the 1754 & 1794 Printings, by Fry & Jefferson 35.00   (713)

Miscellaneous

Virginia Genealogies, by Hayden   15.00   ..... (130)

Index to Hayden's Virginia Genealogies (above) [Available 1975]   .... (13)

Blackstone's Commentaries With Notes of Reference to the Con-
stitution & Laws of the Federal Government of the United
States & of the Commonwealth of Virginia (repr. 1802)   135.00   ..... (756)

Saint-Memin in Virginia: Portraits and Biographies, by
Norfleet [190 Virginiana painted by a Frenchman.]   15.00   ..... (171)

Notes on Southside Virginia, by Watson 8.00   (244)

Biographical Register of Members, Virginia State Convention
of 1861, First Session, by Gaines 1.50   (244)

Historic Virginia Homes & Churches, by Lancaster   24.00   ..... (663)

Historical Collections of Virginia, by Howe   15.00   ..... (130)

The Colonial Virginia Register, by Stanard & Newton   10.00   ..... (130)

Virginia Heraldica, by Crozier (Vol. 5 of Va. County Rec.)   7.50   ..... (130)

Virginia Historical Genealogies, by Boddie   15.00   ..... (130)

Southside Virginia Families, By Boddie. Vol. 1 & 2   Each: 11.00   ..... (130)

NORTHERN NECK

[Included counties of Northumberland, Lancaster, Richmond, Westmoreland, Stafford,
King George, Prince William, Fairfax, Loudoun, Fauquier, Culpeper, Madison, Page,
Shenandoah, Warren, Clark, Rappahannock, Frederick in Virginia & Jefferson, Berke-
ley, Hardy, Hampshire, Mineral, Morgan, Grant in West Virginia.]

Virginia Baron, The Story of Thomas 6th Lord Fairfax, by Brown   7.50   ..... (123)

The Fairfax Line: A Profile In History and Geography, by Morrison [History of the Fairfax grant, its settlers, and the survey
of the line which set it apart from the Colony of Virginia.]

The Fairfax Proprietary, by Dickinson [History and dispositon of
the 5,282,000 acres which made up the "Northern Neck".]

ACCOMACK COUNTY

The Eastern Shore of Virginia, 1603-1964, by Turman

Studies of the Virginia Eastern Shore in the 17th Century, by
Ames (repr. 1940) [Settlement and social history of the region
based on court records of Accomack & Northampton Cos.]

Virginia's Eastern Shore, by Whitelaw [Study of land titles in
Accomack & Northampton Counties.]

Revolutionary Soldiers and Sailors from Accomack County, by
Nottingham (repr. c1927 ed.)

Ye Kingdome of Accawmacke On the Eastern Shore of Virginia In
the 17th Century, by Wise

County Court Records of Accomack-Northampton. Virginia, ed.
by Ames

Marriage License Bonds 1774-1806, by Nottingham

Wills & Administrations 1663-1800, by Nottingham

1810 Federal Census, by Crickard

ALBEMARLE COUNTY

Guardians' Bonds, 1783-1852, by Murphy

1810 Federal Census, by Crickard

AMELIA COUNTY

Marriages 1735-1815, by Williams (repr. 1961)

Will Book 1, With Inventories and Accounts, 1734-1761 (in The
Va. Gen., v.15, #2,3,4; v.16, #1,2,4; Vol. 17, #1,2,3,4;
v.18, #1,2) Average 9pp/issue.   Each iss

1810 Federal Census, by Crickard [Partial list.]

AMHERST COUNTY

Marriage Bonds & Other Marriage Records 1763-1800, by Swe
"   "   "   "   "   "   "

1810 Federal Census, by Crickard

APPOMATTAX COUNTY

Register of Old Concord Presbyterian Church, Appomattox Co
1826-1878, by Chilton

Appomattox Quarterly Meeting Conference Abstracts, Method
Church, 1861-1875, by Chilton

Tax Lists For the Year 1845, by Chilton

ARLINGTON COUNTY

Landmarks of Old Prince William, by Harrison

AUGUSTA COUNTY

Chronicles of the Scotch Irish Settlement in Virginia, by Ch
[Abstracts of original court records, 1745-1800] 3v.

James Patton and the Appalachian Colonists, by Johnson [D
mented acct. of colonization in the Valley & westward by

The Tinkling Spring, Headwater of Freedom, by Wilson [H
Presby. church in the Valley. Names of over 4000 sett
Baptisms 1740-1749; Early cemetery records; Importa
ords 1734-1745; General history of the area.]

1810 Federal Census of Botetourt County, by Crickard 5.00 (47)
1820 Federal Census of Botetourt County - Indexed, by Burton 5.00 (2)
Early Marriages, Wills, Revolutionary War Records, by Worrell 5.00 (130)
Land on the Western Waters, by Schreiner-Yantis [Settlement of
SW Va. 1745-1790 taken from tax, military, survey & other land
records; Loyal & Greenbriar Co.] Publication date: 1976 .... (289)
Colonial Days in the Land That Became Pulaski County, by Smith
Publication date: 1975 .... (597)

BRUNSWICK COUNTY

1810 Federal Census, by Crickard 3.00 (47)

BUCKINGHAM COUNTY

Descendants . . . With Material on Early Methodist History in
Maryland, Virginia & Ohio, by Markham 18.00 ..... (430)
Virginia Tithables From Burned Record Counties, by Woodson
[Buckingham lists for 1773 & 1774 are included.] 10.00 ..... (37)
1810 Federal Census, by Crickard 3.00 (47)

CAMPBELL COUNTY

Register of Old Concord Presbyterian Church, Appomattox County 1826-1878, by Chilton 4.00 (182)
Our Quaker Friends of Ye Olden Time; Being in Part a Transcript
of the Minute Books of Cedar Creek Meeting, Hanover County,
and the South River Meeting, Campbell County, by Bell (1905) 17.50 15.00 (546)
1810 Federal Census, by Crickard 3.50 (47)

CAROLINE COUNTY

Order Book 1732-1740, Parts 1, 2, & 3, by Dorman   Each: 5.00 (500)
Order Book 1740-1746, Parts 1, 2, & 3, by Dorman   Each: 5.00 (500)
Order Book 1746-1754, Parts 1, 2, 3, & 4, by Dorman   Each: 5.00 (500)
Proceedings of the Committees of Safety of Caroline & Southamton
Counties, Virginia, 1774-1776 (Va. St. Lib. Pub., v. 17, #3) 2.00 (244)
1810 Federal Census, by Crickard 5.00 (47)

CHARLES CITY COUNTY

Court Orders 1655-1658, by Fleet [Va. Col. Abs.-Vol. 10] 5.00 (130)
Court Orders 1658-1661, by Fleet [Va. Col. Abs.-Vol. 11] 5.00 (130)
Court Orders 1661-1664, by Fleet [Va. Col. Abs.-Vol. 12] 5.00 (130)
Court Orders 1664-1665; Fragments 1650-1696, by Fleet [Va.
Col. Abs.-Vol. 13] 5.00 (130)
Order Book 1676-1679, by Ayres 10.00 (30)
1800 Tax List (in The Va. Genealogist, v. 15, #1) 6pp. 5.00 (500)
1810 Federal Census, by Crickard 2.50 (47)

CHARLOTTE COUNTY

1800 Tax List (in Va. Genealogist, v. 15, #2 & 3) 15pp. total Both: 6.00 (500)
1810 Federal Census, by Crickard 3.50 (47)
1820 Federal Census, by Crickard 3.00 (47)

CHESTERFIELD COUNTY

Marriages, 1771-1815, by Knorr 5.00 (849)
1800 Tax List (in Va. Gen., v. 15, #4; v. 16, #1, 2)   Three issues: 9.00 (500)
1810 Federal Census, by Crickard 3.50 (47)

CLARKE COUNTY

Shenandoah Valley Pioneers & Their Descendants, by Cartmell 25.00 ..... (123)
History of the Lower Shenandoah Valley Counties of Frederick,
Berkeley, Jefferson, & Clarke, by Norris 32.50 ..... (123)

CRAIG COUNTY

History and Membership of the Gravel Hill (Antioch) Christian
    Church; Sinking Creek Valley, Craig County 1830-1871, com.
    by Miller [Membership record. Frequently mentions place of
    emigration of removed members. Map.] 3.50 (174)

CULPEPER COUNTY

Genealogical & Historical Notes on Culpeper County, by Green	11.00	.....	(130)
Abstracts From the County Court Minute Book, 1763-1764, by			
Prichard [In fire - rebound.]		7.50	(830)
Marriages 1781-1815, by Knorr		5.00	(849)
Abstracts of Will Books B & C, by Wulfeck		12.50	(940)
1800 Tax List (in The Va. Gen., v.16, #3,4; v.17, #1,2) All:		12.00	(500)
1810 Federal Census, by Crickard		7.00	(47)

CUMBERLAND COUNTY

1810 Federal Census, by Crickard 3.00 (47)

DINWIDDIE COUNTY

Dinwiddie County, "The Countrey of the Apamatica", by WPA	16.00	.....	(630)
Births From the Bristol Parish Register of Henrico, Prince			
George, and Dinwiddie Counties, 1720-1798, by Chamberlayne	.....	10.00	(130)
1810 Federal Census [Partial list], by Crickard	.....	3.00	(47)

ELIZABETH CITY COUNTY

1810 Federal Census, by Crickard 2.00 (47)

ESSEX COUNTY

Court Records 1706-1707 & 1717-1719, by Dorman	5.00	(500)
Court Records 1717-1722, by Dorman	5.00	(500)
Deeds & Wills No. 13, 1707-1711, by Dorman	5.00	(500)
Wills & Deeds 1711-1714, by Fleet [Va. Col. Abs., Vol. 8]	5.00	(130)
Wills & Deeds 1714-1717, by Fleet [Va. Col. Abs., Vol. 9]	5.00	(130)
Wills, Bonds, Inventories, etc. 1722-1730, by Dorman	5.00	(500)
Wills No. 7, 1743-1747 (in The Va. Gen., v. 15, #2,3,4; v.16,		
#1,2,3,4) Average 9pp./issue. Each:	3.00	(500)
1810 Federal Census, by Crickard [Partial list.]	2.50	(47)

FAIRFAX COUNTY

Historical Society of Fairfax County Yearbooks:
    Vol. 2 (1952-53) - County history before 1776; Colonial churches;
        Civil War events 1861; Fox hunting; George Mason 2.50 (381)
    Vol. 3 (1954) - Civil War events; Ravensworth; Railroads; Brad-
        dock's Army Treasure; Great Falls; Archives of Burgundy
        Farm 2.50 (381)
    Vol. 4 (1955) - McLean; Centreville; Fairfax-Loudoun County
        Line; Secession Election; General Stoughton's Capture; His-
        tory of Clifton; Barons of Cameron & Fairfax 2.50 (381)
    Vol. 5 (1956-57) - Fairfax County History; Early Courts; St.
        John's Episcopal Church, McLean; Early Vestry Meetings 2.50 (381)
    Vol. 6 (1958-58) - Old Mills in Centreville; Drover's Rest; Rose
        Hill; Sunset Hills Farm; Leeton; Sully 2.50 (381)
    Vol. 7 (1960-61) - Constitutional Conventions; Towlston Road;
        Oakton School; Cornwell Farm; Oak Hill; Ossian Hall 2.50 (381)
    Vol. 8 (1962-63) - Two diaries of Fairfax County families during
        the Civil War 2.50 (381)
    Vol. 9 (1969) - Committee of Safety; Blackburn's Ford; Fairfax
        1906; Manuscript Source Records; Secessionist Sentiment 2.50 (381)

Vol. 11 - Fairfax Resolutions; American Revolution chronology; Official Colonial Records; Truro Rectory; Windy Hill Farm 2.50 (381)
Vol. 12 - (1973) Records of Fairfax County Court for 1771 - complete transcription 3.00 (381)
Landmarks of Old Prince William, by Harrison 25.00 ..... (123)
1810 Federal Census, by Crickard 4.00 (47)

FAUQUIER COUNTY

Fauquier During the Proprietorship. A Chronicle of a Northern Neck County, by Groome 11.00 ..... (130)
Germantown Revived- [An acct. of the colony where the 1st Germanna Colony settled in 1719 after leaving Germanna.] 5.00 (986)
Fauquier County, Virginia Tombstone Inscriptions, by Baird 15.00 ..... (633)
1810 Federal Census, by Crickard 7.00 (47)
1820 Federal Census, by Crickard 7.00 (47)
Landmarks of Old Prince William, by Harrison 25.00 ..... (123)

FINCASTLE COUNTY

James Patton and the Appalachian Colonists, by Johnson [Documented acct. of colonization in the Shenandoah Valley and westward into Southwest Virginia before 1755.] 7.95 ..... (174)
The Committees of Safety of Westmoreland and Fincastle: Proceedings of the County Committees, 1774-1776, by Harwell 4.00 (244)
Soldiers of Fincastle County, 1774, by Kegley [Militia companies pay, public service accts. About 1600 names.] 5.78 (268)
Colonial Days in the Land that Became Pulaski Co., by Smith [Publication date, May 1975.] .... (597)
Land on the Western Waters, by Schreiner-Yantis [SW Va. 1745-1790. Data on early settlers taken from land, tax, military, etc. records.] Publication date, 1976. .... (289)

FLUVANNA COUNTY

1810 Federal Census, by Crickard 2.00 (47)

FRANKLIN COUNTY

Pioneer Families of Franklin County, by Wingfield 12.50 ..... (123)
Marriage Bonds, 1786-1858, With a New Index, by Wingfield 15.00 ..... (130)
1810 Federal Census, by Crickard 5.00 (47)
1820 Federal Census, by Crickard 5.00 (47)

FREDERICK COUNTY

Shenandoah Valley Pioneers & Their Descendants, by Cartmell 25.00 ..... (123)
History of the Lower Shenandoah Valley Counties of Frederick, Berkeley, Jefferson & Clarke, by Norris 32.50 ..... (123)
Hopewell Friends History 1734-1934 [Records of Hopewell Monthly Meetings and Meetings Reporting to Hopewell.] 25.00 ..... (130)
A History of CALVARY Church of the Brethren, by Wine [Origin of Brethren; their beginning in Va.; those who settled in Frederick & Clark Cos.; The Salem Congregation; Biog. of min.] 3.80 (460)
Marriages, 1771-1825, by Davis 10.00 ..... (130)
"   "   "   " 10.00 ..... (123)
Abstracts of Wills, Inventories, & Adms. Accts., by King 10.00 ..... (123)
Obituaries, Vol. 1 & 2 [Fr. Winchester Evening Star, Frederick County Death Register, and other sources.] Each: 8.50 ..... (263)
1810 Federal Census, by Crickard 9.00 (47)
1820 Federal Census, by Crickard 9.00 (47)

GILES COUNTY

History of the Middle New River Settlements, by Johnston (repr.
of 1906 ed.) [Early history, Indian captivities, military rosters, family genealogies. New every-name index.] 17.50 ..... (289)
1810 Federal Census, by Crickard 3.00 (47)
1810 Federal Census, by Schreiner-Yantis [Map of the period.] 2.00 (289)
1815 Personal Property Tax List & Miscelleanous Deed & Survey
Abstracts [Map of the period. Location of residence of most
taxpayers.] 2.25 (289)

GLOUCESTER COUNTY

Records of Colonial Gloucester County, Virginia, by Mason 25.00 ..... (123)
Past is Prologue, Gloucester County, Virginia, by Dabney 3.00 (435)
Six Periods of Gloucester History, by Gloucester Hist. Comm. ..... .50 (435)
Gloucester Court House Historic District ..... .25 (435)
The Vestry Book of Petsworth Parish, Gloucester County, 1677-
1793, trans., annotated and indexed by Chamberlayne 10.00 ..... (244)
Virginia Tithables From Burned Record Counties, by Woodson
[List of tithables of Gloucester for 1770, 1771, 1775.] 10.00 ..... (37)
1810 Federal Census, by Crickard 3.50 (47)
1820 Federal Census, by Crickard 3.00 (47)

GOOCHLAND COUNTY

Goochland County Historical Society Magazine [Published bi-annually.] Subscription per year: 5.00 (584)
The Storyof Goochland, by Wight 5.50 ..... (584)
Facets of Goochland County's History, by Agee 6.20 ..... (584)
Marriages of Goochland County 1733-1815, by Williams 12.50 10.00 (546)
1810 Federal Census, by Crickard .... (47)

GRAYSON COUNTY

1810 Tax List, by Schreiner-Yantis 1.50 (289)

GREENSVILLE COUNTY

1810 Federal Census, by Crickard 2.00 (47)

HALIFAX COUNTY

A History of Halifax County, by Carrington 15.00 ..... (130)
Along the Border; A History of Virgilina, Virginia, and the Surrounding Area in Halifax and Mecklenburg Counties in Virginia
and Person and Granville Counties in N. Carolina, by Mathis 8.00 ..... (123)
1810 Tax List, by Schreiner-Yantis 1.50 (289)

HANOVER COUNTY

Virginia Tithables From Burned Record Counties, by Woodson
[List of tithables of Hanover County for 1763 & 1770.] 10.00 ..... (37)
The Vestry Book of St. Paul's Parish, Hanover County, 1706-1786
trans. and ed. by Chamberlayne 12.50 ..... (244)
Our Quaker Friends of Ye Olden Time; Being in Part a Transcript
of the Minute Books of Cedar Creek Meeting, Hanover County,
and the South River Meeting, Campbell County, by Bell 17.50 15.00 (546)
1810 & 1820 Federal Census, by Chappelear Both: 4.00 (633)
1810 Federal Census, by Crickard 3.00 (47)
1820 Federal Census, by Crickard 3.00 (47)
1850 Federal Census, by Inman & Inman 10.00 ..... (37)

HENRICO COUNTY

Births From the Bristol Parish Register of Henrico, Prince
    George, and Dinwiddie Counties, 1720-1798, by Chamberlayne 10.00 (130)
1810 Federal Census, by Crickard 3.00 (47)

HENRY COUNTY

1778-1780 Tax Lists, by Adams 3.50 (55)
Marriage Bonds 1778-1849, by Dodd 12.50 ..... (123)
1810 Personal Property Tax Lists, by Schreiner-Yantis 1.50 (289)

HIGHLAND COUNTY

A History of Highland County, by Morton 17.50 ..... (130)

ISLE OF WIGHT COUNTY

Seventeeth Century Isle of Wight County, by Boddie 20.00 ..... (130)
1810 Federal Census, by Crickard 3.00 (47)

JAMES CITY COUNTY

A Guide to the Records of James City Co. (in Va. Gen., v.15, #1) 3.00 (500)
Bruton & Middleton Parishes Register 1662-1797, by Chappelear 5.00 (633)
The Vestry Book and Register of St. Peter's Parish, New Kent
    and James City, Counties, 1684-1786, by Chamberlayne 12.50 ..... (244)
The Vestry Book of Blisland Parish, New Kent and James City
    Counties, 1721-1786, by Chamberlayne 10.00 ..... (244)
Virginia Tithables From Burned Record Counties, by Woodson
    [James City tithables for the years 1768 & 1769.] 10.00 ..... (37)
Williamsburg Wills, by Crozier [Va.Co.Rec., Vol. III] 7.50 ..... (130)
1810 Personal Property Tax List, by Schreiner-Yantis 1.50 (289)

KING GEORGE COUNTY

A Guide to the Records of King George Co. (in Va. Gen., v.15, #3) 3.00 (500)
1810 Federal Census, by Crickard 3.00 (47)

KING & QUEEN COUNTY

A Guide to the Records of King & Queen Co. (in Va.Gen., v.15, #3) 3.00 (500)
King & Queen County, Virginia, by Bagby 13.50 ..... (130)
The Vestry Book of Stratton Major Parish, King & Queen County,
    1729-1783, trans., annotated, and indexed by Chamberlayne 10.00 ..... (244)
King & Queen County Records Concerning 18th Century Persons,
    by Fleet [Part of the Virginia Colonial Abstracts]
        Third Collection - Vol. 6 of Va. Col. Abs. 5.00 (130)
        Fourth Collection - Vol. 7 of Va. Col. Abs. 5.00 (130)
        Fifth Collection - Vol. 14 of Va. Col. Abs. 5.00 (130)
        Sixth Collection - Vol. 15 of Va. Col. Abs. 5.00 (130)
        Seventh Collection - Vol. 27 of Va. Col. Abs. 5.00 (130)
        Miscellaneous Records - Vol. 28 of Va. Col. Abs. 5.00 (130)
        Ninth Collection - Vol. 33 of Va. Col. Abs. 5.00 (130)
1810 Federal Census, by Crickard 3.00 (47)

KING WILLIAM COUNTY

A Guide to the Records of King Wm. Co. (in Va.Gen., v.15, #3) 3.00 (500)
Old King William Homes & Families, by Clarke 8.50 ..... (130)
1810 Personal Property Tax List, by Schreiner-Yantis 1.50 (289)
1820 Federal Census, by Crickard 3.00 (47)

LANCASTER COUNTY

A Guide to the Records of Lancaster County (in Va. Gen., v.15, #4) 3.00 (500)
Record Book #2, by Fleet [Vol. 1 of Va. Col. Abs.] 5.00 (130)

Lancaster County Marriage Bonds, 1652-1850, by Lee   7.50   .....   (130)
Abstracts of Lancaster County Wills 1785-1830, by Carlton &
    Tupper [Publication date, April 1975.]   ....   (127)
Virginia Land Causes (Northampton County, 1731-1868) & (Lan-
    caster County, 1795-1848), by Nottingham   8.50   6.00   (546)
Abstracts of Wills, 1653-1800, by Lee   10.00   .....   (130)
1810 Federal Census, by Crickard 2.00   (47)
1850 Federal Census, by Mary Ball Memorial Mus. & Lib. 7.50   (127)

LEE COUNTY

A Guide to the Records of Lee County (in Va. Gen., v.15, #4) 3.00   (500)
Marriage Register No. 1 (1830-1835) (in Watauga Bull., v.1, #2) 5.00   (617)
1810 Personal Property Tax List, by Schreiner-Yantis 1.50   (289)

LOUDOUN COUNTY

A Guide to the Records of Loudoun Co. (in Va. Gen., v.16, #2) 3.00   (500)
Snickersville - Biography of a Village, by Smith [History of the
    village of Snickersville and surrounding farms, with genealogies
    of seven of the prominent families.] 2.15   (205)
Landmarks of Old Prince William, by Harrison   25.00   .....   (123)
Abstracts of Wills, Inventories, and Administration Accounts,
    1757-1800, by King (repr. 1940)   12.50   10.00   (546)
1810 Federal Census, by Crickard 9.00   (47)

LOUISA COUNTY

Abstracts of Will Books 1743-1801, by Chappelear & Hatch 10.00   (633)
1810 Personal Property Tax List, by Schreiner-Yantis 1.50   (289)

LOWER NORFOLK COUNTY

Virginia Land Patents of Norfolk, Princess Anne & Warwick Cos.,
    Patent Books "O" & "6", by Walter 9.00   (199)
Lower Norfolk County, 1651-1654 [Vol. 31 of Va. Col. Abs.] 5.00   (130)

LUNENBURG COUNTY

The Old Free State. A Contribution to the History of Lunenburg
    County & Southside Virginia, by Bell. 2 v. in 1.   32.50   .....   (130)
Sunlight on the Southside. Lists of Tithes, 1748-1783, by Bell   17.50   .....   (130)
Lunenburg County Wills 1746-1825, by Bell   10.00   .....   (123)
Cumberland Parish, Lunenburg County, 1746-1816 [&] Vestry
    Book 1746-1816, by Bell   18.50   .....   (130)
1810 Federal Census, by Crickard 3.00   (47)
1850 Federal Census, by Steltzner & Cutting 8.50   (145)

LYNCHBURG CITY

Behind the Old Brick Wall - A Cemetery Story, by Baber & Moore
    [Data on approx. 3,000 burials in Old City Cemetery in Lynch-
    burg (1806-1913), taken from tombstones, burial records, mor-
    tuary records, newspaper obituaries, etc. Includes names of
    2,701 Confederate soldiers from Ala., Ark., Fla., Ga., Ky., La.,
    Md., Miss., Mo., NC, SC, Tenn., Tex., Va. giving co. & regt.;
    also 187 Union soldiers from Conn., Del., Ind., Me., Md., Mass.,
    Mich., NH, NJ, NY, O, Pa., RI, Vt., Va., Wisc. temporarily
    interred in this cemetery - giving co., regt., & state of each.]   7.50   .....   (569)
Sketches and Recollections of Lynchburg by the Oldest Inhabitant,
    by Cabell & Blunt [A facsimile reproduction of Mrs. Margaret
    Anthony Cabell's 1858 book, enlarged 1 1/3 times the size of the
    original edition, plus supplement by Miss Blunt, and index]   12.50   .....   (604)
Business Firms of 1900 in Lynchburg, by Noell [Gives officers,
    locations, dates of founding and termination.] 10.00   (604)

MADISON COUNTY

1810 Federal Census, by Crickard	.....	3.00	(47)

MATTHEWS COUNTY

The Vestry Book of Kingston Parish, Matthews County (until May 1, 1791, Gloucester Co.) 1679-1796, by Chamberlayne	12.50	10.00	(546)
1810 Federal Census, by Crickard	.....	2.00	(47)

MECKLENBURG COUNTY

Along the Border; A History of Virgilina, Virginia and the Surrounding Area in Halifax and Mecklenburg Cos. in Virginia and Person and Granville Cos. in N.C., by Mathis	8.00	.....	(123)
1795 Personal Property Tax List [Including names of slaves.]	.....	2.00	(531)
1810 Personal Property Tax List	.....	1.50	(289)

MIDDLESEX COUNTY

Marriages Records, 1740-1852, by Virginia Genealogical Soc.	.....	5.00	(13)
The Parish Register of Christ Church, Middlesex County	15.00	.....	(130)
1810 Federal Census, by Crickard	.....	2.00	(47)
1810 Federal Census & 1810 Personal Property Tax List, by Schreiner-Yantis [With comparison of the two.] Both:	.....	1.50	(289)

MONTGOMERY COUNTY

Land on the Western Waters, by Schreiner-Yantis [Settlement of SW Va. 1745-1790. Data from land, tax, military, etc. records. Map.] Publication date, 1976.	.....	.....	(289)
Colonial Days in the Land that Became Pulaski County, by Smith [Publication date, May 1975.]	.....	.....	(597)
A Brief of Wills and Marriages in Montgomery and Fincastle Counties 1773-1831, by Worrell	12.50	.....	(123)
1782 Personal Property & Tax Lists, by Kegley	.....	4.50	(268)
1788 Personal Property Tax Lists, by Schreiner-Yantis	.....	3.00	(289)
Montgomery County – Circa 1790, by Schreiner-Yantis [Tax lists, early surveys, migrational data. Approximate place of residence of virtually every taxpayer given. 16 x 22 map (in color) shows boundaries of the several tax districts; and natural features.]	7.50	5.00	(289)
Map (16x22) [Same as that included in above book sold separately]	.....	1.50	(289)
1790 Personal Property Tax List of that Portion of Montgomery Co. Which Had Been Annexed From Botetourt in 1789	.....	2.00	(289)
1810 Federal Census, by Crickard	.....	4.00	(47)

NANSEMOND COUNTY

Suffolk in Virginia (c1795-1840): A Record of Lots, Lives, and Likenesses, by Norfleet	17.00	.....	(171)
Bible Records of Suffolk and Nansemond County, by Norfleet	.....	12.50	(171)
Nansemond Chronicles Virginia Colony 1606-1800, by Cross [Alphabetical listings of Quaker & Vestry genealogy; land patent & chronological history to 1900.]	25.00	20.00	(462)
The Vestry Book of the Upper Parish, Nansemond County, 1743-1793, ed. by Hall	10.00	.....	(244)
1810 Land Tax List & 1815 Personal Property Tax List Both:	.....	1.50	(289)

NELSON COUNTY

Colonial History of Nelson County, 1734-1807	.....	1.50	(720)
1810 Federal Census, by Crickard	.....	3.00	(47)

NEW KENT COUNTY

The Vestry Book of Blisland Parish, New Kent & James City Counties, 1721-1786, ed. by Chamberlayne	10.00	.....	(244)

The Vestry Book & Register of St. Peter's Parish, New Kent and
James City Counties, 1684-1786, ed. by Chamberlayne   12.50   .....   (244)
The Parish Register of Saint Peter's, New Kent County, From
1680 to 1787, by St. Peter's Parish   10.00   .....   (130)
1810 Federal Census, by Crickard 2.00   (47)

NORFOLK COUNTY

Two Maps with Supplement of Norfolk Town 1636-1682 & Norfolk
Borough 1736-1802, by Walter [Each in 3 colors with a fully
documented supplement of the chains of title.] 10.00   (199)
Vestry Book of Elizabeth River Parish 1749-1761 [Old St. Paul's
Church, Norfolk; 2pp. births & deaths, 1726/7, 1756-1761.] 7.50   (199)
Marriages of Norfolk County (now City of Chesapeake), Vol. 1 -
1706-1792, by Wingo 10.00   (229)
Marriages of Norfolk County (now City of Chesapeake), Vol. 2 -
1788, 1793-1817, by Wingo 10.00   (229)
Revolutionary War and War of 1812 Applications for Pensions,
Bounty Land Warrants, and Heirs of Deceased Pensioners of
Norfolk County, by Wingo 10.00   (229)
Collection of Unrecorded Wills, Norfolk County, by Wingo 10.00   (229)
1810 Federal Census, by Crickard 3.50   (47)
1810 Federal Census of Borough of Norfolk, by Crickard 5.00   (47)

NORTHAMPTON COUNTY

Virginia Land Causes (Northampton County, 1731-1868) & (Lancaster County, 1795-1848), by Nottingham (c1931)   8.50   6.00   (546)
Studies of the Virginia Eastern Shore in the 17th Century, by Ames
(repr. of 1940 ed.) [Study of the settlement and social history of
the region based on court records of Accomack & Northampton.] 17.00   .....   (988)
Virginia's Eastern Shore, by Whitelaw [Study of land titles in Accomack and Northampton Counties.]   30.50   .....   (112)
County Court Records of Accomack-Northampton, Virginia,
1640-1645, ed. by Ames   18.00   .....   (112)
Marriage License Bonds 1706-1854, by Nottingham   10.00   .....   (130)
1810 Personal Property Tax List, by Schreiner-Yantis 1.50   (289)

NORTHUMBERLAND COUNTY

Northumbria Collectanea, 1645-1720, M-Z [v.20, Va. Col. Abs.] 5.00   (130)
Records of Births, 1661-1810, by Fleet (v.3, Va. Col. Abs.] 5.00   (130)
1810 Federal Census, by Crickard 3.00   (47)

NOTTOWAY COUNTY

Index to Old Homes and Families in Nottoway, by Turner 1.00   (13)
1810 Federal Census, by Crickard 2.00   (47)
1850 Federal Census, by Matheny 6.50   (972)

ORANGE COUNTY

A History of Orange County From Its Formation in 1734 . . . to
the End of Reconstruction in 1870, by Scott   15.00   .....   (130)
A History of Orange County, Virginia, by Scott   12.50   .....   (123)
Deed Books 1 & 2 - 1735 to 1738, by Dorman 5.00   (500)
Deed Books 3 & 4 - 1738 to 1741, by Dorman 5.00   (500)
Deed Books 5, 6, 7, & 8 - 1741-1743, by Dorman 5.00   (500)
Will Book 1 - 1735 to 1743, by Dorman 5.00   (500)
Will Book 2 - 1744 to 1778, by Dorman 5.00   (500)
1810 Personal Property Tax List, by Schreiner-Yantis 1.50   (289)

PATRICK COUNTY

Marriages, 1791-1850, by Adams	.....	7.50	(55)
Abstracts of Wills, Inventories & Accounts, 1791-1823, by Adams	.....	7.50	(55)
1810 Personal Property Tax List, by Schreiner-Yantis	.....	1.50	(289)

PETERSBURG CITY

Petersburg, Virginia, Hustings Court, Marriage Bonds, Marriage Reg. & Ministers' Returns, 1784-1854, by Hughes & Standefer	.....	15.00	(38)
1810 Federal Census, by Crickard	.....	3.50	(47)

PITTSYLVANIA COUNTY

The History of Pittsylvania County, by Clement	15.00	.....	(130)
1810 Personal Property Tax Lists, by Schreiner-Yantis	.....	1.50	(289)

POWHATAN COUNTY

1810 Federal Census, by Crickard	.....	2.00	(47)

PRINCE EDWARD COUNTY

History of Prince Edward County, by Bradshaw	10.00	.....	(725)
1810 Federal Census, by Crickard	.....	3.00	(47)

PRINCE GEORGE COUNTY

Virginia Marriages in Rev. John Cameron's Register & Bath Parish Register, by Virginia Genealogical Society	.....	3.00	(13)
Births From the Bristol Parish Register of Henrico, Prince George and Dinwiddie Counties, 1720-1798, by Chamberlayne	.....	10.00	(130)
Abstracts of Wills & Deeds 1713-1728, by Weisiger	.....	8.50	(52)
1810 Federal Census, by Crickard	.....	3.00	(47)

PRINCE WILLIAM COUNTY

Landmarks of Old Prince William, by Harrison	25.00	.....	(123)
1810 Federal Census, by Crickard	.....	3.00	(47)

PRINCESS ANNE COUNTY

. . . Princess Anne County Loose Papers, 1700-1789, ed. by Creecy	8.00	.....	(112)
Marriages, Vol. 2 - 1799 to 1821, by Wingo	.....	10.00	(229)
Genealogical Abstracts From Deed & Minute Books 6 & 7 - 1739 to 1762, by Walter [Available in 1975.]	.....	.....	(199)
1810 Federal Census, by Crickard	.....	3.00	(47)

PULASKI COUNTY

Colonial Days in the Land That Became Pulaski County, by Smith [Period covered, 1742-1781.] Publication date, 1975.	.....	.....	(597)
History of the Middle New River Settlements, by Johnston (repr. of 1906 ed.) [Early history, Indian captivities, military rosters, family genealogies. New every-name index.]	17.50	.....	(289)

RAPPAHANNOCK COUNTY

The Registers of North Farnham Parish 1663-1814 & Lunenburg Parish 1783-1800, by King	15.00	.....	(555)
My Rappahannock Story Book, by Hite	15.00	.....	(123)

RICHMOND CITY

Richmond, Her Past & Present, by Asbury	24.00	.....	(663)
1810 Federal Census, by Crickard	.....	3.00	(47)

RICHMOND COUNTY

Marriages of Richmond County 1668-1853, by King [Annotated, and many genealogical charts appended.]	17.50	.....	(555)
The Registers of North Farnham Parish 1663-1814 and Lunenburg Parish 1783-1800, Richmond County, by King	15.00	.....	(555)
1810 Federal Census, by Crickard	.....	2.00	(47)

ROANOKE COUNTY

Roanoke; Story of County and City, by WPA Writers Program	18.50	.....	(630)

ROCKBRIDGE COUNTY

A History of Rockbridge County, by Morton	15.00	.....	(130)
Old Oxford and Her Families, by Diehl [A Presbyterian Church founded in 1758; organized about 1773. Genealogies of the founding families of the community.]	7.50	.....	(207)
1810 Federal Census, by Crickard	.....	3.00	(47)

ROCKINGHAM COUNTY

Old Tenth Legion Marriages 1778-1816, by Strickler [Rockingham County marriages.] In fire - rebound.	.....	15.00	(830)
1810 Federal Census, by Crickard	.....	5.00	(47)

RUSSELL COUNTY

Archives of the Pioneers of Russell County, by Schreiner-Yantis [Abs. of primary records (tax, military, deeds, surveys, land patents, etc.; Maps; Lineages of descendants of pre-1820 settlers, etc.] (Note: Lineages of qualified individuals are solicited for inclusion - credit given.) To be published in 1978.	.....	.....	(289)
1810 Personal Property Tax List, by Schreiner-Yantis	.....	1.50	(289)

SCOTT COUNTY

1850 Federal Census, by Ball & Shumate	15.00	.....	(123)

SHENANDOAH COUNTY

Shenandoah Valley Pioneers & Their Descendants, by Cartmell	25.00	.....	(123)
History of Shenandoah County, by Wayland	15.50	.....	(717)
Marriage Bonds 1772-1850, by Ashby	15.00	.....	(123)
1810 Federal Census, by Crickard	.....	7.00	(47)
1820 Federal Census, by Crickard	.....	7.00	(47)

SMYTH COUNTY

Smyth County History and Families, by Presgraves [Hardesty's biographies; Harper's Saltville; and Recollections of an Exslave in Marion. Indexed.]	.....	8.50	(830)

SOUTHAMPTON COUNTY

Abstracts of Will Book 1, 1749-1762, by Korich [Includes list of inventories and accounts. Indexed.]	.....	4.00	(220)
Proceedings of the Committees of Safety of Caroline and Southampton Counties, 1774-1776 (Bulletin of Va. St. Lib., v.17, #3)	.....	2.00	(244)
1810 Federal Census, by Crickard	.....	4.00	(47)

SPOTSYLVANIA COUNTY

The History of Fredericksburg Baptist Church, by Darter	3.50	.....	(815)
The History of St. George's Episcopal Church, by Quenzel	.....	1.56	(654)
County Records 1721-1800, by Crozier [Vol. 1, Va. Col. Rec.]	15.00	.....	(130)
1810 Federal Census, by Crickard	.....	4.00	(47)

STAFFORD COUNTY

Virginia Tithables From Burned Record Counties, by Woodson			
[List of tithables of Stafford County 1768 & 1773.]	10.00	.....	(37)
1810 Federal Census, by Crickard	.....	3.50	(47)

SURRY COUNTY

Colonial Surry, by Boddie	10.00	.....	(130)
Births, Deaths & Sponsors 1717-1778 From the Albemarle Parish			
Register of Surry and Sussex Counties, by Boddie	12.50	.....	(130)
1810 Federal Census, by Crickard	.....	3.00	(47)

SUSSEX COUNTY

Sussex County, A Tale of Three Centuries, by WPA	16.00	.....	(630)
Births, Deaths & Sponsors 1717-1778 From the Albemarle Parish			
Register of Surry and Sussex Counties, by Boddie	12.50	.....	(130)
1810 Federal Census, by Crickard	.....	3.50	(47)

TAZEWELL COUNTY

Annals of Tazewell County, by Harman (repr. of 1922 & 1925 ed., 2 v. in 1) [Marriages 1800-1868; Wills 1800-1924; Soldiers of all wars thru WW I; Abs. Deed Bk. 1, 1800-1809; Reprint of History of Settlement & Indian Wars of Tazewell County, by Bickley; Selected entries from Order Bks. 1800-1924; Complete genealogies of many families; New every-name index.]	27.50	.....	(289)
Archives of the Pioneers of Tazewell County, by Schreiner-Yantis [Complete abs. Order Bk. 1, 1800-1810; P.P. & Land Tax lists; Legislative Petitions; Executive Papers; Land Grants, 1800-1820; Wills, Appraisements & Sale Bills, 1800-1832; Petitions; Study of immigration & emigration; Death Records 1853-1871 (of those born prior to 1820); Lineages of individuals descended from pre-1820 settlers; Annotations; Indexed.]	22.50	17.50	(289)
Sketches of Early Burke's Garden, by Greever (1974) [Gen. hist.; sketches, and many photographs. Indexed.] 104pp.	4.00	.....	(660)
History of the Middle New River Settlements, by Johnston (repr. of 1906 ed.) [Early history, Indian captivities, military rosters, family genealogies. New every-name index.]	17.50	.....	(289)
1810 Personal Property Tax List, by Schreiner-Yantis [Map.]	.....	1.50	(289)
1820 Federal Census, by Schreiner-Yantis [Map of the period.]	.....	2.00	(289)
1830 Federal Census, by Schreiner-Yantis [Map of the period.]	.....	2.00	(289)

WARREN COUNTY

The Fairfax Proprietary, by Dickinson [Includes maps.]	10.00	.....	(548)
Shenandoah Valley Pioneers and Their Descendants, by Cartmell	25.00	.....	(123)

WARWICK COUNTY

1810 Federal Census, by Crickard	.....	1.50	(47)
1820 Federal Census, by Crickard	.....	1.50	(47)

WASHINGTON COUNTY

History of Southwest Virginia, 1746-1786; Washington County, 1777-1870, by Summers	19.00	.....	(130)
Land on the Western Waters, by Schreiner-Yantis [Settlement of SW Va. 1745-1790. Data from land, tax, military, etc. records. Map.] Publication date, 1976.	.....	.....	(289)
Marriage Register 1782-1820, by Fleet [Vol. 34, Va.Col.Abs.]	.....	5.00	(130)
1810 Federal Census, by Crickard	.....	7.00	(47)

WESTMORELAND COUNTY

Historical Atlas of Westmoreland County, by Eaton	15.00	.....	(123)
Court Orders, 1653-1657, by Fleet [Vol. 23, Va. Col. Abs.]		..... 5.00	(130)
County Records, 1658-1661, by Dorman		..... 5.00	(500)
County Records, 1661-1664, by Dorman		..... 5.00	(500)
Deeds, Patents, Etc., 1665-1677, by Dorman [In 4 parts] Each:		..... 5.00	(500)
Deeds & Wills No. 2, 1691-1699, by Dorman		..... 5.00	(500)
Deeds & Wills No. 3, 1701-1707, by Dorman		..... 5.00	(500)
Order Book 1690-1698, by Dorman [In 3 parts] Each:		..... 5.00	(500)
Westmoreland County, by Crozier [Vol. 1, New Ser., Va. Col. Rec]	7.50	.....	(130)
Wills, 1654-1800, by Fothergill	10.00	.....	(130)
The Committees of Safety of Westmoreland and Fincastle: Proceedings of the County Committees, 1774-1776, by Harwell		..... 4.00	(244)
Legislative Petitions, 1776 & 1777 (in The Va. Gen., v.15, #1) 14pp		..... 3.00	(500)
1810 Federal Census, by Crickard		..... 3.00	(47)

WINCHESTER CITY

Winchester, Virginia, And Its Beginnings, 1743-1814, by Greene	7.50	.....	(123)

WYTHE COUNTY

Wythe County Chapters, ed. by Presgraves [Reprints of Hardesty's biographies; Boyd's history & geography; Whitman's pamphlets; completely indexed.]	17.50	.....	(830)
1800 Personal Property Tax Lists & Abstract of Deed Book #2 (1796-1800), by Schreiner-Yantis [Map of period.]		..... 3.00	(289)
1810 Federal Census, by Crickard		..... 4.00	(47)
1820 Federal Census & 1821 Boyé Map [shows many residences]		..... 4.00	(904)

YORK COUNTY

Charles Parish, York County, History and Registers: Births, 1648-1789; Deaths, 1665-1787, by Bell (repr. 1932 ed.)	17.50	15.00	(546)
1810 Federal Census, by Crickard		..... 3.00	(47)

Washington

STATEWIDE REFERENCES

From Wilderness to Enabling Act: The Evolution of the State of Washington, by Beckett		..... 2.50	(1022)

Research aids

Origin of Washington Geographic Names, by Meany (1923)	15.00	.....	(233)

Records

Catholic Church Records of the Pacific Northwest, Vancouver Records, Vol. 1 & 2 & Stellamaris Mission, ed. by Warner & Munnick [Bound in one book] (1972)	10.00	.....	(665)

KLICKITAT COUNTY

Index to Ballou's Early Klickitat Valley Days		..... 1.50	(467)
1860, 1870, 1880 Federal Censuses, by Smeltzer All:		..... 5.35	(467)

LEWIS COUNTY

1880 Federal Census, by Smeltzer		..... 4.00	(467)

MASON COUNTY

1880 Federal Census, by Smeltzer		..... 2.00	(467)

PACIFIC COUNTY

1880 Federal Census, by Smeltzer	.....	3.00	(467)
Rolls of Certain Indian Tribes, by McChesney, et al [Consisting in part of depositions given in 1913 by Chinook Indians, some of whom signed the 1851 Anson Dart treaty (not ratified) - has hundreds of Indian names, some photographs.]	10.00	.....	(829)

WHITMAN COUNTY

1880 Federal Census - Indexed, by Tri-City Genealogical Society	.....	5.00	(222)
Pilgrims on the Earth, by Scheuerman [A history of some German families that emigrated to the Ukraine under Catherine in the 1700's and to eastern Wash. State in late 19th century.]	6.00	.....	(829)

YAKIMA COUNTY

1880 Federal Census - Indexed, by Tri-City Genealogical Society	.....	3.00	(222)

West Virginia

STATEWIDE REFERENCES

The Allegheny Frontier: West Virginia Beginnings, 1730-1830, by Rice	10.50	.....	(126)
Virginia Beyond the Blue Ridge, by Gowing (1974) [A pictorial guide which ties the history of this area to today's scenes.]	12.95	.....	(660)
The Old and the New Monongahela, by Van Voorhis	20.00	.....	(130)
Wappatomaka: A Survey of the History and Geography of the South Branch Valley, by Morrison [Describes the settlement of this area, with numerous references to Civil War incidents.]	6.00	.....	(325)
The Fairfax Line: A Profile in History and Geography, by Morrison [History of Fairfax grant, its settlers, & the survey line.]	.....	1.50	(325)
An Outline of the Maryland Boundary Disputes and Related Events, by Morrison [A schematic study - not a text. Deals primarily with disputes along the Potomac River & Preston Co., W. Va.]	.....	3.00	(325)
History of the Early Settlement and Indian Wars of Western Virginia, by DeHass (repr. of 1851 ed.) [Several biog. sketches.]	9.00	.....	(796)
Notes on the Settlement & Indian Wars of the Western Parts of Virginia & Pennsylvania From 1763-1783, by Doddridge (1876)	16.50	.....	(625)

Research aids

Sources For Genealogical Searching in Va. & W. Va., by McCay	.....	3.50	(417)
Check List of West Virginia Imprints 1791-1830	.....	5.40	(624)
A Gazetteer of Virginia & West Virginia, by Gannett	12.50	.....	(130)
West Virginia History, Vols. 1-10 (1930/40-1948/49) Set:	220.00	170.00	(624)
" " " " Each:	.....	16.80	(624)

Records

Virginia Court Records in Southwestern Pennsylvania: Records of the District of West Augusta & Ohio & Yohogania Counties, Virginia, 1775-1780, by Crumrine	20.00	.....	(130)
West Virginia Revolutionary Ancestors Whose Services Were Not Military and Whose Names, Therefore, Do Not Appear in Revolutionary Indexes of Soldiers & Sailors, by Reddy	.....	5.00	(130)
The Soldiery of West Virginia in the French and Indian War; Lord Dunmore's War; the Revolution; the later Indian Wars; the Second War With England, by Lewis	9.50	.....	(130)

Religious and ethnic groups

The Brethern in Virginia, by Sappington [History of the church
of the Brethren in Va. & adj. counties of W. Va.]   7.00   ..... (344)
The Christian Church in West Virginia, 1807-1970, by Cramblet 7.95   ..... (735)

BATH COUNTY

1810 Federal Census, by Crickard 4.00 (47)

BERKELEY COUNTY

Shenandoah Valley Pioneers & Their Descendants, by Cartmell 25.00 ..... (123)
History of the Lower Shenandoah Valley Counties of Frederick,
Berkeley, Jefferson & Clarke, by Norris 32.50 ..... (123)
On this Rock: The Story of St. Peter's Church, Shepherdstown,
1765-1965, by Hartzell [A complete translating from German
of the first register of this Lutheran church. Early baptismal
records and membership lists are included.] 9.25 ..... (754)
American Museum, Vol. 4, by Grove [Baptisimal Register (1836-
1842) of Old St. Joseph's Parish, Martinsburg; Genealogy of the
county from c1634-1820; other items of interest about the area.] 7.75 (889)
1810 Federal Census, by Crickard 5.00 (47)

BROOKE COUNTY

Marriages - Book 1, 1797-1842, by Warrell 4.00 (716)
1810 Federal Census, by Crickard 4.00 (47)

CABELL COUNTY

1810 Personal Property Tax List, by Schreiner-Yantis 1.50 (289)
1815 Personal Property Tax List & Facsimile of John Wood's
Map (made in 1820 and names taverns, ferries, mills, etc.) 2.25 (289)

FAYETTE COUNTY

Historical Notes on Fayette County, by Donnelly (1958) 12.50 10.00 (546)

GREENBRIAR COUNTY

Greenbriar County — Circa 1780, by Schreiner-Yantis [Tax lists,
surveys, etc. of this period. Large map. Approximate location
of residence of most taxpayers given.] Publication date, 1977. .... (289)
1810 Personal Property Tax List, by Schreiner-Yantis 1.50 (289)
1850 Federal Census - Indexed, by Cloninger 7.50 (258)

HAMPSHIRE COUNTY

Shenandoah Valley Pioneers & Their Descendants, by Cartmell 25.00 ..... (123)
History of Hampshire County, by Maxwell & Swisher (repr. 1897) 20.00 ..... (796)
Early Records of Hampshire County, by Sage & Jones 15.00 ..... (130)
Marriage Records (in Gen. Ref. Builders, v. 3, #2) 10pp. 1.50 (931)
Four Years in the Stonewall Brigade, by Casler [Soldier life
under Stonewall Jackson.] 10.00 ..... (848)
1810 Federal Census, by Crickard 7.00 (47)
1820 Federal Census, by Crickard 7.00 (47)

HARDY COUNTY

Shenandoah Valley Pioneers & Their Descendants, by Cartmell 25.00 ..... (123)
1810 Personal Property Tax List, by Schreiner-Yantis 1.50 (289)

HARRISON COUNTY

Marriages (in Gen. Ref. Builders, v. 8, #2) 9pp. 2.00 (931)
1810 Federal Census, by Crickard 5.00 (47)
1820 Federal Census, by Crickard 5.00 (47)

JACKSON COUNTY

A Guide to the Records of Jackson County (in Va. Gen., v. 15, #1) 3.00 (500)
Roster of Jackson County Civil War Soldiers, by Hite [Condensed
    service records; much genealogical data; map of county.] 4.50 (61)
1860 Federal Census, by Hite [Annotated; also list of Jackson Co.
    landowners of 1861 appended; and map.] 10.50 (61)

JEFFERSON COUNTY

A Guide to the Records of Jefferson County (in Va. Gen., v. 15, #2) 3.00 (500)
History of the Lower Shenandoah Valley Counties of Frederick,
    Berkeley, Jefferson, & Clarke, by Norris 32.50 ..... (123)
The Private Journal of Abraham Joseph Warner, ed. by Enderton
    [Rev. Warner, an Episcopal priest, was chaplain of the 12th
    Illinois Cav. in Civil War. He gives an eyewitness acct. of
    Harpers Ferry with supporting documents.] 11.00 ..... (83)
1810 Federal Census, by Crickard 4.00 (47)
On This Rock: The Story of St. Peter's Church, Shepherdstown,
    1765-1965, by Hartzell [A complete translation from German
    of the first register of this Lutheran church. Also early bap-
    tismal records and membership lists.] 9.25 ..... (754)

KANAWHA COUNTY

A Guide to the Records of Kanawha County (in Va. Gen., v. 15, #2) 3.00 (500)
Marriages, 1792-1869, by Wintz 10.00 ..... (796)
West Virginia Estate Settlements, by Johnson & Barnett 15.00 12.50 (688)
1810 Federal Census, by Crickard 3.00 (47)

LEWIS COUNTY

A Guide to the Records of Lewis County (in Va. Gen., v. 16, #1) 3.00 (500)

LINCOLN COUNTY

A Guide to the Records of Lincoln County (in Va. Gen., v. 16, #1) 3.00 (500)

LOGAN COUNTY

A Guide to the Records of Logan County (in Va. Gen., v. 16, #2) 3.00 (500)
1830 Federal Census, by Schreiner-Yantis [Map of the period.] 2.00 (289)

MASON COUNTY

1810 Federal Census, by Crickard 2.00 (47)
1820 Federal Census, by Crickard 3.00 (47)

MERCER COUNTY

History of the Middle New River Settlements, by Johnston (repr.
    of 1906 ed.) [Early history, Indian captivities, military ros-
    ters, family genealogies. New every-name index.] 17.50 ..... (289)
1840 Federal Census, by Schreiner-Yantis [Map of period.] 2.00 (289)
1850 Federal Census - Indexed, by Schreiner-Yantis [Map.] 6.00 (289)

MONONGALIA COUNTY

1810 Federal Census, by Crickard 5.00 (47)
1820 Federal Census, by Crickard 6.00 (47)

MONROE COUNTY

A History of Monroe County, by Morton 17.50 ..... (130)
History of the Middle New River Settlements, by Johnston (repr.
    of 1906 ed.) [Early history, Indian captivities, miliary ros-
    ters, family genealogies. New every-name index.] 17.50 ..... (289)
1810 Federal Census, by Crickard 3.00 (47)

MORGAN COUNTY

Shenandoah Valley Pioneers and Their Descendants, by Cartmell   25.00   .....   (123)

OHIO COUNTY

Virginia Court Records in Southwestern Pennsylvania. Records of
the Dist. of W.Augusta & Ohio & Yohogania Cos., by Crumrine   20.00   .....   (130)
1810 Federal Census, by Crickard 3.00   (47)

PENDLETON COUNTY

A History of Pendleton County, by Morton   16.00   .....   (130)
1797 Assessment List, by Forbes [Includes a supplement on the
population growth of county from 1790-1970.] 3.00   (369)
1810 Federal Census, by Crickard 3.00   (47)

RANDOLPH COUNTY

1810 Federal Census, by Crickard 2.00   (47)
1820 Federal Census, by Crickard 4.00   (47)
1850 Federal Census, by Crickard 6.00   (47)
1860 Federal Census, by Crickard 6.00   (47)

SUMMERS COUNTY

A History of the Middle New River Settlements, by Johnston (repr.
of 1906 ed.) [Early history, Indian captivities, military rosters, family genealogies. New every-name index.]   17.50   .....   (47)

WIRT COUNTY

Warning In Appalachia, by Reed [Social & economic research
with chapter devoted to family names.]   7.00   .....   (77)

WOOD COUNTY

1810 Federal Census, by Crickard 2.50   (47)
1820 Federal Census, by Crickard 3.00   (47)

Wisconsin

STATEWIDE REFERENCES

Wisconsin: The Americanization of a French Settlement, by
Thwaites (repr. of 1908 ed.)   24.50   .....   (630)
A History of Wisconsin, by Nesbit   12.50   .....   (1012)
French Regime in Wisconsin & the Northwest, by Kellogg (1925)   12.95   .....   (985)
Haven in the Woods: The Story of the Finns in Wisconsin, by
Kolehmainen & Hill (repr. of 1951 ed.)   .....   o.p.   (811)
Wisconsin Magazine of History, Vols. 1-20.   Set: 600.00   480.00   (624)
"   "   "   "   Each: 24.00   (624)
Index to Vols. 1-15, Wisconsin Magazine of History (above) 18.00   (624)

Research aids

The Territorial Papers of the United States: The Territory of
Wisconsin, Executive Jour. 1836-1848; Papers, 1836-1839   13.50   .....   (401)
Wisconsin Territorial Papers, County Series (repr. 1941-42)
[Laws, statutes, etc.] 4v.   Set: 110.00   .....   (630)
Wisconsin Territorial Papers, County Series. 4v.   Each: 27.50   .....   (630)
Wisconsin: A Student's Guide to Localized History [#2003-8] 1.50   (762)
The Wisconsin Valley: Guide to Localized History [#1240-X] 1.50   (762)

Wisconsin Historical Collections: Cumulative Index
(repr. of 1915 ed.) 10.00 ..... (811)
Descriptive List of Manuscript Collections of the State His-
torical Society of Wisconsin, Together With Reports on
Other Collections of Manuscript Material For American
History in Adjacent States, ed. by Thwaites (repr. 1908) 17.50 15.00 (546)
Atlas of Wisconsin, by Robinson 20.00 5.95 (1012)
SL #23 - Cartographic Records Relating to the Territory of
Wisconsin 1836-1848, by Kelsay & Ashby ..... free (402)
Wisconsin State Historical Society Collections, 31 vols.
Vols. 1-31 (1903-1931) Partly original ed.
[Vol. 1-10 ed. by Draper. Vol. 21 index to 1-20] ·Set: 904.80 718.80 (624)
Newspaper Collection of the Milwaukee Public Library -
A Listing (in MCGS Reporter, v. 5, #3) 2pp. ..... .75 (596)
The Papers of Robert M. laFollette at the State Historical
Society of Wisconsin: Guide to a Microfilm Edition (1972) 3.00 (811)

FOND du LAC COUNTY

Grafton Hall School for Young Ladies - 1900 [list of students &
graduates] (in MCGS Reporter, v.5, #6) 3pp. ..... .75 (596)

MILWAUKEE COUNTY

Milwaukee County Genealogical Society REPORTER [Publication
of the Milwaukee Genealogical Society which is issued 6 times
per year - 22 pages per issue.] Subscription per year: 2.00 (596)
Note: All of the following are articles which appeared in above.
1840 Federal Census - New Berlin (in v.6, #3) 2pp. ..... .75 (596)
1840 Federal Census - Town of Franklin (in v.6, #1) 2pp. ..... .75 (596)
1840 Federal Census - Kinnekanic (in v.6, #2) 3pp. ..... .75 (596)
1840 Federal Census - Town of Lake (in v.5, #6) 3pp. ..... .75 (596)
Honey Creek Cemetery - West Allis [Index to burials &
map of cemetery] (in v.6, #3) 5pp. ..... .75 (596)
Old Milwaukee - Retail and Fancy Grocers [Biographies]
(continuing article, starting v.5, #2) 4v./$3 or Each: ..... .75 (596)

MONROE COUNTY

Genealogical Branches From Monroe County, by Habelman. Vol. 1
[Obituaries taken from newspapers; church, school, and cem-
etery records. Nearly 2,000 names indexed.] 3.00 (25)
Genealogical Branches From Monroe County, by Habelman. Vol. 2
[Continuation of above. Same sources.] 4.00 (25)

WALWORTH COUNTY

Index to Landowners & Patrons - Walworth County 1873 Atlas, by
Pruett. 2 vols. Both: 5.50 (620)
Cemetery Inscriptions of Old Hudson Cemetery at Lyons
(in MCGS REPORTER, v.6, #1) 3pp. ..... .75 (596)

Wyoming

STATEWIDE REFERENCES

Wyoming: A Student's Guide to Localized History 1.50 (762)
Active Wyoming Pioneers (in Gen.Ref.Builders, v.8, #3) 20pp. 2.00 (931)
Vigilante Days and Ways: The Pioneers of the Rockies, the Makers
and Making of Montana, Idaho, Oregon, Washington, and Wyoming (repr. of 1890 ed.) 2 vols. Each: 18.00 ..... (630)

CONVERSE COUNTY

Index to Morticians Records, Douglas [Gives name, date & place
   of death, many give birthdate & place, parents and birthplace,
   and some give spouses and marriage dates.] 123pp. 3.00 (158)
Fort Fetterman's Cemetery [Soldiers: Regt., Company, circumstances and date of death. Pioneers: all genealogical data
   known, circumstances and events surrounding death.] 1.50 (158)

BIG HORN COUNTY

Big Horn County, by Mercer (repr. 1906 ed.)   10.00   7.50 (814)

LARAMIE COUNTY

Cheyenne: The Magic City of the Plains, 1867-1967, by Cheyenne
   Historical Commissson 5.00 (777)
Cheyenne & Black Hills Stage & Express Routes, by Spring (1965) 2.25 (760)

Regions

MISSISSIPPI VALLEY

Condensed Geography & History of the Western States or the Missi-
   sippi Valley, by Flint. 2 vols. (repr. of 1828 ed.)   Set: 40.00 ..... (922)
History of the Discovery & Settlement of the Valley of the Valley of
   the Mississippi by the Three Great European Powers, Spain,
   France, & Great Britain, & Civil Government by the United
   States Until the Year 1846, by Monette. 2 vols. in 1   50.00 ..... (629)
The French in the Mississippi Valley, 1740-1750, by Dunlap (1974) 12.50 ..... (909)
The Spanish in the Mississippi Valley, 1762-1804, by McDermott
   (1974)   15.00 ..... (678)
Spain in the Mississippi Valley, 1765-1794, by Kinnaird. 3 vols.
   (Annual report for the Am. Hist. Assoc. for 1945)   Set: 125.00 ..... (863)

NEW ENGLAND

New England Diaries, 1602-1800, by Forbes (Repr. of 1923 ed.)
   [A descriptive catalogue of diaries, orderly books, and sea
   journals.]   10.00 ..... (988)
Winthrop Papers, Vol. 1, 1498-1628 [Prepared for the Massa-
   chusetts Historical Society by S.E. Morison, et al] (repr. 1929) 15.00 ..... (988)
Winthrop Papers, Vol. 2, 1623-1630 [Prepared for the Massa-
   chusetts Historical Society by S.E. Morison, et al] Edited by
   Stewart Mitchell. (repr. of 1931 ed.)   12.50 ..... (988)
The Genealogical Advertiser [A quarterly magazine of family history. Collection of previously unpublished genealogical data
   from original sources. Coverage is New England from 17th
   into 19th centuries, with emphasis on Mass.] 4 vs. in 1   21.50 ..... (130)
Directory of the Ancestral Heads of New England Families,
   1620-1700, by Holmes   12.50 ..... (130)
Records of the Colony of New Plymouth, in New England [Print-
   ed by Order of the Legislature . . . of Mass.] 12v. in 6   Set: 437.50 ..... (630)
History of New England, by Palfrey (repr. 1858-1890) 5v.   Set: 140.00 ..... (630)
Apprenticeship and Apprenticeship Education in Colonial New
   England and New York, by Seybolt (repr. 1917)   4.50 ..... (630)
The History of the Indian Wars in New England From the First Set-
   tlement to the Termination of the War with King Philip in 1677,
   by Hubbard. (repr. of 1865 ed.) 2 vols. in 1.   25.00 ..... (624)
Soldiers in King Philip's War. Being a Critical Account of That
   War With a Hist of the Indian Wars of N.E. 1620-1677, by Bodge 15.00 ..... (130)

The Land System of the New England Colonies, by Egleston (1886)	10.25	6.25	(1000)
Church and State in New England, by Lauer (repr. of 1892 ed.)	12.50	8.50	(1000)
The Truth About the Pilgrims, by Stoddard	7.50	.....	(130)
The Puritan Frontier: Town Planning in New England Colonial Development, 1630-1660, by Haller (1951)	10.00	.....	(630)
The Real Founders of New England. Stories of Their Life Along the Coast, 1602-1628, by Bolton	11.00	.....	(130)
Topographical Dictionary of 2885 English Emigrants to New England, 1620-1650, by Banks [Passenger lists.]	12.00	.....	(130)
A Genealogical Dictionary of the First Settlers of New England, by Savage	55.00	.....	(130)
New England Historical & Genealogical Register: Index of Persons, Subjects, Places (Vols. 1-50), by Rayne & Chapman	60.00	.....	(130)
Ancestral Roots of Sixty Colonists Who Came to New England Between 1623 and 1650, by Weis	12.50	.....	(130)
A Genealogical Register of the First Settlers of New England, 1620-1675, by Farmer	13.50	.....	(130)
Transcript of Three Registers of Passengers From Great Yarmouth to Holland and New England, by Jewson	7.50	.....	(130)
Genealogical Notes of N.Y. & New England Families, by Talcott	15.00	.....	(130)
Genealogical Notes on the Founding of New England, by Flagg	15.00	.....	(130)
Result of Some Researches Among the British Archives For Information Relative to the Founders of New England, by Drake	8.50	.....	(130)
Immigrants to New England, 1700-1775, by Bolton	8.50	.....	(130)
Gore Roll of Arms and Positive Pedigrees and Authorized Arms, by Appleton [New England heraldry.]	.....	5.00	(130)
New England Cemeteries: A Collector's Guide, by Kull [How to find & what to look for in the 280 old New England cemeteries most worth a visit.] Available, June 1975.	9.95	5.95	(662)

OHIO VALLEY

A Study of the Local Literature of the Upper Ohio Valley, With Especial Reference to the Early Pioneer and Indian Tales, 1820-1840, by Atkeson (repr. of 1921 ed.)	10.00	.....	(630)
Valley of Democracy. The Frontier versus the Plantation in the Ohio Valley, 1775-1818, by Barnhart	18.00	.....	(624)
The Ohio Valley: A Student's Guide to Localized History (#1044-x)	.....	1.50	(762)
A History of the Manufactures in the Ohio Valley to the Year 1860, by Lippincott (repr. of 1914 ed.)	11.95	.....	(909)
Genesis of Western Culture: The Upper Ohio Valley, 1800-1825, by Miller (repr. of 1938 ed.)	15.00	.....	(863)

OLD NORTHWEST

The French & the British in the Old Northwest, A Bibliographical Guide to Archive & Manuscript Sources, by Beers (1964)	12.95	.....	(902)
Recollections of Philander Prescott: Frontiersman of the Old Northwest (1819-1862), by Prescott (1966)	5.95	.....	(760)
Five Forts, by Ankenbruck [Wilderness wars for the Old Northwest, & the people who held forts at Fort Wayne, 1721-1819.]	.....	1.95	(93)
Fort Wayne, Gateway of the West, 1802-1913: Garrison Orderly Books; Indian Agency Account Book, by Griswold (1927)	24.50	.....	(630)
The Civilization of the Old Northwest: A Study of Political, Social, & Economic Development, 1788-1812, by Bond (repr. 1934)	12.50	.....	(630)

OLD SOUTHWEST
[Louisiana, Texas, Arkansas, Tennessee, Kentucky, Missouri]

Indians & Pioneers: The Story of the American Southwest Before 1830, by Foreman (repr. of 1936 ed.)	7.95	.....	(664)

The Development of Methodism in the Old Southwest, 1783-1824,
by Posey (repr. of 1933 ed.) [Methodist Episcopal Church]   10.00   .....   (909)

NEW SOUTHWEST
[New Mexico, Arizona, Colorado, Utah, Nevada, California]

Spanish Colonization in the Southwest, by Blackmar (repr.1890)   10.25   6.25   (1000)

POTOMAC VALLEY

The Potomac Valley: A Student's Guide to Localized History 1.50   (762)

SOUTH

Southern Colonies in the 17th Century, 1607-1689, by Craven   12.50   4.25   (935)
Southern Colonies in the 18th Century, 1689-1763, by Ver Steeg   ....   (935)
History of the South, by Stephenson & Coulter. 10 vols.   ....   (935)
The Civilization of the Old South: Writings of Clement Eaton, ed.
  by Kirwan [A mosaic of the life of the Old South from the era
  of Jefferson to the Civil War.]   7.50   .....   (126)
Prologue to Democracy: The Federalists in the South, 1789-1800,
  by Rose   8.50   .....   (126)
A Key to Southern Pedigrees, by Crozier [Vol. 8 of Va.Col.Rec.]   6.50   .....   (130)
Subject Index to Southern Historical Society Papers, by Minor
  [An index of authors & titles of articles appearing.] 10.00   (848)
Southeastern Broadsides Before 1877: A Bibliography, by Hummel   15.00   .....   (244)
Special Aids to Genealogical Research on Southern Families
  [Reprints of articles which appeared in the National Genealog-
  ical Society Quarterly. Bound in one book.] Subjects include:
      Oaths of Allegiance for St. Mary's County, Maryalnd
      1800 Census of District of Columbia
      Buckingham County & Lower Albemarle, Virginia
      Lord Fairfax Rent Rolls, Virginia
      Genealogical Research in Kentucky (3 articles)
      Microfilm Records in North Carolina Dept. of Ar. & Hist.
      Genealogical Source Material in South Carolina
      List of Voters in Early South Carolina Elections
      Genealogical Research in Georgia
      Alabama Records for Genealogical Research
      Pension Records of Revolutionary Soldiers in Mississippi
      Also additional titles.   All: 5.50   (616)
Travels in the Old South, 1783-1860, Selected from Periodicals
  of the Times, ed. by Schwaab & Bull   25.00   .....   (126)
Travels in the Old South: A Bibliography. 3 vols. [Vol. 1 - The
  Formative Years, 1527-1783; Vol. 2 - The Expanding South,
  1750-1825; Vol. 3 - The Ante Belleum South, 1825-1860] by
  Clark   Set: 45.00   .....   (664)
Old Southern Bible Records, by Lester (Chiefly 18th & 19th cen.) 18.50   .....   (130)
Colonial Families of the Southern States of America, by Hardy   18.50   .....   (130)
Historical Southern Families, by Boddie. 19 vols.   Each: 15.00   .....   (130)
Notable Southern Families, by Armstrong, 3 vols.   Set: 60.00   .....   (130)
Notable Southern Families, by Armstrong. Vol. 1   12.00   .....   (663)
    "   "   "   "   Vols. 2,3,&4   Each: 15.00   .....   (663)
    "   "   "   , by French & Armstrong, Vol. 5   18.00   .....   (663)
    "   "   "   , by French, Vol. 6   10.50   .....   (663)

Family Genealogies

1   – THE CAPERTON FAMILY by Bernard M. Caperton.
Caperton: Monroe Co, WVa–1774-1900; Madison Co, Ky–1776-   ;
Tenn–1810-   ; N.Ala–1820-   ; N.Miss–1820-   ; Tex–1845-date.
Swope/Soape: Monroe Co, WVa–1776-1790; Madison Co, Ky– 1790-1800
Kelly: Monroe Co, WVa–1776-1790; Morgan Co, Mo–1830-
Gibson: Madison Co, Ky–1790-   ; Tenn–1810-
Townsend: Madison Co, Ky–1700-   ; Tenn–1810-
Cloth–239pp–$12.50 -- Vendor   #1

2   – THE CHRISTIAN HUSS FAMILY TREE AS WRITTEN BY HIS DESCENDANTS
compiled by Fae Elaine Scott
Huss: Chester Co, Pa–1752-1795; Lancaster Co, Pa–1795-1810; York Co, Pa–
1810-1820; Sandusky Co, O–1825-1972
Paper–234pp–$32.00--Vendor   #4

3   – THE DESCENDANTS OF PETER SIMMONS, BRUNSWICK COUNTY, VIR-
GINIA, WITH ALLIED LINES OF HIATT, MILLS, PATTON, JAMES, HARLESS,
AND McGRIFF by Gwen Boyer Bjorkman
Simmons: Brunswick Co, Va–1719-1771; Surry Co, NC–1772-1850; Jefferson
Co, Tenn–1801-1850; Ind–1825-1860
Paper–180pp–$6.00--Vendor   #5

4   – SKETCHES & GENEALOGY OF THE BAILEY - CRADDOCK - LAWSON
FAMILIES by Betsy L. Willis & Martha B. Craddock
Bailey: NC–1755-1973
Paper–218pp–$13.00--Vendor   #6

5   – LETTERS & GENEALOGY OF THE STRUDWICK - ASHE - YOUNG FAMI-
LIES by Betsy L. Willis & Col. J. Webb Strudwick
Strudwick: NC–1764-1900; Ala–1821-1969
Paper–250pp–$12.50--Vendor   #6

6   – CRAWFORD & ALLIED FAMILIES by Andrew J. Crawford
Crawford: Pulaski Co, Ky–1820-1972; Wayne Co, Ky–1820-1972; Calif–
1940-1972; Ind–1940-1972; La–1955-1972
Kindrick: Wythe Co, Va–1750-1824; Wayne Co, Ky–1824-1972
Spiral–298pp–$10.00--Vendor   #9

7   – KNIGHT LETTER, VOLUME I thru VI, by Merle Ganier
Knight: All families, anywhere
Paper–264pp–$24.00--Vendor   #10

8   – THE MAT(T)HEWS FAMILY by John R. Boots, Jr.
Mat(t)hews: Augusta Co, Va–1700-1800; Ga–1780-date; Southeast in general;
Ireland–prior to 18th century
Cloth–800pp–$20.00-- Vendor   #11

9   - A GIVENS-HALL FAMILY HISTORY FROM PRE-REVOLUTIONARY TIMES
TO 1970 by Dorothy Hall Givens
Givens: North Ireland-226-1000; Strathclyde, Scotland-1000-1620; North Ireland-1620-1700's; Southwest Va-1700's to 1970
Hall: Huntingdon Co, Pa-ante 1800-1810; Knox Co, O-1810-1970
Green: Loudoun Co, Va-1755-1788; Licking & Knox Cos, O-1800-1970
Cloth-718pp-$15.50-- Vendor #12

10   - COME OVER INTO MACEDONIA [THE CHARLES THOMPSON LINE
FROM DINWIDDIE COUNTY, VIRGINIA TO RIPLEY COUNTY, MISSOURI]
by Thelma S. McManus & Grace E. Burlison
Thompson: Dinwiddie Co, Va-c1760-c1780; Northampton/Anson Cos, NC-
1781-c1808; Dickson/Benton Cos, Tenn-1808-1855; Ripley Co, Mo-1855-1974
Paper-250pp-$10.50--Vendor #14

11   - THE DARSTS OF VIRGINIA, WITH SKETCHES OF THE CECIL, CHARLTON,
GLENDY, GRIGSBY, LAREW, MILLER, TROLINGER, WELCH, WYGAL AND
WYSOR FAMILIES by H. Jackson Darst
Darst: Shenandoah Co, Va-1755-1790; Goochland Co, Va-1780-1790; Rockbridge Co, Va-1785-1885; Pulaski Co, Va-1839-1972
Cecil: Montgomery Co, Va-1760-1839; Pulaski Co, Va-1839-1972
Charlton: Montgomery Co, Va-1760-1875; Pulaski Co, Va-1839-1900
Glendy: Rockbridge Co, Va-1800-1899; Pulaski Co, Va-1839-1972
Grigsby: Stafford Co, Va-1660-1790; Rockbridge Co, Va-1775-1900
Larew: Frederick Co, Va-1740-1790; Augusta Co, Va-1745-1910
Miller: Montgomery Co, Va-1770-1839; Pulaski Co, Va-1839-1925
Trolinger: Orange Co, Ba-1730-1840; Pulaski Co, Va-1776-1972
Welch: Orange Co, Va-1730-1800; Rockbridge Co, Va
Wygal: Montgomery Co, Va-1770-1839; Pulaski Co, Va-1839-1925
Wysor: Montgomery Co, Va-1780-1839; Pulaski Co, Va-1839-1925
Cloth-574pp-$15.00------------------------------------- Vendor #17

12   - LUCIUS FAMILIES U.S.A., VOL. I, by Ophelia Richardson Wade
Lucius: Seneca Co, O-1854-1971; Allen Co, O-1870-1971; Wyandot Co, O-
1880-1971
Paper-169pp-$12.50---------------------------------------Vendor #19

13   - LUCIUS FAMILIES U.S.A., VOL. II, By Ophelia Richardson Wade
Lucius: Chicksaw Co, Miss-1843-1971; Calhoun Co, Miss-1860-1971;
Choctaw Co, Miss-1860-1971; Webster Co, Miss-1880-1971
Paper-154pp-$15.00---------------------------------------Vendor #19

14   - JACOB LOLLAR FAMILY, 1750-1972 by Ophelia Richardson Wade
Lollar: NC-1750-1790; Pendleton Dist, SC-1790-1830; Walker Co, Ala-
1830-1972; Choctaw Co, Miss-1850-1972
Gaunt: Lincoln Co, NC-1730-1790; Abbeville Dist, SC 1790-1809
Henson: Tuscaloosa Co, Ala-1830-1850; Choctaw Co, Miss-1850-1870
Paper-240pp-$15.00---------------------------------------Vendor #19

15 – KIMBRIEL KITH AND KIN by Ophelia Richardson Wade
Kimbriel: Harris Co, Ga–1840-1855; Choctaw Co, Miss–1850-1974;
Webster Co, Miss–1880-1974; Tex–1880-1974
Forrester: Harris Co, Ga–1842-1850; Troup Co, Ga–1850-1860
Easterwood: Pickens Co, Ala–1830-1840; Webster Co, Miss–1850-1974
Roberts: Itawamba Co, Miss–1840-1870; Choctaw Co, Miss–1850-1880
Lewis: Choctaw Co, Miss–1840-1974; Webster Co, Miss–1880-1974
Paper–202pp–$13.00--Vendor #19

16 – WADE ANCESTORS AND RELATED FAMILIES by Ophelia R. Wade
Wade: Pittsylvania Co, Va–1752-1782; Greene Co, Ga–1788-1790; Pendleton
Dist, SC–1790-1820; Chickasaw Co, Miss–1855-1973
Burford: Pendleton Dist, SC–1790-1817; Ga–1820-1973
Moore: Hall Co, Ga–1820-1830; Tippah Co, Miss–1843-1850
King: Lowndes Co, Miss–1840-1848; Tippah Co, Miss–1850-1860; Chicka-
saw Co, Miss–1860-1973
Aycock: Wake Co, NC–1813-1829; Oktibbeha Co, Miss–1850-1973; Calhoun
Co, Miss–1903-1973
Butler: Wake Co, NC–1813-1829; Greene Co, Ala–1829-1850
Hamilton: Marion Co, Ala–1825-1840; Oktibbeha Co, Miss–1850-1900
Cloth–336pp–$18.00/Paper–$15.00----------------------------Vendor #19

17 – THE FEARNS OF VIRGINIA by Elizabeth Lee Fearn Cabell Ferneyhough &
Elizabeth Lee Lusk
Fearn: Northern Neck, Va–1623-1707; Middlesex Co, Va–1700-1756; Isle of
Wight Co, Va–1760-1833; Buckingham Co, Va–1744-1802; Bourbon Co, Ky–
1786-1800
Paper–90pp–$7.50--Vendor #20

18 – JOHN FLEMING – CAROLINA TO CALIFORNIA – SOME DESCENDANTS
AND IN-LAWS, 1734-1972 by Lee Fleming Reese, M.A.
Fleming: SC–1734-c1800; Ga–1800-1830; Ala–1830-1870; Tex–1870-1974
Frey/Fry/Frye: SC–1790-c1830; Ala–1830-1880
Hendrix/Hendricks: SC–1790-1830; Ala–1830-1974
Lowry/Lowery: SC–1790-1823; Ala–1823-1974
Cloth–560+pp–$30.00-- Vendor #21

19 – PIONEER FAMILIES OF SULLIVAN COUNTY, MISSOURI by Richard Sears
Payne: Sullivan Co, Tenn–1810-1820; Monroe Co, Ky–1820-1970
Baldridge: Ireland–1689-1726; Lancaster Co, Pa–1726-1770; Orange Co,
NC–1770-1800; St. Charles Co, Mo–1800-1844
Sears: Mass–1630-1805; NY–1805-1819
Yardley: St. Charles Co, Mo–1800-1850; Sullivan Co, Mo–1850-1974
Cloth–409pp–$15.00-- Vendor #22

20 – MUDD FAMILY OF UNITED STATES by Richard D. Mudd, M.D.
Mudd: Maryland–1665-date
Cloth–1835pp–$24.00-- Vendor #23

21 — MILLER INDEX compiled by Bette Miller Radewald
Miller: [A research bulletin for the purpose of collecting and preserving Miller family data. Any Miller, any place in the United States. Emphasis is on pre-1899. Number of pages varies; the first three issues averaged 43 pages.]
Subscription: $5 per year/ $9 for 2 years ----------------------Vendor #24

22 — MILLER PATRIOTS IN THE AMERICAN REVOLUTION by Bette Miller Radewald
Miller: [To honer any Miller who served in the formation of our country.]
[In process. Publication date about November 1975]-------------Vendor #24

23 — DIARY OF ALLEN FRANKLIN SCRUGGS . . . 1803-1902 by Judith Allison Walters
Scruggs: Williamson Co, Tenn—1810-1830; Morgan Co, Ill—1832-1836;
Lauderdale Co, Ala—1837-1840; Bourbon Co, Ky—1846-1856
Paper—103pp—$4.00---Vendor #27

24 — JOHNSON-SCRUGGS . . . A COLLECTION OF PHOTOGRAPHS by Judith Allison Walters
Johnson: Fleming Co, Ky—1812-1830; Mason Co, Ky—1830-1857; Pettis Co, Mo—1857-1899; Pierce Co, Wash—1899-1910
Scruggs: Buckingham Co, Va—1770-1804; Davidson Co, Tenn—1804-1830;
Tishomingo Co, Miss—1845-1870
Paper—43pp—$3.00---Vendor #27

25 — ALLISON-SCRUGGS . . . MORE OLD PHOTOGRAPHS AND LETTERS by Judith Allison Walters
Allison: Wilkes Co, NC—1795-1817; Madison Co, Ill—1817-1820; Pettis Co, Mo—1820-present
Scruggs: Johnson Co, Mo—1857-present
Paper—65pp—$4.00---Vendor #27

26 — THOMAS, WALTERS & RELATED WELSH FAMILIES OF SOUTHERN MINNESOTA by Judith Allison Walters
Thomas: Montgomery, Wales—1764-1824; Cardigan, Wales—1824-1865;
Blue Earth Co, Minn—1865-present
Walters: Cardigan, Wales—1800-1840; Jackson Co, O—1840-1852; Blue Earth Co, Minn—1852-present
Paper—57pp—$5.00---Vendor #27

27 — THE 1876 DIARY OF ABRAHAM SPENCER OF CLEARFIELD COUNTY, PENNSYLVANIA by Judith Allison Walters
Spencer: Clearfield Co, Pa—1850-1880
Paper—42pp—$4.00---Vendor #27

28 — STEPHEN PRIDGEN - 1832 to 1864 - LETTERS, MILITARY DATA, GENEALOGY, AND MISCELLANEOUS PRIDGEN RECORDS by Carolyn E. Parker
Pridgen: NC—1790-1820; Ga—1820-   ; Ala-1837-1974; Tex—   -1974
Cloth—131pp—$8.50--- Vendor #31

29   – HOUSE OF MONCURE GENEALOGY (WITH TWO SUPPLEMENTS) by Marion
     Moncure Duncan, Adrian Cather Miller, and Peyton Sagendorf Moncure
     Moncure: Stafford Co, Va–1730's
     Cloth–408pp–$30.00--- Vendor #33

30   – SAGENDORF, SAGENDORPH, SEGENDORF: A GENEALOGY by Peyton
     Sagendorf Moncure and Kathryn Schwartz Callaghan
     Sagendorf/Sagendorph: Columbia Co, NY–1710-   ; NY State–1800-
     Cloth–632pp–$25.00--- Vendor #33

31   – A MASSIE FAMILY HISTORY - DESCENDANTS OF JAMES R. MASSIE by
     Evelyn H. Massie
     Massie: Fauquier Co, Va–1775-1805; Mercer Co, Ky–1805-1972; Fayetteville,
     Ark–1857-1972; Lawrence Co, SD–1880-1972
     Paper–272pp–$7.00---Vendor #34

32   – PREWITT - LIGHT - RINGLER - HOLLOWELL AND ALLIED FAMILIES by
     Lester Dee Prewitt
     Prewitt: Va–1750-1789; Ky–1789-1850; Ind–1850-1876; Ia–1876-1970
     Cloth–65pp–$7.50--Vendor #36

33   – THE DAWKINS AND STEWART FAMILIES OF VIRGINIA AND KENTUCKY by
     Lela Wolfe Prewitt
     Dawkins: Northumberland Co, Va–1680-1746; mid-Va–1746-1768; Frederick
     Co, Va–1768-1789; Ky–1790-1968
     Stewart: Fauquier Co, Va–1720-1800; Henry Co, Ky–1800-1900's
     Cloth–154pp–$8.50--Vendor #36

34   – ANCESTORS & DESCENDANTS OF THOMAS SIMS OF CULPEPER COUNTY,
     VIRGINIA - EDMUND BUTLER OF VIRGINIA AND KENTUCKY WITH ALLIED
     FAMILIES AND OTHER CULPEPER DATA by Lela Wolfe Prewitt
     Sims/Simms: Richmond Co, Va–c1700-1733; Culpeper Co, Va–1734-1973;
     Ky–c1800-1973; and other states
     Butler: Va–1740's-1810; Carolinas–1763-1800's; Ky–c1800-1900
     Cloth–193pp–$12.50---Vendor #36

35   – THE WOLFE - HAWKINS - SHEETS - YATES - WHEELER AND ALLIED
     FAMILIES by Lela Wolfe Prewitt
     Wolf/Wolfe: Shenandoah Co, Va–1760-1803; Harrison Co, WVa–1804-1890
     Cloth–126pp–$7.50-- Vendor #36

36   – THE ABER BULLETIN [The Aber Quarterly in 1971 & 1972, its first two
     years.] by Hugh T. Law and contributors
     Aber/Abers/Abor/Abour: Hampshire Co. & London, Eng–1500's-1870; Morris
     Co, NJ–1745-present; Pa, O, NY–1783-present; All states in U.S.–anytime
     Subscription: $5.00/yr;   2 issues/yr; approx. 32pp/issue------ Vendor #39

37   – THE MARCH OF THE SAGES by Bonnie Sage Ball
     Sage: England–prior 1770's; New England–17th & 18th century; Southwest Va–
     1800's-present; Western Plains States–1800's-present
     Cloth–575pp–$15.00 each/2 for $27.00----------------------- Vendor #40

. . . .

38   – DESCENDANTS OF WILLIAM CAPERS AND RICHARD CAPERS by Dorothy K.
     MacDowell
     Capers: SC–1685–present
     Cloth–134pp–$12.00--- Vendor #41

39   – DuBOSE GENEALOGY by Dorothy Kelly MacDowell
     DuBose: "to" SC in 1685
     Cloth–533pp–$20.00--- Vendor #41

40   – AMES, MEARS AND ALLIED LINES OF ACCOMACK COUNTY, VIRGINIA
     by Lucy Ames Edwards
     Ames: Accomack Co, Va–1670-1956
     Mears: Accomack Co, Va–1655-1956
     Cloth–393pp–$14.95--- Vendor #42

41   – THE VANCE FAMILY SCRAPBOOK by Joseph Harvey Vance
     Vance/Wantz: Bedford & Somerset Cos, Pa–1769-1807; Montgomery Co, O–
     1807-1809; Preble Co, O-1809-1853; Darke Co, O–1853-1958
     Mills: Mt. Holly, NJ–1776-1819; Montgomery Co, O–1819-1970
     Schreel: Germany–1800-1839; Montgomery Co, O–1840-1948
     Cline/Kline/Klein: Germany–1735-1749; Hampshire Co, WVa–1765-1900
     Schweitzer/Switzer/Swisher; Germany–1730-1749; Hampshire Co, WVa–
     1780-1860
     Cloth–227pp–$16.00/Paper–$10.00----------------------------Vendor #43

42   – DESCENDANTS OF MATTISON NATIONS AND CYNTHIA GARRETT by
     Loye E. Nations
     Nations: NJ–   -1711; Va–   -1753; NC–1785-date; SC–1786-date
     Paper–not given–$7.50--------------------------------------Vendor #44

43   – THE WILLIAM A AMSBERRY (AMSBARY) AND RELATED FAMILIES by
     Ruby Roberts Coleman
     Amsberry/Amsbary: Cayuga Co, NY–1800-1824; Mason Co, WVa–1824-1855;
     Marion Co, Ia–1855-1878; Custer Co, Nebr–1878-1970
     Paper–113pp–$12.00---Vendor #45

44   – THE EDMONDSON FAMILY ASSOCIATION BULLETIN by M. Patricia
     Humphreys, Editor/President [Published quarterly since 1968.]
     Edmondson/Edmundson/Edmonson, etc.: Anywhere in U.S. – anytime
     Paper–$3.00 per year/4 issues per year---------------------- Vendor #46

45   – YOUR INHERITANCE by Robbie Lee Gillis Ross
     Ezell: Surry Co, Va–1650-1738; Brunswick Co, Va–1738-1760; Greensville
     Co, Va–1760-1796; Halifax Co, Va–1796-1815; Clarke Co, Ala–1815-date
     Roper/Roaper: Edgecombe Co, NC–1757-1783; Halifax Co, NC–1783-1794
     Harwell: Pr.Geo.Co, Va–1722-1770; Sussex Co, Va–1770-1800
     Wilson: Westmoreland Co, Va–1759-1780; Warren Co, NC–1770-1790
     Halifax Co, NC–1790-1817; Clarke Co, Ala–1817-date
     Rivers: Dinwiddie Co, Va–1782-1784; Warren Co, NC–1785-1801;
     Franklin Co, NC–1802-1816; Monroe Co, Ala–1816-date
     Scott: Pr.Edward Co, Va– ? -1800; Charlotte Co, Va–1801-1804;
     Greensville Co, Va–1804-1806; Wake Co, NC –1806-1819
     Cloth–350pp–$50.00---Vendor #48

46 — LEAVES OF THE JERNIGAN TREE by Verna Thomas Jernigan
Jernigan: Johnston Co, NC—1700's; Wayne Co, NC—1700's; Coffee Co, Tenn—
1805-date; Cannon Co, Tenn—1834-date
Paper—63pp—$3.00--Vendor #49

47 — DESCENDANTS OF CALEB GARRISON, SR. AND HIS WIFE, SARAH FLEM-
ING (1797-1966), co-compiler, editor: Quillian Garrison
Garrison: NC-   -c1795; "Old 96", SC—1795-1803; Franklin Co/W.Ga—c1803-
c1860; E. Tex—c1860-1974
Paper—305pp—$5.50--Vendor #50

48 — TREXLER FAMILY AND RELATED KIN by John Trexler Warren
Trexler: Berks Co, Pa—1719-1972; Rowan Co, NC—1790-1972; Jasper Co,
Ill—1815-1972; Lehigh Co, Pa—1719-1972
Hidy: Fayette Co, O—1811-1972
Haas: Berks Co, Pa—1748-1972
Cloth—339pp—$20.00--Vendor #51

49 — THE DEATS FAMILIES by Edwin R. Deats
Deats: NJ—1747-1900; Deatsville, Ala—1817-1900; Deatsville, Ky—1809-1900;
Northampton Co, Pa—1759-1900
Paper—208pp—$10.00--Vendor #57

50 — TAFT FAMILY BULLETIN [Taft & Allied Families] by Thomas E. Collins
Taft: Clearing house for all Taft families and collateral descendants. Mass—
1640-date; RI—1680-date; Conn, Vt, NY, other U.S.—1710-date
Potter: Mass—1640-1780; NY—1795-1970
Sibley: Uxbridge, Mass—1741-1848; Sutton, Mass—1741-1808
Subscription: $5.00 per year/ 3 issues per year--------------- Vendor #58

51 — ALLEMAN GENEALOGY by Rev. Henry Snyder Alleman
Alleman: Largely Pennsylvania & Utah, with some other states.
Cloth—96pp—$8.00-- Vendor #59

52 — THOMAS ANDREW, IMMIGRANT by Helen R. Andrew
Andrew/Andrews: Watertown & Cambridge, Eng—1629-1647;
Also 100 lineage lines of "distaff side".
Cloth—166pp—$15.00-- Vendor #60

53 — GENEALOGY OF THE SHUMWAY FAMILY IN THE UNITED STATES OF
AMERICA by Asahel A. Shumway [Reprint of a book originally published in 1909]
Shumway:
Cloth—478pp—$18.00-- Vendor #62

54 — HOSKINS OF VIRGINIA AND RELATED FAMILIES by Charles Willard
Hoskins Warner
Hoskins: Jamestowne, Va—1615-1624; Lower Norfolk Co, Va—1624-1660;
King & Queen Co, Va—1683-1912; Essex Co, Va—1853-1965
Hundley: Gloucester Co, Va—1650-1750; Essex Co, Va—1750-1971
Ware: King & Queen Co, Va—1671-1800; Essex Co, Va—1821-1971
Garnett: Essex Co, Va—1690-1971; King & Queen Co, Va—1781-1850
Roy: Caroline Co, Va—1700-1800; Essex Co, Va—1830-1880
Cloth—500pp—$15.00-- Vendor #63

55   — THOMAS CARTER II OF COROTOMAN, LANCASTER COUNTY, VIRGINIA
by Charles Willard Hoskins Warner
Carter: Nansemond Co, Va—1630-1650; Lancaster Co, Va—1642-1800; King &
Queen Co, Va—1785-1830; Pittsylvania Co, Va—1780-1920
Cloth—58pp—$3.50--- Vendor #63

56   — ADAMS ADDENDA co-edited by Ruth Robinson Seibel & Dorothy Amburgey
Griffith
Adams: Clearing house and reference for Adams researchers. Published February, June & October. [Not sold by single issue.]
Subscription: $5.00 per year. Approx. 100pp total per year. -----Vendor #64

57   — FOLLOWING THE BRASWELLS ON THE MOVE WESTWARD IN AMERICA
(1600-1974) by Roy Bennett Braswell
Braswell:

Paper—100+pp—$3.00 ---Vendor #65

58   — BURGARD—HOLLINGER FAMILIES by O.D. & Elizabeth Corbridge
Burgard: La Petite Germany (Alsace-Lorraine)—1100-present; Schuyler Co,
Ill—   —date
Hollinger: Boniswyl, Aargau, Switzerland—1464-1775; USA in 1775; York Co,
Pa—   —date; Ill—1829-date
Cloth—310pp—$10.00/Paper—$8.00-----------------------------Vendor #66

59   — CORBRIDGE-BLACK FAMILIES by O. D. & Elizabeth Corbridge
Corbridge: Northumberland, Eng—1200-present; Lincolnshire & Lancashire,
Eng—1826-1960; Schuyler Co, Ill—to present
Black: Ireland—   —1772; Mecklenburg Co, NC—c1770-1844; Schuyler Co,
Ill—1825-1974
Cloth—500pp—$15.00--- Vendor #66

60   — HINTON & RELATED FAMILY HISTORY - VOL. I, by George W. Hinton
Hinton: England; NC; O; Anywhere—1066-1971
Paper—225pp—$7.50---Vendor #67

61   — HINTON & RELATED FAMILY HISTORY - VOL. II, by George W. Hinton
Hinton: Miss; Ky; NC; Anywhere—1066-1971
Paper—345pp—$10.00--Vendor #67

62   — HISTORY OF THE WEED AND ALLIED FAMILIES by Charles A. Weed
Weed: [Puritan] Mass—1630; Conn; NY; All points West
Cloth—540pp—$9.50--- Vendor #68

63   — THE STUDEBAKER STORY, editor-publisher Mary E. Studebaker
Studebaker: Clearing house for all Studebaker families and Studebaker materials; and lineages for the book.
Subscription: $2.00/yr; 4 issues/yr; Approx. 6pp per issue---- Vendor #69

64 - SKETCHES OF THE AUBREY FAMILY by Olive Seaton Eldred
Aubery/Aubrey: Orange Co, Vt—1775-1815; Erie Co, Pa—1815-1840; Fayette
Co, Ill—1840-   ? ; Welch, OK—1866-1900; Descendants to 1973, many states.
Wetmore: Middletown, Conn—1650-1775; Columbia Co, NY—1775-1837;
Ill—1837-1865
Olmsted: Conn—1636-1785; Green Co, NY—1785-1834
Cloth—103pp—$10.00--- Vendor #70

65 - THE BOSWELL-BUSWELL-BUZZELL GENEALOGIST by Laird C. Towle, Ph.D.
Boswell/Buswell/Buzzell: U.S.A., Anytime.
Subscription: $4.00/yr; 4 issues/yr; approx. 100pp/yr---------Vendor #72

66 - McCONNAUGHEY BULLETIN by Patricia McConnaughay Gregory
McConnaughey & variants
Subscription: $5.00/yr; annual; approx. 64pp/yr---------------Vendor #73

67 - THE JAMES F. MOODY FAMILY HISTORY by Marie Moody Foster & Erma
Melton Smith
Moody: Augusta Co, Va—1750-1790;. Knox Co, Ky—c1800-1840; Fayette Co, Ky—
to 1853; Hunt Co, Tex—to1864
Britton: Knox Co, Ky—to 1834; Vigo Co, Ind—to 1840; Newton Co, Mo—to 1904;
Calif—to present
Coles: Hunt Co, Tex—to 1862; Wilson Co, Tenn—to present
Melton: Newton Co, Mo—to 1932; New Mex—to 1950; Calif—to present
Todd: Gentry Co, Mo—to 1870; Calif—to present
Watson: Madison Co, Ky—to 1870
Lance: N.Mex—1916-present
Cloth—454pp—$17.50---Vendor #76

68 - MY COLBERT COUNTY FAMILIES - LANES, BARTONS, PRIDES, RUT-
LANDS & GOODLOES by Mary Alexander Lollar
Lane: Colbert Co, Ala—1820-date; NC; Tenn
Barton: Colbert Co, Ala—1820-date
Pride: Colbert Co, Ala—1820-date
Rutland: Colbert Co, Ala—1820-date
Goodloe: Colbert Co, Ala—1820-date
Paper—60pp—$10.00--Vendor #78

69 - BUTTON FAMILIES OF AMERICA by R. Glen Nye
Button: Haverhill, Mass—1649-1690; Essex Co, Va—1666- ? ; Waupaca,
Wisc—1864-c1900; Anywhere—anytime
Cloth—944pp—$16.50------------------------------------- Vendor #79

70 - FARNSWORTH MEMORIAL II by Farnsworth & Nye
Farnsworth: All known Farnsworth origins in U.S.
Cloth—948pp—$13.50------------------------------------- Vendor #79

71 - STEPHENS-STEVENS, STEPHENSON-STEVENSON NEWSLETTER by A.
Maxim Coppage
Stephens/Stevens/Stephenson/Stevenson: Anytime, anywhere.
Subscription: $5.00/yr; 4 issues/yr; # of pages varies--------- Vendor #80

· ·

72 — SATTERLEE-LEY-LY & ALLIED FAMILIES GENEALOGIES, by
Goldie Satterlee Moffatt. 3 vols.
Satterlee/Satterley/Satterly: Anytime, anywhere.
Cloth—285 + 342 + 300pp—Each $25.00 ------------------------------Vendor #81

73 — SATTERLEE FAMILY QUARTERLY edited by Goldie Satterlee Moffatt
Satterlee/Satterley/Satterly: Anytime, anywhere.
Subscription: $5.00/yr; 4 issues/yr ------------------------- Vendor #81

74 — RECEIPT FOR AN INHERITANCE by Margery Day Hanson
Fleenor: Washington Co, Va—1750-1974; Sullivan Co, Tenn—c1800-   ;
Brown Co, Ind—1860-1974; Harrison Co, Mo—c1848-   ; Rice/Lecompton
Cos, Kan—1860-1974; Ia; Linn Co, Or; Bucks Co, Pa.
Hope: Southwestern Va—1750-   ; Davidson/Blount Cos, Tenn—pre-1828-
c1850; Iowa—c1850-   ; Rice/Lecompton Cos, Kans—1870-1974
Rude: Pa; Ky—c1824-   ; Brown Co, Ind—c1824-
Whitaker: NC—c1783-c1810; Ky—c1810-c1830; Morgan Co, Ind—c1830-
Cloth—190pp—$10.00 -- Vendor #524

76 — THIS ROBINSON LINE [A beautiful paneled chart printed in brown ink on yel-
low parchment with brown backup — a continuous panel, about 10" x 30", showing unbroken direct line of Robinson from 1520 to 1938.] England-Virginia-
Kentucky - Missouri - Texas. Maternal lines shown. To be used in conjunction
with book below. By E. Viola Robinson Long.
Chart—10" x 30" —$8.00 --------------------------------------- Vendor #82

77 — THIS ROBINSON LINE by E. Viola Robinson Long
Robinson: Yorkshire, Eng—1520-1666; Middlesex Co, Va—1666-1800; King
Wm.Co, Va—1740-1800; western states 1820-1938
Cloth—120pp—$20.00 -- Vendor #82

78 — KNOWING THE BRUNERS by Donald Lewis Osborn
Bruner/Brunner: Schifferstadt, Germany—1679-1729; Frederick Co, Md—
1736-1821; Morgan Co, WVa—1797-1830; Montgomery Co, O—1824-1901;
Wabash Co, Ind—1839-1923; Jasper Co, Ind—1850-1968; Breckinridge Co, Ky—
1814- ? ; Mo—1871-1968; Kan—1885-1968; Okla—1893-1968
Cloth—240pp—$24.95 --- Vendor #84

79 — A FAMILY RECORD: STEPHENS by Donald Lewis Osborn
Stephens: Orange Co, Va—1779-1802; Boone Co, Ky—1823-1953; Cass Co,
Mo—1855-1973; Taylor [in Williamson Co], Tex—1884-1940
Paper—20pp—$4.00 --- Vendor #84

80 — TALES OF THE AMARUGIA HIGHLANDS OF CASS COUNTY, MISSOURI by
Donald Lewis Osborn
Shipley: Tennessee—before 1847; Kentucky—1847-   ; Cass Co, Mo—1847-
1960; Denison Co, Tex—1870's
Paper—20pp—$4.00 ---Vendor #84

81 — GENEALOGY OF EDWARD & SARAH (BURCHETT) OSBORN OF FLOYD
COUNTY, KENTUCKY by Donald Lewis Osborn
Osborn: Charlotte Co, Va–1794-1805; Floyd Co, Ky–1805-1871; Greenwood
Co, Kan–1871-1970; Cass Co, Mo–1890-1970
Paper–12pp–$2.00--Vendor #84

82 — SOME DESCENDENTS OF HEINRICH WHISTLER - 1737 by John Marquiss &
Beulah Wysong Whistler
Whistler: Lancaster Co, Pa–1737-1774; Rockingham Co, Va–1774-1820;
Floyd Co, Ind–1820-1856; Miami Co, Ind–1856-1900; Muscogee Co, Okla–
1909-1923; Lake Co–Fla–1958-1967
Cloth–165pp–$15.00-- Vendor #85

83 — SOME DESCENDENTS OF LUDWIG AND MARY WYSONG, IMMIGRANTS 1740
by John Marquiss Whistler & Beulah Wysong Whistler
Wysong: York Co, Pa–1740-1794; Franklin Co, Va–1794-1818; Preble Co, O–
1818-1865; Noble Co, Ind–1865-1906; Payne Co, Okla–1919-1923
Whistler: Lake Co, Fla–1958-1972
Cloth–193pp–$15.00-- Vendor #85

84 — SOME DESCENDANTS OF HUGH ROE by Frank C. Roe
Roe/Rowe: England–c1617-1642; Weymouth, Mass–1642-1657; Lower & cen–
tral Conn–1657-1671; Suffield, Conn–1671-1800+
Paper–71pp–$3.50--Vendor #86

85 — THE HISTORY AND GENEALOGY OF THE NATHAN P. GOFF FAMILY by
Colonel Joseph Philip Barnes
Goff: Monongalia Co, WVa–1776-1830; Delaware Co, Ind–1833-1863; Madison
Co, Ia–1863-1900
Paper–147pp–$10.00--- Vendor #87

86 — CHANCE FAMILY, ENGLAND TO 48 STATES OF AMERICA by Hilda Chance
Chance: United States–1668-1974
Cloth–141pp–$7.00/Paper–$5.00--------------------------- Vendor #89

87 — THE FAMILIES AND DESCENDANTS IN AMERICA OF GOLSAN, GOLSON,
GHOLSON, GHOLSTON by James M. Black
Golsan/Golson/Gholson/Gholston: Virginia–1680-   ; SC–1730-   ; Ky–
1733-   ; Ala–1710-
Cloth–815pp–$10.00--------------------------------------- Vendor #90

88 — BRUCE FAMILY – DESCENDANTS OF GEORGE BRUCE OF OLD RAPPA–
HANNOCK AND RICHMOND COUNTIES, VIRGINIA by John Goodall Bruce
Bruce: "Berry Hill"; "Staunton Hill"; Kentucky; Tennessee; and other
Cloth–200+pp–[Publication date early in 1975.]----------------- Vendor #91

89 — THE SIBLEY FAMILY IN AMERICA 1629-1972 by James Scarborough Sibley
Sibley: Mass–1629-1972; Ga–   -1972; Mecklenburg Co, NC–1790-1972;
La–1800-1972
Cloth–803pp–$16.25--------------------------------------- Vendor #92

90   - ONE MAN'S FAMILY by John E. Fetzer
      Fetzer: Morgan Co, O−1832-1840; Hocking Co, O−1840-1867; Henry Co, O−
      1864-1965; Wells Co, Ind−1867-1898
      Cloth−212pp−$8.00--- Vendor #95

91   - THE MEN FROM WENGEN AND AMERICA'S AGONY by John E. Fetzer
      Wenger/Winger/Wanger: Bernese, Switzerland−1430-1710; Zweibrucken, W.
      Germany−1710-1718; Lancaster Co, Pa−1718-1836; Green Co, O−1836-1848;
      Darke Co, O−1848-1880; Mercer Co, O−1880-1928
      Cloth−446pp−$15.00--- Vendor #95

92   - LINKS WITH THE PAST by Ethel Evans Albert
      Albert: Montgomery Co, Va−1788-1900; Giles Co, Va−1806-1900; Scott Co,
      Va−1815-1830; Russell Co, Va−1840-1900; Berks Co, Pa−1750-1900's; North-
      ampton Co, Pa−1809-date;
      Ketron: Russell Co, Va−1853-1900; Wythe Co, Va−1770-1900
      Glenn: Montgomery Co, Va−1784-1860; Lee Co, Va−1831
      Tignor: King & Queen Co, Va−1809-   ; Russell Co, Va−1760-date
      Gilmer: Washington Co, Va−1780's; Russell Co, Va−1786-date
      Taylor: Russell Co, Va−1783-date
      Cloth−497pp−$15.00---Vendor #96

93   - EDSON FAMILY HISTORY AND GENEALOGY by Carroll A. Edon
      Edson: Contains all the known male Edson line descendants of Samuel Edson
      and Susanna Orcutt, of Bridgewater, Massachusetts.
      Cloth−1535pp [in 2 vols.]−$35.00-----------------------------Vendor #97

94   - RICHARD CLARKE OF VIRGINIA by James W. Clark
      Clark/Clarke: Gloucester/Fairfax Cos, Va−1732-1792; Montgomery Co, Ky−
      1792-1834; Putnam/Montgomery Cos, Ind−1834-date; Dallas Co, Ia−1849-date
      Cloth−49pp−$6.75--- Vendor #98

95   - HOUGH AND HUFF FAMILIES OF THE UNITED STATES, 1620-1888, VOL. I
      by Granville W. Hough
      Hough/Huff: Anywhere in the U.S.−1620-1880
      Paper−259pp−$12.00--------------------------------------- Vendor #99

96   - HOUGH AND HUFF FAMILIES OF THE UNITED STATES, 1620-1820, NORTH-
      EASTERN STATES, VOL. II by Granville W. Hough
      Hough/Huff/Hoff: Anywhere in the U.S.−1620-1820; Canada−1620-1820
      Paper−153pp−$10.00--------------------------------------- Vendor #99

97   - MISSISSIPPI HOUGHS − FRANK, ZENO, FRANCIS, SAMUEL, AND THEIR
      KIN by Granville W. Hough
      Hough: Wayne Co, Miss−1810-1870; Tombigbee River Area−1803-1815; Smith
      Co, Miss−1850-1970; La−1840-1970
      Paper−155pp−$7.00-- Vendor #99

98 — EARLY OSBORNES AND ALLEYS by Rita K. Sutton
Osborne: Montgomery Co, Va—1700's-   ; Grayson Co, Va—1700's-
Russell Co, Va—1700's-date; Westward states
Alley: Russell Co, Va—1700's-date; Montgomery Co, Va—1700's-
Paper—260pp—$8.00--- Vendor #101

99 — FAVORS FAMILY by Mildred Moody Nutter
Favors/Favour/Faver: Essex Co, Va—prior to 1722-   ; Culpeper Co, Va—
c1783-   ; Nelson/Shelby/Henry Cos, Ky—1785-1810; Jefferson/Decatur Cos,
Ind—1815-
Moody: Albemarle Co, Va—1748-1787; Bedford Co, Va—1748-1787
Surber: Shenandoah Valley, Va—1754-1820
[In process. Publication date approximately 1975.]------------- Vendor #102

100 — CLARA HARMON BRADSHAW: HER AMERICAN ANCESTORS AND HER
DESCENDANTS by Mary Frances Bradshaw Dittrich
Harmon: Springfield, Mass—1644-   ; Suffield, Conn—1670-1759; Rupert,
Vt—1761-1800; Warren, O—1800-1869
Cloth—322pp—$25.00---Vendor #103

101 — RICHARD BAILEY OF TAZEWELL COUNTY, VIRGINIA AND HIS DESCEN-
DANTS by Lewis Bailey
Bailey: Chesterfield Co, Va—1753-1800; Bedford/Franklin Cos, Va—1760-
1786; Southwestern Va & WVa—1782-date; Western migrations—1800's-date
[In process. Publication date approximately 1980.]------------- Vendor #104

102 — THE SHACKLETONS by Bernice Close Shackelton
Shackleton/Shackelton/Shekleton: Yorkshire, Eng—1500-1972; Ireland—1725-
1972; NJ—1700-1820; NY—1822-1850; Kan—1869-1972
Cloth—340pp—$20.00--- Vendor #107

103 — THE WILLIAMS' FAMILY BULLETIN by Richard T. & Mildred C. Williams
Williams: Any family by the name of Williams — anywhere in the United States
Subscription: $5.00/yr; 4 issues/yr.--------------------------Vendor #109

104 — THE McNEEL FAMILY RECORD by Betsy Jordan Edgar
McNeel:
Cloth—496pp—$15.00--- Vendor #110

105 — THE CAMPBELL CLAN IN VIRGINIA by Leslie Lyle Campbell
Campbell:
Cloth—154pp—$10.50---Vendor #112

106 — THE HOUSTON FAMILY IN VIRGINIA by Leslie Lyle Campbell
Houston:
Cloth—77pp—$8.00---Vendor #112

107 – THE FAMILY TREE OF COLONEL LEVEN POWELL'S LINE OF THE
POWELLS OF VIRGINIA by Rosalie (Noland) Ball
Powell:

Paper—75pp—$8.00--Vendor #112

108 – A WILLIAMS CHRONICLE by Frances Hansen Ehrig
Williams: Sullivan Co, NY—1776-1825; Jefferson Co, Pa—1825-date; Green
Co, Wisc—1857-date; Montgomery Co, Ia—1877-date
Cloth—198pp—$7.00-- Vendor #115

109 – DESCENDANTS OF HANS JORGEN THOMSEN & ANE KJERSTINE DITLEVSEN
OF KLEJS, DENMARK by Frances Hansen Ehrig
Hansen: Klejs, Vejle Amt, Denmark—c1825-1864; Ravnholt, Raarup Parish,
Vejle Amt, 1765-1825; Monona Co, Ia—1879-date
Paper—73pp—$3.50--Vendor #115

110 – THE SKOW FAMILY – DESCENDANTS OF HANS CHRISTIAN SCHOU &
KJERSTEN JORGENSEN OF KLAKRING, DENMARK by Frances Hansen Ehrig
Skow/Schou/Skov/Skaw: Hammel Parish, Jutland, Denmark—1800-1850;
Klakring, Vejle Amt, Denmark—1850-1879; Monona Co, Ia—1879-date
Cloth—101pp—$5.50/ Paper—$4.00--------------------------- Vendor #115

111 – EDWARD MORGAN, PIONEER MINISTER OF SOUTHWEST VIRGINIA by
Clarita H. Morgan
Morgan: London, Eng—1751-1767; Montgomery/Giles/Washington Cos, Va—
1769-1844
Paper—140pp—$10.00---Vendor #116

112 – GENEALOGICAL HISTORY OF THE HALLIBURTON FAMILY by William Ken-
neth Rutherford & A. C. Rutherford
Halliburton: Scotland—c1727-   ; Lunenburg/Mecklenburg Co, Va—1746-1767;
NC—1763-   ; Tenn—1796-
Cloth—970pp—$27.50-------------------------------------- Vendor #117

113 – GENEALOGICAL HISTORY OF OUR ANCESTORS: BASS, BEESON, BLED-
SOE, BOONE, GARDINER, BOWEN, PEYTON, HALLIBURTON, RUTHERFORD
AND SIXTY OTHER FAMILIES by W. K. & A. C. Rutherford
Mass—1620-   ; Va—1622-   ; New Netherland [NY]—1630-   ; Md—1630-
Cloth—552—$15.00-- Vendor #117

114 – GENEALOGICAL HISTORY OF THE RUTHERFORD FAMILY by William
Kenneth Rutherford and A. C. Rutherford
Rutherford: Scotland—1140-1969; Colonial America—1621-1776; U.S.—1776-
1969
Cloth—802pp—$27.50-------------------------------------- Vendor #117

115 – SOUTHWORTHS IN ENGLAND AND AMERICA – 1889-1968 by Bess Miner
Johnson
Southworth: Plymouth, Mass—1623-1700's; Bristol, RI—1686-1700's; Mexico,
NY—1808-1843; Hillsdale Co, Mich—1836-present
Paper—131pp—$10.00-------------------------------------- Vendor #118

116 — THOMAS M. LACEY'S FAMILY by Lucile S. Stowell
Lacey/Lacy: Bucks Co, Pa—1698-1768; Loudoun Co, Va—c1790-c1807;
Belmont Co, O—c1807-1841; Steuben Co, Ind—1841-present
Cloth—196pp-$10.00/Paper—$5.00------------------------------Vendor #120

117 — ALTON-ALLTON FAMILY NEWLETTER by Mrs. Elmer Allton & Mrs.
Wilma S. Davis
Alton/Allton: Anywhere-anytime
Subscription: $2.00/yr; 2 issues/yr; approx. 6pp/issue-------- Vendor #121

118 — THE KELLYS OF VEIRGINIA AND KENTUCKY by Anita Pendergrass
Kelly: Lee Co, Va—1760-1800; Harlan Co, Ky—1800-present; Descendants
in all states
Paper—215pp-$5.95--Vendor #124

119 — THE HISTORY AND GENEALOGY OF THE GEORGE W. CANNADY FAM-
ILY by Bruce B. Cannady
Cannady/Canady: Nelson Co, Ky—1791-1809; Harrison Co, Ind—1809-1828;
Vermilion Co, Ill—1828-1846; Davis Co, Ia—1846-1866

120 — WOOD-WOODS FAMILY MAGAZINE by Virginia W. Alexander
Wood/Woods: Clearing House for all Wood-Woods families
Subscription: $6.00/yr; approx. 120pp/yr--------------------- Vendor #128

121 — THE JOHN STEPHEN McFADIN FAMILY OF NORTH CAROLINA, KEN-
TUCKY, INDIANA, AND KANSAS by Maude A. McFadin
McFadin/McFadden: Rutherford Co, NC—c1760-1780's; Barren Co, Ky—
1785-1805; Posey Co, Ind—1805-1855; Lykin Co, Kan—1855-1890
Cloth—105pp-$7.50--Vendor #129

122 — THE GEORGIA DESCENDANTS OF EDWARD NASH OF GREENVILLE COUN-
TY SOUTH CAROLINA AND SOME RELATED FAMILIES by James Henry Nash
Nash: Gwinnett Co, Ga—1830-1972; Atlanta, Ga—1870-1972; Henry/Clayton
Cos, Ga—1830-1900; SC/Ga/Ala/Miss—1782-1972
Paper—111pp-$10.50--Vendor #131

123 — SAVAGE-STILLMAN-ROGERS-LINDSEY-DEVER AND RELATED FAMI-
LIES WITH MAGNA CARTA AND ROYAL LINES by Myrtle Savage Rhoades
Stillman: Hadley, Mass—1684-1703; Wethersfield, Conn—1703-1809; Cole-
brook, Conn—1809-1827; Lamar Co, Ala—1827-present
Cloth—630pp-$25.00-- Vendor #132

124 — ROOTS IN VIRGINIA: CAPTAIN THOMAS HALE, VIRGINIA FRONTIERS-
MAN, HIS DESCENDANTS AND RELATED FAMILIES by Nathaniel C. Hale
Hale: Elizabeth Co, Va—1645-   ; Franklin Co, Va—1774-   ; Adams Co,
Miss—1905
Saunders: York Co, Va—1635-   ; Franklin Co, Va—1767-
Lucke: Richmond Co, Va—1810
Claiborne: Jamestown, Va—1621-   ; Franklin Co, Va—1810-
Lacy: Jamestown, Va—1624-   ; New Kent Co, Va—1756-
Tobin: Barnwell Dist, SC—1790-   ; New Orleans, La—1856-
Cloth—244pp-$20.00 --- Vendor #133

125 ⎿ GENEALOGY OF THE DeBAUN FAMILY by William H. Wallace
DeBaun: New Utrecht, NY—1683-   ; NJ; NY; Ind.
Paper—$10.50--Vendor #134

126 — THE DESCENDANTS OF THE REV. CHRISTOPHER WILKINSON OF
QUEEN ANNE'S COUNTY, MARYLAND by George B. Wilson
Wilkinson: Yorkshire, Eng—1663-1711; Md—1711-date; Ind—1866-date;
Ohio—1730-date
Cloth—135pp—$8.00--- Vendor #135

127 — THE JONATHAN COLLINS FAMILY AND DESCENDANTS OF PENNSYL-
VANIA, VIRGINIA, KENTUCKY, TENNESSEE, AND MO. by Ruby Markland
Collins: Bucks Co, Pa—1738-1760; Sussex (now Warren) Co, NJ—1760-1788;
Grayson (& Parent Cos.) Co, Va—1788-1806; Wayne Co, Ky—1805-1850
Southern Cos, Tenn—1834-1971; Northern Cos, Mo—1850-1971
Cloth—236—$12.50--- Vendor #136

128 — "WHITHER THOU GOEST" by Elnor Stanley Flaherty
Stanley: Henrico Co, Va—1680-1760; Guilford Co, NC—1760-1870; Butler
Co, Kan—1870-1890; Payne Co, OK—1894-1957
Paper—71pp—$6.50--- Vendor #139

129 — CROCKER GENEALOGY by James R. Crocker
Crocker: Anywhere in U.S.A.—anytime
Cloth—246pp—$30.00/Paper—$25.00------------------------- Vendor #140

130 — CLOUD THRASHER BARTON LINEAGES by Jewel Young
Barton: Pickens Co, SC—1804-1838; Marion/Perry Cos, Ala—1837-1839;
Union/Morehouse Parish, La—1839-c1862; Grimes/Bell Cos, Tex—1863-1890
Cloth—215pp[8 x 11]—$17.50------------------------------- Vendor #143

131 — THE HISTORY AND GENEALOGY OF THE WITHERSPOON FAMILY by
Joseph Bailey Witherspoon
Witherspoon: More than 1400 Witherspoons of U.S. and Canada—1400-1972
Cloth—832pp—$25.00-------------------------------------- Vendor #144

132 — THE KINSMAN [Jesse N. Smith Family Bulletin] edited by Oliver R. Smith
Smith: Data on ancestors and descendants of Jesse Nathaniel Smith (1834-1906)
Subscription: $5.00/yr; 4 issues/yr; 16pp/issue-------------Vendor #146

133 — JOURNAL OF JESSE NATHANIEL SMITH — HIS ANCESTORS AND DE-
SCENDANTS edited by Oliver R. Smith
Smith: Essex Co, Mass—1636-1791; St. Lawrence Co, NY—1806-1836;
Iron Co, Utah—1851-1879; Apache (Navajo) Co, Ariz—1879-1970
Cloth—556pp—$15.00------------------------------------- Vendor #146

134 — THE ROYAL FAMILY OF THE PROPHET JOSEPH SMITH, JR. [FIRST
PRESIDENT OF THE CHURCH OF JESUS CHRIST OF LATTER DAY SAINTS
by Thomas Milton Tinney
Smith: Eastern States—1800's-current; Mo—1839-1841; Ill—1841-1847;
Utah—1847-current
Cloth—343pp—$30.50-------------------------------------- Vendor #147

135 - EARLY SOUTHERN FULLERS by Theodore A. Fuller, Col.USAF (Ret.)
Fuller: Va-1685-1730; Md-1655-1670; SC-1670-1800; NC-1730-1850;
Ga-1800-1850; Tenn-1815-1850; Tex-1850-1880
Cloth-207pp-$15.00--- Vendor #148

136 - FAMILY OF JOHN AND ANNA MARGARET LOWALD SNYDER by Vaneta
Thomas Horlacher and Levi Jackson Horlacher
Snyder: Northampton Co, Pa-c1750-1974; Centre Co, Pa-1809-1974;
Marion/Hancock Cos, Ind-1840-1974; Fayette Co, Ky-1918-1974
Paper-175pp-$10.00--- Vendor #149

137 - FAMILY OF HANS MICHAEL AND MARIA VERONICA HORLACHER -
First edition - by Levi Jackson Horlacher & Vaneta Thomas Horlacher
Horlacher: Southeastern Pa-1731-1974; Central Ind-1839-1974; Fayette
Co, Ky-1918-1974; Kan/Colo/Tex-1905-1974
Cloth-326pp-$10.00--- Vendor #150

138 - FAMILY OF HANS MICHAEL AND MARIA VERONICA HORLACHER -
Second edition - by Levi Jackson Horlacher & Vaneta Thomas Horlacher
Horlacher: Southeastern Pa-1731-1974; Central Ind-1839-1974; Fayette
Co, Ky-1918-1974; Kan/Colo/Tex/Mo-1905-1974
Paper-105pp-$10.00--- Vendor #150

139 - CASTLEBERRY AND ALLIED FAMILIES [WITH SEPARATE INDEX] by
Jesse W. Castleberry, M.D.
Castleberry/Casselberry/Casselbury/Castlebury: Pa- 1600's & 1700's;
Ga-1700's
Cloth-335pp-$35.00--- Vendor #151

140 - "THE GAMP TREE": QUARTERLY FAMILY BULLETIN WITH PHOTO-
GRAPHS [A research device] edited & published by Mr. F. E. Castleberry
Castleberry/Casselbury/Castlebury/Casselberry: Pa-1600's & 1700's;
Ga-1700's
Subscription: $5.00/yr---------------------------------- Vendor #151

141 - "BEN'S KIN" - GENEALOGY OF BENJAMIN HYDER by Aline Hyder
Hardwick
Hyder/Hider: Rutherford Co, NC-1790-present
Paper-43pp-$5.50--- Vendor #153

142 - STINSON FAMILY HISTORY 1819-1971 by Lillie & Way
Stinson: Wayne Co, O-1819-1971; Dakota Co, Nebr-1880-1971; Sedgwick
Co, Kan-1885-1971; Bottineau Co, ND-1901-1971
Cloth-400pp-$16.50--- Vendor #154

143 - TO AND FROM JAMES AND CATHARINE PARSHALL by Frank N. &
Homer L. Parshall
Parshall: Normandy/England-896-1620; East tip of Long Island, NY-1620-
1800; Cherry Valley, NY-1800-1856; Western U.S. & Canada-1856-1968
Nellis: Heidelberg, Germany-1694-1710; Otsego Co, NY-1710-1856
Garlock: Heidelberg, Germany-1672-1710; Otsego, NY-1710-1856
Dutcher: Cherry Valley, NY-1805-1848
Granger: Cherry Valley, NY-1820- ? ; Washington, DC- ? -1894
Cloth- $13.75 --- Vendor #155

144 - SOME DESCENDANTS OF JUSTUS HARRIS by Sydney Mike Gardner
Harris: Westchester Co, NY-1746-c1792; St. Joseph Co, Mich-c1835-
c1880; LaSalle Co, Ill-c1853-c1875; Dallas Co, Ia-c1875-1974
Cloth-$10.00--Vendor #156

145 - FROM THE ISLE OF SKYE TO PRINCE EDWARD ISLAND = ARMIGER
NICHOLSON'S CHILDREN by Nettie Gove Nicholson
Nicholson: Isle of Skye: 1600-1840; Prince Edward Island: 1840-1900;
Haverhill, Mass-1904-1930; West Palm Beach, Fla-1954-present
Cantelo: Prince Edward Island-1804-date; British Columbia-1895-date
MacDonald: Prince Edward Island-1804-date; British Columbia-1895-date
MacLean: Prince Edward Island-1804-date: British Columbia-1895-date
Matheson: Prince Edward Island-1804-date: British Columbia-1895-date
Cloth-$18.00/Paper-$12.00-225pp------------------------- Vendor #157

146 - A TENTH GENERATION YANKEE FROM MAINE by Nettie Gove Nicholson
Gove: Hampton, NH-1630-1750; Mass-1630-1750; Edgecomb, Maine-
1771-1921; Haverhill, Mass-1880-1930
Hough/Huff: Bay Colony-1635-1680; Maine-1765-1880
Bulkeley: Line to Charlmagne-   -1632; Boston, Mass-1632-1654
Paper-358pp-$12.50------------------------------------- Vendor #157

147 - GENEALOGICAL SERENDIPITY, VOL. I, by J. Sharon Johnson Doliante
Green/Greene: Tryon Co, NC-c1778; Ky-c1796; White Co, Tenn-mid
1800's; Ill-1800's
Scoggin: Washington Co, Va-early 1800's; White Co, Tenn-mid 1800's
White: Amelia Co, Va-   -1788; White Co, Tenn-mid 1800's
Dyer: York Co, Va-c1727; Lunenburg Co, Va-c1766
Hurt: New Kent Co, Va-   -1728; Amelia Co, Va-c1783
Phillips: Lunenburg Co, Va-c1786
Mackey: Pendleton Dist, SC-c1795; White Co, Tenn-mid 1800's
Cloth-346pp-$20.00------------------------------------- Vendor #160

148 - THE CRAGIN STORY, 1634-1969 by Leslie June Cragin Godley
Cragin: USA-1634-1969 [Starting in Massachusetts.]
Paper-225pp-$15.00------------------------------------- Vendor #162

149 - ANCESTORS AND DESCENDANTS - NASH AND OTHER CONNECTED
FAMILIES - COLONIAL AND REVOLUTIONARY PERIODS TO PRESENT
by Sara M. Nash
Nash: Va-1700's; NC-c1759-1788; SC-1788-1973; Other states

Cloth-197pp-$10.50------------------------------------- Vendor #163

150 - A BRANCH OF THE WRIGHT TREE by Ammerman, Clinton, & Heiss
Wright: Greene Co, Tenn-1790-1830; Madison Co, Ill-1830-1833; Polk
Co, Mo-1833-1900
Paper-170pp-$5.00-------------------------------------- Vendor #164

151 - AUSTINS TO WISCONSIN [RICHARD LINE] by Paul R. Austin
Austin: Suffield, Conn-1674-1783; Shickshinny, Pa-1779-1804; Ohio-
1804-1815; Ind-1815-1818; Ill-1818-1846; Wisc-1835-1963

Woodle: Md—1778-1799; Fayette Co, Pa—1799-1836; Green Co, Wisc—1836-1970
Smith (Col. James): Chester Co, Pa—1720-1748; Franklin Co, Pa—1748-1776; Westmoreland Co, Pa—1769-1788; Bourbon Co, Ky—1788-1812
Cloth—99pp—$6.00-- Vendor #166

152 — THE CRANES OF OWEGO, NEW YORK; MARENGO, ILLINOIS; & MONROE, WISCONSIN by Paul R. Austin
Crane: NJ—1780-1805; Tioga Co, NY—1805-1865; McHenry Co, Ill—1854-1900; Green Co, Wisc—1857-1936; Milwaukee, Wisc—1896-1913
Ely: Lyme, Conn—1666-1798; Tioga Co, NY—1798-1832
Dennis: Union Co, Pa—1800-1845; Green Co, Wisc—1845-1893
Paper—142pp—$6.00--- Vendor #166

153 — ONE MAN'S FAMILY: THE HISTORY AND GENEALOGY OF THE WORLAND FAMILY IN AMERICA, 1662-1962 by Olive Lewis Kolb
Worland: Md—1662-1800; Ky—1790-1840; Shelby Co, Ind—1828-present; East Central, Mo—1840-present
Shocklee: Marion Co, Ky—c1800-   ; Montgomery Co, Mo—1840-date
Clarkson: Washington Co, Ky—1790-date
Abell: Marion Co, Ky—1800-date
Paper—1112pp—$15.00--- Vendor #168

154 — DEVEREUX OF THE LEAP, COUNTY WEXFORD, IRELAND AND OF UTICA, NEW YORK by Clifford Lewis 3rd & John Devereux Kernan
Devereux: Co.Wexford, Ire—1250-1860; Utica, NY—1802-date; Wash. DC—1820-date; Philadelphia, Pa—1799-date
Kernan: Co.Cavan, Ire—1086-1850; Steuben Co, NY—1802-1857; Utica, NY—1837-date
Cloth—116pp—$10.50-- Vendor #169

155 — THE DESCENDANTS OF JOSIAH AND KEZIAH NICHOLS WOOLDRIDGE AND THEIR ANCESTORS by Wright W. Frost
Wooldridge: Chesterfield Co, Va—1749-1795; Madison Co, Ky—1799-1819; Graves Co, Ky—1843-1899; Williamson Co, Tenn—1818-1890
Flournoy: Jamestown, Va—1700- ? ; Chesterfield Co, Va—1749- ?
Nichols: Orange Co, NC—ere 1776; Davidson Co, NC/Tenn—1784-1875; Williamson Co, Tenn—1827-1974
Bolling: Charles City Co, Va—1600- ? ; Pr. Geo.Co, Va—1700- ?
Cloth—221pp—$15.00--- Vendor #170

156 — THE FROSTS AND RELATED FAMILIES OF BEDFORD COUNTY, TENNESSEE [INCLUDES SUPPLEMENT] by Wright W. Frost
Frost: Morristown, NJ—1740-c1755; Rowan Co, NC—1755-1822; Surry Co, NC—1822-1834; Madison Co, Ala—1824-1834; Bedford Co, Tenn—1834-1974
Cloth—375pp—$16.50--- Vendor #170

157 — GEORGE ALDRICH GENEALOGY, VOL. I & II, by A. James Aldrich
Aldrich: Derbyshire, Eng—1629-1631; Dorchester, Mass—1631-1640; Braintree, Mass—1640-1667; Mendon, Mass—1667-death
Cloth—704pp—$39.90--- Vendor #172

158 – WILLIAM & JOHN JOHNSON, COLONIAL FRIENDS OF VIRGINIA by
Lorand V. Johnson, M.D.
Johnson: Va– ? -1800; To midwest & south
Cloth–250pp–$20.00--- Vendor #173

159 – JAMES PATTON AND THE APPALACHIAN COLONISTS by P. Johnson
Patton: Scot/Ire–1692-1735; Augusta Co, Va–1738-1755
Thompson: Augusta Co, Va–c1740; Montgomery/Giles Cos, Va–1776-
Buchanan: Augusta Co, Va–c1740; Montgomery/Wythe Cos, Va–1776-
Cloth–246pp–$7.95--- Vendor #174

160 – THE ILIFF GENEALOGIST by George Ely Russell, C.G.
Iliff/Ayliffe: Eng–1550-1750; USA–1610-1870
Paper–61pp–$5.00--- Vendor #178

161 – CRESWELL-CRISWELL GENEALOGICAL RECORDS by George E. Russell
Creswell/Criswell: Eng/Ire–1550-1750; USA–1610-1870
Paper–119pp–$5.00--- Vendor #178

162 – PRIEST GENEALOGICAL RECORDS, VOL. I by George Ely Russell, C.G.
Priest: Pa/NJ/Md/Va/ & other–1600-1850
Paper–62pp–$5.00--- Vendor #178

163 – HOSKINS FAMILIES OF 17th CENTURY AMERICA by George E. Russell
Hoskins/Haskins/Haskin/Hodgskins: North America–1600-c1720
Paper–21pp–$4.00--- Vendor #178

164 – CRESWELL & CRISWELL FAMILIES OF BALTIMORE, HARFORD, AND
CARROLL COUNTIES, MARYLAND by George Ely Russell, C.G.
Creswell/Criswell: Md–1750-1850
Paper–32pp–$3.50--- Vendor #178

165 – JAMES LUDDEN AND DESCENDANTS by Dr. Wallace Ludden
Ludden: Weymouth, Mass–1630-1670; Braintree, Mass–1670-1730; Wil-
liamsburg, Mass–1730-1795; Herkimer & Wyoming Cos, NY–1790-1974;
Me–1770-1974; Chicago, Ill–1866-1970; Nebr–1840-1974; Tex–1900-1974;
Calif–1900-1974
Clark/Clarke: Dorchester, Mass–1635-1790; Herkimer Co, NY–1790-1828
Thayer: Braintree, Mass–1700-1817; West Point–1817-1833
Vivian: Eng–1213-1846; Wisc–1846-1892
Woodbury: Sommerset, Eng–1579-1750; Beverly, Mass–1750-1910
Cloth–252pp–$10.00--- Vendor #179

166 – THE KLINES OF EVANSTON: 1848-1970 by Faith McClung Kline
Kline: Schenectady, NY– ? -1848; Evanston, Ill–1848-present
Veeder/Vedder: Schenectady, NY–1662-1700; Fonda, NY–1788-1836
Kingsley: Taunton, Mass–1630-1700; Onandago Co, NY–1825-1850
Paper–41pp–$3.50--- Vendor #180

167 - ELIJAH CARR BELDING AND CAPTAIN LEVI BLAKE, THE ANCESTORS
OF - WITH ALLIED LINES by Ruth Leighton Froeberg
Belding/Belden/Baildon: Eng-1066-1641; Wethersfield, Conn-1641-1661;
Hatfield, Mass-1661-1740; Swanzey, NH-1740-1971
Blake: Wrentham, Mass-1640-1800; Swanzey, NH-1800-1900
Cloth-202pp-$20.00--- Vendor #181

168 - THE EDWARDS OF NORTHAMPTON by Bruce Montgomery Edwards
Edwards: Wales-1523-1752; Northampton Co, NC-1752-1973; Southampton
Co, Va-1880-1973
Deloatch: Isle of Wight Co, Va-1663-c1700; Northampton Co, NC-c1700-1883
Cobb: Southampton Co, Va-1613-1973; Hertford Co, NC-c1825-1973
Cloth-316pp-$8.00--- Vendor #185

169 - ANTHONY ROOTS AND BRANCHES by Nancy Vashti Jacob
Anthony: New Kent Co, Va-1704-1750s; Campbell Co, Va-1750s-1974;
Henry Co, Va-1750s-1790; Wilkes Co, Ga-1790-1974
Paper-250pp-$11.00--- Vendor #186

170 - KEY AND COLLATERAL FAMILES 1776-1972 by Edward S. Key & Irene
T. Sevier
Key: Moore Co, NC-1776-1833; Kemper Co, Miss-1833-1860; Lufkin, An-
gelina Co, Tex-1860-1870; Bedias, Grimes Co, Tex-1870-1972
Cloth-300pp-$9.50--- Vendor #187

171 - TRANSATLANTIC SHERMANS by Bertha L. Stratton
Sherman: Dedham, Essex, Eng-1534-1580s; Mass. Bay Colony-1633-   ;
RI/Conn/etc. [emigrants to the various colonies]
Cloth-202pp-$20.00--- Vendor #188

172 - DESCENDENTS OF WILLIAM TILGHMAN MATTHEWS AND ALLIED FAM-
ILIES, 1806-1972 by Ruth Witter May
Mathews/Matthews: Ky-1806-1829; Ohio Co, Ky- ? -1830; Breckenridge
Co, Ky-1830-1834; Wayne Co, Ill-1837-1972
Paper-140pp-$5.25--- Vendor #192

173 - WITTER COUSINS by Doris Ellen Witter Bland & Ruth Ann Witter May
Witter: Breckenridge Co, Ky-1810-1813; Christian Co, Ky-1813-1814;
Ohio Co, Ky-1822-1830; Wayne Co, Ill-1859-1973
Paper-189pp-$8.40--- Vendor #192

174 - LOOKING BACKWARD by Mrs. G. Harold Martin
Rodgers: Bucks Co, Pa-1722-1749; Loudon Co, Va-1749-1790; Bourbon
Co, Ky-1790-1804; Ross Co, O-1804-1974
Mallory: Hanover Co, Va-1790-1796; Bourbon Co, Ky-1796-1823; Ross
Co, O-1823-1974
Paper-46pp-$2.50--- Vendor #193

175 — TUPPER GENEALOGY by Dr. Eleanor Tupper
Tupper: Sandwich, Mass—c1630-date; Nova Scotia—1700's-date; Sussex,
Eng—1500's-date; Maine—1700's-date
Cloth—919pp—$31.00--Vendor #194

176 — AN ABBOTT FAMILY by Ruth Marcum Lind
Abbott: Essex Co, Mass—1643-1750; Hampshire Co, Mass-1770-1815; Cuy-
ahoga Co, O—1815-1833; Hancock Co, Ill—1835-1846; Pottawattamie Co,
Ia—1846-1890; Kings Co, Calif—1890-1960
Paper—59pp—$5.00--------------------------------------- Vendor #196

177 — THE MILWARD FAMILY OF LEXINGTON, KENTUCKY, 1803-1969 by
Margaret Taylor Macdonald
Milward: Lexington, Ky—1803-1969
Cloth—177pp—$9.50---Vendor #197

178 — SOME DESCENDANTS OF NATHANIEL MERRILL WHO WAS IN NEWBURY,
MASSACHUSETTS IN 1635 by Winnifred M. Robinson
Merrill: New Eng—1635-date; Vt—1770-date; Compton, Quebec—1850-1900
Paper—33pp—$3.00-- Vendor #198

179 — THE 17th CENTURY FAMILIES OF JOHN MARTIN & THOMAS KEELING
OF LOWER NORFOLK COUNTY, VIRGINIA by Alice Granbery Walter
Martin: Lower Norfolk Co, Va—c1635-1700s; NC—1704-1716
Keeling: Lower Norfolk Co, Va—c1635-1691; Pr. Anne Co, Va—1691-1700s
Paper—30pp—$15.00--------------------------------------- Vendor #199

180 — JOHN GRANBERY, VIRGINIA by Julian Hastings Granbery
Granberry/Granbery/etc: Devonshire, Eng—1493-1650; Va—1650-1964;
Bermuda; 31 States. Sixteen generations.
Cloth—351pp—$25.00-------------------------------------- Vendor #199

181 — EIGHT GENERATIONS OF GASKINS by Alice Granbery Walter
Gaskins: Lower Norfolk Co, Va—1639-1691; Princess Ann Co, Va—1691-1846
Chart: 11" x 15" —$8.00------------------------------------Vendor #199

182 — FIVE GENERATION CHART OF THE POOLE FAMILY by Alice Granbery
Walter
Poole: Lower Norfolk Co, Va—1650-1691; Princess Anne Co, Va—1691-1768
Chart: 8 1/2" x 11" —$5.00-------------------------------- Vendor #199

183 — CHART OF SIX GENERATIONS OF SOME OF THE DESCENDANTS OF
THOMAS FRANCIS SAYER by Alice Granbery Walter
Sayer: Lower Norfolk Co, Va—c1635-1800; Princess Anne Co, Va—1691-
1800
Chart: 11" x 16 1/2" —$7.00------------------------------ Vendor #199

184 — CHART & FAMILY TREE OF SEVEN GENERATIONS OF WILLOUGHBY,
CAPTAIN THOMAS by Alice Granbery Walter
Willoughby: Elizabeth City Co, Va—1610-c1635; Lower Norfolk Co, Va—
c1635-1800s
Charts [2]: each 8 1/2" x 11" —both for $10.00--------------- Vendor #199

185   – CHART OF THOMAS SCOTT'S & THOMAS HERBERT'S DESCENDANTS by Alice Granbery Walter   Five generations of Scotts, four of Herberts.
Herbert: Norfolk Co, Va–c1700-1794
Chart: 11" x 24" –$7.00--- Vendor #199

186   – FIVE GENERATION CHART OF CARTWRIGHT & SHIPP FAMILIES by Alice Granbery Walter
Cartwright: Lower Norfolk Co, Va–c1635-1691; Pr.Anne Co, Va–1691-c1760
Shipp: Lower Norfolk Co, Va–c1650-1691; Pr. Anne Co, Va–1691-1770
Chart: 11" x 19" –$8.00--- Vendor #199

187   – CHART OF CARRAWAY-FOSTER-WILLIAMSON & BARTHOLOMEW HOSKINS by Alice Granbery Walter
Carraway: Lower Norfolk Co, Va–c1635-1700; Pr.Anne Co, Va–1691-1700
Chart: 11" x 22 1/2" –$7.00-------------------------------- Vendor #199

188   – THREE GENERATIONS OF THE HAPPER FAMILY by Alice Granbery Walter
Happer: Norfolk Co, Va–c1730-1800
Chart: –$3.00-------------------------------- Vendor #199

189   – THE BOOK OF THE WILDERS (revised), by Edwin M. Wilder, M.D.
Wilder: Mass–1638; throughout U.S. [Descendants of immigrants, Thomas and Edward Wilder.] Reprinted from offset masters used in original printing, 1961-1969, by the Wilder Family Foundation. Available August 1975.
Loose leaf, punched for three-ring binder–1100pp–$25.00------ Vendor #356

190   – SEVEN GENERATIONS OF ROBYNS/ROBINS by Alice Granbery Walter
Robyns/Robins: Northampton Co, Eng–1377-1620; Jamestown, Va–1628-   ;
Northampton Co, Va–   -1692; Chincoteague Island, Va–   -1709
Chart: 11" x 15 1/2" –$8.00---------------------------------Vendor #199

191   – GENEALOGY OF THE DEVOL FAMILY & ALLIED FAMILIES: CUDDINGTON, BOYD, BROWN by Elbert E. Boyd
Devol: Mass–1640-   ; RI–1670-   ; O–1793-   ; Ind–1865-
Paper–106pp–$4.95--- Vendor #203

192   – MY ANCESTORS AND GENEALOGICAL HISTORY OF THE SHAMBACH FAMILY by LeRoy F. Shambach
Shambach: Montgomery Co, Pa–1729-1795; Northumberland Co, Pa–1795-date; Snyder Co, Pa–1795-date; Union Co, Pa–1820-date
Cloth–281pp–$7.50-- Vendor #204

193   – SNICKERSVILLE - THE BIOGRAPHY OF A VILLAGE by Jean Herron Smith
Clayton: Loudoun Co, Va–1817-1896
Chew: Loudoun Co, Va–1749-1900
Osburn: Loudoun Co, Va–1712-1900
Throckmorton: Loudoun Co, Va–1777-1950
Lodge: Loudoun Co, Va–1754-1910
Humphrey: Loudoun Co, Va–1742-1882
Paper–107pp–$2.15-- Vendor #205

194 - HISTORY OF THE BURCH FAMILY OF KENTUCKY - INCLUDING ALL
THE DESCENDANTS OF JOHN ARNOLD BURCH & EMILY T. MANNING by
Frank E. Toon, et al
Burch: Charles Co, Md—1664-1797; Melson Co, Ky—1797-1973; Larue Co,
Ky—1812-1973; Union Co, Ky—1872-1973
Paper—175pp [8 1/2 x 11]—$6.00-----------------------------Vendor #206

195 - THE DREAMER: ARCHIBALD DeBOW MURPHEY, by Herbert S. Turner
Murphey: Alamance Co, NC—1777-1832
Cloth—259pp—$7.95--- Vendor #207

196 - DESCENDANTS OF ISAAC VAN TUYL, SR., AND MARY McCARTER OF
BERNARDS TWP., SOMERSET CO., N.J. by Mary Ellenor Stafford Bowman
Van Tuyl: Bernards Twp, Somerset Co., NJ—b1739-d1803
Cloth—100pp—$7.50-- Vendor #211

197 - WAINNER, OVERTON, McMURR(A)Y AND INTERCONNECTING LINES
by Merle W. Jeter & George D. Wainner
McMurry/McMurray: Lancaster Co, SC—c1775-c1810; Rutherford Co, Tenn—
1810's-1830's; Haywood Co, Tenn—1830's-1870's; Reno Co, Kan—1870's-date
Paper—232pp—$9.50--------------------------------------- Vendor #213

198 - SMEDAL FAMILY HISTORY AND GENEALOGY by Erling A. Smedal, M.D.
Smedal: Norway, Denmark, Germany, Scotland & France
Cloth—192pp—$10.00--------------------------------------- Vendor #214

199 - ANDERSON-AMUNDSON-VON KROGH FAMILY by Lester W. Hansen
Anderson/Amundson: Norway-   -1836; Wisc—1836-date; other states
Cloth—323pp—$15.00-------------------------------------- Vendor #215

200 - THE NUTT FAMILY THROUGH THE YEARS by Dr. Merle C. Nutt, P.E.
Nutt/McNutt/MacNutt: Scot, Eng, & N.Ire-   -1635; James City Co, Va—
1635-1660; Northumberland Co, Va—1660-1750; Augusta Co, Va—1750-1811;
Coventry, Eng—1648-1714; County Kent, Eng—1635-1660; County Essex,
Eng—1634-1665; Phoenixville, Pa—1714-1737; Hopkinton, Mass—1726-1788;
Manchester, NH—1735-1843; Troy, Me—1780-1856; Rockbridge Co, Va—
1802-1848; Rodney, Miss—1816-1862; Natchez, Miss—1862-1930; Southing-
ton, O—1814-1875; Hamilton, O—1833-1915; Bloomington, Ind—1860-1875;
Hood Co, Tex—1865-1974; Orange, Conn—1913-1966; Providence, RI—1917-
1942; Moline, Ill—1902-1956; Wakefield, Mass—1923-1947
Cloth-   pp—$10.00-------------------------------------Vendor #216

201 - THE BABERS, BARRON, BUNSON, BROWN, CALDWELL, CASON, COL-
LINSWORTH, COX, CUMMINGS, EASLEY, FOUTS, FRANKS, GRAY, HAYS,
HEDGPETH, HOWARD, JONES, LOE, LOW, MOORE, NELSON, PANKEY,
PARKS, POOLE, POTTS, RENTZ, RODEN, TALBOT, TILLEY, WHITLEY,
WHITLOW, BLACK, CRAWLEY, RABURN, VERNON, WILLIAMS, CRAW-
FORD, FREY, MALONE, PRICE, & SCOGGINS FAMILIES OF BRUSH VALLEY,
FRIENDSHIP, LIBERTY HILL IN BIENVILLE PARISH, LOUISIANA by Eva
Lee McDuffie
Paper—approx. 400pp—$10.00----------------------------------Vendor #217

202 - THE ODYSSEY OF JOHANN CASTOR by Robert H. Peterson
Kastor/Castor: Klotten, Germany—1819-1857; Erie Co, O—1857-1875
[650 photos of descendants included, 32 family tree charts]
Paper—57pp—$4.75--- Vendor #219

203 - THE SWOPE FAMILY BOOK OF REMEMBRANCE by Emily Swope Morse
& Winifred Morse McLachlan
Swope/Schwob/Schwab/Swab: Baden, Germany—1610-1730; Baselland, Swit-
zerland—1560-1750; Lancaster Co, Pa—1720-1800; Lebanon Co, Pa—1750-
1972; Washington Co, Md—1780-1850; York Co, Pa—1750-1800;
Brandt: Lancaster Co, Pa—1717-1750; Lebanon Co, Pa—1750-1800
Gloninger/Kloninger/Cloninger: Lancaster Co, Pa—1740-1750; Lebanon Co,
Pa—1750-1830
Mish/Miesch: Baselland, Switz—1700-1750; Lebanon Co, Pa—1750-1820
Funk/Funck: Baden, Ger—1675-1750; Lebanon Co, Pa—1750-1800
Cloth—1500pp—$30.00------------------------------------- Vendor #221

204 - THE BLEDSOE FAMILY: A GENEALOGICAL HISTORY FROM 1639 to
PRESENT by John T. Bledsoe
Bledsoe: Va—c1630-present; Tenn—c1803-present; NC—c1710-present;
Ky—c1715-present; Tex—c1800-present; NY, Md, & other states—1830-present
Cloth—296pp—$18.91------------------------------------- Vendor #225

205 - DESCENDANTS OF RICHARD KNOWLES, 1637-1973 by Virginia Knowles
Hufbauer
Knowles: Cape Cod, Mass—to most states of the U.S. & Nova Scotia
Cloth—1,000+pp—$40.00----------------------------------Vendor #226

206 - FISHER FACTS by Betty L. Pennington
Fisher/Fischer: Anywhere-anytime
Subscription: $5.00/yr; 4 issues/yr; 25-30pp/issue---------- Vendor #227

207 - THE MAPP FAMILY ON THE EASTERN SHORE OF VIRGINIA by N. Pierce
Eichelberger
Mapp: Accomack & Northampton Cos, Va—1654-1972 [Eight generations of
male & female descent of John Mapp who came to Virginia in 1654]
Cloth—47pp—$12.00/Paper—$8.00-------------------------- Vendor #230

208 - RECORDS OF ROBERT FULLER OF SALEM AND REHOBOTH AND SOME
OF HIS DESCENDANTS by Clarence C. Fuller
Fuller: Salem, Mass—1638-1651; Rehoboth, Mass—1651-1882; Mansfield,
Mass—1882-present
Cloth—347pp—$9.75------------------------------------- Vendor #231

209 - KOOGLER FAMILY OF VIRGINIA AND ALLIED FAMILIES OF AUSTIN,
GOOD, HAHN, HEATWOLE, HEMP, KNICELY, MARTIN, RHODES, SHO-
WALTER, SNEAD, TAYLOR & WITMER by Virginia Koogler Whitney
Koogler: Augusta Co, Va—1770-date; Rockingham Co, Va—1778-date;
Lima, O—1887-date; NM—1878-date
Paper—84pp—$4.00-------------------------------------Vendor #232

210 - WILSONS: ENGLAND TO AMERICA 1600-1970 by Elva Wilson Nyren
Wilson: Denton, Grantham, Lincolnshire, Eng-1600-1870; Upper Sandusky,
O-1847-1856; Hastings, Mills Co, Ia-1856-1974
Cloth-158pp-$6.00--Vendor #236

211 - DESCENDANTS OF WILLIAM KENDALL OF ASHFORD, CONNECTICUT &
CALEDONIA COUNTY, VERMONT by Kendall Laughlin
Kendall: Woburn, Mass-   -1693; Ashford, Conn-   -1760; West Spring-
field, Mass-   -1800; Caledonia Co, Vt-   -1840
Paper-36pp-$4.50-- Vendor #237

212 - THE SANDERS FAMILY OF GRASS HILLS by Anna Virginia Parker
Sanders: Spottsylvania Co, Va-1731-1782; Bryan's Station, Ky-1782-1783;
Fayette Co, Ky-1783-1795; Gallatin Co, Ky-1795-present
Cloth-171pp-$5.25--Vendor #238

213 - A GENEALOGY OF THE MORTONS WITH RELATED GENEALOGIES by
William Markham Morton
Morton: Spencer Co, Ind-1813-1828; Danville [Vermilion Co], Ill-1828-
1840; Green Co, Wisc-1840-1867; Hazelton, Ia-1867-1896
Paper-45pp-$5.00--Vendor #239

214 - THE ROEBUCK FAMILY IN AMERICA by Bette Dickson Casteel
Roebuck: Va-1674-1800; Ohio-1797-1974; NC-1790-1974; SC-1777-1974
Paper-184pp-$10.00--Vendor #240

215 - THE BRAME - BRIM FAMILY IN AMERICA, 1674 to 1974 by Arden H.
Brame, Jr. II
Brame/Brim: Middlesex Co, Va-1674-1860's; Caroline Co, Va-1740-1820's;
Mecklenburg Co, Va-1762-1900's; Granville Co, NC-1770's-1900's; Pitts-
sylvania Co, Va-1760's-1900; Rockingham Co, NC-1790-1900's
Approx. 350pp-to be published 1975 (summer)-----------------Vendor #242

216 - THE NEAL, HARBISON, SNODGRASS, MILLER AND RELATED FAMI-
LIES by Thomas H. R. Neal
Neal: Knox Co, Tenn-1791-1971.
Paper-267pp-$15.00-- Vendor #243

217 - THE SMITH GENEALOGY by Marjorie Little Napoli
Smith: Norfolk Co, Mass-1637-1750; Worcestor Co, Mass-1750-1790; Chesh-
ire Co, NH-1790-1800; Franklin Co, Vt-1800-1974; Franklin Co, NY-1840-
1974; Wyandot Co, O-1840-1974
Royce: New Haven Co, Conn-1637-1770; Cheshire Co, NH-1770-1800;
Franklin Co, Vt-1800-1974
Cloth-198pp-$12.00--Vendor #245

218 - REV. JOHN HAYNIE - ANCESTRY, LIFE & DESCENDANTS, 1650-1963
by Loyce Haynie Rossman
Haynie: Northumberland Co, Va-1650-1786; Botetourt Co, Va-1786-1805;
Knoxville, Tenn-1805-1825; Tuscumbia, Ala-1825-1839; Fayette Co, Tex-
1839-1860
King: Botetourt Co, Va-1786-1805; Bastrop, Tex-1839-1840

Brooks: Savannah, Ga—1787-1805; Fayette Co, Tex—1839-1863
Sweeney: Tenn—1818-1832; Brazoria Co, Tex—1833-
Cloth—260pp—$10.00--Vendor #246

219 — JOSEPH AND ELIZABETH WRIGHT OF BEDFORD COUNTY, VIRGINIA,
AND COLUMBIANA COUNTY, OHIO by Jay B. Wright
Wright: Bedford Co, Va—1786-1802; Columbiana Co, O—1803-1831
Paper—20pp—$3.00--Vendor #247

220 — THE LLOYDS OF SOUTHERN MARYLAND by Daniel B. Lloyd
Lloyd: Wales—5th century-1660; Ire—1660-1795; Southern Md—1795-present
Cloth—324pp—$12.00--Vendor #249

221 — THE MIDDLETONS OF SOUTHERN MARYLAND, AND KINDRED FAMI-
LIES by Daniel B. Lloyd
Middleton: Maryland & nearby states—1650-present
Cloth—390pp—$15.00--[to be published in 1975]---------------- Vendor #249

222 — GENEALOGY OF THOMAS HILL AND REBECCA MILES by Sister M.
Louise Donnelly
Hill: Wiltshire, Eng—1724-1740; St. Mary Co, Md—1740-1785; Washington
Co, Ky—1785-1820
Cloth—380pp—$20.00-- Vendor #251

223 — JOHN BARRICKMAN AND HIS CHILDREN by June B. Barekman
Barekman: Washington Co, Md—1760-1784; Campbell Co, Ky—1784-1812;
Franklin Co, Ind—1812-1845; Shelby Co, Ill—1845-1972
Paper—40pp—$5.00-- Vendor #252

224 — BARRICKMAN OF CRAWFORD CO., PA. by June B. Barekman
Barrickman/Barrackman: Crawford Co, Pa—1800-1964; Monroe Co, O—
1850-1964; Curtis, Nebr—1860-1964; Howard, Kan—1864-1964
Paper—44pp—$5.00-- Vendor #252

225 — OUR BOWLBY KIN, VOLUME I, by June B. Barekman
Bowlby/Bolrie/Bolby/Bowlsby: York, Eng—1553-1633; Nottinghamshire,
Eng—1665-1727; Sussex, NJ—1727-1974
Paper—86pp—$9.00-- Vendor #252

226 — ALLENS OF EARLY ROWAN CO, N.C. by June B. Barekman
Allen: [Transcripts of Rowan Co. sources 1760-1815 relating to Allens]
Paper—10pp—$2.50-- Vendor #252

227 — HUNTER FAMILY SOURCES by June B. Barekman
Hunter: [Transcripts of Rowan Co. records relating to Hunters, 1760-1815]
Paper—21pp—$3.50--Vendor #252

228 — THE DESCENDANTS OF THE MARRIAGE OF SOLOMON & HANNAH
(WELLS) COBB OF CAMBRIDGE, NEW YORK compiled by John L. Cobb
Cobb: Washington Co, NY—1810-1839; Cuyahoga Co, O—1839-present
Fenton: Washington Co, NY—1810-1839; Cuyahoga Co, O—1839-present
Paper—147pp—$3.00-- Vendor #253

229 — BILL-BILLS FAMILY HISTORY by John L. Cobb
Bill/Byll/Bills: [?]Ringstead, Northants, Eng—[?]1611-c1633; Boston-Ips-
wich, Mass—c1633-1667;   New London (Groton), Conn—1667-c1703; Leb-
anon (Goshen), Conn—c1703-c1800; Steuben, Oneida Co, NY—c1800-1814;
Remsen, Oneida Co, NY—1814-1835; (Sandusky), Erie Co, O—1835-1861;
(Cleveland), Cuyahoga Co, O—1861-1930
[To be published about 1977 — over 450pp]---------------------- Vendor #253

230 — THE HICKS NEWSLETTER by Virginia Hicks
Hicks: Anywhere — anytime
Subscription: $6.00/yr; approx. 180pp/yr; 12 issues/yr------- Vendor #254

231 — BARTON-GREEN AND RELATED FAMILIES OF BAKER, CHAMBER-
LAIN, DAVISON, HARTRIDGE AND WRIGHT by Ruth Lincoln Kaye
Barton: Co. Essex, Eng—c1759-1855; Port Elliot, So. Australia—1855-c1868;
Hartford, Conn—c1868-1947
Green: Co. Kent, Eng—1755-1869; Hartford, Conn—1869-1907
Cloth—83pp—$13.00--- Vendor #255

232 — THOMAS LINCOLN OF TAUNTON; JOSEPH KELLOGG OF HADLEY; AND
144 RELATED COLONIAL FAMILIES—ABORNE, ALLERTON, ALLYN, AN-
DREWS, AUSTIN, BANCROFT, BARBER, BARTLETT, BAXTER, BECKWITH,
BEMAN, BENTON, BISHOP, BLANDFORD, BOOSEY, BROWN, BROWNING,
BURNHAM, BURT, CASTLE, CHANDLER, CHATTERTON, CHITTENDEN,
CLARK, COLTON, COOLEY, COOMBS, CUSHMAN, DAVIS, DENNIS, DIGH-
TON, DOWNING, DRAKE, DRURY, DUNHAM, EAMES, ELIOT, ENSIGN, FAY,
FELTON, FILER, FILLEY, FLAGG, FOSTER, FOX, GALE, GARDNER, GIB-
BON, GILBERT, GILLET, GINGELL, GOBLE, GRAY, GREENHILL, GRIS-
WOLD, GUNN, HALE, HAMNORE, HARTWELL, HARVEY, HARWOOD, HAY-
WARD, HICKS, HITCHCOCK, HORN, HUBBARD, JACKSON, JEPSON, KEEP,
KELLOGG, KEYES, KING, LEETE, LEONARD, LINCOLN, LOBDELL, LOCK-
ERT, LOOMIS, LOUGIE, MARSHALL, McFARLAND, MERRIAM, MITCHELL,
MONTAGUE, MOORE, MORGAN, MORTON, MOUSALL, PARLIN, PENNIMAN,
PHILLIPS, PHIPPEN, PORTER, PRATT, PRESCOTT, PRIEST, PYNCHON,
RICE, ROBINSON, ROYALL, SAVAGE, SCARLET, SHAW, SHEAFE, SHELDON,
SHEPARD, SHRIMPTON, SIMONDS, SKELTON, SMITH, SPALDING, STACEY,
STANLEY, STEBBINS, STOCKING, STODDER, STRATTON, SYKES, TERRY,
TIBBALS, TOMPKINS, TRYTTON, WATSON, WESTOVER, WHALE, WHEATE,
WHEELER, WHEELOCK, WHITE, WHITING, WILKINS, WILLIAMS, WILSON,
WILTON, WOLCOTT, WRIGHT, GRIFFIN by Ruth Lincoln Kaye
Lincoln: Hingham, Mass—1635-1649; Taunton, Mass—1649-1759; New
Braintree area, Mass—1759-1770; Oakham, Mass—1770-c1850
Kellogg: Hadley, Mass—1661-1701; Pittsford, Vt area—c1776-1854
Cloth—410pp—$25.75--- Vendor #255

233 — BECHTEL FAMILY ENCYCLOPEDIA compiled by Barbara M. Dalby
Beghton/Bechtel/Bachtel/etc: NJ; Md; Penn; O; Ind; Mich; Ontario, Can;
Ia—[Immigrant through 1880]
Paper—201pp—$7.50-- Vendor #256

234 — FAMILY RECORD OF WILLIAM HENRY SAUER AND MARY SCHAUP
SAUER [AS OF MAY 1, 1973] by Verona M. Marble
Sauer: Dirmstein, Rheinkreis, Bavaria, Ger—1814-1834; Buffalo, NY—1834-
1844; Willoughby Twp, Welland Co, Ont, Can—1844-1974
Paper—52pp—$3.25-- Vendor #257

235 — THE McCLUNGS OF WEST VIRGINIA by Judith A. Cloninger
McClung: Rockbridge Co, Va—1750-1780; Nicholas Co, WVa—1773-
present; Greenbrier Co, Va—1780-present; Bath Co, Va—1780-present
[Publication date about 1977; approx. 250pp------------------- Vendor #258

236 — BALLENGEE TRAILS by Judith A. Cloninger
Ballengee/Belangee: NJ—1720-1780; WVa—1780-present; Mo—1830-1870
Paper—200pp—$6.50--- Vendor #258

237 — THE ANCESTORS AND DESCENDANTS OF ROSWELL NEWCOMB WHITE
AND HIS WIFE JANE OSGOOD OF PLAINVIEW, MINN. by Georgia C. George
White: Hartford, Conn—1636-1683; Middletown, Conn—1652-1736; Lebanon,
Conn—1736-1800; NY St—1800-1838; McHenry Co, Ill—1839-1856; Plainview,
Minn—1856-1898
Osgood: Salisbury, Mass—1638-1780; Gardiner, Me—1789-1811; NYC—
1813-1838
Newcomb: Edgartown, Mass—1687-1780; Hebron, Conn—1727-1787; NY St—
1789-1838
[Publication date about 1976]------------------------------- Vendor #259

238 — THE DESCENDANTS OF WILLIAM AND SARAH MELENDY OF CHARLES-
TOWN, MASSACHUSETTS 1714 to 1977 by Georgia Cook George
Melendy: Charlestown, Mass—1714-1739; Reading, Mass—1740-1761; Am-
herst, NH—1761-1902; Many other states—1772-1977
[Publication date about 1977]------------------------------- Vendor #259

239 — DESCENDANTS OF JOAB D. HINES OF LAUDERDALE COUNTY, ALA-
BAMA by Clara Hines Lanier
Hines: Kershaw Co, SC—1788-1830; Lauderdale Co, Ala—1830-1974
Kirkland: Kershaw Co, SC—1790-1830; Lauderdale Co, Ala—1830-1974
Paper—58pp—$4.00--- Vendor #260

240 — GENEALOGY OF THE ROBERT LUMPKIN FAMILY by Ira W. Hepperly
Lumpkin: K & Q Co, Va—1756-1799; Knox Co, Tenn—1800-1831; Randolph
Co, Ind—1831-11/12/1842 [date of death]
Cloth—240pp—$17.50-------------------------------------- Vendor #261

241 — REV. JOHN KING (1786-1868), HIS ANCESTORS AND DESCENDANTS,
PARTS I & II [bound as one book] by Ira W. Hepperly
King: Loudoun Co, Va—1635-1802; Fayette Co, O—1802-1974; Randolph
Co, Ind—1838-1864; Holt Co, Mo—1864-1974
Hepperly: Fayette Co, O—1821-1842; Stark Co, Ill—1843-1908; Ring Gold
Co, Ia—1866-1888; Madison Co, Nebr—1888-1956
Paper—150pp—$15.00--------------------------------------Vendor #262

242 — A BRIEF FAMILY HISTORY by Theron E. Coffin
Coffin: Nantucket—early-1771; NC—1771-1829; Ind—c1829-
Paper—79pp—$10.00--------------------------------------- Vendor #265

243 — A BOOK OF GARRETTS by Hester E. Garrett
Garrett: Va—1700-1817; Hart/Green/Christian Cos, Ky—1817-1900; Okla—
Paper—444pp—$15.00------------------------------------- Vendor #267

244 - COLLECTED NOTES ON THE FAMILY, ANCESTORS, RELATIVES &
DESCENDANTS OF NATHANIEL GRADELESS OF WHITLEY COUNTY,
INDIANA (Vol. I) compiled by Donald E. Gradeless
Grayless: Caroline Co, Md-1700-1860; Ross Co, O-1790-1840; Whitley
Co, Ind-1830-present; Allen Co, Ind-1830-present
Gradeless: Ross Co, O-1790-1840; Whitley Co, Ind-1830-present
Waugh: Litchfield Co, Conn-1696-1800; Ross Co, O-1800-1860
Paper-113pp-$7.00--------------------------------------- Vendor #269

245 - THE MORT NEWSLETTER by Donald E. Gradeless
Mort: [Clearing house for all Mort families - anytime, anywhere]
Subscription: $2.00/yr; 4 issues/yr; 10+pp/issue-------------Vendor #270

246 - VANDERPOOL NEWSLETTER compiled by Frances R. Nelson
Vanderpool: [Clearing house for Vanderpool families - anytime, anywhere]
Subscription: $5.00/yr; 10 issues/yr; 10pp/issue------------Vendor #271

247 - HEDGPETH NEWSLETTER compiled by Frances R. Nelson
Hedgpeth: [Clearing house for Hedgpeth families - anytime, anywhere]
Subscription: $5.00/yr; 10 issues/yr; 10pp/issue------------Vendor #271

248 - JOHN NEELY OF WARREN COUNTY, OHIO AND SOME OF HIS DESCEND-
ANTS WHO LIVED IN JAY COUNTY, INDIANA by Bonnie Neeley
Neeley: Warren Co, O-1792-c1850; Jay Co, Ind-c1850-1975; Sacramento,
Calif-c1910-1975; Portland, Ore-1900-1975
[Publication date about 1975; approx. 150pp]------------------ Vendor #272

249 - MEADOR FAMILIES OF NORTH CENTRAL TENNESSEE by Victor Paul
Meador
Meador: Va-1630-1809; Tenn-1809-1974; Mo-1830-1974
Cloth-231pp-$9.00--------------------------------------- Vendor #273

250 - LITTELL'S LIVING AGE, [Published by Littell Families of America, Inc.],
edited by Walter W. Littell
Littell/Little/etc: [Clearing house for all who bear the surname Littell (with
various spellings)] Subscription includes membership in the Family Assn.
Subscription: $5.00/yr; 2 issues/yr; 32-40pp/issue---------- Vendor #274

251 - RAYMOND FREDERIC MORIN, FAMILY GENEALOGY by Raymond Fred-
eric Morin
Morin: Ste. Marie Beauce, Quebec, Can-1772-1846; Prescott Co, Ont, Can-
1846-1850; Carleton Co, Ont, Can-1850-1926; Wayne Co, Mich-1926-1970
Therrien: Russell Cou, Ont, Can-1897-1940; Wayne Co, Mich-1940-1974
Paper-25pp-$2.50--------------------------------------- Vendor #275

252 - THE THERRIEN-HOULE HERITAGE, A FRENCH CANADIAN STORY
[Quarterly] by Raymond Frederic Morin
Therrien-Houle: Russell Cou, Ont, Can-1897-1945; Prescott Cou, Ont, Can-
1871-1897; Vaudreuil Cou, Que, Can-1824-1860; Lassomption Cou, Que,
Can-1801-1824
Subscription: $6.00/yr; 4 issues/yr; 12pp/issue-------------Vendor #275

253 — THE MORIN-DELORME STORY [A quarterly] by Raymond Fredric Morin
Morin-Delorme: Cumberland, Ontario, Can—1850-1946; L'Orignal, Ont,
Can—1846-1850; Que, Can—1731-1846
Subscription: $6.00/yr; 4 issues/yr; 12pp/issue--------------Vendor #275

254 — FROM LOUTH TO LOUISIANA by Nicholas Russell Murray
Sharkey: St. Helena Parish, La—1840-date
Paper—42pp—$3.50--- Vendor #277

255 — THESE ARE THE HARDYS by Nicholas Russell Murray
Hardy: Noxubee Co, Miss—1844-1855; Neshoba Co, Miss—1855-date; Kemper Co, Miss—1855-date
Paper—11pp—$1.50--------------------------------------Vendor #277

256 — WOOD AND ALLIED FAMILIES by Edith Louise Wood
Wood: Orange/Culpeper Cos, Va—1746-1789; Several Ky. Cos—1789-1974
Paper—69pp—$9.75-- Vendor #279

257 — SOME FAMILY ORIGINS OF ADAIR-INGALLS by Richard Porter Adair
Adair: Granby, Conn—1780's-1805; Montgomery, Mass—1805-1817;
Genesee Co, NY—1817-1840; Copley, Summit, O—1840-date
Paper—312pp—$17.50--------------------------------- Vendor #280

258 — ADAM & MAGDALENE (MUNCH) RIDENOUR & SOME RELATED FAMILIES by Iva C. Yarlick
Ridenour: Shenandoah Co, Va—1779-1854
Munch: Shenandoah Co, Va—1783-1869
Paper—510pp—$16.00--------------------------------- Vendor #281

259 — THE DEMAREST FAMILY published by The Demarest Family Assn.
Demarest/Demerest/Demorest/Demaray/DeMorier/etc: [This is the second
edition of this work. It is published in two volumes and completely indexed.
Lists the descendants of David desMarets and Marie Sohier, who migrated to
America in 1664. It also contains the male line of the desMarets family from
the Eleventh Century to time of migration to America.]
Cloth—approx. 1,700pp in 2 vols—$38.75---------------------- Vendor #283

260 — THE DEMAREST FAMILY [1972 Supplement to above work] Cambrecis map.
Paper—150pp—$7.75--- Vendor #283

261 — SOME DESCENDANTS OF JOHN MACANTURF, AND ALLIED FAMILIES:
BOYER, MUNCH, RIDENOUR (RITENOUR), ORNDORFF, LICHLITER
(LECHLITER), & O'FHLARETY by H. Eugene McInturff
McInturff/Macanturf: Shenandoah Co, Va—c1780-c1865; Throughout USA
[Publication date approx. 1979]----------------------------- Vendor #284

262 — JOHN ADCOCK OF BUCKINGHAM CO., VA., SOME OF HIS DESCENDANTS, WITH COLLATERAL LINES: CHRISTIAN, McMURTRY, ROBERTSON, INGERSOLL, ETC. by Blanche E. A. Lawless
Adcock: Eng—1226-c1700; Buckingham Co, Va—c1700-1814; Kanawha Co,
Va—1814- ; NC/Ky/Ind/Ill/Mo—1830-
Paper—100pp—$6.00--- Vendor #285

263 - "WE COUSINS", VOLUME II, by Florence Sutherland Hudson
Sutherland: So. & Cen. Va–1698-1804; E. Tenn–1804-1820; N. Ala–1820-
1830; E. Cen. Tex–1830-1895
Rogers: Cen. E. Va–1635-1820; N. Ala–1820-1830; Cen. E. Tex–1830-1900
Hodges: SE Va–1650-1758; Halifax Co, NC–1764-1800; Smith Co, Tenn–
1800-1830
Ward: Norfolk Co, Va–1636-1728; Terrell'/Halifax Cos, NC–1728-1800;
Smith Co, Tenn–1796-1820
Evans: Western Va–1740-1796; Ky–1800-1820; N. Ala–1820-1845
Pride: Va–1693-1763; Vicinity of Orange Co, NC–1763-1785; E. Tenn–
1785-1810; N. Ala–1810-1845
Tinsley: Va–1638-1790; Ky–1790-1800; SC–1780-1815
Morton: Va–1619-1790; Ky–1790-1850
Cloth–340pp–$12.50-- Vendor #286

264 - WILLIFORD AND ALLIED FAMILIES by William Bailey Williford
Ansley: England, NJ, Ga–1715-1950
Bailey: Va, Ga–c1768-1961
Brumby: SC, Ga–c1740-1961
Douglass: Ga–c1734-1911
Elam: Va, Ga–1638-1934
Hall: Ga–1775-1869
Matthews: Ga–1797-1931
Mongin: NJ, SC, Ga–1747-1833
Pearman: Va, Ga–c1780-1886
Pride: Va, SC–c1650-1961
Sandys: England, Va–c1516-c1640
Sitgreaves: NC–1757-1895
Thiot: Ga–1800-1942
Thornton: Va, Ga–1677-1843
Weakley: Va, Ga, Tenn–c1735-1845
Wilhite/Wilhoit: Va, NC, Ga–1728-1836
Wilford/Wilsford/Williford: England, Va, Ga–1499-1962
Worrill: Ga–1782-1923
Cloth–279pp–$15.00-- Vendor #287

265 - THE OWSLEY FAMILY IN ENGLAND AND AMERICA 1635-1890 [Reprint
of work published in 1890] by Harry P. Owsley
Owsley: England–   -1868
Paper–164pp–$7.50--- Vendor #291

266 - ESTEP FAMILY NEWSLETTER by Kathleen Estep Saul
Estep: [Clearing house for all Estep families - anytime, anywhere]
Subscription: $6.00/yr; 4 issues/yr; approx. 30pp/issue----- Vendor #292

267 - COOK'S CRIER by Betty Harvey Williams
Cook/Cooke: [A quarterly for all Cook/Cooke families - anytime, anywhere]
Subscription: $5.00/yr; 4 issues/yr; approx. 25pp/issue----- Vendor #293

268 - THE FRANKLIN FIREPLACE by Betty Harvey Williams
Franklin: [A quarterly for all Franklin families - anytime, anywhere]
Subscription: $5.00/yr; 4 issues/yr; approx 25pp/issue------ Vendor #293

269 - THE VANDENBARK HISTORY by Helen Vandenbark
Vandenbark: NJ- ? -1776; Ohio-1799-date
Clover: NJ- ? -1776
Cossart: NJ- ? -1776
Conine: NJ- ? -1776
Sharpenstein: ? -1776
Jarvis: NY-1638-
Vreeland: NY-1640-
Van Horne: NY-1638-
Cloth-409pp-$20.00---------------------------------------Vendor #295

270 - THE LANDRUM FAMILY OF FAYETTE CO., GEORGIA by Joel P. Shedd
Landrum: Scot-1308-1688; Va-1688-1800; NC-1754-1785; Ga-1774-1972
Cloth-   pp-$6.00---Vendor #296

271 - MARDEN FAMILY GENEALOGY by Sylvia Fitts Getchell
Marden/Mardin: NH-c1664-1974; Me-c1793-1974; Mass-c1740-1974; NY-
c1830-1974; Md-c1834-1974; Ill-c1839-1974
Cloth-631+pp-$25.00---Vendor #301

272 - DESCENDANTS OF THOMAS BRUMFIELD OF BERKS COUNTY, PENN-
SYLVANIA: GENEALOGY & FAMILY HISTORY 1720-1960 by Blackman O.
Brumfield & Ray C. Brumfield
Brumfield: O-c1817-1961; Ind-1821-1961; Ill-1835-1960; Ia-1854-1960
Cloth-493pp-$10.00---Vendor #303

273 - ERI RICH FAMILY TREE by Everett Eri Thomas
Rich: Chester Co, Pa-1714-1757; Guilford/Randolph Cos, NC-1767-1837;
Wayne Co, Ind-1832; Hamilton Co, Ind-1835-1852; Grant Co, Ind-1852-1923
Paper-61pp-$3.00---Vendor #303

274 - CHADWELL HERITAGE by Myrtle W. Braun & Sharon Chadwell Phillips
Chadwell: Henry Co, Va-c1750-1780; Lee Co, Va-1780-1800; Claiborne
Co, Tenn-1800-1833
Ball: Lee Co, Va-1760-1860; Grayson Co, Tex-1860-present
Cloud: Lee Co, Va-1800-1890; Claiborne Co, Tenn-1890-date
Cloth-217pp-$15.00---Vendor #305

275 - BRASFIELD - BRASSFIELD GENEALOGIES by Annabelle C. & Edward N.
McAllister
Brasfield/Brassfield: Va; Southern states; Western states; Other states
Cloth-720pp-Price not given---------------------------------- Vendor #306

276 - ESTES FAMILIES OF OLD CLAY COUNTY, MISSOURI: THEIR ANCES-
TORS AND DESCENDANTS by Edward N. & Annabelle C. McAllister
Estes: K & Q Co, Va; Clay Co, Mo; Calif; Other states
Cloth-335pp-Price not given---------------------------------- Vendor #306

277 - THE MORRISETTES OF N.C. & OTHER SOUTHERN STATES by Edna M.
Shannonhouse
Morrisette: NC-1695-date; Tenn-1790-date; Ala-c1800-date
Cloth-188pp-$10.00---Vendor #308

278 — THE SHANNONHOUSE & RELATED LINES by Edna M. Shannonhouse
Shannonhouse: Lancaster Co, Eng–c1560-1688; Bermuda– ? -1760;
NC–1760-present
Paper–177pp–$10.00--Vendor #308

279 — BURNHAM FAMILY LINEAGE CHARTS, VOL. I by Walter J. Burnham
Burnham: Anytime, anyplace. [Your lineage charts - Burnham or descend-
ants - published for you.
Paper–50 to 100 pp–$5.00 to $8.00---------------------------Vendor #309

280 — POE & UPDIKE FAMILY HISTORY, WITH ALLIED LINES OF HITT, COR-
LEY, CRIM/GRIMM, PARTLOW, SIM & GORE by Pauline A. Brannan
Poe: Culpeper Co, Va–1736-1800; Orange Co, Va–1714-1800; Rappahan-
nock Co, Va–1815-1895; Warren Co, Va–1895-1917
Updike: Fauquier Co, Va–1800-1853; Warren Co, Va–1853-1900
Hitt: Orange Co, Va–1714-1724; Fauquier Co, Va–1724-1900
Corley: Culpeper Co, Va–1767-1830; Rappahannock Co, Va–1830-1922
Crim/Grimm: Rappahannock Co, Va–1740-1767; Fauquier Co, Va–1767-1810
Sim: Richmond Co, Va–1700-1800; Culpeper Co, Va–1800-1850
Cloth–448pp–$28.00---Vendor #310

281 — HALL GENEALOGY by Helen L. Hall
Hall: Aasen, Ger–c1564; Mundelfingen, Ger–c1629; Hiedenhofen, Ger–
c1755; Hochemmingen, Ger–c1794; Buffalo, NY–1886
Cloth–274pp–$10.00-------------------------------------- Vendor #311

282 — STRECKER GENEALOGY by Helen L. Hall
Strecker: Heiligenstadt, Ger–1525; Mulhausen, Ger–1666; Dingelstadt,
Ger–1709; USA–1841
Cloth–700pp–$30.00-------------------------------------- Vendor #311

283 — BRUNGARDT GENEALOGY [2 VOLUMES] by Helen L. Hall
Brungardt: Riga, Russia–1465; Strassburg, Ger–1623; Riba, Russia–
1748; USA–1876
Cloth–777pp & 650pp–$30.00 each----------------------------Vendor #311

284 — THE UPSHAW FAMILY JOURNAL by Ted O. Brooke
Upshaw: [A quarterly, publishing material on Upshaw & allied families - pri-
marily those descended from Capt. William Upshaw of Gloucester/Essex
Cos, Va. 1666-1720]
Subscription: $6.00/yr; 4 issues/yr; 100pp+/yr--------------Vendor #312

285 — BRUBAKER GENEALOGY by Joan Bake Brubaker
Brubaker: Roanoke Co, Va–1777-1848; Preble Co, O–1827-
Paper–34pp–$5.50-- Vendor #313

286 — ROCK FAMILY HISTORY 1807-1969 FROM IRELAND TO UNITED STATES
OF AMERICA by Margaret M. Wagner
Rock: Orange Co, NY–1846-1849; Schuylkill Co, Pa–1849- ? ; Ross Co,
O– ? -1855; Iowa Co, Ia–1855-1969
Cloth–300pp–$12.80--- Vendor #315

287 — MY FAMILY, THE YOUNG-TODD GENEALOGY 1754-1972 by Lois Young
Todd: Lauren Co, SC-1729-1870; Due west SC-1870-1974
Young: Guilford Co, NC-1775-   ; Abbeville Co, SC; Due west-1837-1974
Cloth-100pp-$10.00--Vendor #316

288 — CORNELIUS BARENTSE SLECHT AND SOME OF HIS DESCENDANTS by
Lawrence T. Slaght
Slack/Slaght/Sleght: NY; NJ; Pa; and other-1652-present (in some cases)
Paper-108pp-$5.00-- Vendor #317

289 — GENEALOGICAL SKETCHES OF THE REYNOLDS, FEWELLS, WALLS,
AND KINDRED FAMILIES by John Fewell Reynolds [reprint of 1921 edition]
Reynolds: Pa; Md; NC-1700's; Tenn-1800's; Mo-1800's
Fewells: Pa; Md; NC-1700's; Tenn-1800's; Mo-1800's
Walls: Pa; Md; NC-1700's; Tenn-1800's; Mo-1800's
Paper-56pp-$3.25---Vendor #318

290 — ANCESTORS & DESCENDANTS OF JEREMIAH ADAMS 1794-1883 by Enid
Eleanor Adams, C.G.
Adams: Somersetshire, Eng-1475-1638; Plymouth Co, Mass-1638-1710;
Conn-1710-1807; Sullivan Co, NY-1806-1832; Erie Co, Pa-1832-present;
Mich-1837-present
Bowen: Orange Co, NY-1795-1832; Erie Co, Pa-1832-present
Burd: Erie Co, Pa-1830-1855; Vermilion, O-1855-1880's
Cade: Sturgis, Mich-1830-present
Crispell: Jackson Co, Mich-1830-present
Shadduck/Shattuck: Mass-1640's-1790's; Erie Co, Pa-1790's-present
Cloth-700+pp-$32.00--Vendor #319

291 — OUR BATEMAN ANCESTRY by Enid Eleanor Adams, C.G.
Bateman: Anne Arundel Co, Md-1660's-1800's; Baltimore, Md-1800's-
1830's; Pittsburgh, Pa-1830's-1850; Oregon Territory-1850's-1870's
Edmundson: Md-1800's-1830's; Pittsburgh, Pa-1830's- ?
Cloth-approx. 150pp-[to be published in 1975]----------------Vendor #319

292 — DESCENDANTS OF CORNELIUS MORFORD, SR. 1740-1825 by Enid Elea-
nor Adams, C.G.
Morford: NJ-1740-1800's; Del-1800's; O-c1809-present
[Publication date about 1975]-----------------------------Vendor #319

293 — THE DELONGS OF NEW YORK AND BROOKLYN: A HUGUENOT FAMILY
PORTRAIT by Thomas A. DeLong
Delong/DeLangh/DeLange: Berks Co, Pa-1732-present; Lehigh Co, Pa-
1750-present; NYC-1820-present; Siberia-1879-1882
Weber: Dutchess Co, NY-1708-1736; Lancaster Co, Pa-1736-present
Lopes: NYC-1780-1901; Englishtown, NJ-1850-present
Cloth-203pp-$9.95-- Vendor #321

294 —DESCENDANTS OF RICHARD ALEXANDER SKINNER OF LOUDOUN COUN-
TY, VIRGINIA by Lester Granville Holcombe
Skinner: Loudoun Co, Va; Ky; Ohio
Paper-100pp-$7.50-- Vendor #323

295 — HUEY FAMILY HISTORY, VOL. I (Includes coat of arms) by V.H. Huey
Huey: NC; SC; Ga; Ala; Other states
Paper—75pp—$4.00--- Vendor #326

296 — HUEY FAMILY HISTORY, VOL. II (Includes coat of arms) by V. H. Huey
Huey: Ala; Ark; Ga; Ill; Ky; Pa; Tenn; Other states
Paper—120pp—$8.00-- Vendor #326

297 — A HISTORY OF THE CARLON FAMILY & RELATED FAMILIES by Hugh
Robert Carlon
Carlon/Carlin: Ire—   -1827; Pa—1827-date; Del—1878-date
Blizzard: Pa—1840-date; Del—1757-date
Boyer/Bayer: Ger—1689-1731; Pa—1731-date
Danseisen/Dansiesen: Ger—1821-1857; Pa—1857-date
Dellop: Ire—1830-1851; Pa—1851-date
Effinger: Mannheim, Ger—1756-1776; Pa—1776-date; Va—1785-date
Haddon: Eng—1808-1830; Pa—1830-date
Schobert/Shobert: Bavaria, Ger—1849-c1874; Pa—c1874-date
Powell: Pa—1793—date
Pope: Eng—1807-1840; Pa—1840-date
Cloth—136pp—$6.00-- Vendor #327

298 — MEMOIRS OF MY ANCESTRY by Velma Roades Trant
Roads/Rood/Roodt/Roth: Lancaster Co, Pa—1743-1779; Northampton Co, Pa—
1785-1790; Shenandoah Co, Va—1777-1815; Highland/Ross Cos, O—1813-1833
Paper—200pp—$16.50-------------------------------------- Vendor #329

299 — ONE MAN AND HIS FAMILY: JOHN FRANKLIN SWOFFORD, 1853-1921
by Minnie Ray Bachman Swofford
Swofford: Rutherford Co, NC—1773-1849; Marion Co, Ark—1849-1857; Gray-
son/Johnson/Parker Cos, Tex—1857-1968
Cloth—147pp—$10.00--------------------------------------- Vendor #330

300 — THE DAMERON-DAMRON (DAMARELL) GENEALOGY by Helen Foster Snow
Dameron/Damron/Damarell: Northumberland Co, Va—1652-   ; various states
Unbound—350pp—$25.00------------------------------------ Vendor #332

301 — THE CHRISTOPHER FOSTER FAMILY HISTORY by Helen Foster Snow
Foster: Arrived, Lynn, Mass. 1635; went to Southampton; Long Island, NY;
and various states. [Sections available.]
Unbound—700pp—$25.00------------------------------------ Vendor #332

302 — LINKS OF WALTON HISTORY by Hattie E. W. Heninger
Walton: A brief historical and genealogical account of the Walton family in
the New England states, the Western states, & Canada with notes on allied.
Cloth—429pp—$12.00--------------------------------------- Vendor #333

303 — RECORD OF McMILLAN AND ALLIED FAMILIES by R. H. McMillan
McMillan/McMillian/MacMillan: Scot—1100-1774; Richmond Co, NC—1774-
1804; Camden Co, Ga—1804-1826; Irwin/Berrien/Tift Cos, Ga—1826-1973
Paulk: Wales; Mass; Jefferson Co, Ga; Irwin Co, Ga
Gaskins: Va; NC; SC; Irwin/Berrien Cos, Ga
Cloth—793pp—$23.18--------------------------------------- Vendor #334

304   – DESCENDANTS OF GIRGE FISCHER OF LOBENSTEIN, GERMANY by
     C. W. Fischer
     <u>Fischer</u>: Germany–c1600–date; U.S.A.–1880–date; Austria; Australia
     Publication date: 1975–250pp------------------------------ Vendor #335

305   – NELL, von NELL & NELL von NELLENBURG und DAMANACHER FAMILY
     by C. W. Fisher
     <u>Nell</u>: Holy Roman Empire–c1700–date; East & West Ger; USA; Australia
     Publication date: 1975–300pp--------------------------------Vendor #335

306   – DESCENDANTS OF SOME EARLY SETTLERS OF THE TRUMANSBURG-
     COVERT AREA (N.Y.) – THE SWICK FAMILY by C.W. Fischer & H.J. Swick
     <u>Swick</u>: Seneca Co, NY–c1800–present
     Cloth–$20.00/Paper–$15.00–321pp--------------------------Vendor #335

307   – DESCENDANTS OF THOMAS HORTON OF SPRINGFIELD, MASSACHU-
     SETTS by C. W. Fisher
     <u>Horton</u>:
     Publication date: 1975–300pp------------------------------ Vendor #335

308   – LIVE AND TIMES OF THE NASH FAMILY by Gertrude Nash Locke
     <u>Nash</u>: The story of Nashes from the 12th century on - in colonial times in
     America, especially the New Haven branch.
     Cloth–$5.50 ---Vendor #337

309   – HISTORY OF THE HUNGATE FAMILY (5 vols.) by Carroll P. Hungate, M.D.
     <u>Hungate</u>:
     Vol. I - 250pp–published in 1972
     Vol. II - 450pp–published in 1973
     Vol. III, IV, & V - approx. 450pp each - publication date 1975
     [$50.00/libraries; $40.00/individuals– per volume.] ----------Vendor #338

310   – GONE TO ALABAMA (Vol. 1, part 2) by E. J. Ladd
     <u>Dobbs</u>: NC–1750-1756; SC–1756-1820; Ala–1836-date; Miss–1822-date
     Cloth–871pp–$20.00-- Vendor #339

311   – GONE TO ALABAMA (Vol. 1, part 3) by E. J. Ladd
     <u>Gilbreath</u> (Baxter): SC–1790-1820; Tenn–1820-1830; Ala–1830-date
     Cloth–approx. 1000pp–publication date: 1975–about $25.00----- Vendor #339

312   – GONE TO ALABAMA (Vol. 2, parts 1 & 2) by E. J. Ladd
     <u>Dobbs</u>: SC– ? -1795; Ga–1795-1800; Ala–1800-date
     Cloth–396pp–$15.00-- Vendor #339

313   – THE DAVID SHIPPEE FAMILY GENEALOGY by Lenn Alan Bergsten
     <u>Shippee</u>: RI–1664-1855/84; Mass–1778-1900; Vt–1785-1900; NY St–1793-
     1900
     <u>Ellis</u>: Saratoga Co, NY–1800-1900
     Paper–89pp–$16.00--- Vendor #340

314   – THE FAMILY OF JOSEPH H. AND SALLY (COVINGTON) SMITH OF WAR-
     REN COUNTY, KENTUCKY 1807-1971 by Mildred Hawkins
     <u>Smith</u>: Richmond Co, NC–1784-1807; Warren Co, Ky–1807-1971
     Paper–115pp–$5.50-- Vendor #341

315 — SMALLWOOD FAMILY OF MARYLAND & VIRGINIA by Mildred McDonnell
Smallwood:

Paper—188pp—$15.00--Vendor #342

316 — THE ROMINE FAMILY — Book I by Mildred A. McDonnell
Romine/Romeyn/Romaine/Romyn, etc.

Paper—398pp—$13.00-- Vendor #342

317 — HISTORY OF THE HOPPING FAMILY IN ENGLAND AND GENEALOGY OF
THE JOHN HOPPING FAMILY IN AMERICA by Edward & Louis M. Hopping
Hopping: Suffolk Co, NY—1640-1973; Morris Co, NJ—1730-1973; Southern
O—1790-1973; Dearborn Co, Ind—1820-1973
Paper—$10.00--Vendor #343

318 — A FAMILY HIERARCHY by C. E. Cameron
Cameron: Nova Scotia, Can—1755-   ; US—1872-1972; Many different
states included; Germany—1619
Cloth—320pp—$10.00--------------------------------------- Vendor #345

319 — GENEALOGY OF THE MACY FAMILY FROM 1635-1868 by Silvanus J. Macy
Macy: America—1635-1868
Cloth—500pp—$15.00--------------------------------------- Vendor #346

320 — LUSKS ARE WHERE YOU FIND THEM by John Niles Lusk
Lusk: Scot/Ire/Eng— ? -date; Canada—1600s-date; US—1600's-date
[Collecting data on all of the Lusk name.]
Publication date approx. 1980------------------------------Vendor #347

321 — ALLEN KIN by Clifford L. Allen
Allen: Mifflin Co, Pa—1765-1881; Ottawa Co, Kan—1870-1898; Osceola Co,
Mich—1898-1908; Wexford Co, Mich—1908-1940
Cloth—68pp—$4.00--------------------------------------- Vendor #348

322 — A GENEALOGY OF HENRY JUDSON CHAPIN by Gretchen E. Engel
Chapin: Holyoke, Mass—1836-c1856; NYC—c1856- ? ; Norwalk, Conn—
 ? -1890; Montclair, NJ—1890-1895
Christy: NYC—1844- ? ; Norwalk, Conn— ? -1890; Montclair, NJ—1890-1915
Cloth—192pp—$15.00--------------------------------------- Vendor #350

323 — RICHARD HAINES AND HIS DESCENDANTS, VOL. I by John W. Haines
Haines: Burlington Co, NJ—1682-1832; Chester Co, Pa—1714-1790; Cecil
Co, Md—1714-1858; Frederick Co, Va—1747-1830
Cloth—540pp—$22.50--------------------------------------- Vendor #351

324 — RICHARD HAINES AND HIS DESCENDANTS, VOL. II by John W. Haines
Haines: Burlington Co, NJ—1740-1872; Chester/other Cos, Pa—1750-1908;
Cecil/Carroll Cos, Md—1786-1903; Frederick Co, Va—1750-1864
Cloth—613pp—$15.00--------------------------------------- Vendor #351

325 – MAUD HORN'S ATCHLEY FAMILY HISTORY by P. Atchley & M. Thompson
Atchley: Brunswick, NJ–1750-1786; Loudoun Co, Va–1775-1780; Sevier Co,
Tenn–1786-1974
Cloth–530pp–$25.00--- Vendor #352

326 – A COMPILATION OF GAINES FAMILY DATA WITH SPECIAL EMPHASIS
ON THE LINEAGE OF WILLIAM AND ISABELLA (PENDLETON) GAINES
[Indexed edition.] 3rd printing. by Calvin E. Sutherd
Gaines: Culpeper Co, Va; Descendants migrated mostly to south & midwest.
Cloth–430pp–$14.50--- Vendor #354

327 – THE DESCENDANTS OF HARVEY WILDER AND HIS ANCESTORS TO 1485
IN ENGLAND, WITH A HISTORY OF THE WILDER NAME AND RELATED
FAMILIES OF WARNER, BARNHARD, BENEDICT, HEPWORTH, POORE,
CROCKER AND NEWMAN by Justin E. Wilder
Wilder: Lancaster Co, Mass–1638-1787; Rutland Co, Vt–1787-1842; Kent
Co, Mich–1844-1974; Newaygo Co, Mich–1855-1974
Cloth–271pp–$7.25--- Vendor #356

328 – A GENEALOGICAL REGISTER OF THE DESCENDANTS OF AUGUST D.
KEHN AND SUSANNA JANTZEN by Olney E. Kehn
Kehn: McPherson Co, Kan–1875-1885; Marion Co, Kan–1885-1913; Ford
Co, Kan–1913-1915; Gray Co, Kan–1915-1974
Cloth–151pp–$6.50--- Vendor #357

329 – THOMAS TRACKS compiled by Mrs. Faye Davis
Thomas: Quarterly for all with Thomas surname. Free queries.
Subscription: $6.00/yr–4 issues/yr–25pp/issue-------------- Vendor #359

330 – BACKENSTOSS FAMILY ASSOCIATION OF AMERICA by Elwood Backensto
Bacastow/Backensto(e)/Backenstos(e)/Bagenstos(e)/Baggenstos/Backenstow:
[Descendants of Hans Ulrich Baggenstoss of Rafz, Switzerland. Settled in
Berks Co., Pa. in 1743. Others in Albany, Minn. in 1879 & Tracy City, Tenn.
in 1895.]
Cloth–200pp + index–$15.00------------------------------- Vendor #361

331 – THE STORY OF MOSES COLLINS (1785-1858) AND HIS DESCENDANTS by
Dr. A. O. Collins
Collins: Barnwell Co, SC–1785- ? ; Richmond Co, Ga– ? -1818; Tusca-
loosa Co, Ala–1818-1836; Tippah Co, Miss–1836-1858; Drew Co, Ark–
1856-1973; Union Co, Miss–1836-1973; Grimes Co, Tex–1846-1973
Camp: Grimes Co, Tex–1846-1973; Harris Co, Tex–1900-1973
Cloth–500pp–$22.50-------------------------------------- Vendor #362

332 – ARCHIBALD BINNIE, 1831-1907, AND HIS FAMILY AND THE ANNOTAT-
ED HISTORY OF THE WM. P. HUBBELL, 1811-1890, FAMILY by Lester H.
Binnie
Binnie: State of NY–1830-1867; Monroe Co, Mich–1867-1907
Paper–45pp–$5.00-------------------------------------- Vendor #363

333 – EARLY BRETHREN (DUNKARD) FAMILIES IN THE EEL RIVER CONGRE-
GATION IN KOSCIUSKO AND WABASH COUNTIES, INDIANA: BLICKEN-
STAFF, BUTTERBAUGH, CRIPE, FRANTZ, GROSSNICKLE, HAY, HEETER,
KARN, KREIDER, METZGER, MILLER, MISHLER, OHMART, SHIVELY,

SWANK, ULREY, AND RELATED FAMILIES by Lester H. Binnie
Southeastern Ohio: 1810-1838; Northern Indiana: 1838-1880
Paper—$15.00---Vendor #363

334 — JEAN BELLEVILLE THE HUGUENOT HIS DESCENDANTS by Paul Belville Taylor
Belleville/Belvil/Belveal/etc.: Throughout U.S.A.: from 1670–date
Cloth—532pp—$17.50--- Vendor #364

335 — THE MAY TREE by Aletha May Rowley
May: Charlotte Co, Va—1700-1810; Mercer Co, Ky—1780-1850; Boyle Co, Ky; Montgomery Co, Ind—1825-1832
Paper—75pp—$25.00--- Vendor #365

336 — WILLIAM RENFRO, 1734-1830, SOME DESCENDANTS, RELATIVES AND ALLIED FAMILIES by Josie Baird and Delila Baird
Renfro: Lunenburg/Franklin/Henry Cos, Va—1734-1788; Union/Spartanburg Cos, SC—1789-1807; Maury Co, Tenn—1807-1830; Pa—1707-1736
Crafton: Va—c1740-1807; Tenn—1807-1880
Cloth—$15.50/Paper—$10.50—170pp------------------------- Vendor #366

337 — A MILLER FAMILY TREE GROWS INTO A FOREST by Josie Baird
Miller: SC—c1735-1800; Ga—1800-1965; Ala—1840-1880; Tex—1879-1965
78pp [Out-of-print, but possible reprinting later.] ----------- Vendor #366

338 — A BAIRD FAMILY IN AMERICA AND ALLIED LINEAGES by Josie Baird and Delila Baird
Baird: SC—1780-1800; Tenn—1800-1839; Ark—1836-1970; Tex—1844-1970; Okla—1836-1912·
Cloth—$13.50/Paper—$8.95—71pp-------------------------- Vendor #366

339 — ABRAHAM LESHER, ELIZABETH HUMBERT LESHER, DESCENDANTS AND CONNECTS by Francis L. Wilson and Mrs. Robert Lodge
Lesher: Berks Co, Pa—1790-   ; Fulton Co, Pa— 1846 ; Clearspring, Md—   -1965
Paper—40pp—$2.25--- Vendor #367

340 — WETMORE HISTORY AND SOME MATERNAL LINES by Kathryn W. Stadel
Whitmore/Wetmore: Staffordshire, Eng—900-1970; Conn—1639-1810; NY State—1810-1970; Other states—   -1970
King: New England—1672-1795
Austin (Capt. Anthony's family): Suffield, Conn—1666-1795
Paper—235pp—$10.00------------------------------------- Vendor #370

341 — THE ANCIENT FAMILIES OF DEE AND DAY OF WALES, ENGLAND, AND IRELAND by Leonard F. Day, Sr.
Day: Gloucester, Mass; Many states. [Copy of and additions to the Genealogical Register of Robert Day of Hartford, Connecticut.]
Cloth—380pp—$30.00------------------------------------- Vendor #371

342 — THE GENEALOGY OF HAROLD M. RYDER AND FRANCES B. RYDER by Robert Freese, Sr.
Ryder: Iberville, Quebec—1871; New Haven, Conn—present; Cranford, NJ—present; North Branford, Conn—present
Cloth—24pp—$4.00-------------------------------------- Vendor #372

343   - FOREBEARS AND KIN OF JOHN T. SMITH, SR. & NANNIE M. SKAGGS
by Earl Davis Smith
    Smith: Va-   -1820; Madison Co, Ala-c1820-   ; Pickens Co, Ala-
      -1840s; Harrison Co, Tex-1848-date .
    Skaggs: Russell Co, Va-c1795-c1820; Lee Co, Va-c1820-1876
    Kennard: Sampson Co, NC-c1790-c1816; Madison Co, Ala-c1790-1824
    King: Bertie Co, NC-1753-1812; Madison Co, Ala-1812-1821
    Whitfield: Bertie Co, NC-1723-   ; Gates Co, NC-1728-   ?
    Horton: Russell Co, Va-1771-1792; Lee Co, Va-1792-c1850
    Crumley: Claiborne Co, Tenn-1838-c1848; Lee Co, Va-c1848-1865
    Claiborne : [This family traced to Adam & Eve. Col. Wm. Claiborne im-
    migrant to Am. in 1621.] James City Co, Va-1621-1623; New Kent Co, Va-
    1623-1652; Northumberland Co, Va-1652-1677
    Paper-130pp-$8.50-- Vendor #374

344   - MY HARRISON COUNTY, TEXAS SMITH COUSINS by Earl Davis Smith
    Smith: [To be published by chapters 1975 thru 1978. Each chapter to be
    25 to 50 pages and to sell between $2.50 & $5.00.]
    Paper-- Vendor #374

345   - MY LEE COUNTY, VIRGINIA SKAGGS COUSINS by Earl Davis Smith
    Skaggs: [To be published by chapters 1979 thru 1982. Each chapter to be
    25 to 30 pages and to sell between $2.50 & $3.00.]
    Paper-- Vendor #374

346   - THE NEWSPAPER ACCOUNTS OF B. F. WRIGHT, ESQ. AND OTHERS
OF LOUISA COUNTY, IOWA by Robert Leland Johnson
    Wright: Louisa Co, Ia
    --- Vendor #375

347   - THE AMERICAN HERITAGE OF JAMES NORMAN HALL: THE WOOD-
SHED POET OF IOWA AND CO-AUTHOR OF MUTINY ON THE BOUNTY by
Robert Leland Johnson
    Hall:
    Cloth-161pp-$4.50--- Vendor #375

348   - A PAFFORD LINE IN REVIEW by John Williams Pafford
    Pafford: Eng- ? -1810; Tenn-1820-1841; Ga-1841-present
    Cloth-100pp-$5.00-- Vendor #378

349   - UNDERWOOD ANNALS [Official publication of the Underwood Family Or-
ganization] edited by Glenn E. Underwood
    Underwood: All Underwoods and allied families. Anytime-anywhere.
    Subscription: $6.00/yr-25 to 35pp/issue-4 issues/yr---------- Vendor #379

350   - THE JOHN PERRIN FAMILY OF REHOBOTH, MASS. w/supplement: THE
THOMAS PERRIN FAMILY OF HEBRON, CONN. by Stanley E. Perin
    Perrin: Rehoboth, Mass-1643-1800; Ind-1811-date; Ia-1840-date; Ore-
    1863-date
    Cloth-307pp-$12.50--------------------------------------- Vendor #380

351 — THE McLARTY FAMILY OF KINTYRE SCOTLAND AND MECKLENBURG COUNTY, NORTH CAROLINA AND THEIR DESCENDANTS by Alelaide McLarty McLarty: Scot; NC; Ala; Ga; Miss; Tenn; Ark; Tex; SC; and other states—1700's-date [Over 15,000 names included, many of Old Mecklenburg.] Cloth—962pp—$39.50--Vendor #382

352 — FLORIDA PIONEERS AND THEIR ALABAMA, GEORGIA, CAROLINA, MARYLAND AND VIRGINIA ANCESTORS by David A. Avant, Jr.
Avent/Avant: Surry/Sussex/Brunswick Cos, Va—1701-1809; Chowan/Orange/ Edgecombe/Chatham/Bertie/Nash/Johnson/Northampton/Cumberland Cos, NC—1716-1780; Richmond/Wilkes/Washington/Warren/Montgomery/Tattnall/ Upson/Bibb Cos, Ga—1781-1880; Chambers/Coosa/Elmore Cos, Ala—1840-1928; Gadsden Co, Fla—1907-1974
Boyce: Charles City Co, Va—1617-1663
Britt: Isle of Wight/Southampton/Greensville Cos, Va—1750-1800; Clarke/ Henry/Walton/Muskogee Cos, Ga—1819-1850; Tallapoosa/Coosa/Elmore Cos, Ala—1850-1900
Carpenter: Burke Co, Ga—1786-1840; Leon Co, Fla—1829-1929
Catlett: Rapahannock/Essex Cos, Va—1650-1702
Comer: Lunenburg/Pr. Geo. Cos, Va—1762-1767
Culver: Pr. Geo/Frederick/Montgomery Cos, Md—1679-1770
Davis: Anne Arundel/Pr. Geo./Frederick/Montgomery Cos, Md—1696-1778; Berkley/Newberry/Laurens Cos, SC—1768-1827; Gadsden Co, Fla—1828-1944
Gaines: Rapahannock Co, Va—1682-1686
Gamble: Berkley/Laurens Cos, SC—1771-1830; Gadsden Co, Fla—1828-1907
Gilmore: Johnson/Cumberland/Wake Cos, NC—1749-1846
Glenn: Muskogee/Harris Cos, Ga—1830-1861
Hunter: Spotsylvania/Essex Cos, Va—1736-1785; Hancock/Greene Cos, Ga—1808-1828; Gadsden Co, Fla—1830-1866
Lockett: Pr. Ed. Co, Va—1775
Massey/Massie: Brunswick/Pr. Geo. Cos, Va—1726-1768
Peake/Peek: James City/Charles City/Buckingham/Pr. Charles Cos, Va—1635-1793; Granville/Wake Cos, NC—1759-1801; Hancock, Taliaffero/Greene Cos, Ga—1789-1835
Pearson: Johnson/Wake Cos, NC—1750-1832; Coosa/Tallapoosa/Elmore Cos, Ala—1836-1860
Smith (Maj. Lawrence): Lancashire, Eng—1618-1652; Glouchester Co, Va—1652-1700;
Taliaferro: (Old) Rappahannock/Essex/Spotsylvania/Orange Cos, Va—1666-1782
Tatum: Charles City/Pr.Geo./Surry/Sussex Cos, Va—1619-1780; Orange/ Halifax/Edgecombe Cos, NC—1753-1784; Orangeburg Co, SC—1787-1828; Leon Co, Fla—1825-1973
Townsend: Augusta Co, Va—1746-1755; Anson/Mecklenburg/Tryon Cos, NC—1756-1772; Camden Dist./York/Laurens/Abbeville Cos, SC—1772-1790; Wilkes/Hancock/Greene/Clarke/Jasper Cos, Ga—1785-1811; Tallapoosa/ Coosa Cos, Ala—1835-1851
Underwood: Rappahannock Co, Va—1659-1678
Wood: Charlestowne/Georgetowne Dist/Craven/Berkley Cos, SC—1774-1790; Marion/Sumter Cos, SC—1800-1833; Houston Co, Ga—1834-1840; Gadsden/ Washington Cos, Fla—1831-1973
Yarbrough: Fayette/Jasper/Monroe Cos, Ga—1808-1829; Chambers/Elmore Cos, Ala—1850-1880

Zimmerman: Jasper Co, Ga—c1811; Tallapoosa/Chambers Cos, Ala—1834-1860
Cloth—480pp—Index—$33.00----------------------------------Vendor #383

353 – BIOGRAPHICAL RECORD OF MALONEY FAMILY by Charles A. &
Louise B. Fowler
Maloney: SC—1806; Ga—1830's; Tex—1857-1974
Paper—90pp—$ ---Vendor #384

354 – SOME DESCENDANTS OF JOHN SHEPLEY, SALEM IMMIGRANT, 1635
by Raymond Shepley, Sr.
Shepley: Eng— ? -1635; Salem & Wenham, Mass—1635-1655; Chelmsford,
Mass—1655-1675; Groton, Mass—1675-1885
Paper—32pp—$3.00---Vendor #385

355 – THE JEREMIAH BROWN FAMILY GENEALOGY by Galen Brown Ogden
Brown: Northampton Co, NC—1802-1830; Highland Co, O—1830-1850;
Keokuk Co, Ia—1850-1882
Paper—133pp—$6.00--Vendor #386

356 – DESCENDANTS OF VIRGINIA, KENTUCKY & MISSOURI PIONEERS: IN-
CLUDING BRUBAKER, COOK, CORDRY, GANDER, HUTCHISON, MAIKOW-
SKI, NEALE, OGLESBY, ROBERTSON, SCHLOTZHAUER, SMITH, WEAR/
WEIR, WOOLERY by Eugene Allen Cordry
Cordry: Va—1704-1785; Ky—1785-1830; Mo—1830-1973
Cloth—434pp—$29.00--Vendor #391

357 – THE McGAVOCKS OF TWO RIVERS by Leona Taylor Aiken
McGavock: Antrim, Ire—   -1728; Rockbridge Co, Va—c1754-c1760;
Wythe Co, Va—c1760-c1800; Nashville/Two Rivers, Tenn—1785-c1900
Cloth—[Publication date spring 1975] $10.00-----------------Vendor #392

358 – THE DESCENDANTS OF DANIEL CLARKE OF WINDSOR, CONNECTICUT
by Mrs. Frances B. Todd
Clark/Clarke: Conn—1639-1805; St. Lawrence Co, NY—1805-1819; Pa—1819-1843; Pepin Co, Wisc—1843-1889
Cloth—194pp—$10.00---------------------------------------Vendor #394

359 – ROSE FAMILY BULLETIN edited by Seymour T. & Christine Rose
Rose: Any Rose families-anywhere in U.S.-anytime
Subscription: $4.00/yr—30pp/issue—4 issues/yr---------------Vendor #395

360 – THE TIMES OF STEPHEN MUMFORD by James McGeachy
Mumford: [A brief description of religious persecution in England resulting
in Mumford's move to Rhode Island.]
Paper—18pp—$.50---Vendor #397

361 – ASTERS AT DUSK: THE SMELSER FAMILY IN AMERICA by Polly Pollock
Smelser: Pa—1700's-date; Md—1700's-date; Ky—1700's-date; Ind—1800's-date; Mo—1800's-date
Paper—278pp—$10.00--------------------------------------Vendor #398

362 — THE SOCOLOFSKY FAMILY: A HISTORY by Homer E. Socolofsky
Socolofsky: Dreispitz, Russia—1820-1877; Marion Co, Kan—1876-   ;
Loreburn, Saskatchewan—1907-1950's; Ft. Collins, Colo—1909-   ;
Portland, Ore—1916-
Paper—100pp—$4.00--- Vendor #399

363 — THE HUNTERS OF BEDFORD COUNTY, VIRGINIA by Walter M. Hunter, Jr.
Hunter: Pa—1730-1750; Bedford Co, Va—1750-1765; Rockingham Co, NC—
1765-1820; Rapides Parish, La—1820-date
Cloth—295pp—$15.00--------------------------------------- Vendor #400

364 — BAYNARD: AN ANCIENT FAMILY BEARING ARMS by Annie B. Häsell
Baynard: Normandy, France— ? -1066; Eng—1066-1600's; Del/Md—1600's-
present; SC—1600's-present
Cloth—252pp—$25.00------------------------------------- Vendor #406

365 — THE COOPER FAMILY OF MARYLAND by F. Wm. Cooper
Cooper: St. Marys Co, Md—1674-1765; Harford Co, Md—1765-1788; Cam-
bria Co, Pa—1788-1839; Scott Co, Ia—1839-1936
Cloth—84pp—$10.00------------------------------------- Vendor #407

366 — THE ASA JOINER FAMILY OF MITCHELL CO., GEORGIA by A. H. Clark
Joiner: Mitchell Co, Ga—1852-1896; Nashville, NC—1806-1819;
Pulaski Co, Ga—1819-1829; Stewart Co, Ga—1829-1852
Hilliard: Stewart Co, Ga—1829-1851; Pike Co, Ala—1851-1864; Dooly Co,
Ga—1820-1829; Washington Co, Ga—1799-1815
Powell: Dooly Co, Ga—1824-1855; Washington Co, Ga—1802-1824
Collins: Stewart Co, Ga—1847-1852; Mitchell Co, Ga—1852-1863; Coweta
Co, Ga—1827-1847
Bullard: Stewart Co, Ga—1830-1858; Mitchell Co, Ga—1858-1864; Twiggs
Co, Ga—1811-1830
Cloth—404pp—$14.00--------------------------------------- Vendor #408

367 — ST. JOHN AND HARRIES: THE ANCESTORS AND DESCENDANTS OF
THEODORE EDGAR ST. JOHN AND HIS WIFE JANE CECELIA HARRIES [in-
cluding extensive ancestry of Capt. Thomas Yale of New Haven, Conn., and
of Henry Gregory of Norwalk, Conn.] by Ben LeGrande Cash
St. John: Norwalk, Conn—1650-1841; Wisc—1868-1870; Ia—1882-date;
Independence, Kan-   -1974
Harries: Wales; Buffalo, NY; Wisc.
Gregory: England; Scotland—from ancient times
Yale: Wales; Ireland; Scotland; England—from ancient times
Cloth—$20.00/Paper—$17.50—170pp------------------------- Vendor #410

368 — THE GILLINGHAM FAMILY by Harrold Edgar Gillingham (1901 reprint)
Gillingham: Richland Co, Wisc.1800's; Philadelphia, Pa; migrations to
almost all states—1670-1900.
Paper-   pp—$5.00-- Vendor #412

369 — THE DESCENDANTS OF THOMAS GILLINGHAM. AND ALLIED FAMILIES
MARSHALL, WITHROW, DISON, BARCLAY, NOBLE, STACEY, GALLOWAY,
ANDREWS, DRAKE, FOGO, TRUESDALE & OTHERS by Wm. E. Gillingham
Gillingham: Richland Co, Wisc—1800's-1930; Ohio; other states
Paper-   pp—$6.00-- Vendor #412

370 — DESCENDANTS OF WILLIAM BROWNLOW McCLELLAN by Aubrey
Lester McClellan
McClellan: [William Brownlow McClellan, son of John and Margaret
(Brownlow) McClellan, moved from Abingdon, Va. to Tex. about 1840.]
Cloth—109pp—$4.00--- Vendor #413

371 — CHRISTOPHER GIST OF MARYLAND AND SOME OF HIS DESCENDANTS
1679-1957 by Jean Dorsey
Gist: Baltimore Co, Md; Ky; Tenn; Ala; Mo; & other states—1700's-date
Cloth—296pp—$25.00-- Vendor #414

372 — THE DIARY OF CLARISSA ADGER GOWEN, ASHTABULA PLANATION,
1865, with excerpts from other family diaries and comments by her grand-
daughter, Clarissa Walton Taylor, and many other accounts of the Pendleton-
Clemson area, SC. 1776-1889 compiled by Mary Stevenson
Adger: Pendleton, SC—1852-c1900; Charleston, SC—19th century
Paper—126pp—$7.50-- Vendor #420

373 — THE FIRST 150 YEARS - THE SCHEETZ FAMILY IN AMERICA by Carl
F. Chuey
Scheetz: Noble Co, O—1850-1898; Mahoning Co, O—1898-1930
Freisen: Noble Co, O—1850-1898
Weisent: Noble Co, O—1850-1900
Paper—120pp—$5.00--- Vendor #423

374 — A CHIPMAN GENEALOGY by John Hale Chipmam III
Chipman: Barnstable, Plymouth Colony, Mass; Canada; Australia
Cloth—540pp—$25.00--------------------------------------- Vendor #424

375 — PIONEER, PATRIOT AND REBEL: LEWIS FREDERICK DELESDERNIERS
by Rev. Canon E. C. Royle
Delesderniers: Nova Scotia—1752-1756; Washington Co, Me—1756-1838 [Out
of print, but will be reprinted when 25 orders are received. Mimeographed.]
Paper—45pp—$5.00-- Vendor #425

376 — ROUSSEL REGISTER 1327-1974 by Robert Roussel
Roussel: New Eng—1646-1974; Can—1646-1974; Lowell, Mass—1868-1974;
France—1327-1974
Paper—50pp—$10.00-------------------------------------- Vendor #426

377 — THE JOHN SEAY GREGORYS IN AMERICA 1788-1972 by Judith (Gregory)
Voigt & Dorothy (Cooper) Coombes
Gregory: [The family came from Tennessee around 1831 to Illinois. Most of
them now live in and around Mason Co., Illinois.]
Paper—181pp—$12.00------------------------------------ Vendor #429

378 — DESCENDANTS OF GODFREY GATCH OF BALTIMORE COUNTY, MARY-
LAND AND OTHERS OF THE SURNAME WITH MATERIAL ON EARLY METH-
ODIST HISTORY IN MD., VA., AND O. by Virginia Gatch Markham
Gatch: [Book contains 11 generations, living in all states. Early residences:
Baltimore Co, Md; Va; SC; Clermont Co, O.] [This book won first prize
in the Parker Genealogical Contest, Maryland Historical Society, 1972.]
Cloth—530pp—$18.00------------------------------------ Vendor #430

379 — HEMRICK AND ALLIED FAMILIES (GERMANY TO GEORGIA) 1727-1974
by Grace H. Jarvis, C.G.
Hemrick: Ger— ? -1727; Pa—1727-1780; NC—1780-1840; Ga—1840-date
Buchanan: Ulster, Ire— ? -1740; Pa—1740-1780; NC—1780-1830; Ga—
1830-date
[Projected publication date—1975]---------------------------- Vendor #432

380 — THIS MAN DAVID, A SOUTHERN PLANTER by Juanita Daniel Zachry
Rumph: Switzerland— ? -1835; Orangeburgh Par, SC—1806-1826; Randolph
Co, Ga—1826-1869; Hunt/Grayson/Taylor Cos, Tex—1869-1905
Cloth—243pp—$8.95-- Vendor #434

381 — DUNGANS OF DIXIE by Ruby Finch Thompson
Dungan/Dunnigan/Dunnagan/etc.: [Will start newsletter on Dungans not followed in Justice's Dungan Genealogy of 1922, Pa; SC; Ga; Ala; Tenn; etc. if
sufficient interest. Also will reprint Justice's book.] --------- Vendor #436

382 — FINCH FAMILIES OF DIXIE by Ruby Finch Thompson
Finch: Va— ? -1700; all southern states— ? -present
Cloth— pp—$15.00---Vendor #436

383 — HENRY DUKE, COUNCILOR - HIS DESCENDANTS AND CONNECTIONS
by Walter Garland Duke
Duke: Virginia
Cloth—452pp—$15.00-- Vendor #437

384 — GENEALOGICAL RECORD OF THE CAMPBELL-REA FAMILIES by
Florence Le Van Spicer
Campbell: York Co, Pa—1734-1774; Washington Co, Pa—1774-1850; Harri-
son/Union Cos, O—1848-1858; Peoria/McLean Cos, Ill—1858-1870
Rea: York Co, Pa—1734-1774; Washington Co, Pa—1774-1850; Harrison/
Union Cos, O—1848-1858; Peoria/McLean Cos, Ill—1858-1870
Cloth—200pp—$15.00--------------------------------------- Vendor # 438

385 — MAJOR FRANCIS LOGAN AND WIFE HANNAH TRIMBLE by Katherine
Logan Conley
Logan: Albany, NY—1734-   ; SC; Rutherford Co, NC—   -1826
Paper—85pp—$8.00--- Vendor #443

386 — THE BOSTON FAMILY OF MARYLAND by Matthew M. Wise
Boston: Eastern Shore of Md—1663-date; Baltimore, Md—1847-date; Jef-
ferson Co, Ky—1815-date; Sullivan Co, Ind—1825-date
Byrd: Accomac Co, Va—1664-date
Long: Eastern Shore of Md—1666-date
Payne: Worcester Co, Md—1710-date
Paper—500pp—$14.40------------------------------------- Vendor #446

387 — THE GENEALOGICAL HISTORY OF THE THOMAS DAWSON FAMILY AND
ITS DESCENDANTS IN AMERICA by Everett T. Dawson & Buna R. Dawson
Dawson: Chester Co, Pa—1713-1769; Va—1757-1795; Ross Co, O—1795-
1813; Clark Co, Ky—1795-1826; Henry Co, Ky—1826-1830; Ralls Co, Mo;
Tex—1876 [David Dawson & wife Elizabeth m. and lived in Hampshire Co,
Va. 1772-c1795, then moved to Ross Co, O. They had 7 sons & 7 daus.]
Cloth—265pp—$19.00--------------------------------------Vendor #447

388 — THE GREATER McBRIDE/McBRYDE FAMILY (tenative title) by Benjamin
Ransom McBride, Col. USAF (Ret.)
McBride/McBryde/MacBride: [A fully indexed and comprehensive listing of
all individuals with the surname McBRIDE (and variations) who were born by
1850 and lived some part of their lives in Alabama, Arkansas, Florida, Georgia, Kentucky, Louisiana, Mississippi, Missouri, North Carolina, South Carolina, Tennessee, Texas, Virginia or West Virginia. Vital statistics, official capacities, military service data and genealogical relationships are fully
shown with allied families. Serves as a basic reference for finding any ancestral line of McBRIDES and the corresponding allied family.
In process. Publication date about 1976------------------------Vendor #448

389 — CALL ME HILLBILLY by Gladys Trentham Russell
Trentham: Gatlinburg, Tenn-1793-1974
Paper-92pp-$2.75-- Vendor #450

390 — FOOTE HISTORY AND GENEALOGY by Abram W. Foote (reprint)
Foote: [Nathaniel Foote family of Wethersfield, Connecticut-1633 on. De-
scendants in all states.] Originally printed in 1907.
Cloth-607pp-$30.00-------------------------------------- Vendor #451

391 — GEHLBACH FAMILY RECORD BOOK by Vernon P. Gehlbach
Gehlbach: Logan Co, Ill-1853-1974
Paper-75pp-$3.00-- Vendor #453

392 — GENEALOGY OF THE FAMILY OF HENRY LEWIS, WHO EMIGRATED
FROM WALES IN 1682 Comiler, Walter W. Lewis. Editor, E. R. Lewis
Lewis: Chester Co, Pa-1682-1974; Berks Co, Pa-1799-1957; Belmont Co,
O-c1800-1974; Pendleton, Ind-c1830-c1900; Orange City, Ia-c1850-1900
Scarlet/Scarlett: Chester Co, Pa-1665-1974; Berks Co, Pa-1740-c1890
George: Chester Co, Pa-1736-1751; Berks Co, Pa-1751-1847; Greene Co,
NC-1788-1820 [?], Sevier Co, Tenn-1816-
Cloth-258pp-$15.00-------------------------------------- Vendor #455

393 — HOOSIERS, YANKEES, & ENGLISHMEN, A FAMILY RECORD OF THE
DAVIS, WILCOX, SANFORD, CHITTENDEN, BALDWIN AND ALLIED FAM-
ILIES by James E. Davis
Davis: Conn-1636-1832; NY-1832-   ; Washington Co, Ind-1832-1974;
Ill- ? -1974; Ia- ? -1974
Cloth-100pp-$7.50-------------------------------------- Vendor #456

394 — CHILDREN OF NASHVILLE (Lineages of James Robertson) by Sarah
Foster Kelley
Robertson: Brunswick Co, Va-1740-1750; Wake Co, NC-1750-1770;
Watauga, Tenn-1770-1779; Nashville, Tenn-1779-1814
Cloth-447pp-$16.50------------------------------------- Vendor #457

395 — HILL AND ALLIED FAMILIES OF CENTRAL OHIO by John Neilson Furniss
Hill: Co. Donegal, Ire- ? -c1790; Knox Co, O-1815-1885; Union Co, O-
1880-1900
Ewalt: Bedford Co, Pa-1760-1815; Knox Co, O-1815-date
Gapen: Washington Co, Pa-1760-1790; Greene Co, Pa-1790-1810- Fayette
Co, Pa-1810-1820

Higbie: Dutchess Co, NY–1750-1810; Muskingum Co, O–1815-1825; Knox
Co, O–1825-1885; Hardin Co, O–1885-1900
Douglass: Morris Co, NJ–1750-1800; Knox Co, O–1805-1830; Fountain Co,
Ind–1830-1835
Wheeler: Huntingdon Co, Pa–c1790-1810; Knox Co, O–1810-1840
Keys: Washington Co, Pa–1800-1835; Knox Co, O–1835-1865; Greene Co,
Ind–1865-1890
Varney: Dutchess Co, NY–1770-1841
Cloth–206pp–$10.00--- Vendor #458

396 – MATILDA'S LETTERS by Matilda Appelman Williams, Ed. B.T. Abbott
Williams: Mystic, Conn–1815-1857; Werner, Wisc–c1857-c1867; Freeport,
Ill–1867-1892 [Book is not currently for sale, but Mrs. Abbott solicits
correspondence from related descendants.] 134pp--------------Vendor #465

397 – THE AUSTIN AND ALLIED FAMILIES by Josephine Austin Knight
Austin: Greenville Dist, SC–1761-1972; SC–1776-1972; Ga–1800-1972;
Migrations south, west, north–1800-1972
Cloth–314–$20.00-- Vendor #466

398 – HENRY ALLYN, AUTOBIOGRAPHY by Jean Allyn Smeltzer
Allyn: NY–1784-1810; Washington Co, O–1810-1815; St. Clair Co, Ill–
1815-1830; Fulton Co, Ill–1830-1853; Ore–1853-1880
Paper–98pp–$5.00--Vendor #467

399 – JARBOE FAMILY HISTORY by Bob & Mary Jarboe
Jarboe: St. Mary's Co, Md–1646-1758; Montgomery Co, Md–1758-1795;
Clark Co, O–1799-1828; Greene Co, Ill–1828-1839; Osage Co, Kan–1860-1910
Cleland: Pr. Geo. Co, Md–1719-1768; Clark Co, O–1799-1808
Collins: Winchester, Va–1771-1796; Clark Co, O–1811-1900
Paper–110pp–$ ---Vendor #473

400 – DOWN LUDINGTON LANE by Ruth Ludington Lund
Ludington: NY State–1777- ; Adel, Ia–1865-1874; Merrick/Nance Cos,
Nebr–1874-1927
Cloth–$4.75/ Paper: $3.75–66pp-----------------------------Vendor #474

401 – FOLLOWING McCLUER ANCESTORS [including related lines of Parrill,
LaRue, Moore, and Cox families] by Leon McCluer
McCluer: Orange/Rockbridge Cos, Va–1742-1805; Richland Co, O–1808-
1857; Marion Co, Ill–1857-1896; Hinds Co, Miss–1896-1974 ---------- Vendor #475
Cloth–237pp–$7.80

402 – THE BLASSINGAME FAMILIES by W. Doak Blassingame
Blassingame/Blassingham/Blasingim/etc.: All known lines
Cloth–380pp–$23.00--------------------------------------- Vendor #476

403 – CHAD BROWNE MEMORIAL . . . Genealogical Memoirs of a Portion of
the Descendants of Chad and Elizabeth Browne . . . Appendix Containing
Sketches of Other Early Rhode Island Settlers, 1638-1888 (Brooklyn, N.Y.:
Printed for the Family, 1888) by Abby Isabel (Brown) Bulkley
Brown: RI–1638-1888; Mass–1638-1888; Conn–1638-1888; NY–1638-1888
Cloth–173pp–$65.00--------------------------------------- Vendor #478

404 — THE ANCESTRY OF EDWARD RAWSON OF MASSACHUSETTS BAY
COLONY   by Ellery Bicknell Crane
Rawson: Gillingham, Dorset, Eng–1615-1636; Newbury, Mass–1637-1649;
Boston, Mass–1650-1793
Paper–66pp–$2.00--Vendor #480

405 — DESCENDANTS OF MICHAEL McCLELLAN AND JANE HENRY OF COL-
RAIN, MASSACHUSETTS   by Lois McClellan Patrie
McClellan: Colrain, Mass–1749-1912; Columbia Co, NY–1798-1970;
Chicago, Ill–1867-1900; Mound Prairie, Wisc–1853-1890
Thompson: Colrain, Mass–1749-1970; Nunda, NY–1829-1954
Stewart: Colrain, Mass–1761-1875; Truxton, NY–1797-1857
Holmes: Columbia Co, NY–1832-1902; NYC–1899-1933
Severance: Greenfield, Mass–1750-1800; Truxton, NY–1800-1869
Paper–141pp–$4.50--- Vendor #481

406 — FAMILY HISTORY OF J. F. HEINZE AND J. WEBER AND THEIR DE-
SCENDANTS   by Esther Leona Heinze Miller
Heinze: Germany– ? -1763; Dreispitz, Russia–1764-1875; Marion Co,
Kan–1875-1877; Ellsworth Co, Kan–1877-1879; Russell Co, Kan–1879-1921
Cloth–137pp–$9.95--- Vendor #482

407 — BATCHELOR FAMILY NEWSLETTER   edited by Rosemary E. Bachelor
Batchelor/Batchelder/Bachiler/etc.: [Covers all U.S. branches of family.]
Subscription: $6.00/yr–4 issues/yr--------------------------Vendor #484

408 — CARPENTER FAMILY NEWSLETTER   edited by Rosemary E. Bachelor
Carpenter: [Includes all U.S. families with this surname (or variations).]
Subscription: $6.00/yr–4 issues/yr--------------------------Vendor #484

409 — RICE FAMILY NEWSLETTER   edited by Rosemary E. Bachelor
Rice: [Includes all U. S. families with this surname.]
Subscription: $6.00/yr–4 issues/yr--------------------------Vendor #484

410 — RICHMOND FAMILY NEWSLETTER edited by   Harriet A. Webb
Richmond: [Includes all U.S. families with this surname (or variations).]
Subscription: $6.00/yr–4 issues/yr--------------------------Vendor #956

411 — PALMER – BURLINGHAM GENEALOGY by Dale C. Kellogg
Palmer: Greenwich, Conn–1775- ? ; Salisbury, Conn– ? -1799; Trum-
bull Co, O–1799-1810; New Haven, Huron Co, O–1811-1974
Burlingham: Killingly, Conn–1790-1811; Cayuga Co, NY–1850-1900; Huron
Co, O–1829-1900; LaPorte Co, Ind–1880-1974; Berrien Co, Mich–1903-1974
Cloth–178pp–$10.00------------------------------------- Vendor #487

412 — SOUTHERN TAYLOR FAMILIES   by Albert E. Casey, et al
Taylor:

Cloth–323pp–$25.50------------------------------------- Vendor #488

413 — WEST - BARKER - HODGES, NEW YORK TO WISCONSIN, 1836-1846
West: Salem, Mass–1634-1682; Bradford, Mass–1682-1707; East Windsor,
Conn–1707-1738; Hillsdale, Columbia Co, NY–1738-1793

Barker: Branford, Conn–1667-1776; Brandon, Vt–1776-1803; Rome, NY–1803-c1804; Batavia, NY–c1804-1838
Hodges: Co. Kent, Eng–1799-1831; Oswego Co, NY–1831-1846; Walworth Co, Wisc–1846-1880s; Scattered–1880s-1971
Cloth–   pp–$15.00--Vendor #490

414   – A GENEALOGY OF THE CURTISS - CURTIS FAMILY by Harlow D. Curtiss
Curtis/Curtiss: Stratford, Conn–1639-   ; Many states
Cloth–585pp–$20.00-------------------------------------- Vendor #492

415   – RICHARD CURTICE, MASTER MARINER compiled by Harlow D. Curtis
Curtice/Curtis: Salem, Mass–1654; Southold, NY–1663
Cloth–102pp–$10.00------------------------------------- Vendor #492

416   – JONES - WATSON - HALE by Courtney & Gerlene York
Jones: Union Co, SC–1777-1805; Bedford Co, Tenn–1805-1845; Pike Co, Ark–1845-1930
Watson: Bedford Co, Tenn–1820-1850; Pike Co, Ark–1850-1900
Hale: Bedford Co, Tenn–1820-1850; Pike Co, Ark–1850-1900
Paper–62pp–$5.00---Vendor #497

417   – SOME SANDY BASIN CHARACTERS by Elihu Jasper Sutherland
Austin: Surry/Rowan Cos, NC–1770-1790; Grayson Co, Va–1790-1825; Ashe Co, NC–1825-1857; Wise Co, Va–1857-1974
Beverly: York Co, Va–1700- ? ; NC– ? -1787; Southwest Va–1787-1974
Colley: Washington Co, Va–1780-1787; Russell Co, Va–1787-1974
Counts: Page Co, Va–1765-1789; Russell Co, Va–1789-1974
Grizzle: Pittsylvania Co, Va–1747-17??; Russell Co, Va–1800-1974
Sutherland: Bedford/Page Cos, Va–1781-1807; Russell Co, Va–1807-1974
Cloth–$13.00-- Vendor #498

418   – THE GEORGE MUMMA FAMILY OF WESTMORELAND COUNTY, PENN-SYLVANIA 1732-1971 by Richard Glenn Huffman
Mumaw: Lancaster Co, Pa–1732-1790; Westmoreland Co, Pa–1790-1974; Tuscarawas Co, O–1820-1974; Adams Co, Ind–1840-1900; Indiana Co, Pa–1840-1971; Somerset Co, Pa–1820-1971; Anderson Co, Kan–1870- ? ; Holmes Co, O–1820-1971
Paper–156pp–$15.50--Vendor #499

419   – THE JACOB HUFFMAN (HOFFMAN) FAMILY, UNITY TWP. WESTMORE-LAND COUNTY, PENNSYLVANIA 1767-1968 by Richard Glenn Huffman
Huffman: Adams Co, Pa–1767-1770; Unknown–1770-1785; Unity Twp, Westmoreland Co, Pa–1785-present
Stough: Westmoreland Co, Pa–1800-present; Somerset Co, Pa–1840-1926
Uphouse: Somerset Co, Pa–1840-1900
Paper–70pp–$11.00-------------------------------------- Vendor #499

420   – BARNABAS DAVIS (1599-1685) AND HIS DESCENDANTS by Sumner Augustus Davis
Davis: Mass–1635-1973; NH–1775-1973; Vt–1780-1973; Canada–1900-1973
Cloth: $15.00/Paper: $12.50–380pp------------------------ Vendor #501

421 — THE TINGLEY FAMILY REVISED, VOL. I by Marian McCauley Frye
Tingley: Malden, Mass—1635-   ; desc. in all states and Canada
Cloth—611pp—$15.50 [Disc. to libraries]--------------------- Vendor #502

422 — THE TINGLEY FAMILY REVISED, VOL. II by Marian McCauley Frye
Tingley: Malden, Mass—1635-   ; desc. in all states and Canada
Cloth—609pp—$15.50 [Disc. to libraries]--------------------- Vendor #502

423 — THE TINGLEY FAMILY REVISED, VOL. III by Marian McCauley Frye
Tingley: Malden, Mass—1635-   ; desc. in all states and Canada
Cloth—609pp—$15.50 [Disc. to libraries]--------------------- Vendor #502

424 — FROM MILL WHEEL TO PLOWSHARE by Julia Angeline Drake & James
Ridgely Orndorff
Orndorff: Pa; Md
Cloth—271pp—$6.00-- Vendor #506

425 — THE HOLLYDAY FAMILY & RELATED FAMILIES OF THE EASTERN
SHORE OF MARYLAND by James Bordley, Jr.
Hollyday: Md
Cloth—344pp—$12.50--- Vendor #506

426 — THE MARYLAND SEMMES & KINDRED FAMILIES by Harry W. Newman
Semmes: Md
Cloth—341pp—$12.50--- Vendor #506

427 — WILLIAM GALLOP, REVOLUTIONARY SOLDIER by Louise G. Walker
Gallap/Gallop/Gallup: Boston—1630; Kingston, RI—1720; Scituate, RI—1758-
1779; Pownal, Vt—1779-1793; Otsego Co, NY—1794-1905; Clarence, NY-to 1810
Cloth—289pp—$10.00--------------------------------------- Vendor #508

428 — A GENEALOGICAL HISTORY OF THE WHITMAN, BEDWELL, AND RE-
LATED FAMILIES by Mary Elizabeth Bedwell
Whitman: Long Island, NY—1660-1826; Gallipolis, O—1815-c1820; Yazoo
City, Miss—1840-1925
Medley: Culpeper Co, Va—1759-1792; Madison Co, Va—1792-1810; Choctaw
Co, Miss—1840-1850
Paper—246pp—$15.00-------------------------------------- Vendor #509

429 — MORAGNES IN AMERICA AND RELATED FAMILIES by Nell H. Howard
and Bessie W. Quinn
Moragne: St. Avide, France—prior to 1740-1765; Abbeville Dist, SC—1763-
1974; Etowah Co, Ala—1830-1974; Richmond Co, Ga—1850-1974; Forrest
Co, Miss—1885-1974; Kauai, Hawaii—1898-1974; Tex—1890-1974
Williams: Warsaw Co, Va—1650-1764; Richmond Co, Va—1764-1786; Edge-
field Co, SC—1800-1974; Etowah Co, Ala—1850-1974
Quarles: King William Co, Va—1702-1751
Abernathy: Scotland—9th century-1657; Lincoln Co, NC—1770-1974
Forney: France— ? -1685; Lincoln Co, NC—1754-1974
Hughes: Haywood Co, NC— ? -1830; Etowah Co, Ala—1840-1974
Hodges: Essex Co, Va—1765-1770; Abbeville Dist, SC—1770-1974
Hillsman: Amelia Co, Va— ? -c1770; Knox Co, Tenn—1785-1974
Burns: Rutherford Co, NC—1784-1974; Talladega Co, Ala—1820-1974
Dobbins: Rutherford Co, NC—1784-1974; Talladega Co, Ala—1820-1974

Howard: Newark, NJ–1777-1800; Lincoln Co, Ga–1800-1830; Campbell Co, Ga–1860-1883; Cullman Co, Ala–1883-1974; Cross Keys, SC–1750-1780; Elbert Co, Ga–1780-1792; Baldwin Co, Ga–c1850-1974
Yeilding: Rutherford Co, NC–1795-1810; Blount Co, Ala–1810-1864; Jefferson Co, Ala–1864-1974
Brady: Abbeville Dist, SC–c1830-1870; Hinds Co, Miss–1870-1974
Mynatt: Eng–1729-1750; Pr. Wm. Co, Va–1757-c1770; Botetourt Co, Va–1770-1785; Knox Co, Tenn–1785-1974
Whorton: Va–prior to 1760; Granville Co, NC–1760-c1770; Greenville/Pendleton Dist, SC–1770-1802; Jackson/Hall Cos, Ga–1802-c1840; St. Clair/Etowah Cos, Ala–1815-1974; Blount Co, Ala–1840-1974; Cherokee Co, Ala–1833-1974
McRoberts: Co. Armagh, Ire–1740-c1770; Pa–1770-c1780; Augusta Co, Va–1780-1790s; Lincoln Co, Ky–c1789-1974; Oldham Co, Ky–c1890-1974
Fortune: Holmes Co, O–1870-1900; Fayette Co, Ky–c1900-1974
Thayer: Suffolk Co, Mass–1639/40-1974; Tollard Co, Conn–1840-   ; Marshall Co, Ia–1870-1974; Ventura Co, Calif–c1900-1974
Wilson: Ire– ? -1796; Va–1796-c1803; Buncombe/Henderson Co, NC–1803-c1840; DeKalb/Etowah Cos, Ala–1840-1974
Cloth–522pp–$15.50-- Vendor #510

430 – SOME OF THE DESCENDANTS OF PHILIP SHERMAN by Roy V. Sherman
Sherman: Eng–1493-1634; New Eng–1634-1789; U.S.–1789-1974
Cloth–662pp–$12.50-- Vendor #512

431 – THE NEW ENGLAND SHERMANS by Roy V. Sherman
Sherman: [The other New England lines and a supplement to the Philip Sherman book.]
Cloth–548pp–$12.50-- Vendor #512

432 – MASSEY GENEALOGY by Judge Frank Massey
Massey/Masey/deMascy/Massie/Macy: Eng; Tenn; NC; Va; SC; New Eng; throughout the U.S. [Every Massey immigrant prior to 1700 (and some after) was researched to the beginning of the Civil War - and information included in this work.]
Cloth–417pp–$20.00-- Vendor #513

433 – THE KENAN FAMILY AND SOME ALLIED FAMILIES by Alvaretta Kenan Register
Kenan: NC–1730s-1967; Ga–1794-1967; Southeast USA–1800-1967
Cloth–292pp–$10.50-- Vendor #515

434 – THE TILLINGHAST FAMILY 1560-1971 by Rose C. Tillinghast
Tillinghast: RI–1645-date; NY–1790-date; NC–1804-date; SC–1788-date
Paper–235pp–$10.00-- Vendor #516

435 – OUR HORNER ANCESTORS by Virginia Horner Hinds
Horner: Baltimore/Harford Cos, Md–1700-1800; Fayette Co, Pa–1798-1973; Greene Co, Pa–1803-1973; Washington Co, Pa–1810-1973; Licking Co, O–1815-1973; Adams Co, O–1830-1973
Paper–280pp–$8.50-- Vendor #517

436 — JOHN BRIGGS OF SANDWICH, MASSACHUSETTS, AND HIS DESCEND-
ANTS by Edna Anne Hannibal
Briggs: Mass–1640–present; Me–1783–present; Vt–1783–present
Cloth–152pp–$15.00-- Vendor #520

437 — CLEMENT BRIGGS OF PLYMOUTH COLONY AND HIS DESCENDANTS,
VOL. I & II, by Edna Anne Hannibal
Briggs: Mass
Cloth–580pp–$30.00 for both------------------------------ Vendor #520

438 — THE EARLES AND THE BIRNIES by Joseph Earle Birnie
Earle: Northumberland Co, Va–1642–1653; Westmoreland Co, Va–1653–1746;
Frederick Co, Va–1743–1974; Greenville Co, SC–1766–1974
Birnie: Aberdeenshire, Scot–1722–1857; Charleston Co, SC–1802–1865;
Greenville Co, SC–1865–1925
Cloth–235pp–$15.00-------------------------------------- Vendor #521

439 — MARSH FAMILY BULLETIN, VOL. I, NOS. 1-6, by Warren L. Marsh
Marsh: New Eng/general survey-East–1600–1700; NJ–1665–1900; Pa–1736–
1800 [Published in 1955 (all available).]
Paper–120pp–$6.00------------------------------------- Vendor #527

440 — A GENEALOGICAL HISTORY OF THE FARROW, WATERS, AND RELA-
TED FAMILIES by Audrey Doris Goolsby Farrow
Farrow: Pr. Wm. Co, Va–1731–1773; Old 96 Dist, SC–1775-   ; Miss/
Tenn–1846-1974; Tex–1840–1974
Paper–104pp–$8.00------------------------------------- Vendor #529

441 — THE WRIGHTS OF BLOOMERY by F. Edward Wright
Wright: Federalsburg, Md–1682-   ; O/Ind/Md–early 1800's
Paper–138pp–$12.50----------------------------------- Vendor #534

442 — STOWERS FAMILIES IN AMERICA, VOL. 3, by L. E. Stowers
Stowers: Mass–1629–present; Va–1845–present; Thruout every state-present
Cloth–544pp–$15.00----------------------------------- Vendor #535

443 — RAYNOR FAMILY HISTORY - DESCENDANTS OF EDWARD, PIONEER
WHO CAME TO AMERICA IN 1634 by Clinton E. Metz
Raynor: Nassau/Queens Cos, NY–1644–present; Orange Co, NY–18th cen-
tury-present; Brookhaven town, Suffolk Co, NY–1800-present
Paper–40pp–$3.50------------------------------------Vendor #536

444 — OLIPHANT FAMILY HISTORY, VOL. I: DESCENDANTS OF WILLIAM
OLIPHANT, 1740-1828 by Nancy Hawlick Stein
Oliphant/Ollyphant/Oliphint/etc.: Guilford Co, NC–1783–1828; Greene/
Monroe Cos, Ind–1828-date; Owen Co, Ind–1838-date
Martindale: Greene Co, Ind–1840–1870; Ia–1860-date; Colo–1890-date
Burch: Monroe Co, Ind–1834-date; Ia–1855-date; Kan–1880-date
Paper–150pp–$13.00---------------------------------- Vendor #545

445 — OLIPHANT FAMILY HISTORY, VOL. II: LINES OF THE OLD SOUTH &
WEST OF THE MISSISSIPPI by Nancy Hawlick Stein
Oliphant/Ollyphant; Oliphint/etc.: NC; SC; Va; Ga; La; Kan; & others
Paper [Publication date probably 1975]-----------------Vendor #545

446 – TESTIMONY AND TRIAL – AN AUTOBIOGRAPHY by Luther A. Gotwald
Gotwald: York Springs, Pa–1833-1838; Aaronsburg, Pa–1838-1849; Springfield, O–1852-1855; Gettysburg, Pa–1855-1859; Shippensburg, Pa–1859-
1863; Lebanon, Pa–1863-1865; Dayton, O–1865-1868; Chambersburg, Pa–
1869-1874; York, Pa–1874-1885; Springfield, O–1885-1900
     Cloth: $27.75/Paper: $25.50/Microfilm: $8.50–505pp--------Vendor #546

447 – GAILLARD GENEALOGY - DESCENDANTS OF JOACHIM GAILLARD
AND ESTHER PAPAREL by Dorothy K. MacDowell
Gaillard: SC–1625-1975
     Cloth–385pp–$20.00--- Vendor #41

448 – OUR EGGLESTON AND ALLIED FAMILIES by Elsie B. Kempton
Eggleston: Windsor, Conn–1635-1674; Conn–1635-c1770; Saratoga Co, NY–
by1770-1845; Hillsdale Co, Mich–1845-1975
     Cloth–120pp– $15.00--- Vendor #549

449 – OUR HADLEY AND ALLIED FAMILIES by Elsie B. Kempton
Hadley: Mass–1712-1773; Brattleboro, Vt–1773-1799; Sandy Creek, Otsego
Co, NY–1790-1847; Hillsdale Co, Mich–1847-1975
     [Publication date not set]----------------------------------- Vendor #549

450 – BURGESS - HAINES CONNECTION by Gordon P. Tierney, C.A.L.S.
Burgess: Pa/Md–1600s-1830's; Muskingum Co, O–1815-1835; Seneca Co,
O–1832-date; Delaware Co, Ind–1838-date
Haines: Burlington, NJ–1680's-1730's; Frederick Co, Va–1700-1810;
Greene/Clinton Cos, O–1795-1849; Randolph/Delaware Cos, Ind–1850-date
Terrell: New Kent/Hanover Cos, Va–1680's-1805; southwest O–1805-1861
Clayton: Chester Co, Pa–1680's-1720; Cecil Co, Md–1795-1725
Hunt: Bucks/Chester Cos, Pa–1600's-1730's; Rowan/Guilford Cos, NC–
1740-1820's; Randolph/Grant/Delaware Cos, Ind–1818-date
     [Projected publication date: 1977]----------------------------Vendor #553

451 – DAWES FAMILY NEWSLETTER edited by Merle Ganier
Dawes (John W.): Orange Co, NY– ? -1810; Wayne Co, NY–1810-1837;
Mercer Co, Pa–1837-1857; Waushara Co, Wisc–1857-1864
     Subscription: $3.00/yr–4 issues/yr--------------------------Vendor #554

452 – JAQUITH FAMILY IN AMERICA by George O. Jaquith, M.D.
Jaquith: Mass; NH; upstate NY; Ia   [This is preliminary editon. Author
invites correspondence with members of family for inclusion in later edition.]
     Looseleaf/xerox–400pp–$55.00 [disc. to libraries]------------ Vendor #556

453 – JOHN ATWOOD OF PLYMOUTH, MASSACHUSETTS: The Descendants of
John Atwood of Plymouth, Mass., 1614-1676, and his wife, Sarah Masterson,
1620-1701/2 by Benjamin Shurtleff
Atwood: Plymouth, Mass–1635-1676; Plympton, Carver, Mass;
Middleboro-Bridgewater, Mass; Vt
     Paper–106pp–$9.00--- Vendor #557

454 – JOHN SHAW OF PLYMOUTH, MASSACHUSETTS: The Descendants of John
Shaw of Plymouth, Mass., who died in 1694, and his wife, Alice, who died
in 1654. by Benjamin Shurtleff
Shaw: Plymouth, Mass–1627-1662; Middleboro, Mass–1662-1694;

Vt—c1790-1974; Bremer Co, Ia—1863-1919
Atwood (Nathaniel): Plymouth, Mass; Plympton-Carver, Mass
Fuller (Samuel): Plymouth, Mass; Kingston, Mass
Lucas (Samuel): Plymouth, Mass; Carver, Mass
Shurtleff (Benjamin): Plympton, Mass
Paper—128pp—$9.00-- Vendor #557

455 – JOHN A WASSON, NORTH CAROLINA, GEORGIA, MISSISSIPPI, 1807-
1880 by Sam F. Brewster
Wasson: Iredell Co, NC—1807-1832; Greene Co, Ga—1832-1852; Attala Co,
Miss—1852-1880
Cloth—279pp—$10.00--------------------------------------- Vendor #558

456 – WILLIAM B. BRUSTER, VIRGINIA-TENNESSEE, 1793-1853 by Sam F.
Brewster
Bruster/Brewster: Montgomery Co, Va—1767-   ; Tazewell Co, Va—1793-
; White Co, Tenn- ? -1893
Cloth—121pp—$6.00--------------------------------------- Vendor #558

457 – BEERY FAMILY HISTORY by William Beery & Judith Beery Garber
Beery/Bieri: Berne, Switzerland; Palatinate, Ger- ? -1727; York Co,
Pa—1727-1790; Rockingham Co, Va—1780-present; Fairfield Co, O—1805-
present; All over U.S. and elsewhere in world to present
Cloth—783pp—[Copies in many libraries - not for sale]---------- Vendor #559

458 – ROHRBACH GENEALOGY by Lewis Bunker Rohrbaugh
Rohrbach/Rohrbaugh: Switzerland—1500-date; Germany—1400-date; Pa—
1732-date; NY State—1709-date
Cloth—$20.00--- Vendor #561

459 – THE PEOPLE OF THE MARSH [NEWSLETTER] edited by Charles Recker
Moser/Mosier/Mosser/Musser: From Rhine Valley to Pa. before the Revo-
lution, then to N.C., Va., O., Ind., and points West
Subscription: $2.00/yr—4pp/issue—6 issues/yr-------------- Vendor #565

460 – FANT GENEALOGY by Alfred E. Fant
Fant: All persons of this surname, anywhere in U.S. - contains 2,809 indi-
vidual entries with available biographical data - indexed.
Cloth—278pp—$9.00------------------------------------- Vendor #567

461 – WE VEITCHES, VEATCHES, VEACHES, VEECHES by Laurence R.
Guthrie & Wanda Veatch Clark
Veitch/Veatch/Veach/Veech: Scotland- -1651; Md—1651- ; other states
Cloth—937pp—$12.50------------------------------------- Vendor #568

462 – NICHOLAS YOUNG AND HIS DESCENDANTS by Virgil D. Young
Young: Pa—1775-1815; Washington Co, Ind—1815-1850; Daviess Co, Mo—
1850-1880; Doniphan Co, Kan—1880-1915
Wheaton: Caledonia Co, Vt—1792-1860; Doniphan Co, Kan—1860-1900
Cloth—$10.00--- Vendor #304

463 – CLAN McLAREN SOCIETY QUARTERLY edited by Banks McLaurin, Jr.
McLaren/McLaurin/etc.: U.S.A.; Canada; Scotland
Subscription: $7.00/yr—4 issues/yr------------------------ Vendor #574

464 — THE CONGER FAMILY OF AMERICA by Helen Maxine C. Leonard
Conger: Woodbridge, NJ—1666-present; throughout USA
Cloth—924pp—$25.00--- Vendor #575

465 — JAMES DOUGALL OF GLASGOW (1699-1760) AND HIS DESCENDANTS
THROUGH DOUGALL AND McDOUGALL LINES IN THE UNITED STATES
AND CANADA by Richardson Dougall
McDougall: Manhattan, NY—1774-1810; Essex Co, NJ—1800-1973; Kings'
Co, NY—1856-1905; Morris Co, NJ—1800-1973
Anderson: Lambton Co, Ontario—1840-1973; Pierce Co, Wash—1909-1973
Wark: Lambton Co, Ontario—1839-1973; Thunder Bay Dist, Ont—1910-1973
Young: Lambton Co, Ont—1820-1973; Winnipeg, Manitoba—1873-1973; York
Co, Ont—1894-1973
Smith: Lambton Co, Ont—1838-1973
Dougall: Essex Co, Ont—1832-1973; Montreal, Que—1826-1952; Wayne Co,
Mich—1893-1973; St. Joseph Co, Ind—1925-1973; New York Co, NY—1774-
1805; Lancaster Co, Nebr—1917-1942
Woodruff: Morris Co, NJ—1812-1973; Knox Co, O—1840-1926
Henry: Ontario Co, NY—1812-1964; Jackson Co, Ia—1858-1973
Howell: Morris Co, NJ—1783-1921; Calgary, Alberta—1898-1973
Van Wagenen: Essex Co, NJ—1799-1892; Duval Co, Fla—1937-1973
Robertson: Lambton Co, Ont—1847-1973
Mackenzie: Lambton Co, Ont—1843-1973
Dewar: Essex Co, Ont—1825-1973; Kent Co, Mich—1897-1973
Paper—464pp—$15.00--- Vendor #576

466 — THE BEERS GENEALOGY, VOL. I [The Beers Families of Massachu-
setts and Rhode Island] by Mary Louise Regan
Beers: Boston & Suburbs—1694-1972; Watertown, Mass; Providence, RI;
Newport, RI
Cloth: $15.00/Paper: $12.00—200pp------------------------- Vendor #578

467 — THE BEERS GENEALOGY, VOL. II [The Descendants of Anthony Beers of
Fairfield, Connecticut Through His Son John] by Mary Louise Regan
Beers: Newtown, Conn—1712-1974; Ithaca, NY—1810-1880; Chicago, Ill—
1835-1974; Salt Lake City, Utah—1868-1974
Cloth—247pp—$20.00--- Vendor #578

468 — THE BEERS GENEALOGY, VOL. III [Further Descendants of Anthony
Beers and Descendants of James Beers, also of Fairfield, Ct] by M. L. Regan
Beers: Throughout USA
[Projected publication date: 1976]---------------------------- Vendor #578

469 — A HISTORY OF THE OTSTOT(T) FAMILY IN AMERICA by Charles Math-
ieson Otstot
Otstot/Otstott: Pa—1775-date; O—1820-date; Ill—1840-date; Kan—1890-date
Keller: Pa—1804-date
Dellinger: Pa—1808-date
Jung/Young: Pa—1803-date
Cloth—860pp (including 1974 supplement)—$20.00----------------Vendor #583

470 – ESTES BROTHERS - KENTUCKY TO IOWA AND THEIR DESCENDANTS
by Carl O. Estes
Estes: Caroline Co, Va–1700-1800; Hart Co, Ky–1800-1846; Jefferson
Co, Ia–1846-1974; Garfield Co, Colo–1890-1974
Paper–53pp–$21.00--- Vendor #585

471 – A PLACE IN HISTORY: THE DAVANT FAMILY by Hardin Davant Hanahan
Davant: Savannah/Atlanta, Ga–1733-date; Knoxville/Memphis, Tenn–1877-
date; Beaumont/Houston/other towns, Tex–1900's; Roanoke, Va–1892-1974;
many states throughout U.S. [This book was awarded third prize in Heart-
of-America Genealogical Society book contest.]
Cloth–216pp–$15.50-------------------------------------- Vendor #589

472 – THE COFFIN FAMILY by Louis Coffin
Coffin: Nantucket, Mass–1609-1962
Cloth–575pp–$10.00-------------------------------------- Vendor #590

473 – WADE - WAID - WAIDE by Mrs. Jeff Wade, Jr.
Wade/Waid/Waide: [A basic book of vital records for these surnames.]
Paper–260pp–$11.00------------------------------------- Vendor # 19

474 – SOME DESCENDANTS OF NATHAN SPICER (1735-1811) OF CONNECT-
ICUT AND NEW YORK by Jean Burt Grube
Spicer: Litchfield Co, Conn–1735-1760's; Amenia, Dutchess Co, NY–1760's-
1770's; Columbia Co, NY–1770's-1794; Rensselaer Co, NY–1794- c1810
Wells: Rennselaer Co, NY– ? -1810's; Richland Co, O–1819-1838; Van
Wert Co, O–1838-18--
Bishop: Pompey, NY–1790's-180–; Oswego, NY–1806-1860
Doty: Ft. Ann, NY–180-to1814; Allegheny Co, NY–1814-1860
[Projected publication date: 1976]-------------------------Vendor #592

475 – DELPS GALORE by Leonard Arnold Delp
Delp: [A cataloging of thirteen family lines, tracing them from Pennsylvania
as they migrated across the United States.]
Paper–120pp–$7.00------------------------------------- Vendor #593

476 – FARRALL AND FRAZELL (FRASER) FAMILIES WITH INFORMATION ON
SPECK, YOUNG, MYER, BUCK AND KNOX FAMILIES by Arthur W. Farrall
Frazell: Northfield, Mass–1766-1817; West Liberty, O–1817-1845; Har-
vard, Nebr–1899-1922
Cloth–191pp–$14.50-------------------------------------- Vendor #594

477 – FRANCIS MARION FARLEY AND LULU CAIN FARLEY, THEIR ANCES-
TORS AND DESCENDANTS by Lucille Farley Speer
Farley: Virginia to Indiana–1623-1957
Cain (Benjamin): Md; S.E. Ohio; Green Co, Ind– -1874
Elgin (Robert): Md; Pr. Wm. Co, Va; Abbeville Dist, SC–c1808
Elliott (Thomas): Morgan Co, Ind–1838
Cloth–214pp–$16.50-------------------------------------- Vendor #598

478 – WILLIAM BEAN PIONEER OF TENN. & HIS DESC. by Jamie Ault Grady
Bean: Va–1742-1769; Washington Co, Tenn–1769-1800; Hawkins Co, Tenn–
1800- ? ; Mo; Tex; Ark
Cloth–350pp–$12.50------------------------------------- Vendor #600

479 — BOWENS OF VIRGINIA AND TENNESSEE by Jamie Ault Grady
Bowen: Wales— ? -1698; Montgomery Co, Pa—1698-1730; Augusta Co,
Va—1730-1779; Tazewell Co, Va—1779-1795; Grainger Co, Tenn—1795-
1837; Boliver, Mo—1837-1861
Cloth—150pp—$12.50--- Vendor #600

480 — A LARKINS GENEALOGY: ELDRIDGE LARKINS & ELIZABETH BLEDSOE
AND THEIR DESCENDANTS by Winniferd Eyrich Perrigo & Lyle D. Perrigo
Larkins: Hawkins Co, Tenn— ? -c1867; Orange Co, Ind—1867-1882; Iro-
quois Co, Ill—1882-1883; Orange Co, Ind—1883-1884
Paper—63pp—$4.50--- Vendor #602

481 — SAMUEL MAY & DESCENDANTS by Lyle D. Perrigo & Dalene T. Perrigo
May: Astabula Co, O—c1810-1859; Grant Co, Wisc—1859-c1870;
Cass Co, Nebr—c1870-1876; desc. elsewhere in Nebr. to the present
Paper—7pp—$1.00--- Vendor #602

482 — SOULE NEWSLETTER, magazine of the Soule family published quarterly
since 1967 by Soule Kindred in America, Inc.
Soule/Sowle/Sole/Soules/Sowles/Soles: Includes all of surname in U.S. A.-
1620-1975.
Subscription: $5.00/yr—4 issues/yr—approx. 50pp/issue------- Vendor #606

483 — THE GOOLDY GRAPEVINE edited by Walter R. & Patricia A. Gooldy
Gooldy—Va—1700's-1800's; O—1700's-1800's; Ind—1818-date; Mo—1867-date
Subscription: free—4 issues/yr—approx. 10pp/issue----------- Vendor #607

484 — THE VAN TREESE FAMILY NEWSLETTER edited by Harold W. Van Treese
Van Treese (all spellings): Pa—1788-1800; Ky—1800-1825; O—1825-1860;
Ind—1860-date; points West—1860-date
Subscription: free—4 issues/yr—approx. 10pp/issue----------- Vendor #608

485 — AMBROSE N. COX, SR. DESCENDANTS 1772-1972 by Elza B. Cox
Cox: Botetourt Co, Va—1772-1779; Montgomery/Floyd Cos, Va—1776-1848
Floyd Co, Va—1831-1848; Other areas
Reed: Franklin Co, Va—1775-1790; Montgomery Co, Va—1790-1831; Floyd
Co, Va—1831-1854
Phillips: Pittsylvania Co, Va—1765-c1800; Montgomery Co, Va—c1800-1828;
Grayson Co, Va—1828-c1862
Bishop: Montgomery Co, Va—1755-1831; Floyd Co, Va—1831-1839
Wilson: Montgomery Co, Va—1776-1831; Floyd Co, Va—1831-1848; Hancock
Co, Ill—1835-1930
Wade: Goochland Co, Va, 1739-1790; Montgomery Co, Va—1790-1831; Floyd
Co, Va—1831-1864
Cloth—630pp—$20.00--- Vendor #610

486 — THE GENERATIONS OF THE WHITE FAMILY FROM 1624 to 1884, PAR-
TICULARLY THE DESCENDANTS OF NATHANIEL AND NANCY WHITE by
Imogene N. Marshall [Reprint of 1890 edition]
White: Del—1600's-1700's; Md/Va—1700's-1800's; Ohio—1800's; various
mid-west states—late 1800's
Paper—44pp—$3.95--- Vendor #318

487 — THE WILLIAM FOWLER FAMILY OF GARLAND COUNTY, ARKANSAS –
HIS ANCESTORS AND DESCENDANTS by Charles A. & Louise B. Fowler
Fowler: Floyd Co, Ga–1830's; Ark–1840's-1975; Hunt & Fannin Cos, Tex–
1880's-1975
[In Process]-- Vendor #384

488 — THE THOMAS A WHITE FAMILY OF SALINE COUNTY, ARKANSAS –
HIS ANCESTORS AND DESCENDANTS by Charles A. & Louise B. Fowler
White: Chester Co, SC–1801-1847; Saline/Hot Springs/Garland Cos, Ark–
1847-1975; Fannin/Hunt Cos, Tex–1880's-1975
[In Process] -- Vendor #384

489 — DAVID SPENCE OF NEW JERSEY, NORTH CAROLINA, AND TENNESSEE
by Louise B. Fowler
Spence: NJ–1759-1780's; Surry Co, NC–1780's-'790's; Robertson/Hickman
Cos, Tenn; Ill; Okla; Tex.
[In Process] -- Vendor #384

490 — THE COLEMAN FAMILY OF NORTH CAROLINA AND TENNESSEE by
Louise B. Fowler
Coleman: Craven Co, NC–1780's-1817; Hickman Co, Tenn–1817-1975;
Tex; Okla
[In Process] -- Vendor #384

491 — THE DAVID BISHOP FAMILY OF TAZEWELL COUNTY, VIRGINIA –
HIS ANCESTORS AND DESCENDANTS, by Louise Bishop Fowler
Bishop: Russell/Tazewell Cos, Va–1780-1850's; Lawrence Co, Ky–1840-
1975; W.Va; Okla; Tex.
[In Process]-- Vendor #384

492 — AMONG FIRST FAMILIES IN AMERICA [INCLUDING CARPENTER, DI-
MOCK, GURLEY, HAND, HULL, LITTON, MILLHOUSE, MURDOCK,
NICKEY, REDICK, RUDISILL, STORRS, SOUTHWORTH, WILDMAN] by
George W. Guirl. [Compiling a book for Bi-centennial slating entitled
"Among First Families in America". A history/genealogy. Three hundred
fifty years, 12 generations, of Gurley direct and collateral ancestors. May-
flower Pilgrim descendants. Thousands of indexed names. Gurley from
1174 A.D. to present. Data to exchange before publishing.]
[In Process]-- Vendor #389

493 — REV. ROBERT ROSE OF SCOTLAND, ESSEX COUNTY, VIRGINIA, AND
ALBEMARLE COUNTY, VIRGINIA – THE FIRST FIVE GENERATIONS IN
AMERICA, compiled by Christine Rose [A research booklet - includes es-
tate abstracts, census records, etc. Corrects much of the previously pub-
lished information on this family. Fully indexed.
Paper–55pp–$4.00--- Vendor #395

494 — CAPTAIN JOHN SINCLAIR OF VIRGINIA by Claude O. Lanciano
Sinclair: Hampton/Isle of Wight Cos, Va—c1728-c1796; Gloucester Co,
Va—1796-1820; Gloucester/Hampton Cos, Va—1820-present
Cloth—301pp—$7.50--- Vendor #435

495 — THE WINE FAMILY IN AMERICA, Section Three, by Jacob David Wine
(1881-1968) & Joseph Floyd Wine
Wine: Germany—1747-1749; York Co, Pa—1749-1776; Frederick Co, Md—
1776-1782; Forestville, Shenandoah Co, Va—1782-present
Cloth—591pp—$14.00--- Vendor #460

496 — GEORGE ALFRED TRENHOLM AND THE COMPANY THAT WENT TO
WAR by Ethel S. Nepveux
Trenholm: Allerton, Eng—1765; Charleston, SC—to present [Story of Tren-
holm, his antecedents, his & his company's role in the Civil War.]
Cloth—132pp—$10.00--- Vendor #486

497 — LAYNE-LAIN-LANE GENEALOGY by Floyd B. Layne
Layne/Lane/Lain: Amherst Co, Va—1700-1955; Sequatchie Valley, Tenn—
1788-1958; Hanover Co, Va—1683-1962; Randolph, Ill—1766-1953
Cloth—336—$10.00--- Vendor #522

498 — LAYNE GENEALOGY by Floyd B. Layne
Layne/Lane/Lain
Cloth—251pp—$8.00--- Vendor #522

499 — OUR SIMMONS FOREFATHERS AND THEIR DESCENDANTS by Georgia
Crosthwaite & Bennett L. Smith
Simmons: Muhlenberg Co, Ky—1800-1874; Parker Co, Tex—1874 to date
Luce: Martha's Vineyard, Mass—1670-1700; Suffolk Co, NY—1700-1789
Muhlenberg Co, Ky—1800-1874
Rhoads: Bedford/Somerset Cos, Pa—1760-1780; Muhlenberg, Ky—1780-1874
Studebaker/Baker: Westmoreland Co, Pa—1770-1800; Muhlenberg Co, Ky—
1800-1874
Paper—450pp—$11.00--- Vendor #533

500 — DANIEL HAND OF MADISON, CONNECTICUT, 1801-1891, by Oedel
Hand: Madison, Ct; Richmond Co, Ga.
Paper—58pp—$1.75--- Vendor #577

501 — DESCENDANTS OF JOSEPH OGDEN (b.1796/98), by Ella Stover
Ogden: Pa— to after 1796/98; Ind—1820-1830; Fulton Co, Ill—1830-1880
Cloth—144pp—$14.50--- Vendor #611

502 — ROBERT MCKAY CLAN NEWSLETTER by Wallace & Dorothy Chipp
[Periodical issued 3 times a year/ 8 pp. per issue concerning descendants of
Robert McKay of Warren County, Virginia. Published since 1965.]
Subscription: Voluntary donation --------------------------- Vendor #613

503 — LUMPKIN FAMILY OF VIRGINIA, GEORGIA, & MISSISSIPPI, compiled
and edited by Martha Neville Lumpkin
Lumpkin: Va—c1640-1800; Ga—1784-1850; Miss—1837-1970; NC—1740-1800
Paper-[punched for 3-ring binder]-150pp—$8.00--------------- Vendor #614

504 — MINOR, SCALES, COTTRELL, AND GRAY FAMILIES OF VIRGINIA,
NORTH CAROLINA, & MISSISSIPPI compiled by Martha Neville Lumpkin
Minor: Va—1640-1845; Miss—1840-1970
Scales: Va—c1750-1845; Miss—1845-1970
Cottrell: NC—c1800-1835; Miss—1836-1970; Md—c1767-c1800
Gray: NC—c1790-c1820; Tenn—c1820-c1840; Miss—c1840-1970
Paper-[punched for 3-ring binder]-162pp—$8.00-------------- Vendor #614

505 — DEAR DARLING LOULIE: [Letters written during the Civil War by Cordelia
Lewis Scales, a teenager in Marshall Co., Miss.] ed. by Martha N. Lumpkin
Scales: Va—1770-1845; Miss—1845-1915
Gray: Miss—1840-1915   [Some of the families mentioned in these letters
include Arthur, Clayton, Crump, Gilmore, Irby, Mickle, O'Meara, Top.]
Paper-165pp—$8.00--------------------------------------- Vendor #614

506 — DATA ON DEMERS/DUMAIS FAMILIES IN QUEBEC 1648-1835: BACK-
GROUND FOR EMIGRATION TO THE UNITED STATES, by Virginia DeMarce
Demers/Dumais/DeMarce: Quebec Province, Canada—1648-1835
Paper-183pp—$10.00------------------------------------- Vendor #618

507 — THE FAMILY AND ANCESTRY OF HERMANN JOSEPH JONGEBLOED
AND HIS WIFE MARIE EMMA ZUHLKE IN GERMANY & AMERICA by
Virginia Easley DeMarce
Jongebloed: Papenburg, Ger—1650-1895; New York City—1895-present
Paper-86pp—$2.00------------------------------------- Vendor #618

508 — A TENTATIVE OUTLINE OF U.S. EASLEY LINES, PRIMARILY TO THE
YEAR 1800 by Virginia Easley DeMarce
Easley: Va—1688-1800; Ky—1780-1800; NC & SC—1750-1800; Tenn—1780-1800
Paper-310pp—$7.50------------------------------------- Vendor #618

509 — THE TUNIS HOOD FAMILY: ITS LINEAGE AND TRADITIONS (From
1695) by Dellmann O. Hood
Hood: NY—c1695-   ; Mecklenburg Co, NC
Cloth-666pp—$15.00------------------------------------- Vendor #626

510 — THE BEVILLE FAMILY OF HUNTINGDONSHIRE, ENGLAND, AND SOME
ALLIED FAMILIES: INCLUDING THE FIRST THREE GENERATIONS IN HEN-
RICO COUNTY, VIRGINIA by Asselia Strobhar Lichliter
Beville: England—pre-1066-   ; Henrico Co, Va—
Carew: Pembrokeshire & Surrey, Eng—1066-1611
Hoo: Bedford & Sussex, Eng—1000-c1460
Sanders: Surrey Co, Eng—c1450-1611
Bowerman: Isle of Wight, Eng—c1129-1559
[In Process. Projected publication date, 1975. Approx. 400pp] -Vendor #627

511 — THE MARTZES OF MARYLAND by Ralph Fraley Martz
Martz: Gettysburg, Pa; Harrisonburg, Va; Ky; Frederick Co, Md.
Cloth-210pp—$12.00------------------------------------- Vendor #628

512 — THE McINTURFFS (McInturf/McEntarfer) by Raymond L. Kringer
McInturff/McInturf: Va—1750-1860; Tenn—1785-1875; Ohio/Ind—1800-1860;
Ill—1820-1900; West—1820-1900
Cloth-150pp—Approx. $12.50-[Publication, fall 1975]---------- Vendor #652

513 — DAVID BIRGE MARRIES ABIGAIL HOWLAND, THEIR ANCESTORS & DE-
SCENDANTS by George & Opal Birge Pixley
Birge: Hartford Co, Conn–1625-1720; Litchfield Co, Conn–1720-1786;
Chittenden Co, Vt–1799-1869; Bond Co, Ill–1819-1931; Addison Co, Vt–
1831-1851; Kenton Co, Ky–1847-1874; Wash. DC–1850-1975
Howland: Plymouth Co, Mass–1620-1673; Barnstable Co, Mass–1658-1778
Cloth–272pp–$15.00--- Vendor #634

514 — A HISTORY OF ONE BRANCH OF THE GEORGE FAMILY IN THE UNITED
STATES by Dora B. George
George: Haverhill, Mass–1700-1778; Conway, NH–1779-1840; Burton (now
Albany), NH–1805-1930; Garden Plain, etc. Ill–1840-date
Paper–74pp–$10.00--- Vendor #655

515 — DESCENDANTS OF JOHN WISMER AND HIS WIFE AGNES HONSBERGER
OF LINCOLN COUNTY, ONTARIO, CANADA by Orpha McChesney Smith
Wismer: Lincoln Co, Ont, Can–1804-1974; Bucks Co, Pa–1726-1974
Cloth–110pp–$10.00--- Vendor #656

516 — McCLUNG FAMILY ASSOCIATION JOURNAL ed. by Judith A. Cloninger
[Published 3 times a year. Approximately 40 pages per issue. Includes
all families of the McClung surname.]
Subscription: $5.00/yr ------------------------------------ Vendor #682

517 — THE HORNE FAMILY OF BLOOMINGDALE - ROAD by Philip Field Horne
Horn/Horne: Ulster Co, NY–1685-1692;   New York Co, NY–1700-1959;
Westchester Co, NY–1845-1975; Riverside Co, CA–1912-1962
"Binder"–88pp–$13.00--------------------------------------- Vendor #691

518 — THE CURREY FAMILY IN THE HUDSON HIGHLANDS by Philip F. Horne
Currey/Cury/Currie: Westchester Co, NY–1703-1975; Queens Co, NY–
1783-1975; Sullivan Co, NY–1795-1975; Kane Co, Ill–1853-1975
Paper–189pp–$12.50-- Vendor #691

519 — CERTAIN TOPICS ON THE INGHAM, WATERHOUSE AND ALLIED FAM-
ILIES by Carmack Waterhouse
The Family Group: NJ–1710-date; Pa–1730-date; Ia–1850-date; Calif–
1870-date
Cloth–274pp–$8.95--- Vendor #699

520 — ARNOLD FAMILY ASSOCIATION OF THE SOUTH QUARTERLY, ed. by
Hazel A. MacIvor [Published since 1970. Number of pages varies.]
Subscription: $11.00/yr ---------------------------------- Vendor #705

521 — LOVE'S VALLEY by Jolee Love
Love: Hampshire Co, Eng–1327-1650; Chester Co, Pa–1699-1720;
Chester Co, SC–1760-1791; DeKalb Co, Tenn–1797-1974
Cloth–556pp–$20.00-- Vendor #711

522 — A GENEALOGY OF THE LITTLE - ODOM FAMILY OF GEORGIA AND
NORTH CAROLINA by Lawrence L. Little & Margaret M. Little
Little: Rowan Co, NC–1800-   ; Lincoln Co, NC–1820-   ;
Wilkes Co, NC–1840-   ; Union Co, Ga–1885-
Paper–191pp–$4.25---------------------------------------Vendor #714

523 – THE FAMILY OF PETER RUETER AND AMELIA SCHLUETER by Berdena E. Rosenow Koehler
Rueter/Rüther: Glüsingen, near Lüneburg, West Ger–1860-1874; Murdock, Nebr–1874-1912; Anaheim, Calif–1912-1932
Paper–100pp–$4.50--- Vendor #715

524 – THE FAMILY OF DOROTHEA E. RUETER AND CHRISTIAN DAVID KUNZ, SR., by Berdena E. Rosenow Koehler
Kunz: Granau, Wuertemberg, Ger–1839-1857; Ill–1857-1875; Elmwood, Nebr–1875-1913
Paper–90pp–$4.50--- Vendor #715

525 – THE FAMILY OF MARGARETHA E. RUETER AND AUGUST A BORNE-MEIER by Berdena E. Rosenow Koehler
Bornemeier: Detmold, West Ger–1841-c1870; Murdock, Nebr–c1870-1918; Elmwood, Nebr–1918-1933
Paper–80pp–$4.50--- Vendor #715

526 – THE FAMILY OF KATHERINE E. RUETER AND SIMON F. BORNE-MEIER by Berdena E. Rosenow Koehler
Bornemeier: Detmold, West Ger–1851-c1870; Murdock, Nebr–c1870-1922; Elmwood, Nebr–1922-1931
Paper–60pp–$4.50--- Vendor #715

527 – THE FAMILY OF MAGDALENA E. RUETER AND JURGEN HEINRICH F. OEHLERKING by Berdena E. Rosenow Koehler
Oehlerking: Near Lueneburg, West Ger–1827-c1860; Murdock, Nebr–c1860-1905; Elmwood, Nebr–1905-1924
Paper–90pp–$4.50--- Vendor #715

528 – JAMES DAWSON FROM WALES AND HIS DESCENDANTS by Carol R. Dawson
Dawson:
Cloth–204–$7.95--- Vendor #719

529 – DAWSONS IN THE REVOLUTIONARY WAR [AND THEIR DESCENDANTS] Vol. 1, by Carol R. Dawson
Cloth–176pp–$20.00--- Vendor #719

530 – GENEALOGIE DE LA FAMILLE JUNEAU [GENEALOGY OF THE JUNEAU FAMILY (WITH GENEALOGICAL TABLE)] by Connerton & Landry
Juneau: Canada–1652-1965; Wisc–1816-1965; La–1755-1965; Kan–1850-1965
Paper–748pp–$10.00--- Vendor #748

531 – AN INDIANA SOJOURN - THE MILHOUS FAMILY - 1854 to 1904 by Crawford [A biographic history.]
Milhous: Ire–1720- ; Pa–1729-1803; O–1803-1854; Ind–1854-1904
Paper–59pp [8 1/2 x 11]–$3.95----------------------------- Vendor #761

532 – THE CHRONICLE OF A SOUTHERN FAMILY by William H. Sebastian
Sebastian: Md–1649-1689; Va (northern neck)–1689-1780; NC–1778-1975; Ky–1780-1975
Cloth–$10.50/Paper–$8.00–142pp-------------------------- Vendor #765

533 — THE GENEALOGY OF THE FAMILY OF JOSEPH ALEXANDER
      KINSMAN by Donald M. Kinsman
      Kinsman: Ipswich, Mass—1634-1760; Cornwallis, Nova Scotia—1760-1850;
      Lakeville, Nova Scotia—1850-1974
      Spiral binding—70pp—$10.00----------------------------------Vendor #766

534 — THE FAMILY OF DANIEL AND MARY McEACHERN by Sally S. Trotter
      McEachern: Robeson Co, NC; Union Church, Miss; Holmes Co, Miss;
      Carroll Co, Miss—1832-present
      Paper—120pp—$6.00--------------------------------------- Vendor #775

535 — THE CANNON FAMILY by Edward P. Cannon
      Cannon: Newberry Co, SC—1734-1820; Lauderdale Co, Ala—1820-1870;
      Carroll Co, Tenn—1871-1974; Lincoln Co, Mo—1800-1940

536 — VAN TASSEL AND ALLIED LINES 1574-1974 by Mary Van Tassel Pazurik
      Van Tassell:
      Cloth—535pp—$90.00-------------------------------------- Vendor #791

537 — THE SIMMS FAMILY OF STAFFORD COUNTY, VA. by Hall & Chappell
      Simms: Stafford Co, Va—1750-1820; Clay Co, Mo—1829-1969; Montgom-
      ery Co, Ind—1817-1969; Ralls Co, Mo—1817-1969
      Cloth—248pp—$15.00-------------------------------------- Vendor #793

538 — WOODRUFF CHRONICLES, A GENEALOGY. 2 vols. by C.N. Woodruff
      Woodruff: Fordwich, Kent, Eng—1639-   ; Southampton, Long Island—
      1665-   ; Elizabeth Town, NJ; Seneca Co, NY
      Cloth—360 & 268pp—$23.50 + $15.75—Set: $36.00-------------- Vendor #794

539 — COLONEL PATRICK McGRIFF, HIS CHIDREN & GRANDCHILDREN by
      Joseph Edward Hill, Sr.
      McGriff: Chester Co, SC—1799; Montgomery Co, Ga—(death 1810)
      Paper—66pp—$5.00--- Vendor #795

540 — AS I FIND IT by Emma Plunket Ivy
      Butler: Ire—1066-1600's; Va—1600's-1700's; SC—late 1700's; Newton Co,
      Ga—1900's; States west—1900's
      Cloth—200 + index—$10.50------------------------------------- Vendor #806

541 — TEN THOUSAND PLUNKETTS. 2 vols. by Emma Plunkett Ivy
      Plunkett: Ire—1638-1655; Va—early 1700's; SC—c1700-c1900; Ga—late
      1800's to present; States west—late 1800's to present
      Cloth—628 + 377pp—Each vol. $15.75------------------------- Vendor #806

542 — GENEALOGY . . . OF . . . STEINER, STONER, BAIR, GAUMER,
      BARRICK by Robert T. Stoner
      All families in title: Eastern Pa—1700-1972
      Paper—125pp—$5.00--------------------------------------- Vendor #826

543 — THE LINCOLNS IN VIRGINIA by John W. Wayland [Limited to 500 copies]
      Lincoln: Rockingham Co, Va—1768-1900
      Cloth—300pp—$30.00-------------------------------------- Vendor #830

544 — THE DESCENDANTS OF ANDREW FORD OF WEYMOUTH, MASSACHU-
SETTS. Part 1: The First Six Generations by Elizabeth Cobb Stewart
Ford: Weymouth, Mass—c1642-present; Abington, Mass—c1680-present;
Morris Co, NJ—c1720-present; Windham Co, Conn—c1712-present
Cloth—169pp—$10.26--- Vendor #828

545 — HENRY SHARP (c1737-1800) OF SUSSEX COUNTY, N.J. & FAYETTE
COUNTY, PA. AND HIS WIFE LYDIA MORGAN AND SOME OF THEIR DE-
SCENDANTS INCLUDING DEPUY, CHALFANT, SILVERTHORN, AND
WHEATLY FAMILIES by Eastwood & Wickliffe
Sharp: Clinton Co, Ill—1809-present; Washington Co, Pa—1808-present;
Jefferson Co, O—1835-present; Greene Co, O—1839-present
Cloth—approx. 250pp—$20 to $25—[Publication date, 1975]-------Vendor #828

546 — SELDEN & KINDRED OF VIRGINIA by Edna M. Selden
Selden: Va—1690-1940
Cloth—224pp—$17.50--- Vendor #830

547 — THE SKELTONS OF PAXTON, POWHATAN COUNTY, VIRGINIA by
Baskervill P. Hamilton
Cloth—119pp—$15.00--------------------------------------- Vendor #830

548 — JOHN BUSHMAN: HIS LIFE & LABORS by Derryfield N. Smith
Bushman: Nauvoo, Ill—1843-1846; Lehi, Utah—1851-1876; Joseph City,
Ariz—1876-1916; Salt Lake City, Utah—1918-1926
Cloth—approx. 325pp—$12.00—[Publication date, late 1975]----- Vendor #839

549 — THE CARTER, ALKIRE, KENNEDY, AND WILLIAMS FAMILIES by
Judge James M. Carter
Carter: Va—1796-   ; Lewis Co, WVa—1821-1850; Los Angles Co,
Calif—1900-present
Alkire: Lewis Co, WVa—1793-1850; Va—1720-1900
Kennedy: Lewis Co, WVa—1839-1850; Los Angeles Co, Calif—1900-present
Williams: Highland Co, Va—1790-1850; Lewis Co, WVa—1850-
Linger: WVa—1792-1850
Gillespie: Braxton Co, WVa—1850
Woods: WVa—1850
[In Process. To be published in 1975/6.]-------------------- Vendor #840

550 — THE SAWYERS, HAY, HICKS, & KING FAMILIES by Judge J.M. Carter
Sawyers: Shelby Co, Ky—c1745-1835; Clark Co, Mo—1835-1854;
Mendocino Co, Calif—1854-present
Hay: Shenandoah Co, Va—1782-1831; Page Co, Va—1831-1835; Clark Co,
Mo—1835-1854
King: Shelby Co, Ky—c1773-1844; Trimble Co, Ky—1844-c1852
Hicks: Spottsylvania Co, Va—1777-1870; Rockbridge Co, Va—1850-1856;
Linn Co, Mo—1856-1863; Santa Barbara Co, Calif—1868-present
Paper—285pp—$6.50--------------------------------------- Vendor #840

551 — THE GENEALOGY OF SIX GERMAN-SWISS FAMILIES: HARTEL, HES-
SEL, IRMINGER, NEUDECK, NOLTING, WEBER by Orin F. Nolting
All surnames in title: Clay Co, Mo—c1800-1972
Plastic—110pp—$9.00------------------------------------- Vendor #846

552 — THE FOLKS by D. Ray Wilson
Green (William): Mercersburg, Pa—1785-1819; Bono, Ind—1819-1846;
Carroll Co, Ill—1846-1850
Diffendaffer/Daffer: Fayette Co, O—1835-1855; Poweshiek Co, Ia—1855-1874
Wilson (Stephen): Morgan Co, O—1809-1891
Roberts (Mark): Tenn—1807-1851; Woodburn, Ia—1851-1872
Carpenter: Westerly, RI—1803-1829; Caro, MI—1870-1888
Hatfield: Cabell Co, WVa—1810-1829; Fayette Co, O—1829-1855;
Shellsburg, Ia—1855-1882; Huron, SD—1882-1892
Cloth—430pp—$15.00-- Vendor #856

553 — THE FISHER SCRAP BOOK 1730-1972 by William L. Jones
Fisher: Pa—   -1754; Anson/Mecklenburg Cos, NC—1756-1777; Washing-
ton Co, Va—1777-1782; Tenn—1808-present
Cloth—353pp—$10.00-- Vendor #861

554 — PATILLO, PATTILLO, PATTULLO & PITTILLO FAMILIES by Crosse
Patillo/Pattillo/Pattullo/Pittillo: Southern states, Canada, Scotland-1716-1972
Cloth—382pp—$19.50-- Vendor #862

555 — THE DESCENDANTS OF JAMES JEFFERSON KEY by Harmon & Key
Key: SC—(b.1826); Decatur Co, Ga—(m.1846); Newton Co, Tex—1850;
Natchitoches Parish, La—1860-1902
[Unfinished mss. A copy was donated to St. Hist. Soc., Wisc.]--Vendor #869

556 — THREE HUNDRED YEARS OF CECILS IN AMERICA 1665-1971 by Koch
Cecil: Md—1665-c1800; NC—1800-1971; Mo—1850-dispersal
Iiams: Md—1600's-1800; NC—1800-1856; Mo—1856-dispersal
Kennedy: NC—1800-present
Russell: Pa—1740-c1800; NC—c1800-1850; Mo—c1850-dispersal
Paper—160pp + index—$7.50-------------------------------- Vendor #874

557 — THE SPARKS QUARTERLY by Sparks Family Association
[Four issues/yr. Approx. 10pp/issue. Back issues available at 75¢ per.
Indexes (4) available at $1.00 each. Complete file of back issues with 4 in-
dexes are $51.00. All of Sparks surname invited to subscribe.]
Subscription: $3.00/yr-------------------------------------- Vendor #921

558 — THE LIFE AND CHARACTER OF THE REV. BENJAMIN COLMAN, D.D.
by Ebenezer Turell (repr. of 1749 ed.)
Colman: Boston, Mass—1673-1747
Cloth—269pp—$12.50--- Vendor #922

559 — THE IRTON-IRETON FAMILY by Judith S. Ireton
Irton/Ireton: Cumberland Co, Eng—1225-1900; Derbyshire Co, Eng—1192-
1900's; NJ—1680-1972; Irelad—1770-1972
Paper—183pp—$10.50-- Vendor #941

560 — HISTORY AND RECORD OF THE CLAN OF RUDOLPH BOLLINGER
FROM SWITZERLAND by Noah Bollinger
Paper—200pp—$10.00-- Vendor #965

561 — HIGHSMITHS IN AMERICA - DESCENDANTS OF DANIEL HIGHSMIGH OF
HALIFAX COUNTY, NORTH CAROLINA WITH APPENDICES OF UNCONNECT-
ED HIGHSMITH FAMILIES by Annette P. Highsmith. Ed. by Chris H.
Bailey Highsmith: NC-1744-date; Ga-1785-date; Ill-1812-date; Tex-1827-date
Cloth-690pp-$25.00--- Vendor #1135

562 — THE RAUCH FAMILY 1763-1973 by Betty Harrington
Rauch: Pa; O; later settlements
Alspack: Pa; O; later settlements
Cloth-225pp-$10.00-------------------------------------- Vendor #1136

563 — A ROACH FAMILY HISTORY: JAMES & MALINDA McCONNELL ROACH
& THEIR DESCENDANTS by Frank W. & Ruth D. Roach Medley
Roach: Pendleton Dist, SC-1793-c1804; West Ky-c1804-1824; Gibson/adj.
Cos, Tenn-c1825-1848; Lamar/Red River Cos, Tex-1848-1975
Cloth-400pp-$25.00------------------------------------- Vendor #1138

564 — THE ADVENTURES OF MY GRANDFATHER [with appendix "PEYTON FAM-
ILY GENEALOGY"] by Col. John Lewis Peyton (repr. of 1867 ed.)
Peyton: Va-1654-1798+; Suffolk, Cambs., Eng-1069-1675; Normandy-1069
Cloth-218pp-$10.00------------------------------------- Vendor #1155

565 — STEPHEN TATOM & HIS DESCENDANTS by J. Green & W. Tatom
Tatom/Tatum: Spottsylvania Co, Va-1721-1771; Granville Dist/Orange Co,
NC-1771-1790; Dickson Co, Tenn-1790-1846; Benton Co, Tenn-1846-1908
Cloth-$17.50/Paper-$12.50-150pp------------------------- Vendor #1157

566 — GENEALOGIES AND FAMILY HISTORIES: A CATALOG OF DEMAND RE-
PRINTS. [Electrostatic (paper) copies of these books are produced on demand
from microform masters. Prices are based on number of pages in the book
and range from $6.00 to $45.00. Cloth binding is also available for an additional $2.50 per volume. Microfilm copies are available on 34mm. positive
silver halide film. Copies of this catalog are available from the publisher for
$1.00 each pre-paid. Quotations on individual books are provided free of
charge.] Books on the following families are listed in the catalog:
      Adams (4), Aiken, Alexander, Alger, Alis, Allen, Al(l)ison, Almy, Al-
tizer, Anderson (2), Andrews (2), Andrus, Anthony, Antrim, Arbuckle, Arch-
er, Armistead, Armstrong, Arnold, Ashton, Aspinwall, Austen, Austin, Bacon,
Baker (2), Baldwin, Balfour, Ball, Banta, Barber, Barbour, Barrett, Barthol-
omew, Baskerville, Bass, Bassett, Bates, Baxter, Beaman, Beaver, Beebe,
Beerbower, Beery, Beeson, Belcher, Bell, Bemis, Benner (2), Berry, Bev-
erly, Bickerton, Biddle, Bierbauer, Bill, Bishop, Blackbird, Blair, Blake (2),
Blakeney, Bliss, Blunt, Blythe, Boarman, Bogardus, Bolton, Bonner, Boone,
Borden, Borneman, Borton(2), Bowie, Bowling, Bowman, Bowser, Boyd,
Boynton (2), Branham, Brashear (2), Brayton, Brereton, Brewer, Brewster,
Brinckerhoff/Brinkerhoff, Briscoe, Broaddus, Brockman, Brooks, Broomhall,
Brown(e) (5), Brownell, Brownlee, Brubacher, Bryan, Bryson, Buck, Buckner,
Buffington, Burgess, Burgner, Burnham, Burr, Burris, Burroughs, Burwell,
Bush (2), Butler (2), Bywaters, Cady, Calkins, Callaway, Calvert, Calkins,
Calvert, Cameron, Campbell, Cantrell, Capron, Carhart, Carothers, Carpen-
ter (4), Carr, Cary (3), Cessna, Chandler, Chappell, Chenault, Chenoweth,
Chipman, Chisholm, Chiswell, Church, Churchill, Claiborne (3), Clapper,
Clark(e) (5), Clay (3), Claypoole, Clendinen, Cleveland, Cochran, Coe, Coffin-
berry, Coggeshall, Cogswell, Cole, Colegrove, Coleman, Collins, Colver,

566
cont.
 — Conant/Connet, Conger, Conway, Corbin, Corley, Corless, Cornell, Countryman, Courtright, Craig (2), Crane, Crawford (3), Creigh, Creighton, Crockett, Crosby, Culber(t)son, Cunningham, Curd, Current, Curtis, Custer, Cutler, Dabney, Danforth, Dann, Dare, Darling, Dashiel, Davidson, Davis (4), Dawes, Day, Dean, DeCou, Deppen, Dewees, Dewey (2), Dial, Dickenson/Dickinson (2), Dickey (2), Dickie, Dixon, Donnell, Donnom, Donnell, Doolittle, Dorsey, Doty, Douglass, Drake, Draper, DuBois, Dudley, Dungar, Dunklin, Dunlap, DuPuy (2), Dutton, Duvall, Dyer, Ebersol(e), Eckles, Eden, Edwards, Egerton, Eggleston, Elkins, Ellis, Elson, Embry, Emerson, Engle, Erwin, Estabrook/E(a)sterbrook, Ettleman, Evans (2), Everard, Eversole/Ebersole, Eves, Ewing, Fay, Fell, Fellows, Fenn, Ferris, Field (3), Finkle, Fishback, Fitch, Fitz-Elys, Fitz-Randolph, Flagg, Flegg, Flippin, Fogg, Fontaine, Forbes/Forbush, Forney (2), Foulke-Hughes, Fox (2), Fraser, Freeman, Freese, French, Frey, Frisel, Frost, Fulkerson, Fulton, Fun(c)k, Gaither, Gardiner (2), Garretson, Garth, Gary, Gault, Gay, Gaylord, Gentry (2), Gernhardt, Gilbert, Gill, Gist, Glanville, Glover, Goodrich/Goodridge (2), Goodwin, Goss, Gould, Grady, Graff, Granger, Grant, Gray, Greenberry, Green(e), Greenlee, Greeve, Gregory, Griffith, Groome, Grove, Grubbs, Gunn, Gunnison, Gwinn, Gwydir, Haggard, Haines, Hale (2), Hall, Halste(a)d, Hamilton, Hammond (2), Hanna (3), Hardaway, Harington, Harlan, Harmon (2), Harris (4), Harrison, Hart (2), Harvey (2), Harwood, Haskins, Has(s)ler, Hastings, Haviland, Hawkins (3), Hayman/ Haymond (2), Hazard, Headington, Hearne, Heathley, Heatwole, Heckendorn, Helles, Hericke, Herr, Herrick, Hersey, Hertzler, Hibbard, Hieronymous, Higby, Hill, Hillegas, Hines, Hitchcock, Hoagland, Hobson, Hoffman, Hoge, Hogg, Holder, Hollister, Hollon, Holmes, Holmsley, Hoogland(t), Hooper, Hope, Hopkins (2), Hornblower, Horne, Hosmer, Hostetter, Houghton, House, Howard, Howell, Howland (2), Hubbell, Huckins, Hull, Hume, Huntington (2), Hurlbu(r)t, Huston, Hutchins, Hůtwole, Hyatt, Ingalls, Ingraham, Irwin, Isham, Jacobs, Jameson, Jarratt, Johnes, Johnston, Jones (3), Jordon, Kagy, Keller, Kelly, Kelsey, Kemmerer, Kemp(e), Kemper, Kennedy, Kennon, Kester (2), Ketel, Ketelhuyn, Kettelle, Keyes (3), Keyser (2), Kidder, Kilgore, Killingsworth, Kincheloe, King (3), Kingston, Kinkead, Kite, Kniss, Kool, Küster, Kuykendall, Kyle, Lac(e)y (2), Ladd, Lamar, Lane, Lantz, Larison, Latham, Lauffer, Leake, Lee (2), Leftwich (2), Leiter, Lemar, Lemon, Lent, Leonard, LeVan, Lewis (6), Lincoln (4), Lindl(e)y, Lindsay/ Lindsey, Linnell, Linville, Littlepage, Littler, Loockermans, Loomis, Lovejoy, Lovelace, Loveland, Lucy, Luttrell, Lynn, McAllister,(2), McCoy, Maccubbin, McCue, McDowel(l), McElroy, MacGregor, Macintosh, Mackey, MacLaughlin, McPherson, Macy, Madison, Maltby, Manley, Mansperger, Mansur, Maris, Marks, Marsh, Marshall, Martin, Mason (2), Massie, Mast, Maulsby, Maury, Mayberry, Mays, Mead(e) (5), Meador, Meadow, Merriam, Merrick, Merritt, Metherd, Metcalf, Miller, Miscampbell, Mobley, Moncrief, Montague, Montgomery (3), Moodie, Moore(s) (3), Morgan (2), Morris, Moulton, Mount, Mullins, Murray, Musick, Nance, Nash(3), Nesbitt, Newsome, Newton, Noble, Oak(e)(s), Ogden, Old(s), Oliphant, Olmste(a)d, Olney, Opdyck(e), Orr (2), Orton, Otis, Overmyer, Overton, Owen (2), Owings, Pabodie/Pa(y)body, Paine, Palmer, Parks, Parshall, Paxton, Payne, Peabody,. Pearce, Pearson (2), Pease (3), Peirson, Pendleton (2), Perkins, Perrin(e), Perry, Pettus, Phelps (2), Pierson (2), Pilcher, Poage, Polk, Pollock, Pomeroy, Porter, Post, Potts, Pound (2), Powell (2), Powers (2), Pratt, Price (2), Prichard, Prickett, Puckett, Pynchon, Quarles (2), Quisenberry, Ramsey, Randall, Randolph, Rankin, Rapaje, Rathbone, Rawson, Raymond, Read(e) (2), Reading, Readle, Reber, Reichner, Remey, Reynolds,

566 — Richards, Richardson, Rickey, Ridg(e)way, Rigby, Rigg, Riggs (2), Ring (2),
cont. Ripley, Rix, Roades, Robeson, Robertson (2), Robinson (2), Rohrer, Root(s),
Rose(n)krans, Ross, Ruchty, Rucker, Rudulph, Run(n)el(l)s, Rush, Russell,
St. Johns, Sackett, Salmans, Sampson, Sanborn, Sanford, Sappington, Sayre,
Schnebele, Scholl, Scott (2), Scruggs, Scudamore, Seagrave, Searcy, Sears,
Seawell, Sea(w)right, Segar, Serven, Sharp (2), Sheldon, Sherman, Shinn,
Shirley, Shotwell, Shouse, Shreve, Sill, Sims, Sizer, Skidmore, Slagle, Slaw-
son, Slayton, Slonaker, Smith (3), Smollett, Smoot, Smute, Snively, Snowden,
Southwick, Southworth/Southards, Spangler, Sparhawk, Spear, Speece, Speed,
Springer, Spurgeon, Stamm, Stark, Steele, Stephens (2), Stevens, Stewart (2),
Stiles, Stillman, Stith, Stockton (3), Stockes, Stone, Stoner, Stratton, Straw,
Street, Stribling, Strickland, Strother, Strycker, Study, Sturm, Sutton, Swain,
Swartwout, Swearingen (2), Swift (2), Swope, Swyft, Sykes, Syng(e) (2), Talia-
ferro, Tallman, Tandy, Tappan, Tarleton, Taylor (2), Terrell/Tyrrell (3),
Thorley, Thornton, Threlkeld, Throckmorton (2), Thurston (3), Tiffany,
Tilley, Tillinghast, Tindall, Toler, Torrey, Tower, Towne, Trabue, Traill,
Troth, Truby, Trumbo, Tucker, Turner (2), Underhill, Utterback, Vale,
VanBibber, Vance, VanCleve, Vanden, Vanderbilt, Vanderpoel, VanDuzee,
VanHorn, Van Kortryk, VanLent, VanNess, Van Nuys/Vannice, Van Sweringen,
Van Voorhees/Van Voorhis, Van Winkle, Varian, Vaux, Vawter, Veeder, Venn,
Vose, Vreeland, Vrooman, Wade, Wadsworth, Waitman, Wakefield, Waldron,
Walker, Wallace, Wander/Wanderer, Wanzer, Ward, Warfield, Wardlaw,
Waring, Warne, Warner, Washburn, Washington, Waters, Watkins (2), Wat-
son, Watt(s) (2), Way, Weaver, Wedgwood, Weightman, Weiser, Welch,
Weld (2), Wells, Welsh, West, Westervelt, Wheatley/Wheatleigh, Whittelsey,
Whittinghill, Widener, Wight (2), Wightman, White, Whit(e)man, Whitney,
Whitten, Whytman, Wilcox (2), Willet, Willey, Williams, Wills, Wiltsee,
Winans, Winship, Winder, Winn, Winship, Winston, Wintermute, Wise, Wise-
man (2), Withers, Witherspoon, Wolfensberger, Wood(s), Woodside, Wright
(2), Wyatt, Wyghtman, Wynn, Yeager, Yeakley, Yerkes, Zug.
Catalog with annotation on each of above books: $1.00. Information on individ-
ual books: No charge.--- Vendor #546

Index to Family Genealogies & Newsletters

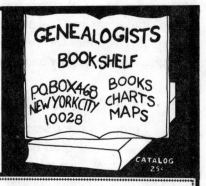

Names and Addresses of Vendors

[1]
Bernard M. Caperton
1113 West Main Street
Charlottesville, VA 22903

[2]
Charles T. Burton
Rt. 2, Box 191
Troutville, VA 24175

[3]
Elizabeth Potts Koleda
P.O. Box 27
Princeville, OR 97754

[4]
Fae Elaine Scott
2890 North Scott Court
Genoa, OH 43430

[5]
Gwen Boyer Bjorkman
4425 - 132nd Avenue, S.E.
Bellevue, WA 98006

[6]
Betsy L. Willis
104 Commonwealth Avenue
Alexandria, VA 22301

[7]
Nancy H. Day
7505 - 203 Vernon Square Drive
Alexandria, VA 22306

[8]
Martha Porter Miller
Box 4894
Washington, DC 20008

[9]
Andrew J. Crawford
312 South Second Street
Fairborn, OH 45324

[10]
Merle Ganier
2108 Grace
Fort Worth, TX 76111

[11]
John R. Boots, Jr.
P.O. Box 1341
Ocala, FL 32670

[12]
Dorothy H. Givens
1258 Flintlock Drive
Daytona Beach, FL 32014

[13]
Virginia Genealogical Society
Jefferson Hotel, Box 1397
Richmond, VA 23211

[14]
Thelma S. McManus, G.R.S.
507 Vine Street
Doniphan, MO 63935

[15]
Jean Stephenson
c/o 2255 Cedar Lane
Vienna, VA 22180

[16]
Grace D. Bales
1829 Cherry Road
Springfield, IL 62704

[17]
Dr. H. Jackson Darst
210 Indian Springs
Williamsburg, VA 23185

[18]
Carol Willsey Bell, C.G.
4649 Yarmouth Lane
Youngstown, OH 44512

[19]
Mrs. Jeff Wade, Jr.
Route 1 - Box 66
Bragg City, MO 63827

[20]
Mrs. James F. Ferneyhough
18360 Sharon Road
Triangle, VA 22172

[21]
Lee Fleming Reese, M.A.
6042 Fenimore Way
San Diego, CA 92120

[22]
Richard Sears
108 Hillside
Berea, KY 40403

[23]
Dr. Richard D. Mudd
1001 Hoyt Avenue
Saginaw, MI 48607

[24]
Bette Miller Radewald
RE: Genealogy, 639 Sandalwood Ct.
Riverside, CA 92507

[25]
Mrs. Robert L. Habelman
Rt. 3 - Box 177A
Black River Falls, WI 54615

[26]
First United Methodist Church
606 Main Street
Pennington, NJ 08534

[27]
Judith Allison Walters
10917 East Riverside Drive
Bothell, WA 98011

[28]
Mrs. Gerald B. McLane
112 Leach Street
Hot Springs, AR 71901

[29]
St. Louis Genealogical Society
1617 S. Brentwood Blvd., Suite 268
St. Louis, MO 63144

[30]
The L.B. Gardiners
1863 Cowden Avenue
Memphis, TN 38104

[31]
Carolyn Edwards Parker
P.O. Box 584
Auburn, AL 36830

[32]
Michael J. Denis
P.O. Box 253
Oakland, ME 04963

[33]
Mrs. Richard C.L. Moncure
"Glen Killie"
Clifton, VA 22024

[34]
Evelyn H. Massie
6214 West Victoria
Kennewick, WA 99336

[35]
June Baldwin Bork
17352 Drey Lane
Huntingon Beach, CA 92647

[36]
Lester & Lela Prewitt
501 Carpenter Street
Fairfield, IA 52556

[37]
Joseph F. & Isobel B. Inman
910 Pine Ridge Road
Richmond, VA 23226

[38]
Thomas P. Hughes, Jr.
4140 Chanwil Avenue
Memphis, TN 38117

[39]
Aber Family Association
1216 Lillie Circle
Salt Lake City, UT 84121

[40]
Bonnie S. Ball
606 Wood Avenue
Big Stone Gap, VA 24219

[41]
Dorothy K. MacDowell
113 Gregg Avenue
Aiken, SC 29801

[42]
Mrs. Ray O. Edwards
1400 LeBaron Avenue, Apt. 1213
Jacksonville, FL 32207

[43]
Joseph H. Vance
310 N. Garfield Street
Lombard, IL 60148

[44]
Loye Eugene Nations
1110 Edgefield Street
Columbia, SC 29201

[45]
Mrs. Ruby Coleman
1002 Highland Drive
Ogallala, NB 69153

[46]
M. Patricia Humphreys
13181 E. Lampson Avenue, Sp. 111
Orange, CA 92668

[47]
Madeline W. Crickard
Rt. # 1 - Box 218
Beverly, WV 26253

[48]
Mrs. Grady Ross
2138 Sherwood Avenue
Charlotte, NC 28207

[49]
Mrs. V. H. Jernigan
Box 366
Manchester, TN 37355

[50]
Quillian Garrison
705 North Willow
Angleton, TX 77515

[51]
Trexler Family and Related Kin
P. O. Box 68
Trexlertown, PA 18087

[52]
Benjamin B. Weisiger III
8 Glenbrooke Circle, East
Richmond, VA 23229

[53]
Bobbie Richardson
Rt. # 1
Bragg City, MO 63827

[54]
Joseph W. Watson
406 Piedmont Avenue
Rocky Mount, NC 27801

[55]
Mrs. Lela C. Adams
Rt. # 5, Box 26-B
Bassett, VA 24055

[56]
Charles H. Bricknell
63 Palmer Road
Plympton, MA 02367

[57]
Edwin R. Deats
20 Tonnele Avenue, Apt. 6B
Jersey City, NJ 07306

[58]
Thomas E. Collins
1111 Army Navy Drive
Arlington, VA 22202

[59]
Rev. Henry Snyder Alleman
Rt. # 1 - Box 265
East Berlin, PA 17316

[60]
Mrs. L. C. (Helen) Andrew
96 Highland Street
Portland, ME 04103

[61]
Delmer R. Hite, Secretary
Jackson County Historical Society
Star Rt. # 1 – Box 34
Statts Mills, WV 25279

[62]
George Shumway Publisher
R.D. 7
York, PA 17402

[63]
Charles Willard Hoskins Warner
P.O. Box 882
Tappahannock, VA 22560

[64]
Ruth R. Seibel
7530 Westmoreland
St. Louis, MO 63105

[65]
Dr. Roy B. Braswell
1723 Dogwood Lane
Pampa, TX 79065

[66]
O. D. Corbridge
3003 Greenwood Avenue
Rockford, IL 61107

[67]
George W. Hinton
5116 Dogwood Drive
Everett, WA 98203

[68]
Charles Allison Weed, Ph.D.
P.O. Box 196
Rio Grande, OH 45674

[69]
Mary E. Studebaker
781 West Drive, Woodruff Place
Indianapolis, IN 46201

[70]
Olive S. Eldred
702 West Locust Street
Princeton, KY 42445

[71]
Esther O. Powell
36 North Highland Avenue
Akron, OH 44303

[72]
The Yankee Genealogist
3602 Maureen Lane
Bowie, MD 20715

[73]
Patricia McConnaughay Gregory
5410 S. Meridian St. – P.O. Box 46227
Indianapolis, IN 46227

[74]
Joseph T. Maddox
Box 157
Irwinton, GA 31042

[75]
Pemiscot County Historical Society
c/o Mrs. Jeff Wade, Jr.
Rt. # 1 – Box 66
Bragg City, MO 63827

[76]
Erma Melton Smith
702 Lakeside Drive
Carlsbad, NM 88220

[77]
Louis Reed
Beulah Hill
Elizabeth, WV 26143

[78]
W. Rutland Cunningham
Box 732
Florence, AL 35630

[79]
R. Glen Nye
9369 Loren Drive
La Mesa, CA 92041

[80]
A. Maxim Coppage
707 Wimbledon Road
Walnut Creek, CA 945 98

[81]
Goldie Satterlee Moffatt
689 Altura Drive
Perris, CA 92370

[82]
E. Viola Robinson Long
2837 1/2 San Gabriel
Austin, TX 78705

[83]
Col. Herbert B. Enderton
16769 Diego Drive
San Diego, CA 92128

[84]
Donald Lewis Osborn
322 Willow Way
Lee's Summit, MO 64063

[85]
John M. Whistler & Beulah W. Whistler
255 Eustis Road, Eustis Heights
Eustis, FL 32726

[86]
Frank C. Roe
1001 North Union Street
Kennett Square, PA 19348

[87]
Col. J. P. Barnes
2346 Outlook Drive
St. Louis, MO 63136

[88]
Daniel Lynn Bolin
211 Pearl Street
Irvington, KY 40146

[89]
Hilda Chance
R.D. 1 - Box 141
Liberty, PA 16930

[90]
Wheelwright Lithographing Company
975 Southwest Temple
Salt Lake City, UT 84101

[91]
John G. Bruce
1801 Braeburn Drive
Salem, VA 24153

[92]
Col. James S. Sibley
2695 Lakeshore Drive
College Park, GA 30337

[93]
Lion's Head Publishing Company
4415 Karen Avenue
Fort Wayne, IN 46805

[94]
Sandra H. Boyd
5768 Firwood Drive
Troy, MI 48084

[95]
John E. Fetzer
590 West Maple Street
Kalamazoo, MI 49001

[96]
Mrs. Ethel Albert
2217 Cypress Street
Kingsport, TN 37664

[97]
George W. Edson
9 East Elizabeth Street
Skaneateles, NY 13152

[98]
James W. Clark
1761 Delwood
Abilene, TX 79603

[99]
Granville W. Hough
1026 North Richman Avenue
Fullerton, CA 92635

[100]
Dorothy Williams Potter
804 Westwood Drive
Tullahoma, TN 37388

[101]
Southwest Virginia Historical Society
c/o Emory L. Hamilton, Secretary
Wise, VA 24293

[102]
Mildred Moody Nutter
Wynhunter - R.R. # 7
Rushville, IN 46173

[103]
Mary Frances Bradshaw Dittrich
Box 529 - Ogden Dunes
Portage, IN 46368

[104]
Lewis Bailey
5454 Wisconsin Avenue, Suite 1050
Chevy Chase, MD 20015

[105]
Mrs. Howard W. Woodruff
1824 South Harvard
Independence, MO 64052

[106]
Missouri Pioneers
c/o Mrs. Howard W. Woodruff
1824 South Harvard
Independence, MO 64052

[107]
Bernice C. Shackelton
1016 West Euclid
Pittsburg, KS 66762

[108]
Mrs. Taney Brazeal, Editor
Northampton County Cousins
Rt. # 2 - Box 50
Fairhope, AL 36532

[109]
Mr. & Mrs. Richard T. Williams
P.O. Box 307
Danboro, PA 18916

[110]
Mrs. Betsy J. Edgar
Box 86
Hillsboro, WV 24946

[111]
OWENS & TANCO
1307 South Davis Drive
Arlington, TX 76013

[112]
Virginia Historical Society
P.O. Box 7311
Richmond, VA 23221

[113]
Darla M. Jones
674 North Clifford Avenue
Rialto, CA 92376

[114]
Nancy Gaillard Chadwick, G.R.S.
6336 Burgundy Road South
Jacksonville, FL 32210

[115]
Mrs. Jack W. Ehrig
Rt. # 1 - Box 191
Richland, WA 99352

[116]
Clarita H. Morgan
Rt. # 2 - Box 195
Radford, VA 24141

[117]
Kenneth Rutherford
P.O. Box 85
Lexington, MO 64067

[118]
Constance L. Crowe
300 North Rampart Street - Space 2&
Orange, CA 92668

[119]
Margaret J. Watson
906 Calhoun Avenue
Greenwood, SC 29646

[120]
Lucile S. Stowell
4817 91st Avenue, S.E.
Mercer Island, WA 98040

[121]
Mrs. Kent J. Davis
6311 Joyce Drive
Camp Springs, MD 20031

[122]
Shirley Linder Rad
2904 Rebel Drive
Midland, TX 79701

[123]
Virginia Book Company
Berryville, VA 22611

[124]
Anita Pendergrass
Box 52
Keokee, VA 24265

[125]
Bruce B. Cannady
824 Southeast 205th
Gresham, OR 97030

[126]
The University Press of Kentucky
Lexington, KY 40506

[127]
The Mary Ball Memorial Museum
& Library, Inc.
P.O. Box 97
Lancaster, VA 22503

[128]
Virginia W. Alexander
903 Myers Avenue
Columbia, TN 38401

[129]
Maude A. McFadin
The Hillcrest - Apt. 2B
115 South Rutan Street
Wichita, KS 67218

[130]
Genealogical Publishing Company, Inc.
521-523 St. Paul Place
Baltimore, MD 21202

[131]
James H. Nash
P.O. Box 391
Somerville, TN 38068

[132]
Mrs. William L. Rhoades
270 South Harrison Street
East Orange, NJ 07018

[133]
Hale House
Box 181
Wynnewood, PA 19096

[134]
William H. Wallace
3237 Third Street
Oceanside, NY 11572

[135]
George B. Wilson
3212 Guilford Avenue
Baltimore, MD 21218

[136]
Mrs. Ruby Markland
933 S. Wolcott
Casper, WY 82601

[137]
Helen B. Anthony
P.O. Box 3855
Dallas, TX 75208

[138]
Pat Isabel Brown
2013 Park Street, S.E.
Decatur, AL 35601

[139]
Elnora Stanley Flaherty
2219 Granada
Irving, TX 75060

[140]
James R. Crocker
8781 Raejean Avenue
San Diego, CA 92123

[141]
Irvin D. Hess
500 East County Club Drive, Apt. 15
Yuma, AZ 85364

[142]
Lucie Clift Price
2527 Harris Boulevard
Austin, TX 78703

[143]
Jewel Young
2003 North O'Connor
Irving, TX 75061

[144]
J. B. Witherspoon
P.O. Box 257
Weatherford, TX 76086

[145]
Mildred White Steltzner
4037 Tanglewood Trail
Chesapeake, VA 23325

[146]
Jesse N. Smith Family Association
2465 North 820 East
Provo, UT 84601

[147]
American Jewish Archives
Hebrew Union College
Cincinnati, OH 45220

[148]
Theodore A. Fuller
12 Ridgeway
Sylva, NC 28779

[149]
Vaneta T. Horlacher
639 Maxwelton Court
Lexington, KY 40508

[150]
L. J. Horlacher
639 Maxwelton Court
Lexington, KY 40508

[151]
F. E. Castleberry
P.O.. Box 651
Washington, DC 20044

[152]
V. Joy McCall Kay
303 Wheatland Avenue
Logansport, IN 46947

[153]
Aline Hyder Hardwick
1201 Indian Hills Drive
Bristol, TN 37620

[154]
Col. Leroy D. Lillie
808 Douglas Avenue
Ames, IA 50010

[155]
Frank Nellis Parshall
1500 Pierre Street
Manhattan, KS 66502

[156]
Sydney Mike Gardner
1604 East Turin Avenue
Anaheim, CA 92805

[157]
Nettie Gove Nicholson
156 Beacon Lane
Jupiter, FL 33458

[158]
Sharon Lass Field
5005 Greybull Avenue
Cheyenne, WY 82001

[159]
Johnson Historical Publications
2409 Gaboury Lane, NE
Huntsville, AL 35811

[160]
Mrs. William J. Doliante
380 Sheffield Drive - Montecito
Santa Barbara, CA 93108

[161]
Prince George's County Genealogical Soc.
P.O. Box 819C
Bowie, MD 20715

[162]
June C. Godley
33 Kingwood Drive
Little Falls, NJ 07424

[163]
Sara M. Nash
Rt. # 1 - Box 330
Fountain Inn, SC 29644

[164]
Phyllis M. Heiss
1511 Southwest 65th Terrace
Boca Raton, FL 33432

[165]
Summit Publications
P.O. Box 222
Munroe Falls, OH 44262

[166]
Paul R. Austin
2327 West 18th Street
Wilmington, DE 19806

[167]
Mrs. Charles W. Durrett
403 North Pawnee Drive
Springfield, TN 37172

[168]
Olive Lewis Kolb
3016 Covington Street
West Lafayette, IN 47906

[169]
The Devereux Enterprise
222 Blake Road
Hamden, CT 06517

[170]
Mrs. Wright W. Frost
730 Cherokee Boulevard
Knoxville, TN 37919

[171]
Fillmore Norfleet
2012 Minor Road
Charlottesville, VA 22903

[172]
A. James Aldrich
273 Windsor Drive N.E.
Cedar Rapids, IA 52402

[173]
Lorand V. Johnson, M.D.
17600 Parkland Drive
Shaker Heights, OH 44120

[174]
Patricia Givens Johnson
6905 Westchester Drive
Camp Springs, MD 20031

[175]
Virginia S. Wood, C.G.
230 Payson Road
Belmont, MA 02178

[176]
Georgia E. Morgan
714 South Hillward Avenue
West Covina, CA 91791

[177]
Pomona Valley Genealogical Society
c/o Georgia E. Morgan, President
714 South Hillward Avenue
West Covina, CA 91791

[178]
George Ely Russell, C.G.
3800 Enterprise Road
Mitchellville, MD 20716

[179]
Dr. Wallace Ludden
113 East Pine Street
Rome, NY 13440

[180]
Faith M. Kline
163 Burr Oak Street
Spring Arbor, MI 49283

[181]
Ruth L. Froeberg
364 Park Terrace S.E.
Cedar Rapids, IA 52403

[182]
Harriett A. Chilton
3108 Annandale Road
Falls Church, VA 22042

[183]
Prudence Groff Michael
64472 U.S. 31, No. 1
Lakeville, IN 46536

[184]
Bonnie Neeley
318 North Water Street
Chesterfield, IN 46017

[185]
Montgomery Publishing Company
P.O. Box 5504
Knoxville, TN 37918

[186]
Vashti Jacob
2400 McCutcheon Avenue
Shreveport, LA 71108

[187]
Edward S. Key
8402 Meadowview
Houston, TX 77037

[188]
Mrs. William J. Stratton
79 Sommers Lane
Staten Island, NY 10314

[189]
Accredited Researchers
254 East 1300 North
Bountiful, UT 84010

[190]
The Tennessee Genealogical Society
P.O. Box 12124
Memphis, TN 38112

[191]
Genealogical Forum of Portland
Rm. 812, Neighbors of Woodcraft Bldg.
1410 Southwest Morrison
Portland, OR 97205

[192]
Bland Books
401 Northwest 10th Street
Fairfield, IL 62837

[193]
Mrs. G. Harold Martin
1611 Southeast Second Street
Fort Lauderdale, FL 33301

[194]
Tupper Family Association, Inc.
375 Hale Street
Beverly, MA 01915

[195]
Mary Elizabeth Sanders
P.O. Box 1864
Baton Rouge, LA 70821

[196]
Ruth Marcum Lind
704 College Avenue
Dinuba, CA 93618

[197]
Margaret Taylor Macdonald
308 Laurel Hill Road
Chapel Hill, NC 27514

[198]
Herbert W. Merrill, Jr.
9 Broadway Place
Normal, IL 61761

[199]
Alice Granbery Walter
116 B Pinewood Road
Virginia Beach, VA 23451

[200]
James F. Morgan
P.O. Box 771
Pinellas Park, FL 33565

[201]
Mrs. H. R. Gentry
3311 Clearview
Austin, TX 78703

[202]
Mrs. Theodore Murphy
1837 Fendall Avenue
Charlottesville, VA 22903

[203]
Mrs. L. F. Brown
3306 Huron
Kalazazoo, MI 49007

[204]
LeRoy F. Shambach
R.F.D. # 2
Middleburg, PA 17842

[205]
Jean Herron Smith
301 South School Street
Fairhope, AL 36532

[206]
Frank E. Toon
130 Spring Road
Nevada City, CA 95959

[207]
The McClure Press
White Marsh, VA 23183

[208]
Iowa Genealogical Society
P.O. Box 3815
Des Moines, IA 50322

[209]
Iowa Genealogical Society
Attn: Mrs. Ronald R. Woodin
P.O. Box 3815
Des Moines, IA 50322

[210]
Kalamazoo Valley Genealogical Society
c/o A. H. Kerr, Publications Comm.
3628 Market Street
Kalamazoo, MI 49001

[211]
Mrs. Mary S. Bowman
Edgewater Pines #119
10399 - 67th Avenue North
Seminole, FL 33542

[212]
Raymond B. Clark, Jr.
Box 352
St. Michaels, MD 21663

[213]
Mrs. Robert M. Jeter
308 Fraser Drive
Beaufort, SC 29902

[214]
Ohio Genealogical Society, ORPF
P.O. Box 2625
Mansfield, OH 44906

[215]
Lester W. Hansen
6345 Burlington Avenue North
St. Petersburg, FL 33710

[216]
Dr. Merle C. Nutt, P.E.
2119 West Edgemont Avenue
Phoenix, AZ 85009

[217]
Eva Lee McDuffie
1107 Auburn Avenue
Monroe, LA 71201

[218]
Morris Genealogical Library
228 Elberon Avenue
Allenhurst, NJ 07711

[219]
Robert H. Peterson
2828 Stonehill Drive
Altadena, CA 91001

[220]
Barbara Faircloth Korich
8511 Yorkshire Lane
Manassas, VA 22110

[221]
Winifred M. McLachlan
2609 Keddington Lane
Salt Lake City, UT 84117

[222]
Tri-City Genealogical Society
Rt. # 1 - Box 191
Richland, WA 99352

[223]
Avery E. Kolb
6417 Julian Street
Springfield, Va 22150

[224]
Joy Reisinger
1020 Central Avenue
Sparta, WI 54656

[225]
John T. Bledsoe
7101 Hillwood Road
Little Rock, AR 72207

[226]
Virginia Knowles Hufbauer
1001 Avenida Amantea
La Jolla, CA 92037

[227]
Betty L. Pennington
6059 Emery Street
Riverside, CA 92509

[228]
Charmaine Burdell Veronda
P.O. Box 505
Petaluma, CA 94952

[229]
Mrs. William B. Wingo
5916 Powhatan Avenue
Norfolk, VA 23508

[230]
N. Pierce Eichelberger
Quinby, VA 23423

[231]
Clarence C. Fuller
70 Granite Street
Foxboro, MA 02035

[232]
Virginia K. Whitney
502 Orchard Street
Aztec, NM 87410

[233]
Gale Research Company
Book Tower
Detroit, MI 48226

[234]
Rev. Donald J. Hebert
P.O. Box 31
Eunice, LA 70535

[235]
Gertrude L. Soderberg
1954 Columbia Road, N.W. - Apt. 710
Washington, DC 20009

[236]
Elva Wilson Nyren
Henderson, IA 51541

[237]
Kendall Laughlin
Apt. 6, Bldg. E, Oaklawn Villa Apts.
Manor Drive
Hot Springs, AR 71901

[238]
Ann Virginia Parker
Ghent, KY 41045

[239]
William Markham Morton
4700 Northwest Barnes Road
Portland, OR 97210

[240]
Bette Dickson Casteel
Star Rt. - Box 192 C
Alameda, NM 87114

[241]
Gloria D. Chaston
1348 North 380 West
Provo, UT 84601

[242]
Arden H. Brame, Jr. II
1690 N. Altadena Drive
Altadena, CA 91001

[243]
East Tennessee Historical Society
Lawson McGhee Library
500 West Church Avenue
Knoxville, TN 37902

[244]
Virginia State Library
11th and Capitol Streets
Richmond, VA 23219

[245]
Kathleen Smith
17 Second Street
Swanton, VT 05488

[246]
Loyce Haynie Rossman
Box 146
Fredericksburg, TX 78624

[247]
Jay B. Wright
418 Buffington Road
DeWitt, NY 13224

[248]
William Eldridge
832 Hillside
Liberty, MO 64068

[249]
Daniel B. Lloyd
5010 Rockmere Court
Bethesda, MD 20016

[250]
Mary H. Stancliff
12235 Sharpview
Houston, TX 77072

[251]
Louise Donnelly
8360 Forrester Boulevard
Springfield, VA 22152

[252]
June B. Barekman
3302 West Diversey
Chicago, IL 60647

[253]
John L. Cobb
11913 Hamlen Avenue
Cleveland, OH 44120

[254]
Virginia Hicks
Rt. # 2 - Box 207
Corning, CA 96021

[255]
Ruth Lincoln Kaye
708 Braxton Place
Alexandria, VA 22301

[256]
Dalby Associates, Inc.
P.O. Box 66
Hazel Crest, IL 60429

[257]
Verona M. Marble
201 East Maple Avenue
Newark, NY 14513

[258]
Judith A. Cloninger
Rt. # 2
Ozark, MO 65721

[259]
Georgia Cook George
13371 Danbury Lane 136G
Seal Beach, CA 90740

[260]
Clara H. Lanier
P.O. Box 732
Luray, VA 22835

[261]
Order from any of below
Robert Lumpkin Ass'n.
Elmer E. Lumpkin
Phillipsburg, KS 67661

or

Mrs. Ray Lumpkin
Modoc, IN 47358

or

Ira W. Hepperly
1100 Industrial Avenue, Sp. I-55
Chula Vista, CA 92011

[262]
Order from any of below
Mrs. J. G. Pearson
61 Jade Avenue
Walla Walla, WA 99362

or

Richard D. Hepperly
615 West 9th
Concordia, KS 66901

or

Ira W. Hepperly
1100 Industrial Avenue, Sp. I-55
Chula Vista, CA 92011

[263]
Wilma Dunlap
6380 Devonshire Avenue
St. Louis, MO 63109

[264]
Decatur Genealogical Society
P.O. Box 2068
Decatur, IL 62526

[265]
Willard Heiss
4828 North Illinois
Indianapolis, IN 46208

[266]
State of Maryland - Hall of Records
P.O. Box 828
Annapolis, MD 21404

[267]
Hester Garrett
1619 Clifton Street
Lansing, MI 48910

[268]
Mary B. Kegley
P.O. Box 1093
Dublin, VA 24084

[269]
Gradeless Research
1721 Edgewood Avenue
Racine, WI 53404

[270]
Mort Newsletter
c/o Donald E. Gradeless
1721 Edgewood Avenue
Racine, WI 53404

[271]
Frances R. Nelson
4000 Pierce Street - Space #90
Riverside, CA 92505

[272]
Bonnie J. Neeley
101 Holly Acres Mobile Court
Woodbridge, VA 22191

[273]
Victor Paul Meador
12402 East 33rd Street
Independence, MO 64055

[274]
Judge Noble K. Littell
5912 - 5th Avenue South
St. Petersburg, FL 33707

[275]
Raymond F. Morin
1908 Cambridge Road
Berkley, MI 48072

[276]
Sam McDowell
Rt. # 1
Richland, IN 47634

[277]
Nicholas Russell Murray
306 South Oak Street
Hammond, LA 70401

[278]
The Havilah Press
807 Clearwater Drive
Richardson, TX 75080

[279]
Edith Louise Wood
221 South Madison Avenue
Middletown, KY 40243

[280]
Richard Porter Adair
Box 390
Dobbs Ferry, NY 10522

[281]
Iva C. Yarlick
2404 North Kensington Street
Arlington, VA 22205

[282]
Barbara J. Brown
6583 South Downing Street
Littleton, CO 80121

[283]
The Demarest Family Association
188 Euclid Avenue
Hackensack, NJ 07601

[284]
H. Eugene McInturff
Box 1111
Front Royal, VA 22630

[285]
Blanche E. A. Lawless
410 North Capitol Avenue
Mt. Sterling, IL 62353

[286]
Mrs. Charles E. Hudson
787 North Houston Boulevard
San Benito, TX 78586

[287]
Cherokee Publishing Company
P.O. Box 1081
Covington, GA 30209

[288]
Indiana Historical Society
140 North Senate Avenue
Indianapolis, IN 46204

[289]
Netti Schreiner-Yantis
6818 Lois Drive
Springfield, VA 22150

[290]
Edgar Gray Publications
P.O. Box 181
Kalamazoo, MI 49005

[291]
Richard P. Owsley
Box 180
Salem, OH 44460

[292]
Estep Family News
Rt. # 3 - Box 103
Louisa, KY 41230

[293]
Betty Harvey Williams
410 Eighth Street Terrace
Warrensburg, MO 64093

[294]
Stephenie H. Tally-Frost
3909 Live Oak
Corpus Christi, TX 78408

[295]
Helen Vandenbark
515 McConnell Avenue
Zanesville, OH 43701

[296]
Joel P. Shedd
3705 North Woodstock Street
Arlington, VA 22207

[297]
American Library Association
50 East Huron Street
Chicago, IL 60611

[298]
Hoenstine Book Mart
P.O. Box 208
Hollidaysburg, PA 16648

[299]
Dr. Alice Catt Armstrong
1331 Cordell Place
Los Angeles, CA 90069

[300]
National Genealogical Society
1921 Sunderland Place, N.W.
Washington, DC 20036

[301]
Sylvia Fitts Getchell
51 North Main Street
Newmarket, NH 03857

[302]
Mrs. Verle H. Parrish
Rt. # 2 - Sebree Road
Stamping Ground, KY 40379

[303]
Hoosier Heritage Press, Inc.
520 North Campbell Street
Indianapolis, IN 46219

[304]
Western Heraldry Organization
P.O. Box 19281
Denver, CO 80219

[305]
Sharon Chadwell Phillips
4455 Palos Verdes Drive N.
Rolling Hill's Estates, CA 90274

[306]
Mrs. Edward Nevill McAllister
10622 South Evers Park Drive
Houston, TX 77024

[307]
Howard Donald Criswell, Ph.D.
5711 Nebraska Avenue, N.W.
Washington, DC 20015

[308]
Edna M. Shannonhouse
402 North Road Street
Elizabeth, NC 27909

[309]
Walter J. Burnham
315 Castlegate Road
Pittsburgh, PA 15221

[310]
Pauline S. Brannan
1 East Ring Factory Road
Bel Air, MD 21014

[311]
Helen L. Hall
Rt. # 1
Hutchinson, KS 67501

[312]
Ted O. Brooke
79 Wagonwheel Court, N.E.
Marietta, GA 30062

[313]
Joan Bake Brubaker
Rt. #3 - Box 159
West Alexandria, OH 45381

[314]
Hyde History, Inc.
Box 85
Fairfield, NC 27826

[315]
Margaret M. Wagner
2820 - 12th Avenue Southwest
Cedar Rapids, IA 52404

[316]
Lois Young
2310 Whitehall Avenue
Anderson, SC 29621

[317]
Dr. Lawrence T. Slaght
69 Winston Drive
Somerset, NJ 08873

[318]
The Printery
Box 353
Clinton, MO 64735

[319]
ANCESTOR HUNTERS
c/o Mrs. Harold L. Adams, C.G.
R.F.D., Fox Creek Road
Victor, ID 83455

[320]
Mrs. S. F. Webster
206 West Hunter Street
Madison, NC 27025

[321]
SASCO ASSOCIATES, Publishers
P.O. Box 335
Southport, CT 06490

[322]
Augusta County Historical Society
Box 686
Staunton, VA 24401

[323]
Mrs. C. B. Deaver
Box 491
Lone Star, TX 75668

[324]
Mrs. Leister E. Presley
1708 West Center
Searchy, AR 72143

[325]
Charles Morrison
1117 Moler Avenue
Hagerstown, MD 21740

[326]
V. H. Huey
1750 Mayfair Drive
Birmingham, AL 35209

[327]
Hugh R. Carlon
11 McGregor Way
Bel Air, MD 21014

[328]
Wilkes Genealogical Society
P.O. Box 1629
North Wilkesboro, NC 28659

[329]
Velma Roades Trant
911 Robert Street
El Campo, TX 77437

[330]
Mrs. Raymond P. Swofford
2010 33rd Street
Lubbock, TX 79411

[331]
Wayne County Genealogical Section
c/o Mrs. Paul Liggett
722 Quinby Avenue
Wooster, OH 44691

[332]
Helen F. Snow, C.G.
148 Murgertown Road
Madison, CT 06443

[333]
Hattie E. W. Heninger
Box 441, Lethbridge
Alberta, Canada T1J 3Z1

[334]
R. H. McMillan, Jr.
417 North Park Avenue
Tifton, GA 31794

[335]
Carl W. Fischer
214-57 33rd Road
Bayside, NY 11361

[336]
Marjorie Churchill
7138 Sandy Mountain Road
Scottsdale, AZ 85253

[337]
Gertrude Nash Locke
15 B Sagamore Way
Waltham, MA 02154

[338]
Hungate Family Historical Society
522 Professional Building
Kansas City, MO 64113

[339]
E. J. Ladd
Box 29
Ft. Payne, AL 35967

[340]
Lenn Alan Bergsten
19 Woodside Drive
Topsfield, MA 01983

[341]
Mildred Hawkins
Hickory Heights, Rt. #3, Box 175B
Bowling Green, KY 42101

[342]
Mildred A. McDonnell
19100 SW 354 Street
Homestead, FL 33030

[343]
Louis M. Hopping
18165 Jamestown Circle
Northville, MI 48167

[344]
Shenandoah District Office
Church of the Brethern
1029 South High Street
Harrisonburg, VA 22801

[345]
C. E. (Cameron) Riefschnider
4816 Reith Road
Kent, WA 98031

[346]
Macys of Ellinwood
606 North Main Street
Ellinwood, KS 67526

[347]
John Niles Lusk
1008 Goode Drive
Killeen, TX 76541

[348]
Clifford L. Allen
7957 Hathon
Detroit, MI 48213

[349]
John J. Tyne
14 Siver Street
Sidney, NY 13838

[350]
Gretchen E. Engel
223-B Heritage Village
Southbury, CT 06488

[351]
John W. Haines
134 Apache Trail
Medford Lakes, NJ 08055

[352]
Dr. Paul L. Atchley
2311 Magnolia Avenue
Knoxville, TN 37917

[353]
Alsa F. Gavin
Box 452
Southport, NC 28461

[354]
Calvin E. Sutherd
2709 N.W. 52nd Court
Fort Lauderdale, FL 33309

[355]
Roberta Liles Zachary
635 Sycamore Avenue
Shafter, CA 93263

[356]
Justin E. Wilder
1322 East Douglas Street
Goshen, IN 46526

[357]
Olney E. Kehn
1006 East Lawn Drive
Teaneck, NJ 07666

[358]
M. Juliette Magee
c/o Advance-Yeoman
Wickliffe, KY 42087

[359]
Thomas Tracks
c/o Mrs. Faye Davis
6060 Humble Street
Riverside, CA 92509

[360]
Donald A. Lapham
Box 361
Wolfeboro, NH 03894

[361]
Elwood Bruce Backensto
37 North Girard Street
Woodbury, NJ 08096

[362]
Dr. A. O. Collins
7902 Edgemoor
Houston, TX 77036

[363]
Lester H. Binnie
Rt. # 4
Albion, IN 46701

[364]
Paul B. Taylor
705 Brubaker Drive
Kettering, OH 45429

[365]
Aletha May Rowley
1105 York Street
Denver, CO 80206

[366]
Josie M. Baird, C.A.L.S.
909 East Johnston
Rotan, TX 79546

[367]
Francis L. Wilson
General Delivery
Ellsworth, KS 67439

[368]
J. Orton Buck
301 East 38th Street, 4-A
New York, NY 10016

[369]
Amanda A. Forbes
1209 Magnolia Road
Ednor, MD 20904

[370]
Kathryn Lee Wetmore Stadel
5603 Fox Run Drive, Princeton Meadows
Plainsboro, NJ 08536

[371]
Leonard F. Day
68 Matthews Street
Pontiac, MI 48058

[372]
Robert Freese, Sr.
104 Long Avenue
Framingham, MA 01701

[373]
Pendleton District Historical and
   Recreational Commission
125 East Queen Street, P.O. Box 234
Pendleton, SC 29670

[374]
Earl Davis Smith
406 East Methvin Street
Longview, TX 75601

[375]
Robert Leland Johnson
705 West Eighth Avenue
Denver, CO 80204

[376]
GEN-RE-PUT, Genealogical Research
3624 Guadalupe Road
Ft. Worth, TX 76116

[377]
Ruby J. Fears
P.O. Box 71
Princeton, KY 42445

[378]
J. W. Pafford
P.O. Box 185
Statenville, GA 31648

[379]
Glenn E. Underwood, President
The Underwood Family Organization
763 Crescent Drive, S.W.
Largo, FL 33540

[380]
Stanley E. Perin
3722 South Wigger Street
Marion, IN 46952

[381]
The Historical Society of Fairfax County
P.O. Box 415
Fairfax, VA 22030

[382]
Mary Adelaide McLarty
P.O. Box 249
Lexington, NC 27292

[383]
L'AVANT STUDIOS
Box 1711
Tallahassee, FL 32302

[384]
Louise B. Fowler
6117 Nashville
Lubbock, TX 79413

[385]
Raymond Shepley, Sr.
212 Dyer Road
West Palm Beach, FL 33405

[386]
Galen B. Ogden
387 Hubbard Avenue
Elgin, IL 60120

[387]
Eastchester Historical Society
Box 37
Eastchester, NY 10709

[388]
Jayne K. Sweger
Rt. # 2 - Box 242-A
Nowata, OK 74048

[389]
George William Guirl
1600 East Roger Road, Box 28
Tucson, AZ 85719

[390]
W. Earl Merrill
1916 North Country Club Drive
Mesa, AZ 85201

[391]
Eugene Allen Cordry
P.O. Box 11102
Fort Worth, TX 76109

[392]
Leona Taylor Aiken
509 Green Meadow Drive
Kingsport, TN 37663

[393]
Nancy W. Simpson
Rt. #3 - Box 59
Wilkesboro, NC 28697

[394]
Frances B. Todd
P.O. Box 98
Maple Falls, WA 98266

[395]
ROSE FAMILY BULLETIN
Seymour T. & Christine Rose, Eds.
1474 Montelegre Drive
San Jose, CA 95120

[396]
Mrs. R. P. Dryden
1764 Swallow Drive
El Cajon, CA 92020

[397]
Seventh Day Baptist Historical Society
510 Watchung Avenue, P.O. Box 868
Plainfield, NJ 07061

[398]
Polly Pollock
36 Sunderland Drive
Vandalia, OH 45377

[399]
H. E. Socolofsky
1314 Fremont Street
Manhattan, KS 66502

[400]
Hunter Book Fund
546 Old Academy Road
Fairfield, CT 06430

[401]
Superintendent of Documents
U.S. Government Printing Office
Washington, DC 20402

[402]
Publications Sales Branch (NEPS)
Room G-6
National Archives & Record Service
Washington, DC 20408

[403]
Cashier
National Archives (GSA)
Washington, DC 20408

[404]
Bureau of Census
Washington, DC 20233

[405]
Library Research Associates
Dunderberg Road
Monroe, NY 10950

[406]
Mrs. Samuel M. Hāsell
22 Tradd Street
Charleston, SC 29401

[407]
F. William Cooper
700 Jerusalem Road
Cohasset, MA 02025

[408]
A. H. Clark
P.O. Box 401
Waycross, GA 31501

[409]
Chi-Ga-U Enterprises
P.O. Box 2241
Norman, OK 73069

[410]
Ben L. Cash
211 Montclaire Drive, N.E.
Albuquerque, NM 87108

[411]
Shelby County Historical & Genea-
    logical Society
Box 86
Shelbyville, IL 62565

[412]
Phyllis Gillingham Hansen
Grass Roots Drive - Rt.1
Richland Center, WI 53581

[413]
A. L. McClellan
2711 Oak Street
Shreveport, LA 71104

[414]
Marguerite S. Dorsey
730 Wildcat Canyon Road
Berkeley, CA 94708

[415]
Williard Memorial Library
6 West Emerald Street
Willard, OH 44890

[416]
Tuscarawas County Genealogical Society
Box 141
New Philadelphia, OH 44663

[417]
Betty L. McCay
6702 East 46th Street
Indianapolis, IN 46226

[418]
Fulton County Historical Society
c/o Shirley Willard
Rt. # 1 - Box 130
Rochester, IN 46975

[419]
Hendrick Hudson Chapter NSDAR, Inc.
113 Warren Street
Hudson, NY 12534

[420]
Research & Publication Committee
Foundation for Historic Restoration
P.O. Box 444
Pendleton, SC 29670

[421]
ABSTRACTS OF S.C. WILLS
307 Stono Drive
Charleston, SC 29412

[422]
Olive P. Wetherbee
R.F.D. #2
Pomfret Center, CT 06259

[423]
Carl F. Chuey
214 Wildwood Drive
Youngstown, OH 44512

[424]
Mildred B. Chipman
P.O. Box C
Norwell, MA 02061

[425]
Rev. Canon E. C. Royle
Box 423 - Hudson Heights
Quebec, Canada JOP 1JO

[426]
Robert L. Roussel
107 Dow Avenue
Arlington, MA 02174

[427]
Mary Carter
P.O. Box 1028
Albany, GA 31702

[428]
Central Texas Genealogical Society
Dept. G, Waco-McLennan County Library
1717 Austin Avenue
Waco, TX 76701

[429]
Mrs. E. Voigt & Mrs. E. Coombes
4135 North 47th Drive
Phoenix, AZ 85031

[430]
Virginia Gatch Markham
P.O. Box 573
Baldwin City, KS 66006

[431]
Mildred S. Wright, G.R.S.
140 Briggs
Beaumont, TX 77707

[432]
Grace H. Jarvis, C.G.
4589 Amherst Street
Jacksonville, FL 32205

[433]
Mrs. Fred Young
420 North Bradshaw Street
Denton, TX 76201

[434]
Juanita D. Zachry
502 East North 16th
Abilene, TX 79601

[435]
Gloucester Bicentennial & Histor-
ical Committee
Gloucester, VA 23061

[436]
Finch Families of Dixie
P.O. Box 7192 - North Station
Arlington, VA 22207

[437]
Irving T. Duke
King George, VA 22485

[438]
Florence L. Spicer
2380 Olive Street
Eugene, OR 97405

[439]
Peter E. Randall
Box 68
Hanover, NH 03755

[440]
American Jewish Historical Society
2 Thornton Road
Waltham, MA 02154

[441]
Putnam County Historical Society
c/o Audrey S. Carroll
R.R. #1 - Ottawa Drive
Ottawa, OH 45875

[442]
Robert G. Cowan
1650 Redcliff Street
Los Angeles, CA 90026

[443]
Mrs. J. W. Conley
Rt. #2 - Box 138
Rutherfordton, NC 28139

[444]
Mrs. John Kerr, Jr.
P.O. Box 569
Warrenton, NC 27589

[445]
Yesteryears Magazine
Box 52 - Dixon Road
Aurora, NY 13026

[446]
Dr. Matthew M. Wise
315 Sunset Road
Salem, VA 24153

[447]
Everett T. Dawson
4107 Jefferson Street
Austin, TX 78731

[448]
Benjamin R. McBride
1113 Seabrook Avenue
Cary, NC 27511

[449]
Lola B. Taylor
P.O. Box A
Olney, IL 62450

[450]
Russell Publishing Company
P.O. Box 253
Alcoa, TN 37701

[451]
Mrs. C. W. Beekman
5236 Geer Road
Hughson, CA 95326

[452]
Bedford Town Historian
Bedford Hills, NY 10507

[453]
Vernon P. Gehlbach
307 Third Street
Lincoln, IL 62656

[454]
Ruth B. Mapes
5323 Southwood Road
Little Rock, AR 72205

[455]
Walter W. Lewis (or)
   Eleanor R. Lewis
1675 Wendell Avenue
Schenectady, NY 12308

[456]
James E. Davis
R.R. - Box 53
Seaton, IL 61476

[457]
Sarah Foster Kelley
567 Whispering Hills Drive
Nashville, TN 37211

[458]
John Neilson Furniss
Box 81350
Memphis, TN 38152

[459]
Bettie Carothers
1510 Cranwell Road
Lutherville, MD 21093

[460]
J. Floyd Wine
924 Woodland Avenue
Winchester, VA 22601

[461]
Barbara E. Grether
14022 Margate Street
Van Nuys, CA 91401

[462]
Evelyn H. Cross
1600 Westwood Avenue
Richmond, VA 23227

[463]
Harrodsburg Historical Society
Box 316
Harrodsburg, KY 40330

[464]
Colorado Genealogical Society
P.O. Box 9654
Denver, CO 80209

[465]
Barbara Trueblood Abbott
151 Shore Road
Old Greenwich, CT 06870

[466]
Mrs. James L. Knight
31 Muscogee Avenue, N.W. - Apt. 1
Atlanta, GA 30305

[467]
Jean Allyn Smeltzer
4327 N.E. Glisan Street
Portland, OR 97213

[468]
Cass County Genealogy Society
c/o V. Joy Kay
303 Wheatland Avenue
Logansport, IN 46947

[469]
Graham Historical Society, Inc.
c/o Letha Marie Mowry, Secretary
Graham, MO 64455

[470]
Hampton Dunn
10610 Carrollwood Drive
Tampa, FL 33618

[471]
West-Central Kentucky Family Re-
    search Association
P.O. Box 1465
Owensboro, KY 42301

[472]
Questing Heirs Genealogical Society
4112 Walnut Grove Avenue
Rosemead, CA 91770

[473]
Robert A. Jarboe
1205 Ridgeway Drive
Richardson, TX 75080

[474]
Mrs. Elmer Lund
Genoa, NB 68640

[475]
Leon McCluer
P.O. Box 14
Jacksonville, AL 36265

[476]
The Blassingame Family Archive
P.O. Box 131
Denison, TX 75020

[477]
Laurence K. Wells
Box 694
Kingstree, SC 29556

[478]
Rhode Island Historical Society
52 Power Street
Providence, RI 02906

[479]
A. P. Robbins
801 Chestnut Street - Apt. 610
Clearwater, FL 33516

[480]
K. O. Rawson
49 - 20th Street
Clintonville, WI 54929

[481]
Lois M. Patrie
207 Pawling Avenue
Troy, NY 12180

[482]
Esther L. Heinze Miller
1113 West Maple Street
Independence, KS 67301

[483]
Dr. Jack D. L. Holmes, Editor
Louisiana Collection Series
520 South 22nd Avenue
Birmingham, AL 35205

[484]
Rosemary E. Bachelor
Box 398
Machias, ME 04654

[485]
Dr. Harold J. Dudley
2726 Anderson Drive
Raleigh, NC 27608

[486]
George Trenholm Book
717 Parish Road
Charleston, SC 29407

[487]
Dale C. Kellogg
221 Lexington Avenue
Elyria, OH 44035

[488]
Albert E. Casey, M.D.
2011 Southwood Road
Birmingham, AL 35216

[489]
William Perry Johnson
Box 1770
Raleigh, NC 27602

[490]
Murle R. Seitz
214 West Van Buren Street
Janesville, WI 53545

[491]
Leon E. Lowry
716 North 8th
Kansas City, KS 66101

[492]
National Society of the Descendants
    of John & Elizabeth Hutchins Curtiss
Richmond H. Curtiss, Secretary
Joshua Point - Leetes Island
Guilford, CT 06437

[493]
P. A. Casey
1945 Columbine Street
Baton Rouge, LA 70808

[494]
Mrs. L. E. Shelton
2616 Poplar Street
Montgomery, AL 36107

[495]
Ore H. Vacketta
Box 3
Westville, IL 61883

[496]
John F. Blair, Publisher
1406 Plaza Drive
Winston-Salem, NC 27103

[497]
HOUSE OF YORK
1323 Wylie Way - Dept. C
San Jose, CA 95130

[498]
Hetty S. Sutherland
Sunset Hill
Clintwood, VA 24228

[499]
Richard Glenn Huffman
P.O. Box 221
Whitney, PA 15693

[500]
John Frederick Dorman
2022 Columbia Road, N.W.
Washington, DC 20009

[501]
Sumner A. Davis
367 Pinehurst Drive
Talladega, AL 35160

[502]
Marian M. Frye
R.F.D. #3 - Box 168
Elkton, VA 22827

[503]
Ann Evans Alley
Rt. #1 - Box 76
Adams, TN 37010

[504]
Texas State Historical Maps
P.O. Drawer 3885
San Angelo, TX 76901

[505]
Hammond Historical Society
260 - 165th Street
Hammond, IN 46324

[506]
Maryland Historical Society
201 West Monument Street
Baltimore, MD 21201

[507]
Arthur C. M. Kelly
Box 79A - R.D. 1
Rhinebeck, NY 12572

[508]
Mrs. L. G. Walker
536 Arlington Place
Chicago, IL 60614

[509]
Mary Elizabeth Bedwell
403 Progress Street, N.E., Apt. 1
Blacksburg, VA 24060

[510]
Manly Yeilding
927 Brown Marx Building
Birmingham, AL 35203

[511]
Mrs. Lester E. Taylor
2706 West Road
Mobile, AL 36609

[512]
Roy V. Sherman
840 Warren Way
Palo Alto, CA 94303

[513]
Judge Frank Massey
c/o Civil Courts Building
Fort Worth, TX 76102

[514]
The Pemberton Press
Box 2085
Austin, TX 78767

[515]
Alvaretta K. Register
307-A College Blvd.
Statesboro, GA 30458

[516]
Rose C. Tillinghast
715 Randolph Street, N.E.
Washington, DC 20017

[517]
Virginia Horner Hinds
334 Robin Road
Waverly, OH 45690

[518]
Mrs. Joe T. Clark
602 LaFayette
Ringgold, GA 30736

[519]
Thomas H. Davenport
11 West Street
Westboro, MA 01581

[520]
Edna Anne Hannibal
650 Coleridge Avenue
Palo Alto, CA 94301

[521]
Joseph Earle Birnie
Trust Dept., National Bank of Georgia
P.O. Box 1234
Atlanta, GA 30301

[522]
Linda L. Layne
747 North Huntington Street
San Fernando, CA 91340

[523]
McClure Press
P.O. Box 936
Verona, VA 24482

[524]
Russell Farnsworth, Publisher
35 Alfred Terrace
Burlington, VT 05401

[525]
Mary N. Speakman
706 Denver Street
Wichita Falls, TX 76301

[526]
Illiana Genealogical & Historical Society
Box 207
Danville, IL 61832

[527]
Warren L. Marsh
5 Windsor Court
Old Saybrook, CT 06475

[528]
Bedford County Historical Society
Shelbyville, TN 37160

[529]
Doris G. Farrow
Rt. # 1 -
Ripley, MS 38663

[530]
Mrs. Tania S. Ham
1073 Murray Drive
Jacksonville, FL 32205

[531]
Don Simmons
1397 Johnson Boulevard
Murray, KY 42071

[532]
Minnesota Historical Society
Order Department
1500 Mississippi Street
St. Paul, MN 55101

[533]
Bennett L. Smith
2529 Stadium Drive
Fort Worth, TX 76109

[534]
Fred F. Wright
RFD 3 - Box 166
Denton, MD 21629

[535]
L. E. Stowers
8820 State Avenue
Kansas City, KS 66112

[536]
Clinton E. Metz
213 North Long Beach Avenue
Freeport, NY 11520

[537]
ROADMAPS-THRU-HISTORY
P.O. Box 90622
Los Angeles, CA 90009

[538]
THE EVERTON PUBLISHERS, INC.
P.O. Box 368
Logan, UT 84321

[539]
Charles M. Hall
157 North State Street
Salt Lake City, UT 84103

[540]
Patricia Packer Bronson
Hopkins Hall, Box 81
Wye Mills, MD 21679

[541]
Geography & Map Division
Library of Congress
Washington, DC 20540

[542]
Agricultural History Center
University of California
Davis, CA 95616

[543]
Nortex Press
P.O. Box 120
Quanah, TX 79252

[544]
DeKalb County Historical Society
P.O. Box 72
Auburn, IN 46706

[545]
Oliphant Family History
Nancy Hawlick Stein
631 Central Avenue
Wilmette, IL 60091

[546]
University Microfilms
300 North Zeeb Road
Ann Arbor, MI 48106

[547]
Attakapas Historical Association
P.O. Box 107
Martinville, LA 70582

[548]
Mrs. J. L. Dickinson
400 North Royal Avenue
Front Royal, VA 22630

[549]
Elsie B. Kempton
530 St. Andrews Road
Saginaw, MI 48603

[550]
Joida Whitten
5314 Emerson
Dallas, TX 75209

[551]
San Joaquin Genealogical Society
621 East Garner Lane
Stockton, CA 95207

[552]
AREA KEYS
P.O. Box 19465
Denver, CO 80219

[553]
Gordon P. Tierney, C.A.L.S.
1810 Thomas Atkinson Road
Inverness Countryside
Palatine, IL 60067

[554]
James L. Watson
11825 Wakeley Plaza, Apt. 5
Omaha, NE 68154

[555]
George H. S. King, F.A.S.G.
1303 Prince Edward Street
Fredericksburg, VA 22401

[556]
George O. Jaquith, M.D.
Box 511, 116 North Plaza
Brawley, CA 92227

[557]
Margaret Johnson Drake
643 Park Drive
Kenilworth, IL 60043

[558]
Sam F. Brewster
230 East 4075 North
Provo, UT 84601

[559]
Judith Beery Garber
P.O. Box 887
San Francisco, CA 94101

[560]
Kentucky Publishing Committee, DAR
153 Cherokee Park
Lexington, KY 40503

[561]
Lewis Bunker Rohrbaugh
Sea Street
Rockport, ME 04856

[562]
Allstates Research Company
P.O. Box 25
West Jordan, UT 84084

[563]
Dade County Missouri Historical Society
207 McPherson
Greenfield, MO 65661

[564]
Vermont Historical Society Bookshop
Pavilion Office Building
Montpelier, VT 05602

[565]
The People of the Marsh
819 Franklin Avenue
Las Vegas, NV 89104

[566]
Xerox University Microfilms
300 North Zeeb Road
Ann Arbor, MI 48106

[567]
Alfred E. Fant
3902 Edgerock Drive
Austin, TX 78731

[568]
Wanda Veatch Clark
6060 S.W. Coyote Avenue
Redmond, OR 97756

[569]
N.S. of Col. Dames - Lynchburg
c/o Mrs. J. Duval Lee
3030 Ravenwood Drive
Lynchburg, VA 24503

[570]
Lida Flint Harshman
Box 556
Mineral Ridge, OH 44440

[571]
Lyman County Historical Society
c/o Mrs. Claire Murphy, Secy.
Reliance, SD 57569

[572]
Mesquite Hist. & Gen. Society
P.O. Box 165
Mesquite, TX 75149

[573]
Mrs. William Wood
Box 204 - R.R. # 2
Godfrey, IL 62035

[574]
Banks McLaurin, Jr., Editor
Clan McLaren Society, USA
5843 Royalcrest
Dallas, TX 75230

[575]
Helen Maxine C. Leonard
West Barrick Road
Janesville, IA 50647

[576]
Richardson Dougall
3309 Highland Place, N.W.
Washington, DC 20008

[577]
Madison Historical Society
P.O. Box 17
Madison, CT 06443

[578]
Mary Louise Regan
246 North Plum Grove Road
Palatine, IL 60067

[579]
Genealogical Reference Company
Box 1554
Owensboro, KY 42301

[580]
Polyanthos, Inc.
811 Orleans Street
New Orleans, LA 70116

[581]
Craighead County Historical Society
P.O. Box 1011
Jonesboro, AR 72401

[582]
Dorothy R. Morton
Moscow, TN 38057

[583]
Charles Mathieson Otstot
5124 North 33rd Street
Arlington, VA 22207

[584]
Goochland County Historical Society
Attn: Margaret Henley
Goochland, VA 23063

[585]
Carl O. Estes
111 West 9th Street
Storm Lake, IA 50588

[586]
Fulton County Hist. & Gen. Society
c/o Mr. Charles V. Petrovich
1040 North Main Street
Canton, IL 61520

[587]
Society for German-American Studies
7204 Langerford Drive
Cleveland, OH 44129

[588]
Alvin D. White
R. D. # 1
Hickory, PA 15340

[589]
Mrs. Hardin Davant Hanahan
5100 Kesterwood Road
Knoxville, TN 37918

[590]
Nantucket Historical Association
Box 1016 - Old Town Building
Nantucket, MA 02554

[591]
American Society of Genealogists
c/o Donna R. Hotaling, Agent
2255 Cedar Lane
Vienna, VA 22180

[592]
Jean B. Grube
2834 Ruby Avenue
Fairbanks, AK 99701

[593]
Mrs. L. A. Delp
P.O. Box 353
Monticello, FL 32344

[594]
Arthur W. Farrall
1858 Cahill Drive
East Lansing, MI 48823

[595]
Mid-Michigan Genealogical Society
Dr. Donald J. deZeeuw, Pres.
1965 Bloomfield Drive
Okemos, MI 48864

[596]
Milwaukee Co. Genealogical Soc, Inc.
916 East Lyon Street
Milwaukee, WI 53202

[597]
Pulaski County Library
60 West Third Street
Pulaski, VA 24301

[598]
Mrs. Ferrel C. Speer
1012 Lake George Drive
Hobart, IN 46342

[599]
Historic Lyme Church Association
R.R. # 1 - S.R. #113 E.
Bellevue, OH 44811

[600]
Jamie Ault Grady
4404 Holston Drive
Knoxville, TN 37914

[601]
Cass County Genealogical Society
c/o A. R. Stanley
Rt. 2 - Box 33 C
Diana, TX 75640

[602]
Lyle D. Perrigo
2345 Camas
Richland, WA 99352

[603]
Lee County Genealogical Society of Iowa
P.O. Box 303
Keokuk, IA 52632

[604]
Lynchburg Historical Foundation, Inc.
P.O. Box 3154 - Rivermont Station
Lynchburg, VA 24503

[605]
Linn County Heritage Society, Inc.
P.O. Box 175
Cedar Rapids, IA 52406

[606]
Soule Kindred in America, Inc.
P.O. Box 1146
Duxbury, MA 02332

[607]
Walter R. Gooldy
9430 Vandergriff Road
Indianapolis, IN 46239

[608]
Harold W. Van Treese
9350 Vandergriff Road
Indianapolis, IN 46239

[609]
Melvin R. Matthew
P.O. Box 253
Blue Mound, IL 62513

[610]
Elza B. Cox
P.O. Box 186
Southmont, NC 27351

[611]
Naomi Giles Chadwick
ES: Genealogy
3375 Celeste Drive
Riverside, CA 92507

[612]
Athens Historical Society
c/o Mrs. George O. Marshall, Jr.
402 Riverview Road
Athens, GA 30601

[613]
Wallace E. Shipp
5319 Manning Place, N.W.
Washington, DC 20016

[614]
Ben Gray Lumpkin
Route 3, Box 391
Clarksville, TN 37040

[615]
Margaret D. Falley
1500 Sheridan Road
Wilmette, IL 60091

[616]
National Genealogical Society
1921 Sunderland Place, N.W.
Washington, DC 20036

[617]
Watauga Assoc. of Genealogists
Sherrod Library - Room 301
East Tennessee State Library
Johnson City, TN 37601

[618]
Virginia Easley DeMarce
2508 North Kenilworth Street
Arlington, VA 22207

[619]
San Diego Genealogical Society
Studio #30 - Spanish Village - Balboa Park
San Diego, CA 92101

[620]
Dorothy D. Pruett
916 East Lyon Street
Milwaukee, WI 53202

[621]
Currituck County Historical Society
c/o Roy E. Sawyers, Jr.
P.O. Box 305
Jarvisburg, NC 27947

[622]
Magna Carta Book Company
5502 Magnolia Avenue
Baltimore, MD 21215

[623]
Lorain County Historical Society
331 Fifth Street
Elyria, OH 44035

[624]
Kraus-Thompson Organization, Ltd.
Rt. 100
Millwood, NY 10546

[625]
Burt Franklin
235 East 44th Street
New York, NY 10017

[626]
Binford & Mort, Publishers
2536 S.E. 11th Avenue
Portland, OR 97202

[627]
Asselia S. Lichliter
2122 Massachusetts Avenue, NW
Washington, DC 20008

[628]
Ralph Fraley Martz
Route #8
Frederick, MD 21701

[629]
Arno Press
330 Madison Avenue
New York, NY 10017

[630]
AMS Press, Inc.
56 East 13th Street
New York, NY 10003

[631]
Mrs. Stahle Linn, Jr.
Box 978
Salisbury, NC 28144

[632]
University of Oregon Books
Eugene, OR 97403

[633]
Nancy C. Baird
Route # 1 - Box 89
Delaplane, VA 22025

[634]
George & Opal Birge Pixley
9339 Grove Avenue
Norfolk, VA 23503

[635]
Frontier Press
Box 4149
Memphis, TN 36104

[636]
Books for Libraries
50 Liberty Avenue
Freeport, NY 11520

[637]
Kennikat Press, Inc.
90 South Bayles Avenue
Port Washington, NY 11050

[638]
Broadman Press
127 Ninth Avenue, North
Nashville, TN 37234

[639]
Henry R. Timman
RFD #1 - Medusa Road
Norwalk, OH 44857

[640]
University of Texas Press
Box 7819
Austin, TX 78712

[641]
Ira J. Friedman, Inc.
c/o Kennikat Press Corp.
90 South Bayles Avenue
Port Washington, NY 11050

[642]
Haskell House Publishers, Ltd.
280 Lafayette Street
New York, NY 10012

[643]
Barnes & Noble, Inc.
Division of Harper & Row
Scranton, PA 18512

[644]
Shrewsbury Historical Society
Box 333
Shrewsbury, NJ 07701

[645]
Texas State Historical Association
Richardson Hall 2/306 University Street
Austin, TX 78712

[646]
Society of Ohio Archivists
Bowling Green State University Library
Bowling Green, OH 43402

[647]
Watts Powell, G.R.S.
605 Sixth Street
Vienna, GA 31092

[648]
Vista Royse Allison
Columbia, KY 42728

[649]
Harriet Stryker-Rodda
421 Summit Avenue
South Orange, NJ 07079

[650]
University of North Carolina Press
Chapel Hill, NC 27514

[651]
Bernice C. Richard
2771 Lincoln Avenue
Chicago, IL 60614

[652]
Raymond L. Kringer
16 Quinton Hill Court
St. Louis, MO 63137

[653]
G.P. Stout
1209 Hill Street
Greensboro, NC 27408

[654]
St. George's Episcopal Church
905 Princess Anne Street
Fredericksburg, VA 22401

[655]
Dora B. George
Illinois P.E.O Home
Knoxville, IL 61448

[656]
Mrs. Edward A. Smith
Rt. 1 - Box 191A
Richland, WA 99352

[657]
Charles E. Tuttle
Rutland, VT 05701

[658]
Southern Historical Press
P.O. Box 229
Easley, SC 29640

[659]
Historical Publications Section
N. C. Division of Archives & History
109 East Jones Street
Raleigh, NC 27611

[660]
Commonwealth Press, Inc.
1st & Berkeley Streets
Radford, VA 24141

[661]
Kent State University Press
Kent, OH 44242

[662]
Stephen Greene Press
Box 1000 - Fessenden Road
Brattleboro, VT 05301

[663]
The Reprint Company, Publishers
P.O. Box 5401
Spartanburg, SC 29301

[664]
University of Oklahoma Press
1005 Asp Avenue
Norman, OK 73069

[665]
French Prairie Press
St. Paul, OR 97137

[666]
Mobile Genealogical Society, Inc.
P.O. Box 6224
Mobile, AL 36606

[667]
Harbor Hill Books
P.O. Box 407
Harrison, NY 10528

[667]
Harbor Hill Books
P.O. Box 407
Harrison, NY 10528

[668]
Jenkins Publishing Company
P.O. Box 2085
Austin, TX 78767

[669]
Auerbach Publishers, Inc.
121 North Broad Street
Philadelphia, PA 19107

[670]
William A. Yates
P.O. Box 1687
Rifle, CO 81650

[671]
Texas Christian University Press
Box 30783
Fort Worth, TX 76129

[672]
Banner Press
2305 Harmony Lane
Bluff Park Area
Birmingham, AL 35209

[673]
J. S. Canner & Company
49 - 65 Lansdowne Street
Boston, MA 02215

[674]
Globe Publishers International
2205 Maryland Street
Baytown, TX 77520

[675]
Purdue University Studies
South Campus Courts-D
West Lafayette, IN 47907

[676]
KTAV Publishing House, Inc.
120 East Broadway
New York, NY 10002

[677]
Accelerated Indexing Systems
P.O. Box 1214
Provo, UT 84601

[678]
University of Illinois Press
Urbana, IL 61801

[679]
Katherine W. Ewing
124 West Tyne Drive
Nashville, TN 37205

[680]
Arco Publishing Company, Inc.
219 Park Avenue South
New York, NY 10003

[681]
The Pennsylvania Historical Junto
6303 20th Avenue - Green Meadows
West Hyattaville, MD 20782

[682]
McClung Family Association
c/o Patricia Francis
Route # 2 - Box 174
Attica, KS 67009

[683]
Helen Bullard
Ozone, TN 37842

[684]
John DeGraff, Inc.
PROFESSIONAL BOOKS
Clinton Corners, NY 12514

[685]
Southern Methodist University Press
Dallas, TX 75275

[686]
Bookcraft, Inc.
1186 South Main Street
Salt Lake City, UT 84101

[687]
International Scholarly Book Service, Inc.
Box 4347
Portland, OR 97208

[688]
Miran Publishers
3327 Winthrop Avenue
Fort Worth, TX 76116

[689]
Desert Book Company
P.O. Box 659
Salt Lake City, UT 84110

[690]
University of Wisconsin Press
Box 1379
Madison, WI 53701

[691]
Field Horne
3 Greenwood Lane
Valhalla, NY 10595

[692]
Elizabeth Easley Ross
RFD #1 - Box 403
Clayton, NC 27520

[693]
Hope Farm Press
Strong Road
Cornwallville, NY 12418

[694]
Pergamon Press, Inc., Sales Dept.
Maxwell House - Fairview Park
Elmsford, NY 10523

[695]
John Wiley & Sons, Inc.
c/o Eastern Distribution Center
1 Wiley Drive
Somerset, NJ 08873

[696]
Utah State University Press
Dept. of English & Journalism
Logan, UT 84321

[697]
Edith V. Howard
1905 Valley Glen Road
Topeka, KS 66615

[698]
Oma Dee Phillips
Box 615
Lamesa, TX 79331

[699]
Carmack Waterhouse
108 Orange Lane
Oak Ridge, TN 37830

[700]
Elizabeth Becker Gianelloni
Longwood Plantation
Route 3 - Box 114
Baton Rouge, LA 70808

[701]
Brent Holcomb
Drawer 889
Clinton, SC 29325

[702]
Brigham Young University Press
205 University Press Building
Provo, UT 84602

[703]
Houghton Mifflin Company
2 Park Street
Boston, MA 12107

[704]
Thomas E. Partlow
816 West Spring Street
Lebanon, TN 37087

[705]
Arnold Family Association of the South
6600 Placid Street
Falls Church, VA 22043

[706]
James Logan Morgan
314 Vine Street
Newport, AR 72112

[707]
Rutherford County Historical Society
c/o Dorothy Matheny
1434 Diana Street
Murfreesboro, TN 37130

[708]
Hastings House Publishers, Inc.
10 East 40th Street
New York, NY 10018

[709]
Roanoke Historical Society
P.O. Box 1904
Roanoke, VA 24008

[710]
Ursula Smith Beach
512 Madison Street
Clarksville, TN 37040

[711]
Jolee Love
3900 Woodmont Boulevard
Nashville, TN 37215

[712]
The American Genealogist
1232 - 39th Street
Des Moines, IA 50311

[713]
University Press of Virginia
Box 3608 University Station
Charlottesville, VA 22903

[714]
Lawrence L. Little
1600 Renoir Lane
Creve Coeur, MO 63141

[715]
Berdena E. Koehler
Elmwood, NE 68349

[716]
Mary Freese Warrell
398 National Road
Wheeling, WV 26003

[717]
Shenandoah Publishing House
Strasburg, VA 22657

[718]
Wava Rowe White
P.O. Box 1746
West Palm Beach, FL 33402

[719]
Carol R. Dawson
2112 Third Street
Eau Claire, WI 54701

[720]
Amherst Publishing Company
Amherst, VA 24521

[721]
Jerome S. Ozer Publishers, Inc.
475 Fifth Avenue
New York, NY 10017

[722]
Asher L. Young
Box 56
Bellevue, TN 37021

[723]
Grand Lodge of New Hampshire
P.O. Box 299
Concord, NH 03301

[724]
New Hampshire Publishing Company
1 Market Street
Somersworth, NH 03878

[725]
Dietz Press, Inc.
109 East Cary Street
Richmond, VA 23219

[726]
Stinson House
Rumney, NH 03266

[727]
United Church of Christ in Keene
23 Central Square
Keene, NH 03431

[728]
Courier Printing Company
102 Main Street
Littleton, NH 03561

[729]
New York Public Library
Readex Books
101 Fifth Avenue
New York, NY 10003

[730]
University of Nevada Press
Reno, NV 89507

[731]
John Knox Press
Box 1176
Richmond, VA 23209

[732]
Piedmont Press
Box 3605
Washington, DC 20007

[733]
Eunice Pennington
Pennington Trading Post
Fremont, MO 63941

[734]
Macmillan Company
866 - 3rd Avenue
New York, NY 10022

[735]
The Bethany Press
Beaumont & Pine Blvd. - Box 179
St. Louis, MO 63166

[736]
Associated University Presses, Inc.
Box 421
Cranbury, NJ 08512

[737]
McGill - Queens University Press
1020 Pine Avenue, West
Montreal, Quebec, Canada H3A 1A2

[738]
Augustus M. Kelley, Publisher
305 Allwood Road
Clifton, NJ 07012

[739]
Hunterdon House
38 Swan Street
Lambertville, NJ 08530

[740]
The Institute of Early American History
and Culture
Box 220
Williamsburg, VA 23185

[741]
McGraw-Hill Book Company
1221 Avenue of the Americas
New York, NY 10020

[742]
British Book Centre, Inc.
966 Lexington Avenue
New York, NY 10021

[743]
Barre Publishers
South Street
Barre, MA 01005

[744]
Indiana University Press
Tenth & Morton Streets
Bloomington, IN 47401

[745]
Texian Press
P.O. Box 1684
Waco, TX 76703

[746]
Durham Ward
c/o Bishop James L. Bennett, Jr.
2804 Coventry Road
Durham, NC 27707

[747]
Filter Press
Box 5
Palmer Lake, CO 80133

[748]
Association of Juneau Families
4478 North 26th Street
Milwaukee, WI 53209

[749]
Illinois State Historical Library
Old State Capital
Springfield, IL 62706

[750]
Bismarck - Mandan Hist. & Gen. Soc.
P.O. Box 485 - 218 North 8th St.
Bismarck, ND 58501

[751]
Brethren Press
1451 Dundee Avenue
Elgin, IL 60120

[752]
Heritage House
Rt. 1 - Box 211
Thomson, IL 61285

[753]
Pruett Publishing Company
Box 1560 B
Boulder, CO 80302

[754]
St. Peter's Lutheran Church
Box 325
Shepherdstown, WV 25443

[755]
Rio Grande Press, Inc.
Glorieta, NM 87535

[756]
Rothman Reprints
c/o Fred B. Rothman & Company
57 Leuning Street
South Hackensack, NJ 07606

[757]
South Illinois University Press
Box 3697
Carbondale, IL 62901

[758]
University of Missouri Press
103 Swallow Hall
Columbia, MO 65201

[759]
Nebraska State Historical Society
1500 R Street
Lincoln, NE 68508

[760]
University of Nebraska Press
901 North 17th Street
Lincoln, NE 68508

[761]
Frieda F. Crawford
1615 Rocky Ford Road
Columbus, IN 47201

[762]
Teachers College Press
1234 Amsterdam Avenue
New York, NY 10027

[763]
Southern University Press
130 South 19th Street
Birmingham, AL 35223

[764]
Yale University Press
92 A Yale Station
New Haven, CT 06520

[765]
William H. Sebastian
P.O. Box 362
Catlettsburg, KY 41129

[766]
Donald M. Kinsman
45 Moulton Road
Storrs, CT 06268

[767]
Northeast Missouri State Teachers
   College
Kirksville, MO 63501

[768]
Montezuma Press
P.O. Box 202
Bessemer, AL 35020

[769]
Mrs. Chester C. Nash
102 East Vandercook Drive
Jackson, MI 49203

[770]
Ramfre Press
Southeast Missouri State College
1206 North Henderson
Cape Giradeau, MO 63701

[771]
Loyola University Press
3441 North Ashland Avenue
Chicago, IL 60657

[772]
United Church Press
1505 Race Street
Philadelphia, PA 19102

[773]
Yankee Peddler Book Company
38 Hampton Road - Drawer O
Southampton, NY 11968

[774]
University of Toronto Press
33 East Tupper Street
Buffalo, NY 14203

[775]
Mrs. W. C. Trotter, Jr.
1276 Kirk Circle
Greenville, MS 38701

[776]
Jeffries Abstract & Title Ins. Co., Inc.
Lebanon, MO 65536

[777]
Vic Press
Box 883
Cheyenne, WY 82001

[778]
Parchment Press
P.O. Box 3909
Birmingham, AL 35208

[779]
Century Enterprises
P.O. Box 607
Huntsville, AR 72740

[780]
Walker & Company
720 Fifth Avenue
New York, NY 10019

[781]
Chatham Press, Inc.
15 Wilmot Lane
Riverside, CT 06878

[782]
Mountain Press Publishing Company, Inc.
279-287 West Front Street
Missoula, MT 59801

[783]
Potomac Stake of LDS
P.O. Box 89
Annandale, VA 22003

[784]
Copyright Office
Library of Congress
Washington, DC 20559

[785]
National Society of Daughters of the
American Revolution
1776 "D" Street, N.W.
Washington, DC 20006

[786]
Jim Comstock
West Virginia Hillbilly
Richwood, WV 26261

[787]
Edward P. Cannon
P.O. Box 83
Poplar Bluff, MO 63901

[788]
University of Alabama Press
Drawer 2877
University, AL 35486

[789]
San Francisco Historical Records
1204 Nimitz Drive
Colma, CA 94015

[790]
Transatlantic Arts, Inc.
North Village Green
Levittown, NY 11756

[791]
Mrs. Bonny Bennett
Van Tassel Trust Fund
R.R. # 1 - Pratt Road, Gibsons
British Columbia, Canada VON IVO

[792]
University of Arizona Press
Box 3398
Tucson, AZ 85722

[793]
William K. Hall
33 Westmoreland Place
St. Louis, MO 63108

[794]
A. H. Clark Company
1264 South Central Avenue
Glendale, CA 91204

[795]
J. E. Hill, Contractor
P.O. Drawer 1356
Leesburg, FL 32748

[796]
McClain Printing Company
Parsons, WV 26287

[797]
Sanford C. Gladden
1034 Spruce Street
Boulder, CO 80302

[798]
Chronicle Books
54 Mint Street
San Francisco, CA 94103

[799]
Taplinger Publishing Company, Inc.
200 Park Avenue, South
New York, NY 10003

[800]
Barbara Ferree Barden
98 Sarles Lane
Pleasantville, NY 10570

[801]
Battleground Historical Society of
Monmouth County
P.O. Box 1776
Tennent, NJ 07763

[802]
R & E Research Associates
4843 Mission Street
San Francisco, CA 94112

[803]
University of New Mexico Press
Albuquerque, NM 87131

[804]
Peter Smith, Publisher, Inc.
6 Lexington Avenue
Magnolia, MA 01930

[805]
Margaret Dale Masters
Syracuse, NE 68446

[806]
Mrs. J. Swanton Ivy
924 Rockinwood Drive
Athens, GA 30601

[807]
Larry D. Mart
621 Fairfield Drive
Lima, OH 45805

[808]
Syracuse University Press
1011 East Water Street
Syracuse, NY 13210

[809]
Valley Publishers
1759 Fulton Street
Fresno, CA 93721

[810]
University of Chicago Press
11030 South Langley Avenue
Chicago, IL 60628

[811]
State Historical Society of Wisconsin
Business Office
816 State Street
Madison, WI 53706

[812]
Pequot Press
Old Chester Road
Chester, CT 06412

[813]
Abingdon Press
201 Eighth Avenue, South
Nashville, TN 37202

[814]
Shorey Publications
815 - 3rd Avenue
Seattle, WA 98104

[815]
Fredericksburg Baptist Church
1019 Princess Anne Street
Fredericksburg, VA 22401

[816]
Scholarly Resources, Inc.
1508 Pennsylvania Avenue
Wilmington, DE 19806

[817]
Rowman & Littlefield
81 Adams Drive
Totowa, NJ 07512

[818]
Unigraphic, Inc.
1401 North Fares Avenue
Evansville, IN 47711

[819]
University of Florida Press
15 Northwest 15th Street
Gainesville, FL 32601

[820]
Loretta E. Burns
B & R Publications
1804 Zapp Lane
Pasadena, TX 77502

[821]
Kentucky Historical Society
Box H
Frankfort, KY 40601

[822]
Pitman Publishing Corporation
6 East 43rd Street
New York, NY 10017

[823]
The Shoe String Press, Inc.
995 Sherman Avenue
Hamden, CT 06514

[824]
Holmes Book Company
274 Fourteenth Street
Oakland, CA 94612

[825]
Benjamin E. Achee
1414 Fox Street
Bossier City, LA 71010

[826]
Robert T. Stoner
126 Locust Street
Shiremanstown, PA 17011

[827]
Bantam Book, Inc.
666 Fifth Avenue
New York, NY 10019

[828]
Mrs. Robert L. Eastwood
2 Bratenahl Place
Cleveland, OH 44108

[829]
Ye Galleon Press
Box 400
Fairfield, WA 99012

[830]
Bookworm & Silverfish
James S. Presgraves
Box 516
Wytheville, VA 24382

[831]
University of California Press
2223 Fulton Street
Berkeley, CA 94720

[832]
Huntington Library Publications
San Marino, CA 91108

[833]
Ernest L. Ross
2114 Oakland Drive NW
Cleveland, TN 37311

[834]
DOR Company
Box 647
Williamstown, MA 01267

[835]
Cornell University Press
124 Roberts Place
Ithaca, NY 14850

[836]
Cambridge University Press
32 East 57th Street
New York, NY 10022

[837]
Louise Lyon
23121 Highway 65 NE
East Bethel, MN 55005

[838]
Aurora C. Shaw
2525 Oak Street
Jacksonville, FL 32204

[839]
John Bushman Family Association
c/o Derryfield N. Smith
854 Park Lake Circle
Maitland, FL 32751

[840]
Judge James M. Carter
U.S. Courthouse
San Diego, CA 92101

[841]
Ward Ritchie Press
3044 Riverside Drive
Los Angeles, CA 90039

[842]
California Historical Society
2090 Jackson Street
San Francisco, CA 94109

[843]
G.K. Hall & Company
70 Lincoln Street
Boston, MA 02111

[844]
Benjamin Blom, Inc.
2521 Broadway
New York, NY 10025

[845]
The Genealogical Society
50 East North Temple
Salt Lake City, UT 84150

[846]
Orin F. Nolting
6601 Blue Jacket Avenue
Shawnee, KS 66203

[847]
Negro Universities Press
51 Riverside Avenue
Westport, CT 06880

[848]
Morningside Bookshop
P.O. Box 336
Forest Park Station
Dayton, OH 45405

[849]
Mrs. H. A. Knorr
1401 Linden Street
Pine Bluff, AR 71601

[850]
The Bookmark
On the Historic Town Square
P.O. Box 74
Knightstown, IN 46148

[851]
Edwin F. Lochner, C.G.
P.O. Box 12873 - Commerce Station
Philadelphia, PA 19108

[852]
Dover Publications
180 Varick Street
New York, NY 10014

[853]
Rhea Cumming Otto
8816 Ferguson Avenue
Savannah, GA 31406

[854]
Gregg Press, Inc.
70 Lincoln Street
Boston, MA 02111

[855]
Pauline Jones Gandrud
311 Caplewood Terrace
Tuscaloosa, AL 35401

[856]
"The Folks" Book
1507 Laurel Court
Dundee, IL 60118

[857]
Chicago Genealogical Society
P.O. Box 1160
Chicago, IL 60690

[858]
Wesleyan University Press
Middleton, CT 06457

[859]
Pelican Publishing Company, Inc.
630 Burmaster Street
Gretna, LA 70053

[860]
Mrs. John Vineyard
Rt. 2 - Box 141D
Ozark, MO 65721

[861]
William L. Jones
10 Tanglewood Drive
Milan, TN 38358

[862]
Melba C. Crosse
631 Bryn Mawr Drive, N.E.
Albuauerque, NM 87106

[863]
Da Capo Press
227 West 17th Street
New York, NY 10011

[864]
Grossman Publishers, Inc.
c/o Viking Press
625 Madison Avenue
New York, NY 10022

[865]
University of Southwestern Louisiana
P.O. Box 831
Lafayette, LA 70501

[866]
Lawrence Verry, Inc.
Mystic, CT 96355

[867]
Schuyler County Jail Museum
Corner Congress & Madison Streets
Rushville, IL 62681

[868]
Mississippi Genealogical Society
408 Dunbar Street
Jackson, MS 39216

[869]
Mrs. M. G. Harmon, Jr.
Rt. # 10 - Box 275-A
Tyler, TX 75701

[870]
Historic Frankfort Press
P.O. Box 775
Frankfort, KY 40601

[871]
Hermosa Publishers
P.O. Box 8172
Albuquerque, NM 87108

[872]
National Society United States
   Daughters of 1812
c/o Cleo Warren
1461 Rhode Island Avenue, NW
Washington, DC 20005

[873]
University of Tennessee Press
293 Communications Building
Knoxville, TN 37916

[874]
Alta Cecil Koch
Rt. 1 - Box 477
West Terre Haute, IN 47885

[875]
W. W. Norton & Company, Inc.
500 Fifth Avenue
New York, NY 10036

[876]
Bond Wheelwright Company
Porter's Landing
Freeport, ME 04032

[877]
University of South Carolina Press
Columbia, SC 29208

[878]
Oceana Publications, Inc.
Dobbs Ferry, NY 10522

[879]
Ohio University Press
Administrative Annex
Athens, OH 45701

[880]
The Gazetteer Press
415 Chesterfield
Nashville, TN 37212

[881]
Greenwood Press, Inc.
51 Riverside Avenue
Westport, CT 06880

[882]
Statesman Books
Columbia, KY 42728

[883]
Ruby Lacy
P.O. Box 628
Ashland, OR 97520

[884]
Mrs. Clyde Lynch
Rt. # 5
Franklin, TN 37064

[885]
Publications Sales Committee
Maryland Genealogical Society, Inc.
201 West Monument Street
Baltimore, MD 21201

[886]
Mid-Continent Book Store
North 15th & Dunbar
Mayfield, KY 42066

[887]
Oregon Historical Society
Western Imprints
1230 S.W. Park Avenue
Portland, OR 97205

[888]
Ohio Historical Society
c/o Order Clerk
Columbus, OH 43211

[889]
Max W. Grove
P.O. Box 4345
Silver Spring, MD 20904

[890]
American Association for State &
Local History
1315 Eighth Avenue, South
Nashville, TN 37203

[891]
The Centennial Press
P.O. Box 4765
Memphis, TN 38104

[892]
Howell-North Books
1050 Parker Street
Berkeley, CA 94710

[893]
State Printing Company
1305 Sumter Street
Columbia, SC 29201

[894]
Octagon Books
19 Union Square, West
New York, NY 10003

[895]
University of Minnesota Press
2037 University Avenue, S.E.
Minneapolis, MN 55455

[896]
Reader Services Staff
Division of Public Library Services
Georgia Dept. of Education
Atlanta, GA

[897]
Columbia Historical Society
1307 New Hampshire Avenue, NW
Washington, DC 20036

[898]
College of Arts & Sciences
University of Kentucky
Lexington, KY 40506

[899]
Scholarly Press
22929 Industrial Drive, East
St. Clair Shores, MI 48080

[900]
The Historical Society of Delaware
Old Town Hall
Wilmington, DE 19801

[901]
New York Gen. & Biog. Society
122 East 58th Street
New York, NY 10022

[902]
Wayne State University Press
5980 Cass Avenue
Detroit, MI 48202

[903]
Kansas State Historical Society
Memorial Bldg., 120 W. 10th
Topeka, KS 66612

[904]
Van A. Stilley
718 9th Street, S.E.
Washington, DC 20003

[905]
Cumberland County Historical Society
P.O. Box 626 - 21 N. Pitt Street
Carlisle, PA 17013

[906]
Henry Stewart, Inc.
249 Bowen Road
East Aurora, NY 14052

[907]
R. L. Bryan Company
Greystone Executive Park
Columbia, SC 29210

[908]
Jacobs Press, Inc.
P.O. Box 150 - #1 Clay Street
Clinton, SC 29325

[909]
Porcupine Press, Inc.
1317 Filbert Street
Philadelphia, PA 19107

[910]
Beverly Yount
2414 Northwest B Street
Richmond, IN 47374

[911]
Augsbury Publishing House
425 South 4th Street
Minneapolis, MN 55415

[912]
Ethel W. Williams
730 Parker Avenue
Kalamazoo, MI 49008

[913]
The Genealogical Society of New Jersey
c/o Dorothy A Stratford
132 West Franklin Street
Bound Brook, NJ 08805

[914]
Georgia Department of Archives & Hist.
Div. of the Office of Sec. of State
Atlanta, GA 30334

[915]
Pennaylvania State University Press
215 Wagner Building
University Park, PA 16802

[916]
Pennsylvania Historical & Museum Comm.
Box 1026
Harrisburg, PA 17120

[917]
University of Georgia Press
Waddell Hall
Athens, GA 30602

[918]
Historical Society of Michigan
2117 Washtenaw Avenue
Ann Arbor, MI 48104

[919]
Caxton Printer, Ltd.
312 Main Street - Box 700
Caldwell, ID 83605

[920]
Scarecrow Press, Inc.
52 Liberty Street - Box 656
Metuchen, NJ 08840

[921]
Russell E. Bidlack
1709 Cherokee Road
Ann Arbor, MI 48104

[922]
Scholars' Facsimiles and Reprints
Box 344
Delmar, NY 12054

[923]
Bluegrass Printing Company
Danville, KY 40422

[924]
Georgia Historical Society
501 Whitaker Street
Savannah, GA 31401

[925]
Herald Press
Mennonite Publishing House
616 Walnut Avenue
Scottdale, PA 15683

[926]
Dorrance & Company, Inc.
1617 J.F. Kennedy Boulevard
Philadelphia, PA 19103

[927]
William Morrow & Company, Inc.
6 Henderson Drive, West
Caldwell, NJ 07006

[928]
Plenum Publishing Corporation
227 West 17th Street
New York, NY 10011

[929]
Order of the Crown of Charlemagne
c/o Robert George Cooke
761 Linwood Avenue
St. Paul, MN 55105

[930]
Henry Clay Press
Box 116A
Lexington, KY 40501

[931]
Elaine Walker
P.O. Box 248
Post Falls, ID 83854

[932]
New Haven Colony Historical Society
114 Whitney Avenue
New Haven, CT 06510

[933]
Jean O. Morris
P.O. Box 8530
Pittsburgh, PA 15220

[934]
Stephenson County Historical Society
1440 South Carroll Avenue
Freeport, IL 61032

[935]
Louisiana State University Press
Baton Rouge, LA 70803

[936]
Genealogical Enterprises
P.O. Box 232
Morrow, GA 30260

[937]
Oxford University Press, Inc.
1600 Pollitt Drive
Fair Lawn, NJ 07410

[938]
University & College Press of Miss.
3825 Ridgewood Road
Jackson, MS 39211

[939]
Somerset Publishers
200 Park Avenue - Ste. 303 East
New York, NY 10017

[940]
Dorothy Ford Wulfeck
51 Park Avenue
Naugatuck, CT 06770

[941]
Mrs. John E. Ireton
6441 Brushwood Court
Dayton, OH 45415

[942]
The Eastern Shore News
Accomac, VA 23301

[943]
Princeton University Press
Princeton, NJ 08540

[944]
Granby Town Clerk
Granby, MA 01033

[945]
Weybright & Talley, Inc.
c/o David McKay, Inc.
750 Third Avenue
New York, NY 10017

[946]
Janlen Enterprises
2236 South 77th Street
West Allis, WI 53219

[947]
Ballantine Books, Inc.
201 East 50th Street
New York, NY 10022

[948]
Harvard University Press
79 Garden Street
Cambridge, MA 02138

[949]
Root & Tree Publications
18013 Armitage Court
Homewood, IL 60430

[950]
Rutgers University Press
30 College Avenue
New Brunswick, NJ 08901

[951]
Massachusetts Historical Society
1154 Boylston Street
Boston, MA 02215

[952]
Atheneum Publishers
122 East 42nd Street
New York, NY 10017

[953]
Carole Kastner
P.O. Box 51
Denville, NJ 07834

[954]
V.C. Bergling
Box 523-T
Coral Gables, FL 33134

[955]
Salem County Historical Society
79-83 Market Street
Salem, NJ 08079

[956]
Harriet A. Webb
P.O. Box 398
Machias, ME 04654

[957]
Essex Institute
132 Essex Street
Salem, MA 01970

[958]
Bangor Chamber of Commerce
23 Franklin Street
Bangor, ME 04401

[959]
Tennessee Valley Genealogical Society
P.O. Box 1512
Huntsville, AL 35807

[960]
Claitor's Book Store
3165 South Acadian Thruway
Baton Rouge, LA 70806

[961]
End of Trail Researchers
Rt. # 1 - Box 138
Lebanon, OR 97355

[962]
Publications Department
The Western Reserve Historical Society
10825 East Boulevard
Cleveland, OH 44106

[963]
G. R. Clark Press, Inc.
561 Blankenbaker Lane
Louisville, KY 40207

[964]
Argosy-Antiquarian, Ltd.
116 East 59th Street
New York, NY 10022

[965]
Harry R. Bollinger
R. R. # 1 - Box 54
South Whitley, IN 46787

[966]
Lee Academy
Lee, ME 04455

[967]
New American Library
1301 Avenue of the Americas
New York, NY 10010

[968]
International Publications Service
114 East 32nd Street
New York, NY 10016

[969]
Betty Crume
2415 - 30th Street
Lubbock, TX 79411

[970]
Pikeville College Press
Pikeville, KY 41501

[971]
Genealogical Society of Cumberland
& Coles County, Illinois
c/o Violet E. McCandlish
Rt. #1 - Box 141
Toledo, IL 62468

[972]
Emma Robertson Matheny
1718 Glenview Road
Richmond, VA 23222

[973]
Heraldic Publishing Company, Inc.
305 West End Avenue
New York, NY 10023

[974]
Holt, Rinehart & Winston, Inc.
383 Madison Avenue
New York, NY 10017

[975]
Phoenix Publishing
Woodstock, VT 05091

[976]
Fernhill - Humanities Press, Inc.
450 Park Avenue, South
New York, NY 10016

[977]
Range Genealogical Society
P.O. Box 726
Buhl, MN 55713

[978]
L. B. Lincoln
79 Garden Street
Cambridge, MA 02138

[979]
Corner House
Green River Road
Williamstown, MA 01267

[980]
Div. of History & Cultural Affairs
Hall of Records
Dover, DE 19901

[981]
Gordon Press
Box 459 - Bowling Green Station
New York, NY 10004

[982]
Columbia University Press
136 South Broadway
Irvington-on-Hudson, NY 10533

[983]
Crown Publishers, Inc.
419 Park Ave., South
New York, NY 10016

[984]
Bicentennial Hdqrs., Citizens Bank
425 West Dixie Avenue
Elizabethtown, KY 42701

[985]
Cooper Square Publishers, Inc.
59 Fourth Avenue
New York, NY 10003

[986]
The Memorial Foundation of the
    Germanna Colonies, Inc.
Box 693
Culpeper, VA 22701

[987]
The Hist. Soc. of Western Pennsylvania
4338 Bigelow Boulevard
Pittsburgh, PA 15213

[988]
Russell & Russell, Publishers
122 East 42nd Street
New York, NY 10017

[989]
University of Pennsylvania Press
3729 Spruce Street
Philadelphia, PA 19104

[990]
Iowa State University Press
Ames, IA 50010

[991]
University of Pittsburgh Press
127 North Bellefield Avenue
Pittsburgh, PA 15260

[992]
Harper & Row Publishers, Inc.
Scranton, PA 18512

[993]
Parnassus Imprints
Yarmouth Port, MA 02675

[994]
Barron's Educational Series, Inc.
113 Crossways Park Drive
Woodbury, NY 11797

[995]
Beehive Press
321 Barnard Street
Savannah, GA 21401

[996]
Hunt-Morgan House
201 North Mill Street
Lexington, KY 40507

[997]
Oklahoma Historical Society
2100 North Lincoln
Oklahoma City, OK 73105

[998]
The Christopher Publishing House
53 Billings Road
North Quincy, MA 02171

[999]
Institute of Genealogical & Histor-
    ical Research
Samford University Library
Birmingham, AL 35209

[1000]
Johnson Reprint Company
111 Fifth Avenue
New York, NY 10003

[1001]
State Historical Society of Iowa
402 Iowa Avenue
Iowa City, IA 52240

[1002]
Arizona State Genealogical Society, Inc.
P.O. Box 6027
Tucson, AZ 85733

[1003]
A.B. Markham
215 East Markham Avenue
Durham, NC 27701

[1004]
History Publications
South Dakota State Historical Society
Memorial Building
Pierre, SD 57501

[1005]
Historical Society of Pennsylvania
1300 Locust Street
Philadelphia, PA 19107

[1006]
Princeton University Library
Princeton, NJ 08540

[1007]
Mrs. Weynette P. Haun
243 Argonne Drive
Durham, NC 27704

[1008]
Long Island Historical Society
128 Pierrepont Street
Brooklyn, NY 11201

[1009]
Fay Maxwell
712 South Chesterfield Road
Columbus, OH 43209

[1010]
The Sergeant Newton Chapter - DAR
c/o Mrs. Edgar M. Lancaster
Shady Dale, GA 31085

[1011]
City Archives
City Hall - Room 790
Philadelphia, PA 19107

[1012]
University of Wisconsin Press
Box 1379
Madison, WI 53701

[1013]
AHM Publishing Company
1500 Skokie Boulvard
Northbrook, Il 60062

[1014]
Mifflin County Historical Society
53 North Pine Street
Lewistown, PA 17044

[1015]
Bancroft Press
27 McNear Drive
San Rafael, CA 94901

[1016]
Brown University Press
71 George Street
Box 1881
Providence, RI 02912

[1017]
Countryman Press
Taftsville, VT 1017

[1018]
Freneau Press
P.O. Box 116
Monmouth Beach, NJ 07750

[1019]
Harcourt Brace Jovanovich, Inc.
757 Third Avenue
New York, NY 10017

[1020]
Johnson Publishing Company
P.O. Box 317
Murfreesboro, NC 27855

[1021]
John P. Dern
950 Palomar Drive
Redwood City, CA 94062

[1022]
Washington State University Press
Pullman, WA 99163

[1023]
The Johnstown Genealogy Society
P.O. Box 345
Johnstown, OH 43031

[1024]
Cornell University
Regional History & University Archives
Ithaca, NY 14850

[1025]
Sandlapper Store, Inc.
P.O. Box 841
Lexington, SC 29072

[1026]
Prospect Presbyterian Church
c/o Mavis C. Chappell
Rt. 3 - Box 340
Mooresville, NC 28115

[1027]
Vio-Lin Enterprises
2358 East Johns
Decatur, IL 62521

[1028]
Social Concerns Committee
First United Methodist Church
29 North College Street
Washington, PA 15301

[1029]
Rapid City Soc. for Gen. Research
P.O. Box 1495
Rapid City, SD 57701

[1130]
Western Pennsylvania Genealogical Soc.
c/o Elizabeth J. Wall
310 Scotia Street
Pittsburgh, PA 15205

[1131]
Historical Soc. of Monmouth County
P.O. Box 1776
Tennent, NJ 07763

[1132]
Asbury Park Public Library
500 1st Avenue
Asbury Park, NJ 07712

[1133]
Virginia Mennonite Church Offices
1151 Greystone
Harrisonburg, VA 22801

[1134]
Ohio Genealogical Society - ORPF
P.O. Box 2625
Mansfield, OH 44906

[1135]
Chris H. Bailey
100 Maple Street
Bristol, CT 06010

[1136]
Betty Harrington
611 Belle Aire
Carthage, MO 64836

[1137]
Mrs. Mary M. Curry
1510 Kentucky
Joplin, MO 64801

[1138]
Ruth Roach Medley
2701 20th Street
Lubbock, TX 79410

[1139]
Mrs. Louis F. Ison
Lexington Road - Rt. 4
Harrodsburg, KY 40330

[1140]
Norman E. Gillis
P.O. Box 9114
Shreveport, LA 71109

[1141]
Gloucester County Historical Society
58 North Broad Street - Box 409
Woodbury, NJ 08096

[1142]
Pulaski County Historical Society
Public Library Building
Somerset, KY 42501

[1143]
The Genealogical Society of Old Tryon Co.
P.O. Box 745
Spindale, NC 28160

[1144]
The Pennsylvania German Society
Rt. 1 - Box 469
Breinigsville, PA 18031

[1145]
Pastor Frederick Weiser
425 George Street
Hanover, PA 17331

[1146]
Mrs. J.R. Carter
406 East 5th Street
Sedalia, MO 65301

[1147]
Maryland Bicentennial Commission
2525 Riva Road
Annapolis, MD 21401

[1148]
First Baptist Church
205 West Hamlet Avenue
Hamlet, NC 28345

[1149]
City Clerk
113 South Main Street
Lodi, WI 53555

[1150]
Gendex Corporation
P.O. Box 299
Provo, UT 84601

[1151]
Cdr. J. H. Bronson Smith, Treas.
5601 Seminary Road - Apt. 510N
Falls Church, VA 22041

[1152]
Massachusetts Mayflower Descendants
101 Newbury Street - 3rd Floor
Boston, MA 02116

[1153]
Rhode Island Mayflower Descendants
128 Massasoit Drive
Warwick, RI 02888

[1154]
Mayflower Society
c/o Edith K. Zuber
4501 Druid Lane
Dallas, TX 75205

[1155]
Bernard Chamberlain, Secretary
The Peyton Society of Virginia
224 Court Square
Charlottesville, VA 22901

[1156]
Barbara Smith Buys
R.D. #1 - Sunset Hill East
Fishkill, NY 12524

[1157]
Walter J. Tatom
544 Parkhurst
Dallas, Texas 75218

[1158]
Library of Congress - CDS Division
Building # 159, Navy Yard Annex
Washington, DC 21541

[1159]
J.W. Edwards, Publisher, Inc.
2500 South State Street
Ann Arbor, MI 48104

FAMILY SHEET

Do not write in this space

Husband's Code . . . .
Wife's Code . . . .

HUSBAND'S NAME _____

Date of Birth _____ Place _____

Date of Death _____ Place _____

Present Address (or) Place of Burial _____

His Father _____ His Mother's Maiden Name _____

Date of Marriage of HUSBAND and WIFE on this sheet _____ Place _____

Check here if there was another marriage: By husband ☐ By Wife ☐   Was this couple divorced? Yes ☐ No ☐   When? _____

WIFE'S MAIDEN NAME _____ (Use separate sheet for each marriage)

Date of Birth _____ Place _____

Date of Death _____ Place _____

Present Address (or) Place of Burial _____

Her Father _____ Her Mother's Maiden Name _____

Items of interest about the above couple (occupations, hobbies, achievements; social, civil, and political activities; physical descriptions—include photos if possible; military service; cause of death):

Do not write in this space   Do not write in this space   Use reverse side for additional information

Have family sheet		CHILDREN (Arrange in order of birth)	Code	Birth Information	Death Information	Marriage Information
	1			ON AT	ON AT	ON TO
	2			ON AT	ON AT	ON TO
	3			ON AT	ON AT	ON TO
	4			ON AT	ON AT	ON TO
	5			ON AT	ON AT	ON TO

Check here if there are additional children ☐

Footnoting. To substantiate the information recorded on this page, please use the footnotes listed below. One of these numbers should be placed in the circle provided next to each answer on the questionnaire. If you got the information from a source not listed, place that source on a vacant line and use the number next to which it has been placed as your footnote number.

Use ① only if you have filled in the blank from personal knowledge (such as the name of your brother). If you must look up his marriage date, give as the source wherever you looked it up. If you asked him, give his name as the source.

① Name and address of person filling in this sheet. _____ Date _____

② _____

③ _____

④ _____

⑤ _____

⑥ _____

⑦ _____

⑧ _____

Form B-100

© 1969 Netti Schreiner-Yantis, 6818 Lois Drive, Springfield, Virginia 22150

THE MARK ✓ OF A GOOD GENEALOGIST IS CAREFUL DOCUMENTATION.
THE FORM WHICH PROVIDES SPACE FOR CAREFUL DOCUMENTATION IS ABOVE.

The continuation sheet for the above form contains space for 10 additional children; plus space for additional documentation. Ratio received with 1st order is as below. Subsequent orders may specify exact number of each sheet.

8½ x 11:
| 100 FORMS – 75/25 --- $ 3.55 |
| 250 FORMS – 200/50 -- 5.95 |
| 500 FORMS – 400/100 - 10.95 |
| 1000 FORMS – 800/200 - 19.95 |

8½ x 14:
Similar format
| 100 FORMS – 75/25 --- 3.85 |
| 250 FORMS – 200/50 -- 6.25 |
| 500 FORMS – 400/100 - 11.25 |
| 1000 FORMS – 800/200 - 20.25 |

ORDER FROM: GENEALOGICAL BOOKS IN PRINT, 6818 LOIS DRIVE - SPRINGFIELD, VIRGINIA 22150

ORDER FROM CATALOGUE OF GENEALOGICAL BOOKS IN PRINT

Title: _____

If periodical: Vol. _____ No. _____   Enclosed: $ _____
                                                 [In-state residents, please add sales ta

Send to: _____

_____

_____

ORDER FROM CATALOGUE OF GENEALOGICAL BOOKS IN PRINT

Title: _____

If periodical: Vol. _____ No. _____   Enclosed: $ _____
                                                 [In-state residents, please add sales ta

Send to: _____

_____

ORDER FROM CATALOGUE OF GENEALOGICAL BOOKS IN PRINT

Title: _____

If periodical: Vol. _____ No. _____   Enclosed: $ _____
                                                 [In-state residents, please add sales ta

Send to: _____

_____

_____

ORDER FROM CATALOGUE OF GENEALOGICAL BOOKS IN PRINT.

Title: _____

If periodical: Vol. _____ No. _____   Enclosed: $ _____
                                                 [In-state residents, please add sales ta

Send to: _____

_____

ORDER FROM CATALOGUE OF GENEALOGICAL BOOKS IN PRINT

Title: _____

If periodical: Vol. _____ No. _____   Enclosed: $ _____
                                             [In-state residents, please add sales tax]

Send to: _____

_____

_____

- -

ORDER FROM CATALOGUE OF GENEALOGICAL BOOKS IN PRINT

Title: _____

If periodical: Vol. _____ No. _____   Enclosed: $ _____
                                             [In-state residents, please add sales tax]

Send to: _____

_____

_____

- -

ORDER FROM CATALOGUE OF GENEALOGICAL BOOKS IN PRINT

Title: _____

If periodical: Vol. _____ No. _____   Enclosed: $ _____
                                             [In-state residents, please add sales tax]

Send to: _____

_____

_____

- -

ORDER FROM CATALOGUE OF GENEALOGICAL BOOKS IN PRINT

_____

ol. _____ No. _____   Enclosed: $ _____
                                             [In-state residents, please add sales tax]

_____

_____